THE GREAT WAR IN THE AIR

Smithsonian History of Aviation History

Von Hardesty, Series Editor

On December 17, 1903, on a windy beach in North Carolina, aviation became a reality. The development of aviation over the course of little more than three-quarters of a century stands as an awe-inspiring accomplishment in both a civilian and a military context. The airplane has brought whole continents closer together: at the same time it has been a lethal instrument of war.

This series of books is intended to contribute to the overall understanding of the history of aviation—its science and technology as well as the social, cultural, and political environment in which it developed and matured. Some publications help fill the many gaps that still exist in the literature of flight; others add new information and interpretation to current knowledge. While the series appeals to a broad audience of general readers and specialists in the field, its hallmark is strong scholarly content.

The series is international in scope and includes works in three major categories:

SMITHSONIAN STUDIES IN AVIATION HISTORY: works that provide new and original knowledge.

CLASSICS OF AVIATION HISTORY: carefully selected out-of-print works that are considered essential scholarship.

CONTRIBUTIONS TO AVIATION HISTORY: previously unpublished documents, reports, symposia, and other materials.

ADVISORY BOARD: Roger E. Bilstein, *University of Houston;* Horst Boog, *Militärgeschichtliches Forschungsamt, Germany;* DeWitt C. Copp, *Author and air historian;* Tom D. Crouch, *National Air and Space Museum;* Sylvia Fries, *National Aeronautics and Space Administration;* Ben Greenhous, *Historian;* John F. Guilmartin, Jr., *Ohio State University;* Terry Gwynn-Jones, *Author;* Richard P. Hallion, *Secretary of the Air Force's Staff Group;* James R. Hansen, *Auburn University;* Von Hardesty, *National Air and Space Museum;* Robin Higham, *Kansas State University;* Lee Kennett, *University of Georgia;* Nick Komons, *Federal Aviation Administration;* William M. Leary, *University of Georgia;* W. David Lewis, *Auburn University;* Air Vice-Marshal R. A. Mason, CBE MA RAF (Ret.); LTC Phillip S. Meilinger, *HQ USAF/XOXWD;* John H. Morrow, Jr., *University of Georgia;* Dominick A. Pisano, *National Air and Space Museum;* Air Commodore H. A. Probert, MBE MA RAF (Ret.); General Lucien Robineau, *Service historique de l'armée de l'air, France;* Alex Roland, *Duke University;* F. Robert van der Linden, *National Air and Space Museum*

THE GREAT WAR IN THE AIR

Military Aviation from 1909 to 1921

John H. Morrow, Jr.

Smithsonian Institution Press
Washington and London

Editor: Jenelle Walthour
Designer: Linda McKnight

Library of Congress Cataloging-in-Publication Data
Morrow, John Howard, Jr., 1944–
The great war in the air: military aviation from 1909 to 1921 /
John H. Morrow, Jr.
    p.   cm.
    Includes bibliographical references and index.
    ISBN 1-56098-238-1 (alk. paper)
    1. World War, 1914–1918—Aerial operations.   I. Title.
D600.M565   1993
940.4′4—dc20   92-17437

British Library Cataloguing-in-Publication Data is available

Manufactured in the United States of America
00 99 98   5 4 3 2

∞ The paper used in this publication meets the minimum requirements of the American National Standard for Permanence of Paper
for Printed Library Materials Z39.48-1984

To my wife, Diane Batts Morrow, with love
In memoriam: Dr. James A. Batts, Jr. [1913–1992]

Contents

List of Abbreviations and Acronyms

ABC All British Company (engine factory)

AEF American Expeditionary Force

AEG Allgemeine Elektrizitäts Gesellschaft (General Electric Company) [Germany]

AH *Airpower Historian*

AHB Air Historical Branch [England]

AID Aeronautics Inspection Department [England]

Airco Aircraft Manufacturing Company

AOK Armeeoberkommando (Austro-Hungarian High Command)

AR Avant Renault

BA Bau-Aufsicht (Construction Inspectorate) [Germany]

BAO Brieftauben Abteilung Ostende

BEF British Expeditionary Force

BFW Bayerische Flugzeugwerke (Bavarian Aircraft Works)

BHP Beardmore-Halford-Pullinger (English engine company)

BMW Bayerische Motorenwerke (Bavarian Motor Works)

CFS Central Flying School [England]

CID Committee of Imperial Defense [England]

CIGS Chief of the Imperial General Staff [England]

CinC Commander in Chief

CMTD Chief Military Technical Directorate [Russia]

CRFC Command Royal Flying Corps [England]

DAeM Direction de l'Aéronautique Militaire (Directorate
of Military Aeronautices
[France]

DAO Director of Air Organization [England]

DD Donnet-Denhaut (flying
boat company)

DFW Deutsche Flugzeugwerke
(German Aircraft Works)

DMA Director(ate) of Military
Aeronautics [England]

DP, MdA Dorand Papers, Museé de
l'Air

FF Flugzeugbau Friedrichs-
hafen (Friedrichshafen
Aircraft Construction
Company)

FHS *French Historical Studies*

Flik Fliegerkompagnie (Flight
Company)
[Austria-Hungary]

FBA Franco-British-Aviation
(flying boat company)

GAN French Army Group
North

GAR French Reserve Army
Group

GC Peter Grosz Collection

Gotha Gothaer Waggonfabrik
AG (Gotha Railroad
Factory)

GQG Grand Quartier Général
(French High Command)

Jastas Jagdstaffeln (Fighter
Units) [Germany]

JWAC Joint War Air Committee
[England]

KAdL Kriegswissenschaftliche
Abteilung der Luftwaffe

**Kogen-
luft** Kommandierender General
der Luftstreitkräfte (Commanding General of the
Air Force) [Germany]

LFG Luftfahrzeuggesellschaft
(Aircraft Company)
[Germany]

LVG Luftverkehrsgesellschaft
(Air Transport Company)
[Germany]

MD Ministry of Defence
[England]

MdG Ministère de Guerre (War
Ministry) [France]

MLG Motorluftfahrzeuggesellschaft (Motor Aircraft
Company) [Austria]

NACA National Committee for
Aeronautics [United
States]

**NASM,
SI** National Air and Space
Museum, Smithsonian
Institution

OHL Oberste Heeresleitung
(German High Command)

Öffag Österreichische Flugzeugfabrik AG (Austrian Air-
craft Factory)

PRO Public Record Office
[England]

RAF Royal Air Force [England]

RAFM Royal Air Force Museum

REP Robert Esnault-Pelterie or
the aircraft factory

RFC Royal Flying Corps
[England]

RHA *Revue Historique des
Armées*

RHMC *Revue d'histoire moderne et
contemporaine*

RNAS Royal Naval Air Service [England]

SBAC Society of British Aircraft Constructors

SCFA Service Centrale des Fabrications Aéronautiques (Central Service of Aviation Production) [France]

SEA Société d'études aéronautiques

SFA Service des Fabrications Aéronautiques (Aviation Production Service) [France]

SHAA Service Historique de l'Armée de l'Air (Air Force Historical Service) [France]

SI Industrial Section [France]

SIA Società Italiana Aviazione (Fiat's aircraft branch)

SIT Società Italiana Transaerea

SPAD Société pour l'Aviation et ses Dérivés

SSW Siemens Schuckert Works

STAé Section Technique de l'Aéronautique (technical branch or section of the SFA)

Stavka Russian High Command

SVA Savoia-Verduzio-Ansaldo

TP Trenchard Papers

Ufag Hungarische Flugzeugfabrik AG (Hungarian Aircraft Factory)

WAF Wissenschaftliche Auskunftei für Flugwesen (Scientific Information Office)

ZfM *Zeitschrift fur Militärgeschichte*

Preface

The Great War in the Air: Military Aviation from 1909 to 1921 is a comprehensive study of the development and significance of airpower in World War I. This history of the rise and decline of military aviation from 1909 to 1921 compares various military, political, technological, industrial, and cultural aspects of airpower in the major combatant powers—France, Germany, England, Italy, Russia, Austria-Hungary, and the United States.

The years 1909 to 1921 held great significance for airpower. Military aviation and the aviation industry began in 1909. Only four years later, when the European great powers went to war for the first time in nearly a century, military establishments had no proof of the value of aviation. The Great War provided that proof. From 1914 to 1918, air warfare became important as combatants amassed and used aircraft sufficient in quantity and quality to affect the outcome of engagements.

World War I forged military aviation, within a decade of its origins, into an important weapon. Then, in three years of postwar contraction, the air forces and aviation industries plummeted from the pinnacle of wartime expansion to the verge of extinction in some countries. Yet if postwar military aviation and industry shrank to mere shadows of their wartime selves, the shadows cast were long and dark, and the fears they engendered endured. Prewar circumstances spawned wartime developments whose legacy persisted in the postwar era. This nexus necessitates examining wartime aviation in the context of its prewar antecedents and postwar aftermath.

The few general histories of airpower in the Great War are invariably popular, anecdotal, and insufficiently analytical to capture the significance and complexities of the development of aviation in the first major conflict of the twentieth century. They concentrate on the battlefront, in particular aerial combat, air aces, and fighter planes, to the near exclusion of the equally important though less spectacular homefront. These anecdotal narratives tend to gloss over the different national contexts in which aviation evolved, either by concentrating on one or two countries such as England and Germany, or by seizing salient examples from various countries in a haphazard fashion. Such treatments have perpetuated myths about one of the most highly romanticized subjects of military history and have ensured that military aviation in World War I remains primarily a popular but unscholarly subject.

The famous pilots and airplanes of the war are the focus of popular and technical works; the doctrine, politics, and industry of airpower are the subjects of scholarly studies. There often seems to be an implicit assumption that the audience for one realm is disinterested in the other—that the frontline exploits are exciting and of interest to many, while the developments in the rear are dull and of interest to few. Yet the spheres of front and rear, of destruction and construction, are so interrelated that neither can be adequately understood apart from the other. This book consequently seeks to appeal to and enlighten both the general reader and the scholar. Air warfare is exciting, heroic, and dramatic, and it seems to possess an intrinsic hold upon our imagination. Yet its destructiveness, its cost in human lives and material resources, and our persistent tendencies to glamorize it require us to penetrate the veil of the romantic myth. This can be done by examining the air war in its totality through the comparative study of the combatants' development of air forces and aviation industries.

The air war of World War I evokes romantic images of valiant young aviators clad in long leather coats and helmets, with silk scarves about their craning necks as they peer from the open cockpits of their fragile wooden biplanes in search of prey or predator. Darting about the heavens in their lightly armed and unarmored planes and pouncing on one another in individual combat, they fight tenaciously, win gallantly, or die heroically, their flaming craft plunging to earth like meteoric funeral pyres, extinguishing their equally meteoric careers with scorching finality. Their names—Boelcke, Ball, Richthofen, Guynemer, Mannock—are legend; their lives, terribly short; their exploits, the material of myth. They are the symbols of the first war in the air, its heroes and victims, and the focus of most studies of the subject.

This concentration on the "knights of the air" stems from a natural tendency to emphasize the heroic. The very circumstances of the conflict encouraged a mythologizing of the air war into a single image of individual combat, deadly but chivalrous. Mass slaughter on an unprecedented scale was rendering individuals insignificant. Aerial heroes provided a much-needed, though misleading, affirmation of the importance of the individual and of youth in a slaughter of both. The fighter pilots consequently became not only the symbols of aviation but also the ultimate heroes of World War I. They were the darlings of the press and civilians, the perfect symbols of an upstart arm that displayed many of the wayward tendencies of youth, in particular a lack of discipline.

Yet anecdotal narratives of wartime aviation that concentrate on the exploits of fighter pilots give the impression that in this mass war of technology and industry, the air arm was merely an atavistic appurtenance in which a few exceptional aces were the dominant feature. This approach robs World War I airpower of its genuine military and industrial significance. The air arms did more than just provide the warring nations with individual heroes, for their individual exploits occurred within the context of an increasingly mass aerial effort in a war of the masses. Aviation played a significant role, first in rendering ground forces more effective through reconnaissance or artillery observation. Later its effectiveness as a weapon for fighting, bombing, and strafing required that it be brought to bear en masse against the enemy.

Concentration on the individual exploits of a few fighter pilots has thus given an archaic, anachronistic image to the most advanced and innovative technological arm of warfare, the one that epitomized the new total warfare in its requirement of meshing the military, political, technological, and industrial aspects of war—the front and the rear, the military and the civilian. The fighter arms and their aces were the icing on the cake of World War I aviation; the unheralded crews of two-seat observation, ground support, and bombing aircraft were the supporting layers.

Military and political leaders had to make crucial decisions to expand the tiny air arms and mobilize the embryonic supporting industries, for in airpower more than in any other realm of combat in the First World War, technological and industrial superiority essentially determined the outcome of the struggle. Critical determinants of the success of airpower were the quality and quantity of materiel. Producing masses of aircraft that would be reliable combat machines was a unique and exceedingly difficult task.

The nature of air warfare necessitated frequent innovations and changes in production, and the race for aerial superiority had to be won first in design offices and then on factory floors, as the airplane evolved from an experimental vehicle into a weapon in the arsenals of all combatant powers.

The airplane exemplified the harsh demands and enormous waste of modern industrial warfare, as the intensifying air war necessitated increased production to replace destroyed craft and to meet the front's incessant demands for more aircraft. It had to be sufficiently simple to lend itself to serial production, yet of sufficient reliability and performance to be effective under rapidly changing frontline conditions, despite its limited combat life. It demanded much higher standards of precision and reliability than the automobile, as many an automotive manufacturer who entered aviation production learned. Airplanes were not like small arms or artillery, which were of standard types that changed infrequently and could be produced by state-run arsenals. Airplane types obsolesced in months, and airplane designs underwent modifications frequently.

Even more demanding than aircraft design was engine technology. The engine is the heart of the airplane, and the invention of certain engine types, as much as or even more than airplane types, ushered in particular eras of powered flight and of military aviation. Yet with the exception of a few works on engines that do not relate their development to other aspects of military aviation, historians have overlooked engines. This study, however, gives aero engines a prominent place, one more reflective of their actual importance than previous histories of World War I airpower acknowledge.

The English have set the standard and tone for works on aviation in the Great War. Their official history, *The War in the Air,* remains the sole official history of the air war. The Germans completed only fragments of theirs, the French compiled an official history of military aviation in 1980, and in the 1970s the United States issued four volumes of edited documentary materials on the air service in World War I. Furthermore, British and Dominion aviators have left far more reminiscences about their experiences than aviators from other countries. British or Commonwealth historians have done much of the best—in some instances the only—work on airpower from 1914 to 1918.

The plethora of British memoirs contrasts with a relative paucity of French and German accounts. The few German memoirs are often matter-of-fact recountings of exploits. The few French memoirs, unlike British, German, and American narratives, are occasionally melodramatic or gory and often morbid. Yet, among historical accounts published soon after the war, only a French study, Georges Huisman's *Dans les coulisses de l'avi-*

ation, published in 1921, both concentrates on the politics and industry of aviation and criticizes its country's aerial effort. His account contrasts sharply with the laudatory semiofficial tomes that appeared in England, France, and Germany after the war.

Works in English have essentially ignored the French aerial effort, except for the great aces, because the British carried the brunt of the fighting on the Western Front for the war's last two years. The Germans usually receive more attention than the French because they were the enemy, and giving one's defeated enemy his due enhances one's own victory. Historical writing on American aviation in World War I has examined either the air service or the industry, but not both together. I. B. Holley's fine study of American aviation mobilization, *Ideas and Weapons*, advances the thesis that the absence of a guiding doctrine flawed American development of the air weapon. Yet the formulation of a doctrine for an embryonic weapon rapidly evolving in a complex web of military, political, technological, and industrial factors proved extremely difficult.

A comparative assessment combining the various secondary accounts with primary evidence from archives and museums yields enlightening insights about the evolution of airpower. This study's inclusion of industrial production among its emphases necessarily entails significant attention to France, the world's leading manufacturer of aircraft and engines. Its discussion of all the major combatant powers redresses the general tendency to ignore military aviation in Italy, Russia, and Austria-Hungary. Its study of the air forces and the aeronautics industries presents a more complete picture of aviation's development in all powers than studies that focus on either the front or rear. The synthesis in *The Great War in the Air* aims to enable a new appreciation of airpower's importance in the First World War and its intricate evolution in the respective combatant powers.

Acknowledgments

During many years of research for this book, I have received invaluable assistance from numerous institutions and individuals. I sincerely hope that I have overlooked no one in these acknowledgments.

I thank the National Air and Space Museum in Washington, D.C., for welcoming me as the Lindbergh Professor in 1988–89. During that time I accomplished much research and writing on the manuscript and made a legion of friends and colleagues: Martin Harwit, the director of the museum; Von Hardesty, Peter Jakab, Joanne Gernstein, Tom Dietz, Karl Schneide, and Howard Wolko, all Aeronautics Department staff; and Tami Biddle Davis, Ted Robinson, and Jacob Vander Meulen, the museum's visiting staff and fellows. I am indebted to Peter M. Grosz for his friendship, gracious hospitality, and unrestricted access to his extensive archive in Princeton. I also thank the National Archives, my friends and colleagues at the Office of Air Force History, particularly Dick Kohn (now at the University of North Carolina, Chapel Hill) and Dan Mortensen. At the Air Force Historical Research Center at Maxwell Air Force Base, chief Elliot Converse was especially helpful.

In London the resources of the Public Record Office, the Imperial War Museum, the Air Historical Branch of the Ministry of Defense, and the Royal Air Force Museum Hendon were crucial to my research. I am indebted to my friend Sebastian Cox of the Air Historical Branch for his hospitality and invaluable assistance there and at Hendon. In Paris the Service Historique de l'Armée de l'Air (in particular my colleague Patrick Facon), the Musée de l'Air, the Archives Nationales, and historian Emmanuel Chadeau all rendered significant aid. I have acknowledged those who have given me assistance in Germany and Austria in previous books, but again I express gratitude to the staffs of the Bundesarchiv in Koblenz, the Bundesarchiv-Militärarchiv in Freiburg, the Deutsches Museum and the Bayerisches Kriegsarchiv in Munich, and the Osterreichisches Kriegsarchiv in Vienna.

I thank the University of Tennessee and the University of Georgia and my department heads at those respective institutions, professors Sarah Blanshei and Lester Stephens, for their support. Friends and colleagues Lee Kennett and William Leary of the University of Georgia, James Laux of the University of Cincinnati, and Robin Higham of Kansas State University have offered encouragement and directed me to valuable sources. The office manager of the history department at the University of Tennessee, Susan Felker, typed drafts of early chapters. Ultimately, I am indebted to the Smithsonian Institution Press, to its director, Felix C. Lowe, and to editors Jenelle Walthour and Jan McInroy for their work and advice on the book.

Finally, I thank my family. My parents, Ann Rowena and John, Sr., have stood by me through the years, as have my mother- and father-in-law, Ruth and James Batts. My two children Kieran and Evan and my wife Diane have always given me their unfailing support and understanding. In addition to managing the responsibilities of school, career, and family, Diane has been variously a researcher, proofreader, editor, and general adviser through three books. She has made it all possible, and I dedicate this book to her.

CHAPTER ONE

To 1914

"Flying has been brought to a point where it can be of great use in . . . scouting and carrying messages in time of war."

THE WRIGHT BROTHERS TO CONGRESSMAN M. NEVIN, 18 JANUARY 1905[1]

"Everything presently serves war, there is no invention whose military use the military does not contemplate, no single invention that it will not endeavor to use for military ends."

NICHOLAS FEDOROV, 1906[2]

From its origins flight offered the prospect of a new arena of warfare. Within 10 years of the Montgolfier brothers' first ascent in a hot air balloon in 1783, the French Revolutionary army had formed an airship company of captive balloons for observation. In July 1849 Habsburg unmanned balloons launched from ships bombarded Venice, though lightly and ineffectively, before the city was subdued by artillery. Both sides in the American Civil War used tethered balloons for observation, while in the Franco-Prussian War the French used free balloons to lift mail and people over the

1

Prussian siege of Paris in 1871. Yet free flight in balloons was a difficult and unreliable proposition, since the balloon was completely at the mercy of capricious wind currents and weather. While such flight could satisfy a thirst for adventure, it had limited military potential. By the 1890s the European armies' airship units employed only captive observation balloons, of which the preferred type was the German sausage-shaped Drachen. The British army used captive balloons in its 1880s African campaigns and during the Boer War; the French used them in colonial campaigns in Tonkin in 1884 and on Madagascar in 1895; the Americans used them in Cuba during the 1898 Spanish-American War.

The Military and Powered Flight to 1909

The military's adoption and use of observation balloons paved the way for its later acceptance of powered flight. The military units in charge of balloons usually assumed the responsibility for powered flight. Their operational mobility requirement—the capability to launch or dismantle ships within 30 minutes to incorporate them into an army's line of march—foreshadowed the early demands that the military would place on dirigibles and airplanes. Ballooning also gave rise to a network of aviation technology societies—composed of soldiers, scientists, and engineers promoting technology—and aeronautical clubs—consisting of supporters of practical balloon flight. Both types of organizations later sponsored powered flight. Historian Lee Kennett points out that in 1883, one year before the dirigible's invention, Albert Robida's *War in the Twentieth Century* envisaged a sudden, crushing air strike, while Ivan S. Bloch's 1898 treatise on warfare expected bombardment from airships in the near future.[3] By the end of the nineteenth century, balloon flight had provided a foundation of civilian and military institutions and established certain expectations for military powered flight.

The French army pioneered military powered lighter-than-air flight in dirigibles. In 1884 French army officers Charles Renard and Arthur Krebs invented the first successful nonrigid dirigible, which was powered by an 8-hp electric motor. Renard, a graduate of the École Polytechnique and in 1877 instrumental in establishing the world's first aeronautical laboratory at Chalais-Meudon, became the head of the army's new Directorate of Military Aerial Ballooning in 1888. The absence of a suitable engine thwarted his later efforts to build a 100-hp dirigible and prompted the army to wait until private industry could furnish dirigibles. Overworked and burdened by this failure and the rejection of his candidacy to the French Academy of

Sciences in 1904, Renard committed suicide on 13 April 1905. This tragic figure had laid the experimental foundation for French military aviation at Meudon.

The invention of the gasoline engine in the 1880s and the development of more reliable and efficient high-speed gasoline engines in the 1890s made powered flight a definite possibility by the turn of the twentieth century. The French army bought the first military airship, a nonrigid dirigible, from the Lebaudy brothers in 1906 and issued the first contract for a military airship from them later that year. By the end of 1907 the French army was developing a fleet of transportable dirigibles like the Lebaudy ship La Patrie, which was 3,500 cubic meters in volume, 60 meters long, and smaller, cheaper, and easier to handle than the Zeppelin—a newer and more frightening behemoth east of the Rhine.[4]

In Germany in the early 1890s Swabian Count Ferdinand von Zeppelin had proposed a rigid airship that would be able to fly for a week, tow transport vehicles in an "aerial express train," explore the African interior, fly over the North Pole, and serve as a vehicle for long-range reconnaissance, bombardment, and troop and supply transport. After checkered beginnings—an 18-minute flight in 1900 by his first Zeppelin and an abortive second dirigible—in 1907 Zeppelin's third ship, the LZ3, flew 350 kilometers in under eight hours. The German General Staff and the Imperial Office of the Interior overruled a reluctant Prussian War Ministry, granted Zeppelin more funds, and challenged him to cover at least 700 kilometers in 24 hours of uninterrupted flight with his airship. The LZ3's 11,300 cubic-meter volume and 128-meter length dwarfed other airships, but its greater flexibility and load would be partially offset by its dependence on bases in Germany.

A 12-hour round trip by Zeppelin's LZ4 on 1 July 1908 unleashed such a clamor in the German press that the War Ministry awarded Zeppelin more funds. The LZ4's fiery destruction on 5 August 1908 while attempting the 24-hour voyage spurred a popular campaign that raised over seven million marks for Zeppelin construction, enabling the count to establish airship and engine companies. The resulting enthusiasm of the General Staff, civilian agencies, and the Kaiser, who had encouraged Zeppelin and would proclaim him "the greatest German of the twentieth century" before its first nine years elapsed, forced the War Ministry to accept the LZ3 as army airship Z1 early in 1909, before the Zeppelin had met its performance stipulations.[5] By 1909 the army had also accepted a Parseval airship of some 2,500 cubic meters in volume and 50 meters in length, with its own semirigid dirigible.[6]

In England, as historian Alfred Gollin has shown, the flight of the LZ4 portended a new avenue of assault on the island nation: the air.[7] Press magnate Alfred Harmsworth, the Lord Northcliffe, had recognized that "England was no longer an island" when Alberto Santos-Dumont flew in 1906, although his conception of the threat as "aerial chariots of a foe descending upon England" indicated no realistic appraisal of its nature.[8] R. B. Haldane, who became Secretary of State for War in 1906, was interested in aviation and in 1907 monitored British experiments carefully. H. G. Wells's *The War in the Air*, published in 1907, dramatically portrayed the destruction of cities and, ultimately, of civilization by gigantic airships and planes in the first major aerial conflict.[9] After Zeppelin's flight of 1908, Lord Northcliffe's *Daily Mail* carried speculations about Germany's use of airships to invade England. In October 1908 the Committee of Imperial Defense (CID) established a subcommittee on aerial navigation, before which the Honorable Sir Charles Rolls of Rolls Royce testified in December that "England will cease to be an island."[10] A General Staff memorandum on the subject in November noted other nations' efforts in aviation and acknowledged that airships would likely be used for reconnaissance and, possibly, for bombing in future conflict. The subcommittee's final report was due shortly after the new year. Meanwhile, at the Government Balloon Factory at Farnborough, the semirigid airships, Nulli Secundus I and II, failed to live up to their portentous names in 1907 and 1908.

By the end of 1908 airships had not emerged from the experimental stage. Germany and France led the other powers in military lighter-than-air aviation. In Italy a dirigible built by two lieutenants of the Italian War Ministry's Engineers Brigade, who had been assigned the task by their commander in 1904, flew over Rome in October 1908. In the United States the U.S. Army Signal Corps accepted its first dirigible in 1908.

At the end of 1908, therefore, the military effectiveness of the dirigible was still questionable, and the suitability of the various types for warfare remained undetermined. At this crucial juncture, when armies were beginning to acquire airships, the airplane burst upon the stage of European aviation. The French army had been interested in heavier-than-air flight before it was practical. From 1892 to 1894 the French War Ministry subsidized inventor Clément Ader with 550,000 francs to develop a steerable flying machine capable of carrying passengers or explosives at a speed of 55 kilometers per hour at an altitude of several hundred meters—a performance that would be some 15 years in advance of aviation technology. In stipulating a military vehicle, the War Ministry was not guiding Ader along paths that he was loath to tread. Like future aviation inventors, he believed that aviation should be used first and foremost in the national defense, and he regarded the military establishment as a source of subsidies and contracts. The early aviation inventors did not balk at their creations' potentially bellicose applications. They actively sought the military's attention, often with claims that their inventions would end war. In Ader's case the army, disappointed at the lack of results, ceased its aid, and in 1898, at the age of 58, Ader abandoned his experiments to write about aviation. Like other aeronautical experimenters before the twentieth century, he had been defeated by the absence of a light, powerful, and reliable engine.[11]

That same year, 1898, the only other military establishment to sponsor heavier-than-air flight—the U.S. War Department's Board of Ordnance and Fortification—granted $50,000 for the airplane project of Smithsonian scientist S. P. Langley, whose abject failure in 1903 made the War Department wary of future winged projects.

The only significant heavier-than-air flights before 1908 were Wilbur and Orville Wright's experiments. After their first flight at Kitty Hawk on 17 December 1903, they remained far ahead of European competition through 1908. Yet European skeptics, particularly the French, believed either that the Wright brothers had not flown or that their exploits were insignificant. French seaplane designer Antoine Odier and aviator and inventor Albert Etévé acknowledged that the Wrights had flown but were convinced that their achievements were ignored until the Wrights appeared in Europe in 1908, by which time French aviators believed they had technologically surpassed the Wrights. On the contrary, however, the Wrights' exploits had not been ignored, and French aviators had not surpassed their efforts as of 1908.[12]

Despite their efforts, the Wrights had no military contracts. Although they advised Congressman Nevin on the flying machine's usefulness in January 1905, the U.S. War Department's Board of Ordnance and Fortification rejected their offer of a "Flyer." The brothers then conducted intermittent negotiations with the British, French, and German armies between 1905 and 1908. The British War Office insisted on flight demonstrations with no prior commitment to purchase, while the brothers, afraid of piracy, insisted on an advance guarantee of purchase if the plane met its advertised performance. French performance stipulations remained beyond attainment, and the Prussian War Ministry found the price too high. The Wrights were unwilling to haggle over their $200,000 price for the machine and patent rights because they were convinced that no one else could develop a practical airplane within five years. Confident of their achievement, yet confronted with these impasses and dogged by the fear of patent espionage, the

Wrights dismantled their aircraft and did not fly from October 1905 until May 1908.[13]

Neither the interest nor the negotiations ceased, however. German General Staff Captain Hermann von der Lieth-Thomsen advised his superiors early in 1907 that it was dangerous merely to observe foreign aerial progress, but General Staff negotiations with the Wrights foundered on the War Ministry's continued objections to the price. German interest rekindled French ardor, but once again French stipulations—the ability to take off from any location, to clear uneven terrain, and carry an observer to a minimum 300-meter altitude—stymied the brothers. By 1907 British army balloon chief Col. J. E. Capper, who had earlier been interested in buying a Wright plane, had become more interested in sponsoring the aviation experiments of Britain's resident American wild West showman Samuel Cody and British Lt. John Dunne. The pressures of the arms race in the early twentieth century kept the European powers, particularly the French and Germans, interested in the Wrights, but not sufficiently to meet the brothers' demands.[14]

The foreign interest may have had some effect in the United States. In 1907 the U.S. War Department sent Maj. G. O. Squier to Europe to study aviation progress and established an aeronautical division in the office of the chief of the Signal Corps, which requested bids for both an airplane and an airship (which it received in 1908). The Wright brothers won the airplane contract, and when Congress failed to appropriate the $200,000 requested by the Signal Corps for aviation in 1907, the U.S. Board of Ordnance and Fortification covered the contract's cost. Although at flight trials at Fort Myer, Virginia, the plane surpassed the contract's performance requirements, its crash on 17 September 1908, severely injuring Orville Wright and killing Lt. T. E. Selfridge, delayed acceptance of the U.S. Army's first airplane until August 1909.[15]

In 1908, while the Wrights negotiated, a small coterie of French inventors began to make significant strides in winged flight. After the turn of the century, France had emerged as the European center of winged flight. French army Capt. Ferdinand Ferber, a polytechnician and artilleryman whom Renard brought to Meudon in 1904, managed a powered glide in 1905 similar to the Wright brothers' first flight in 1903. Brazilian emigré Alberto Santos-Dumont, the toast of Paris since a 1901 dirigible flight, flew a box kite-like machine 220 meters in November 1906. Although neither accomplishment deserved much military note, in 1905 engineer Gen. Joseph Jacques Césaire Joffre recognized the necessity of continuing aeronautical research, although he had reservations about the army's practical use of airplanes.[16]

By then the French possessed the best-known early European airplane engine, engineer Léon Levavasseur's V8 Antoinette of 24 and then 50 horsepower. The Wright brothers' four-cylinder engine had produced 12 and later 30 horsepower at 180 pounds. The 50-hp Antoinette weighed only 110 pounds because Levavasseur, through trial and error, determined the minimum admissible engine weight by reducing the parts' thickness until they broke under tests.[17]

The 24-hp Antoinette had powered Santos-Dumont's hop in 1906, the year that Gabriel and Charles Voisin founded the first aircraft workshop making planes for sale in the Parisian suburb of Billancourt. Capable craftsmen as teenagers, the Voisin brothers, then in their 20s, had built everything from guns to kites. After Clément Ader's early experimental craft Avion lured Gabriel irretrievably from architecture to aviation, he founded his own firm with 60,000 francs of capital. After an attempt in 1905 to collaborate with another early inventor, Louis Blériot, foundered within the year, he joined forces with his younger brother.[18] On 13 January 1908 the 50-hp Antoinette powered a Voisin biplane flown by French aviator Henri Farman over the first officially monitored closed-circuit kilometer at Issy-les-Moulineaux. The official French history of military aviation proclaims this event "the true birth of practical aviation" because Farman, flying the wheeled Voisin, was the first to manage to take off under the plane's own power, while the Wright biplane lacked wheels and required a launching apparatus.[19]

Farman had managed to stay airborne for 30 minutes by August 1908, when Wilbur Wright arrived in France to show the brothers' wares. By December Wright had astounded French spectators by easily outdistancing French competition and raising the duration record to two hours and 20 minutes. That month French businessmen Henri Deutsch de la Meurthe and Lazare Weiller founded the Compagnie Générale de la navigation aérienne to exploit the Wright patent. Yet the official French history of military aviation suggests that Farman's exploit in the Voisin during the fall held more significance for military aviation than the Wrights' achievements.[20] Perhaps French pride led them to denigrate the Wrights' achievements and exaggerate Farman's successes.

On 30 October 1908 Farman made the first cross-country flight, some 27 to 30 kilometers from Bouy to Reims. The Technical Section of the German General Staff reported that "with this flight of 30 kilometers, a new epoch in aviation has dawned. Farman is the first aviator to leave the maneuver field and undertake a flight to a distant destination—admittedly over flat but nonetheless built-up terrain."[21] This assessment confirmed Farman's importance to military aviation in a crucial sense: as long as the airplane's takeoff was tied to a launching apparatus and its flight bound by a maneuver field, the military perceived it to be of little practical use. In 1908 overland flight demonstrated the airplane's potential for reconnaissance and communications, and thus its military significance.

In the summer of 1908 the Prussian War Ministry's Transport Inspectorate, which was in charge of aviation, debated whether to build its own airplane or to aid domestic inventors, deciding to wait until inventors showed more promise. In the fall the War Ministry and General Staff agreed that airplanes would be useful for reconnaissance and communication, but the War Ministry—ironically in view of its reservations about the Zeppelin—believed that the Zeppelin enabled the German army to wait until private initiative perfected a military airplane. The War Ministry obviously preferred to wait for both, while the General Staff desired to forge ahead with airplane and airship development. By the fall some 10 private enterprises around Germany were building airplanes. In October former bicycle and automobile manufacturer August Euler founded the first German airplane company in Darmstadt, followed by a second in November established by Edmund Rumpler in Berlin.[22]

In Austria-Hungary, as in Germany, the General Staff wished to take the initiative in aviation, while the War Ministry exercised restraint because of the cost and the embryonic nature of the technology. In 1907 General Staff chief Franz Conrad von Hötzendorff, who was observing foreign developments, was already pressing for aviation forces. In October 1908 Conrad advocated the support of any inventor who had a useful aircraft project, but the War Ministry was interested only in proven machines. Its negotiations with a Wright representative, however, collapsed over price.[23]

In Britain J. E. Capper continued to sponsor airplane inventors Cody and Dunne at Farnborough, while individuals like Alliott V. Roe and the three Short brothers, Horace, Oswald, and Eustace, were experimenting on their own. In September 1908 the War Office issued aircraft specifications, which included the ability to rise from the ground under the craft's own power, thus effectively eliminating the Wrights' flyer from consideration.[24]

By the end of 1908 the Wrights' exploits had also kindled interest in Italy, where the commander of the War Ministry's Engineers Brigade proposed to establish a flying school in Rome, and in Russia, where the War Ministry considered buying Wright biplanes only months after its Main Engineering Directorate had concluded in April that aviation, while it might be important in the future, was not then suitable for military use. The future seemed to be fast arriving, and with it came heightened hopes and fears about aviation's military potential.

Even in these early days of aviation, international jurists deemed its destructive potential significant enough to attempt to delineate the ramifications of aerial warfare for international law. There was little agreement among them on the legitimate uses of aviation in warfare—some were willing to allow aerial bombing but not fighting; others were willing to permit reconnaissance, communications, and exploration but not bombing. Peace conferences at the Hague in 1899 and 1907 included discussions of air warfare. In 1899 concern for the dirigible's potential as a bomber had led to five-year prohibitions against the discharge of projectiles and explosives from balloons and against bombing undefended towns and cities. Yet this decision was obtained only in the absence of effective and proven bombers, since the French, German, and Russian representatives would not foreclose using new weapons in warfare. In 1907 the Hague conferees agreed only not to bomb undefended towns and villages.[25] The closer the aerial machine drew to usefulness as a weapon, the closer international jurists edged to acknowledging its legitimacy as a weapon. Admittedly, within four years British international lawyers would lament the very existence of flying machines, as did some British military figures. Yet such anomalous wishful thinking undoubtedly reflected the aerial weapon's potential to affect Britain more profoundly than the continental powers, since it made the British vulnerable to a threat with which they had always contended—attack and invasion from their neighbors.

In France and Germany a popular clamor for aviation, particularly military aviation, became more apparent in 1908. Edmond Petit pointed out that during 1908 aviation became a "universal preoccupation" in France and aviators became popular heroes.[26] While he attributed this change in public attitude to the aviation press, also underlying the publicity were the recent dramatic achievements of Zeppelins and airplanes. As airships and airplanes impressed the public, military aviation leagues formed in Germany and France. The German Air Fleet League, modeled after the German Navy League, was formed to promote military aviation in the summer of 1908. By 1909 it had 3,000 members and a board of prominent military, industrial, and political figures including Ernst Bassermann, parliamentary leader of the National Liberal Party. In France in September 1908 propagandist René Quinton formed the National Aviation League, whose vice president was Paul Painlevé, a future prime minister and war minister. By February 1909 the Senate and Chamber of Deputies contained groups on aerial locomotion, the latter having 82 members. Farsighted civilians began to envisage the possibilities of military aviation. In late 1908 Prince Pierre d'Arenberg, president of a provincial automobile club in the department of Cher, conceived of making the department an aviation center. From this seed, through civil-military cooperation, would grow France's largest prewar flying school and famous wartime training field at Avord.[27]

The circumstances surrounding the German army's acceptance of the Zeppelin Z1 in 1908, when the public had actively intervened to promote the Zeppelin to the War Ministry, indicated that governments would have to contend with public opinion—a new factor in their decisions on military aviation. Previously military aviation had aroused virtually no public interest, and the military had been able to approach aviation in relative isolation. By the end of 1908, flight was being drawn into the web of increasingly bellicose popular attitudes encouraging militarization, and these formed the context for European aviation's development in the five-and-one-half years left before the war.

Historians have often judged European military establishments to have been conservative in their attitudes toward technological innovation, and have faulted the military leadership for its alleged reluctance to adopt the airplane.[28] Yet no sponsors stood ready to develop aviation for commerce or sport beyond the prizes for distance flights offered by the press or interested individuals. The military response was certainly less conservative than that of other European institutions.

The French army, true to its long aeronautics tradition, led other armed forces in its support of powered flight. Aviation historian Lt. Col. René Chambe, writing before World War II, claimed that "in many cases the army, by rational utilization, was able to give inventions a practical quality and to enable a development to which their inventors could never have aspired if left to their own devices."[29] Yet Ader's example suggests some exaggeration of the army's constructive role on Chambe's part. The French War Ministry had supported Ader handsomely, but its requirements were not practical. In its zeal to have a military instrument, the War Ministry's stipulations were far beyond the current aviation technology. In fact, the military essentially capitalized on the initiatives of the successful early inventors like Zeppelin, the Wrights, Levavasseur, and Voisin. Nevertheless, the French War Ministry—especially when compared to the more cautious attitude of other European war ministries—deserves much credit for its sponsorship of aviation inventors at the early stages of powered flight.

Within both the military establishment and the aviation industry, individuals who would prove instrumental to World War I aviation had already begun to play significant roles by 1909. German General Staff Capt. Hermann von der Lieth-Thomsen, who encouraged the army's active espousal of aviation in 1907, would become the key figure in wartime German aviation and the architect of the German army's air service. Lieth-Thomsen's superior in 1908, Erich Ludendorff, an ardent advocate of aviation, would be commander in 1916 to 1918, as the Chief Quartermaster General who directed the war effort in its final two years. In France Gen. J. J. C. Joffre, who chaired the commission on Ferber's experiments in 1905, commanded the army during the first two years of the war. The military aviation research institute at Meudon had become a repository of aviation expertise. Lieutenant J. B. E. Dorand, for example, who was first assigned to Meudon in 1894, would be a wartime chief in the French aviation procurement bureaucracy. Within the aviation industry, both Voisin and Farman became important to the war effort.

The invention of suitable engines determined the boundaries of achievement of flight. In the heyday of the Antoinette and the Wrights' engine, firms such as the Gnome engine company and the Renault automobile firm were already at work on superior designs that would raise flight to higher plateaus. Succeeding years would witness the rise of the aero engine industry and its production of more reliable and powerful engines, enabling flying machines to become practical instruments of warfare.

In 1908, however, such reliability lay in the future. The airship and the airplane were still in their infancy and their suitability for military use was more a matter of conjecture than proven fact. Aviation everywhere was of low military priority, which was compounded in countries such as Austria-Hungary and Russia by the relative lack of a substantial industrial base and government funding. By the end of the year aeronautics was on the verge of acceptance by the military establishments; 1909 to 1914 would witness its transformation into an instrument of modern warfare.

The Military and the Origins of the Aviation Industry, 1909–1911

"In 1909 powered aviation came of age. The aeroplane became technically mature and established in the public mind . . . , and the beginnings of national aircraft industries, as well as government concern for aviation, were now to be seen throughout Europe."

CHARLES R. GIBBS-SMITH[30]

In 1909 French achievements—Louis Blériot's crossing of the English Channel in July and the Reims aviation week in August—stimulated aviation development and military interest everywhere. The workshops of a small coterie of talented aviator-designers, particularly the two Voisin and three Farman brothers, Louis Blériot, Louis Breguet, Alfred de Niéport, and Robert Esnault-Pelterie (known by his initials REP) formed the nucleus of France's prewar aircraft industry. As bourgeois, they enjoyed a certain material ease that enabled their pursuit of the fanciful goal of flight. The Voisins had inherited their grandfather's wealth; REP, who held a degree in physics, was the heir of a wealthy cotton manufacturer; Niéport was the son of an army colonel; Blériot, who had managed a Paris automobile headlight factory, was an engineer and mathematician trained at the École Centrale; Breguet was an engineer working in his father's electrical equipment factory; and Henri and Maurice Farman, who had gravitated from bicycle racing and automobile sales to aviation, were the sons of a British journalist residing in France. They were all independent inventors and test pilots and all, except Dick Farman, earned aviator's brevets in 1909, the first year of the aviator's license. Voisin's firm, the oldest, had fewer than 20 employees in 1909. This small work force, which included the owners, built each part of the plane successively, acquired parts they could not produce from the sawmills, foundries, and lathe shops of Paris, and then, using primarily hand tools, assembled the planes one at a time on a frame in the middle of the workshop. These shops' financial condition remained precarious as the inventors struggled to find a lucrative market.[31]

Equally crucial to French aerial ascendancy were the engine manufacturers. Blériot's monoplane vaulted the Channel powered by a light, compact three-cylinder "fan-type" air-cooled engine of 24.5 horsepower. It was designed and built by Italian Alexander Anzani, a temperamental self-taught mechanic and former motorcycle racer, who fired workers when engine tests failed with "le direct," the jab, ejecting them bodily from his employ and leaving them with black eyes or missing teeth as severance pay.[32] Anzani also developed the first practical air-cooled radial engines, three-cylinder types, producing first 22.5 and then 35 horsepower in 1910. Before and during the coming war these engines would equip nonflying French trainers, called "rouleurs" or "pingouins," that accustomed student pilots to the feel of a plane on the ground and on the verge of flight.

Perhaps the single most important prewar engine was the famed Gnome rotary, which gave tremendous impetus to European aviation. Invented by Laurent Séguin, the Gnome first appeared in 1908 in a five-cylinder version but evolved quickly into its classic forms, a 50-hp, 165-pound seven-cylinder engine in 1909 and a later 80-hp nine-cylinder model. Gnome, the Séguin family's firm, had been founded in 1905 to build internal-combustion engines but had lost money until its beautifully crafted little engine dominated the Reims air meeting.

In the usual engine configuration the cylinders are fixed around (in the radial or fan-type engine) or along (in the in-line) the crankcase, in which the crankshaft rotates. In the rotary the cylinders whirled around a fixed crankshaft with the propeller, creating gyroscopic movements that initially frightened some aviators. Rotaries had no carburetor to regulate fuel flow and thus engine speed, so the pilot reduced power for landing by intermittently cutting the ignition, relying on the continued whirling of the engine and unabated fuel flow to restart as necessary. A cowl kept the unused, sometimes flaming, oil and gas that shot out of the revolving cylinders from setting the plane on fire, but nothing could protect the pilot from the fumes of castor oil, the sole lubricant capable of withstanding the heat and pressure inside a rotary. If this seemed rather hazardous, early flight was fraught with hazards, and Gnomes compensated with their light weight, power, and reliability. They would be imitated by many builders and exported to all countries, as early fliers soared to new heights powered by their whirling pistons.[33]

French feats increased the soaring popularity of flight, already evident in 1908. The cradle of French aviation, Issy-les-Moulineaux along the Seine outside Paris, became the rendezvous of the social elite, who arrived fashionably attired in their automobiles. These aerial meetings attracted gigantic crowds—an estimated 250,000 delirious spectators at Reims in 1909, another 200,000 at the races at Issy-les-Moulineaux in 1911— whose infatuation with and faith in aviation electrified French builders. Aviation became the newest sport, attracting former bicycle, motorcycle, and automobile racers. The aviator, the newest daredevil, worshipped by crowds of adoring followers—particularly women—possessed an allure that carried over into wartime. In this heady milieu, the aviator had to be the essence of sangfroid, as Gabriel Voisin demonstrated when he impudently suggested to an impatient and unruly mob, "You have waited ten thousand years to see man fly; you can certainly wait ten minutes more."[34] This national passion for aviation was the essential context for the French army's adoption of the airplane.

The Reims air meeting provided the catalyst for French military aviation.[35] Before that the small air arm of the War Ministry's Engineers Directorate under General Roques had considered the airplane potentially useful. After Reims the engineers bought two Farmans, two Wrights, and one Blériot to familiarize their officers with the "sport." By then they were not alone in their interest in airplanes. At Reims French artillery officers conceived of using airplanes to locate targets for their vaunted 75mm cannon, and in November the artillery established an air service at Vincennes with five airplanes under the command of an inventive and aggressive officer, Lieutenant Colonel Estienne. Although the War Minister, an artillery general, expediently attempted to justify the division by assigning short-range spotting to the artillery and longer-range reconnaissance to the engineers, this dichotomy was potentially disruptive. From its origins French military aviation would be dogged by bureaucratic fragmentation and infighting between engineers and artillerymen.

Coinciding with the rise of the airplane, the fiery crash of the dirigible le République on 25 September 1909, killing its crew of four, convinced some observers that the dirigible was obsolete. Yet the army bought three airships in 1909, including one after the crash, because the airplane's exact use was uncertain, and the dirigible's superior range and load compensated for its cumbersome characteristics on the ground. Furthermore, the acquisition of airplanes and training of pilots were subject to delays.

The civilian aircraft industry delivered first to private buyers who paid higher prices than the state, thereby delaying military procurement and forcing the army to train pilots at the industry's schools. There sportsmen and wealthy foreign officers, who paid their own way, received priority in training and aircraft over French officers, who in turn resolved to begin the army's own flight-training program.[36] In the summer of 1910 Roques assigned the first breveted military aviators to run new military flight schools at Châlons and Vincennes, which trained 52 army and 6 navy pilots, primarily on Farmans and Blériots, by the end of the year. The military brevet examination, like the civilian, entailed three closed-circuit flights of five kilometers, but the military emphasized cross-country flights. After graduation the officers participated in civilian competitions to hone their skills and stoke the public's interest in military aviation, encouraging such grants as a subscription from the newspaper *Le Temps*, which bought the army four airplanes and a dirigible, and banker Lazare Weiller's 25,000-francs award for the longest nonstop flight by a military aviator with a passenger.

Early in 1910 the struggle within the military bureaucracy for control of aviation extended into the parliament, where under interpellation the War Minister found the division of aviation difficult to justify. In March the senate and government adopted Senator Reymond's proposal that the War Ministry group aviation units as quickly as possible in one autonomous service. On 9 June, two days after the War Minister announced his intention to place the entire aeronautical service under the Engineers Directorate, two artillery fliers staged a spectacular long-distance flight that was designed to mobilize political opinion against the engineers' absorption of the artillery air arm. The fliers became the first airplane pilots to receive the cross of the Legion of Honor, and their feat provoked a challenge to the proposed reorganization from the artillery lobby in the Chamber of Deputies on 20 June, but the War Minister advised that the new arrangement would save some 200,000 francs and might prepare the way for aviation's autonomy.

In September, in Picardy where deep valleys and apple orchards made landing and observation difficult, and constant, strong, and occasionally violent winds made even flight hazardous, the tiny French air arm became the first to participate in military maneuvers. Dirigibles could not fly, but the eight airplanes, piloted by active officers and civilian reservists, sortied on five of the six days despite crashes, clearly demonstrating, to the praise of aviation publications and Le Temps, that airplanes could be used effectively for reconnaissance and liaison.[37] Before the maneuvers, Roques was uncertain of aviation's future; afterward he observed to the War Minister that "airplanes are as indispensable to armies as cannon or rifles."[38]

On 22 October 1910 the War Ministry established in the Engineers Directorate a permanent Inspectorate of Military Aviation over all aviation agencies, although artilleryman Estienne at Vincennes continued to report directly to the War Minister until the fall of 1912. General Roques, now fully convinced aviation's merits, relinquished command of the Engineers Directorate to become the first inspector and promptly set out to improve the quality of planes and pilots. On 7 November he announced a 300-kilometer speed competition for three-seat military airplanes. The prizes of contracts for 10, 6, and 4 planes for the first three finishers, respectively, were designed to stimulate competition in the industry to build heavier military types, although a year would elapse before the competition was held.

In 1911 the army imposed more stringent demands on its pilots. On 13 July 1911 Colonel Hirschauer, commander of the Flying Troops, observed that individual exploits, such as long-range flights to impress the public, were less important than the abilities to follow orders, to fly in weather that civilians would not risk, and to function as a team under a single command.[39] A new military brevet in 1911 that required three flights of 100 kilometers was passed by only 31 pilots, the first of whom was Lt. Tricornot de Rose, the commander of the first French Pursuit Group during the coming war. The aircraft competition's stipulation of three-seat airplanes, Hirschauer's memorandum, and the new military brevet indicated the growing divergence of military from civilian aviation by 1911.

The fall maneuvers demonstrated that airplanes could locate an enemy's exact position at 60 kilometers and that two-seaters were superior to single-seaters for reconnaissance, and also suggested the need for squadrons of similar airplanes, which were introduced in 1912. General Roques further contemplated the need for airplanes equipped with weapons to fight aerial adversaries and projectiles to bomb and demoralize enemy troops. He was not alone in conceiving of the airplane as a weapon. In 1909 Clément Ader, envisaging a short war, foresaw that airplanes would be used to create terror by raids on cities, attacks that could only be prevented by the formation of an independent air force. In 1910 Lt. Albert Etévé of Meudon had contemplated the potential effects of bombing attacking skirmishers. In the *Revue générale de l'aéronautique militaire* in 1911, Belgian officer Lieutenant Poutrin suggested that the aerial bombardment of urban centers and government capitals could disorganize a nation's life and weaken its morale. The artillery flyers had already attempted the first bombings with shells and fléchettes (metal antipersonnel darts) when Roques and the War Ministry in November 1911 ordered bombing exercises, anticipating "the offensive use of airplanes . . . for attacking and using projectiles against troops in dense formation."[40]

While such speculations might be considered the germ of aerial doctrine, Col. Félix Marie, writing in 1924 about the early years of French military aviation, wisely pointed out that ideas greatly preceded realization in aviation and what counted was the realization.[41] Doctrinal debates surrounded French aviation from its inception and would affect its future direction; yet technology and industry, through their creation of the implements of doctrine, determined the extent to which any doctrine could be realized. General Roques, a practical man, considered doctrine premature.

The realization of present and future aims lay ultimately with the aviation industry, whose lifeblood consisted increasingly of military contracts. After the Seine flooded and wrecked the Voisin factory in April 1910, only an order of 35 planes from Meudon prevented its financial collapse. The army ordered 208 planes in 1910 to 1911, of which 157 were delivered by the end of 1911. The military preferred Farmans, Blériots, Voisins, and REPs, in that order. The engines in these planes were Renaults (51.8% of the total), Gnomes (22.3%), Anzanis (22.3%), and REPs (3.8%). Selection by aircraft manufacturers determined an engine's success: the Farman brothers preferred Renaults, which also powered a few Voisin planes, while the Gnomes were beginning to equip a variety of types, displacing, for example, the Anzani at Blériot.[42] At the fall 1911 military competition near Reims, three monoplanes, all powered by Gnome rotaries, won: Nieuport received a total subsidy of 780,000 francs, for a speed of 117 kilometers per hour; Breguet received 345,000 francs; and Deperdussin won 218,000 francs. The Gnomes' domination was complete, and the Renault 70-hp air-cooled V8 also performed well. As the success of Breguet and

Deperdussin at the military competition indicated, new airplane firms were supplementing or supplanting the original builders. Breguet, who specialized in steel tube fuselage construction, built 7 to 8 planes in 1910 and some 30 in 1911, the year he founded his firm with 800,000 francs of capital, 12 staff members, and 50 workers. In 1910 Deperdussin, a wealthy, debonair, and freewheeling silk broker, had established engineer Louis Béchereau in business at Betheny near Reims.[43] The industry continued to produce planes and engines by handicraft procedures. Lucien Coupet, aero-engine mechanic at the automobile firm of De Dion Bouton in 1911, recalled, "I was brought all the pieces of an engine loose in a box. To assemble a motor took a full month. That was the work of the time."[44] The work of Coupet and other skilled craftsmen enabled the ascendancy of French aviation.

In 1909 to 1911 the German army made crucial choices about dirigibles and airplanes.[45] The press and popular scientific literature had represented the Zeppelin as a symbol of German inventive spirit and greatness, a peerless wonder weapon. The Zeppelin's most notable feature was its rigid airframe of thin aluminum girders. The airframe, covered with waterproof cotton containing the gas cells, gave the ship its streamlined form and provided a strong anchor for the gondola and control surfaces. The outer form of the smaller nonrigid Parseval was maintained by the air pressure within its gas bags, since it had no rigid parts except the detachable stabilizers and a gondola that hung from the ship by a cable system. It could be emptied under field conditions and transported on two vehicles. The semirigid military airship was similar to the Parseval except that it had a keel. In November 1909 at airship battalion maneuvers, a joint War Ministry–General Staff commission, stipulating that airships be as independent of wind and weather as possible so that they might reconnoiter and bomb strategic targets, found all three types inadequate.

During the resulting suspension of military contracts, the Zeppelin firm founded a civilian airship line, Delag, on 16 November 1909 with three million marks. The army subsidized the line, which trained military airship crews, and an airship school established in October 1910 in Friedrichshafen at the initiation of the German Air Fleet League. Although commercial Zeppelins would carry over 35,000 passengers some 170,000 miles without a fatality or injury between 1910 and 1914, accidents in 1910 and 1911 shook the general faith in airships. In April 1910 army airship Z2 was destroyed; two months later the commercial Zeppelin Deutschland was wrecked; by May 1911 two more commercial airships were lost; and in September 1911, the army airship M3 burned at the Kaiser maneuvers.

Airships had not measured up to military expectations in 1910 and 1911 maneuvers. They continued to exhibit inadequate reliability, speed, load, and ceiling, and excessive dependence on the weather. Successful flights of the Delag ship Schwaben in the second half of 1911 encouraged new hope for the military use of Zeppelins, but airplanes were displacing the smaller Parseval and army ships for tactical reconnaissance duties, and the substantial increases in volume and length necessary for the smaller ships to be effective in strategic reconnaissance and bombing would deprive them of their greatest advantages of transportability and collapsibility.

From 1909 to 1911 the airplane progressed enough to threaten the airship's ascendancy in Germany. The Air Fleet League and Aviators Association were instrumental in persuading the army to attempt its own airplane construction in 1909 and also to subsidize the operation of the airfield at Johannisthal near Berlin, where early companies like Rumpler, Wright, and Albatros were located. The early firms copied Austrian, U.S., or French designs and attempted to secure a foothold with the army through pilot training. The founding of the Wright company in May 1909 was apparently sponsored by Walther Rathenau, director of the giant electric company Allgemeine Elektrizitäts-Gesellschaft (AEG), with the encouragement of the Kaiser. Wright's backing from powerful firms like AEG, Krupp, Stinnes, Borsig, and Loewe gave it an extraordinarily large capital of 500,000 marks in 1909 when other firms had no more than 100,000 marks. While the Wright company trained some military pilots, it sold only one plane to the German army in 1911, as other craft had quickly surpassed its airplane's performance. In February 1910 General Staff Chief Helmuth von Moltke recommended that the army train officer pilots. In March the Transport Corps' expert on airplanes—who envisioned their use for reconnaissance, communications, and the destruction of airships by dropping explosives or acid on them from above—suggested the need for a special military organization to stimulate an industry and ensure that it produced planes and engines that would operate under field conditions.

Although some observers believed that a paucity of orders prevented the German aircraft industry from overtaking the French, the industry's condition—its reliance on foreign designs and the inferior performance of its aircraft—warranted circumspection. German flight competitions were won by French pilots until August 1910, when they were closed to planes built outside Germany. The German motor industry's neglect of aircraft engines forced reliance on French Gnomes and Antoinettes and Austro-Daimler engines, until German Daimler's production of the Austrian design in 1911 gave the German army a domestic source of reliable aero engines.

In the fall of 1910, when Moltke suggested that the army form a military aviation agency and purchase the best airplanes, the same joint commission that had examined airships in 1909 upgraded the Transport Inspectorate to a General Inspectorate and established a subordinate Inspectorate for Aviation and Motor Vehicles with a small allocation—130,000 marks—for airplane procurement.

The German airplane manufacturers, most of whom had formed a trade association in March 1911, looked to the army for contracts. Yet the army's limited aircraft procurement—30 airplanes by the end of 1911—was not sufficient for the industry's survival. Military policies of buying the winners of flight competitions favored the few larger firms such as Albatros, Rumpler, and Aviatik that had the automobiles, technicians, and craftsmen for repairing and refueling aircraft at forced landings. Although Germany's "national awakening" in fall 1911 after the Moroccan crisis prompted some companies' expansion, military contracts remained meager. The German Air Fleet League, which had about 12,500 members in 1912, had pressed for a national fund for the airplane industry since July 1911, while the Aviators Association, with some 70 member associations and 60,000 members, staged contests. Since there was no civilian market for airplanes, however, the investment of significant private capital in the industry depended on military interest, and the military proceeded cautiously.

The German army preferred stolid, slow, stable airplanes—the Taube, a birdlike, Austrian designed monoplane, and large biplanes. The General Staff liked airplanes because they were easier to handle, service, house, and prepare for flight, and were faster and harder to shoot down, than airships. In the *Vierteljahrshefte für Truppenführung und Heereskunde*, Major Lieth-Thomsen warned against overestimating the capabilities of airships, and he expected that the surprisingly rapid development of airplanes would soon render them more suitable for strategic and tactical reconnaissance than airships. He further anticipated that aerial reconnaissance would lead to aerial struggle, just as cavalry reconnaissance had led to clashes on the ground. The War Ministry insisted that the longer-ranged airship was safer and more suitable for reconnaissance. In the fall of 1911 Moltke recommended using the funds designated for smaller airships to purchase airplanes, as the army's three Zeppelins, with the Schwaben in reserve, would suffice for strategic reconnaissance. War Minister August von Heeringen and transport General Inspector Alfred von Lyncker preferred to continue all three systems, given the army's sizable investment in contracts, trained personnel, and dockyards. On 25 October the War Minister emphasized to Kaiser Wilhelm the importance of preserving Germany's advantage in airships over France at all costs, especially given France's supremacy in airplanes, and with the Kaiser's agreement the army continued its emphasis on airships and the division of airship funds among all three types.

The reasons for this questionable decision were many. Ruling circles, who regarded the airship as a symbol of German aerial superiority and a political and military means of pressure on foreign countries, were reluctant to admit failures. Airship manufacturers Zeppelin and Maj. August von Parseval, and subcontractors, who had hired former officers of the airship battalion, had excellent connections in the War Ministry and further threatened to sell airships abroad to potential enemies Britain and Russia. The decision to continue the emphasis on airships was based on a combination of military, political, and economic factors.

In November 1911, when General Staff Chief Moltke proposed the purchase of 112 additional planes by October 1912, the War Ministry intended to procure only 34 and had no plans to support a larger industry at the end of 1911. The French army had allocated 9.7 million francs for aviation in 1911, most of which went to airplanes; the German army designated 4.38 million marks, of which 2.25 million went to airplanes. Nineteen eleven was the only prewar year in which funds for airplanes exceeded those for airships in Germany, and the War Ministry's decisions at the end of the year ensured it would not happen again. Yet its policy of strict frugality had led to an impasse: while the War Ministry and General Inspectorate insisted on making their investment contingent on the industry's prior development of warplanes, the industry needed the state's money to develop its products.

The years 1909 to 1911 preceded the concrete development of British military aviation.[46] The 28 January 1909 report of the aerial navigation subcommittee of the Committee of Imperial Defense (CID) concluded that since large-scale aerial attack was not an immediate danger, an allocation of 35,000 pounds for the navy's development of a rigid airship would suffice for the present. As the subcommittee deemed airplane experiments better left to private enterprise, the army abandoned sponsorship of inventors John Dunne and Samuel Cody and continued only a small airship construction program. The only private enterprise then consisted of a few experimenters such as A. V. Roe, the Short brothers, Frederick Handley Page, and Geoffrey de Havilland, all engineers embarking on new careers in aviation.

Others were more concerned about the aerial threat than the government. Lord Northcliffe launched a campaign for aviation through an article in the 15 February 1909 *Times* that discussed how air raids could assist a foreign invasion force. The Aerial League of the British Empire, founded in January, held a large meeting in London on 5 April with extensive press coverage that emphasized British aerial unpreparedness compared to German readiness. In a speech of 21 April, published prominently in the *Times*, Lord Montagu of Beaulieu proclaimed London, the nerve center of government, defenseless and open to strategic air attack. This fear was echoed in a May editorial of the aviation journal *Flight*, the official organ of the Aero Club. R. P. Hearne's book *Aerial Warfare*, published in 1909, proclaimed that everything was at the mercy of the Zeppelin, whose raids would destroy morale and disable military forces. Spurred by this "airship scare," a few members of parliament formed the Parliamentary Aerial Defense Committee to press for military aviation. At the end of April the government established the Advisory Committee for Aeronautics for aviation research, while the National Physical Laboratory at Teddington formed an aviation department. In October, at the recommendation of the Advisory Committee for Aeronautics, the gifted and flamboyant Irish engineer Mervyn O'Gorman was appointed superintendent of the Government Balloon Factory, which would be renamed first the Army Aircraft Factory then the Royal Aircraft Factory.

In 1910 the British government continued to observe aviation. A Committee of Imperial Defense note of 6 October declared that the government was ready to purchase airplanes and train officer pilots. Yet the government's sentiment was more aptly captured in a General Staff comment in July, explaining that although it could not "arrest or retard the perhaps unwelcome progress of aerial navigation," it would be a while before it would be necessary to develop aircraft to defend the island.[47] Britain's two airplane companies—the Short brothers' firm and Sir George White's British and Colonial Aeroplane Ltd. of Bristol lobbied the government for contracts through the press, but the army merely bought two Farmans from Lord Northcliffe's wealthy friend George Holt Thomas for examination. By early 1911 there were four small airdromes in operation: Brooklands, the home of small aircraft workshops; Eastchurch, the future home of naval aviation; Hendon, the future location of Thomas's Aircraft Manufacturing Company (Airco), producing Farmans under license; and Larkhill, where the army and White's Bristol Aircraft Company would locate.

In 1911 both the army and navy displayed somewhat more interest in aviation. The Royal Aircraft Factory emerged under O'Gorman as an experimental institute intended to assist in aircraft design improvements but not to compete with private industry. Yet the factory's very existence symbolized the focus of the British government's aeronautical policy on a state agency at the apparent expense of private inventors and firms. The army's Balloon School became the Engineers Air Battalion, which acquired 13 planes and

3 small airships by winter. The Army Council determined that the battalion needed 80 to 100 aviators, but potential aspirants first had to secure a Royal Aero Club certificate at a private flight school at their own expense. The Vickers's naval airship Mayfly, built with the 1908 allocation and allegedly labeled "the work of a lunatic" by Admiral Sturdee,[48] broke its back before flying, thus ending airship work until another Zeppelin scare. The navy began to train its first officer pilot candidates on Short airplanes at its new naval flight school at Eastchurch airdrome. Naval airmen already considered long-range aerial scouts potentially useful for reconnaissance, bombing, gunfire direction, antisubmarine patrol, and locating enemy minefields, although the Admiralty's interest was essentially in their defensive use to protect the British fleet. Late in the year the new First Lord of the Admiralty, Winston Churchill, showed a keen interest in aviation and establishing a "new corps of airmen."

In 1911 the press and the members of parliament in the Parliamentary Aerial Defense Committee increased the pressure for aviation on the government. *Flight* praised the airplane's value for reconnaissance and its role in French and German maneuvers, and decried the "hopelessness" of the British government's attitude toward air defense, its neglect of aviation compared to the continental powers' advances, and particularly its failure to support a domestic aviation industry.[49] A mid-May flying meeting at Hendon airdrome demonstrated the use of planes for reconnaissance and bombing to members of parliament, Churchill, and others, and in the fall the members of parliament challenged the War Office to buy more airplanes. Undersecretary of State for War Col. J. E. B. Seely explained that the War Office was waiting to select the best plane in a military aircraft competition scheduled for the next summer. *Flight*, unappeased, found the War Office's tentative rewards "parsimonious and unsatisfactory," insufficient to stimulate a domestic industry.[50] Secretary of State for War Richard Haldane later claimed that insular Britain required a smaller air service than France or Germany. But under mounting pressure in November, Prime Minister Herbert H. Asquith asked the CID to consider the future of aviation for naval and military purposes and to propose measures necessary to establish an efficient air service. The aviation budget rose from 9,000 pounds in 1909–10 to 131,000 pounds in 1911–12.

In 1909 growing interest in airplanes in Austria-Hungary was reflected in the formation of a Flight Technology Association by various aviation groups, with the participation of the military chancellery, the highest military agency under the emperor.[51] The joint efforts of city officials, businessmen, and army officers enabled Wiener Neustadt to establish a flying field that became the center of Austrian aviation, while Austrian civilians presented the army with its first three airplanes—a Voisin, a Wright, and a Blériot. On 23 November Igo Etrich became the first Austrian to fly his own machine successfully, while two small aircraft firms—rubber magnate Camillo Castiglioni's Motorluftfahrzeuggesellschaft (MLG) and the aircraft department of the Lohner chassis factory—were established but with no planes ready for the market.

The airplane's reception in the Austro-Hungarian army varied. That fall an aspiring pilot, artillery Lt. Emmanuel Quoika, who had returned from flight school in Paris with his own Blériot and mechanic, was asked pointedly by his colonel, "Do you want to become an aerial acrobat or an artillery captain?" and then ordered to sell the plane.[52] Unlike Quoika's colonel, General Staff Chief Conrad was pressing—albeit unrealistically—for 180 airplanes, 360 pilots, and a domestic industry sustained by the army's aircraft contracts, only to be blocked by the War Minister Gen. Franz von Schönaish, who was reluctant to invest in untested technological inventions and content to rely on gifts until private enterprise could develop a successful warplane. The Austro-Hungarian General Staff and War Ministry thus assumed the same attitudes of promoter and restrainer toward airplanes as did their German counterparts at the time.

In 1910 the rapid improvement of airplanes evident at the Budapest air week in June so impressed the War Ministry's Transport Brigade observers that they recommended buying domestic airplanes to promote the industry and steer it from sport to military uses. In September at the Wiener Neustadt flying meeting, where Conrad flew for the first time, Igo Etrich's Taube monoplane, powered by a 60-hp, 220-pound six-cylinder in-line engine designed by Ferdinand Porsche, technical director of the Austro-Daimler works, performed impressively against foreign competition. Conrad's urgent request to the emperor in November for 200 planes and 400 pilots was effectively checked by Schönaish and Finance Minister Aehrenthal.

In March 1911 the only plane to pass the first army trials was the Taube, which was built by Lohner and delivered by MLG, to whom Etrich had sold the Austrian rights in 1910. The War Ministry's Transport Brigade bought eight. The "Taube" proved effective in fall military maneuvers, and in October the Transport Command formed an aviation unit. By the end of the year the Taube, now equipped with a 120-hp Daimler engine, was joined by a new biplane, the Lohner Pfeilflieger (Arrow-flyer) with a 90- or 120-hp Daimler engine. In the fall of 1911 Conrad urged the procurement of more planes and their development for long-range reconnaissance, bombing, and troop transport. In September War Minister Schönaish stepped down, to be replaced in January 1912 by Gen. Moritz von Auffenberg, who considered aviation essential for a modern army. It remained to be seen how this change would affect Austro-Hungarian military aviation.

Russian military aviation was under the control of the Electric Service Section of the War Ministry's Engineer Department from 1909 to 1911.[53] In 1909, as membership in the Imperial All-Russian Aero Club increased, the War Ministry allotted funds to buy foreign airplanes, established an aviation branch, and bought its first domestic dirigible. Blériot's cross-Channel flight had so impressed Grand Duke Aleksandr Mikhailovich that he became Russia's royal patron of aviation, coordinating civilian and military activities such as flight exhibitions and competitions. Convinced that an aerial fleet would be essential for victory in a future war, he petitioned the tsar to solicit public subscriptions for buying planes and hiring instructors from the Blériot and Voisin firms and to have selected army and navy officers trained abroad. With military flight schools at Sevastopol and at Gatchina in the Crimea to enable year-round flight, the army training program had 10 planes and 30 engineer officer pilot trainees by September 1910. In 1910 the Duma insisted on an increased aviation budget, and mobilization plans entailed a future total of 17 airships. By the end of 1911, the first year that airplanes participated in Russian military maneuvers, the army had 30 training planes, primarily Farmans and Blériots. In 1910 and 1911 French capital laid the industrial foundations for Russian aviation with small firms such as the Duks company in St. Petersburg. From the beginning the French aviation industry was instrumental in Russian aviation's development.

In Italy the Ministry of War's Engineers Brigade, under the command of Maj. Maurizio Moris, had successfully manufactured its own dirigibles in 1908 and 1909 and detached its officers as advisers to private dirigible construction ventures.[54] Moris headed an Italian Aviators Club founded in February 1909 and partially funded by the war and naval ministries, and he contracted with the Wright brothers to train an army and a navy pilot in Italy. The Italian Society of Aviation sponsored the first aerial circuit in September at Brescia, where the futurist poet Gabriele d'Annunzio flew for the first time in a Curtiss biplane, piloted by Glenn Curtiss himself. D'Annunzio marveled that "until now I have never really lived. Life on earth is a creeping, crawling business. It is in the air that one feels the glory of being a man and of conquering the elements."[55]

In 1909 the Engineers Brigade established its own aviation unit; in 1910 it founded its first aviation school. The brigade, which had become an Engineers Battalion, used its first notable aviation allocation of 10 million lire in mid-1910 to order 9 dirigibles, all Italian-made, and 10 airplanes, all French-made. By the end of 1910, when the army had 8 airplanes, an officer, Giulio Douhet, was predicting future aerial struggles and the importance of an air force for conquest of the air. Douhet, former General Staff captain and commander of a Bersaglieri battalion, had written enthusiastically of military aviation possibilities in the service journal *La Preparazione*.

Powered flight was first used for war in the Italian military. In April 1911 the War Ministry established an aviation inspectorate under Moris. In August aircraft participated successfully in maneuvers, just in time for the September mobilization of an aeroplane flotilla of 9 planes and 11 pilots for the war in Libya. The planes were all foreign-made—Blériots, Nieuports, Farmans, and Taubes. In addition to the Tripoli flotilla and three dirigibles, a Benghazi squadron was formed in November and two more squadrons at Derna and Tobruk in 1912. In these fragile craft Italian aviators performed the first tactical reconnaissance, cartographical and artillery observation, day and night bombardment, and propaganda leaflet dropping missions, exacting praise from foreign war correspondents. Much of the future of air warfare, except aerial combat, was prefigured, if writ very small, in this colonial conflict of 1911 and 1912 in places that later became famous during World War II's North African campaign.

Compared to the strides in European military aviation, U.S. military aviation lagged behind. Congress provided no funds for it in 1909 or 1910, apparently because of congressional suspicion after the Wright crash in 1908 and the War Department's priorities of reforms and fundamental necessities such as field guns and ammunition.[56] In late 1909 the army had only one plane, a Wright biplane, and one active pilot, Lt. Benjamin D. Foulois, to whom the chief of the Signal Corps granted a shoestring budget of $150 for operations in San Antonio through the beginning of 1910.

The American public continued to be interested in aviation, although some observers suggested that American spectators came hoping to see "blood." There were significant air meetings in the United States: at Belmont Park on Long Island the two major U.S. companies, Wright and Curtiss, sent six and five contract pilots respectively to a contest that included such luminaries as Cornelius Vanderbilt among its spectators. Only at the beginning of 1911, however, was a military flight school established near Washington and an airfield built in San Antonio, while both civilian and military pilots registered significant overland flights. The navy bought its first Curtiss airplanes that year, and Congress appropriated $125,000 for aviation for fiscal year 1912.

In 1909 and 1910, as aviation publicists observed the rapidity with which the military responded to aviation, the airplane's potential for peace or war came under increasing discussion, evoking ambivalent responses, as Felix Ingold's work on aviation literature amply demonstrates.[57] Blériot's flight, for example, while arousing British fears of the end of their island security, also became an act symbolic of a new technocratic heroism. Blériot himself, circulating from one banquet to the next, was elevated in the press first to national hero, then to cosmopolitan genius, the founder of a new epoch, the bearer of technological progress.[58] As Jean Aicard wrote in *Le Figaro* on 26 July 1909:

> Because your glory is for all; French, it is human;
> The conquest of the air requires struggles without hate,
> It needs truly great hearts;
> It raises all eyes to the stars
> It should abolish all war and its disasters,
> Honors of conquerors of old.[59]

Blériot's feat and other aeronautical achievements unleashed an enthusiasm for new technology. The press commented that "flying fever," which caused such mass hysteria, also promoted pacifist and international strivings and gave an impetus to optimism about progress and science's ability to create a better world. French industrialist Ernst Archdeacon, a grand promoter of aviation, also endorsed the propagation of Esperanto, an artificial world language that was intended to help overcome national boundaries.[60] Engineers, Blériot included, did not believe that the plane would be used for war. German engineer N. Stern in his book *Die Eroberung der Luft* (1909) found the airplane's significance not in its military but in its cultural effects, proclaiming that it would help avoid war and promote thoughts of peace, that it would bind nations to each other and unify diverse peoples.[61]

In a more fearful variation on this theme, German author Paul Scheerbart's work, *Die Entwicklung des Luftmilitarismus und die Auflösung der Europäischen Land-Heere, Festungen, und Seeflotten* (1909), calculated that aerial militarism would lead to the dissolution of armies and navies through fears of aerial war,[62] an idea echoed in a pacifistic poem "Aviation" written in 1912 by the Frenchman Lucien Jeny, who believed that air war would be so gruesome that war would die "of its own excesses."[63] German Wilhelm Kress thought that "the flying machine will become a frightful weapon of war and will thus help to make wars more seldom."[64] In these interpretations, the authors acknowledged the tendency toward the military application of the airplane, but counted on fearful expectations of air war, or air war itself, to end war or at least lessen its occurrence. In 1909 Ferdinand Ferber assumed a far more balanced stance than those above:

> A curious circumstance: most inventors of flying machines think only and alone of its military use! Even the Wright brothers have not escaped such errors. On the other hand dreamers do not refrain from affirming that just the emergence of the flying machine will eliminate war.
>
> We, however, believe that it ought to be used primarily for peaceful goals—like the automobile; still, like the automobile, the airplane will be a wonderfully useful machine for military purposes.[65]

In a more military vein, Englishman R. P. Hearne's book *Aerial Warfare* discussed the use of aviation for war and described a German air attack on London,[66] while French naval lieutenant Levaillant in a July 1909 article in *L'Aéronaute* demonstrated how shipboard aircraft could be used for reconnaissance in naval warfare.[67]

For some observers, the airplane's role as an instrument for heroic achievement tied the technological to the heroic with Nietzschean overtones. After watching flights in 1909 and 1910, Russian storyteller and playwright Leonid Andreev penned a story, as an epitaph for a crashed record-setting pilot, depicting the ecstatic union of man with machine, his hero endowed with the heroic fatalism of a Nietzschean superman whose goal can be attained only in death.[68] In his novel *Forse che si, forse che no* (1910), D'Annunzio began to propound a "mythology of flight with a clearly nationalist accent," in which he conceived of the airplane as an "aristocratic" machine that served to elevate his hero, who represented the Italian nation, to the realm of the superman. Such elevation was inextricably bound to death, the justification and goal of life, because truly superhuman existence began only with the afterlife following a hero's death.[69]

A critical factor in the rise of military aviation from 1909 through 1911 was the rapid improvement of aircraft performance effected by the French, as they raised the speed record from 48 mph in 1909 to 83 mph in 1911. Distance also increased from 146 miles to 449 miles, and height increased from 1,468 feet to 12,828 feet. By 1911 the three basic types of airplane— pusher and tractor biplanes, and tractor monoplanes—were far more efficient than they had been two years before. Yet flight remained a hazardous undertaking, a danger that undoubtedly added to its appeal. Concern about aircraft safety grew, as prewar aviation journals carried graphic accounts of bloody crashes in which fliers and passengers were killed, their spines crushed, their brains and bodies pierced by broken petrol pipes or chassis struts, and their bodies occasionally so burned that "nothing . . . was left but ashes and two unrecognisable trunks of burnt flesh."[70] Even spectators were at risk. On 21 May 1911 at Issy-les-Moulineaux aviator Émile Train lost control of his plane, which plunged into the crowd, killing French Minister of War Berteaux and injuring the prime minister.[71]

The very presence of the two government ministers reflected the interest of influential civilians—press lords, reporters, politicians, and royalty—in aviation. Within the military establishment, opinions on aviation's value varied; there was no monolithic front for or against the new technology. In all countries aviation was assigned to the military agencies responsible for technology. Aviation gained advocates within military bureaucracies, and by 1911 its adoption by the military in France and Germany forced the military establishment in other European countries to follow suit. Only in the United States, where there was no threat or sense of an impending major conflict, did little pressure arise to develop military aviation. But even in the States experiments equipping airplanes with rifles, machine guns, and bombs were proof that in 1911 some soldiers were thinking beyond reconnaissance to actual combat with airplanes.

Germany was the only nation to rely primarily on the dirigible, because no other had a ship to match the Zeppelin's size, load, and range. Despite its susceptibility to weather, the airship held potential as a naval scout because operation at sea would enable it to escape ground fire. The British government built airships from fear of the Zeppelin rather than from recognition of its potential at sea, while the French army kept a few smaller ships for longer-range reconnaissance to supplement its airplanes. Since the Zeppelin was still better suited for long-range reconnaissance than airplanes in 1911, the German General Staff's recommendation to concentrate on airplanes and Zeppelins and relinquish smaller airships was wise. Yet the War Ministry's reluctance to select among the airships of the various firms, which may have been prompted by fears of a Zeppelin monopoly, bound it to even greater future expenditures on dirigibles.

Airplane industries everywhere were in dire need of funds, but their only potential market was the military establishment because the airplane was not ready for commercial use and only the wealthy few could afford sport aviation. The military everywhere relied essentially on private industry and predicated its investment upon the industry's development. French commitment to and superiority in military aviation, though flawed by the artillery's and engineer's competition for control of the tiny air arm, was based on a superior aircraft industry, which owed its success to French achievements in aero engine development. The French industry exported its craft throughout Europe and virtually controlled its tiny Russian counterpart. Only Austria-Hungary and Germany possessed alternative sources of capable airplanes in 1911. The Gnome surpassed other engines, although the Austro-Daimler gave the central European powers a more fuel-efficient, though heavier, alternative in 1911. The military consequence of France's industrial leadership was the successful participation of airplanes in French military maneuvers in 1910, a year before other countries.

Military minds had not fully comprehended the airplane's military potential until cross-country flights. But by 1911, if reconnaissance appeared to be the airplane's niche, to some the possibilities of its military use seemed boundless. The future evolution of military aviation was contingent on military-industrial ties to develop the instruments of these designs. Military writers have praised such relationships unequivocally, claiming that the military's development of planes, when no one else was prepared to do so, benefitted all of aviation because of its concentration on fundamentals such as speed, load, ceiling, and safety. This assertion is essentially correct, but as early as 1910 the French, German, and Austrian armies clearly perceived the difference in emphasis between military and sport aviation—on teamwork rather than individuality, on reliability, sturdiness, load, and allweather performance more than high speed and high performance—and the consequent need to deflect the industry's focus from sport to military airplane production. The military's control of the aviation market enabled it to do exactly that in the next two years.

Military Aviation and Looming War, 1912–1914

"Nothing but the supreme stimulus of war considerations, and nothing but the large and generous flood of money which the taxpayer can provide, will carry aviation forward to the foremost place in the world."

WINSTON CHURCHILL SPEAKING TO THE ROYAL AERO CLUB DINNER
AT THE SAVOY, EARLY 1914[72]

After the 1911 Moroccan crisis, war was expected in Europe. It would be a short offensive campaign that would end in decisive triumph for the victor. The question was when, not if, conflict would occur, and in this increasingly pressured atmosphere, Europe's armies and navies sought to develop their embryonic air arms.

From 1912 to 1914 the French army needed to maintain the airplane supremacy it had established by the end of 1911. General Roques departed as aviation inspector in April 1912, to be replaced later by Colonel Hirschauer, former commander of Flying Troops. In September 60 aircraft—the largest number to that date—participated in fall maneuvers. At year's end the General Staff advised the War Ministry that planes were especially suitable for reconnaissance, rapid liaison, and possibly for attacking dirigibles and troops in dense formations, although effective battlefield operations at altitudes below 800 meters risked serious losses—unless, as Colonel Estienne suggested, airplanes were armored.

In 1913 and 1914 the French army wasted precious time with debilitating administrative struggles, an abortive policy on armored airplanes, and indecision on aircraft armament. Aviation units' placement under Army Corps commanders in 1913 diminished the permanent inspector's authority and unleashed a long debate between proponents of aviation's autonomy and those who regarded it as an instrument of the land army units. Then the War Ministry's assignment of artillery General Bernard to investigate the state of aviation proved too much for General Hirschauer, who resigned, to be replaced by Bernard in September 1913.

Rumors of grave abuses under Hirschauer's autonomous inspectorate, stemming from the "paramount" and "pernicious" influence of the great aircraft manufacturers, flew furiously in November 1913. Bernard and the Army Corps commanders intended to expunge them through more rigid military discipline and inspection. Furthermore, the War Ministry, pressured by army engineers, was allegedly considering two drastic measures to increase its control over the aircraft producers: building all except one hundred aircraft at Meudon, where Dorand was designing airplanes; and striking seven principal manufacturers from the list of government contractors for inefficiency and delays in past deliveries.[73]

There was fire beneath this smoke. French manufacturers were in arrears, but this situation was as much the army's fault as it was theirs. France continued to possess a more substantial aviation industry than other states, but the aircraft industry found itself hard-pressed to keep up with the army's orders because the army tended to rely primarily on its original suppliers— Farman, Blériot, Voisin, and the Caudron brothers' firm. Nieuport, Breguet, and Deperdussin, the 1911 military competition's winners, received far fewer orders, limiting their potential for expansion. The army justified its choice by citing the original manufacturers' larger production capacity, forgetting that its contracts were what had endowed those early factories with that ability. The army failed to develop some of the newer firms' manufacturing capability by distributing its contracts too narrowly.[74]

The War Ministry's economic doctrine was to divide the market among several producers to avoid such potential abuses as delayed deliveries, poor quality, and ultimately, monopolies. Yet in his determination to keep prices low and disperse contracts, Hirschauer was confronted with the delays that he hoped to avoid, and the firms found themselves in greater debt and unable to hasten or expand deliveries. Under these conditions, only the so-called big three—Blériot, Farman, and Gnome—prospered. They did so, as French historian Emmanuel Chadeau has shown, not just because of the quality of their products but also because of the success of their directors in personally relating to the military, presenting their factories as well organized, and in exporting their wares abroad—Farman to Russia in particular, Blériot to England, and Gnome to all countries. While Bernard inappropriately reproached them for retarding their domestic deliveries in favor of export and impugned their patriotism, the exports gave them a certain independence from and leverage vis-à-vis the army.[75]

The military establishment's desire to control the private aircraft industry was not peculiar to France; it also was evident in Germany and England. Dorand at Meudon was probably urging increased control over design and production for his establishment. Senator Reymond was concerned early in 1914 about the reputed tendency of Meudon designers to work on their own experiments rather than test submitted inventions.[76] Clearly certain officers there had grander designs, perhaps along the lines of the Royal Aircraft Factory in England. But Dorand's designs were unexceptional, and the army, despite its difficulties with the situation, was dependent on the private aircraft firms.

As the artillery-engineer struggle flared anew, Bernard's appointment proved debatable because the coterie of artillery aviation officers around him specified that all airplanes were to be armored, in accord with Estienne's ideas of 1912. After the delays resulting from this program change, the three armored aircraft prototypes presented to Joffre in June 1914 were too heavy for the army's low-horsepower engines. French aircraft firms had wasted valuable time developing impractical aircraft, and the French army bought only 350 airplanes in the year before the war, when the German army had procured over four hundred. Amid these delays, the War Ministry and General Staff decided that aviation was ready for autonomy, and by April 1914 the new aviation service had been placed under a Twelfth Directorate of Military Aeronautics directly subordinate to the War

Ministry, with separate technical inspectorates for airplanes *(aviation)* and airships *(aérostation)*. General Bernard was the first director, but two months after the war began Hirschauer would be recalled to head the Twelfth Directorate.

In 1913 and 1914 the French army high command also appointed commissions to study arming aircraft with machine guns and bombs. A high commission on military aeronautics chaired by Joffre established a further commission in May 1913 to study attacks by armed aircraft against ground targets and dirigibles. The results of tests with machine guns and incendiary grenades, similar to those with photographic and wireless equipment, were still too fragmentary to determine correct uses of these weapons. In mid-June a War Ministry commission studying aviation's practical uses concluded that bombing troops with fléchettes and buildings with shells posed interesting prospects. This was a reserved and belated judgment, considering that such testing had begun as early as 1910.

The high command reserved judgment about armed airplanes, but aviation officers and civilian industrialists were far more sanguine about such possibilities and were developing ideas and staging tests that laid the groundwork for future doctrine and practice in air warfare. The Michelin brothers, who were aware of Poutrin's 1911 article on bombing, launched an annual bombing competition in 1912 and published brochures that proposed bombing troops and supplies beyond the range of artillery. The Blériot, Deperdussin, and Voisin firms tested 37mm cannon on their planes with the assistance of junior aviation officers, but higher commanders judged the tests of cannon-armed Voisins as savoring "more of Jules Verne than of reality."[77] Morane-Saulnier was studying a synchronized machine gun installation on its monoplane and considering the possibility of protecting propeller blades from bullets with steel wedges. These tests and studies were done without high-level military support because the high command believed that armament might deflect crews from their primary mission of reconnaissance.

Despite these problems in the military-industrial relationship, the bedrock of France's strength in military aviation continued to lie in the aviation industry. In March 1914 Farman employed some 1,000 workers in plants at various locations around Paris, including Issy-les-Moulineaux, where Caudron and Nieuport had located, and Billancourt, where Voisin was established.[78] By 1914 both Nieuport and Deperdussin had lost their owners: Alfred and Charles de Niéport were killed in crashes in 1911 and 1912, and Deperdussin, whose wealth apparently was partially gained from speculation or gambling, was imprisoned in 1913 for bank fraud. But the two firms remained successful, as their talented designers assumed control. Deperdussin, for example, led by Louis Béchereau, whose midwinged monoplanes with monocoque fuselage had won the Gordon Bennett and the Schneider trophy races in 1911 and set world speed records before 1914, would become the vaunted Spad factory. Morane-Saulnier and REP completed the ranks of French aircraft manufacturers. Although the REP firm was no longer significant, Esnault-Pelterie himself was instrumental in organizing the industry's trade association.

The aero engine industry remained French aviation's ultimate strength; its nucleus was the firms Gnome-Rhône, Renault, Salmson, Clerget, and Anzani. Compared to airframe manufacturers, these companies required more capital and more industrial and technological experience to surmount the complexities of engine production. Laurent Séguin of Gnome, and Georges Canton, R. Unné, and Emile Salmson of Salmson were all École Centrale graduates, while Pierre Clerget was a university engineer.

Gnome, the most successful engine manufacturer, delivered nearly two-thirds of the army's prewar engines. In 1913, when its main plant at Paris-Gennevilliers employed 650 to 800 workers, it built some 1,400 rotaries. By May 1914 it possessed the latest U.S. machine tools, which were operated by unskilled labor, but assembly was accomplished primarily by skilled metal workers, some of whom were trained in the factory's school. The location of successive construction processes in widely separated portions of the shop required much transport of material within the plant. The principal elements of the Gnome rotary were forged from cast steel, and it took three hours to cut a 6-kilogram crankcase from a 49-kilogram steel block and eight hours to build a 2.8-kilogram cylinder from a 37-kilogram piece.[79] While such arrangements were not as efficient as the United States assembly-line production, they were typical of handicraft construction, which sufficed to meet the relatively limited prewar demand. In June 1914 Gnome fused with its nearest competitor, Le Rhône, which built a small number of 80-hp rotaries with better fuel consumption.

France's second leading engine producer, Renault, supplied about one-third of the army's prewar engines, introducing air-cooled V8s of 80 horsepower in 1913. Clerget had begun rotary-engine production, and the Salmson firm, which had started in the pump business, moved successfully into aero engine production in 1913 with Canton-Unné water-cooled radial engines in first seven-cylinder 90 horsepower and then nine cylinder 110-hp versions.

The development of French military aviation and the aviation industry occurred within a context of intense civilian scrutiny and support. In fall

1912 a press campaign by *Le Temps* and *Le Matin* led to the creation of a National Aviation Committee, chaired by Georges Clemenceau, that engineered a national subscription raising four million gold francs for aviation. A veritable web of political figures, newspapers, and aviation associations had arisen around military aviation. Military-political links, for example, were evident in Avord's development into France's largest military flight school. In a visit with General Joffre in 1912, the new prime minister, André Millerand, an early supporter of aviation, gave Avord his blessing. When the school opened in August, its first commander was Capt. Georges Bellenger, a polytechnician and artillery officer, the army's youngest captain, and aviation adviser to Senator Reymond, a staunch aviation advocate in the parliament.[80] In January 1914 War Minister General Moulen formed a Superior Council of Aeronautics, comprising politicians, engineers, and War Ministry representatives, to consider the applications of aeronautical research to military aviation.[81]

In Europe's increasingly bellicose atmosphere after 1911, all aspects of aviation, including civilian pilots' exploits, became indissolubly tied to the military. France's great civilian aviators like Roland Garros, master of the distance flight, and Adolphe Pégoud, who performed the first intentional aerobatics—including loops and upside-down flight in a Blériot—were national heroes, defenders of French honor, asked to sacrifice their lives for France, as the following verse by Maurice Olivaint in *la Revue des annales politiques et littéraires* indicates:

Come! Faithful aviators,
France needs your wings!
France needs your hearts!
France needs your lives!
They will die deserving of envy
Who die for our rights triumphant![82]

The Circuit of Anjou in 1912, which the French army used as a test, occurred in such dreadful weather that only Roland Garros completed the course. Journalist René Bazin commended the participants in *L'Illustration:* "You risk yourselves for France. For that reason, when you appear, all France is stirred. And she loves you, applauds you, thanks you, because in you, who have no fear, she recovers the knight who made her history, nation of the avant-garde, elegant in peril."[83] The notion of an elite was evident before the war. After an aviator's death in a crash at Avord, the mourning was celebrated in a large funeral and extensively covered in the aviation press, which set the precedent for the wartime mourning, or *deuil*, of the fallen and ascended heroes of the air. Even civilian aviators became linked with the military, patriotism, and heroism.

In August 1914 the French army's air service went to war with 141 airplanes—primarily Farmans, Blériots, a few Voisins, Deperdussins, Breguets, Caudrons, Nieuports, and REPs—in 21 squadrons. The army also had 126 airplanes in its general reserve and 50 more in flight schools. In August it had 220 service pilots to fly the biplanes and monoplanes, whose performance had changed little since 1912. As the army command was not interested in aerial combat, speed was not essential. It preferred heavy, slow airplanes, although it had some rapid, light single-seat Blériots. The planes were made for average pilots, those that might have to be trained quickly in case of war. The army had not pressed armament development between 1912 and 1914, and the bureaucratic wrangling had delayed its airplane production. It could ill afford delays in production and development with war looming on the horizon and the Germans forging ahead in aviation.

Aviation was not universally accepted within the army, even in the climate of impending war. Ferdinand Foch, future Allied commander in chief in 1918, reputedly stated in March 1913 that "aviation is fine as sport. I even wish officers would practice the sport, as it accustoms them to risk. But, as an instrument of war, it is worthless [c'est zéro]."[84] Yet if the commander of Twentieth Corps did not appreciate aviation's value, General Galliéni, commander of the Paris garrison, did.

French naval aviation remained an afterthought in the prewar era, although Frenchman Henri Fabre had invented the first successful seaplane in 1910, and François Denhaut had created one of the first flying boats in 1912. A naval aeronautical service was officially instituted in March 1912 under Capt. René Daveluy, and a seaplane carrier, the Foudre, was commissioned the same year, but by August 1914 the Foudre's deck had been dismantled and the French navy had only eight planes.

The steady expansion of the German army air arm and its aviation industry continued from 1912 through 1914.[85] Both the army and navy divided their resources between the rigid airship and the airplane, and the General and Admiralty Staffs held high expectations of their Zeppelins' performance.

By April 1912 the army had 10 airships, including 2 Delag Zeppelins, and in September the General Staff planned to have 15 ships for bombing in 1914, although it had yet to test their effectiveness for this mission. Improvements in the Zeppelins' range, climb, and load still did not assure their ability as bombers. Officers' rides in army and Delag ships, Count Zeppelin's exaggerated claims, and particularly the General Staff's own determination to stay ahead of France shaped its plans more prominently than did hard evidence. General Staff Chief Moltke wanted to have the most possible airships operational for a future war and held exaggerated notions of the Zeppelins' "first-strike capability." On 24 December 1912 he informed the War Ministry that "in the newest Z-ships we possess a weapon that is far superior to all similar ones of our opponents and that cannot be imitated in the foreseeable future if we work energetically to perfect it. Its speediest development as a weapon is required to enable us at the beginning of a war to strike a first and telling blow whose practical and moral effect could be quite extraordinary."[86] Such sentiments were echoed in aviation journals, as 1913 articles in the *Deutscher Luftfahrer Zeitschrift* anticipated pinpoint and unstoppable Zeppelin attacks on enemy targets in the dark of night.[87] German war plans in 1913 placed dirigibles directly under the high command and army commands for strategic reconnaissance and bombing missions. In preparation for a future conflict, military and Delag ships participated in maneuvers and tested installations of machine guns and wireless sets, but performed only one bombing trial before the war.

The General Staff remained convinced of the airships' suitability for bombing and reconnaissance, although in 1913 a ballistics expert, General Rohne, warned that dirigibles would be vulnerable to incendiary shells, and by 1914 Zeppelins met the army's minimum performance standards only under the most favorable weather conditions. In summer of 1914, the army still had only 10 airships, of which three were Delag Zeppelins that were fit only for training.

The inability to keep to the General Staff's plan should come as no surprise. Zeppelins were monstrous vehicles, expensive and difficult to build. The Z9 delivered in July 1914 was 158 meters long, 22,740 cubic meters in volume, and powered by three 200-hp engines. It cost 860,000 marks, the equivalent of 34 biplanes. The Prussian War Ministry had ceased building the army's own airship to save funds, but it had bought Schütte-Lanz wooden airships in an attempt to promote competition with the Zeppelin. Small wonder that the Bavarian War Ministry, subordinate to and far less wealthy than its great Prussian counterpart in the hierarchy of imperial Germany's war ministries, wondered in May 1914 whether airplanes might not replace airships.[88]

The German General Staff, however, considered the airplane suitable for shorter-range reconnaissance, communications, and artillery spotting. In early 1912 Moltke, who also wanted all the airplanes possible for his air arm, had been dismayed with the joint War Ministry–General Staff commission's decision to proceed slowly with airplanes. Early in 1912 the War Ministry planned to buy only 200 planes annually and insisted that any future airplane factories be diversified, large-scale, and financially sound to survive on few contracts. As airplanes became more effective, the War Ministry increased its airplane contracts from 130 in 1912 to 432 in 1913, and the number of manufacturers rose from 9 to 11, as it encouraged large diversified enterprises such as AEG and the Gothaer Waggonfabrik (Gotha) to enter aircraft production. The heyday of the solitary inventor and small builder yielded to the age of the larger company, with sufficient capital and skilled workers to develop better airplanes and survive the rigors of competition.

In 1914 the army's aircraft firms, in order of productivity, were Albatros, Aviatik, Luftverkehrsgesellschaft (LVG), Rumpler, Deutsche Flugzeugwerke (DFW), Euler, Gotha, Jeannin, AEG, Fokker, and Luftfahrzeuggesellschaft (LFG). Mechanization and serial production were common in the larger factories, of which Albatros and Rumpler employed 745 and 400 workers respectively. Early in 1914 the army estimated that its eight best firms could produce more than 100 planes monthly, which meant that they possessed surplus capacity for wartime expansion. The companies relied on skilled craftsmen, working in the same pattern as in France, though called *Platzarbeit* in Germany, where "machines were grouped by type . . . and the pieces were moved from one post to another until they were finally brought together for fitting in the assembly shop."[89]

Yet these firms relied on one aero engine company, Daimler, producing one engine type, the 100-hp six-cylinder water-cooled in-line. The engine was excellent—sturdy, reliable, and fuel efficient—but the monopoly was unhealthy. In June 1914 the War Ministry included Benz in its orders of six-cylinder in-lines in a belated effort to lessen its dependence on Daimler. On the eve of the war the army was anxiously awaiting the Oberursel company's copy of the Gnome rotary for diversification of engine type. The army's prewar role in engine development had been at worst a detriment to and at best no factor at all in aero engine development. In accord with its emphasis on reliability and de-emphasis on speed, it had set an upper limit of 125 horsepower for the engines on its large and stable Taubes and biplanes, and the 1912 Kaiser's award, which was intended to spur aero engine development, had stipulated a maximum of 115 horsepower for its competitors. The inspectorate lacked aero engine experts and merely checked the engines on delivery of the airplanes until April 1914, when it permanently assigned an officer to Daimler to accept engines at the factory.

In the absence of alternative markets for airplanes, the army controlled the destiny of its aircraft manufacturers. The General Inspectorate gave "Taubes" to firms as production prototypes to foster standardization and licensed production, and after crashes in the fall of 1913 the army monitored its manufacturers more stringently to improve detailed construction techniques and safety. Yet standardization of monoplane manufacture meant ossification, as most manufacturers concentrated on Taube production, while only Anthony Fokker, a maverick young Dutchman who in 1912 had established his first aircraft factory in Germany, built new though primitive light monoplane types during this period.

The army also effectively steered civilian aviation ventures to its own ends through its pervasive influence in German society, playing upon chauvinistic notions of cultural supremacy to bolster military aviation. In 1912 a National Aviation Fund was organized by the government and industry under the aegis of the patron of German aviation, Prince Heinrich of Prussia. The fund's proclamation preached that in "this hour of national danger," Germany had to protect its preeminence in applied science and assure its honored place in history by making the German nation the "powerful engine that would drive her planes to victory in peace and war." The "pioneers in a great new cultural task" who "risk their lives in the patriotic endeavor to secure for Germany in this area an equal place in the universal struggle of nations" deserved the entire nation's active support. Postcards, medals, parades, and photos celebrated German aviators' feats; a *Kladderadatsch* cartoon portrayed a winged Germania soaring above a uniformed Gallic cock glaring up from a dunghill.

The fund raised over 7.2 million marks, which bought 62 airplanes for the army, financed the training of 162 field pilots by August 1914, and built airfields that the military would control in wartime. It provided partial funding for the civilian German Research Institute for Aviation, a central research agency that performed stress tests on military aircraft and sponsored civilian competitions that became virtually long-range reconnaissance flights for slow, stolid military two-seaters and their crews. Some manufacturers' efforts to use these contests to promote sport aviation and a market for light, fast craft were effectively thwarted by civilian aviation sport associations' zealous defense of the army's priorities. The army's interest in the Oberursel 80-hp rotary engine reflected its belated recognition of light planes' potential, which might have been developed by the very sport competitions that its sycophants had quashed.

Although the General Staff planned to use its airplanes primarily for reconnaissance, Maj. Wilhelm Siegert, a dynamic and imaginative Flying Troops commander, expected aerial combat and anticipated bombing and strafing raids. In 1913 the General Staff ordered tests with 5- and 10-kilogram bombs; by 1914 it was considering arming some planes with Parabellums—light machine guns that had been available since early 1913—although the guns' weight significantly reduced the maximum ceiling of the army's low-hp craft.

Aviation's growing importance was reflected in the General Inspectorate's October 1913 creation of separate inspectorates, each with five battalions of troops, for airships and airplanes. The airships would be assigned to the high command and army commands, the airplanes would be allotted to armies and fortresses in units of six planes each. Yet on two counts—size and independence—this aviation establishment fell far short of the 26 September 1912 General Staff proposals submitted shortly before the formation of the Prussian Flying Troops in October. The memorandum had recommended the formation of an inspectorate of military aviation separate from transport and with sufficient flying stations to allot one to each army corps by April 1914, but the War Ministry rejected such radical and expansive steps.

In August the German army went to war with 10 dirigibles and 245 rugged, dependable two-seat reconnaissance craft with reliable water-cooled in-line engines, and 254 pilots and 271 observers to operate them. The Germans had thus overtaken the French through their single-minded development of reconnaissance planes.

The German naval air arm was still in an embryonic state by July 1914. The Imperial Naval Office had begun airplane tests before 1911 and initiated contacts with the aircraft industry in 1911, but seaplanes were more difficult to develop than landplanes. The German navy ultimately found the floatplane suitable for the North Sea's rough waters, and by 1914 it had two firms specializing in seaplane construction—Flugzeugbau Friedrichshafen, founded on Lake Constance in 1913 by Count Zeppelin's friend and co-worker Friedrich Kober, and Hansa-Brandenburg, founded on the war's eve by Camillo Castiglioni—expanding his industrial empire from Austria-Hungary to Germany—and directed by Ernst Heinkel, formerly of Albatros and LVG. The navy further encouraged the development of engines of more than 100 horsepower for its heavy craft, and some of its 24 aircraft in July 1914 had 150-hp Mercedes in-lines. In 1914 the Admiralty Staff regarded airplanes as useful for reconnaissance (to compensate for the navy's lack of cruisers) and for defense against enemy airships and airplanes.

In 1912 the Naval Office and Admiralty Staff agreed that Zeppelins would be cheaper substitutes for cruisers and potentially useful for reconnaissance against submarines and bombarding enemy coastal installations.

A naval airship detachment bought its first Zeppelin in October 1912. In July 1914 the staff still planned to use Zeppelins for strategic reconnaissance and bombarding the British fleet and coast. Yet the Naval Airship Division had only one airship besides a Delag ship for training, and had conducted no bombing tests. Its first two airships had crashed in September and October 1913, killing almost an entire crew, including the division commander. The program survived only because its demise would have seriously damaged national prestige and its new commander, Capt. Peter Strasser, was a dynamic individual who would not let it die.

The disjunction between the fantastic goals for Zeppelins, and the paucity of ships, repeated disasters, their inability to meet minimum performance standards, and the failure to develop bombing techniques or bombs was common to both the army and navy. To the army high command, its few airships remained wonder weapons. The airplane, in contrast, was considered a tool expected to perform useful battlefield tasks, and the airplane arm was well prepared for the war. The aircraft industry was comparable to France's but dependent upon an engine industry more narrowly based in firms and types than France's. To the navy, the airship and seaplane were reconnaissance and attack vehicles, although in 1914 neither could perform the tasks envisaged for them.

British military and naval air services were officially formed in 1912. Amid agitation from the press and parliament for larger aviation forces, they grew slowly in the two years before the war. Parliamentary deputy William Joynson-Hicks's attacks on the War Office's aviation policy grew steadily more acrimonious, while in *The Daily Mail* articles H. G. Wells speculated whether Britain, behind in submarines, airships, and airplanes, was not "backward, unorganized, unimaginative, [and] unenterprising" compared to the continent.[90]

Prime Minister Asquith's request to examine aviation in November 1911 led to the creation of a technical subcommittee of the CID, whose key members were Brig. Gen. David Henderson, director of military training, and General Staff Capt. Frederick Sykes, both of whom had earned their civilian pilots' brevets in 1911. The subcommittee's 28 February 1912 report, which Asquith approved in April, recommended forming a Royal Flying Corps (RFC) organized in military and naval wings, based on a Central Flying School (CFS), and monitored by an advisory CID air committee. Sykes commanded the military wing from 1912 to 1914, and Henderson, often labeled the father of the RFC, became director general of a separate Directorate of Military Aeronautics in September 1913. The most prominent officer in the future British air arm, Capt. Hugh "Boom" Trenchard, learned to fly in 1912 at age 39 (the age limit for admission to the CFS was 40) and became a CFS instructor. Sykes and Henderson could envisage artillery observation, the prevention of aerial reconnaissance, attacks on an enemy field army, and aerial combat as possible tasks for an air arm. The subcommittee even received predictions of wars for aerial supremacy, but circumspectly concluded that military airplanes were essentially a reconnaissance auxiliary for land armies. In the 1912 army maneuvers airplanes successfully performed reconnaissance missions, convincing Gen. J. T. Grierson of their military value. The army also tested planes equipped with bombs and a new lightweight machine gun, the Lewis automatic, which was not available for infantry use until late 1914.

The RFC's military wing sought to obtain a standard reconnaissance plane in military trials in the summer of 1912. The judges, who included Henderson, Sykes, and O'Gorman of the Royal Aircraft Factory at Farnborough, found no winner from private industry. The best participant was Farnborough's own unofficial entry, Geoffrey de Havilland's stable BE2 biplane. Despite mounting criticism from private manufacturers and the aviation press of a government factory's influence on aircraft procurement policies, Farnborough began to issue contracts for the production of BE2s by private companies. The factory and the National Physical Laboratory used the BE2 to coordinate mathematical research, wind tunnel experiments, and full-scale flight tests, although the research results contained in the 1912–1913 report of the Advisory Committee for Aeronautics had still not been released to the wider aviation community by May 1914. While Farnborough was not intended to compete with the aircraft industry, it came dangerously close to supplanting private aircraft manufacturers. The CID air committee actually considered having the Royal Aircraft Factory build all army craft, a decision that would have crushed the developing private industry.

This reliance on Farnborough and failure to foster the aviation industry became the focal point of the press's concern about War Office policy. The War Office's inattention to industry is exemplified by its devotion of only a small segment of the "miscellaneous" section in its April 1912 White Paper on military and naval aviation to "the encouragement of private enterprise."[91] Charles Grey, the editor of *The Aeroplane*, labeled the Royal Aircraft Factory "the most scandalously mismanaged civilian department that has ever existed" and in 1914 accused it of controlling the War Office's aviation procurement policy and pirating the ideas of others. Articles in *The Times* defended the factory, praised the BE2 as "unsurpassed," and condemned the trade's slowness in delivery.[92] *Flight* was more balanced in its judgment, pointing out that the BE2 had not been copied in its details and that the factory had been willing to encourage the trade, which did not produce sufficient planes. Yet *Flight* remained uneasy about the factory's continued airplane construction.[93]

While *The Aeroplane*'s attacks may have been extreme, the CID's consideration of Farnborough's near usurpation of aircraft production validates the aviation press's criticisms and fears. The Royal Aircraft Factory was impeding the private industry's growth by corralling designers, controlling licensed production, and producing some of its own airplanes. Although its original guidelines had not allowed aircraft construction, it had received permission to rebuild them, a procedure the army and navy liberally employed to evade the necessity of including new constructions in their annual estimates. Its ambiguous position of producing its own airplanes and judging private industry's changed only with the December 1913 formation of the Aeronautics Inspection Department (AID). One of its own designers, Geoffrey de Havilland, worked for the AID, but held his position for only a short time before entering private industry. O'Gorman used his position to protect the factory fiercely, rejecting any complaints of shoddy workmanship or negligence from the military wing to the extent that Maj. E. M. Maitland, commander of the First Squadron, believed that O'Gorman regarded the wing officers as "potential, if not actual, hostile critics."[94] Additional evidence of the factory's power was provided later when Maj. G. P. Bulman of the wartime AID indicated that O'Gorman—a man of tremendous drive, enthusiasm, ambition, pride, wit, and persuasion—had created a "nursery" of gifted designers and "dragooned" the War Office into concentrating on factory products.[95] The Royal Aircraft Factory, despite its contributions to British aviation, was a political and industrial liability to military aeronautics' development.

In 1913 the military air estimates rose to 501,000 pounds, and the army bought BE2s from Vickers and Handley Page, Farmans from Airco, and three-seaters from Sopwith, founded by wealthy aviator and former motor boat racer T. O. M. Sopwith. The Royal Aircraft Factory, while improving its inspection and test techniques, was developing prototypes: de Havilland's FE2, a pusher biplane potentially armed with a machine gun in the nose; Frank Gooden's sleek tractor biplane SE2, the predecessor of famous wartime fighters; and a 100-hp in-line engine by Fred Green. At the 1912 military airplane competition, all the entries had been powered by foreign engines—primarily the Gnome—and the judges had acknowledged the overwhelming importance of establishing a British aero engine industry. In

June 1913 the government offered a prize for 90- to 200-hp engines of over four cylinders and scheduled tests for February 1914.

The naval wing had taken a different approach to aviation. The CID subcommittee's February 1912 report had directed the naval wing to concentrate on airplanes and cease development of the expensive rigid airship. The Admiralty appointed Capt. Murray F. Sueter as director of its Air Department. Sueter was a member of the Advisory Committee for Aeronautics and the inspector captain of airships from 1908 to 1911. He planned to use airplanes for fleet and coastal reconnaissance, submarine and mine detection, and defense against enemy aerial incursions. The navy chose to rely on private industry for its airplanes, and Sueter's request for a twin-float seaplane drew the Short brothers to naval production, while in the summer of 1912 Sopwith sold its first plane to the navy. Sueter was responsible to no specific member of the Admiralty board, but in Winston Churchill, the First Lord of the Admiralty, he had a staunch supporter.

Churchill became the darling of the aviation press, *The Aeroplane* labeling him the "fairy godfather" of naval aviation in January 1914.[96] In 1913 he became the first cabinet minister to control an airplane in flight, a feat that the *Pall Mall Gazette* applauded but the *Westminster Gazette* found "thoroughly ill-advised and mischievous."[97] As the principal guest of the Royal Aero Club dinner at the Savoy early in 1914, Churchill noted that aviation's "great driving power is derived from its military aspect and utility," and that "the Navy and the Army . . . must be the main propulsive force of aviation in this country."[98]

In July 1912 the CID subcommittee, overcome by another Zeppelin scare, reversed its February decision and concluded that while airships were expensive, they were cheaper than warships and thus worth active naval development. After a CID meeting in February 1913, the navy in July ordered two rigid and six nonrigid dirigibles. Yet these intermittent flurries of effort, prompted more by Zeppelin scares than by a fundamental appreciation of the airship's potential for scouting, would not suffice to develop airships, nor would the naval air estimates of 230,000 pounds for 1913. Though Churchill supported airships, he was never really convinced of their merits, regarding them as suitable vehicles for overage pilots. The navy thus had seven nonrigid dirigibles in August 1914, most of them acquired from the army in 1914 when its airship program ceased.

Churchill believed that airplanes could supersede small cruisers and reconnaissance vessels and protect naval ports. By October 1913 he desired three aircraft types—a scout seaplane, a ship-based fighter seaplane, and a home service fighting airplane for defense and patrol. The naval wing's interest in more than just reconnaissance led to its collaboration with Short, Avro, and Sopwith in prewar experiments with wireless telegraphy, machine guns, bombs, and torpedoes. In efforts to counter Zeppelins it even tested a Vickers 1.5-pound semiautomatic cannon—whose recoil was so great that the plane stopped dead in the air and fell 500 feet—and shotguns firing chain shot and grenades on grapples. For aerial defense the Admiralty and War Office also proposed an "aerial minefield" with mines hoisted aloft by balloons on a cable. Churchill quashed the idea with the statement, "Since Damocles there has been no such experiment."[99] The Royal Navy also tested a seaplane carrier, the British cruiser Hermes, equipped with Short seaplanes with folding wings, whose planes made 30 flights during a three-month period in 1913. It then ordered the Ark Royal, a merchantman design transformed on the drawing boards to a seaplane carrier and launched in September 1914.

By 1914 the divergent approaches to aviation of the RFC's military and naval wings—the former preoccupied with standard reconnaissance planes for a land army and primarily reliant on the Royal Aircraft Factory, the latter interested in a variety of planes from private industry for reconnaissance and fighting—led to a split. Early in 1914, and officially in July, the naval wing became the Royal Naval Air Service (RNAS) with its own school at Eastchurch.

On the war's eve the British aviation industry was not prepared for conflict. Naval contracts had not sufficed to support the domestic aircraft industry, and the military wing had given its few orders primarily to the Royal Aircraft Factory and a few large armaments firms. Fortunately, some of Britain's small aircraft companies were potentially topnotch. Avro was already developing its long-lived biplane series, the 504, for the RFC and the RNAS, and Sopwith's small biplane, the Tabloid, whose seaplane version won the Schneider trophy race at Monaco in April 1914, exhibited the maneuverability and climb for which its wartime fighters would become famous. Yet Britain's Achilles heel in aviation was aero engines. The aircraft industry was almost totally dependent on French engines, and Farnborough's 100-hp six-cylinder engine, which had won the government's engine award, was large and heavy.

In June 1914 the RFC staged an intensive program to assemble its few BE2s, Farmans, Avro 504s, and Sopwiths with their crews, not for "promiscuous" flying but for reconnaissance exercises.[100] The *Morning Post* said of the fliers present, "They are curiously alike in type—quiet, keen, interested faces, foreheads narrow rather than wide, and eyes set somewhat close together. . . . Their heads may well be the new fighting type, as unlike the old bullet face as possible, tenacious and determined rather than aggressive and obtrusive."[101] Prewar doggerel proclaimed the dashing and audacious "Lieutenant Icarus Daedalus Brown, RFC pilot of fame and renown, . . . unsullied and pure," though "erratic and wild" in deed.[102] A different type of warrior, a new hero, had arisen, though there were far fewer of them in Britain than in France or Germany.

British aviation historian R. A. Mason has asserted that by 1914 fundamental ideas of airpower had been formulated in Britain: its contribution to land and sea operations, the necessity of air command and an independent service to achieve it, air power's ability to strike at targets in the enemy homeland, and the consequent forced diversion of enemy resources to air defense.[103] Yet these were the ideas of a handful of civilians or aviation officers such as engineer F. W. Lanchester and army Capt. C. J. Burke, who commanded the RFC's Second Squadron RFC in 1914. These early notions bore no relationship to the actual state of British aviation in August 1914. Aviation officers such as Lt. Col. Frederick Sykes and Maj. W. S. Brancker agreed more circumspectly that the airplane's fundamental role was reconnaissance, which ultimately would lead to a struggle for aerial command.[104] The RFC sent four squadrons of 50 planes to France with the British Expeditionary Force (BEF) in August; all the planes had French engines and nearly half were foreign designed; perhaps half of the 75 military planes left in Britain were fit to fly. The RNAS had 50 usable airplanes and seaplanes built by eight different manufacturers, including one German.

As elsewhere, councils on the usefulness of airplanes were divided in the British military establishment. According to Sykes, within the army the air arm counted among its supporters Sir John French, commander of the BEF, and General Grierson. Among its detractors was Douglas Haig, French's successor, who allegedly commented in July 1914 that "I hope none of you gentlemen is so foolish as to think that airplanes will be able to be usefully employed for reconnaissance purposes in war."[105] Haig and others seemed to overlook the evidence from the maneuvers of the previous two years.

In Austria-Hungary grand designs continued to contrast with meager state finances and industrial development from 1912 through 1914.[106] An Austrian Air Fleet Fund initiated in early 1912 by the Aeroclub would eventually raise 1.5 million crowns, which was presented to the army on 30 July 1914, too late to help prewar aviation. More critically for military aviation, on 24 April 1912 Lt. Emil Uzelac, a capable Croatian officer who earned his field pilots' badge in three months at age 45, became commander of the aviation branch, a position he would retain throughout World War I. An aviation budget of 7.9 million crowns partially reflected War Minister Moritz von Auffenberg's pride in his officer pilots, whose achievements included a new world altitude record set on a Lohner Arrowflyer.

Yet in 1913 individual achievements (by the end of 1912 Austria was second only to France in the number of world aviation records held by its pilots) and demands from the General Staff for the expansion of military aviation contrasted starkly with the Austro-Hungarian aircraft industry's actual state. As tension in the Balkans exploded into war, General Staff Chief Conrad von Hötzendorff sought to expand aviation rapidly. Maneuvers in fall 1913 with four participating flying companies increased trust in the airplane, but the War Ministry refused to place large serial orders. The Lohner company was the army's sole supplier and provided the military with its only plane, the Arrow biplane, as the Transport Brigade's excessive demands for modification had proved too much for the Taube. As late as 1913 the brigade continued to overlook the industry's importance. As it threatened to build airplanes in its own workshops, it forced harsh terms on its manufacturers. Though Porsche's Austro-Daimler engine was the prototypical six-cylinder in-line and had become the engine of choice in Germany, Austro-Hungarian industry could not mass-produce it.

Lohner biplanes were banned in March 1914 after post-crash investigations indicated that Arrowflyers could survive break tests of only 2.5 times the plane's weight, although an advisable and generally accepted minimum was considered four to five times the plane's weight. As the press attacked Austro-Hungarian aviation's deplorable state, into the vacuum rushed German firms, who saw a much-desired market for expansion. DFW, Albatros, LVG, and Aviatik all founded factories in Austria-Hungary before the war, though too late to be a factor in mobilization. At the war's outbreak the army had 40 planes and 85 trained field pilots. The dearth of planes was the result of both aircraft prohibitions and the state's refusal to fund aviation adequately. Early in 1914 state Finance Minister Teleszky had labeled aviation an "amusement," a "worthless military fad."

By 1914 the naval section of the Austro-Hungarian War Ministry, which had been interested in special naval airplanes as early as 1910, had settled on the flying boat for the Adriatic Sea. Late in 1913, after buying Donnet-Lévêque and FBA (Franco-British Aviation Company) boats from France and Curtiss boats from the United States for its arsenal and as prototypes for its domestic industry, the navy procured the first of the Lohner E- boats, a reliable machine that was powered either by an 85-hp

Hiero or a 100-hp Mercedes engine. By the war's beginning the navy had some 25 pilots and perhaps 10 to 15 usable seaplanes.

In contrast to Austria-Hungary's meager numbers, by 1914 its arch-rival Russia had developed an air arm seemingly comparable even to Germany's.[107] By 1 April 1913 the Russian air arm had 13 dirigibles and 150 modern airplanes. In August 1914 it had 15 to 22 dirigibles and some 250 airplanes in 39 aviation sections, but no reserves. This appearance of strength was misleading. The Russian War Department transferred aviation from the Chief Engineering Directorate to the General Staff in July 1912. Then after a reorganization of the directorate into a Chief Military Technical Directorate (CMTD) in December 1913, the War Department divided responsibility for aviation, leaving the organizational functions under the General Staff and placing the technical and training aspects under the CMTD. The transfer and division of the authority on aviation and the lack of cooperation between the General Staff and CMTD precluded a well-planned system of aviation command.

The Russian War Department had no clearcut policy regarding aircraft manufacture. It procured its airplanes from nearly 24 different manufacturers and had 12 engine types from five countries. Many of the 16 aircraft types operating in 1914 were useless and without spare parts. In March 1914 the CMTD selected the French Deperdussin, Morane Parasol, and Voisin for production as its preferred aircraft and ordered 292 airplanes in May, but production would take time.

In the aircraft industry, the Duks factory produced Farmans, Voisins, and Nieuports; the Russko-Baltiiskii Rolling Stock Company manufactured Farmans; and the Lebedev factory built Deperdussins, Farmans, Voisins, and Moranes. The factories were little more than workshops, with a total monthly output estimated at 30 to 40 planes and five engines. As did German industry, they produced copies of French aircraft that were inferior to the original prototypes. The factories did not alleviate Russia's most severe deficiency, its shortage of aero engines and the absence of indigenous engine types that caused complete reliance on French or German power plants.

The Russian army used aero club schools for its pilots' primary training, but the number of these schools decreased in 1913. In March 1913 Russia had 72 military and 40 private pilots. Although several hundred pilots were supposedly trained during the year before the war, no power could have adequately trained pilots in such numbers at that time.

Although the aviation industry had not stabilized before the war, Russia possessed talented individuals in aviation. Nikolai Zhukovskii, engineering professor at Moscow Technical College, established a power-operated wind tunnel in 1902 and later an aerodynamics laboratory. He also did significant research on airfoil profiles and lift. Igor Sikorskii, the son of a prominent Kievan psychology professor and a student at the St. Petersburg Polytechnical Institute, began building small aircraft in 1910 and then in 1911 worked for M. V. Shidlovskii of the Russko-Baltiiskii Rolling Stock Company, which would allow him to construct a giant airplane. Sikorskii's Grand model, with a 92-foot wing span and weighing 9,000 pounds, flew on 13 May 1913 powered by four 100-hp German Argus engines. Sikorskii's Il'ia Muromets, of 102-foot span, flew six hours and thirty minutes with seven persons on board and then to Kiev and back, a distance of 1,600 miles, in June 1914. In April 1914 the army ordered 10 Sikorskii airplanes from the Russko-Baltiiskii company, 3 dirigibles, and 326 airplanes, although such an order was unrealistically large for the industry.

By 1913 the Russian navy had an air service, but like the army, it had pursued no systematic procurement policy and so had various types—foreign and domestic, land and seaplanes, including a Muromets. Its acquisition of FBA boats provided the prototypes for Russian designer Grigorovich's wartime flying boats, which became the backbone of naval aviation, but by the war's outbreak, some 24 Glenn Curtiss floatplanes constituted the naval air arm.

Aviation exploits in the Libyan campaign stimulated Italian aviation in 1912, when an air fleet fund raised three million lire for military aviation, indicating a burgeoning aviation consciousness there as elsewhere in Europe.[108] That summer the army established an aviation inspectorate with airship and airplane battalions and an experimental institute. Turin's Mirafiori field, where the airplane battalion located, became the center of Italian aviation. The Turin Polytechnical Institute founded an aeronautical laboratory in the winter of 1912–1913, and the first Italian aircraft factory, Società Italiana Transaerea (SIT), was founded there with French and Italian capital to build Blériots and then Farmans under license. SIT received contracts for the majority of the 150 planes ordered by the War Ministry in 1912 and 1913. In December Major Douhet, soon to be the commander of the airplane battalion, proposed an air arm of 25 squadrons of 94 planes and 150 pilots.

At a military competition for airplanes and engines held in April 1913, the judges, among them Douhet, declared no winners, finding that no domestic products equaled French machines, not a surprising conclusion given the primitive state of the Italian aviation industry. By default SIT remained the army's essential supplier, since its 150 employees and potential monthly production of 10 to 14 planes monthly made it larger than the rest of the Italian aircraft industry. Despite the small size of the industry and its firms, Italian aviation's pioneer age was beginning to fade in 1913, as artisanal airplane builders, no longer able to compete in sporting events and distance flights, which required substantial financial backing, dwindled.

Giulio Douhet, in his continued press advocacy of aviation, was urging Italian industry to support airplane development. If the campaign availed little, Douhet supported a close friend, the young aircraft designer Gianni Caproni, in his efforts to establish a factory. In June 1913, when Caproni was near financial ruin, Douhet persuaded Moris to make the factory part of the War Ministry's administration, although Caproni resigned the post in 1914 because of inadequate government support for his experiments. By August 1914 Caproni had raised enough money to reopen his factory.

While Russia had Sikorskii, Italy possessed Caproni, who was convinced of the importance of a fleet of multi-engine bombers for tactical and strategic purposes. In 1913 he produced the first plane expressly conceived as a bomber, a trimotored craft powered by Gnome 80-hp rotaries, which Douhet had encouraged and perceived as a potential means of making aviation the decisive element of modern warfare.

By 1914 the Italian air arm comprised 11 squadrons of Blériots, Nieuports, and Farmans. The Italian aviation industry, like its counterparts in Russia and Austria-Hungary, was tiny and underdeveloped compared to the German and French industries. SIT lacked even a design office, while Caproni was concentrating on simplifying his bomber design for production. In 1914 the Italian War Ministry asked the engine industry for new projects to make Italy independent of foreign suppliers. Fortunately, Fiat, which had begun designing aviation engines in 1907 and had built dirigible engines since 1909, quickly developed the A10, a water-cooled 100-hp six-cylinder in-line patterned after German and Austrian types, and began its mass production in the fall. (Fiat had not previously encouraged aircraft engine orders because of the demands of automobile production.) Italian naval aviation was created only early in 1913 and remained insignificant in August 1914. Italy's decision to remain neutral in the summer of 1914 meant that its air arm and industry would have until May 1915 before they faced the test of war.

Without the threat of war to spur its evolution, aviation in the United States stagnated.[109] By November 1912 the Signal Corps, using its first congressional appropriation of $125,000 for aviation, had 12 officers, 39 men, and 12 planes. That year the secretary of war asked Congress for $2 million to build a 120-plane force to keep pace with European powers. Congress again gave $125,000, a sum barely adequate to maintain or even increase its small air operations. Assistant Secretary of War H. S. Breckinridge and even army aviation enthusiasts like Lt. Benjamin Foulois, Lt. Henry H. "Hap" Arnold, and Capt. William "Billy" Mitchell considered aviation a subordinate service in the Signal Corps. It was not surprising that Congress, faced with other military priorities, did not grant increased funds.

By the summer of 1913 the army had only six active aviators and 15 planes. Colonel Samuel Reber, chief of the Aviation Section, lamented that the U.S. government and public did not support military and sport aviation or aeronautical laboratories as their European counterparts did, and that Europe had surpassed the United States in all realms of aviation, with the exception of seaplane development. The public had lost interest in sport aviation, and with fewer civilians flying there would be no reserve pilots for wartime. At least the chief of the Signal Corps, General Scriven, did acknowledge the airplane's value for reconnaissance and artillery spotting. March 1914 field service regulations included using the single aero squadron for reconnaissance in advance of the cavalry, and a 1 July 1914 law formed the Aviation Section of the Signal Corps.

The U.S. navy's active interest in aviation began in the fall of 1910 with the General Board, specifically Adm. George Dewey. But the officer placed in charge of aviation, Capt. Washington Irving Chambers, had no power. Aviator Eugene Ely flew Curtiss planes from a platform on the scout cruiser Birmingham on 14 November 1910 and then landed and took off from a special deck on the cruiser Pennsylvania on 18 January 1911. Early in 1911 the first naval aviators began training. In March Congress approved $25,000 for naval aviation experiments. Yet Glenn Curtiss's invention of an operable seaplane in 1911, and then his introduction of the flying boat in early 1912, turned the attention of Chambers and other naval officers from planes using ship decks for landing and takeoff—functions that impeded the operation of a warship's guns—to seaplanes. Then naval aviation stagnated for the next two years. Only on 1 July 1914, after naval aviators had flown over Vera Cruz in April, was an Office of Naval Aeronautics officially established. When the war began, the naval air service had only a few pilots and airplanes. The U.S. aircraft industry, which received few government contracts, employed 168 workers in 1914, placing it last in the ranks of those powers that would figure prominently in the world war.

In *The Culture of Time and Space, 1880–1918,* historian Stephen Kern observed that at the turn of the twentieth century, aviation engendered ambivalent visions—aerial warfare's terrifying potential and a great technological revolution transcending old boundaries and uplifting human consciousness.[110] While premature expectations of the apocalyptic or the transcendent had surrounded aviation from infancy, what actually occurred in prewar Europe was the militarization of flight. Sport aviation was languishing, the era of great races and tournaments was over, and accidents had cooled public enthusiasm for air transport. In an atmosphere of heightening nationalistic bellicosity, and in the absence of substantial sport or commercial markets, military aviation's supporters molded popular attitudes to benefit their cause. Civilian aviators, lionized as defenders of national honor, were sponsored by successful aircraft manufacturers, who were in turn indissolubly tied to the military, their essential if not sole source of contracts by 1912. In Europe, even in the poorest nations, military establishments funded aviation's growth. In the United States where funding and the fears of war were absent, the aircraft industry was virtually insignificant.

In Europe the competition for national superiority took hold with the attendant stereotypes. French accounts often depicted German aviators as fat, florid types in large, slow planes, while proclaiming that the energy and initiative necessary to use airplanes accorded marvelously with traditional Gallic audacity. The Germans lorded the Zeppelin over other powers as a symbol of their presumed cultural superiority. The British, who had little to gloat about until Sopwith's 1914 performances, then quickly claimed that the mantle of leadership in aviation had passed to them.

The British were the first to understand the implications of the airplane for colonial domination and white supremacy. In 1910 the CID directed the War Office to consider the use of the airplane "in war against uncivilized countries such as the Sudan, Somaliland, and the north-west frontier of India."[111] Charles Grey stated in 1912 that a few airplane squadrons could possibly restore British prestige, and he wanted to use the airplane "for impressing European superiority on the enormous native population."[112] A possible joint project of the Colonial Office and the navy endorsed by Churchill in March 1914 entailed plans to have the white population employ aircraft to control and threaten the empire's native populations in the event—considered a "distinct possibility"—of black uprisings.[113] Flight thus assumed a nationalist, imperialist, and militarist appearance.

The Zeppelin was actually used for commerce, but only in the absence of the military contracts so sought after by Count Zeppelin. Even the commercial venture was inextricably intertwined with German military and naval aviation. The drive toward larger Zeppelins was grounded in technological and military reasons, since the ship's size determined its load and ceiling. The dirigibles prompted tremendously inflated expectations of German military capability and a recurring dread of airship attacks in Britain.

Although scornful French aviators swore to expose Zeppelins as "soap bubbles,"[114] Germany's possession of them compelled France and Britain at least to attempt dirigible construction. Meanwhile, the Germans could not allow any pragmatic reservations to impede Zeppelin development, lest their symbol—and thus their sense of military, technological, and cultural superiority—be deemed impotent. The German military establishment's unrealistic expectations that its minuscule Zeppelin fleet could deliver a telling blow revealed a great gap between belief and reality. No doubt the prospect of crushing an enemy quickly with a wonder weapon, which reinforced the prevailing concept of a short war, further nourished such fantasies.

The airplane had generated much popular excitement, but it had not inspired such premature expectations for the immediate future within the military. Notions of mass destruction caused by airplanes in the sky were clearly beyond the small, fragile machines of the day, whose engine horsepower was barely adequate to lift the crew, much less a weapon. Although World War I aviation was not likely to equal the direst prewar predictions, which were far beyond the time's technological capability, the essential foundation of wartime developments was laid by 1914. Small air services had participated in maneuvers as reconnaissance or liaison vehicles since 1910 and had experimented with wireless and photography, bombs and machine guns.

If high commands understood that air services would reconnoiter and spot for artillery, visionaries anticipated bombing, ground strafing, and aerial combat. The cadres of officers and other ranks in military aviation and the many designers and craftsmen in the aviation industry were wartime aviation's essential human foundation. These men—supported or tolerated by some of their superiors, with allies in the parliaments, the press, and among other industrialists—saw potential where others saw little or nothing, and it was their initiatives that moved military aviation forward.

The military bureaucracies did not function monolithically or systematically in accepting aviation. Within the military establishment various salient bureaucratic divisions affected the adoption of aviation: in Germany and Austria-Hungary there was the dichotomy between the general staffs and war ministries; in France there was the struggle between engineers and artillerymen; and in Britain, where the navy was the senior service, there was the division between the navy and the army. With the air arm's growth came questions of its autonomy within the army. In France, for example, it achieved autonomy in the War Ministry's Twelfth Directorate, though the engineer-artillery struggle simply continued within the directorate. In Germany, despite efforts by some General Staff officers and Flying Troop commanders, the air arm remained subordinate to transport.

In prewar Europe the high commands' doctrine, that aviation would serve for reconnaissance and communications, was limited and convenient. Viewing the air arm as a supplement to the cavalry disturbed no current notions of warfare. Experiments that might have upset this equilibrium and led to the airplane's transformation into a weapon did not percolate up the military hierarchy. Many commanders who praised the airplane for its performance on maneuvers probably retained doubts about its ability in an actual war among the major European powers, and they would not have included the Balkan War of 1912–13, in which the combatants engaged a few foreign aviators to perform reconnaissance missions, in their assessment.

Military aviation's origins indicate the necessity of linking doctrine and aircrew training and technological and industrial developments. It was one thing to proclaim that the airplane would be used for reconnaissance; it was another to realize that observers required specialized training. By 1914 all the powers had trained small cadres of pilots. They would have been larger except that military aviators were still posted to flight units on a temporary basis in 1914, and in France they continued to wear the uniforms of their original branch of service, making for a colorful array of varying outfits.

Yet if posting to the air services was temporary, the services themselves were there to stay. France and Germany began training observers in 1911; in Germany the generic names Emil and Franz—pilot and observer—denoted the sense of a team in which the observer, a commissioned officer, commanded his noncommissioned officer pilot. In Germany a few young General Staff officers were trained as observers before the war, and in January 1914 50 officers from the war academy were assigned to observation training so that the aviation troops would have tactically trained officers. The prewar RFC did not train observers. Initially it believed that the pilot was merely a chauffeur to fly a trained General Staff officer, and it planned to create a force of officer and noncommissioned pilots. In the absence of firm policy decisions, the pilots did the observation and almost all were commissioned officers. Only in 1914 was the notion of training staff officers as observers resurrected, and 11 reported for an RFC course on 27 July 1914.[115] None of the armies appears to have deemed it necessary to train army commanders to appreciate and understand aviation.

With regard to doctrine, in relation to technology and industry, Thomas Keaney's work on prewar British air doctrine suggests that these two elements evolved on different and sometimes unconnected planes.[116] Without a war to force them together—to test doctrine with reality, to determine if the materiel could execute the doctrine—there was little to prevent this dichotomy. On the whole a limited doctrine restricting the airplane's use to reconnaissance and communications accorded well with the technological and industrial realities of the moment. Doctrine led to dead-ends and wasted effort if it exceeded the state of the technology—as in the French efforts to develop the armored airplane—or inflated expectations if it were not tested with actual maneuvers—as in the Zeppelin's case. The German air arm's development of a standard reconnaissance plane, on the other hand, linked early doctrine closely to materiel procurement, as it focused the industry's efforts, perhaps too narrowly, on a single type.

The concentration on reconnaissance and artillery spotting led armies to prefer slow, stable two-seat airplanes whose top speed in 1914 was 65 to 75 mph, far below the 1913 world speed record of 126.67 mph set by a Deperdussin monoplane. By 1914 most military aircraft were biplanes, partly because of their superior sturdiness and lift in an era of externally braced wings, and partly because the French and British militaries had suspended and banned monoplanes after crashes in 1912. Even though the monoplane design was exonerated of having inherent flaws, the setback exacerbated the trend toward biplanes.

Armies clearly distinguished between sport and military aviation in airplane type and pilot training, and the untrammeled individualism and daredevilry associated with aviation sport were anathema to the military's emphasis on the disciplined fulfillment of one's mission as part of a unit. Prewar military aviation agencies had sought to minimize flight risks through standardization of aircraft controls, installation of instruments, surveillance of construction, and the introduction of safety standards and stress tests.

The aviation science institutes in the powers—the National Physical Laboratory and the Royal Aircraft Factory in Britain, the Eiffel laboratory and Meudon in France, and the German Aviation Institute and the Kaiser Wilhelm Institute in Germany—were all connected to or part of the military, while their ties to the industry, which was run by practical flier-designers with little or no concern for aviation science, were limited or nil. These institutes could advise the military procurement agencies on such matters as break tests for aircraft, but they were not positioned for direct influence on the industry's affairs.

Ultimately the military sought to acquire slow stable planes for average pilots, not the great and gifted sport fliers whom some officers regarded as acrobats. Somewhat ironically, the war would catapult the flying machine again into the forefront of public imagination, as a vehicle of the greatest individual heroes, the aces, who were reminiscent of those prewar aviators who had mastered the skies. Wartime aerial combat, the realm of aviation in which there had been the least prewar experimentation, would reintroduce some aspects of sport aviation that the military had sought to escape—the individualism and the individual pilot's exploits, and the high-performance airplane, faster, more maneuverable, riskier to fly, occasionally even dangerous to its own pilots. The aura of prewar sport would return, though in a context so deadly that it altered the nature of the game.

The army's relationship to the aviation industry was determined not only by its military doctrine but also by economic doctrine. As the experience in France, Germany, and England indicates, the military sought to control aviation production, most fundamentally through its position as the prominent or sole consumer in the prewar market. All the armies professed a preference for relying on a private aviation industry. In France the army dispersed its contracts among its major producers. In Germany the army, requiring more aircraft producers than it had, further lured large industrial combines like AEG and the Gotha Rolling Stock Factory to aircraft production, though its efforts to increase engine production and avoid a Daimler monopoly were belated. The War Ministry also encouraged the Schütte-Lanz factory to compete with Zeppelin in dirigible construction. In Britain the War Office, relied first on the Royal Aircraft Factory and then on the trade, which it severely disadvantaged by 1914. In part these relationships were determined by timing: the French firms antedated military interest in aviation, as did the Zeppelin in Germany; elsewhere the aviation industry formed in response to military interest in flight. Consequently the French army was preoccupied with controlling the industry and the German army was concerned with control and expansion of industry, while the British army, with little industry at all, stated the wish to rely on the trade, but in practice thwarted its development.

In aircraft production the French industry, with some 3,000 workers in 9 firms, was larger than Germany's 11 firms that employed 2,500 workers, while a British industry of 12 firms employed only 1,000 workers. Both the French and German air arms had limited their industries to a few proven companies, while British reliance on the Royal Aircraft Factory had restricted the domestic industry's growth. The French eschewed standardization and obtained variety of type at the expense of uniformity of production, supply, and repairs. The Germans, relying solely on private industry and allowing firms to produce standard monoplane or biplane types diverse in construction, secured neither uniformity of production nor variety of type.

The British, far behind both, were going to need French assistance in aircraft supply until their industry could expand. Among the lesser powers, Russia and Italy possessed individual designers of merit but were dependent on France, while Austria-Hungary relied on Germany. The United States, land of aerial pioneers such as the Wright brothers and Glenn Curtiss, had the smallest aircraft industry of all.

By 1914 international connections had been significant in the development of national aviation industries. These ties allowed aircraft and engine acquisition for prototypes, unrestricted investment and the founding of subsidiaries throughout Europe, and the monopolization of key items by certain countries—Germany's magneto production for example. Designers and other innovators were mobile. The Italian Anzani established himself in France, the Swiss Franz Schneider and the Dutchman Anthony Fokker settled in Germany. Entrepreneurs, always quick to proclaim their patriotism, were equally quick to sell their craft abroad and to use that threat to pry more government contracts. The war would reduce or break ties between enemies, strengthen them among allies, and force the development of alternative sources for crucial items.

The aviation industry's dependence on a small pool of highly skilled craftsmen meant that a potential reservoir of trained talent would be indispensable to future expansion, particularly in engine production. The only alternative would be an alteration of the nature of construction, an unlikely prospect rendered nearly impossible under wartime pressures. France, already the leading aero engine producer, might turn to the plants and skilled craftsmen of its vaunted automobile industry—which was a distant second to the United States in prewar output—since firms such as Renault and De Dion Bouton were already producing aviation engines. The Daimler monopoly rendered German aero engine supply more precarious, and the rest of the German automobile industry, third in the world, was less productive than its French counterpart. Furthermore, while the fuel efficiency and long service life of German six-cylinder, liquid-cooled in-lines ideally suited them for states that might experience wartime labor, materiel, and fuel shortages, they did not offer the potential for diversity that French in-lines, rotaries, and radials did. As for the other future combatants, Britain, despite its industrial potential, depended on France; Italy possessed Fiat, which gave it the greatest manufacturing potential among the lesser powers; Austria-Hungary, home of Porsche's in-lines, probably lacked the industrial foundations to exploit its production substantially; Russia, like Britain, was dependent on France but lacked the industrial potential of its Western allies; and the United States, while it had the world's greatest automobile industry, possessed virtually no aero engine industry.

France and Germany were clearly beyond other nations in military aviation, but it is debatable which one was ahead. The official history of French military aviation published in 1980 concluded that the Germans, with both airplanes and Zeppelins, had wrested qualitative leadership from the French.[117] In the 1930s two German historians, one military and the other popular, concurred that the French were ahead. Hilmer von Bülow considered France about one year ahead of Germany in the tactical use of airplanes for artillery spotting and bombing, while popular writer Peter Supf believed that France was two years ahead.[118] It seems difficult to substantiate even the claim of a one-year advance, much less two years, although the proclamation of such a substantial lead increased the heroism of German wartime aviation efforts and warned against a repetition of such circumstances to Nazi audiences. Some British authors' claims that Sopwith's victory in the Schneider trophy race in April 1914 demonstrated that the lead in aviation was moving to Britain are best considered premature.[119]

Germany went to war with some 250 of 450 airplanes considered frontline materiel; French frontline squadrons had only 141 of some 600 military airplanes. Yet in 1913 the French had expanded their general reserve, which was comprised of frontline materiel, to nearly the same size as the frontline squadrons. The air services were thus nearly equal in size, and if the Germans had marginally more active-duty field pilots—254 to 220— the French probably had more reservists available given their earlier start and larger number of civilian pilots. Finally, the size of the air service was only the first part of preparedness in a branch based on technology and industry. If the Germans had the Zeppelin, the French led in aero engines, and without resorting to hindsight to determine that the engine would be far more crucial than the airship for wartime aviation, one can say that the two powers were about equal and were the nuclei of their respective alliances' aerial strength in 1914.

By 1914 technological and industrial progress in aviation, harnessed by the military, portended the fulfillment of the intention to fight from and in the air. Military commanders did not necessarily relish such a prospect, yet supreme commanders, even if not convinced, recognized that they could not afford to be without aviation in the coming war. The imperative of the arms race was perhaps best summarized in the British General Staff's July 1910 acknowledgement of the inability to "arrest or retard the perhaps unwelcome progress of aerial navigation." And unwelcome it undoubtedly was to many, as aviation injected a new factor into the equation of military balances, which generals could ignore only at peril to their states' security. In World War I air warfare would become significant, as combatant powers mustered progressively greater air arms in their struggle for victory.

August to December

1914

Into the Fray

Men were going to die in the air as they had died for centuries on the ground and on the seas, by killing each other. The conquest of the air was truly accomplished."

RENÉ CHAMBE[1]

In August 1914, when European air services answered the call to arms, they had existed for no longer than four years. In their fledgling state, they faced the herculean tasks of evolving daily air operations and mobilizing the aviation industry. Had the war been over in six weeks or six months, as many contemporaries predicted, the campaign would have ended before the necessity for industrial mobilization or technological evolution had arisen. Yet the conflict soon assumed an unprecedented nature. The demands of the fighting front far surpassed anything envisioned by the belligerents, necessitating the mobilization of the homefront just to continue, much less win, the war. The first months further witnessed two disparate modes of conflict on far-flung fronts. In the west the war of movement before the Battle of the Marne in early September gradually yielded to a stationary war of trenches in the fall, when the French and British fought the attacking Germans to a standstill. In the east a cataclysmic Sisyphean struggle over a vast expanse of often uncharted territory began when Germany and Austria-Hungary failed to overwhelm Russia. Italy's decision to remain neutral and ultimately to declare war on the Central Powers in May 1915 granted its aviation arm and industry a reprieve. Thus discussion of Italian aviation begins in 1915.

Of what use would the air arms prove in actual warfare? Performing peacetime maneuvers over familiar territory and airdromes was one matter; finding enemy targets and troops by reconnaissance over unfamiliar land while under fire from the ground was quite another. The success of aviators would depend not only on their execution of their missions for skeptical ground commanders, but also, and no less critically, on logistics (the military's ability to supply the front with new materiel) and ultimately on production (the domestic industry's ability to furnish the military with supplies). All these tasks were made more difficult by the rudimentary state of prewar plans for mobilizing the aviation industry. The air services had performed well in peacetime maneuvers; now the acid test of men and materiel—war—was upon them.

On 2 August 1914 the French army went to war with 4,342 officers and men in aviation and 23 squadrons totaling 141 airplanes. Squadrons were organized according to aircraft type, thereby avoiding problems of supply from mixing the types within units.[2] Thirteen squadrons flew biplanes, primarily Farmans, and 10 flew monoplanes, mostly Blériots. Eight firms supplied airplanes: Farman, Voisin, Caudron, and Breguet furnished biplanes; Blériot, Deperdussin, REP, and Nieuport provided monoplanes. Most of the aircraft used the 80-hp Gnome rotary; the Maurice Farmans had 70-hp Renault air-cooled in-line engines; and the Breguets were powered by 85-hp Salmson Canton-Unné water-cooled radial engines. The monoplanes and the Breguet and Caudron biplanes were tractor machines; the rest were pushers; and none of them could exceed 110 kilometers per hour (70 mph). Another 136 airplanes waited in the General Aviation Reserve at St. Cyr, while a few more were at training centers and factories. These planes were sufficient to form three additional squadrons in August.

At mobilization General Bernard, Director of Military Aeronautics in charge of the War Ministry's Twelfth Directorate, was certain that the war would be over quickly. He promptly curtailed flight training, closed the aviation schools, and decided to order no more airplanes during the war. Hostilities would not last more than six weeks, he observed, so what was the use of training new pilots and building new airplanes?[3] Because Bernard closed the aviation schools, their precious mechanics were inducted into the infantry and lost, some permanently, to aviation. When he curtailed plane orders, aviation factories also lost critical personnel. The aeronautical laboratory at Chalais-Meudon ceased experimental work in August when its officers rejoined their original units, although in August and September it did produce nine aircraft designed by its director, Captain Dorand. Bernard posted all officer pilots in the procurement bureaucracy as reserve pilots in the squadrons, leaving only three nonflying officers to procure airplanes.[4] Bernard acted unilaterally because he had no liaison with the high command (Grand Quartier Général, GQG) at the front and made no attempt to consult them.

Authors writing on French aviation have unequivocally condemned Bernard's shortsighted policies.[5] Yet he was merely acting upon the widely shared, though erroneous, premise of a short war, and like many of his contemporaries, he never envisioned the possibility of a protracted conflict. Bernard and others believed that reduced labor forces could complete airplanes ordered before hostilities; there would be no time to build more. Only the immediate future—when the greatest weight of arms possible had to be brought to bear on the attacking enemy—mattered, so all who could fly hastened to participate in the glorious fray. In the trying months ahead others would have occasion to regret the severe disruptions of personnel training and aircraft production and procurement that resulted from Bernard's policies, but at the time his actions seemed warranted.

The War Ministry's aviation procurement hierarchy—the Twelfth Directorate (Directorate of Military Aeronautics), Aviation Production Service (SFA), and the Airplane Service—did take last-minute steps to ensure a reduced flow of supplies. According to the following rather apocryphal statement by Louis Renault:

> On mobilization day this factory was not classed among those to remain open, and as all directors were subject to mobilization, we were preparing to flee our creditors when Gen. Bernard, director of aeronautics at the war ministry, deferred twenty men so that we could continue the production of some aviation engines under construction at the factory.[6]

It would have been surprising if prewar mobilization plans, however rudimentary, had not included Renault, an important producer of engines and motor vehicles. In fact a plan to operate the factory at reduced capacity existed two weeks before mobilization. Renault's total work force declined from 5,000 in July 1914 to 1,200 on 17 August, but staff and 200 workers remained at Billancourt to produce its durable in-line engines and "fléchettes," five- to seven-inch metal darts that aviators dropped on infantry below.[7] Other factories, among them Blériot, Farman, Breguet, and De Dion Bouton, which built motor vehicles and some aero engines, remained open with reduced work forces by military order. The army requisitioned all of Salmson's Canton-Unné engines in production. At Gnome and Rhône the mobilization of reservists in August took much of its labor force and reduced its production to 15 engines in September 1914, considerably below its prewar monthly production of 125 rotary engines.[8]

Bernard's subordinates, Commandant Stammler of the SFA and Captain Destouches of the airplane service, did all they could to ensure supplies. Stammler requisitioned all available airplanes. Destouches, who conducted acceptance tests from the passenger seat of airplanes with a bowler perched upon his head, practically single-handedly stabilized the factory monitoring system and aircraft procurement. In August the aviation industry delivered 50 planes, mainly Blériots and Farmans, and only 40 engines, primarily Gnome rotaries and Renault in-lines, evidence that the beginning of the war disrupted engine far more than airframe manufacture.[9]

Supplying these planes to a French army in rapid retreat was no easy task. Regular deliveries became a dead letter after 20 August. Frontline pilots could be found at storehouses in the rear at St. Cyr and Dijon, attempting in vain to commandeer airplanes. In this confusion the War Ministry occasionally displayed a narrow bureaucratic mentality. On 26 August it complained to GQG that frontline units were taking parts from some engines to repair others and then sending the incomplete ones to the rear for repairs. The ministry prescribed that only complete engines should be sent back for repairs, although if urgent situations did require cannibalization, units at least needed to account for the parts. The frontline units, suffering from irregular supply in the face of the German juggernaut, undoubtedly were not concerned with such administrative niceties.[10]

As the German army approached Paris at the end of August, the rear agencies retreated with the government from Paris to Lyon. Leaving only sufficient personnel in Paris to accept planes from the Parisian aircraft factories, Stammler's SFA moved from Meudon to Lyon and there formed a new procurement annex staffed with retired officers. At Stammler's invitation, Farman, Voisin, Caudron, REP, Salmson, and Gnome and Rhône began to organize factories in the vicinity of Lyon. In September their Paris factories, while struggling to reclaim inducted workers, delivered to the army 62 planes that replenished the general reserve and equipped five new squadrons. In two months the engine manufacturers delivered 145 engines—

76 rotaries, 60 Renault in-lines, and 9 Salmson radials—an increase of 105 over August, though still dismal compared to prewar production.[11]

While the rear struggled to regain its feet, the aviation units at the front served as best as they could in the war of movement. GQG's air chief Colonel Voyer and his aide Captain Jaillet, both dirigible pilots, responded flexibly to the disappointing performance from their fragile airships in the first days of the war by working to improve the use of airplanes. Crews performed their reconnaissance missions diligently, and individual airplanes even undertook bombing missions against the Zeppelin hangars at Metz. Yet Commander in Chief Joffre and his staff received information gleaned by aerial reconnaissance with surprise, skepticism, and even irritation.[12]

On 30 August as the Germans approached Paris, the aviation units of the Paris fortifications, which included volunteer Corp. Louis Breguet flying his own airplane, were placed on alert. On 2 September Breguet returned from a mission to report that the German army was turning to the east of Paris. That day and the next Captain Bellenger, the Sixth Army aviation commander, received similar reports from his squadrons. When the intelligence chief of the Sixth Army refused to believe him, Bellenger went straight to the commander of the Paris fortifications, General Galliéni, who had been favorably disposed toward aviation since 1910. The outcome of the general's suggestion that Joffre take advantage of the German maneuver by striking Klück's flank was the Battle of the Marne—a victory for the French and the beginning of the stalemate on the Western Front.[13]

On 8 September during the Marne battle, aerial observation enabled the French artillery to strike the German artillery of the Sixth Army near Triaucourt so effectively that it elicited Joffre's praise in his daily communiqué of 10 September. Although Joffre commended such collaboration on 3 and 27 September, this incident was the exception, as the artillery was usually reluctant to entrust spotting to airplane crews. In August and September 1914 French aviators flew reconnaissance missions and seized any occasion to drop 90mm shells and packets of fléchettes on the Germans. The airplane's role in the Marne battle impressed Joffre enough for him to determine that aviation needed someone with initiative to organize it at the front. GQG selected Commandant Joseph Barès, a volunteer aviator in the Balkan War of 1912–13 and the sole superior officer pilot who flew regularly. The bearded and mustachioed Barès became GQG's aviation chief on 25 September, a post he would hold until February 1917.[14]

With the end of September the first phase of the history of French aviation in World War I closed. In helping the French army survive the

German onslaught, the aviation squadrons had begun to demonstrate their potential for reconnaissance and bombing before the war settled into a stalemate. The rear, disorganized and disrupted first by Bernard's policies and then by the retreat, had managed to maintain some semblance of production and supply. By September the factories were beginning to recover from the chaos, although pilot training schools were still closed.

Barès assessed the first two months of the war, and on 8 October GQG proposed its first wartime plan for the development of military aviation. On 1 October there were 31 squadrons at the front. GQG hoped to raise the number to 65 with 384 airplanes in three months. Furthermore, the plan called for specialization of functions: 16 bomber squadrons in four groups; 16 reconnaissance and pursuit squadrons at the army level; 30 observation squadrons at the army corps level; and 3 cavalry squadrons, which would have four rather than the usual six planes per unit. In order to simplify supply and eliminate unsuitable airplanes, the number of service types would be reduced to four: the Morane-Saulnier monoplane with the 80-hp Le Rhône rotary for pursuit; the Maurice Farman biplane with the 80-hp Renault in-line for reconnaissance; the Caudron biplane with the 80-hp Le Rhône for artillery spotting; and the Voisin biplane with the 130-hp Salmson radial for bombardment.[15]

The plan's provisions represented a clear step forward. Specialization according to task and the assignment of units to the armies and army corps they served meant a clearer delineation of the air arm's role. Despite the mediocrity of artillery shells as bombs, the addition of fins and new detonators that caused them to explode on impact prompted GQG to advocate on 27 September the use of the airplane as an instrument of direct combat, bombing artillery batteries, troop concentrations, and communications that were beyond the range of French cannon.[16]

The creation of pursuit squadrons indicated that some French aviators preferred attacking their German counterparts to the more mundane tasks of observation. The first recorded aerial victory occurred on 5 October, when Sgt. Joseph Frantz and his mechanic Quénault shot down an Aviatik biplane from their Voisin, whose structural rigidity and pusher configuration allowed a machine gun to be mounted in the front cockpit. The squadron's captain had arranged for André Voisin himself to bring the guns directly from the Hotchkiss factory. Death in the air proved gruesome. An infantry lieutenant who witnessed the victory reported that the German plane, having caught fire and crashed, left its occupants "one burning under the machine, the other, who could be pulled away, wounded in the chest and partially burned."[17] The riveted attention of observers on the ground showed that air combat attracted spectators, and aerial victories provided the occasion for medals. General Franchet d'Esperey personally congratulated and decorated the fliers.[18]

If the Voisin was successful, other planes failed the test of war and were eliminated in the plan. The First Army aviation commander labeled the Blériot "one of the most mediocre of military airplanes," its poor climb and gliding characteristics so inadequate and dangerous that its crews were asking to be retrained on other airplanes.[19] Although the few cavalry squadrons would retain it because of its ease of transport, both the units and the Blériots were not long for the Western Front.

In the rear on 8 October a new Director of Military Aeronautics, General Hirschauer—Bernard's predecessor and now his successor—reported on the state of aviation and future production plans to War Minister Alexandre Millerand at the Elysée Palace. Bernard's relationship with GQG had been less than cordial, but Hirschauer's prewar experience in aviation and his fine relationship with Joffre had prompted Millerand to select him. Hirschauer proposed to have three of the four standard types produced under license—the Caudron by Blériot and Deperdussin, the Voisin by Nieuport, REP, and Breguet, and the Morane by Breguet—and he was prepared to requisition the workshops of Breguet, Nieuport, and Deperdussin if they refused to cooperate. The aeronautical laboratory halted the production of Colonel Dorand's airplane to concentrate on aircraft acceptance and tests. Hirschauer planned to eliminate gradually the production of lower-hp engines, favor the production of the Le Rhône over the more fragile and thirstier Gnome, and speed the production of Salmson and De Dion engines. The army requisitioned the Hispano-Suiza automobile factory at Bois-Colombes to manufacture Rhônes, while the Darracq and Peugeot automobile factories would build Salmson and Renault engines respectively by the agreement with the Third Directorate to partition work in these automotive factories. To compensate the firms for the shift to licensed production, Hirschauer guaranteed them contracts for 2,300 airplanes, 3,400 engines, and 1,050 transport vehicles in order to have 400 aircraft in line and another 200 in the general reserve by the planned spring offensive.[20]

Potential problems loomed—accelerating production would take time, and Caudron's lack of plans for its aircraft would delay licensed production until early 1915—but Hirschauer forged ahead. With the issue of such large orders, Hirschauer negotiated prices with the firms and attempted to restore order to supply. Renault, for example, requested an increase in price from 11,200 to 12,800 francs for its 80-hp engine to compensate for the cost of its move to Lyon, rising labor and material costs, and difficulties procuring special steel for engine production. The directorate accepted Renault's request, reasoning that while the Renault cost more than rotary engines of comparable horsepower (the Gnome at 9,500, the Le Rhône at 10,200, and the Clerget at 10,500 francs), its crankcase was more voluminous and difficult to manufacture and its crankshaft was larger and more expensive. Its maintenance was also more economical since its interval between overhauls was three times that of a rotary.[21]

As of mid-October aviation officers were still traveling directly to Parisian firms to acquire aircraft and parts. This practice should have ceased once the front stabilized because it played havoc with accurate inventories of supplies. English pilots who journeyed to Paris to obtain replacement airplanes found that the trip offered certain diversions and delights, with which French pilots were undoubtedly familiar. Hirschauer consequently threatened to return future offenders to their original branch of the service.[22]

With the onset of winter's inclement weather, aerial action slowed, giving the aviation service the late fall and early winter to prepare for the coming year. Because of the closing of the flight schools, only 134 pilots were breveted in 1914, and Pau and Avord did not reopen until December. As the French government returned to Paris, the SFA returned to Chalais-Meudon on 4 December, leaving a procurement annex in Lyon. In the last three months of 1914, aircraft and engine deliveries rose steadily (100, 137, and 192 airplanes; 137, 209, and 374 engines) to total 541 planes and 860 engines during the first five months of the war. Despite these increases, GQG advised the War Minister on 13 December that deliveries of 77 Voisins, Morane Saulniers, and Maurice Farmans in November had been far below the 183 planes it had anticipated. This was the first of many similar charges from the front, as in the months ahead deliveries would often fall below the front's expectations in both quality and quantity.[23]

Engine factories increased production of current types and developed higher-hp engines simultaneously. Renault delivered 150 80-hp engines ordered on 1 October by 1 January and had received a further order for 420 engines on 13 December. Meanwhile the company was developing a 130-hp V12 engine, building foundries for malleable cast iron for its engine cylinder heads and aluminum for engine crankcases, and producing machine tools to save the expense of importing them. Salmson also expanded. It received an order for 600 140-hp radial engines on 24 November while developing a new Canton-Unné 200-hp radial for an order of 100 engines. Historian James Laux attributed Salmson's large orders not merely to the superior power of its engines but also to the patronage of shareholder Charles Humbert, an influential Parisian journalist and member of the Senate's Army Commission. At the end of 1914 Gnome and Rhône received orders for 315 engines, and the factory had increased production from 15 engines in September to 215 in December. Rotary engines, compared to 200 in-lines and 138 radials, constituted the majority of the 860 engines delivered to the army in the war's first five months.[24]

Although Hirschauer was intent on increasing engine production, in November he was not interested in having the engine manufacturers form an interest group like those the Comité des Forges had established in September 1914 to work with the War Ministry. Renault already headed the Comité's Paris group of 10 shell-producing automobile factories and could easily have done the same for the Twelfth Directorate. But Hirschauer probably feared that an association might give the manufacturers too much power against the directorate. Wartime pressures for increased production would make him more amenable to such proposals in 1915.[25]

The year thus ended in France with the implementation of GQG's production plan in the rear, the production of aircraft and engines rapidly increasing, and the aviation agencies in the front and rear under new commanders, who would have to coordinate frontline demands and the industry's capacity to fulfill them. At the front, French aircrews were beginning to use cameras for reconnaissance while they staged an occasional bombing raid or attack on German reconnaissance planes. In November GQG began to consider the strategic bombardment of German industrial centers. As early as 2 August, Paul Painlevé at the War Ministry and industrialists such as the Michelin brothers and aircraft builder Paul Schmitt had expressed interest in bombing Essen, but such a mission had exceeded the capacity of the tiny air arm. Now, with Paris bombed by German Taubes in August—however lightly and ineffectively—and the war stalemated, GQG, encouraged by British raids and "the need to fill the empty pages of the communiqué and sustain the morale of the rear," formed four squadrons on 23 November into the First Bombardment Group (GB1) of 18 Voisins under the command of Commandant de Goÿs.[26] Barès and de Goÿs first struck Germany with this force on 4 December with a raid on the railway station at Freiburg, and by the end of the year they were drawing up a list of vulnerable and important targets.

At 1830 hours on 1 August 1914 the German army received its mobilization orders, and the next day its aviation units were activated. Each of the eight German armies received an airship and airplane unit with a supporting aircraft park; each of the 25 army corps headquarters was given an airplane unit. Ten fortress-flight units of four airplanes each were deployed to Metz, Strasbourg, and Cologne in the west and Posen, Königsberg, Graudenz, and the military bases at Boyen, Breslau, and Glogau in the east.[27]

The army high command (OHL) had airships, but no airplanes, at its direct disposal.[28] It planned to use its fleet of six ships in the west, Zeppelins Z6–8 and three former Delag ships, the Sachsen, Hansa, and Viktoria Luise, to support the army with reconnaissance and bombing attacks, and its three in the east, the older Zeppelins Z4–5 and the Schütte-Lanz SL2, for reconnaissance. In fact, the three Delag ships were suited only for training purposes, so the OHL began the war in the west with three combat ships, receiving a fourth, the Z9, on 10 August. The Z6 promptly attacked Lüttich on 6 August, dropped 200 kilograms of bombs, was hit by groundfire, and was forced to land in a forest near Bonn where it was dismantled. The OHL then ordered the Z7 and Z8 on 21 August to bomb the French forces attacking from Alsace. The Z7 dropped 500 kilograms of bombs, but to satisfy the General Staff officer on board it circled the French twice in the morning light at 800 meters altitude. Hit by ground fire, it landed in Lorraine. The Z8, hit first by German and then French troops, dropped 160 kilograms of bombs and then descended out of control. By the end of September the Z9 had dropped 3,750 kilograms of bombs in three attacks on Antwerp and 1,100 on Ostende and had flown reconnaissance missions to Calais. On 21 August it attacked five cities in a raid down the coast—Antwerp, Zeebrugge, Dunkirk, Calais, and Lille—with 1,200 kilograms of bombs. It was lost in a British bombing attack on its shed in Düsseldorff on 8 October.

On the Eastern Front the Z4, the army's oldest ship, performed only night missions until early October, when it was grounded because of the weather. The Z5, used for reconnaissance missions in August, was shot down in a bombing attack, while the SL2 was sent to the Austrian army in September. The Zeppelins' initial wartime performance had thus been disastrous; of seven military airships, five had been destroyed by early October, four by fire from the ground. The policy of having General Staff officers lacking in technical knowledge accompany and command the ships on missions had resulted in the loss of the Z7, and the Z8 need not have been lost on the Eastern Front if the command had heeded the losses of ships on bombing missions in the west. The Zeppelins were proving to be liabilities. They could be used over the front only on dark nights, and replacement of their losses was slow. Only three new Zeppelins entered service by the end of 1914.

Airplanes, on the other hand, acquitted themselves well on both the Eastern and Western Fronts. In the war of movement in the west in August, they kept track of the French retreat. Although the Aviation Inspectorate received numerous complaints about the obsolescent Taubes, the biplanes served well and the standard of crew training paid dividends. While aircrews initially overlooked the presence of the British army corps, their detection of the French withdrawal from positions at Maas on 21 and 24 August enabled changes in the direction of the German attack. They played an important role in the German victory at Neufchâtel and then detected Joffre's counteroffensive at the Marne on 4–5 September coming from northeast of Paris and not directly from Paris as expected. According to Hilmer von Bülow, a retrospective collection of the handwritten reports of German fliers gives a full overview of enemy movements in the west. Individual pilots bombed Lunéville on 3 August and then Paris at the end of August. On 29 August Hermann Dressler flew around the Eiffel Tower, dropped a bomb on Paris, and then managed to outrun two Gallic "cocks" in his dove, a remarkable feat probably accomplished only with a substantial lead. Lieutenant Hiddessen dropped a note on 30 August advising Parisians that "The German Army stands before the gates of Paris. You have no choice but to surrender."[29] The Germans, though prepared to bomb, seem to have been slower than the British or French in attempting to down their opposite numbers.

On the Eastern Front, aviation may have been even more important than in the west because the Russian cavalry greatly outnumbered the German. Aviators were instrumental in the German victory at Tannenberg, locating the Russian army, providing a clear picture of its advance in mid-August, and then detecting the Russian attempt to spring Samsonov from the German encirclement. Baron Elard von Loewenstern's memoir of these early days on the Eastern Front emphasizes the difficulty of observation in this unfamiliar and uncharted territory. If the weather was cloudy, he and his pilot had difficulty observing and keeping their bearings. They often would not have seen troops on the ground if the excited Russian soldiers had not fired at them. At Tannenberg they were so preoccupied with following a distant Russian column that they remained unaware of an entire Russian division directly beneath them until bullets began smacking into their Taube. Loewenstern saw little of the Battle of Tannenberg because the masses of troops simply disappeared into the land.[30]

By the end of August the airplane had developed from "a supplementary means of information relied upon principally for confirmation" to "the principal means of operational reconnaissance—an important factor in forming army commanders' decisions."[31] Instrumental in preparing the victory at Tannenberg and in preventing a more serious defeat at the Marne, air operations, if not completely successful, had shown the airplane's potential.

Inadequate organizational, logistical, and industrial underpinnings prevented a rapid realization of aviation's potential. The OHL and army commands lacked central aviation agencies to collect and assess the fliers' reports, and the subordination of the German aviation troops to the War Ministry's transport corps deprived them of direct access to the front command. This organizational gap, in an army noted for its organization, meant that many reports simply went unassessed or unheeded. Similarly, Prussian aviation lacked a single authority to coordinate the frontline units with the Aviation Inspectorate and the War Ministry in Berlin. The inspector, Col. Walther von Eberhardt, had noted on 12 August in his diary that without aviation staff officers at the various army commands, the flying troops lacked central agencies in the field to collect and evaluate frontline experience for technical and operational use. Eberhardt actually went to the field on 15 August to attempt to regain control over his troops, but during his absence the inspectorate in Berlin suffered while his temporary presence in the field did not restore order. Yet at the end of the month, when Eberhardt recommended the creation of a chief of air forces in the field with staff officers at each army headquarters, Minister of War Erich von Falkenhayn, averse to such an extensive measure, demurred.[32]

Organizational deficiencies further threatened to disrupt the supply of aircraft to the front. The practice of equipping a unit with different aircraft types unnecessarily complicated the distribution of spare parts. Intermediate airparks often had no liaison with their frontline units. For the German army's right wing on the Western Front, lengthening distances to the depots so ruptured supply that the airpark commander at Liège, Belgium, let his planes be used for active service. Pilots who had crashed their planes at the front could be seen lounging around factories in Germany, waiting their turn for new airplanes. Unit leaders zealously sent flying officers in lorries to aircraft factories to commandeer airplanes and drive them to local railway stations for shipment to the front. Frequently the frames arrived broken or crushed; in their haste the officers often forgot that Belgian railway tunnels lacked the clearance of those in Germany. The flying officers' expeditions home, in flagrant defiance of Eberhardt's orders, impeded the formation of new units and the inspectorate's surveillance of available materiel. Major Wilhelm Siegert, commander of Aviation Park 7, unilaterally attached himself to the headquarters of the Seventh Army's 14 Corps, encouraged the Aviatik factory in Freiburg to equip a wildcat flight unit, and then began flying at the front in utter disregard of orders. Such enthusiasm, though well-intentioned and, in Siegert's case, later rewarded with greater responsibility, was disruptive in this instance. Ruthless stopgap measures—requisitioning airplanes from firms, even planes designated for naval or Bavarian units—failed to alleviate the shortage. These logistical problems were solved primarily by the stabilization of the Western Front in September.[33]

The aircraft and, particularly, the aero engine industries were not prepared to meet the high loss rate of airplanes. One flight unit was requesting two planes daily in August, and overall losses for the month have been estimated at 40 percent of the army's frontline strength. As of 4 August, with the factories delivering 50 airframes and 12 engines weekly, Eberhardt could not replace anticipated losses, much less equip new units. Although engine deliveries had increased to 24 by the end of the month, field units could still expect to receive less than one airplane weekly.[34]

Within 48 hours of mobilization, industry representatives were requesting three-month contracts, aid in materials procurement, exemptions for employees, and an increase in airplane prices. The army promised assistance with material and exemptions, but not with contracts or prices because it feared premature agreements might prevent lowering prices later and lead to the industry's "unjustified enrichment." On 5 August seven members of the Reichstag's center and right-wing parties convened on their own initiative to help the military develop the aircraft industry and a large air fleet to offset English naval superiority; this offer of consultation was accepted by the Prussian War Ministry and the Imperial Naval Office. At meetings of military, industrial, and political representatives during the next two days, the aircraft industry agreed to deliver some 200 airplanes monthly after mid-September, and the engine industry promised to provide 170 engines. Hastily assembled, the manufacturers were persuaded to sacrifice lesser patent rights and price increases in return for the assurance of contracts, exemptions, and pupils for their flying schools—concessions they would have won as the war continued. While the army feared that the manufacturers might use the favorable market to their advantage, the manufacturers were so grateful for the change in the market that they neglected to press their advantage. Throughout the first months of the war, the army would dispense exemptions to the industry parsimoniously while it refused to raise aircraft prices despite increases in material prices.[35]

The parliamentary deputies, who offered themselves as arbiters in future disputes, were generally interested in industrial affairs and reflected a sentiment in military, diplomatic, and business circles for "breaking British resistance" through air warfare. In late August the German minister in Stockholm, Franz von Reichenau, hoped "with all his heart" that "Germany would send airships and aircraft cruising regularly over England dropping bombs" until "the vulgar huckster souls" of those "cowardly assassins" would forget "even how to do sums." Walther Rathenau also advocated "systematically working on the nerves of the English towns through an overwhelming air force." Their plan to use air weapons to offset naval power indicated some perception, however vague and inflated, of the potential to strike directly at England through the air.[36]

The stabilization of the Western Front temporarily frustrated the grandiose designs of bringing England to its knees through aerial bombardment. Major Wilhelm Siegert, who became aviation adviser to the high command on 19 October, formed the command's flying corps, which was later called the Brieftauben Abteilung Ostende (Carrier Pigeon Unit Ostende), with the aim of bombing England from Calais. The Germans never captured Calais, and since existing aircraft could not reach England from Ostende, the force had to content itself with raids on Dunkirk and French harbors and railroad junctions. Its value was thus much less than intended, and it actually weakened other units of the air service by absorbing many of the most experienced pilots when the service was confronted with a new type of warfare in the west.[37]

Trench warfare, which made cavalry sorties impossible, shifted the burden of reconnaissance to the airplane. Given prewar expectations, German aviators had been trained for the long-range reconnaissance of the war of movement. With the war of position in September and October the major tasks gradually shifted to short-range reconnaissance and artillery spotting over and behind the lines. The new assignments were difficult but potentially quite useful. In early September a wounded French infantry lieutenant told a French pilot how a German aircraft had spotted his Moroccan division hidden behind an embankment and unleashed a terrible barrage 20 minutes later that reduced their battalion from 750 to 220 men and killed or wounded 13 of their 20 officers.[38]

Artillery spotter Maximilian von Cossel flew three flights daily for two days to direct German artillery shoots of British batteries at Fort Condé between Reims and Soissons. He used a flare pistol to signal the German batteries, although such flare systems were rudimentary, employing either direction or color of flare for different instructions. Such spotting enabled more accurate shooting and thus saved shells in a war whose profligate use of them led to severe shortages. Air-ground communications by means of shooting flares, dropping weighted messages, or landing to deliver them were not particularly efficient, so in September the army initiated wireless tests, contracted with the firms Telefunken and Huth to deliver sets suitable for airplanes, and the first German planes with wireless arrived at the front in December 1914.[39]

Aviators on the Eastern Front encountered other difficulties in covering the entire front with only four or five flight units having an average strength of three airplanes. Erich Ludendorff, chief of staff of Germany's Eastern Front armies, advised aviators on 16 October that their reports on what they saw must be absolutely precise, and if conditions made reliable observation difficult, then their reports needed to acknowledge these circumstances. Loewenstern admitted that it was difficult for the observers to formulate such clear messages, and their General Staff chiefs often desired more specificity than they could provide.

In the rear, the military bureaucracy and the aviation industry were hard-pressed to keep up with the front's demands even after the war settled into the trenches. Although the firms at the 5 August conference had promised to deliver 200 airplanes monthly, the air service received only 462 new airplanes between 3 August and 29 November, and the first new aviation units formed since 3 August did not depart for the front until 28 September. In the first months of the war, planes arriving at the front were often defective, so in the fall the inspectorate enforced its construction and delivery guidelines more stringently. While the Taube's low ceiling and poor climb rendered it obsolete, Anthony Fokker's small factory delivered its first production M8 monoplanes in October. Oswald Boelcke, destined to become one of the war's great fighter pilots, observed that the Fokker's speed, climb, and maneuverability made it the best aircraft for the air service's major task of artillery spotting. The plane's poor serviceability, however, prompted inspection visits to the factory and units at the front from the inspectorate's team of civilian engineers, who discovered only that the Fokker factory's use of steel tubing and welding by Fokker chief technician Reinhold Platz was further advanced than the inspectorate's guidelines required it to be. In December, to keep pace with the front's demands, the inspectorate raised its minimum climb rate from 800 meters in 15 minutes and 2,000 meters in 60 minutes to 800 meters in 10 minutes and 2,000 meters in 35 minutes, though it consented to transitional times of 12 and 40 minutes when the firms complained that they could not meet such demands overnight.[40]

By early December the firms were also complaining vehemently about prices. Although the parliamentary commission advised them that the profits from substantial wartime contracts had offset the rise in production costs, the firms retorted that aircraft prices by January were lower than they had been at the war's beginning, while raw material prices had risen from 20 to 100 percent and wages for skilled workers had risen 14 percent. Only in February 1915 did the War Ministry consent to increase the price of all aircraft delivered after 1 January by 3 percent.[41]

The Prussian War Ministry thus resisted aircraft price increases four months longer than did the French War Ministry, which had consented to price increases in October when it issued extensive aircraft contracts to prepare for the coming spring offensive. The Prussian army took until February 1915 to acknowledge the following: that the extensive induction of skilled workers and the concomitant use of unskilled hands had lowered per capita output and increased losses from ruined material; that many airplane factories had entered the war with sizable deficits and now faced the daunting expenses of enormous expansion and the continual conversion of production to new types; and that factories would have to pay off as much of their wartime investments as possible during the war because after the war much of their plants would be useless.

The army bureaucracy had also been reluctant to acknowledge the industry's right to lay claim to potential soldiers. On 5 October the head of the War Department, Gen. Franz von Wandel, had reprimanded the deputy general commands about the necessity of exempting personnel whom the aircraft manufacturers considered essential and trusting the industry not to abuse the privilege, since denial of or failure to fulfill the exemptions policy would release the firms from responsibility for reliable work or prompt delivery.[42]

The structure of the German empire complicated aviation mobilization because, while the Prussian War Ministry dominated the military bureaucracy, the existence of ministries in some of the smaller states, Bavaria in particular, impeded the most efficient and unified mobilization of the aviation industry. The Bavarian War Ministry was as preoccupied with maintaining its independence from Prussia and north German firms as it was with obtaining sufficient airplanes, although it remained dependent upon Prussia for its supply of the precious Mercedes engine. The Bavarian air arm relied upon two small firms, the Gustav Otto works of Munich and the Pfalz factory in Speyer am Rhein. Otto delivered some 50 planes during the first five months of the war. Pfalz manufactured only 14, but at the end of the year it created a successful copy of the French Morane parasol, which began to replace the Fokker in Bavarian artillery spotting units.[43]

German naval aviation was also subordinate to military aviation, as the Prussian army insisted on priority of claims upon the aircraft industry. Anthony Fokker recalled that in August army and navy commanders dashed up to his factory daily, "warring with each other" over his aircraft, until a visit from Inspector Eberhardt persuaded him to grant priority to the army.[44] The General Staff then stopped all landplane deliveries to the navy, forcing the Imperial Naval Office to acquire them through the War Ministry and the Aviation Inspectorate, which controlled all landplane and aero engine production. A Chief of Naval Flight Units (Befehlshaber der Marine-Flieger Abteilungen), Rear Admiral Philipp, was appointed on 29 August 1914, though he had only 20 seaplanes in his command. Rear Admiral Starke headed a new aviation section for the development and procurement of aviation materiel in the Imperial Naval Office's dockyard department. The navy relied primarily on Flugzeugbau Friedrichshafen (FF) for its early patrol floatplanes, receiving 21 of the slow but reliable and seaworthy craft from August through December. None of its firms—FF, Rumpler, Albatros, Gotha, and Hansa-Brandenburg—could produce more than half their assigned orders, with production times ranging from one week to three months. The navy could not supplement these orders with its own efforts because, despite orders in December to undertake aircraft construction, the dockyards at Wilhelmshaven and Danzig found that experienced aircraft designers and skilled workers were impossible to obtain. The navy approached Albatros, Hansa-Brandenburg, FF, and Gotha about torpedo plane construction in 1914.[45]

The naval airship unit had only one Zeppelin, 12 officers, and 340 men at mobilization. Its commander, Strasser, concentrated on developing the infrastructure necessary for a dirigible fleet, and by December he had 3,740 officers and men at nine bases. They had received 50-kg bombs in October and tested a 300-kg bomb for use in dirigibles in December. Now the unit was waiting for the larger airship under construction at the Zeppelin works and due to appear in the spring. The dirigible had failed the army, but the navy, considering it a cheap substitute for reconnaissance cruisers, and imbued with the idea of striking England, expanded the airship unit.

While the dirigible had yet to measure up to expectations, the German army's airplane service had succeeded in establishing itself as the reconnaissance arm, although the aviation industry, particularly the aero engine producers, had experienced great difficulty keeping abreast of the front's demands.

In August 1914, the Royal Flying Corps's chief planner, commander of the military wing Colonel Sykes, was convinced, like his continental counterparts, of a short and glorious war. He threw nearly every man and machine into the fray, believing that neither could stand more than three months in the field. He sent four squadrons, the Second through Fifth, with 105 officers,

755 persons of other ranks, 63 airplanes, and 95 transport vehicles to support the British Expeditionary Force (BEF) on the continent, leaving a home reserve of 41 officers and 116 aircraft, of which only 20 were fit for service. This sweep of England nearly paralyzed the RFC's later development by taking pilots from the reserve, the CFS, the depot, and even from the embryonic Sixth Squadron's nucleus. Major General Henderson assumed direct command of the field force with Sykes as his chief of staff, leaving the Directorate of Military Aviation at home under the command of Sefton Brancker, a junior lieutenant colonel, and the remnants of the military wing at Farnborough under Major Hugh Trenchard, formerly second in command of the CFS. The RFC force comprised two squadrons of BE2c's and a motley collection of Vickers and Farman two-seat pushers, Avro two-seat tractors, and Blériot monoplanes. The squadrons flew across the Channel to Amiens, arriving on 13 August, and then on to Maubeuge aerodrome two days later, suffering four fatalities on the way. They arrived just in time for the retreat from Mons.

The RFC's effectiveness in 1914 has occasioned some historical debate. Early accounts, the official history, and the Air Ministry's official synopsis of the wartime aerial effort praised the RFC's regular, rapid, and accurate reconnaissance in the retreat. Sykes's memoir credits aerial reconnaissance on 21–22 August with saving the army and on 3 September with leading to the Battle of the Marne.[46] More recently historians David Divine and Malcolm Cooper have emphasized the RFC's flaws in August and September 1914. Divine condemned its insufficient airplanes, inaccurate navigation, indeterminate observation, general failures of interpreting information, and the General Staff's injudicious rejection of the information gained from aerial reconnaissance.[47] Cooper concluded that such problems meant airplanes had only slightly aided the army in the war of movement and that aerial reconnaissance did not save the army at Mons or lead directly to the victory at the Marne.[48] It is ironic that Divine and Cooper give the RFC less credit for its performance than did the BEF command.

After painting Union Jacks on the undersides of their wings at Maubeuge to discourage friendly ground fire, the RFC entered action on 19 August. Its first sorties were abortive; two pilots flying without observers lost their way. On 22 August, as the RFC moved into position at Mons, 12 reconnaissance missions informed Gen. John French for the first time of the French Fifth Army's defeat and withdrawal. The RFC steadily retreated, moving for the fifth time to 20 miles northeast of Paris on 31 August, when its reports of Klück's swing to the southeast, which corroborated those of

French aircraft, helped the French Fifth Army prepare for the Marne battle. General French's dispatch of 7 September paid particular tribute to the RFC for its "admirable work," "skill, energy, and perseverance," commending it for providing him with "the most complete and accurate information, which has been of incalculable value in the conduct of operations." In a difficult retreat the RFC, like the BEF, gave a creditable account of itself.[49]

In these adventurous early days on the wing, RFC pilots were not content to observe and report. During the retreat they had dropped hand grenades and gasoline bombs on the advancing Germans. They were determined to assert their ascendancy over the German pilots. On 22 August six RFC craft vainly pursued an Albatros over Maubeuge, one of them armed with a machine gun that so weighed the Farman down that it was still climbing long after the German had left. Yet the British would down five German aircraft by mid-September, essentially by harassing them from above and forcing them to land. Supply collapsed during the war of movement, so unit commanders had to replace their severe losses of 40 aircraft in two months from French firms. Captain Philip Joubert de la Ferté of the Third Squadron recalled traveling to Paris, where he would take a bath, buy clean clothes, and eat several good meals in civilized restaurants.[50] Major H. R. M. Brooke-Popham, Joubert de la Ferté's squadron commander and Deputy Assistant Quartermaster-General of the RFC, kept a traveling bag of gold under his Daimler's seat with which to buy the planes.[51]

With the advance to the Aisne River and the end of mobile warfare, the airplane was gradually incorporated into the routine of trench warfare. Particularly from October on, during the relative lull in activity after the first Battle of Ypres, the RFC began to evolve the rudiments of air-ground cooperation and offensive operations, especially bombing. It mapped out the front and immediate rear and began to experiment with wireless and aerial photography, crews taking some 40 negatives in November at Neuve-Chapelle. By the end of the year Sykes's instructions to training commander John Salmond to study the French aerial photography organization had led to the formation of an experimental British aerial photography section.[52]

The squadrons received sufficient reinforcements to replace their losses and to permit the formation of two more squadrons by the end of November, when the RFC was divided into two wings of three squadrons each. Yet early in August Secretary of State for War Kitchener had instructed Brancker to raise five additional squadrons. The formation of these new squadrons did not constitute any real increase in the RFC. By the end of the year the corps still had only 61 airplanes—essentially the same number with which it had begun the campaign in August—because the small British aviation industry was not prepared to meet the RFC's wartime needs.

Early in the war the War Office and the Admiralty urged maximum production from the industry and provisionally allocated all airplanes and engines of 100 horsepower or less to the War Office and all seaplanes and higher-hp engines to the Admiralty. Both asked the Rolls Royce firm to enlist the help of the Royal Aircraft Factory in developing a 250-hp engine for the Admiralty. Commander Wilfred Briggs, the Admiralty's chief of aero engine design, actually towed a Mercedes Grand Prix racer from its showroom and presented it to the Rolls Royce factory with instructions to place top priority on making a series of in-line water-cooled engines using Mercedes cylinder and valve construction. [53]

The army selected the BE2c for mass production, since the Royal Aircraft Factory had its drawings ready and was prepared to train managers and foremen from suitable companies that lacked aircraft manufacturing experience. The factory had also designed BE wings to be interchangeable with the outer-wing bays of its FE2 pusher for further ease of design and manufacture. The RFC's standardization of the BE2c would later come under fire on the fighting fronts and homefronts when it became fodder for German fighters. In 1914, however, its stability seemed ideal for reconnaissance, and its readiness for production appeared a great advantage in meeting the unexpectedly high wastage of wartime flying.

The eight or nine British contractors capable of production manufactured only 193 aircraft in 1914, 60 of which were experimental types. Confronted with this inadequate supply, the War Office in October opened aircraft design and assembly to the trade, giving the industry the opportunity it had sought but failed to achieve before the war. Early in December the RFC also requested the attachment of small parties of RFC men to aircraft and engine works for rigging and engine fitting instruction, in preparation for training more military personnel.

The near absence of an engine industry in Britain compounded the difficulties of aircraft production. In the last five months of 1914 British companies manufactured only 99 engines, compared to 894 produced by French firms, leaving the RFC dependent upon French Renaults and Gnomes. Magneto shortages delayed the plans of Holt Thomas of Airco to produce the Gnome monosoupape. Also, a prewar recommendation by Thomas and Capt. J. B. D. Fulton of the Aircraft Inspection Department to produce the Rhône engine in Britain had been rejected because simplifying production would have required concentration on a single rotary. This situation left only the Royal Aircraft Factory's 90-hp engine—a reliable derivative of the French Renault—in domestic production, as designs by Fred Green and the Sunbeam engine company were still too heavy for efficient use in airplanes. The factory asserted priority in engine supply and informed its former employee Geoffrey de Havilland in December 1914 that all 100-hp Green engines would be allotted to its 12 FE2a pushers. De Havilland had to settle for the old 70-hp Renault for his new design at Airco.[54]

In December, in the midst of shortages, expansion plans for the RFC were being forged and the struggle for its future command began. Brancker suggested an air arm of thirty squadrons for Kitchener's proposed force of six armies with three corps each, or one squadron for each army headquarters and each army corps at the front and six squadrons for RFC headquarters. On 21 December Kitchener deemed Brancker's estimates too conservative and doubled the proposal to accord with his notion of a mass volunteer army.[55] The RFC was clearly subordinate to the BEF, but there were further thorny interrelated questions of the arm's future organization, commander, and relationship to the BEF. With the Battle of Ypres in October, the RFC, according to David Divine, abandoned the principle of centralized control and independence to one of subordination to the various army corps' headquarters.[56] Each army commander thereby gained a private air force, leaving only a small unit, the ninth wing, at RFC headquarters for strategic reconnaissance. Sykes averred that he and Henderson prevented an even worse scenario by defeating attempts of Trenchard and Brancker to leave only an RFC adviser at General Headquarters.[57]

According to historian Neville Jones, Sykes was about to assume command of the RFC late in 1914 when his nemesis, Trenchard, protested to the War Office. In response Kitchener, who favored Trenchard, decided that Sykes, whom he deemed too inexperienced to command the RFC, and Trenchard, whose combat experience in South Africa he valued, were both to remain at their posts.[58] Capt. Philip Joubert de la Ferté's trenchant observations about his superiors shed further light on the likely role of personalities in the selection process. To him Major General Henderson was a quiet gentleman of great intelligence and integrity, but lacking in ruthlessness. Sykes was a deep thinker and most competent staff officer, but lacking in strength—too cold to secure men's affection and too calculating to inspire enthusiasm. Joubert de la Ferté found Trenchard and Kitchener very much alike, "blunt to the point of rudeness, intolerant of human weakness and indecision, averse to politics and intrigue, and single in purpose." If Trenchard lacked the intellectual capacity to state his case clearly, Joubert de la

Ferté "learned to respect his integrity, his drive, and his extraordinary power of coming to a correct conclusion by a complicated and sometimes erroneous series of arguments."[59]

Trenchard and Kitchener agreed on the RFC's subordination to the BEF, while Sykes and Henderson would advocate increasing the RFC's independence. Trenchard was a "thruster," the aggressive, forthright, and unwavering type of commander that Kitchener at the War Office and French and later Haig in the BEF command appreciated. He was close to Kitchener in location, temperament, and policy. Of course, if Jones is correct that Trenchard intervened against Sykes in 1914, then Joubert de la Ferté's perception of Trenchard's "aversion to intrigue" was incorrect, although aversion need not necessarily entail a refusal to indulge. Both Sykes and Trenchard intrigued, but the BEF command and the War Office would favor Trenchard's efforts, and they could provide Trenchard with a staff that could articulate intelligibly what he intuited was necessary first for the BEF and then the RFC. At home Brancker virtually ran the General Directorate of Military Aviation until 1917, even after Henderson returned from the continent in 1915. Trenchard and Brancker, the two officers advocating the RFC headquarters' reduction to near insignificance in the fall of 1914, thus emerged to direct the RFC on the continent and at home.

Their hands full with the rapidly expanding commitment to the BEF, the RFC and the War Office had to ask the Admiralty for aid, first in September to divest itself of the responsibility for home defense, and again in December, when Brancker asked the navy for airplanes. In the meantime, the Royal Naval Air Service (RNAS), searching for a mission, had pursued its own tack. On 4 August 1914 the RNAS, with 93 seaplanes and airplanes and a complement of 138 officers and 589 men, was closer in strength to its military counterpart than continental powers' naval air arms.

Home defense was not a welcome task, since no means to intercept Zeppelins existed at a time of rampant "Zeppelinmania," when rumors of Zeppelin raids and new types of Zeppelins abounded. In mid-October the *Daily Telegraph* correspondent at Harwich related that a steamer's crew reported a Zeppelin flying on the surface of the North Sea while surrounded by British destroyers.[60] It turned out to be a dead whale. In late November the editor of *Flight* dismissed the Zeppelin invasion scares, claiming that the dirigibles were too slow and unwieldy and would be no more successful over Britain than over the continent.[61] Yet the fear—and the fad among London insurance agents for selling antibomb insurance—did not disappear so easily.

In September Churchill proposed to control the air for a 100-mile radius around Dunkirk and to attack the Zeppelins in their sheds, thereby preventing them from reaching the British coast. Commander Samson had taken his Eastchurch squadron to the continent and, in buccaneering fashion, had sent armored cars marauding through Belgium. Now he undertook to bomb the Zeppelin sheds at Cologne and Düsseldorf from Antwerp with his motley force of airplanes. After a first raid on 22 September, a second on 8 October destroyed the Z9 in its shed in Düsseldorf. No more than four airplanes, each carrying a few 20-pound bombs, participated in each of the raids, and individual craft also attacked railway junctions and stations at Cambrai and Bruges and the submarine pens at Ostende. When retreat from Antwerp placed him out of range of the Rhine dirigible sheds, Samson had his men attack the Zeppelin factory at Friedrichshafen and the sheds at Ludwigshafen from Belfort on 21 November.[62] A violation of Swiss neutrality in this raid provoked angry cries of outrage from the Swiss parliament, eliciting Churchill's response, "tell them to go milk their cows."[63] On Christmas day nine RNAS seaplanes transported on carrier steamers staged an abortive raid on the Zeppelin shed at Nordholtz. It would be hyperbole to label these small efforts a strategic bombing campaign, but they apparently incited the French to plan a more substantial effort late in the fall of 1914. The RNAS, interpreting its home-defense mission aggressively, was striking at Germany, while the RFC concentrated on support of the BEF on the Western Front. Both depended on an aviation industry that was hard pressed to supply one force, much less two. Shortly after the war began, Lt. Richard Davies, who had been Winston Churchill's flight instructor, said of naval skeptics toward aviation, "They have pissed on Churchill's plant for three years—now they expect blooms in a month."[64] Technological plants require deep roots and constant nurturing, and they do not blossom readily, even in the hothouse of war.

Russia's front-line strength of 244 airplanes and 14 dirigibles at the war's outbreak looked impressive, but the planes were obsolete or obsolescent, reserves were almost entirely lacking, and spare parts were in short supply. Only four airships were potentially ready for combat. In August the high command (the Stavka) divided the aviation command between Grand Duke Aleksandr Mikhailovich on the Southwestern Front and General Kaulbar on the Northwestern Front. Army headquarters used aircraft for close-range reconnaissance and communications within 100 to 120 kilometers and the cavalry for long-range surveillance. Russian naval aviation in the Black and Baltic seas performed reconnaissance and mine-laying missions, and even attempted to disrupt shipping, but its small and diverse roster of airplanes rendered it, in historian Jacob Kipp's view, more a "toy" than a weapon.[65]

Historian Petr Duz stated that Russian generals did not pay attention to aerial reconnaissance and that Samsonov's army was defeated when it ignored air observers' reports of Mackensen's movements.[66] Yet some Russian generals did heed their aviators and pointed to the aircraft shortage as the problem. Early in the war, on the Southwestern Front, Gen. A. A. Brusilov observed that "because of the short supply and poor quality of aircraft, air reconnaissance was quite weak, nevertheless, our information was mainly through this channel."[67] Aerial reconnaissance detected Austrian troop movements toward Grodsk against Brusilov's army on 24 August, enabling him to reinforce his units. The few Russian aviators found that their troops often fired on them. General Vasili Gurko, a cavalry commander, explained that most Russian soldiers "seriously thought that such a cunning idea as an aeroplane could only emanate from, and be used by, a German."[68] Russian generals appreciated their aerial inferiority to the Germans. General Iurii Danilov concluded that "as a consequence of our lack of sufficient airplanes, the enemy could maneuver as he wished by using his highly developed railroad network and be certain that his plans would not be discovered by us very quickly. At the same time, with considerably better aviation facilities, the enemy was able to observe each of our steps with complete impunity."[69]

Given the great distances on the Eastern Front, the initial air force policy of units staying in permanent billets at aircraft depots was superseded on 30 September, when the Stavka ordered the Southwestern Front headquarters to attach air units to the armies directly under the chief of the army staff's control. But movement of the units posed serious logistical problems, since the Russian army, like its Austro-Hungarian opponent, relied primarily on horse- or ox-drawn carts to move weapons and ammunition.[70]

Russia possessed the Sikorskii Muromets, a craft capable of long-range reconnaissance of up to 300 to 400 kilometers, but only two were ready when the war began, and the high command did not trust them and underestimated their value. One of the giant planes was hastily assigned to reconnaissance missions on the Northwestern Front, and the Chief Military Technical Directorate (CMTD) ordered 32 Muromets from Russko-Baltiiskii on 2 October to be completed by August 1915 and gave the factory a 3.5-million-ruble advance. As the factory was expanding to begin construction, the Muromets aircraft commander, who apparently preferred small, single-engine planes, complained that the plane could not maintain the required operational altitude and possessed unreliable engines. Based on his report, Northwestern Front headquarters refused to accept the second Muromets, occasioning a Stavka directive to the CMTD on 29 October canceling the order and the advance because the Muromets was "unfit for carrying out combat missions."[71] Duz attributed the decision to German army commanders and the German clique involved with Grand Duke Nikolai, which argued that the army could buy 10 Voisins for 1 Muromets. Faced with this setback, Igor Sikorskii persuaded Shidlovskii, the chairman of the board at Russko-Baltiiskii, to request that the War Ministry allow a squadron under Shidlovskii's command to test the Muromets in action at the factory's expense. Permission was given, and the squadron was formed on 10 December and sent to the Northwestern Front in the Pskov region to begin operations early in 1915.[72]

The Russian General Staff placed no importance on air combat early in the war, so it made no serious attempts to arm its aircraft. Despite the paucity of planes on the Eastern Front, as reconnaissance expanded into artillery spotting and bombing, air combat became more likely. Near Sholkiev in August, P. N. Nesterov, commander of the 11th Corps Air Unit against the Austrians, decided to ram an Austrian craft. "Even if the airplane breaks," he reasoned, "this is nothing, because sooner or later one has to fall all the same, and to sacrifice one's life is the duty of every soldier."[73] Nesterov, of course, calculated that he could survive the collision. On 8 September he rammed an Albatros, but fell with his aircraft, his body separating from the airplane 25 feet from the ground. Though hailed as a hero, Nesterov thus demonstrated that ramming was a measure to be taken only in desperation, not as a calculated risk.

The Stavka had seriously underestimated pilot and aircraft losses. Pilots lacked sufficient flight practice, so air units of the 3rd, 5th, 8th, and 9th Armies lost 91 of their 99 planes in the first three months of the war. Its calculation that two pilots sufficed for each airplane had not accounted for the poor pilot training and exploits such as Nesterov's. On 15 October Supreme Commander Nikolai Nikolaevich permitted the admission of men and women volunteer pilots "provided that they come with their personal machines."[74] As of October some units on the Southwestern Front had volunteer pilots under contract and others flying without salary, though at year's end they fixed remuneration at 300 rubles monthly, by which time the military was discouraging civilian volunteers. By mid-December the commander of a squadron attached to 9th Army staff had four planes but only two fit pilots in the unit, prompting him to request only two missions daily. Pilot training was insufficient to cover losses, resulting in critical shortages. The need to accelerate training led inevitably to lower standards, heightened inefficiency, and ultimately higher losses—a vicious circle that Russia would not be alone in experiencing.[75]

High aircraft losses negated the previous four years' airplane accumulation, and by 1 September only 145 machines remained in service. The lack of reserves, an aircraft wastage rate of 37 percent monthly, and inadequate domestic production and foreign procurement combined to restrict Russian aerial activity severely from the start. The Deperdussin monoplane quickly proved too slow and light, and its midwing monoplane configuration was an impediment to observation. The army halted Deperdussin procurement after 63 planes and relied primarily on Moranes and Voisins. With a monthly productive capacity of some 30 aircraft, and with engine supply capricious, the industry would have severe difficulties meeting the front's demands for quality airplanes.[76]

Duz's assertion that the Russian air arm was not the weakest of the European air arms is correct; it was in better condition than its Austro-Hungarian opponent. The Austro-Hungarian army assembled 13 flight companies (Fliks) and 5 aircraft depots, with 48 operational and 27 training planes and 114 military pilots, sending 9 Fliks to the Russian Front and two to the Serbian/Montenegrin Front. German aircraft deliveries enabled the formation of 7 more companies, but by the end of the year, plagued by problems of supply, the Austro-Hungarian army still had only 14 flight companies, 10 on the Russian Front and 4 on the Serbian/Montenegrin Front, with 147 operational airplanes (64 Lohners, 41 Aviatiks, 22 Albatroses, 13 DFW, 1 Lloyd, and 6 other biplanes). Plans to discourage ground fire from friendly troops by painting red-white-red markings on the planes were modified to the simple expedient of using the German iron cross to identify planes, since so many Austro-Hungarian planes came from German factories. The German high command also gave the Austrian high command the dirigible SL2, which performed successful reconnaissance flights in August and September. The Austro-Hungarian army was testing machine guns on aircraft in August and dropped fléchettes late in October in the southern campaign. Flik 1 began using the first wireless sets in the fall. The importance of aerial reconnaissance grew as the war continued, although with the onset of winter, flying diminished dramatically.[77]

The navy, which began the war with 5 operational and seventeen training planes, quickly began operations in Lohner E-boats. In August it made 39 flights on reconnaissance, artillery, and bombing missions, and 3 E-boats made squadron and night attacks in October and November before winter weather limited flight operations.[78]

The Austro-Hungarian aviation industry was inadequate and dependent upon Germany. At mobilization the entire aircraft industry employed only 218 workers, and 150 worked at the Lohner factory. The recently founded branches of German firms—Aviatik and Albatros and the Lloyd firm in Budapest—were merely workshops. When German deliveries of 48 aircraft from August to December did not meet front-line demands, army aviation commander Colonel Uzelac raised the requisite minimum domestic production from 46 to 60. Such production was not remotely possible. Although the Austrian industry's labor force quadrupled to 824 by the end of the year, it produced only 64 aircraft from August through December, and monthly deliveries actually declined from 24 to 7 planes because of the transition to new types. Given these figures, Austrian aviation historian Col. Erich Kahlen's assessment that "it was extremely difficult to raise monthly production to forty-six planes by the end of 1914" displays a mastery of the art of understatement.[79]

Some of the army's policies actually compounded these inadequacies. Although Uzelac wisely ordered the expansion of the airship unit's small installation at Fischamend into an aviation arsenal, the airship unit contracted with domestic firms for the development of twin-engine G-planes in August, despite the industry's total inability to develop such a sophisticated aircraft. The War Ministry's refusal to authorize the training of sufficient test pilots, for fear of creating a postwar surfeit of pilots, delayed aircraft acceptance. Finally, the absence of a prepayment system until mid-1915 hindered the firms' procurement of raw materials and thus slowed deliveries. It is not surprising that the official history of the World War I Austro-Hungarian Army mentions 1914 aviation troops once, and then only to observe their embryonic state. The army's air arm and the aircraft industry had failed to meet even minimal expectations.[80]

Conclusion

After five months of warfare—as winter weather reduced operations, allowing time for recuperation and refitting—the air services had demonstrated their usefulness to the military machine. Although the Zeppelin had failed to measure up to the expectations of the German army, the airplane had established itself as a primary reconnaissance tool in all armies, especially on the Western Front with the onset of trench warfare. It had further demonstrated potential for bombing and aerial combat. French and British pilots had shown a penchant for aggressively seeking out the enemy, thereby making a hazardous occupation more so. All the air arms had experienced an unexpected attrition of men and machines due to human error, mechanical failure, and the general difficulties of wartime flight, particularly indiscriminate ground fire.

Initially the armies encountered severe difficulties with logistics and production. Supplies collapsed in the war of movement, causing disruptions that did not subside until the fronts stabilized and military bureaucrats could cope with the chaos. In the west units were moved by rail, and primarily, by truck, linking the two innovations based on the gasoline piston engine. In the east the logistical problem was more fundamental. No more striking contrast can be drawn than the one in pictures of the Russian or Austro-Hungarian army aviation units moving to the front, their aircraft dismantled and pulled by horses or oxen—the most modern of innovations dependent on the most ancient of civilization's beasts of burden.

The onset of the war disrupted aviation production everywhere, and the French responded most quickly to the new challenges. In October they began specializing their aircraft types, and gearing up aircraft and particularly aero engine production to prepare for the anticipated campaign in 1915. The German army, perhaps more complacent because it was on French soil, waited until the winter to take comparable steps in production, thereby giving the French a lead. British production was so small as to be more similar to that of Russia or Austria-Hungary than France and Germany, although the two eastern empires, with few actual and potential facilities for production, could not contemplate the kind of expansion that Britain could undertake to reduce its dependence on France.

Naval aviation on the continent was even more embryonic than military aviation. The French naval air arm, for example, had only eight seaplanes in August 1914. In Britain the RFC and RNAS were nearly comparable in size. The RNAS's exploits on the continent and the missions of the Austro-Hungarian Lohner boats over the Adriatic were harbingers of naval air services' future contributions to the war effort.

The airman's essential contribution to warfare in 1914 was reconnaissance. Aerial observers could detect with the naked eye individual men at 1,200–1,500 meters and troop columns at 2,500–3,000 meters altitude. Such observation sufficed in the war of movement, but with trench warfare it became necessary to obtain minute details of the opponent's trench system, its occupants, artillery batteries, and the immediate rear. The camera secured these details, while the wireless enabled their speedy transmission. The airplane, a new implement of technology, required further technological advances in photography and wireless telegraphy to make it an efficient observation instrument.

Required to locate an enemy in alien territory while keeping their own bearings, and becoming potential prey to the weather, ground fire, or mechanical malfunction, junior officer aviators played a new and significant role in warfare. They could spot previously undetectable enemy movements, forcing armies to conceal their activity more extensively. A French artilleryman, indicating a German Taube over Péronne road near Albert early in October, commented to a British reporter, "There is that wretched bird which haunts us."[81] In 1914 the bird of war had spread its wings, casting its shadow over the battlefields of Europe. In 1915 it would grow fierce talons, to become a bird of prey, and the skies, like the earth and seas below, would become an arena of mortal combat.

CHAPTER THREE

1915

"As long as one stays calm and deliberate, an air fight in my fast, maneuverable Fokker is scarcely more dangerous than driving an automobile."—

OSWALD BOELCKE TO HIS PARENTS IN NOVEMBER 1915[1]

"I felt very sorry for him when he fell in flames, but war's war and they have been very troublesome of late."

LANOE HAWKER TO HIS FAMILY AFTER DOWNING A GERMAN OVER YPRES,

SUMMER 1915[2]

The shocking and costly initial battles of 1914 and the epic struggles of Verdun and the Somme in 1916 often overshadow 1915. Yet in 1915 the war continued to grow, and the west's siege warfare and the east's seesaw battles continued with no end in sight to the stalemate. New arenas of conflict were added to the Eastern and Western Fronts: the Southwestern Front with Italy's entry into the war against the Central Powers in May 1915; and far-flung theaters in Asia Minor, the Middle East, and Africa. As the conflict spread to these distant arenas, so did aviation. On the European Fronts, the consumption of materiel exceeded expected levels, causing significant and highly publicized shell and skilled-labor shortages. The powers had not only to continue the grinding effort but also to make critical decisions regarding mobilization, if they were to remain effective combatants. The new air arm, based on a rapidly changing technology and industry, required mobilization policies that would have far-reaching implications for the air war's future course. In 1915 the air powers fell into two categories: the greater ones— France, Germany, and England; and the lesser—Russia, Austria-Hungary, and Italy. Potential for technological and industrial development, as much as actual strength, determined this division.

The Greater Powers

France

In France during 1915, military aviation grew in importance, while an embryonic naval air arm remained no more than an afterthought. The naval air service, which had been formed in July 1914 with only eight seaplanes, ordered FBA flying boats in early 1915 and stationed its first squadron of coastal patrol seaplanes at Dunkirk in April. By July it had 54 aircraft, a number that limited its effectiveness and reflected the French government's emphasis on the land war.[3]

French military aviation underwent significant administrative and political changes in the winter and spring of 1915. The army opened four new flight schools by March. Captain Destouches of the Airplane Service was killed in a December 1914 aircraft accident. His successor, Capt. Albert Etévé, appointed officers to monitor the production of the five basic airplanes—Voisin, Caudron, Farman, Nieuport, and Morane—to ensure the standardization of manufacture. In March Colonel Stammler was replaced as head of the SFA by his assistant Commandant Grard. In March the parliamentary army commissions' aviation subcommissions convened to hear testimony on aviation, an indication of some politicians' increasing interest in powered flight.[4]

Early in 1915 French aircraft and engine production rose rapidly (262, 280, and 431 airplanes and 307, 370, and 696 engines monthly through March). Some planes went to France's allies, since a January 15 agreement provided England and Russia each with one-fifteenth of each French factory's total production. As production climbed, GQG twice increased its program from 65 squadrons ultimately to 75 squadrons for the spring to meet the front's rapidly rising demands.[5]

By 30 March GQG had 51 squadrons at the Western Front (and two more in Serbia and the East) with 390 planes. The air service comprised 130 officers, 500 pilots, 240 observers, and 4,650 other personnel. Having standardized its types in October, the air arm relied on increases in engine power for improved performance: the Voisin now had a 130-hp Salmson radial instead of the 80-hp Gnome; the Caudron G4 had two Rhône rotaries in comparison with the G3's one; and the Farmans and Morane Saulniers had slightly larger engines. Although squadron chiefs complained of numerous defects from careless construction and poor materials, these types would give France what author Georges Huisman labeled "absolute mastery of the air" in spring 1915, when the pace of aerial operations quickened.[6]

During 1915, particularly in the latter half, observation, pursuit, and bombing became distinct specialties.[7] The air arm, the army's eyes, concentrated on reconnaissance and artillery spotting. Pursuit aviation and air combat, despite significant strides, remained less developed. GQG's focus, aerial bombardment, could potentially carry the war to the enemy. Observation crews operated their Farmans and Caudrons with little threat from the air far into 1915. When German fighters appeared in the summer of 1915, French crews were forbidden to venture over French lines because their slow, cumbersome Caudrons and Farmans would have been easy prey. Artillery spotting improved during the year. Fliers' reports in the fall offensives enabled the neutralization of enemy artillery, although French artillerymen still showed a reluctance to heed them. Perhaps the last blatant fiasco that resulted from ignoring aerial reports occurred at the "Tranchée des Tentes" in the September 1915 Artois campaign, when French artillery refused to believe air reports that a French company remained in German lines after an otherwise successful German counterattack. Only after a three-day bombardment could a company officer escape to confirm the survival of remnants of the unit.

French pursuit operations began in late spring, as two-seater crews used carbines to down German planes. Three Morane-Saulnier squadrons—MS23, MS12, and MS3—commanded by future fighter leaders Lieutenants Vergnette, Tricornot de Rose, and Félix Brocard, were particularly successful at seizing aerial ascendancy with these improvised pursuit planes. In fall 1914 MS23's Roland Garros, famed prewar flier and Morane-Saulnier test pilot, renewed Raymond Saulnier's unsuccessful prewar attempts to develop and patent a synchronizing gear for a machine gun to fire through the propeller arc. By that November Garros and his mechanic, Jules Hue, experimenting with a Hotchkiss gun fixed to fire through the arc of a specially armored propeller, had found that only 10 percent of the bullets hit the airscrew. Although that 10 percent caused breakages on the ground that would have wrecked the plane in flight, Garros remained confident of his scheme's feasibility and was released from MS23 during the winter to work with Saulnier to improve the steel deflectors on the propeller blades. In the spring he entered MS26 at Dunkirk, equipped with a Morane with channeled deflectors. Within three weeks, from 1 to 18 April, he shot down three German airplanes, an astounding feat for the time. When Garros himself fell victim to antiaircraft fire, the Germans captured him and his plane and quickly produced a Fokker monoplane armed with a synchronized machine gun, which appeared at the front in July. Though few in number (only 40 at the front by December), the Fokkers gave the Germans aerial ascendancy. The French lacked a synchronizing gear, the Morane was outclassed, and Garros's daredevil contraption was too dangerous for widespread use.[8]

Garros was gone, but on 8 June a 20-year-old, so frail that his father had had to use his influence to secure the youth's entry into the air service, arrived at MS3. After entering the service as an assistant mechanic, he had begun pilot training at the end of January, first flown on 10 March, and was breveted on 26 April. He achieved his first victory on 19 July. By his 21st birthday on Christmas eve 1915, he had been promoted to sergeant and made a Knight of the Legion of Honor after four victories and two special missions behind enemy lines. Remarkably tenacious and unafraid of danger, Georges Guynemer had begun to make his indelible mark on the French air service.[9]

In fall 1915 the French developed the Nieuport 11, named the Bébé for its small size. Gustav Delage, chief designer at Nieuport, had created a smaller version of his successful two-seat reconnaissance craft powered by an 80-hp rotary. Despite frequent early breakdowns from inadequate motor mounts, the Nieuport's fine flight characteristics made it a match for the Fokker, though its Hotchkiss gun, mounted on the top wing above the propeller arc, fired only 25 rounds a clip, at a slower rate than the Fokker's LMG machine guns. Most of the few Bébés delivered in the fall formed France's first true pursuit squadron, N65, which was assigned to defend the city of Nancy, while the rest were dispersed to various units.[10]

In 1915 GQG's aircraft programs strongly emphasized bombardment, although the bomber posed significant technological problems. On 20 August 1914 the Michelin brothers, convinced of the effectiveness of bombing railroads, had offered the government to build 100 airframes at cost in their Clermont-Ferrand factories, stipulating only that the plane had to carry 400 kilograms of bombs with a 400-kilometer range. GQG's choice, the Voisin, could not lift the weight, so on 16 January 1915 the War Ministry offered a prize for bomber designs. In February Louis Breguet began constructing a pusher craft powered by a single 200- to 220-hp engine. Industrialists' interest in bombing enabled the War Ministry to raise 1.1 million francs from various firms for bomber production.[11]

Technical experts within the SFA disagreed about the wisest course of bomber development. Captain Dorand at the aeronautical laboratory advised against studying engines of over 200 horsepower for war planes until engine weights decreased. In April he informed the War Ministry of his own project for a bomber with a 200-hp engine, which he wanted to build immediately in the laboratory.[12] Dorand's tendency to promote his own projects led nowhere in this instance.

Early in 1915 C. Martinot-Lagarde, chief of the engine service, pressed for the development of fixed, water-cooled 200-hp engines for a strategic bomber, recommending the V engine or radial as the lightest types possible because of their shorter crankcase and crankshaft in comparison with in-line engines. The higher the horsepower, the less feasible the rotary became because of cooling difficulties, the rotating cylinders' stress on metal and absorption of almost 30 horsepower for a 200-hp rotary.

Martinot-Lagarde understood that increasing engine production in 1915 posed grave problems in securing materials and accessories such as special steels, aluminum, magnetos, and spark plugs that France, like the rest of Europe, had imported from Germany before the war. French companies now had to manufacture the accessories, while firms like Renault and Salmson had just begun to build new forges to produce the steels, which incorporated other metals—nickel for increased elasticity, chrome for strength, and tungsten for resistance to high temperatures.[13] Despite their differences, Dorand's and Martinot-Lagarde's preoccupation with linking bomber and engine development confirmed that bombers and engines would be French aviation's emphasis in 1915.

In so many accounts of World War I aviation, the fighter arm takes precedence, yet in 1915 and again in 1918, French bomber forces would be the focus of GQG's attention.[14] Aware that the war was becoming a conflict of materiel, GQG selected industrial targets for a strategic bombing campaign intended to shorten the war. The first bomber group, GB1, was equipped with the simple and robust Voisin. The bombs were artillery shells with fins; the early techniques were primitive. Pilots departed for the target when they chose, bombing on an individual basis. The observer used a nail on the fuselage as his sight and threw the 90mm shells overboard from an altitude of 1,500 to 2,000 meters. GB1's commander, de Goÿs, began training in unit operations, and manufacturer Gabriel Voisin, during his visits to the units, helped the crews create bomb racks under the planes that enabled them to drop 40-kilogram 155-mm artillery shells, too heavy for an observer to manage. GB1, stationed on the plain of Malzéville above the city of Nancy, was ready for operations in May.

Its first target was the Badische Anilin Company of Ludwigshafen, which produced explosives and poison gas. For several mornings the crews arrived at the field at 0200 hours only to have the raid canceled because the prevailing high winds would have prevented the return of the ponderous Voisins at their speed of 80 kilometers per hour. On 27 May the wind abated; at 0300 hours GB1 took off to bomb Ludwigshafen. By 0855 hours all the crews had returned, except de Goÿs himself. The commander's plane had an engine breakdown and he was captured, to languish in captivity until he escaped in 1918. The raids continued, as GB1 was joined by GB2, GB3, and GB4. Twenty-three planes attacked Karlsruhe on 15 June, 62 attacked Dillingen on 25 August. Trier and Saarbrücken were bombed. By August almost 100 Voisins were stationed at Malzéville.

In July German armed Aviatik biplanes and antiaircraft batteries began to take a higher toll of the attackers. In an August attack on Saarbrücken, Fokkers destroyed nine French bombers. The bombers countered with tighter formations, because even with improved engines and armament, the Voisin's 90 to 95 kilometer-per-hour speed and pusher configuration, which impeded rearward defense (the observer stood on his seat, braced his body against the top wing, and fired over it with a carbine) made it vulnerable prey. The Farman 11s that supplemented the Voisins were equally deficient, although commanders like Capt. Maurice Happe of MF25, who had invented group flights and the V formation to improve their defense, used them daringly.

Happe was a colorful character over six feet tall. An impressive, bushy, black beard and eyebrows, piercing black eyes, and his black artillery uniform gave him a forbidding countenance that cloaked a rather lighthearted individual with a lively sense of humor. Happe lost his two formation mates in a 25 September attack on a gunpowder factory at Rottweil and returned with his Farman shot full of holes. Undaunted, especially when he heard that the Germans had placed a 25,000 mark price on his head, he painted the wheels and part of his wings red and dropped a message on Habsheim challenging the Germans to spare his wingmen and attack him. Élan alone, however, could not arrest the rising losses, and by fall momentum had swung against the French.

GQG increasingly sent the bombers on night raids against military targets right behind the front, using them as extra long-range artillery.

Night missions complicated navigation, and decreased the attacks' precision and intensity but enabled surprise and the sacrifice of speed for heavier bomb loads. Gasoline fires in a triangular arrangement pointed toward the target, and the Voisins were equipped with electric landing lights. GQG dispersed the bomber groups to aid in the fall offensives in Artois and the Champagne, then regrouped them at Malzéville in December for further night operations.

After a successful spring and early summer, the decline of French bomber aviation stemmed as much from stagnation in plane production and development as it did from stiffening German defenses and the Fokker's appearance. Aircraft and engine production peaked at 431 and 696, respectively, in March, then leveled off until the winter. By March the October 1914 program was two months behind. The dichotomy between the front and rear was causing communication problems. In testimony before the parliamentary commissions in April, Director of Military Aeronautics Hirschauer confessed that "we don't know what there is at the front," as the front units took what they desired from the supply reserve without informing the rear.[15] Insufficient material supplies, and continuous aircraft- and engine-type modifications accounted for delays.

In June Hirschauer took measures to spur production. According to historian Patrick Fridenson, the alliance with the automobile industry that "Hirschauer had initially disdained became the foundation of his programs," as he drew auto firms to engine production. The Chambre Syndicale des industries aéronautiques, the trade association of the aeronautical industry, under president Robert Esnault-Pelterie and secretary general André Granet, became the liaison between military and industry. The association's commissions on technical, economic, and legislative affairs set guidelines standardizing aircraft construction and distributing primary materials to the firms. Hirschauer also began bimonthly meetings with manufacturers.[16] On 9 and 10 June 1915 the War Ministry allowed the industry to reclaim its labor force as of 1 August 1914 and threatened to take disciplinary action against commanders who did not comply. German aero engine historian J. A. Gilles believed this uncompromising attitude enabled France to overcome the industry's wartime labor shortages better than other powers.[17] Such steps would increase the front's immediate materiel supply, but would not supply newly developed reconnaissance planes—besides the Nieuport—and bombers to supersede the Voisins and Farmans.

On 6 June GQG informed Hirschauer that it desired 50 squadrons (500 bombers) to attack Essen, and on 29 June Hirschauer anticipated developing such a program in six months, once GQG selected a bomber. The

Breguet-Michelins, however, were not ready; their Salmson 220-hp radials were unreliable; and their pusher configuration was vulnerable to rear attack.

In July a bomber commission convened industry representatives to set an August aircraft competition, which was then postponed until November. In November only the Breguet-Michelin and a tractor craft designed by Paul Schmitt, both powered by 200-hp Renaults, flew the requisite 600 kilometers. Despite reservations, GQG ordered some Breguet-Michelins, which crews found more difficult to fly than the Voisins. The Schmitt firm had to build its plant before beginning serial production, and Schmitts finally arrived for service in 1917, thoroughly obsolete. In November, to avoid a Renault monopoly on powerful bomber-engine production, the army opted for the construction of various bombers with various engines.[18]

During the summer observation squadrons complained about defective and inadequate equipment.[19] In late August the squadron officers of the Third Army's air service, after having met with officers from the production services, complained to Barès about the factories' lack of research and the production services' failure to monitor or spur them sufficiently.[20]

In September GQG accused the rear bureaucracy of falling into a peacetime routine, inadequately developing aviation, and retarding innovation by issuing contracts on a trimester basis. The trimester orders, which enabled firms to accumulate needed materials, applied only to existing types, although the directorate acknowledged that builders with months of orders demonstrated a certain inertia toward researching improvements or new types.[21] Yet when the Directorate attempted to force improvements from Voisin by halting contracts for 1915's last trimester, GQG, after all its complaints about the Voisins, insisted on further production to keep the factory operating, thus undermining the War Ministry's attempt to meet GQG's very demands for improvements.[22]

GQG's needs for more powerful craft were met when the Renault 110-hp engine yielded 130 horsepower in July; now the Farmans and Caudrons would have to be modified to receive the engine. GQG, dissatisfied with the Gnome rotary since fall 1914, on 2 August judged its rotaries deficient in the necessary security for a military aero engine. The rotary's shorter service time between overhauls (40 hours) compared unfavorably to that of more durable radials and in-lines (100 hours). GQG was planning to cease their production entirely when the industry developed and produced powerful, safe engines, but it had a prospective engine in mind.[23]

In December 1914 Marc Birkigt, technical director of the automobile firm Hispano-Suiza in Barcelona, had decided to design a V8 aero engine that would emphasize a simplicity and ease of construction ideal for wartime use. In 1915, at GQG's request, Hirschauer sent Grard and Martinot-Lagarde to Barcelona to buy one for tests in France. July bench tests were so impressive that Grard urged immediate contracts. Gnome therefore vacated the Hispano-Suiza factory in Bois-Colombes outside Paris that it had rented since the mobilization.[24]

The Hispano-Suiza 150-hp V8 engine has been labeled "the outstanding engine of World War I from a technical standpoint" and a "revolution in liquid-cooled engine design."[25] Instead of individual cylinders in a row along the crankshaft, as was the case in separate-cylinder in-line engines, the Hispano-Suizas had "*en bloc* cylinder construction with a cast aluminum water jacket containing steel cylinder barrels and with enclosed and lubricated valves and valve gear."[26] The aluminum cylinder blocks with screwed-in steel sleeves saved weight and stiffened the crankcase; and the jacket protected the engine's moving parts. Powerful, rigid, light, and durable, the Hispano-Suiza could certainly be enlarged to give 200 horsepower in time. The French command initially envisaged it as a bomber engine, then as a panacea for French aviation. Once perfected, it would become one of the war's great fighter engines.

In July the French parliament's aviation subcommissions completed their first interpellation quite annoyed with Hirschauer's inability to provide basic information on manufacturers and supplies. The politicians suggested a reorganization of the air service to remedy the lack of communication between the front and rear, and the development of bombers for strategic attacks on Germany's war industry. On 5 July before the army commission, deputy Pierre Etienne Flandin not only denounced the rear's deficiencies but severely criticized the army's bomber deployment as "useless or disastrous," demanding the bombardment of German industrial centers and the construction of large, long-range bombers for the task.[27] The commission's vote to this effect was the opening barrage in a war behind the front. Some observers believed that the report did not draw enough attention to the high prices and mediocrity of some materiel. They wanted the government to draw established manufacturers, such as the automobile factories, to the large-scale production of a few standardized aircraft types.[28]

Politicians were not the only ones with such ideas. In August Professor A. Le Châtelier of the Collège de France, in a memorandum on aviation to the government, reasoned that if it was impossible to break the German Front on land, then it could be crossed and dominated by the rear, through an aviation arm of 1,000 planes each carrying 300 to 400 kilograms of bombs. Attacking German communications, stations, supply parks, and munitions depots in the Rhine zone by day and night would result in "a victory, by shock, in the rear of the German front."[29] Michel Corday, a novelist with strong ties to aeronautical circles, referred in his diary to "those who see in an intensified aerial struggle the resolution of the war,"[30] at a time, ironically, when the high command was renouncing its hopes for strategic aviation because of cost and materiel deficiencies, as well as its awareness that Paris, the only one of the three capitals within relatively easy reach of the front lines, would be Germany's prime target for reprisal raids in any strategic air war.

In a report of 23 September 1915, the aviation subcommission scathingly condemned French aerial inferiority 10 days after the government replaced Hirschauer by appointing Senator René Besnard, reporter of the war budget, to the new position of undersecretary of state of aviation in charge of the Twelfth Directorate in the War Ministry. The report proclaimed the situation in aviation "grave," attributing the problems to the absence of close cooperation between GQG and the directorate and the directorate's failure to manage the coordinated expansion of labor and equipment reserves.[31] Flandin sought a massive production program of bombers, bomber escorts, and powerful engines to strike German industrial production, but the complicated nature of mobilization—securing raw materials and labor, and harmonizing delivery, personnel training, and frontline preparations—required a unified program directed by an able and energetic directorate with organizational skills, a view of the whole, and control of the aeronautical industry.[32] The appointment of an undersecretary, comparable to those for artillery, munitions, and provisions, mollified the politicians, but only until November, when GQG proposed a new program for military aviation.

GQG's 21 November program drastically revised two previous plans presented in August and September by proposing an air arm of 128 squadrons for spring 1916, decreasing bomber units and increasing pursuit squadrons. It also planned to stop producing ancient observation planes and 80- to 100-hp engines. Yet its most controversial aspect was its proposal to equip combat units with some 800 "omnibus" or all-purpose, twin-engine three-seat craft powered by Hispano-Suizas.

The parliamentary commissions were astounded; the proposed all-purpose plane defied the trend toward specialization. They objected strongly to the reduction of the bomber force from 575 to 310 planes and warned against basing the program on engines that were not yet ready for service. The manufacturers also protested the plan, which would mean abandoning their materiel. Despite these objections, Undersecretary Besnard determined to execute the program. He believed the rear's role was to support the front, not offer alternative views on aerial programs and tactics.[33]

In mid-December Birkigt began constructing a large factory at Courbevoie for V8 serial production, while the prototype of the Caudron R4–R5 series, which would be the foundation of Besnard's program, crashed on 15 December, killing Gaston Caudron. After an inquiry ascertained that inadequate numbers of bolts along its longerons had caused the crash, the Airplane Service assigned a young designer, Henri Potez, to assist René Caudron with modifications. A commission in January 1916 agreed to continue production of the strengthened R4, but they decided to suspend construction of the more powerful R5, which would have needed the Hispano-Suizas.[34]

While the parliamentary deputies were correct in objecting to the omnibus aircraft and a program based on untested and unperfected planes and engines, they erred in proposing to continue the production of 80- to 100-hp engines and ancient observation craft that GQG sought to terminate. However, Albert Etévé and Georges Huisman, both authorities on French aviation, believed that wartime aviation's later development vindicated the GQG and Besnard, not their parliamentary opposition, who had merely created an unnecessary crisis.[35] Huisman even asserted that GQG was instituting a necessary military and industrial revolution.

To execute GQG's controversial program, Besnard proposed the formation of an inspectorate of materiel. Barès then informed Besnard that he could form an inspectorate for the rear, but his inspectors would have no authority over the front. A compromise later established both front and rear inspectors.

Besnard drastically reorganized the SFA, divesting it of many functions and placing them in autonomous services subordinate to his own office. He detached the Industrial Service from the SFA, made his staff responsible for planning and monitoring production and supplies, and reassigned Commandant Grard from head of the production service to chief of the industrial service, despite protests from parliamentary deputies and industrialists. Grard's replacement at the production service, artillery Colonel Raibaud, proceeded to replace the aircraft, engine, and armament services with a single general inspectorate of aviation production patterned after the artillery inspectorate and divided into regional subinspectorates. Previously, officers had specialized in major aircraft types. Now the same officers had to monitor the production of various aircraft types and other materiel, and it became more difficult to ensure the interchangeability of parts with firms producing the same plane under different regional subinspectorates. The remaining three services—research, provisions, and buildings—formed a separate general services group.[36]

While Georges Huisman considered the reforms wise, Albert Etévé thought many were motivated by the mistaken drive to fit aviation into the same bureaucratic mold as the artillery's.[37] Besnard's removal of planning from production with only himself to unify them was questionable given the caprice of French politics. The subinspectorate arrangement was certainly debatable, as aircraft and engine technology changed rapidly, unlike the relatively static technology involved in firearms production. Finally, placing the technical service with the lesser supply services suggested a wrongheaded denigration of research.

Parliamentary deputy D'Aubigny wrote Besnard on 27 December that his reforms had "stupefied" the aviation world, imploring him:

> One does not destroy or rebuild under the guns of the enemy; one does not disturb departments managing 50 million francs with a stroke of the pen; at a moment of intensive labor, one does not replace competent chiefs with incompetents. The future of aviation is in your hands, Mr. Undersecretary. Save it today; it will be too late tomorrow.[38]

Besnard then attempted to negotiate price discounts with the firms, as a subcommission report of 5 July had criticized the high cost of aviation materiel. The engine manufacturers resisted, complaining that the state did not guarantee sufficient contracts for them to immobilize their capital. Following an 8 December commission report on Renault, the directorate asked Renault to reduce its prices 2,000 to 3,000 francs. Renault refused, leaving the SFA to lament that "the state is suffering the unreasonable demands of the contractor."[39]

Besnard's policies endeared him to neither politicians nor manufacturers, but he held firm in his endeavors despite their protests. When Salmson 150-hp radials experienced several serious breakdowns from poor materials and defective assembly, Besnard confronted Salmson. The firm took refuge behind shareholder and senator Charles Humbert, who unleashed a bitter press campaign to discredit Besnard. A 14 December article in *Le Journal*, for example, decried the "savage war" in French aviation, described conditions in the French air service as anarchic and chaotic, and declared Besnard too weak and disorganized to manage the bureaucracy. During this crisis, which was sparked immediately by Humbert's malignant use of his power and more generally by Besnard's reforms and endorsement of GQG's program, the army saddled the undersecretary with another program: the

Chief of the General Staff General de Castelnau chaired a commission proposing a program of 1,430 planes that would have eliminated pursuit squadrons and reduced artillery spotting squadrons to prepare for the introduction
of all-purpose combat squadrons. This "Castelnau Conference," supporting
GQG and Besnard, thus proposed an even more extreme program, but despite Besnard's assurances of its feasibility, its prospects of achievement by
1 April 1916 were nil.[40]

In any case, Besnard was finished. On 8 February, after a Zeppelin
raid on Paris and his third offer of resignation, Besnard left office. Nearly
a year later, in December 1916, a Chamber of Deputies committee recognized his contribution to aviation and judged that he had been the victim
of political rivalries and industrial interests. He could console himself with
having departed 13 days before the Germans unleashed their attack on
Verdun.[41]

Besnard's fall demonstrated the difficulties in bridging the schism between the front and rear. At the front the army, hierarchically organized
and based on authority and subordination, confronted a clear and immediate
enemy, the Germans. In the rear a multiplicity of interdependent interests
and agencies—military, political, and industrial—interacted and clashed.
The rear's intrigues, entanglements, and failure to meet the front's demands
prompted Huisman's simplistic assessment, which blamed the rear primarily
for wartime aviation's problems.

The air arm under Barès had acquitted itself well in reconnaissance,
artillery spotting, pursuit, and strategic bombing. It had become less sanguine about bombing when confronted with technical limitations and rising
losses in the latter part of 1915. Its stipulation of materiel, however, had
been less effective. GQG's rapid-fire succession of programs, while certainly a reflection of the development of aviation, was too demanding. In a
January 1916 memorandum to the undersecretary, Captain Dorand recalled
that several times in 1915 his department had advised that the programs
were based solely on military considerations and had ignored aviation's technological limits. French manufacturers, despite their "remarkable ingenuity,"
needed more time to realize successful new types. While Dorand attributed
to the Germans "an inventive genius of zero," he credited their industry with
the tenacious and successful refinement of inventions without the spur of military programs, thereby implying that GQG's programs hindered rather
than promoted progress.[42]

GQG desired total compliance with its plans, but without assisting the
rear or understanding the complexities of industry, technology, or politics.
When it obtained a staunch supporter in Besnard, it presented him with an

unrealistic program that upset politicians and industrialists and then left him at the mercy of powerful political and industrial interests. GQG's rising distress with the quality and quantity of materiel as the year continued was legitimate, but its November program, particularly the emphasis on an all-purpose craft, was detrimental.

Despite the uncertainties and crises, the aviation industry was expanding to provide the materiel. Caudron's turnover rose from 560,000 francs in 1914 to 15.7 million in 1915; Nieuport's sales increased from 285,000 francs in 1914 to 12.2 million in 1915. Five firms—Peugeot, Panhard, Michelin, Borel, and Burlat—entered aviation production partially or entirely in 1915. In 1914 to 1915 13 aviation firms earned 59.7 million francs in gross profits based on a turnover of 192 million for a remarkable rate of 32 percent, and they reinvested those profits into their plant and used them to pay their prewar debts.[43] Aircraft manufacture, after fluctuating between 350 and 450 craft monthly since the spring, reached 501 in January, the industry having delivered 4,489 planes in 1915.[44]

Engine production, after leveling off during the summer, climbed steadily during the fall and winter, totaling 7,096 for 1915 and reaching 1,001 in January 1916. By 1916 the French were producing nearly two engines to every one aircraft, a ratio they sustained for the rest of the war and which other countries found impossible to duplicate. Of the 7,096 engines produced in 1915, 3,256 were rotaries, 2,013 were radials, and 1,827 were in-lines. The French aero engine manufacturers had established an ascendancy in production. Salmson expanded its plant from 8,000 square meters in 1914 to 24,000 square meters in 1915; its labor force from 300 to 1,500. In October it began to build its own magnetos and in December its own airplanes.[45]

By 1 February 1916 the French army had 1,149 planes—826 observation planes, 135 pursuit craft, and 188 bombers—but the aircraft standardization so early in the war had a major drawback: by 1916 many of those planes were obsolete or obsolescent. Most of the observation craft, Farmans and Caudrons, were potentially easy prey for enemy pursuit craft. The 120 two-seat reconnaissance Nieuports and the Bébés, which were the backbone of the pursuit force, remained effective. Most of the bombers were Voisins, with a few Breguet-Michelins and seven Caproni trimotor bombers powered by French engines and built by REP under license at its Lyon annex.

French aerial ascendancy had lasted through the summer of 1915. The success in engine production notwithstanding, the second half of the year had been increasingly difficult at the front and in the political arena, culminating in Besnard's resignation. The political cauldron had engulfed him just as the cauldron at the front was about to boil over at Verdun, to engulf an entire generation of Frenchmen. The mettle and materiel of the French air service would be sorely tested in 1916.

Germany

In 1915 the German army had to mold its air service into an efficient fighting machine, and its navy had to further its airplane arm, while both services sought to bring their Zeppelin forces to bear on Britain. Major Siegert, the OHL's bomber chief and aviation adviser, considered the winter of 1915 the nadir of German military aviation. The poor morale of the flight crews (some still flew obsolete and unarmed Taubes), winter's limited aerial activity, and the influx of inexperienced fliers as the air service expanded— all impaired efficiency at the front. The absence of a central aviation organization impeded the air arm's overall development in both the front and the rear.[46]

Operations continued, of course, even in the dead of winter. The elite bomber units of the Brieftauben Abteilungen Ostende (Carrier Pigeon Units Ostende [BAO]) had been badly hurt in daylight attacks in December 1914, but they made the first German squadron attack on Dunkirk on the night of 28 January. In their 100-hp craft carrying 123 bombs, they flew at 1,100 meters altitude in below-freezing temperatures. The sight above Nieuport awed their chief, Siegert:

> Moonlight shone on the surf of the North Sea; a factory near Firmeny was ablaze, the artillery fire on both sides looked like chains of glowing beads; hundreds of thousands of star shells of all colors seemed to be bubbles dancing in black champagne. . . . There above lay the roots for the understanding of cubism and expressionism.[47]

Siegert referred to the scene as a "cosmic fireworks," the air as a "flaming brew." The bombing of Dunkirk was uneventful, almost incidental, since no planes collided or dropped their bombs on each other. Later the BAO and its successor unit at Metz would expand to become the OHL's battle wing (Kampfgeschwader). Its aircraft would include the few early AEG twin-engine bombers built in 1915.

In 1915 the reconnaissance fliers' reports were often ignored, in part because they lacked air staff officers at headquarters to transmit information. In February inattention to reports of French preparations for an attack around the Reichsackerkopf caused the loss of the position and meant that German units had to retake the lost ground in March.

A primary difficulty the air service faced was its own organization. Major Siegert echoed aviation inspector Eberhardt's 1914 complaints about the absence of one overarching authority and of staff officers at army headquarters and suggested to the OHL the formation of a unified aviation command. On 9 February 1915 the OHL recommended to the Prussian War Ministry the establishment of a chief of field aviation (Feldflugchef) to direct all aviation affairs, including industrial production. The War Ministry finally conceded control over the inspectorate to the Feldflugchef on 26 April, so he could "organize a systematic mobilization of the aviation industry." The army commands, which directed the operations of the field units, now employed a staff officer of fliers as their liaison with the front. Colonel Hermann von der Lieth-Thomsen became the new chief, Siegert his deputy, and with a small staff of 10 officers and 28 other ranks at general headquarters at Charleville, they assumed command of the German air service.[48]

As the year proceeded the German air arm recovered, buoyed primarily by the appearance in May of C-planes and later of single-seat fighters. The C-planes were the standard two-seat 100- to 120- hp biplanes of late 1914, equipped with 150-hp engines and a machine gun for the observer, who now sat in the rear seat behind the pilot instead of in front. The units greeted them with enthusiasm, since the armament would now enable German crews to strike back.

The air arm was just recovering from winter doldrums when the French attacked in Artois in May. While the armed two-seat C-planes helped restore morale mid-year, the service remained outnumbered in July and August when the French attacked again in Champagne and Artois. Forced on the defensive, the Germans resorted to an aerial blockade, using all aircraft, regardless of suitability, as combat planes in defensive patrols to protect German airspace. By August, however, they possessed a significant new weapon, if only in limited numbers.[49]

Roland Garros's armed Morane monoplane had posed an immediate challenge for the German air arm and aircraft industry in April. German fliers fled precipitately, unaware of the contraption's risky nature. As morale threatened to collapse, Garros was forced to land in German territory on 18 April. The Prussian authorities shipped his craft to Berlin and summoned Anthony Fokker from his factory at Schwerin to adapt Garros's system for German use. The army selected Fokker because he specialized in light-airplane construction and was then building a modified copy of the Morane powered by an Oberursel rotary, a licensed copy of the Gnome.

Fokker's adaptation—a mechanical interrupter gear enabling a machine gun fixed to the fuselage to fire through the arc of the revolving propeller in the direction of flight—revolutionized air warfare and gave German pilots the opportunity to become as aggressive as their British and French counterparts. While Fokker claimed that he conceived of the gear in a brilliant flash of inspiration,[50] it is more likely that the inspectorate provided him with the details of a synchronizing gear patented by LVG engineer Franz Schneider in 1913 and promised to protect him from lawsuits, thus enabling him to develop a mechanism so quickly.[51]

After May the E-plane (Eindecker, or monoplane) began to appear at the front—2 by June and 11 by mid-July. The gun occasionally shot off the propeller. German pilots, used to heavy, stable craft, had difficulty flying the light, maneuverable monoplane. After three fatal crashes in July and August, the inspectorate forbade its use and disbanded the Fokker training unit at Döberitz. But by that time the intrepidity of early Fokker pilots, particularly the most famous, Oswald Boelcke and Max Immelmann, had made the Dutchman and his monoplane legends.[52]

Immelmann, on 1 August the first to score on the Fokker, had just come to the front in May, been promoted to second lieutenant on 14 July, and had only flown the Fokker for three days when, after firing 500 rounds in a combat of 8 to 10 minutes, he downed an unarmed British reconnaissance craft. He would continue to score throughout the year. On 14 December he shot down a British plane from within 100 meters range, hitting both the pilot (four times in the head, leg, and chest) and the observer, whose body fell from the plane to be impaled on the branches of a tree.[53]

Boelcke, the more experienced of the two, had been a pilot at the front since September 1914. With 42 flights over enemy territory by January 1915, the young Boelcke was the acknowledged "old master" of the unit, Abteilung 62, at Douai. Assigned to pilot the unit's first C-plane in June, he and his observer had shot down their first plane on 6 July. Equipped with the Fokker in July, he wrote his parents: "With the singleseater my ideal is achieved: now I can be pilot, observer and fighter all at the same time."[54] He also decided, unlike other Fokker pilots, that since he could find no prey over his own lines, he would violate instructions and roam beyond the lines, reasoning that "one must not wait until they come, but search them out and hunt them."[55] Boelcke got his first kill on the Fokker on 19 August, and he and Immelmann often flew together, the first hunting pair in German aviation history.

Immelmann had noted in his diary on 27 May that Boelcke was "extraordinarily calm and deliberate, . . . never nervous," and flew "admirably."[56] Boelcke possessed a sense of humor, a reticence about publicity beyond mention in the army reports, and a flair for romantic escapades. Early in November he was invited to general headquarters in Charleville to meet air chief Lieth-Thomsen, who introduced him as "the famous Boelcke" to the General Staff, then feted him and discussed matters at the front. The twenty-four year-old's star was ascending rapidly.[57]

When Anthony Fokker demonstrated the plane to frontline units, he established an immediate rapport with Boelcke, Immelmann, and other Fokker pilots. Their offensive and aggressive use of the machines created the success that led to demands for more Fokkers. The inspectorate relented and resumed training in October, but entirely at the Fokker factory in Schwerin.

Ironically, the inspectorate had sought to sever ties between frontline pilots and factories to avoid the confusion of August 1914; now such ties were reestablished in extravagant fashion. On leave in Berlin the fliers could bask in the luxury of the best hotels, coddled by the manufacturers who rented the facilities and sought their advice. Immelmann, now known as "the Eagle of Lille," was a teetotaler and physical fitness fanatic, so he shunned the Berlin frivolities to spend his November leave as Fokker's guest in Schwerin, where they discussed building a more heavily armed E-plane especially for Immelmann.[58]

Fokker production did not exceed 32 per month through December, and no more than 50 were in service at any moment even in early 1916. This limited production restricted the Fokker's impact on the air war. The Fokkers were dispersed among other types, precluding the effect they might have had as a unit. The Siemens Schuckert Works (SSW) and Pfalz also produced armed monoplanes—both inferior to the Fokker in performance—in limited numbers.[59] The inspectorate did not have the fighters license-produced by larger firms, probably because it required more of its mainstay, the standard two-seat biplane (the C-plane), now armed with a synchronized machine gun and a ring-mounted gun for the observer, for indispensable tasks of reconnaissance and tactical bombing. The air arm and industry, which had been accustomed to dealing with a single aircraft type, were now adjusting to the construction, testing, and production of a variety of types using new construction methods and requiring different training. Now some German fliers were seeking combat, and their efforts did enable German reconnaissance fliers to secure information about enemy intentions during the rest of the year, although they remained outnumbered on the Western Front.

On the Eastern Front, the few flight units, receiving less materiel than those of the Western Front, had to cover great distances and watch not only the Russians but also their own troops, given the inadequate communications. Stretched to the limit, they received praise for everything from artillery spotting to cooperation with the cavalry. For General von Mackensen's attack in Galicia in early 1915, the army amassed three flight units and the OHL's battle squadron for a total of 54 planes, which were used to gain an overview of the front, sight artillery, and then to follow and harass the withdrawing Russian forces. In the heavily wooded Carpathian Mountains, only aerial photographs enabled the detection of Russian artillery hidden in dense forests and gorges, and the airplane became the only means to maintain contact with enemy forces. [60]

The German navy developed its own small airplane force in 1915 within the limits set by the army's control of engine distribution. The naval air service expanded from 82 officers and 2,755 other ranks to 225 officers and 3,342 other personnel. A new aviation department in the Imperial Naval Office established its procurement apparatus. The naval seaplane arm grew, though not as fast as its officers desired. In February 1915 it had 59 seaplanes, not the 120 it had sought; in December it had 143 and not its desired strength of 236. Flugzeugbau Friedrichshafen delivered 84 seaplanes, and Hansa-Brandenburg sent 28 in 1915 in response to the navy's contracts, which were issued intermittently either because of the firms' inability to produce more or because of difficulties in securing engines from the army. The small size of the force, most of whose planes were unarmed, explains why the English reported few encounters with German seaplanes along the Belgian coast in 1915. [61]

Naval aviation diverted precious resources to the cautious development of torpedo plane prototypes by Albatros and Hansa-Brandenburg during 1915. The navy's first landplane unit, formed in the fall, expanded from 64 craft in February (35 under the desired amount) to 115 in December (8 over the targeted amount), because firms could produce them more readily and cheaply than seaplanes. On 15 December the naval and military flight chiefs arranged to exchange flying officers to ease any friction in procurement. [62]

In the winter of 1914–15 the German army and navy jockeyed for the undertaking of strategic attacks on England using dirigibles. [63] The army proposed a joint offensive under its control; the navy demurred. The Kaiser, concerned for his royal cousins and London's historical monuments and residential areas, disliked the entire proposition. In late 1914 German naval memoranda had urged that the material and moral results of concentrating on London could "diminish the enemy's determination to prosecute the war." In January, after the French had bombed German cities, the chief of naval staff, Adm. Hugo von Pohl, pushed by his deputy Adm. Paul Behncke and flight chief Admiral Philipp, managed to gain the Kaiser's consent to bomb the English coast, docks, and military establishments on the lower Thames. After an abortive attempt on 13 January, the navy's Zeppelin L3 became the first dirigible over England on 19 January, when it and the L4 bombed the British coast. Exaggerating the significance of this first raid, a 21 January *Kölnische Zeitung* editorial exulted: "The most modern air weapon, a triumph of German inventiveness and the sole possession of the German Army, has shown itself capable of . . . carrying the war to the soil of old England! . . . This is the best way to shorten the war, and thereby in the end the most humane."[64] The L3 and L4 were lost on a 16 February scouting mission over the Skagerrak.

Just as the army was preparing to bomb London with airships, the Kaiser forbade any attacks on London. Wilhelm and his chancellor, Theobald von Bethmann Hollweg, were concerned about world opinion and the unfavorable impression on foreign neutrals—particularly the United States—that bombing undefended cities would make. In a 20 March attack on Paris, two of the three attacking airships were damaged.

At the end of April the Kaiser consented to attacks on parts of London. His reservations were outweighed by the various arguments for bombing as a means of material destruction, demoralization of the population and consequent damage to war production, and diversion of British aircraft from the continent that might ultimately prompt the British to reconsider their war commitment. His consent came just as the army and navy began to receive the first of the million-cubic-foot Zeppelins, the "p" and "q" class, of which 22 and 12 would be built, respectively. The p ships were 536 feet long, with a diameter of 61.35 feet, a maximum speed of 60 mph and a cruising speed of 40 mph, and a volume of 1,126,000 cubic feet. Powered by four six-cylinder 210- and later 240-hp Maybach engines, these dirigibles carried a crew of up to 19 people, seven or eight machine guns, and a bomb load of over 2 tons. The q class, which would begin to arrive in December, was longer—over 585 feet—and larger—with a volume of 1,263,000 cubic feet—than the p ship. Two additional gas cells (18 compared to 16 for the p ships) raised its ceiling 1,500 feet over the p ship's maximum of 11,600 feet.

The army's first p ship, the LZ38, bombed British coastal towns in April and May and then staged the first air attack on London the night of 31 May–1 June. After such a rapid start, however, on 6 June the army lost the LZ38 on the ground to bombing by British Farmans from Dunkirk, and the LZ37 with its crew—the first army Zeppelin crew lost in the war—to an in-flight attack near Ghent by British flight sub-Lt. Alexander Warneford, who bombed it from his Morane parasol. These losses deflated the army's dirigible assault in the west. Although the LZ74 and the SL2 would bomb London in July, the high command transferred most of its ships to the Eastern and Balkan Fronts. In the latter part of 1915 military airships supported Hindenburg's offensive in Poland with raids on railroad lines.

Zeppelin operations, even successful missions, were difficult. On 15 July Maj. Viktor Gaissert and his crew took command of the LZ79 at the Zeppelin dockyard in Potsdam. Before completing their test flights, they were ordered to fly immediately to Poland and bomb the railroad yards and bridges near Brest Litovsk. He attacked the night of 10 August, following the brightly lit Russian trains on the railroad line to Brest and bombing the fortress from 4,000 meters with 12 100-kilogram bombs. The return was the most difficult part of the mission because a strong head wind forced them to descend into fog and fly at 400 meters altitude for hours, after which they located their position only with some difficulty. The 1,400 kilometer round-trip had taken 17 hours. Returning from a later mission against rail lines east of Brest Litovsk, they required over two hours to land after a first unsuccessful attempt because of engine problems.[65]

As the army retreated from its Zeppelin offensive in the west, the navy was placing increasing emphasis on airships for attacking England and scouting for the fleet. In April the German Admiralty, buoyed by the exaggerated estimates of damage done in the first raids, ordered a six-engine Zeppelin airship of nearly two million cubic feet in volume. In May Zeppelins located and bombed, albeit unsuccessfully, British submarines. On 4 June Admiral Pohl wrote a memo emphasizing the value of airships to combat submarines, locate mine fields, protect minesweepers from surprise attack, and, most crucially, scout in the absence of suitable fast cruisers. The Admiralty and naval staff approved Pohl's proposal of a fleet of 12 operational ships, which would necessitate a total of 18 dirigibles. Construction of giant double hangars—790 feet long, 197 feet wide, and 110 feet high—began that summer.

Admiral Bachmann, Chief of the Admiralty Staff, with the agreement of General Staff Chief Erich von Falkenhayn, persuaded the Kaiser to approve unrestricted airship attacks in July. The night of 9 August the navy sent four p ships to bomb London, losing one to antiaircraft damage and missing the target because of faulty navigation, a common occurrence given the current state of navigation. On 8 September Heinrich Mathy, considered to be a virtuoso airship navigator, bombed London with two tons of bombs, setting off fires in textile warehouses and causing more than a half million pounds of damage, the greatest monetary loss of any air raid during the war. On 12 September General Staff Chief Falkenhayn cautioned the navy to avoid residential areas and excessive civilian damage in London, for fear of British and French reprisal raids.

Although the p ship L10 was lost (the first navy crew to fall) in a thunderstorm near Cuxhaven after a 3 September reconnaissance mission, in the year's last raid on 13 October five p ships attacked London in one of the war's deadliest raids, killing 71 and injuring 128. The raiders encountered increased antiaircraft fire and the first interceptor, a BE2c that the Zeppelin easily outclimbed. With the onset of winter weather, the raids ceased and the naval airships faced the ravages of high humidity, mold, and putrefaction in their hangars. Although the navy lost a new p ship to fire in its shed, it received its first q ship, the L20, on 21 December, as it prepared for another year of raids on Britain.

With the appointment of an air chief, the Prussian army was developing its aviation bureaucracy to manage the growth of the air service. In the rear it assumed a larger role in the aircraft industry's affairs, hoping to improve productivity, aircraft quality, and coordination of the Prussian, Bavarian, and German naval aviation bureaucracies. Although the Bavarian army retained its autonomy in aviation administration, the Prussian army's control of engine distribution enabled it to buy monoplane scouts directly from Bavaria's Pfalz factory and then distribute Bavaria's share to Bavarian field units.[66] The army faced an enormous task in replacing the unplanned daily efforts of the individual factories with a coordinated industrial mobilization to supply sufficient aircraft for reconnaissance, artillery observation, bombardment, and incipient air fighting.

Before the chief assumed command, the Inspectorate of Flying Troops had been separated from the Inspectorate of Aviation and Motor Vehicles, and three army airparks had been created for supply and repairs. The Inpectorate of Flying Troops recommended the formation of its own central acceptance commission and four subordinate commissions to control aircraft procurement from the fliers' replacement units, which had previously managed aircrew training and aircraft acceptance. From February to December flight schools increased from 11 to 20, with 4 additional schools for observer training. The acceptance subcommissions' formation, however, took until the winter of 1915–16 because of the shortage of technicians and the inspectorate's difficulty in retaining them due to competition with the industry.[67]

The manufacturers had been producing designs that taxed the army's ability to assess aircraft. In August 1914 Zeppelin and his associate, Claudius Dornier, had begun work on a huge multi-engine aircraft, whose first successful test flight in 1915 changed the inspectorate's initial opinion that the craft was too large. After Zeppelin flew in the giant ship on 1 August, he had another factory built in Friedrichshafen to manufacture them. In August 1914 SSW, the leader of the German electrical industry, had reactivated an aviation department dormant since 1911 to build two giant airplanes, one of which passed acceptance tests in June 1915. The inspectorate ordered six more, and in November the army designated these craft R-planes (Riesenflugzeuge, or giant planes) and stipulated that their engines be repairable in flight.[68]

In perhaps the most significant development for the future of aviation science and technology, Hugo Junkers, a prolific inventor, had begun preparations to develop an all-metal airplane in his bath-heater factory. Although the armed forces initially took no interest, he built a test institute in Dessau in early 1915 and in February offered to develop an all-metal plane for the War Ministry. After a May visit a War Ministry commission issued him a contract for a prototype.

Junkers, determined to create an instrument that could affect the war's course, had ascertained that a thick airfoil offered little more resistance to airflow and better stability than the thin profiles in use, and he selected steel for his building material. His design, he believed, opened entirely new paths for aircraft construction, using materials that would make aircraft more resistant to weather and fire. After a wing section successfully completed its first break test in early July, War Ministry representative Maj. Paul Oschmann grew concerned about lower-cost mass production based on materials that were easier to procure and required fewer skilled workers. Junkers found his project delayed by insufficient labor and was prepared to place his entire operation under military supervision to obtain the War Ministry's support in securing additional staff. By October the project was some six weeks behind schedule, but Oschmann promised to find sufficient staff only when the airplane proved "viable." In December 1915 Junkers finished the prototype, which would be ready to fly in the coming year.[69]

The inspectorate monitored plant processes and set aircraft prices more stringently after the War Ministry's decision to grant a price increase of three percent in February. After a War Ministry audit of most firms' books and several conferences, the ministry decided that the increased profits from serial orders of 50 to 100 planes offset the higher production costs at major firms and did not honor the price increase. Yet twice in 1915, in May and in September, the War Ministry mediated between the Berlin aircraft manufacturers and their wood and metal workers, pressuring the industrialists toward collective bargaining and wage increases to meet the higher cost of living. The manufacturers of the Convention of Aircraft Industrialists then persuaded the War Ministry to make the September wage increases conditional on an increase in aircraft prices. In October the army granted the price increase promised in February and further accorded the industry's labor exemptions the same high priority as the Krupp armaments and Zeiss optic firms. By mid-1915 the aircraft industry had become extremely important to the war effort.[70]

Spurred by more contracts, the aircraft factories expanded their production from two to eight times, their labor force from one-half to three times, and aircraft deliveries to the army from 1,348 in 1914 to 4,532 in 1915. Engine factories delivered 5,037 engines—4,544 stationary in-lines and 493 rotary engines. The increased production enabled the air arm's expansion from 74 flight units in March 1915 to 96 units, 6 combat squadrons, and 40 single-seat fighters, for a total of 764 planes by the year's end.

Yet German engine manufacture, after increasing to 309 engines in December 1914, stagnated below 500 monthly until the last quarter of 1915, when it rose to 650. Erroneous decisions by the inspectorate, which lacked engine experts, compounded the limitations posed by Daimler's near monopoly of production. During the war's first year its engine section comprised one civilian engineer, Walter Simon, who managed procurement, acceptance, tests, new designs, and material supply in a "peculiar and arbitrary" manner.[71] On 16 November 1914 it had decided against the development of engines greater than 150 horsepower to avoid disturbing production. This decision, while prompted by limited production capacity, delayed the evolution of more powerful engines. In 1915 the inspectorate declined a Benz eight-cylinder 240-hp engine because it did not conform to the standard six-cylinder engines, but then allowed production of a Daimler eight-cylinder in-line 220-hp engine after its December 1915 bench test. It halted production after 429 units because the engine's length resulted in a lack of stiffness in its crankshaft. Skilled-labor and machine tool shortages kept crankshaft production insufficient to increase overall engine production, so the entire year was spent expanding plant capacity. Inadequate production thus condemned the German air service to, at the very best, a temporary aerial superiority over a circumscribed area of the front.[72]

Early in June air chief Lieth-Thomsen sought to attract large industrial enterprises to give aircraft manufacture a firmer financial basis, enable greater experimentation, and increase competition. In the summer the inspectorate drew the Hannoversche Waggonfabrik A.G., with its skilled labor force, excellent woodworking capacity, and large stocks of seasoned timber, to aircraft production for propeller construction and aircraft repairs.

The firm established an aircraft construction department, which in November received contracts from the inspectorate for the licensed production of Aviatik C-planes. The War Ministry and inspectorate also engineered the Benz motor company's acquisition of the Leipzig Aviatik factory, persuaded Daimler to undertake aircraft production, and loaned the Rumpler and LVG firms substantial funds for expansion. The Waggonfabrik Linke-Hoffmann in Breslau began R-plane construction. On 20 November Lieth-Thomsen informed the OHL that the air arm would need 1,000 planes in service during 1916, sought ratification for measures to increase production, and requested further exemptions for the industry's skilled workers.[73]

In 1915 the German army air service had rebounded from its early 1915 depression and ended the year with an aviation commander, who used improved aircraft to pursue a defensive strategy. Its rear bureaucracy was developing an aviation industry that was based on inadequate engine production. The German navy concentrated on airships for fleet escort and strategic bombing, and used successively larger airships to assault England. The army, chastened by its attempts at these attacks, withdrew, leaving the navy to press on in 1916.

England

In England the RFC and the RNAS faced increasing commitments but lacked adequate supplies. The RFC, with only 85 to 90 frontline aircraft in March, 106 in June, and 153 in September, remained small compared with the French and German air arms. In the winter of 1914–15, it prepared to support the BEF in more offensive operations. In mid-February RFC headquarters directed one flight per squadron to specialize in bombing in addition to its normal duties. The RFC gave no systematic guidance on techniques or tactics, suggesting only that accuracy might require low flying. Before the BEF attack on Neuve-Chapelle in March, the RFC systematically photographed the region and flew tactical bombing raids over the lines. When the attack began on 10 March, mist and cloud impaired air-ground cooperation. Despite plans for the infantry to use white strips of cloth to mark their progress for aerial observers, there was little effective battle coordination between the army and the air arm. Low-level bombing attacks concentrated on German communication lines, particularly railroad stations and junctions, but with negligible results. Of 141 attacks on railroad junctions and stations, RFC headquarters judged only three successful.[74]

Among the losses suffered in these raids was the RFC's and British aviation's first Victoria Cross, Lt. W. B. Rhodes-Moorhouse. On 26

April Lt. Rhodes-Moorhouse attacked the railroad station at Courtrai from 300 feet with a 100-pound bomb. Mortally wounded from ground fire, he flew the 35 miles back to his aerodrome and insisted on reporting before receiving medical attention. He died the next day. In April Trenchard, whom Brancker's biographer Basil Collier accused of pressing his First Wing so hard that "it suffered losses wholly disproportionate to any good achieved,"[75] reported to Henderson that he was limiting his operations to a few short-distance reconnaissance and bombing missions and eliminating long-distance reconnaissance entirely in order to reduce losses.[76]

Trenchard considered the seven squadrons under General Henderson's command for the Battle of Aubers Ridge in May insufficient and the army's skill in using airpower inadequate. Wartime personnel losses at the front reportedly totaled 100 by June 1915, when the frontline force in France was only 106 fliers. By the end of July Lt. Col. C. J. Burke, commander of the RFC's Second Wing, estimated the average flight time of his serviceable aircraft at one hour a day. The army command still had not integrated aerial operations with attack plans. Battery commanders, annoyed with the technical difficulties of air-ground cooperation, ignored air reports; infantry officers seldom marked forward positions for aerial identification.[77] Yet in June BEF commander Sir John French commended the RFC's "invaluable assistance," which was "becoming more and more an indispensable factor in combined operations."[78]

The RFC's dissatisfaction with bombing was evident at a 7 August conference between British and French air representatives, when it perceived little material result from 4,062 bombs dropped in 483 operations on the Western Front between 1 April and 18 June. Late in July RFC headquarters limited bombing to strikes on targets within the army's close reconnaissance area. By then, the RFC's most committed bombing advocate was no longer in Europe. Colonel Sykes, rejected by Kitchener as Henderson's successor, alienated Henderson by conspiring to succeed him when Henderson was home on sick leave. Sykes was exiled to the Dardanelles, supposedly to command the naval air operations there. Yet Henderson himself had been under pressure to return to England since early 1915. In July Colonel Brancker, who had been managing the Directorate of Military Aviation, insisted that Henderson's leadership at the directorate was urgently required to defend the interests of the air arm, which some still considered "an expensive and precocious innovation." Henderson returned to the War Office on 19 August, and Hugh "Boom" Trenchard, promoted to brigadier-general, assumed command of the RFC on the continent.[79]

In September the BEF staged its first large-scale offensive, the Battle of Loos, supported by a three-wing RFC totaling 12 squadrons. The RFC completed its preliminary photoreconnaissance missions and registered artillery targets, but smoke, rain, cloud, and gas impeded reports on the attack's progress. Aircrews struck the Lille-Douai-Valenciennes railway line as far as 36 miles behind the lines, dropping nearly 5.5 tons of bombs from 23 to 28 September.[80]

The fall battles saw the introduction of the clock code for artillery spotting developed by Capt. Baron T. James and Lt. Donald S. Lewis, two former Royal Engineers who had adapted the wireless for British aircraft. The code was a transparent celluloid trace with 12 radial lines emanating from its center and eight concentric circles, the lines representing direction, the circles distance from the target to 500 yards. The observer estimated the point of the shell burst and transferred it to his map, placing the center of the trace over the target and determining the burst's position. Used with a lightweight wireless transmitter, the code facilitated artillery shoots.[81]

Early in 1915 the RFC's aggressive pilots tried to engage the Germans in combat, but their intended foes declined to fight when possible, fleeing when chased and usually flying higher than the British. Pilot Lewis Strange engaged a German Aviatik biplane on 10 May with near disastrous consequences. The empty drum of the Lewis gun mounted on his Martinsyde scout's top wing jammed. Just as Strange tried to repair it, his climbing plane stalled and spun. He next found himself in midair dangling from the gun's drum and praying that it would remain jammed, as his plane descended upside down in a flat spin. Grabbing a strut, he managed to swing his feet and then his torso into the cockpit. Then in righting the plane he smashed his seat so badly that bits of it jammed his controls, which he managed to free just in time to avoid a crash.[82]

The aviator who early emerged as the RFC's premier fighter pilot was the Sixth Squadron's Lanoe Hawker, a small, sensitive, and introspective former Royal Engineer, endowed with great determination and willpower but subject to bouts of depression. Alternating reconnaissance, bombing, and scouting duties, Hawker fixed a Lewis gun on the side of his Bristol that was aimed to fire forward at an oblique angle to miss his propeller. On 25 July he attacked three German planes, shooting one down and forcing a second down in German lines, thus adding a Victoria Cross—the RFC's second and the first for aerial fighting—to his Distinguished Service Order. Combat flying severely strained his health and nerves, but he lived for the moment and rarely thought of the future. In September Strange, the last of his original squadron of August 1914, and Hawker, the last of his squadron formed in October 1914, were posted to Home Establishment, Strange to form the 23rd Squadron and Hawker to the 24th. Hawker nearly collapsed under the strain of command in Britain, but he returned to France with his new squadron at the end of 1915.[83]

In 1915 the limited performance of the few fighting aircraft meant that encounters were few and usually indecisive. When the German Fokkers entered the war, they affected the RFC's morale, since the RFC had been accustomed to pursuing poorly equipped, fleeing Germans. The Fokker had its first success in the British sector on 1 August. By 25 October Trenchard was advising the War Office to train pilots and observers in air fighting at home, while winter losses of 7 planes in November, 11 in December, and 10 in January 1916 prompted RFC headquarters' doctrine of heavy escort over the lines in 1916. By the end of 1915, the RFC had lost control of the air over its sector of the front.[84]

The training of RFC aircrew, particularly observers, was inadequate to the increasing demand.[85] By May 1915 234 officers under instruction at 11 air stations in Britain encountered instructor and training-aircraft shortages. Some pilots were sent overseas with as little as five hours of solo flight time. Observer training was worse. The RFC treated the observer's demanding and essential role casually and encouraged observers to become pilots, as the early careers of James McCudden, one of Britain's great aces, and Sholto Douglas, later Air Marshal, illustrated.

McCudden had left the Royal Engineers in 1912 to join the RFC, following his older brother, who by 1914 was a rarity in the RFC: a noncommissioned officer pilot. The younger McCudden began as an air mechanic, taking every occasion to ride with his brother. A noncommissioned officer by 1915 and still a mechanic, McCudden occasionally flew as a gunner in Moranes. His older brother William was killed while an instructor at Gosport in May, and McCudden, though recommended for flight training in June, was held at the front because of the dire need for engine mechanics. To mollify him somewhat, he was assigned to observation duties. Although McCudden flew a great deal, his pilot did most of the work—ranging on targets and reporting by wireless—since it was the pilot's task to obliterate the gun positions. McCudden noted the time and place of gun flashes but was essentially there to watch for Fokkers, with which he had two indecisive encounters in December.[86]

Douglas, an artillery lieutenant who had volunteered for observation duties early in 1915, received only a sketchy definition of the observer's role and "extraordinarily little training," nearly all of it with a squadron at the front. He left observation to learn to fly in May. When he returned to France he had 40 hours and 5 minutes of flight time, while the average pilot that he encountered in the summer of 1915 had only 20 hours and some as few as 14 hours, a policy he later described as "sheer murder." Douglas, despite his inexperience, was lucky to have survived the fall and winter. Fighting Fokkers and the prevailing westerly winds always made fliers' returns from missions over the German lines an enervating proposition. In December Douglas barely escaped Oswald Boelcke when his violent, evasive maneuvers sickened his observer, who vomited on him before sinking into the fuselage. After that encounter, Douglas returned to England to prepare a new squadron for combat in France.[87]

This small force—a "company of individualists," "eccentric and even downright crazy," as Douglas referred to them—was not easily daunted.[88] The RFC sought public school and university youths who had participated in sports or officers' training. Ideal RFC candidates were like Cecil Lewis, author of *Sagittarius Rising*, who had joined the RFC at the age 17 in 1915,[89] and Sholto Douglas, who had enrolled in the Officers Training Corps in public school and at Oxford and had subscribed to notions of war as a great adventure—views he later called "unrealistic."[90] In fall 1915 Lt. M. F. Powell, a member of actor Robert Loraine's B flight of the Fifth Squadron, threatened to lead a revolt in the unit when he found headquarters mechanics fitting bomb racks on his plane without his permission. Powell explained that "in those days the Flying Corps was a highly individual service. Each officer had his own machine, housed in its own tent, with his own rigger and his own mechanic to attend to it. He regarded himself as a separate fighting unit. As a unit he was willing to co-operate, but he certainly could not be bossed about as though he were an air taxi-driver."[91]

The RFC's characterization of air combat as a sport stemmed from its composition—a corps of commissioned officers who were recruited as much as possible from the ranks of public school sportsmen and drawn to war flying for the adventure. Theirs was, at least initially, a "marvellous life, a sport, a game," as Cecil Lewis bubbled. R. M. Neill wrote to his school newspaper urging Westminster boys to join the RFC, advising that "any sportsman will realise that, apart from fighting, there is absolutely nothing to touch flying as a sport. . . . It is the public schoolboy who very often makes the best pilot." Six weeks later Neill was killed in action.[92]

The RFC rejected the notion, advanced by *The Aeroplane* in November, that most pilots should enter as noncommissioned officers and be promoted on the basis of meritorious work.[93] In the war's first year the RFC's waiting list had enabled it to reject applications for commission.[94] When it had exhausted the list, it was slow to modify its criteria. The French and Germans used noncommissioned officers as pilots from the start, but the RFC persisted in its belief that only officers from the educated middle and upper classes made effective aviators.

Army council letters of 25 August and 10 December ordered that the RFC's three wings be formed into a brigade, with additional brigades formed until there would be one for each army. Until 1918 each brigade would comprise a corps wing for general army-related duties of close reconnaissance, photography, and artillery cooperation, and an army wing (which received the best airplanes) for long-range reconnaissance, bombing, and air fighting. On 23 November, when the RFC had 18 service squadrons abroad (14 in France), with another 13 at home, General Henderson authorized the organization of 60 service squadrons with a strength increased from 12 to 18 planes and pilots, 20 reserve squadrons, and four airparks. The first three brigades would be formed by mid-February.

The RNAS, though saddled with home defense, thought in strategic terms even after the May replacement of Churchill and Sir John Fisher at the Admiralty by the more traditional, prudent, and less dynamic regime of First Lord H. A. Balfour. In June Churchill suggested the formation of an air department over both military and naval aviation, which many presumed he desired to head. In July the Admiralty declared the RNAS an integral part of the Royal Navy and in September appointed the "unoriginal" nonaviator Rear Adm. C. L. Vaughan-Lee as the first director of admiralty air services, relegating Murray Sueter, who was considered "brilliantly inventive, extremely impatient of authority, and highly prone to 'hubris,' " to superintendent of aircraft construction.[95] In the 13 October *The Globe* Sueter proposed the formation of a Royal Air Service; he would ultimately be "exiled" to the Mediterranean.[96]

In the spring the RNAS continued its bombing raids on Belgian targets, particularly Zeppelin bases, while the RFC was retreating from its disastrous bombing efforts. The RNAS sustained low losses for reasonable success. In April they reduced the number of targets, limited the range of the raids, and began planning a strategic bombing campaign against Germany and the expansion of the naval air arm to 1,000 landplanes and 300 seaplanes by the end of 1915. The Admiralty and the French made tentative arrangements in the fall for future joint bombing operations, and at a meeting on 17 December the French representative ordered six Sopwith $1\frac{1}{2}$ strutter biplanes as potential bombers.

The Zeppelin menace posed the greatest problem because the RNAS was generally unable to intercept the dirigibles. Between January 1915 and

January 1916 21 Zeppelin raids dropped 1,900 bombs totaling just over 36 tons, killing 277, wounding 645, and causing an estimated damage of 870,000 pounds. Given this overall failure to deter the Zeppelin raids, RNAS flight sub-Lt. R. A. J. Warneford received much attention in the press, when he destroyed the first Zeppelin in the air over Ostende by dropping a 20-pound bomb on it from his Morane on 6 June. On the night of 16–17 May RNAS craft had intercepted the LZ39 above Ostende, damaging it with bombs, but Warneford had sent his down in flames. Warneford became the first naval airman to win the Victoria Cross, but he had little time to enjoy his success. Ten days later, in Paris to collect a new Farman, Warneford crashed to his death when the plane broke up in the air. His commanding officer had warned him to fly with more care, an admonition that the young flier apparently disregarded.[97]

The RNAS, like the RFC, attracted able but often "highly idiosyncratic characters,"[98] types like the buccaneer commander Charles R. Samson, whose strong personality, courage, rudeness, and "blackbearded piratical appearance," as one of his men, Richard B. Davies, described him, made for good prewar press and aggressive and fearless wartime leadership.[99] Samson's early continental naval operations had shown initiative and drive. His Third Naval Wing went to the Dardanelles for the assault on Gallipoli, where air support became a small but integral aspect of operations. The seaplane carrier Ark Royal and other seaplane tenders were part of the fleet, and a naval airship unit arrived in August. The navy's seaplanes and landplanes performed photoreconnaissance and artillery and submarine spotting missions, and bombed railroad bridges and junctions on the Berlin-Constantinople line. During these raids Davies won the Victoria Cross by landing his single-seat Nieuport in enemy territory to rescue a downed airman. RNAS seaplanes also torpedoed three ships during the campaign.

The Air Ministry's synopsis of the Gallipoli campaign attributed the success of the evacuations from Suvla and Helles—the most successful part of the Gallipoli venture—to the RNAS's reconnaissance and patrol work. Yet supplies were short, repairs were difficult, and the planes suffered from sand, dust, and intense heat that warped the wings, weakened the airframes, and overheated the engines. In May Samson complained that the BE2c climbed "rottenly" with an observer and that the Avros "waste money." Seaplanes could not take off if the water was either too rough or calm, and water seeping into damaged floats lowered their ceiling to within range of Turkish ground fire.[100]

Operations in hot climates were difficult for both the RFC's and the RNAS's personnel and materiel. In East Africa early in 1915 aircraft located the German cruiser Königsberg in the Rufiji River delta, where it had hidden in fall 1914, and spotted for the monitors that battered the cruiser into submission that summer. The seaplanes suffered from warped wood, melted glue, and peeling float bottoms, although two Farmans and two Caudrons that arrived in June managed the climate better. During 1915 two landplane squadrons replaced the seaplanes and did valuable reconnaissance work over dense bush country. In Southwest Africa Farmans spotted for the British and colonial forces, pursuing the German and colonial forces of Col. Paul von Lettow-Vorbeck, who would lead them on a merry chase for the war's duration. In fall 1915 the British sent a squadron to the first Tigris campaign in Mesopotamia, which the history of the Australian Flying Corps (four Australian corps officers participated in the Kut operations) described as a "deplorable muddle." Aircraft were too few in number, poorly supplied, and equipped with unreliable engines.[101]

In 1915 politicians and civilian publicists were increasingly dissatisfied with and occasionally hysterical about the aerial war effort. At a 24 February War Council meeting participants contemplated aerial attacks on Germany. Lt. Col. Maurice Hankey suggested an air attack to distribute a "blight" on Germany's next grain crop, which he considered no worse than indiscriminate submarine use. O'Gorman preferred to burn it using thousands of little discs of gun cotton. Churchill preferred the crop burning, regarding the blight as analogous to poisoning food, while David Lloyd George, then minister of munitions, averred that the blight "did not poison, but merely deteriorated the crop." Balfour advised that they should work out the proposition in detail, but use it only under extreme provocation.[102]

In public, air advocates Noel Pemberton-Billing and William Joynson-Hicks were concerned with the air attacks on Britain and Britain's inexcusable loss of air command. On 21 May *Flight* advocated government internment of enemy aliens, fearing that they would light fires or organize attacks during Zeppelin raids, although others believed that the presence of enemy aliens in London was all that stood between the city and destruction. *Flight* also feared the use of incendiary or chemical clouds to cloak Zeppelin movements.[103]

In June members of parliament advocated destroying Essen and other vital German centers with daily massed raids. In a patriotic manifesto in the *Daily Express*, H. G. Wells argued that 2,000 planes could demolish Essen, and even if 1,000 were lost, it would be cheaper than the Battle of Neuve-Chapelle or the loss of a battleship. Wells demanded 10,000 planes with reserves and personnel. When Undersecretary of War Tennant was queried in the Commons about the possibility of Britain's producing 3,000 planes in six months, he replied that no good purpose would be served by it, private industry could not deliver them, and the proportion of the air service to the army was adequate.

Joynson-Hicks, however, identified himself with the 10,000- , even a 20,000- , plane scheme to end the war, accusing the government of neglecting the RFC's supplies. He wanted a fleet of large, powerful planes to bomb Prussian communication lines. In an October public meeting organized by *The Globe*, Joynson-Hicks pushed for reprisal raids, and the meeting voted for the speedy formation of an air ministry. The agitation over inadequate British air defenses, the inability to retaliate against the German homeland in response to the Zeppelin raids, and the awareness of British materiel inferiority to the Fokkers on the Western Front coalesced in a demand for the formation of an air ministry or air department. Various people, from members of parliament to Churchill and Sueter, were beginning to perceive the division between the RFC and the RNAS as deleterious to effective aerial operations.[104]

The War Office complained that friction with the Admiralty over aviation had begun as early as October 1914. Admiralty representatives accused the army of exaggerating the problem and the Royal Aircraft Factory of production failures. General Henderson could cite numerous examples to counter the navy's claim. For its engine supply the Admiralty now depended on four firms that the army had first lured to engine production—Rolls Royce, Daimler, Peter Hooker, and Wolseley. Large Admiralty orders for BE2cs and Avros at prices higher than War Office standards had inflated their prices between 16 and 50 percent since the war's outbreak. While the Admiralty had no compunction about ordering from firms on the army list, it refused to allow the War Office to approach its firms for military design competitions. The competition between the War Office and the Admiralty was greatest in the bidding for French aircraft and engines, as the navy, despite a relatively light demand for materiel, regarded France as its main supply source and outbid the army. Clearly at a disadvantage, in June 1915 the War Office suggested an interdepartmental conference on aeronautical supplies, which the Admiralty postponed.[105]

In 1914 33 percent of all aircraft had needed to be replaced each month. In 1915 the monthly wastage dropped to 26 percent, the lowest ever, but aircraft supplies to the RFC did not increase sufficiently to meet the arm's rapidly growing demands.[106] Only five firms built more than 100 planes, of which Bristol (British and Colonial) delivered 335, although Airco prepared for expansion by adopting the French "système global," in which smaller firms made minor parts for assembly at the Airco factory. In 1915 34 British manufacturers produced 1,680 aircraft, including 710

BE2cs, which were reaching maximum output by late 1915, when the introduction of German Fokkers made them obsolete. Private manufacturers' disregard of drawings, which would have allowed licensed production of their prototypes, contributed to the dependence on the BE2c. The Sopwith designers continued to draw planes full scale in chalk on the floor of the experimental shop. Moving production to less experienced firms was expected to cause severe dislocation, so the RFC risked reliance on an obsolete craft far into 1916.

By 1915 the Royal Aircraft Factory, still criticized by *The Aeroplane*, had 5,000 employees and continued its multifaceted aircraft and engine design regimen, along with its investigations of aircraft dope, instruments, propellers, inspection methods, and metallurgical problems fuselages. The factory was militarized in October, O'Gorman became a lieutenant colonel, and 1,600 workers were taken from its ranks to form airparks in the field.[107]

General Henderson called a manufacturers conference in October to review design and performance requirements. As demand far outran supply in 1915, the RFC dropped its competitive contracts for cost-plus contracts. At the end of 1915 it advanced manufacturers 20 percent of the total aircraft and engine contracts for them to buy materials; the next 60 percent was advanced when the Aircraft Inspection Department (AID) certified that the materiel was ready for testing, and the rest was paid when materiel was accepted.[108]

Conditions in engine production were even more problematic. British firms delivered 1,721 engines that year, the largest supplier, British Daimler, producing 801, of which 25 percent were licensed-built Gnomes. At the end of 1915, and for the rest of the war, the most serious supply problems remained high-powered engine production and the difficulty of matching engine type with airplane class.[109] Five firms had begun production of the RAF's eight-cylinder air-cooled RAF 90-hp engine, which like its aircraft, the BE2c, did not attain maximum output until the first quarter of 1916, when it was already quite outmoded.[110]

Despite problems in production, there was progress in engine and aircraft development. Rolls Royce's 250-hp engine, the Eagle, ran on the test bench on 1 March, and the first batch was delivered on 18 October. The firm also designed a 75-hp engine, the Hawk, and a 200-hp engine, the Falcon. Negotiations for British manufacture of the Hispano-Suiza under license led to the selection of the Wolseley Company, while the Royal Aircraft Factory was instructed to design a fighter for the French engine. Murray Sueter's rejection of Frederick Handley Page's early drawings of a bomber for the RNAS with the words, "Look, Mr. Page—what I want is a bloody paralyser, not a toy," galvanized Handley Page to design a giant twin-engine bomber in January.[111] The prototype Handley Page 0/100 required 300 design weeks and 295 drawings for production and would fly in December.[112]

With increased production, the RFC and the industry required the same skilled trades. In November the trade union executive committees of seven unions, primarily woodworkers, convened to object strongly to piecework wages in the aircraft factories, insisting on hourly wages, and requesting information about the industry's employment of women.[113] At the end of 1915 the Ministry of Munitions, formed to surmount materiel shortages, began to tighten restrictions on the enlistment of labor, while the army opposed the transfer of soldiers with skills from the frontline units.

The British relied on the French to counter their production inadequacies, and the French until the end of 1915 supplied one-third of the RFC's engines. From August through November the British contracted nearly 12 million francs of aircraft, engines, parts, and accessories from France. These large orders and friction in the Paris aviation supplies department between the RFC and RNAS representatives forced Trenchard and the RFC representative to make several visits to bargain with French firms. Both the French and the British began to delay orders until the other side fulfilled its obligations. In October the French suggested that the aviation representatives meet monthly to discuss supplies. In December Trenchard asked Henderson to allow the French government to order raw materials from British firms only if the British received the 150 Rhône 110-hp rotaries, 50 Hispano-Suizas, Gnomes, Clergets, spare parts, and other accessories requested as early as June 1915. Beginning in 1916, the British would place all orders through the French government and not directly with French firms, while the French government would control the distribution of British raw materials to its manufacturers. The French government thus gained stronger authority over its manufacturers and could begin to establish a balance between the material supply from England to France and the aircraft and engine supply from France to Britain.[114]

The Lesser Powers

Russia

On 5 January 1915 the Stavka unified the aviation command under Grand Duke Aleksandr Mikhailovich. The Russian air arm grew from about 350 planes midyear to 553 by the end of 1915, although the number of service-able planes is uncertain. In early 1915 the army formed Russia's first fighter force, a special aviation detachment, for Warsaw's defense against enemy air raids, and in the spring it began to use aircraft for artillery spotting. The air arm remained inferior to its enemies' air services, especially during the German offensive and the disastrous Russian retreat from March through May. Its Voisins and Moranes were inadequate in comparison with enemy planes, while its growth to 49 aviation sections by September did not keep pace with the army's expansion.[115]

In 1915 the navy continued and increased its operations over the Baltic and Black seas from stations at Reval and Sevastopol, using seaplanes operating from seaplane tenders, and even Il'ia Muromets, for reconnaissance and bombing missions against ships and fortresses.[116]

The singular achievement in Russian military aviation was the performance of the Sikorskii Grand airplane of the Squadron of Flying Ships, a self-contained unit that trained its own crews.[117] The Stavka, the Russian high command, had appointed Shidlovskii, the chairman of the Russko-Baltiiskii factory, to command the squadron with the rank of major general. The only other general in aviation was the field inspector of aviation, who opposed the appointment. Thus the squadron was resented, mistrusted, and isolated.

Beginning operations in February, the squadron was performing reconnaissance, photoreconnaissance, and bombing missions over East Prussia by March. Flying at 3,200 meters altitude, the planes could carry fuel for a five-hour flight with three crew members, two machine guns, and a half-ton of bombs. In March the Stavka was so impressed that it assumed direct control of the Sikorskii airplanes from the field inspector. The headquarters staff of the First Army praised the planes' "awe-inspiring" armament and impressive bomb load. On a 31 March mission to monitor German army troop movements, the plane covered 533 kilometers at 3,200 to 3,600 meters altitude. The Stavka withdrew its October 1914 order that banned the planes and revived the contract with Russko-Baltiiskii for 32 Sikorskii airplanes, ordering 30 more for October 1915.

In spring 1915 two Sikorskii airplanes assigned to the Third Army reconnoitered the German and Austrian spring offensive and flew reconnaissance and bombing missions as the army retreated through the Carpathians. The giant could withstand enemy fire. In its first air battle on 19 July, a Sikorskii returned damaged by 60 rounds from three German craft that wounded the pilot and knocked out both engines on one wing. By late August the squadron had six giants. By year's end, after more than 100 sorties dropping nearly 20 tons of bombs on railroad stations, junctions, bridges, and fuel dumps, the squadron was a small heavy-bomber force with 1,350 personnel, workshops, a flight school, photo laboratory, antiaircraft battery, and meteorological station. The army had ordered 76 giants by the end of the year.

Trained personnel and materiel supply remained the Russian air service's fundamental problem. It received only 190 pilots during the year, and they were poorly trained. Russian aircraft manufacturer M. Lebedev estimated that fewer than 20 percent of Russian pilots performed their duties effectively. Their 30 percent casualty rates reflected their inadequate training. [118]

Although aircraft production in Russian factories rose from 37 planes monthly in 1914 to 205 per month in 1915, it did not satisfy the front's demands. The aviation command had held four special conferences to determine the army's aviation needs, which the CMTD presented to the War Council. By the end of 1915 the army received 851 of 1,970 planes ordered in 1914 and 1915. Thus, there was no reserve to replace wastage. The CMTD reported that it expected to receive 557 aircraft fewer than the 1,995 it needed by late 1916. Also by September 1915, the shortage of experienced engineers and skilled workers had prevented the CMTD from founding much-needed aircraft factories, which would have manufactured high-grade steel and various implements. The urgent need for improved aircraft, which the CMTD hoped to resolve through a competition, conflicted with the necessity of placing orders immediately. [119]

Deliveries from France were slow, and the materiel was obsolescent. The commander of the Russian unit defending Warsaw complained that the machines he received early in 1915 had already seen action on the Western Front. In the fall the German offensive through Serbia blocked the shortest supply route from France, further delaying deliveries for 1916, when 306 of 586 planes ordered arrived. In June the War Council decided to build Nieuports and Farmans in Russian factories.

Engine supply was even more inadequate than aircraft deliveries. In 1915 Moscow's Gnome rotary-engine factory delivered at least 15 engines monthly and by the year's end it delivered 30, but engine construction was unreliable. The Paris firm maintained the Moscow branch without an independent technical office and in "total technological and administrative chaos" as described by a War Department representative. [120] After a 10-month argument between the CMTD and the French director of the Moscow firm, the latter was recalled to Paris only to be placed in charge of relations with the Moscow branch. The Sikorskii Squadron of Flying Ships also experienced engine shortages. Unable to secure more German Arguses and saddled with inferior French Salmsons and British Sunbeams, the Russko-Baltiiskii firm had to produce its own engines, which were only slightly inferior to the Arguses in quality.

Austria-Hungary

In early 1915 Austro-Hungarian aviators fought on the Eastern (Russian) and Southern (Balkan) Fronts. The army required faster, more maneuverable, and better-climbing airplanes to fight enemy planes and evade anti-aircraft fire. On the Eastern Front, army aviators flew 33 missions from January through March carrying messages to the besieged garrison at Przemyśl before the fortress surrendered to the Russians.

With the Italian declaration of war on Austria-Hungary on 23 May, the focus of the Austro-Hungarian air war shifted to a new arena, the Southwestern Front. Hazardous flying from small airfields in the Alps and the Balkans led Colonel Uzelac to advise the War Ministry that the industry needed to increase its monthly production from 45 to 60 airplanes and improve its aircraft types. The army established two more flight companies (bringing the total to 18), pilot-training facilities, and in October a special school for observers. The number of officer pilots grew from 89 in August 1914 to 120 by the beginning of 1916. Also noncommissioned pilots increased from 4 to 155, and observers rose from 30 to 78, while at the beginning of 1916 an additional 26 officers and 273 noncommissioned officers were training as pilots and 100 officers as observers.[121]

The Lohner L-boats dominated the air over the Adriatic Sea throughout 1915. Equipped with engines from 145 to 185 horsepower, the two-seat L-boat, when powered by an Austro-Daimler 165-hp engine, could fly seven hours with 150 kilograms of bombs and one machine gun, and its top speed was 125 kilometers per hour. This superiority apparently lulled the Austrians into complacency. Satisfied with the boat's superiority, the Austro-Hungarians did not pursue its development with any intensity, although the Italian firm Macchi successfully copied a captured Lohner by fall 1915. Austro-Hungarian naval aviators had already flown more than 100 missions over the Balkans and the Adriatic in their Lohner boats before the Italian war declaration. The day after the Italian declaration they attacked targets in Italy, including the arsenal at Venice. Naval aviators reconnoitred, searched for submarines and mine fields, and attacked military and naval targets as well as enemy planes and airships. One crew shot down in a night attack on 27 June formed a sail with the linen from the bottom wing and floated far enough for a friendly submarine to find them the next day. From October 1915 naval fliers sortied in squadron strength of 7 to 8 boats against Venice, Brindisi, and Rimini. They had begun the war with 64 planes and received 44 more through December 1914, but had only 65 planes at the end of November, including 32 L-boats. [122]

The capabilities of the Austro-Hungarian aviation industry set limits to the quality and quantity of the air services' materiel. During 1915 the industry, laboring under delays in material procurement and rising material prices and wages, never delivered more than 46 airplanes monthly, while German deliveries arrived erratically. In May Colonel Uzelac went to Germany to order planes from Camillo Castiglioni's Hansa-Brandenburg factory, which the German army had released for German naval and Austro-Hungarian production. After severe prewar difficulties with monopoly in the aircraft industry, the Austrian authorities might have been concerned that Castiglioni already controlled two domestic firms: the Austrian Albatros works in Vienna and the Hungarian Aircraft Factory in Budapest. If they were disturbed, they said nothing, silenced by their desperation to procure planes. [123]

From July through November the army ordered 156 planes from Hansa-Brandenburg, which delivered orders punctually, sending 148 craft by the year's end. By December the Austro-Hungarian aviation command was dependent upon the firm for modern, fast planes, a dependency that Hansa-Brandenburg used to dictate comparatively high prices to the Austro-Hungarian army. Some months Hansa-Brandenburg delivered more planes than the entire Austro-Hungarian aircraft industry, a circumstance the monarchy could ill afford in the face of a rapidly expanding air war. The army and navy were competing for limited resources, and during the latter half of the year they sought unsuccessfully to set procurement norms, dividing aircraft and engine production between them. By the end of 1915 Austria-Hungary's seven aircraft and engine factories in operation had delivered 281 planes and 440 engines—another 186 planes and 72 engines had come from Germany—numbers barely sufficient for replacement and training, much less expansion. [124]

Italy

In Italy Royal Decree number 11 of 7 January 1915 formed the Military Aeronautical Corps with a general directorate in the War Office, two commands for dirigibles and planes, and a central aeronautical inspectorate. [125] A government decree of 25 October 1914 had planned to use aviation for strategic and tactical reconnaissance. The decree was followed with plans in November and December to acquire first 21 and then 90 planes. When the Italian government declared war on 23 May, the army air service had 150 frontline planes (mostly obsolescent French types), 91 pilots, 20 observers, and 200 student pilots training at five schools. The naval aviation school at Taranto had 50 students and 15 obsolescent Curtiss craft, and naval aviation had 19 seaplanes or boats and 6 semirigid dirigibles of 10,000 to 23,000 cubic meters in volume.

At the beginning of 1915 the Italian aviation industry employed only 100 skilled workers; plant machinery, special steels, tubes, wires, and linen and cotton fabrics were lacking. In February 1915 the government sent designer Ottorino Pomilio of the Technical Directorate of Military Aviation in Turin to the United States to obtain raw materials for aircraft production. The 20 workers at the Italian branch of Gnome could produce one engine monthly, while Italy's five aircraft firms—SIT, Savoia, Nieuport-Macchi, Oneto, and Caproni—each had 10 to 12 skilled workers and produced 6 to 10 planes annually. As war loomed, the work force rose to 1,500 and monthly production increased to 15 planes, while a few new factories appeared. The key to Italian aero engine production lay with Fiat, which had begun the mass production of its 100-hp A10 engine in fall 1914. Fiat also established an aircraft department, which in 1915 became the Società Italiana Aviazione firm (SIA), to build the technical directorate's copies of the Maurice Farman. [126]

Italian aviation began the war with 58 planes in comparison with Austria-Hungary's 96, but the destruction of 70 of the 100 planes assigned in May and June 1915 prevented the intended drastic increases in the force's size. The Italian fliers, well-trained and ready for flight, were hampered by their obsolescent French planes. [127] Toward the end of August artillery spotting squadrons had received their first planes with radiotelegraphic apparatus from France, and on 7 October 14 reconnaissance planes dropped 27 bombs totaling 350 kilograms on Castagnevizza in their first "mass" bombing mission.

Italy, with the Caproni Ca1, was the sole country to have a plane expressly designed as a bomber. Starting late in August, Ca1s powered by three Fiat 100-hp engines staged bombing raids on the Austro-Hungarian aviation camp at Aisovizza. Eight were at the front by the end of September. During the third and fourth Battles of the Isonzo from October to December, the Capronis bombed various targets and were ultimately placed at the Supreme Command's disposal for long-range reconnaissance missions and bombing railroad junctions and stations. [128]

The Supreme Command and the General Directorate of Aviation, preoccupied with enemy superiority and aviation's inadequate organization in relation to the front's demands, proposed programs to develop the industry despite problems in securing raw materials. Despite substantial plane losses, they planned to double the number of squadrons and to secure higher-hp engines. Italian aircraft production in 1915 totaled 382 planes and 606 engines. With the exception of 28 Capronis, the remaining craft were primarily French designs and a few German Aviatiks.

The two most notable individuals affiliated with Italian aviation were nationalist poet and author Gabriele D'Annunzio and airpower theorist Giulio Douhet. Fifty-two years old when the war began, D'Annunzio asked Prime Minister Antonio Salandra on 30 June for full discretion to wage war as if it were his individual crusade. Though not a pilot, D'Annunzio joined the air service, flew with his pilot over Trieste in August and September to drop propaganda leaflets on the city, and from August to December 1915 did aerial reconnaissance in naval aircraft over the enemy coast. [129]

Behind the front Giulio Douhet, convinced by November 1914 of the airplane's potential as a strategic bomber to destroy enemy material and morale, continued to promote aviation. But Douhet's superiors removed him as commander of the aviation battalion and sent him to be chief of staff of an army division in Lombardy to discipline him for exceeding his authority in authorizing Caproni's bomber. Before he left for this exile in December 1914, he wrote a series of articles in the *Gazzetta del Popolo* urging Italy to prepare to win command of the air. By July 1915 Douhet was commenting in his diaries that Italian aviation was "encumbered by waste" and advocating the formation of a huge group of heavy planes for strategic operations against the enemy war machine, attacking military and industrial centers, railroad junctions, arsenals, and ports. He also proposed the formation of an Allied bomber fleet to strike Constantinople and open the straits. When his superiors suggested that antiaircraft fire could stop bombers, he countered that the only defense against warplanes was strategic attack. Douhet was sowing the seeds of strategic bombing doctrine, however infertile the soil. [130]

Conclusion

In 1915 air arms became more sophisticated, performing specialized functions at the front and adapting types to perform these tasks. As the demands for new and improved aviation materiel grew, technological and industrial mobilization in aviation became crucial for the combatant powers. Both the greater and the lesser powers confronted problems in eliciting rapid technological advances from industry and providing small industries with the skilled labor, plants, and materials for expansion in the midst of pressures to develop other, more fundamental weaponry.

Bombardment and pursuit, the air arm's new roles, required the appropriate machines. As most aircraft in service had not been designed for these specialized purposes, the most suitable available aircraft types were adapted to perform these roles—light craft such as Moranes, Nieuports, and Fokkers for fighting and heavier craft such as Voisins and Aviatiks for bombing.

In 1915 the absence of higher-hp engines, enabling large airplanes to carry defensive armament and greater bomb loads over longer distances, limited bomber development. While designers strove to develop bombers, the French strategic campaign expired for want of suitable aircraft, and the RNAS carried out its raids with poorly suited materiel. Russia, Italy, and Germany had a few operational large planes whose range and load indicated their potential for development as strategic bombers with more powerful engines. The German dirigible was the only craft capable of carrying enough bombs to make strategic raids a worthwhile consideration. Though airships could climb fast and high enough to escape aerial interception in 1915, the costly giants were vulnerable to ground fire and weather.

A major development in 1915 was the beginning of fighter aviation. Initially a plane armed with a machine gun sufficed for aerial fighting, regardless of its flight characteristics, but by the end of 1915 an effective fighting machine required speed and maneuverability as well as fixed-forward, firing machine guns. The early pursuit pilots—Garros, Immelman, Boelcke, Guynemer, and Hawker—though varied in temperament, displayed tenacity, determination, courage, and aggressiveness. Aware of the risks, they minimized them by calculating how to pursue and attack an opponent without being downed themselves. This new breed of warrior mounted on a technological steed evolved new fighting tactics and recommended improvements for fighter planes. Their efforts would make the skies over Europe's battlefields far more dangerous in the coming year.

CHAPTER FOUR

1916

"Modern warfare has shown itself to be at least as much an affair of industrial organisation as of purely military operations in the field. . . .

Taking aerial warfare alone, the industrial capacity *of a country at war is only capable of deciding the issue in the long run."*

AERONAUTICS, 17 MAY 1916[1]

In 1916 the three major combatant powers—France, Germany, and Britain—were locked in desperate battles of attrition on the ground and had amassed so many aircraft over the battlefields of Verdun and the Somme that aerial mastery became the crucial issue. In the east General Brusilov's fall and summer offensives were imperial Russia's last major military efforts, in which the effectiveness of the Austro-Hungarian army was destroyed. On the Southwestern Front Italy and Austria-Hungary battled along the Isonzo River and in the Tyrol. The war grew larger and more intense, an intensity epitomized in the aerial struggle. All the powers had to mobilize their industries sufficiently to keep pace with the front's increased demand for more and better aircraft.

The Greater Powers

France

If 1915 had been the year of the high command's emphasis on bombing, 1916 became the year of the fighter, partially because of France's bomber and observation craft development and partially because of the emphasis on the fighter necessitated by the first major struggles for aerial control at Verdun and the Somme. The number of pursuit aircraft at the front rose steadily from 133 in February to 325 in October and December, while bombers increased from 160 in January to only 216 by December.[2] The focus on pursuit aviation was relative, since most French aviators were engaged in army corps duties in stolid two-seat observation aircraft. In February the quality of France's 1,149-plane force was varied. Most of its 188 bombers were obsolescent, and 379 of the 826 reconnaissance craft were pushers—slow and vulnerable prey to the Fokkers. Yet 90 of the 135 pursuit planes were maneuverable Nieuport Bébés.[3]

The French naval air arm continued to grow steadily in 1916. It comprised 159 planes and 4 dirigibles for patrol duties at its stations along the Atlantic and Channel coasts as well as along the Asia Minor and Red Sea coasts. It used either FBA or Donnet-Denhaut (DD) two-seat flying boats, armed with machine guns and light bombs, equipped with radiotelegraphy, powered by 150-hp Hispano-Suiza engines, and capable of three to four hours flight time.[4] Naval aviation remained secondary to the Western Front's land war, which intensified in February with the German attack on Verdun.

Over Verdun the Germans seized the initiative, concentrating their fighter strength to prevent French observation, and secured local aerial mastery from the beginning of the battle on 21 February. The French realized quickly that aerial control was the essential precondition to their own reconnaissance and artillery spotting. Before Verdun they had given priority to observation and bombardment and dispersed pursuit planes over the front to protect other craft. In 1916 a doctrine of aerial combat to organize the deployment of pursuit planes was necessary, since the Battle of Verdun changed the nature of the war.[5] On 29 February the Second Army's aviation commander established offensive reconnaissance patrols to find and destroy the enemy. This tactic required that French aviators, who considered aerial combat an individual affair, operate in groups.[6]

In response to the desperate situation, GQG aviation commander Barès concentrated his forces at Verdun. He gave Commandant Tricornot

de Rose, commander of squadron MS 12, full discretion to wrest the initiative from the Germans. In the Verdun sector de Rose assembled all the
Morane-Saulnier and Nieuport units and the best pilots, forming 15 elite
squadrons. GQG established an aeronautical command on 21 March under
Barès to coordinate and concentrate aviation and secure aerial mastery. The
chain of command proceeded directly from Joffre to Barès to de Rose's
fighter units, which were not assigned to a particular army and were
amassed for specific operations.[7] GQG intended its reserve fleet of combat
craft for attacks against the enemy, not for the direct protection of its own
craft or ground troops.

The French relinquished close protection of their planes for "permanent" or constant patrols by sectors. Operating in units of four to five
planes, the French fighters swept the skies clear of the Germans' three to
four plane patrols to enable observation with reconnaissance planes and
tethered balloons. Since it was difficult to surprise the Germans with these
patrols, some aces flew alone or in groups of two or three above the patrols,
using them as lures. Although the patrols initially lacked regular formations
and well-defined tactics, by late May they were performing group attacks on
tethered German observation balloons using le Prieur rockets. Despite severe losses, including de Rose, who was killed in an accident, after April
the French virtually closed their airspace to German observation.

Verdun showed that aerial mastery was essential and required concentrated forces. However, as the aviation commander at Vaux-Douaumont indicated on 3 May, aerial control was transitory and incomplete. A momentary enemy concentration could gain superiority at a particular location,
or isolated aircraft could cross the lines at low altitude. Absolute security
for reconnaissance craft was thus impossible to attain, but a fighter offensive over enemy lines could offer some "indirect cover" to army reconnaissance planes.[8]

Pursuit aviation at Verdun inspired the legends of aces such as Jean
Navarre (the "sentinel of Verdun"), Georges Guynemer, and Charles
Nungesser, as well the combat pilots of Escadrille N124, whose American
volunteer pilots gained their first victory in May. American physician Edmund L. Gros and French Senator Gaston Menier, an avid aviation supporter, had sponsored N124 to capitalize on the political value of the handful of American volunteers who had been serving in the French air arm since
1915. Director of aeronautics Col. Henri-Jacques Régnier approved N124
in mid-March 1916, and in May the squadron, equipped with Nieuports,
arrived at Verdun to fly protective cover for the bombers of Capt. Maurice
Happe's Fourth Bombardment Group (GB4). Only five days after the

first sortie, Kiffin Rockwell gained the squadron's first victory in his first aerial combat.[9]

Combat over Verdun was personal and at close range. French pilots often experienced a savage joy when they shot down a German. Albert Deullin, a cold, calm, and reserved individual, avenged the death of his friend Lieutenant Peretti when he attacked a Fokker over Verdun and put 25 rounds in the cockpit at less than 10 meters range: "The fellow was so riddled that vaporized blood sprayed on my hood, windshield, cap, and goggles. Naturally, the descent from 2,600 meters was delicious to contemplate."[10]

With bloodthirsty hunters on both sides, reconnaissance and artillery spotting became more dangerous. The struggle over Verdun was grim and brutal, as Bernard Lafont's *Au Ciel de Verdun,* one of the few books on the air war to dwell on its horror, graphically recounted. After a Caudron landed with the observer shot in the head, the pilot was found unhurt but "very shaken, very enervated, . . . covered with blood, [his] clothes and face, for in the wind of the motors, the blood that poured out of the passenger's wound lashed him."[11] On squadron burial detail Lafont witnessed the fate of two aviators who had fallen from their Farman:

> "The first of the two men is impaled on the iron gate. There is the pierced body, a bloody rag. The wounds are enormous. Purple streams flow onto the clothes; drops hang and fall one by one, in the large puddle on the ground below . . .
> The second fell on the roof of the house. I clearly heard the dull sound of the body when it was crushed in a heap. Flouc! . . . The body was recovered from the roof, entirely broken, shattered and shapeless and without rigidity like a heap of ooze. . . . They filled a coffin with it.[12]

On the night after a burning crash, they retrieved the bodies of the two crew members:

> It is Senain. He received three bullets in the head, which exploded like a rotten fruit; brains and blood trickle on the face and clothes. The helmet moves on the broken skull.
> Both are horribly crushed. The stretcher bearers who pick them up have only a bloody pulp in their hands.
> Life is a mere trifle.

Lafont concluded, finding refuge in patriotism:

> Thus we go toward death. . . . But why do we complain? When the hour comes, will we not have lived an intense and lofty life! And will not France survive, to perpetuate a little of us?[13]

Artillery observer Lieutenant Carayon related that his pilot and he often spent three and a half hours over the lines spotting long-range artillery and although they always sought to evade enemy fighters and antiaircraft fire, they had "terrible losses." From 21 February to 1 July the French lost over 100 pilots and observers, 51 of whom were killed or missing.[14]

By 1 June the French had 1,120 planes at the front—60 army corps squadrons of 10 planes each, 24 artillery squadrons of 5 aircraft each, and 19 combat and 21 bomber squadrons, each with 10 planes. They maintained aerial superiority through August with the formation of a group of 8 fighter squadrons in June at Cachy, just before the Somme offensive. The 1 June orders of French Army Group North concentrated aviation for the offensive and advised that observation planes work in groups for protection. The Cachy group, which was initially subordinated to the attacking Sixth Army, staged fighter sweeps over the lines. French observation crews, despite inadequate aircraft, were able to execute their missions. The Germans, confronted with the French offensive, were not.[15]

With the 10th Army's August attack, French Army Group North (GAN) ordered that the Cachy group be placed directly at its disposal, removing fighter aviation from the armies' control. Thus, the armies did not always receive the fighter support they requested for their observation planes, a circumstance that led to discontent and recriminations. The Somme posed the crucial organizational problem of whether combat aviation should be the army's or the army group's organ. Toward the end of August the Cachy group began to escort more observation craft, despite the diversion from its offensive operations, and in September and October the Germans' use of combat groups employing new fighters forced the French to provide more protection for their observation craft. In October 1916 the French air arm created combat pursuit groups Numbers 2, 3, and 13 under Commanders A. le Révérend, who had succeeded de Rose, Brocard, and Philippe Féquant, which enabled them partially to offset the Germans' introduction of the new Albatros fighter. With fighter aviation's more offensive attitude, observation planes on both sides suffered disquieting losses.[16]

Yet a 10 October GQG order continued to emphasize the offensive, with the protection of observation craft as only an accessory or indirect result of the aviation battle. In exceptional cases it did allow for the immediate and direct protection of observation craft by assigning squadrons specifically for that to the aviation commander of a particular army. At the very end of the year, however, observation crews in the 10th Army were still requesting close-pursuit protection for their outclassed planes. Historian André Voisin observed two tendencies in wartime French air doctrine: the offensive destruction of the enemy air force in aerial battle and close liaison with the individual army to protect reconnaissance aviation. The first tendency prevailed in 1916.[17]

The Somme was a glorious epoch for French fighter aviation. Captain Brocard of N3 commanded the fighter squadrons assembled at Cachy and proceeded to gain aerial mastery from July through mid-September. N3, the famous Storks (Cigognes), included aces Brocard, Guynemer, Alfred Heurtaux, Deullin, and René Dorme, while N65 had Nungesser. Flying the Nieuport 17 with a Lewis gun mounted on the top wing, they thrust the Germans completely on the defensive until the Albatros fighters appeared in the fall. Despite the emphasis on concentration and patrols, the tactics of the great fighter pilots remained individual.[18]

Guynemer won 21 victories in 1916, including a triple kill one day in March. A crash in January left Nungesser with two broken legs, one partially paralyzed, but he was back in the air over Verdun by April and finished the year with 21 victories. Others, like Heurtaux, a 1914 graduate of St. Cyr and a decorated lieutenant of Hussars, joined the ranks of the famed aces. Heurtaux initially had become an observer because he regarded aviation as a "dangerous sport." He later became a pilot, after complaining to his superiors that his pilot was dangerous and should he wish to be killed in an airplane, he would rather do it himself.[19] Heurtaux survived the war to become a general in the French air arm. Even when the Albatros appeared with its superior armament, the Nieuport's superior maneuverability and a new 100-cartridge drum for the Lewis gun enabled pilots such as Guynemer and Heurtaux to challenge the Germans over their own airfields. Yet the appearance of the Albatros signaled the French loss of technological superiority in fighter aviation.[20]

The Americans of N124, after having gained considerable experience in aerial combat, arrived at Cachy to join the fight in October as part of Combat Group 13. Their first serious casualty, H. Clyde Balsley, retired from the service after being hit by an explosive bullet that shattered his pelvic bone, partially severing his sciatic nerve and leaving fragments in the lower part of his body. Kiffin Rockwell, its first victor, died in September from an explosive bullet that left a gaping hole in his throat. During the summer Raoul Lufbery, an itinerant French-American adventurer before the war, had established himself as its leading pilot. In December N124 became the Lafayette Escadrille.[21]

These fighter pilots' task might have been easier had they had Louis Béchereau's new Hispano-Suiza-powered Spad 7, which the Storks tested in the summer. Béchereau used the engine mounts to cradle the Hispano-Suiza engine and the pilot's seat, thus forming a strong and rigid fuselage.

But the new plane suffered from engine crankshaft ruptures and problems with the synchronizing gear of the Vickers gun. Heurtaux recalled that when the Spads first began to arrive at squadron N3 in late July, pilots were reluctant to fly them because they were accustomed to the Nieuport rotary engine, which could take three or more rounds without stopping. The Storks had flamed so many German planes with inline engines that they feared a similar fate with the Spad. Colonel Barès designated Lt. Armand Pinsard to test the Spad at the front, and on 13 August he gained his first victory in the new mount. When Georges Guynemer received his on 27 August, he found it "marvelous" and spent the entire day in his "taxi." It was strong, fast, and maneuverable, and it possessed sufficient fuel for two hours and thirty minutes of flight at full-engine power. The Hispano-Suiza water-cooled engine enabled better speed control than the rotary, despite its vulnerability to a bullet through the water circulation system.[22] The Spad promised to be excellent, but it would not appear at the front until 1917.

Despite the delays in the Spad, French fighter aviation excelled in 1916, while bomber and observation aviation, which lacked quality craft such as the Nieuport or the Spad, foundered. Bombardment aviation was already in crisis at the beginning of 1916, and during the year daylight bombing ceased because of the heavy casualties exacted by German fighters. During Verdun GQG, which considered night bombing too inaccurate, was reducing the bomber fleet's size and reassigning some squadrons to army corps aviation. For day missions against railroads behind Verdun, it sought in vain for transition aircraft such as the British Sopwith 1½ strutter. After May, however, the French planes' inadequate performance and their inability to defend themselves necessitated a shift to night bombing and retraining crews for night flight.[23]

The diary of a pilot-bombardier killed in combat in October reflected bombing's checkered course. He considered the long-range daylight raids on railroad stations in February "idiotic." At the end of March he judged that the future of bombing lay in night missions, since daylight bombardment was "in a depression, a little like all of our aviation, except the fighter squadrons." In May annoyance, boredom, and demoralization reigned because the crews were not allowed to bomb the Germans, although the idea of a daylight raid 40 kilometers behind enemy lines uncomfortably reminded him of an infantry assault.[24]

In 1916 the GQG's bombardment program targeted German industrial centers—first chemical and powder production works and metallurgical shops, and then munitions and arms plants. In 1916 the First and Second Bombardment Groups (GB1 and GB2) raided economic targets within a 300-kilometer radius of their Malzéville base, bombing railroad stations at Metz, blast furnaces in Lorraine, and factories in the Saar, but with no decisive results. During the Battle of the Somme the bombers attacked railroads, stations, bivouacs, camps, and even German airfields, as the diehard Capt. Maurice Happe continued to stage large raids in daylight despite heavy losses. Finally, in a 12 October joint attack with the RNAS against the Mauser factory at Oberndorf, 14 of the mission's 23 bombers with pursuit protection reached the target and 5 were lost. After these losses the French turned exclusively to night bombing.[25]

A December 1916 bombardment program included furnaces and factories in Luxembourg, Lorraine, and the Saar, along with French factories that had not been on previous lists. The new program was less ambitious than earlier ones, since it renounced distant objectives such as Mannheim, Ludwigshafen, the Main River area, and Cologne to concentrate on the metallurgical shops of the Saar-Luxembourg-Lorraine region, which were within 100 miles of Nancy. Those targets were barely within reach of French bombers, and the air arm lacked the planes to strike them effectively.[26]

In 1916 the French had no satisfactory bomber. The old Voisins and Farmans were obsolete. The Breguet-Michelin pusher that appeared in early 1916 was slow, difficult to fly, required a long runway with a full load and, after October 1916, could be used only at night. The new Voisin that arrived at the year's end was mediocre. None of these planes could carry large bomb loads. Foreign imports like the few Italian Capronis, which were built under license by REP, proved too delicate, while the Sopwiths were too light and fragile for sustained use and carried a 60-kilogram bomb load, too small to cause much material destruction.

The year was probably more difficult for observation than bombing. Unlike bombing, the army could not dispense with or reduce artillery spotting and observation. Inadequate planes made observation crews most vulnerable, just when French air doctrine preached that they needed little immediate protection from fighters.

In 1916 the observation units, like the bomber squadrons, suffered from the use of outmoded and outclassed Farmans and Voisins, though they perfected their photography and wireless techniques. On 21 April Joffre informed the war minister that the Farmans were "poorly armed toward the rear" and that information from Verdun affirmed that they could not perpetuate this type indefinitely.[27] German ace Oswald Boelcke observed that the Farmans burned easily because of the gas tank's location above the pusher engine. If he hit the tank, the gas poured out over the hot engine and ignited.[28] Pilots on the Northeast Front no longer wanted Voisins or Salmson engines because they flamed easily.[29] Squadron V210 pilots and observers, who flew Farmans and Salmson-powered Voisins, chose a winged snail as their emblem. Their Farmans were "not famed for their solidity," and one collapsed in midair in September, confirming the crew's lack of confidence in their planes. When Barès visited them, they complained of the Farmans' poor construction and unsuitability for wartime operations.[30] GQG ultimately concluded that "it is preferable to have no planes than to have a mediocre type like the Farman."[31] A parliamentary commission report in December, written by deputy and aviator Daniel Vincent, attested that pilots had lost confidence in the Farmans, which were slow, fragile, and incapable of crossing the lines without falling prey to the enemy.[32] Despite such condemnation, Henri Farman, saying that he had received no complaints about his airplanes, rebuffed the attempts of the Director of Military Aeronautics to reorient his production to tractor aircraft.[33] Eight hundred Farmans on contract through June would still be arriving at the front in the fall and serving in the beginning of 1917.[34]

By the year's end the French air arm had regularized the structure of its corps squadrons. Each squadron had 12 pilots, 3 of them officers, and 12 observers, all of whom were artillery officers. Six observers were permanent squadron members and moved with the squadron, while six belonged to the army division. Three squadrons worked for an army corps— one for trench and contact work, a second for counterbattery and artillery work, and a third for photography and special tasks—and formed a sector with four kite balloons.[35]

As air warfare cost more personnel and materiel, the military began to keep more precise casualty and wastage lists. In October 14 pilots were killed, 12 wounded, and 23 missing at the front, while 14 pilots and student pilots were killed at the front and 4 injured in the rear. Six of the 14 pilots killed at the front and 8 of the 12 wounded were involved in accidents. Thus, in October the overall number of pilots killed in accidents in the front and rear (20) exceeded the number killed in combat (8). Nearly half of the casualties (49) occurred on Caudrons and Farmans. Furthermore, while the air arm lost 25 airplanes, these were only a fraction of the total, which included 144 airplanes and 871 engines received for repairs and 180 airplanes and 150 engines scrapped. In 10 months, from January to November, the air arm lost 837 pilots and observers who were killed or missing.[36]

The air service's expansion and replacement of its losses required an extension of the training system. In 1916 newly breveted pilots no longer went to units but to "transformation" schools where they learned to fly different types. By the fall aspiring combat pilots received dual-control training in large biplanes and then short solo flights in a smaller machine. United States pilot Sgt. James R. McConnell, later killed in combat, described France's pursuit-pilot training in a 1 November article in *Aviation and Aeronautical Engineering*.[37] According to McConnell, pilots began on a dual-control "rouleur" or "pingouin" (roller or penguin) trainer and drove faster ones as they learned to steer a straight line. Then they gradually flew better and faster Blériots to higher altitudes, first in straight lines and then in curves. They learned how to cut and restart the engine in the air and spiral down to earth near a fixed point. After three military brevet trips, the first two to designated towns an hour away and the last a triangle, the pilots attended an "école de perfectionnement" where they trained on fighters, steadily graduating to higher-powered Moranes. After machine gun school and battle tactics and stunt flying at combat school, the pilots went to reserve school, where they practiced on the available planes. Finally, after some months in reserve training, the pilots went to the front.

Behind the front the administration and politics of French aviation remained riven with conflict. The struggle over aircraft programs between the parliament and the high command continued, with the War Ministry caught between the two. The parliamentary subcommissions scrutinized aviation closely, especially after the omnibus aircraft of the January 1916 Castelnau program failed to materialize by the projected 1 April date.

A crisis in May led to secret committee meetings and commissions of inquiry. The number of frontline squadrons, after increasing from 30 to 80 between November 1914 and May 1915, had reached only 100 with 10 planes each by May 1916. Aircraft production was stationary, engine production had not increased substantially, and largely obsolescent airplanes equipped the frontline units. Parliamentary deputy Gabriel Veber, upon hearing a secret committee report of 16 June that gave the army's strength as 1,299 frontline and 231 reserve planes, suggested the numbers were insufficient. The War Minister replied that they would always be insufficient, and the chamber did not pursue deputy Raoul Anglès's demand for an interpellation.[38]

In June the parliamentary subcommission proposed that the government increase its 10 January (Castelnau) program from 1,430 planes to 2,190, including 800 fighters and 500 bombers. On 3 August GQG limited the program to 1,770 planes, including 480 fighters. The War Ministry's 20 September program proposed 1,950 planes, including 660 fighters and 400 bombers as a compromise. On 24 October the subcommission raised the number to 2,690 planes, including 1,000 bombers, recommending an autonomous chief of bomber aviation, and blaming delays in the bomber arm's development on GQG aviation chief Barès. In the fall GQG sought 1,950 planes, and politicians criticized the high command for lacking ambition and neglecting bombardment.[39]

While French aviation lurched from crisis to crisis and program to program in the political arena, the War Ministry's procurement bureaucracy struggled to meet the front's demands through its dealings with the aviation industry.

In a letter to Georges Clemenceau published in the 5 February *L'Homme enchaîné*, Louis Blériot charged that aviation was in "if not a crisis, at any rate a retarded development," and complained that builders and active service pilots, the people who had created aviation, were excluded from technical committees and the study of aviation programs, and thus eliminated from policymaking decisions.[40] The administrative changes about to occur in aviation procurement did little to answer his complaint.

With the resignation of Undersecretary Besnard on 8 February, War Minister Galliéni, who had not been a partisan of the undersecretariat, restored the Twelfth Directorate of Aeronautics and chose as its chief Col. Henri-Jacques Régnier, an artilleryman. Although Georges Huisman considered Régnier inexperienced in aviation and only interested in it for the artillery,[41] Albert Etévé, who served in the directorate, recalled that Régnier had been an adjutant to the director of aeronautics, General Bernard, and had returned to the artillery to direct the pyrotechnical school at Bourges when Bernard left aviation in 1914.[42] Régnier would direct aviation for a year because, according to the recent official history of French aviation, as a soldier he represented the military's reassertion of its power against the civilians and the War Ministry protected him from political attacks.[43] Yet it was not simply a matter of civil-military tension, because Régnier's desire to implement a procurement policy for aviation similar to the artillery's contradicted GQG's instructions and led to increasing hostility between Régnier and Barès at GQG.

In the 24 February *Le Matin* Jacques-Lois Dumesnil, a deputy serving in the air service at the front, advocated the closest liaison between front aviators and manufacturers.[44] Later, in October, when the War Ministry proposed the establishment of an inspector of frontline materiel subordinate to an inspector general in the rear, GQG insisted that its materiel inspectorate remain separate and independent.[45] The War Ministry's attempt to institutionalize the liaison and control materiel inspection had failed.

While Régnier could not change the structure of GQG-War Ministry relationships, he promptly reorganized his procurement bureaucracy. On 28 February he created two new departments: the Technical Section of

Aeronautics (STAé) for new planes and the Industrial Section (SI) for supplying builders with primary materials, separating them from the Aviation Production Service (SFA), which he assigned to control the serial production of established types.

Commandant Dorand, the chief of the aeronautical laboratory at Chalais-Meudon, was called to direct the STAé and brought his office staff, which included Captain Lepère as head of his research office. The STAé's mission was to direct, coordinate, and centralize new studies on military aeronautics, and to establish a liaison between GQG, the War Ministry, and the manufacturers to meet the military demands for new and better planes. Dorand construed the STAé as a construction and technical service. Having designed aircraft until 1914, he envisaged building them again. His guiding principles were to stay within the current technology's limits while clearly defining the areas that needed development. Dorand personally took charge of the design and research offices and an office for the Spad. The former chiefs of the engine, airplane, and armament offices in the SFA, most critically engine expert Martinot-Lagarde, were assigned to the STAé on 15 March.[46]

Perhaps the major task that Dorand confronted was developing a tractor reconnaissance craft to replace the Farman. In a 15 March memorandum, he asked the manufacturers to build a tractor craft powered by the same Renault 160-hp engine that the Farman used and advised them that only planes showing marked progress over types currently in service or undergoing tests would be adopted.[47] The builders were not interested; some had sufficient orders, while others believed the engine power was too low. With Régnier's assent, Dorand charged Lepère to design a tractor biplane. In tests on 24 September the plane proved to be only 10 kilometers faster than the Farman's speed of 135 kilometers per hour. Without waiting for frontline tests, the Directorate of Aeronautics ordered 650 ARs (Avant Renaults, or Renault tractors) from Renault on 4 October, increasing the order to 725 in November and to 1,435 on 1 January 1917. GQG, desperate for a new plane and confronted with a fait accompli, declared itself satisfied after tests on 18 October. When the French production of Sopwiths that Dorand had planned encountered delays, he had the Renault 190-hp engine installed in the AR to improve its performance.[48]

While AR production seemed necessary in the absence of other aircraft, Dorand had violated his 15 March policy of producing only markedly superior types. In December aircraft builders claimed that Dorand had infringed on their patents and ideas to perfect his plane.[49] Later the continued production of 190-hp engines for the AR delayed Renault's production of the larger 300-hp engine for the Breguet 14 reconnaissance bomber.[50] Daniel Vincent's report of December 1916 reproached the directorate for ordering too few Spads and too many ARs and criticized the STAé for building airplanes and thus competing with the industry, rather than remaining a technical organ to advise the manufacturers. Despite these rebukes Dorand took credit for resolving the crisis of early 1916 by creating the AR.

Dorand admitted, however, that bomber development eluded the STAé. He attributed the failure to improve bomber production to a lack of powerful engines and the French manufacturers' preference for building small observation and pursuit planes. By late February, the Twelfth Directorate attributed the looming delays in bomber production to the poor organization or complacency of certain builders. Joffre advised the War Ministry to encourage production in the rear.[51] On 21 August bomber Captain Adrian noted that only designers Paul Schmitt and Louis Breguet were studying bomber development. Although powerful engines were becoming available, most builders were reluctant to commit to the unprofitable and arduous task of bomber development. Ironically, the army discouraged Nieuport's pursuit of bomber design because such a deflection of effort might halve the firm's production of essential pursuit craft.[52]

In 1916 one of the war's best reconnaissance bombers—the Breguet 14—was designed. GQG and the Twelfth Directorate were encouraging manufacturers to use the Hispano-Suiza in bomber designs, but Breguet was designing a tractor biplane around the heavier 12-cylinder 220-hp Renault. Historian Jacques Mortane deemed this success one "of circumstance imposed by necessity" and not of a clear conception, precise directives, or lengthy estimations.[53] Breguet's tractor biplane design, however, was no accident.

Breguet had decided to use a light metal, duralumin, an aluminum alloy that the Germans used on dirigibles, instead of steel tubing. A 21 February War Ministry notice on acceptance criteria for metals used in aircraft construction had not mentioned aluminum or duralumin. The alloy, which was three times lighter than steel, could replace soft steel parts, but its tendency to crack under alternating stresses meant that it had to be used with care. Breguet consequently used wiredrawn duralumin tubes for the fuselage and wings, and steel tubes for parts that were subject to vibrations or alternating stresses like the tail, ailerons, and landing gear. He designed the plane in June, and it flew for the first time on 21 November. Both GQG and the STAé wanted Breguet to adapt his airframe to the lighter Hispano-Suiza 220-hp engine, which had only been tested in prototype form, but Breguet refused. In advising the STAé of the new plane's

TABLE 1.

Monthly Aircraft and Engine Production in France During 1916

	1/16	2/16	3/16	4/16	5/16	6/16	7/16	8/16	9/16	10/16	11/16	12/16
Aircraft	501	422	505	526	603	541	664	745	814	731	752	745
Engines*	1,001	965	1,178	1,249	1,262	1,295	1,522	1,561	1,579	1,727	1,624	1,792

*Of the engines, 6,252 (37 percent) were rotaries and 3,561 (21 percent) were radials.

excellent performance in its first tests, Breguet reiterated that he could not have obtained the same results with the Hispano-Suiza. He promised to present the Breguet 14 prototype for tests in January 1917.[54]

In the manufacturing realm, Régnier replaced Raibaud at the head of the SFA with another artilleryman, Lt. Col. Stammler, who had directed the SFA in 1914 and would be the last artilleryman to direct the service. Despite the manufacturers' protests, the SFA retained the general inspectorate and territorial subinspectorates, but Stammler improved relationships with the manufacturers by naming Captain Camerman, a well-known aviator, as general inspector of production and designating certain officers as the sole intermediaries between the builders and the SFA's territorial subinspectorates. This organization remained, as did Stammler and Régnier, until the end of February 1917, as it sought to improve its relationship with the manufacturers and orchestrate increases in airplane and engine production.[55]

Aircraft production, which totaled 7,549 in 1916, increased erratically, while engine production, which totaled 16,875 in 1916, offered the primary evidence of the success of the French industrial effort in aviation (see Table 1).[56] The number of engines in service rose so much that in October the directorate relieved St. Cyr of Renault and Salmson engine repair and requested that each firm organize its own repair shop.[57]

As the demand for materiel rose, the Directorate and the SFA attempted to tighten procedures on contracts, prices, and payment that they had allowed to lapse for the war's first 18 months. Yet establishing a firm contract required determining a firm price. The Undersecretary of State for Aeronautics had resorted to provisional price agreements in February because of the constantly changing nature of aeronautical materiel. These agreements allowed payment of advances on existing orders to give the industrialists the funds necessary to continue production. Firm contracts were occasionally set only at delivery time.

After the undersecretary's departure, the directorate continued to use provisional price agreements with the understanding that contracts would follow shortly. On 9 May, however, a parliamentary markets commission noted that the directorate was also using provisional conventions for established materiel due for delivery in three weeks, a clear indication of laxness in procurement procedures. By 30 May the directorate was to restrict the use of conventions only to very exceptional cases and to reduce the number of conventions still in force.[58]

To curtail the agreements, which left the state at the builder's mercy, a commission was established to determine materiel prices. The commission initially considered Gnome and Rhône's prices too high and Salmson's prices "scandalous." The price commission asked the undersecretary on 8 February 1916 to provide it with information on Renault engines, but over two months later on 21 April, the Directorate of Military Aeronautics replied that it could neither locate its documents on Renault contracts nor obtain them from Renault.[59]

While the directorate managed in the spring and summer of 1916 to get discounts on certain spare airframes and engines, it had to struggle to reduce basic engine prices.[60] Renault consistently refused to lower its engine prices, alleging successive increases of materiel and labor costs. Yet in June the SFA believed that orders for some 2,000 Renault 220-hp engines in 1915 and 1916 should have enabled the firm to reduce its price by 2,000 to 3,000 francs. Ultimately the commission won a 1,000 franc price reduction to 26,500 francs and similar price reductions in Peugeot's and Panhard's 200- and 220-hp engines. Over a year of pressure, from January 1916 to May 1917, would elapse before Lorraine-Dietrich would even release production information. Gnome and Rhône, Hispano-Suiza, and Salmson did not provide price justifications, although the commission accepted Salmson's radial engine prices because they were cheaper than in-line engines of comparable power.[61] The firms' leverage against the directorate enabled them to fend off its efforts to secure production information.

Huisman condemned French industry for stagnating aircraft production and effecting insubstantial increases in engine production, thus failing the French air arm and its allies. He believed that the basic problem was the aircraft manufacturers' relatively small size and little capital, which prompted them to try to recoup their peacetime losses through mediocre and routine production instead of introducing night shifts, more intense work habits, and other means to improve production. The aircraft factories needed to attract more large companies that could lure talented engineers.[62]

Huisman's picture of the industry in May is not in accord with Emmanuel Chadeau's recent work on the French aviation industry. Although the July 1916 parliamentary war profits tax penalized pioneer firms by determining excessive profits based on prewar profits, the French aviation industry was thriving, its deliveries steadily growing. Caudron's sales rose from 560,000 francs in 1914, to 15.7 million in 1915, and to 34.8 million in 1916; Nieuport's sales increased from 285,000 francs in 1914, to 12.2 million in 1915, and to 26.4 million in 1916; Voisin's sales grew from 4.5 million in 1915 to 47 million in 1916. Five firms had entered aviation in 1915; 12, primarily automotive companies, entered in 1916. By the year's end the industry had 49,200 workers, 22,000 of whom were mobilized workers and 12,000 were women. Some firms had become modernized, in particular Renault, Nieuport, Salmson, and Spad. Thirteen pioneer aviation firms earned 59.7 million francs in gross profits based on sales of 190 million in 1914–15, a remarkable rate of 32 percent; in 1916 they made 81.4 million gross profits on sales of 277 million francs (a rate of 29 percent). They invested these profits in plant expansion. The industry's work force had grown from 12,650 in 1914, to 30,960 in 1915, and to 68,920 in 1916.[63]

Gnome and Rhône, Renault, and Salmson exemplify the engine industry's development. By December 1916 Gnome and Rhône had 3,200 workers and occupied 106,000 square meters of factory space in three factories, one of which was in Lyons. It produced 4,864 engines in 1916, of which it exported 1,720 (35 percent) to the Allies. Gnome and Rhône's assets had more than trebled since 1914 and more than doubled since 1915 to 84,289,000 francs. Yet the firm did not look to the future. In 1916 when the army questioned the rotary's future suitability for combat because of its loss of efficiency above 150 horsepower, the firm's directors continued rotary engine production and did not devote resources to the development of alternative types such as the radial.[64]

In 1916 Renault's position among engine producers continued to rise from third behind Gnome and Rhône and Salmson to second behind Gnome and Rhône, and by the beginning of 1917 Renault and Hispano-Suiza would become the leading engine manufacturers. Renault far surpassed other automobile firms that converted to engine production such as Peugeot, Panhard, Brasier, and Lorraine-Dietrich. In 1916 Renault produced 3,680 engines (22.8 percent of French engine production) and in November, at the STAé's request, it began constructing the AR army corps airplane. Of the 19,697 workers at Renault in December, 3,209 (16.3 percent), including 525 women, were building aero engines.[65]

Salmson's plant covered 51,352 square meters at the end of 1916, and daily production had risen from one motor in March 1915 to six motors a year later. In 1916 Salmson delivered 2,881 engines, up from 1,776 in 1915, and it could produce seven planes daily by the year's end. It was producing its own magnetos, oxygen and hydrogen for metalwork, aluminum and copper, and machine tools.[66]

Chadeau's figures indicate that the aircraft manufacturers were profiting more than Huisman suspected, and that aircraft and engine producers were increasing production. Huisman's charges of mediocre and routine production seemed to apply to certain pioneer firms, like Farman, Voisin, and Gnome and Rhône, who were unwilling to develop in new directions.

Judgments on the outcome of French aviation in 1916 differ. In parliament the year ended on a grim note with the 6 December release of deputy Daniel Vincent's report, which painted a depressing picture of the frontline air service, portraying a front and rear that could not cooperate and a rear that was incapable of increasing production. Of 1,418 frontline craft, 328 were fighters, of which 82 were obsolescent and only 25 were Spads. Of 837 reconnaissance craft, 802 were obsolete, while all 253 bombers were mediocre. The air arm needed at least 1,000 Spads and had only ordered 629. For reconnaissance it had ordered 724 ARs, which Vincent judged as not much better than the Farmans they were replacing.[67]

Huisman believed that administrative anarchy had lost France aerial mastery and that what was needed was an autonomous air arm with an air ministry and GQG's aviation commander as the arm's chief. He viewed industrial structures as essentially unchanged since 1915, as manufacturers had failed to invest or increase production and justified their reluctance with GQG's continual program changes and the directorate's failure to give guidance. The new directorate sought only to meet the GQG's demands rather than doubling or tripling production, and it also refused to admit that quality in aviation was more important than quantity. It needed, Huisman asserted, aviators, not artillerymen, on its staff.[68]

Albert Etévé, on the other hand, asserted that in the second half of 1916 French aviation overcame its crisis and recaptured the advantage. By the year's end lighter and more powerful French engines were becoming available. Renault had increased the power of its 160-hp engine to 190 horsepower and its 220-hp motor to 300 horsepower; Clerget pushed its 110-hp rotary to 135 horsepower; and the Lorraine-Dietrich got 220 horsepower from its 160-hp power plant. Hispano-Suiza was working on a 220-hp geared engine; Salmson was experimenting on a 250-hp radial. Aircraft under development included day bomber and reconnaissance craft such as the Breguet 14 and the Salmson 2A2, which would be powered by the firm's radial. The Spad was nearly ready for the front. Yet the French still lacked decent heavy bombers. Those that it had were inadequate and suitable at best for night missions.[69]

The year had been difficult and disappointing for the French air arm, except in fighter aviation. Huisman's blanket condemnation of the French military bureaucracy and the aviation industry for losing aerial mastery was too negative. He was certainly correct in perceiving the schism between GQG and the War Ministry, with neither ultimately in control, as a serious problem. The new directorate and its SFA were proving more successful at encouraging quantity than quality, although the responsibility for the situation lay as much with aviation advocates like Dorand in the STAé as it did with the artillerymen in charge. Yet eliciting technological advances was a more difficult task than pushing the enlargement of industrial capacity. Some firms such as Farman and Voisin were stagnating technologically. But Huisman's blanket condemnation of the industry for failing to invest or rationalize did not apply to most of the major firms, which were expanding and rationalizing their production and developing new types, some of which would appear in 1917. Aircraft design sprang from a variety of factors, from military demand to the predilections of aircraft engineers, and the French failed to pursue effectively the design of multiengine aircraft because GQG and most aircraft designers accorded it the lowest priority among aircraft types, if for differing reasons. The command might desire strategic bombers, but it needed tactical aircraft more. Most manufacturers, aware of this circumstance, naturally gravitated toward the smaller planes, which promised greater return from investments of time and expertise. Only the politicians pressed urgently for a strategic bomber.

If Huisman's judgments were too harsh, Etévé, from his perspective in the STAé, was premature in asserting that French aviation had overcome the crisis by the year's end. It remained to be seen whether the planes and engines under development would reach mass production in 1917. Furthermore, French aviation's political-military context was problematic. The resignation of Commander in Chief Joffre and his replacement by Gen. Robert Nivelle in December meant further instability at the top of the military bureaucracy in 1917.

Germany

In 1916 the German air arm on the Western Front was hard-pressed to compete against an enemy superior in number and often in aircraft quality.

In the winter of 1915–16 Field Aviation Chief Lieth-Thomsen proposed to strengthen the German army air service by removing flight units from the corps headquarters' control and attaching them to army headquarters, where staff officers would have more control over the aviation squadrons. Army headquarters declined this proposal.[70]

Although Lieth-Thomsen's organizational proposals were unsuccessful, he did strengthen the service for the Battle of Verdun. In December 1915 the air arm began preparations for the Verdun attack by concentrating fighter units to prevent enemy observation and then adding reconnaissance flight units in early February. The high command's battle squadrons (Kampf-geschwadern der OHL, or Kagohl) were the nucleus of German aerial might. Their single-engine, two-seat C-planes served as a tactical weapon for fighting or bombing military targets behind enemy lines. These mobile squadrons could be transported throughout the front by rail, and the German air arm positioned two strengthened Kagohl at Verdun to bomb railroad junctions, bridges, supplies, and airdromes behind the French lines.[71]

With the attack on Verdun, the air war began in earnest. The Germans staged strong fighting patrols, though bad weather often kept fighters on the ground and infantry support was inadequate because the troops were not yet used to the practice. The 10 flight units that had previously photographed the area now staged defensive patrols to prevent enemy reconnaissance planes' access to German territory. There also were six artillery flight units for observation, 21 single-seat fighters to help the two-seaters with patrols, two G-planes (twin-engine large planes or Grossflugzeuge) for air fighting, and four army high command airships to attack targets in the rear. This concentrated force secured aerial superiority, and in the first few days the battle groups dropped nearly 4,500 pounds of bombs on French-controlled railroad junctions, hindering supplies and reinforcement.[72]

The French responded so quickly with their own concentration of forces that they surprised the Germans and regained air mastery by May, despite the efforts of Fokker pilots such as Max Immelmann and Oswald Boelcke. By March the Fokker monoplane had reached the peak of its development, and if the French and English lacked the synchronized gun, they had comparable aircraft in the British pushers DH2 and FE2b with their forward-mounted guns, and a superior craft in the French Nieuport, which outclassed German planes in speed and maneuverability. To supplement the Fokker, the German units had only its less reliable duplicates, the Pfalz and Siemens-Schuckert monoplanes. After almost falling prey to a Nieuport in March, Boelcke judged the latest Fokker monoplane, the 160-hp E4, deficient in climb above 3,000 meters and suggested the development of modern, light biplane fighters to counter the Nieuport.[73] After flying the E4, Immelmann reverted to the E3. Forced on the defensive, the Germans resorted to stronger defensive patrols over their own lines and limited their reconnaissance. The Kagohl concentrated on patrols and defensive flights and limited their bombing missions. Although five Kagohl were ready for service in March 1916, from the beginning of April four of them were stationed at Verdun to fly defensive air patrols and suffered high losses in planes and crew despite help from single-seat fighters.[74]

By June the German air service desperately needed a new fighter plane. It had responded to the French ascendancy with the inadequate policy of barrage flying in ineffective defensive patrols, and the French Nieuports outclassed the few new Fokker and Halberstadt biplanes reaching the front that month. Boelcke quickly ascertained that the Fokker biplane was too stable for aerobatics, and poor workmanship further impaired the plane's quality.[75]

To add to Fokker's difficulties, on 18 June Max Immelmann fell to his death in an E3. Immelmann, who had been promoted to lieutenant on 24 April, noted in May that the demands for combat were greater and the flight conditions were more stressful. Initial reports stated that his machine fell apart in midair. Some believed that his synchronizer had malfunctioned; others thought that the vibration from a broken propeller had torn the plane apart. The British FE2b crew firing at him thought they were responsible. With the factory's reputation at stake, Fokker and his assistants examined the wreckage and reported that the control wires had been shot through. Whatever its cause, the death of Max Immelmann, "the eagle of Lille," damaged Fokker's position and spelled the monoplane's demise. Furthermore, his death, according to Boelcke, boosted British morale and lowered that of the Germans.[76]

By spring Boelcke had emerged as a careful assessor of airplanes and combat tactics. After Immelmann's death, just as Boelcke was to assume command of a trial six-plane Fokker squadron intended to combat the larger French units, the Kaiser, fearing Boelcke's loss, forbade him to fly and sent him to the rear. Annoyed, Boelcke flew again and shot down another plane before he left. He visited several days with the air chief's staff, and Lieth-Thomsen asked him to summarize his lessons on air fighting. Boelcke's response, labeled the "Dicta Boelcke," set guidelines for aerial fighting that still apply today: Seek the advantage before attacking; attack from the rear, and if possible place the sun at one's back ("beware the Hun in the sun" was standard advice for Allied fighter pilots in the two world wars); once attacking, carry it through, keep the opponent in sight, and fire only at close range; if attacked from above, turn and meet the adversary; over enemy territory, never forget the line of retreat. Boelcke was prepared to organize air combat, and discussed attacking with a fighter unit of four to six planes cooperating in a disciplined fashion. Instead, banned from the air, he went east to visit units, departing just before the Battle of the Somme.[77]

In June German reconnaissance units detected British forces massing for an attack on the Somme. The British struck on 1 July, completely overwhelming the German air service. English and French aircraft outnumbered the Germans by a three-to-one ratio—185 English and 201 French planes to 129 German craft. Verdun had been a difficult and trying time for the German air service, as it developed from a reconnaissance to a battle arm; through the summer, the Battle of the Somme was even more trying.[78]

By mid-July enemy aerial superiority was overwhelming. German aircraft were driven from the skies, and German ground forces cursed the British, French, and German air services in the same breath. The infantry was defenseless against machine-gun fire from low-flying planes, while the artillery was losing its aerial spotters. Aerial mastery now gravely affected the land struggle. The diary of German Lt. Karl Bopp of the 127th Infantry Regiment noted that in August French aviators circled over the regiment at 200 meters altitude as if "parasites . . . attached to them without respite from daybreak into the night," but they did not fire on them for fear of attracting French artillery fire.[79] German 7 August estimates credit the Allies with a two-to-one superiority (500 planes to Germany's 251) and qualitative ascendancy, and Field Aviation Chief Lieth-Thomsen could not promise much relief. German aviators were nowhere to be found, the Allies ruled German airspace, and the German air service was ill-prepared for it.[80]

Deputy Chief of Field Aviation Wilhelm Siegert considered the Somme a lesson that critically influenced aviation's organizational and technical development throughout the rest of the war. The criticism of German aviation before and during the battle brought issues to the foreground in the Reichstag, where parliamentary deputies accused aviation officers of failing to discover enemy offensive preparations. On the contrary, air observation had detected preparations from February through May, but the German First Army did not heed its warnings. Most army commanders regarded the aviation staff officers (Stofl) as technical advisers, and the air officers lacked an organization at the army commands to review the aerial observers' reports and a direct means to report them to the General Staff.[81] Siegert believed German infantry, untrained in defending against low-flying planes, panicked and overestimated the capability of enemy planes, while the First

Army continued to lose opportunities to retaliate and deflect the enemy aerial offensive by deeming the bombing of enemy troops a subordinate task.[82]

After this dismal setback, German aerial strength at the Somme recovered steadily in the summer and fall. It increased from 9 flight units on 1 July to 34 in September and to 46 in October. Battle units rose from one to four Kagohl by the end of August and then to the equivalent of Kagohl organized in smaller units called Kasta (battle squadrons). Instead of striking the Allied rear areas, the Kastas had to concentrate on protecting artillery observation planes.

Fighter organization also changed during the Somme. The single-seat fighter command increased from 16 to 60 fighters between July and August and was then reorganized into Jagdstaffeln (Jastas), or hunting units, of which there were two in September and four in October. Despite these changes, the Germans could not reclaim aerial superiority against the intense enemy offensive.[83]

Meanwhile the German army and air service received new leadership. On 29 August Paul von Hindenburg replaced Falkenhayn as chief of the OHL. Hindenburg appointed Erich Ludendorff, a long supporter of aviation, as the chief quartermaster general. In the air arm Siegert, the dynamic Deputy Chief of Field Aviation, returned to the rear as aviation inspector to mobilize the aircraft industry. The air service concentrated its strength at the Somme, gradually abandoning the Verdun theater, where they had attempted to maintain some degree of "aerial blockade." Finally, during these dark days for German aviation, the German air service could no longer allow Oswald Boelcke to languish, unused, in the rear.

In mid-September German aerial resistance stiffened noticeably, since Boelcke had returned to the front in late August to command and train one of the new fighter units, Fighter Flight 2 (Jagdstaffel 2). The September arrival of the new twin-gun Albatros fighter D1 immensely aided Boelcke's efforts to mold his squadron into an effective fighting unit. He trained his handpicked fighters to understand that the squadron came first, that they had to stick together, and that the individual's victory tally did not matter, so long as the Jagdstaffel won. Before each unit flight, he issued instructions; afterward he gave a severe critique of the unit's performance. He emphasized the importance of thoroughly knowing the enemy aircraft's strengths and weaknesses. By formulating and teaching the rules of organized fighter aviation, Boelcke set the pace in combat flight as he continued to score steadily, often having "an Englishman for breakfast" in lone early-morning sorties.

Boelcke was a born leader, idolized by his subordinates. He bore his adversaries no malice, preferring to count downed planes rather than fliers.

With 40 kills to his credit, he crashed to his death on 28 October after a collision with his friend Erwin Boehme, as the two pursued the same British machine. Boelcke was not tightly strapped into the Albatros, and he seems to have been killed on impact with the ground. The war's first great aerial combat leader and one of its greatest aces was dead, and Germany mourned, immortalizing him in story and verse proclaiming that every German boy wished "to be a Boelcke." Boelcke's legacy was his example, his advice, Jagdstaffel 2, and in particular his most adept pupil, Manfred Freiherr von Richthofen.[84]

Germany's other great aces included Rudolf Berthold, an aviator obsessed with duty, who like France's Charles Nungesser, possessed an indomitable will that refused to let him succumb to repeated and severe injuries. An observer in 1914 and then a G-plane pilot in 1915, Berthold had suffered a nervous breakdown in June and then was wounded on a mission in October during which both his observers were killed. He then switched to single-seaters. Assigned to the single-seat command at Vaux near Verdun, he gained his first victory on 2 February. Testing a Pfalz monoplane on 22 May, he survived a potentially fatal crash with a broken leg and nose, a skull fracture, concussion, and injury to his optic nerves. Berthold returned to the air in August to find the losses in aviation "frighteningly high," the wastage of fliers "enormous." His left leg now shorter, weak, and stiff, his wounded eye in pain, he nevertheless claimed his sixth victim and became commander of Jagdstaffel 14 in October. On 2 October he was lightly wounded in his left hand, and his left thigh was injured again in the ensuing crash, but Berthold continued to fly.[85]

By mid-October, of the 885 German aircraft on the Western Front, 540 flew for the German First and Second Armies on the Somme.[86] Concentrating strength enabled the Germans, though numerically inferior overall, to achieve temporary aerial superiority at the focus of an attack, with the Albatros D-planes wresting aerial superiority from the enemy. The Jastas replaced the Kagohl as the air service's elite, and pilots from the battle groups often transferred into the fighter units.

In accordance with Lieth-Thomsen's late-1915 proposal, the flight formations were removed from corps headquarters and placed under the armies. Flight units were now divided into two types: long-range reconnaissance units for army headquarters that flew fast C-planes with special cameras, and army cooperation units for artillery observation. The Kagohl, reduced in number to three and equipped with twin-engine planes for bombing, epitomized the new specialization of duty and type that had previously been lacking in the use of twin-engine planes. Finally, in the fall the

Kastas, the smaller battle units, became protective units (Schutzstaffeln) to safeguard infantry- and artillery-cooperation planes and, if necessary, to perform those same duties and support local offensives. The increasing numbers of Jastas were intended specifically for aerial fighting. To complete these organizational measures, on 20 November the air force was separated from the transportation inspectorate, and on 29 November, based on Lieth-Thomsen's October memorandum, the flier staff officers became flier commanders at the army commands with authority to use their units tactically, while air group officers were stationed at army corps headquarters.[87]

The year witnessed the steady growth of the German army's airplane force. Although most German army fliers were located on the Western Front, the force on the Russian Front included test units of giant multiengine R-planes (Riesenflugzeuge); two flight units combined into one (unit 300 Pascha) in the Middle East; a command in Sofia, Bulgaria, with one flight unit; and three flight units in Turkey. On 1 October, the air arm had 24 G-planes, 910 C-planes, and 210 D-planes for a total of 1,144 planes with 423 in reserve.[88] Its airship force, along with the navy's, was intended as a strategic weapon.

With the attack on Verdun the army had planned to increase its night airship operations. It had staged a Zeppelin raid on Paris at the end of January in which it lost one ship, so on 22 February the high command assigned four airships to attack Nancy. One succeeded, dropping 3,000 pounds of explosives, but two ships, visible to the naked eye on the moonlit night, were lost to antiaircraft fire. After another sortie on 7 March by one ship against Bar-le-Duc near Verdun, the last of a series of unsuccessful strikes against railroad junctions near Verdun, problems with the airships combined with snow and fog in February and March to prompt the army to forbid Zeppelins to cross the Western Front.[89]

The army sent one ship to the Eastern Front and the others to reconnoiter and bomb the French and English coasts, where they would be over the sea and thus avoid ground fire. This policy had some success. On 1 and 26 April five airships bombed England, as the army and navy staged uncoordinated attacks. Army ships raided the French and British coasts until October, when worsening weather and British air attacks on the Belgian Zeppelin sheds halted their depredations. In long-range reconnaissance and bombing missions on the Russian Front, only one of five ships was extensively damaged by antiaircraft fire. On the Southeastern Front two airships operated from Jambol, Bulgaria, against Salonika and the Black Sea until both were lost and replaced by one ship. OHL commander General Falkenhayn was convinced that the airships were effective, but Field Aviation

Chief Lieth-Thomsen believed that their high losses and cost and negligible results pointed inescapably toward abandoning their operations. With Falkenhayn's replacement by Hindenburg and Ludendorff, who had worked with Lieth-Thomsen on the prewar General Staff, Lieth-Thomsen's view would prevail. The army would substantially downgrade the airships' importance in the coming months.[90]

The navy's airships continued to raid England during 1916. On 8 January 1916 Vice Adm. Reinhold Scheer replaced Admiral Pohl as Commander in Chief of the High Seas Fleet. Vice Admiral Scheer and Naval Airship Commander Strasser were friends, so Scheer's office supported the Naval Airship Division. On 18 January Scheer approved Strasser's plans for a new airship offensive against England. Nine Zeppelins raided The Midlands on 31 January, forcing the RFC to send a BE2c squadron home for anti-Zeppelin duties. The Chief of the Naval Staff prepared to increase the pressure on England.[91]

On 30 May, the day before the Battle of Jutland, the first "r" class Zeppelin, the L30, which had been commissioned in February, arrived. The L30 had six Maybach engines for a total of 1,440 horsepower, was nearly 650 feet long, 91 feet high, and 78.5 feet in diameter, with a volume of 1,949,600 cubic feet. It had a maximum speed of 62 mph and could carry nearly five tons of bombs. This type, with modifications, would continue in production until the war's end. One of them, the L33, after a forced landing in Britain on 23 September, would provide the model for the first successful British rigid airships, the R33 and R34, while the later L49 would be the model for the United States' dirigible, Shenandoah. After the losses of four cruisers at the Battle of Jutland, the navy justified the new airships as scouts for the fleet. Now the airships set out to destroy England, as Strasser was convinced that Britain could be "overcome by means of airships, inasmuch as the country will be deprived of the means of existence through increasingly extensive destruction of cities, factory complexes, dockyards, harbor works with war and merchant ships lying therein, railways, etc. . ."[92]

Goaded by such grandiose expectations, the navy staged major efforts against England between 20 August and 6 September, with a raid of 13 ships on 24 August and the war's biggest raid, with 12 naval and 4 army ships, on 2 September. In the second raid, the only joint army-navy raid on London, weather scattered the attackers. The one ship to reach London, the army SL11, fell in flames to the Brock explosive and Pomeroy incendiary bullets of Lt. William Leefe Robinson's BE2c. In the 23 September 12-ship raid against London and The Midlands, the navy lost the L33 and the

L32 to antiaircraft fire and airplanes. On the 1 October raid of five r class ships, Lt. W. J. Tempest shot down the L31. In his words, the Zeppelin "went red like an enormous Chinese lantern and then a flame shot out of the front part of her. . . . She then shot up about 200 feet, paused, and came roaring down. . . . She shot past me, roaring like a furnace."[93] L31's commander, Heinrich Mathy, the division's operational leader, jumped to his death rather than be roasted alive. His body was found half buried in the ground. This string of tragedies enervated morale in the Naval Airship Division. In the 27 November raid on The Midlands, the year's last raid, RFC pilots downed two of nine airships, clear evidence that the RFC had achieved an ascendancy over the Zeppelins. The height of the Zeppelin raids on England had passed, although Strasser was determined not to relinquish the campaign.

In 1916 Zeppelins were more effective scouts for the High Seas Fleet than airplanes. They were present at the various 1916 naval battles, including Jutland. In August, when Vice Admiral Scheer wanted to bomb Sunderland, Zeppelins sighted and later relocated the main British forces involved. No airship was brought down while scouting at sea, which, despite the notoriety of their operations against England, remained their major occupation. They performed 283 scouting flights compared to 202 raiding sorties.[94]

The German navy's airplane arm became independent of the airship service in June under a Chief of Naval Flight Units (Befehlshaber der Marine-Flieger Abteilungen), Capt. Kranzbühler. This force slowly expanded, based primarily on the aircraft deliveries of FF and Hansa-Brandenburg. The need to respond to the aggressive forays of English naval aviators determined the navy's operational demands. In summer 1916 marauding English patrol planes drove German machines from the skies over the English Channel and the lower North Sea, and by the fall the English were inflicting losses on German dirigible patrols over the North Sea. To counter these assaults the navy sought larger seaplane forces, including fighters and multi-engine seaplanes. Naval aircraft development consequently focused on these two types from 1916 until the war's end.

In response to the Admiralty's July request for single-seat floatplane fighters, Albatros, Hansa-Brandenburg, and Rumpler produced twin float versions of landplanes in relatively small numbers. In the fall, however, German seaplane stations requested a defense fighter, a two-seater that could defend itself against rear attacks. Rear Admiral Starke, head of the aviation department in the Imperial Naval Office, discussed the type, which would have to use either the 160-hp Mercedes or the 150-hp Benz, with the manufacturers in his periodic two-hour conferences in Berlin. Hansa-Brandenburg's chief designer, Ernst Heinkel, had a small floatplane built in eight weeks and shipped to Warnemuende for tests. When the firm's chief test pilot discovered that the plane was tail-heavy, Heinkel had a factory crew remove the top wing and set it 35 centimeters to the plane's rear to correct the center of gravity. The result justified his belief that construction was best done "über den Daumen gepeilt"—literally, by taking one's bearings over one's thumbs—that is, by trial and error. The W12 (Wasserflugzeug, or seaplane) proved to be a superior airplane, as fast and maneuverable as a single-seater, though larger and heavier. The British were in for a rude shock over the Flanders coast in 1917.[95]

In the rear, two topics assumed considerable importance in 1916: the reorganization of the German aviation bureaucracy and the further development of the aviation industry. On 10 March Lieth-Thomsen proposed to Chief of the General Staff Falkenhayn the unification of all German aviation in an imperial air arm directed by a state secretary who would be independent of the army and navy. Lieth-Thomsen believed that the aircraft industry's needs were important reasons for unification: "It cannot be beneficial to the development and most extensive use of the industry, which is still embryonic, if the demands and claims placed upon it come from two independent agencies. Rather, it must be directed according to unified and planned principles."[96] Although Falkenhayn favored the idea, the various War Ministries and naval authorities did not, on the grounds that extensive reorganization in wartime would disrupt efficiency and that the constitution had not foreseen the creation of a higher agency over the armed forces.

Although the Bavarian army had lost complete control of procurement to Prussia, it clung fiercely to the remnants of its bureaucratic autonomy. The Prussian army already managed aircraft procurement through its control of engine distribution. Bavaria's two aircraft firms, the Bavarian Aircraft Works and Pfalz, produced licensed Albatros and LFG craft respectively for north German firms. Yet in July, when confronted with Prussian initiatives for a unified air force, the Bavarian War Ministry, though firmly convinced of the need for a separate organization for aviation, clung to its nominal autonomy and control of personnel exemptions for the aircraft factories.[97]

The navy objected to unification ostensibly on technological grounds, emphasizing the irreconcilable difference between seaplanes and landplanes, the former requiring seaworthiness and range, the latter requiring speed, climb, and maneuverability. To no avail Siegert countered that the differences between giant planes and single-seaters were greater than those between seaplanes and landplanes, and that Rumpler, Albatros, and other firms built both types.[98]

Further interservice friction lessened any chance for acceptance of Lieth-Thomsen's proposal. On 12 May the inspectorate objected to the navy's procurement of seaplanes at the LFG factory, and in response the Chief of Naval Flight Units urged defeat of the inspectorate's attempt to gain control of naval landplane coastal units. The navy had to concede the army's control of supply to these units in August, but it retained control of the landplane force. In 1921 Wilhelm Siegert still found it inconceivable that Lieth-Thomsen's "pioneering and imperative" idea was allowed to be quashed by the "petty" sentiments of naval and state particularism.[99] In reality, it would have been more amazing had the Bavarian army and the German navy acquiesced in the surrender of their bureaucratic autonomy in aviation.

Lieth-Thomsen's far-reaching organizational plans had been thwarted, but Verdun and the Somme necessitated some change in army aviation. On 8 October the high command issued the following order of council over the emperor's name:

> The increasing importance of the air war requires that all air-fighting and defense forces of the army, in the field and in the hinterland, be united in one agency. To this end I command:
> The centralized improvement, preparation, and employment of this means of warfare will be assigned to a "Commanding General of the Air Forces" who will be directly subordinate to the Chief of the General Staff. The "Chief of Field Aviation," with the dissolution of that post, becomes "Chief of Staff to the Commanding General of the Air Forces."[100]

This culmination of the organizational development of the army air arm brought Gen. Ernst von Hoeppner, a cavalry officer commanding the 75th Infantry Division, to the position of Commanding General of the Air Forces, or Kogenluft. The triumvirate of Hoeppner, Lieth-Thomsen, and Siegert, who had become aviation inspector on 31 July, would be responsible for improving the effectiveness of the German air force and the aircraft industry.

In "The Expansion of the Flying Troops in the Winter 1916/17," a memorandum dated 31 August and released in early October, Lieth-Thomsen noted that despite more powerful C-planes and the D-planes, the Allies supported by the "world raw material market and the American motor and aircraft industry," had increased their "oppressive" numerical aerial superiority, causing severe losses to Germany's best and most experienced fliers.[101] Since the air service could not rely on the sheer weight of numbers to gain superiority, it had to improve its organization and equipment to assert aerial control at the decisive points of future battles. He proposed further development of C-, D-, and R-planes, more fighter groups and flight units on the Western Front, and the establishment of flier commanders to coordinate operations. In September, based on the experience gained in the Somme, the inspectorate also issued a specification for a new type, the CL—fast, light, and maneuverable two-seaters for attack and fighter roles in the new Schutzstaffeln.

In fall 1916 the German air force had 1,544 planes—910 C-planes, 210 single-seaters, 24 G-planes, and reserves of 400 craft in the airparks. Lieth-Thomsen planned to expand this force to 2,322 planes by spring 1917, increasing C-planes by only 100 but quadrupling G-planes to 108 and trebling fighter strength to 638. To furnish this growth of over 600 planes, production was to rise to 1,000 planes monthly by spring 1917. Lieth-Thomsen could alter the air service's structure to achieve his ends, but securing technological development and the expansion of industrial production posed more complex problems.

The appointment of a commanding general and a new title—Luftstreitkräfte, the air force—coincided with the proclamation of the Hindenburg Program, which decreed total mobilization in an all-out effort to win the war. The military bureaucracy for total mobilization granted aviation procurement special status. At Lieth-Thomsen's request, Ludendorff opted to keep aircraft procurement separate from the new Weapons and Munitions Procurement Office, which was supposed to control all procurement and eliminate fragmentation and conflicts among procurement agencies.[102] This special position complicated overall aircraft acquisitions and impaired the new office's effectiveness, but it assured aircraft procurement's total subordination to Hoeppner and Lieth-Thomsen and enabled Siegert to function independently.

Lieth-Thomsen and Siegert in effect reorganized the aviation procurement bureaucracy in the latter part of 1916. Faced with ongoing shortages and temporary production disruptions, the inspectorate revised its procurement procedures and production guidelines in the fall, confirming changes that had been in process since the summer. Siegert's 19 September directive officially established a new procurement hierarchy. Just beneath the inspectorate's aircraft depot, a Central Acceptance Commission (Zentral-Abnahme-Kommission), which had existed since May 1915, monitored all production, acceptance, and delivery of airplanes for the depot. It would transmit advice from the front to the factories through construction inspectorates (Bau-Aufsichten or BAs) at the firms. The BAs were to accept airplanes, to monitor production, the allocation of raw material and manpower, and labor affairs, and to mediate among management, labor, and the military. Inspection committees had functioned at individual firms such as Fokker since late 1915, but now the BAs became the official organs of aircraft acceptance at all aircraft factories. The inspectorate secured a "controlling" influence on construction and production through the BAs, whose powers "meant an infringement on the rights of private industry that was justified only by the severity of the war." The BAs would increase from 19 in September 1916 to almost 50 before the war's end. [103] With these permanent surveillance agencies at the firms, the procurement hierarchy was complete, and the institutional prerequisites for the aviation industry's expansion to meet the war of attrition were in place.

Legal prerequisites for offsetting materiel attrition were established in early 1916. The question of patent protection had lain dormant in the political arena since August 1914, when eight major aircraft firms had agreed to allow the military the license-free use of "lesser" patents and to allow patent disputes to be arbitrated by a parliamentary commission. During that time the army resisted paying license fees if the parliamentary commission considered a patent of limited importance. In 1916, when the growth of the German air service and the aircraft industry necessitated clarification of patent guidelines, the parliamentary commission called a conference on the subject between the military and industry for 20 January 1916. Though no settlement was reached, the conference had clearly delineated the positions of the parties involved. The War Ministry considered its license free use of lesser patents reasonable—in light of the more drastic option of expropriation by decree—and a small price for the industry to pay in return for the large contracts and extensive frontline advice the army provided.

The parliamentary representatives essentially agreed with the army, though for varying reasons. The conservative Baron Karl von Gamp-Massaunen, the army's most rabid supporter, believed that the military's interpretation of the national interest took precedence over any laws; the socialist Albert Südekum believed that the industry was attempting to profit unjustly from the war and was prepared to threaten nationalization of factories and induction of manufacturers. National Liberal Dr. Hermann Paasche sought a cooperative solution on the army's terms, since he believed that the industry's wartime profits more than compensated for the license-fee forfeiture. Only Catholic Center party member Count Hans Georg von Oppersdorff, who worked in the War Department's central aviation agency, sympathized with the aircraft manufacturers' position. The industry, however, was divided: older pioneering firms supported maintaining patent laws; recently established firms, which built and repaired planes under license, had everything to gain from an abrogation of patent rights.

After six months of protracted maneuvering, manufacturers, military bureaucrats, and parliamentary deputies reconvened on 20 June and decided that while claims arising from industrial patents were legal, the firms would waive such claims against the army under three conditions. If military workshops built the part, the army would negotiate special agreements with the firm; if firms copied patented parts under contract with the military, they would pay a fabrication right to the original company. Finally, the August 1914 agreement to relinquish lesser patent rights would still apply to the participating manufacturers. Thus the manufacturers' trade association had essentially preserved the rule of patent law and normal judicial processes. The army paid disputed claims over "lesser" patents to firms who had not participated in the August 1914 agreement.

The War Ministry was generally exploiting the wartime situation by using its experts in the patent office to prevent the publication of certain patents that it deemed of military value. After capitalizing on the invention, the ministry refused to discuss license fees or indemnities with the inventor on the grounds that he had no rights until the patent was published. The laws' fragility under wartime pressures was evident, as the War Ministry had settled such questions of patent rights to proceed with standardized and licensed construction, the key to production expansion.[104]

Further mobilization measures followed. On 6 October the aircraft depot ordered a "significant reduction of present aircraft types" and planned to select the best available types for licensed production to meet the increased demand for aircraft in the coming winter. It then requested the exemption from induction of 3,655 skilled workers for the aircraft and engine firms, and in November the War Ministry's Aviation Department instructed the deputy general commands and Bavarian and Swabian War Ministries to assign workers immediately—even from the ranks of frontline troops, if necessary. In wage disputes, the Prussian War Ministry continued to mediate in the workers' favor. In a fall confrontation of the Berlin aircraft industrialists with the unions, Count von Oppersdorff of the War Ministry's Aviation Department summoned labor and management to his office and insisted upon more concessions to the workers. When the manufacturers protested that such concessions to the aviation industry's 7,000 workers would lead to similar demands from the 60,000 workers in other Berlin war industries, Oppersdorff replied that he had to have the airplanes, regardless of the possible repercussions.[105]

The industry advanced rapidly toward its goal of 1,000 planes monthly—the factories delivered 900 in December and a total of 8,182 aircraft in 1916. The Rumpler works grew from 700 workers in 1915 to 1,200 in 1916; its yearly production rose from 210 to 486 planes. Fokker's work force rose from 480 to 950 workers; its annual deliveries increased from 260 to 675. In October Halberstadt doubled its capital to 400,000 marks. The Prussian and Bavarian aviation inspectorates arranged for Edmund Rumpler and the Riedinger Balloon Factory of Augsburg to form the Bavarian Rumpler works in Augsburg in October. Aviatik, which Daimler owned, raised its capital to one million marks. In December the Gothaer Waggonfabrik raised its capital from one to three million marks to produce G-planes, while AEG bought another factory in Johannisthal and established an R-plane construction department at its original plant in Hennigsdorff. [106]

Germany's most important aircraft factory in 1916, the Albatros works, averaged 1,500 employees for seven months and then expanded its work force to some 2,000 workers in August, which enabled an increase in production from 90 aircraft in July and August to 120 in September and 135 in October. The expansion of the work force and production coincided with the introduction of Albatros's new twin-gun biplane fighters, the D1 and D2. The prototype had been ready in the spring; the inspectorate had ordered 12 prototypes powered by the Mercedes 160-hp engine in June; and the fighter that would restore German qualitative supremacy in fall 1916 through spring 1917 was arriving at the front in September. In the fall the inspectorate distributed French Nieuports to three firms, including Albatros, and requested an improved copy of the highly maneuverable French sesquiplane, whose bottom wing was much smaller than the top. Albatros designer Robert Thelen produced a sesquiplane version of the D2, and tests of the new D3 in September and October were so successful that Albatros received the largest single aircraft production contract—for 400 planes—to that date. [107]

While discussions of the Albatros's innovative nature usually focus on the Mercedes engine and its twin synchronized guns, the plywood construction of its fuselage, inspired by prewar Russian techniques, was crucial to the plane's superiority. Albatros had adopted the Steglau method, named after the Russian designer who in 1913 crafted the first airplanes made completely of plywood. The new fighter used longerons over ply bulkheads and enclosed the frame with plywood sheets formed to the frame's curves and fastened to the longerons and bulkheads with screws or nails.

The British and French used primarily fuselages of longerons trussed with wooden and wire struts and ties and covered with linen. When they used plywood, it was to cover flat or slightly curved areas. In crashes, a wrecked truss body became "a crumpled mass of kindling wood," while the Albatroses often held together well after crashes even when riddled with holes. On the Albatros, the plywood skin, molded and united as an integral part of the structure, added strength and stiffness to the frame and minimized wind resistance. The Mercedes thus drove the Albatros 20 percent faster than had been practicable with earlier forms of fuselage construction. Furthermore, the new construction avoided the difficulties of "truing up" trussed fuselages to make certain they were straight, and of obtaining a large supply of thoroughly seasoned spruce. This method suited Germany, which lacked large numbers of workers and the access to American spruce that was the source for the French, British, and Italian aircraft industries. Wood fuselages by other German factories such as Pfalz and LFG demonstrated strengths similar to Albatros bodies.[108]

Despite such success, serious deficiencies remained in the German industrial sector. Skilled labor was still in short supply, and the exemption of skilled aircraft workers from the armed forces proceeded slowly. The quality of aircraft construction material was steadily deteriorating, as the industry rapidly consumed the best wood. Increasing labor and material shortages affected not only current production but also the development of new aircraft types. Plywood was one alternative to spruce; metal construction was an alternative to both.

Hugo Junkers had begun development of his all-metal aircraft in 1915, but in 1916 he was beset by manifold problems.[109] The Junkers test institute finished the first test monoplane with a Mercedes 120-hp engine and received a contract from the inspectorate for six fighters on 31 January. Yet, upon completion in July, the steel plane's climb was inadequate, so Junkers began work on reducing the plane's weight. In November 1916 the army gave him a contract for three prototype J-planes, or infantry aircraft, for use with the 200-hp Benz engine, and he decided to use a biplane configuration for the armored plane.

Junkers was caught in a vicious circle. In February the inspectorate had expressed its interest in production of the plane once it passed frontline tests, but shortages of engineers, skilled labor, materials, and capital were delaying Junkers's completion of the prototypes. By June problems with the metal's inelasticity caused tears in highly stressed parts of the plane, necessitating consideration of an entirely new material. By August Junkers despaired, commenting that if the plane failed, the fault lay not in the design but in problems obtaining administrative support, workers, engines, materials, orders, and capital. Yet in the same month he was already discussing another innovation, the thick wing without bracing, with the inspectorate. In

November the new wing form was successful in test planes. Now Junkers only had to decrease the plane's weight. In the fall he feared losing his enterprise for want of military support and worried that he and his institute would be reduced to "slaves of purely income interests," "raped by capital." At the end of October he complained about having to devote most of his time to business, though he considered himself no businessman. To hasten the process of development and mass production, the inspectorate had considered tying Junkers to Zeppelin in May; in December it decided to make orders contingent on Anthony Fokker's judgment. Thus, Junkers's metal plane amply demonstrated the vicissitudes of wartime innovation.

The most serious industrial problem was inadequate aero engine production.[110] In 1916 German aero engine firms delivered 7,823 engines, rising from a low point of 370 in February to a peak of 1,008 in November. Peacetime engine manufacturers Daimler, Benz, Oberursel, and Argus continued to be the sole aero engine producers until Opel joined their ranks in mid-1916. In April the inspectorate was negotiating with seven engine manufacturers to copy the Rhône, as the Oberursel-Gnome performed poorly at high altitudes compared to the French Rhône and Clerget engines. Although Germany was running out of the rotary's essential lubricant, castor oil, and ersatz oils had not given satisfactory performance, at year's end Oberursel was developing a nine-cylinder 120-hp rotary. Meanwhile Siemens and Halske were experimenting on a counterrotating nine-cylinder rotary engine.

Until fall 1916 other German engine firms concentrated on improving the parts and increasing production of the six-cylinder in-line engine. Benz developed its Bz3 engine into the extremely reliable 200-hp Bz4, of which 6,400 were built after tests in February. Daimler modified its D3 engine into the 260-hp D4a in June and into the 160-hp D3a later that year. After tests in December, 12,000 D3as were manufactured, making it the war's most-produced German engine. The inspectorate and the Imperial Naval Office considered the D3a and the Bz4 their most reliable engines.

The early 1916 capture of a Renault prompted air force chief of staff Lieth-Thomsen on 27 March to order the inspectorate to test powerful engines of more than six cylinders, while the test of a captured Hispano-Suiza prompted the inspectorate in October to instruct firms to develop a similar engine. It issued developmental contracts for high-speed 8- and 12-cylinder V engines with transmissions, though it recommended adhering to the standard German practice of separate cylinders. The air arm also captured examples of the Rolls Royce at the Somme, but its complexity thwarted the Germans from copying it. Although the front declined high-compression engines because it considered their throttle arrangements too complicated, in August the inspectorate ordered Benz and Daimler to equip a six-cylinder engine with large pistons and a better carburetor, and Maybach was testing a high-altitude engine for service in airships and larger airplanes.

What had been a difficult year for the French air arm was even more so for the Germans, who began and finished 1916 well on the Western Front but took a chastening beating in between. They responded by reorganizing their bureaucracy and preparing for total mobilization in the Hindenburg Program. The German aero engine industry perfected six-cylinder in-lines of 150 to 250 horsepower, but German authorities had not drawn additional firms to engine production or pushed the production of higher-hp engines the way the French had. The aircraft industry remained competitive, building sophisticated aircraft like the Albatros and the Junkers, but the German aero engine industry was unable to keep pace with domestic aircraft production, much less its French counterpart. Germany's future aerial prospects were not pleasant, as Lieth-Thomsen was already resigned to occasional and limited aerial ascendancy from a defensive posture. In 1916 it was questionable if efficient organization and technology, two realms in which Germany traditionally excelled, would suffice to offset the Allies' mounting numerical superiority.

Britain

In 1916 the RFC expanded to support the growing BEF, in accordance with the Army Council's December 1915 guidelines, which provided for a new RFC brigade for each army. Each brigade comprised a corps wing for general cooperation duties and an army wing for longer-range reconnaissance, bombing, and aerial fighting. From April through August the command concentrated the scout planes from the corps squadrons, thus differentiating offensive fighting from corps work. The first three brigades were formed by mid-February, and another for the newly organized Fourth Army in April. An RFC Headquarters wing, the Ninth Wing, became operational just before the Somme offensive, and a fifth brigade for the Fifth Army became active during the Somme battle. This expanding force would be heavily engaged over the Somme battlefield from July through November.

The RFC prepared to take the offensive in 1916, a decision that Maj. Gen. Hugh Trenchard and his French counterpart Commandant Jean du Peuty had made in fall 1915. An RFC headquarters 14 January 1916 order instituted formation flying to combat the Fokker scourge. Three fighters would escort each British observation craft in close formation on reconnaissance missions.[111]

The British profited from news of French military advances transmitted through du Peuty's liaison officer with the RFC on 20 February. In April they copied French aerial photography practices at Verdun by decentralizing photographic operations from the wing headquarters to small development sections in reconnaissance squadrons. On 17 April the French established general instructions for contact patrols cooperating with attacking infantry. The British followed suit in May, thereby preparing for perhaps the most significant innovation in air operations during the Somme battle. From German machines captured by the French the British copied the disintegrating separate metal links on German machine gun belts. Their canvas ammunition belts had caused gun jams from the belts' occasionally freezing at high altitudes or their empty part fouling the unused portion. The British also adopted and built French Besonneau hangars, which consisted of a light detachable wooden frame covered with 85×90 feet canvas.[112]

According to historian Malcolm Cooper, the air war at the front was successful just before the Somme offensive.[113] The pusher fighters, the single-seat DH2 and the two-seat FE2, had proven capable of competing against the Fokkers and protecting army cooperation patrols. In the year's first and second quarters most of the low monthly aircraft wastage—17 percent for BE2cs, 22 percent for FE2bs, and 30 percent for DH2s—was due primarily to takeoff and landing accidents, and enemy action accounted for a low percentage of losses. Airplane wastage in 1916's second quarter totaled 198 craft—134 from accidents, 33 from deterioration, and 31 from enemy aircraft or ground fire.[114]

Yet the relative calm before the Somme battle should not obscure Trenchard's repeatedly expressed concerns about inadequacies in crews and machines. Even before the Somme, keeping up with the BEF's expansion proved difficult. In mid-March General Brancker in the Directorate of Military Aeronautics informed General Trenchard that he would be lucky to secure his expanded program of 32 squadrons with 18 to 20 pilots (up from 27 squadrons with 12 pilots) by the end of September, and in September they were still one squadron short of those requirements. In addition to two new squadrons in December 1915, the RFC received two in January and three each in February and March, but its slender support organization left Trenchard still 100 pilots short of the guidelines' requirements in March and 70 pilots short in mid-April, and limited further expansion to three more squadrons in Europe by July.[115]

Throughout the spring Trenchard and Brancker found the deficiency of pilots "very serious" and "very depressing." Pilot reinforcements in March and April either had no experience or were inadequately trained in using the Lewis gun. In May crews had such inadequate training in wireless telegraphy that they were losing large numbers of antennae by just extending or retracting them. Brancker believed that they were "paying for too rapid growth" and acknowledged that they had trained the new squadrons too quickly. Yet when he suggested slowing the process, Trenchard insisted that he had to have the pilots.[116]

Trenchard hoped to secure 40 naval pilots to ease the shortage, but in March the 14 naval pilots detailed to come to the front refused to fly the obsolescent BE2cs and persuaded Major General Henderson to allow them to bring four or five 80-hp Nieuports. When the craft arrived the pilots wanted 110-hp Nieuports, a request Trenchard refused.[117] The naval aviators were used to flying better equipment and their refusal to fly the BE2cs, while inappropriate, showed a certain wisdom on their part. As Trenchard himself admitted, the craft were obsolescent. The incident showed the imbalance of resources between the two air arms: the RFC desperately needed all the pilots and planes it could obtain, while the navy had pilots to spare and could equip them with superior aircraft.

The RFC could have sought more pilots in the ranks of noncommissioned officers, as the continental air arms did, but Major General Henderson believed that noncommissioned officer pilots broke too many machines and took longer to train.[118] Thus the RFC retained its prewar emphasis on commissioned officer pilots and middle- and upper-class youth, and as the quality of the recruits declined it turned to the Dominions as a reservoir of talent.

In early 1916 the lack of trained men posed serious concerns. The average of 10 pilots weekly reaching the front barely sufficed to replace even the rather low casualties, and those replacements often had only the minimum legally allowable 15 hours of flight time.[119] In March, when Lt. Col. John M. Salmond returned to Britain to command the training brigade, he improved the flow of training planes to the air arm by shipping them directly from the factory to training stations by truck, rather than by train through AID inspection at Farnborough, where they were unpacked, dismantled, reassembled, and repacked at every stage. Salmond's system necessitated more inspectors, but it doubled the supply of aircraft to the training stations. He also expedited the training facilities' expansion. The training aerodromes increased rapidly, from 11 stations with 234 officers under instruction in May 1915 to 15 stations with 963 officers and other personnel in training and another 10 stations under construction by the year's end. [120]

In March Trenchard reported to Brancker that British aircraft were inferior to German planes. Unreliable British monosoupapes were a "beast of an engine" in the DH2s, which aircrews occasionally labeled "spinning incinerators" because of engine problems. Poor woodwork often marred the De Havillands and Martinsydes, especially the latter. Brancker was "hopelessly depressed" about the BE2s. The new BE2d was only a small improvement over the BE2c, a circumstance that on 17 April provoked a tirade from Trenchard, who condemned Mervyn O'Gorman at the Royal Aircraft Factory for failing to keep pace with design alterations. Late in April Brancker informed Trenchard that the new RE7 was also a failure as a fighting aircraft. Though Britain was gaining the advantage in the front-line war, the condition of the RFC's aircrews, aero engines, and aircraft offered no grounds for complacency. [121]

On 1 July, at the beginning of the Somme, the RFC had 410 aircraft and 426 pilots in 15 corps squadrons for army cooperation work and 12 army squadrons for offensive duties behind German lines. Trenchard was determined to fight the Germans over their own territory. The RFC seized the initiative early in the battle, dropping 13,000 pounds of bombs in four days. It dominated the skies over the battlefield, and in late July the German prisoners' refrain of the diminished prestige of their absent flying corps delighted Trenchard.

British pilots constantly flew "contact patrols" to support the infantry and reconnaissance and photographic and bombing missions to keep the Germans on the defensive. The RFC's artillery spotting was particularly critical to the BEF, which relied on artillery fire far more than infantry tactics for success in battles. By 1916 aerial photographs provided most of the artillery's information, enabling them to construct detailed maps of German positions for fire missions. Aerial supremacy enabled the RFC to execute its reconnaissance and artillery work without interference from the Germans during most of the battle, to prevent the Germans from carrying out similar work for 10 weeks, and to limit them to only a proportion of the RFC's work in the last two months of the Somme. [122]

Yet the RFC also suffered unparalleled casualties in the battle's early days. In June, the month before the battle, 98 aircraft had been written off ("struck off the lists") from all causes, including 25 from enemy action. In July 210 were struck off, with 97 from enemy action. The early July RFC communiqué reported 24 aircraft downed and 39 aircrew killed or missing; the late July communiqué reported 9 planes and 12 aircrew downed. Trenchard and Brancker, however, were not overly concerned. Trenchard observed that they were doing two to three missions daily for 2 percent losses, while Brancker presumed that casualties would not continue at that level. Yet the RFC lost 20 percent of its force during the first days of fighting at the Somme, and though the losses did drop, they remained sufficiently high—111 aircrew in the four weeks ending 28 July—to make it debatable whether replacements could cover them.[123]

The offensive took a particularly severe toll of units in the battle. The 70th Squadron of the Ninth Wing, which flew long-distance reconnaissance and fighting patrols on the new Sopwith 1½ strutter, Britain's best two-seater, experienced casualties in August through October that set records in the RFC. After nine weeks only 9 of the original 36 pilots and observers remained. The rest, plus 20 of their replacements, were either dead, missing, captured, or disabled. They had ranged in age from 17 to 22.[124]

In the bombing offensive against German communications and headquarters, distant targets fell to the Ninth Wing's 21st squadron. It flew the RE7 biplane, which, similar to early versions of the BE2c, placed the observer and his machine gun in the front cockpit, severely restricting his field of fire and increasing the plane's vulnerability. After initial losses, Lt. J. A. Brophy of the 21st Squadron related that Lt. Col. Hugh "Stuffy" Dowding, the wing commander, decided to lead the raid on 11 July to show how it was done. Dowding gained altitude by circling above the lines where the Germans could see them. A larger force of Germans attacked them, hitting Dowding in the hand and his observer in the face, and striking his machine 12 times. Brophy concluded laconically, "He probably won't try to lead us out again."[125]

Dowding, in fact, was not long for the front. The tall, spare, quiet 34-year-old professional soldier, a graduate of public school and the Royal Military Academy, had served as an observer in Blériots in October 1914. By the summer of 1915 he was commander of the 16th Squadron; a year later he became commander of the Ninth Wing. In July Dowding asked Trenchard for relief of the 60th Squadron because of the excessive frequency of its patrols and its 50 percent casualties. Trenchard complied but probably regarded the request as a sign of weakness. Dowding was promoted to colonel and sent home to a training brigade. The future commander of RAF fighter command in the Battle of Britain would spend the rest of the war away from the Western Front.[126]

Cecil Lewis, author of the classic memoir, *Sagittarius Rising*, was over the Somme from May until November in FE2s, the RFC's two-seat pusher and multi-purpose craft. His squadron's main functions were artillery observation and contact patrols, the latter of which, he commented, were worthless in the first phase of the attack until aircrews flew so low to observe the troops that they took losses from direct hits by their own shells.

According to Lewis, "pilots, in 1916, were lasting, on an average, for three weeks." Lewis survived—though in a "shaky and good for nothing" condition—350 hours in the air in eight months (four over the Somme battle) overseas before he was posted home to a testing squadron. He left convinced that no pilot could stand the strain of frontline flying indefinitely because of the various fears and the sense of being always "at the mercy of machine and the unreliability of the engine." If they were not downed, they cracked up and lost their nerve. Lewis portrayed the legendary RFC airmen as "very brave, very daring, very gallant . . . birdmen" who lived riotously, womanized, and drank excessively. Such "adventurous spirits, the devil-may-care young bloods of England, the fast livers, the furious drivers . . . were not happy unless they were taking risks."[127]

Like Lewis's memoir, published wartime dispatches compared the air war to a medieval tournament or dangerous rugby game. From RFC Headquarters Philip Gibbs's column, "Daily Chronicle," which appeared in *Flight* in February and August, depicted the RFC as "Knights-Errant of the Air," recalling the Black Prince in Flanders. In a war with precious little romance, he found it in the "daily tourneys in the air." In August he praised the fearlessness of British fliers, who attacked unequal odds "with the gusto of schoolboys who fling themselves into a football scrimmage."[128]

The RFC espoused a direct, aggressive approach to combat, exemplified by Lionel W. Brabazon Rees, commander of the 32nd Squadron flying DH2s, who won one of two VCs awarded to fliers in 1916 for attacking an enemy formation on the first day of the Somme and driving them away, though hit in the leg. In June 1916 before the Somme, Lanoe Hawker ordered the 24th Squadron to "attack everything."[129] Capt. R. E. A. W. Hughes Chamberlain, one of Hawker's flight commanders, engaged several Germans late in August, only to be caught in a cross fire. Shot in the foot, his limb spurting blood, he required 20 minutes to descend from 11,000 feet at 90 to 100 mph. Two days and three operations later, he lay in agony, unable to sleep, afraid that he might lose his foot.[130]

The British strategy of seeking combat regardless of location or odds in an unrelenting offensive over enemy lines was alien to German fighter tactics. German Lt. Baldamus, downed by the British on 11 December, 1916, commented on the contrast in style between British and German aviators:

You seem to be magnetically attracted to any German aeroplane you see, and never weigh the situation. I saw one of your machines take on one Fokker, then two Fokkers, then three Fokkers, before being shot down at Lille. We do not look for fights unless it is our duty. With us a machine should return without a fight, unless it is specifically sent up to fight. To return without a fight and with our work done, is the task with us.[131]

The British, on the other hand, interpreted the German mode of operation as a lack of courage.

Britain had to struggle to maintain aerial command against a determined foe. As late as 10 September combat reports suggested that the RFC was still destroying more German planes than it lost, but by mid-September Trenchard realized that the Germans were regaining aerial superiority. On 9 September he confided to Brancker that he was "very uneasy about next year," since the number of German craft at the front was increasing and taking a severe toll of British planes. On 17 September the RFC lost 10 machines in a half day, and on 30 September Trenchard reported to Gen. William Robertson in the War Office that the heavy casualties since new German aircraft had appeared in the last fortnight had tipped the balance of losses in Germany's favor, and he stressed the necessity of more efficient fighters.[132]

Despite the fall resurgence of German fighter forces, Trenchard did not retreat from his offensive doctrine. Instead, the RFC headquarters' late September memorandum, "Future Policy in the Air," indicated a hardening of Trenchard's resolve that the airplane was primarily an offensive weapon.[133] He believed that the French experience at Verdun had demonstrated the value of the offensive. The British policy during the Somme of "relentless and incessant offensive" had forced the Germans on the defensive, and if the Germans took the offensive, the RFC would become more aggressive. He also believed that the value of the RFC during the Somme was its assistance to the ground forces and its offensive actions. He refused demands for the direct protection of army cooperation craft and instead advocated an even more vigorous offensive policy of bombing raids and patrols 20 miles behind the lines, a policy whose value he considered proven by the fact that fighter losses were five times those of corps aircraft, who could perform their work without interference.[134]

As the Somme continued, the RFC's existence became much grimmer than the jaunty tone reflected in Gibbs' dispatches and Lewis' memoir. One way British pilots coped with their circumstances was to trivialize them in song. As the song "It's a Long Way to 8,000" made light of the capabilities of their aircraft, the famous song "The Dying Airman" poked fun at death:

The young aviator lay dying,
And as in the hangar he lay, he lay,
To the mechanics who round him were standing
These last parting words he did say:

Take the cylinders out of my kidneys
The connecting rod out of my brain, my brain,
From the small of my back take the camshaft,
And assemble the engine again. [135]

The song's dark humor alludes to the RFC's use of many pusher aircraft, in which the crew was likely to be crushed from behind by the engine in violent crashes.

The 24th Squadron's DH2 pushers, though outclassed by new German scouts in the fall, continued in service because the RFC could not secure sufficient superior scout craft like the Sopwith Pup or the French Nieuport. As losses mounted the RFC command's orders discouraged squadron commanders from flying. Lanoe Hawker's administrative and command duties kept him increasingly on the ground, but he persisted in flying occasional offensive patrols. In October he was pleased that the 24th Squadron's victories had mounted to 55, but by late that month he was becoming depressed again at the incessant losses. [136]

A week after the Somme's official end, on 23 November Lanoe Hawker, flying over German territory on patrol, encountered a less-experienced German flier mounted on the new Albatros. The combat lasted 30 minutes, but the Albatros's advantage in speed and climb enabled the German to get above and behind Hawker. When Hawker bolted for his own lines, zigzagging at altitudes below 100 meters, his foe pursued him, firing relentlessly. After evading some 900 rounds, Lanoe Hawker, struck in the head, plummeted from an altitude of 30 meters to the Somme battlefield, about 50 meters behind the German lines. Manfred von Richthofen had claimed his eleventh victim. [137]

Yet the critical factor here was the fatal combination of British technological inferiority and aerial policy. The strategy of unrelenting offensive patrols thrust British pilots deep into enemy territory in inferior craft, and they flew determined to give combat regardless of the grim circumstances.

Hawker had nearly succeeded in escaping, but in aerial combat "nearly" was the difference between life and death. The hunters of 1915 had become the hunted of 1916.

Even a robust youth like Albert Ball, Britain's first popular ace, was not immune to the severe stresses of air combat. A precise marksman, he was a short (5 feet 6 inches), stocky, strong public school graduate and a 20-year-old apprentice engineer who possessed a "natural lack of fear." He was enthusiastic about and relished the prospect of flying and fighting in France. In France in mid-February, by May 1916 Ball was "always tired" and found the work "rather a nerve pull." In July he requested a rest from "all this beastly killing."[138]

Ball returned to fly the Nieuport in the fall. He invented and perfected tactics adopted by most RFC Nieuport pilots, attacking from underneath and pulling down the Lewis gun on the plane's top wing to fire up into his adversary. By the year's end Ball had amassed some 30 victories.[139]

Ball, like Hawker, possessed immense courage and individual prowess. Unlike Hawker, who enjoyed the youthful brawls in the squadron mess, Ball was a loner, withdrawn, uncommunicative, and unsociable. A pilot in the 60th Squadron referred to him as an "introspective little chap" whom they called "lonely testicle, or pill,"[140] while another flier in the 11th Squadron later observed:

> There was in his attitude none of that sporting element which to a certain extent formed the basis of many scout pilots' approach to air fighting. Ball never made jokes about it. In the nature of things he was bound to be killed sooner or later as he always looked for and never refused a fight.[141]

In September Ball once again informed his commanding officers that he needed a rest, since his nerves were failing and causing him to take unnecessary chances. He was sent home in October to a basic weapons course and ground instruction. By the year's end, he was ready to return to the front.

During the Somme 499 British aircrew were killed, wounded, or missing, compared to German losses of 359, totals which historian Christopher Cole somehow judged relatively equal.[142] During the battle up to 17 November, 592 planes were wrecked, shot to pieces, or worn out and 190 were missing, for a total of 782. According to other figures 308 pilots were killed, wounded, or missing and 268 were struck off the lists from sickness or exhaustion, for a total of 576. The RFC had lost more planes and pilots than its complement of 410 planes and 426 pilots at the start of the battle.

It had destroyed 164 hostile aircraft and driven down 205 damaged planes, while dropping 292 tons of bombs in 298 raids on definite targets.[143]

In November RFC staff guidelines for aerial combat in single-seater scouts stressed fast, maneuverable, well-armed planes and specially selected pilots who were fit, courageous, and determined to shoot down as many adversaries as possible. While emphasizing the element of surprise and recommending flying in units of two and no more than six planes, the report observed that in encounters with equal numbers of enemy scouts, the Germans "as often as not, scatter before such an attack" or the German team "breaks up under the threat of attack."[144]

Such disparaging commentary on the Germans did not accord with the toll the enemy was exacting and its effect on pilot training or life expectancy at the front. Increased demand for aircrew made adequate training more difficult. Late in October the Air Board discussed the "grievous" number of British training casualties, noting that in the fortnight ending 30 September, 31 officers and other ranks had been killed and 33 had been injured abroad, while 12 had been killed and 15 had been injured at home. Colonel Salmond assured the board that they took no "undue" risks, given the urgent demand for pilots, and explained that the 14 fatal casualties in early October were a small proportion of the 1,800 aircrew in training. When Adm. Frederick Tudor suggested that army air casualties at the front were partially due to the brevity of training, Trenchard explained that while the RFC had suffered 100 percent casualties in 18 weeks, it took only one casualty for every hundred times a plane crossed enemy lines, compared to one in three for the infantry when it crossed the lines—a strong argument for joining the air corps but not an answer to Tudor's challenge. Henderson asserted that "short training was a consequence of the number of casualties and not the casualties of the shortness of training," a most peculiar form of reasoning that, in effect, encompassed only 180 degrees of the vicious circle in which the RFC found itself.[145]

In November RFC headquarters' Third Brigade reported that most new scout pilots were sufficiently trained only to take off and land without damaging their machines. Crossing the lines in this condition posed personal risks and diminished the efficiency of other pilots. The report concluded by recommending France's example of establishing an air school for frontline training and also the introduction of dual-control trainers.[146] Late in November Trenchard noted that if on every fine winter day he lost an average of 8 to 12 pilots he would need more pilots from the navy, obviously not too pleasant a prospect after his first encounter with navy pilots in early 1916.[147]

By December complaints about aircrew training finally prompted a revision of pilot training procedures. In November Maj. Robert Smith Barry, flight commander of the 60th Squadron, had written a paper advocating the use of dual-control trainers with an instructor in the passenger's seat, the fitting of two-seat scouts with dual controls, and the establishment of a school where pilots would hone their flying skills. He considered instructors the key to the problem, as they regarded the whole business as drudgery and called student pilots "odious Huns." In late December 1916 he returned to England to revamp training procedures.[148]

The RFC also planned to use the winter months for training artillery crews by arranging visits to artillery batteries in December. Early in December Trenchard had commented that new observers often required elementary instructional work at the front, since they arrived after long spells in the trenches without leave and thus were unfit for observation work. By January 1917 observers would be sent home for a month's course, which indicated that the RFC still denigrated the value of trained observers.[149]

By the year's end, as the Germans were rallying in the air, RFC pilots paid the consequences of their reckless attitudes. Trenchard refused to acknowledge that materiel and manpower imposed very real limitations on doctrine. While he complained vociferously and constantly about inadequate aircraft and poorly trained crews, he persisted in an offensive policy that severely strained those inadequate resources, ultimately at his aircrews' expense. In September, with the technological tide turning against the RFC, he obstinately proposed to swim against it. A policy that would have allowed the RFC respite to refurbish offered many advantages, but Trenchard and his superior Douglas Haig, whom he had convinced of the importance of aerial support, were unrelenting. In the big push at the Somme the RFC, like the army in general, aimed to prove that it could survive a war of attrition. The proof, as was so often the case in World War I, lay in the sacrifice of its own people.

While the RFC's war on the Western Front remained the main theater of aerial engagement, it also engaged in operations beyond Europe. In the Khartoum region, the British used a few airplanes to attack the forces of Sultan Ali Dinar with machine guns and small antipersonnel bombs, despite problems of transport and maintenance common to tropical operations. In the Middle East in April aircraft dropped 19,000 pounds of supplies in 140 flights to Major General Townshend's beleaguered garrison at Kut before it surrendered.[150]

The RNAS continued its operations over both sea and land. Small seaplane carrier forces attempted unsuccessfully to bomb airship sheds on the island of Sylt and at Tondern in March and May. The Battle of Jutland witnessed one ineffectual flight by a Short seaplane from the carrier accompanying Adm. David Beatty's battle cruiser fleet. In the eastern Mediterranean Sopwith and Short floatplanes were used for various purposes—spotting for naval guns, reconnoitering and bombing railroads, and escorting a lone blimp on antisubmarine and mine patrols.

The blimp was one of several nonrigid airships the British used for coastal antisubmarine patrols. The largest and most powerful type, the North Sea class of 360,000 cubic feet powered by two 250-hp engines, appeared in 1916. These blimps were suitable for patrolling mine barrages and coasts, but they were no substitute for rigid airships in fleet reconnaissance and Atlantic patrols. Churchill had canceled the rigid airship program before his departure from the Admiralty in 1915, while Lloyd George, as Minister of Munitions, was reluctant to allocate machine tools and skilled labor to airships. Balfour reinstated the airship program when he became First Lord, and in 1916 Admiral Beatty wanted rigid airships for scouting, in the erroneous belief that Zeppelins had enabled the German fleet to escape at Jutland. The Vickers R9 rigid airship of 890,000 cubic feet powered by four Wolseley copies of the 180-hp Maybach engine finally flew in November 1916. By then the Admiralty had ordered two copies of the Zeppelin L33 (downed in September) from other firms. Yet it was unlikely, after all the delays, that Britain could establish even a small airship fleet. [151]

By spring 1916 the RNAS had three wings totaling 72 aircraft on the continent. On the French coast the Fifth Naval Wing's new Sopwith 1½ strutters attacked Zeppelin sheds in Belgium and German airfields in the spring. For joint operations with the French, the Admiralty placed the Third Wing at Luxeuil, near Nancy and Belfort, where it staged its first big raid with the French—a joint venture of 55 planes—on 12 October against the Mauser factory at Oberndorf. After moving to Ochey, however, the Third Wing conducted only four more raids in 1916, due to weather, the field's muddy condition, and the wear and tear on the Sopwiths' Clerget 130-hp engines.

The navy's acquiescence to Trenchard's requests for aircraft and pilots for the Battle of the Somme prevented operations at Luxeuil from fully materializing, while Vice Adm. Reginald Bacon of Dover Patrol suspended the Dunkirk units' long-range bombing operations to help the RFC. Historian Neville Jones regretted the suspension of these strategic plans, since he considered the French-Admiralty plan of striking chemical, explosives, iron, and munitions works in the industrial centers of the Saar, Lorraine, and Luxembourg eminently feasible, given the speedy Sopwiths' ability to strike with impunity. Naval bombing could have shaken industrial and popular morale and forced the Germans to divert planes, labor, and materials to home defense, just as the Zeppelin attacks forced their diversion in Britain.[152] Yet Jones's premise, that the formation of a large bomber force at the expense of other priorities would have promoted the British war effort, is unprovable and doubtful. The Sopwiths were incapable of enduring a taxing campaign and could not have remained invulnerable after a German defensive response. Like the Zeppelin campaign, they would certainly have caused diversion of resources to defense, but not enough to change the war's course.

In Britain the army assumed responsibility for air defense on 16 February. The equipping of aircraft with luminous instruments, the Lewis gun, and efficient incendiary and explosive bullets; the improvement and increased production of antiaircraft shells and weapons; and a more reliable warning system based on gun belts and lights all ultimately enabled the Zeppelins' defeat in September and October. The defeat was symbolized by the award of the Victoria Cross on 5 September to public school and Sandhurst graduate William Leefe-Robinson for shooting down a Zeppelin on the night of 2–3 September. By the year's end the government had diverted personnel and guns from other areas, and 12 squadrons of some 200 officers, 2,000 other ranks, and 110 aircraft were stationed in the United Kingdom for its aerial defense.[153] In 1916 the Zeppelin campaign had brought the air war home to Great Britain, and with it came much political agitation over aviation.

In politics and industry the year was tense and difficult—in naval historian S. W. Roskill's words, "a year of discord and frustration."[154] Despite public pressure in late 1915 for the coordination of the two air services and the outrage provoked by the Zeppelin raid of 31 January–1 February, the government was not prepared to take drastic measures in aviation organization. *Flight* suggested that only an air ministry could provide the necessary unified control of the allocation of skilled labor and materiel.[155] In March, Noel Pemberton-Billing, a flamboyant former RNAS pilot, succeeded in his second bid for election to parliament as an air representative from East Hertfordshire and then promptly charged that Britain's gallant air officers were being murdered. *Flight* editor Stanley Spooner compared this "unnecessarily vehement language" to the "irresponsible ravings of third-rate sensational journalism,"[156] although the *Aeroplane*'s acerbic editor Charles G. Grey interpreted the murder charge merely as "an exasperated effort to awake M. Tennant [Undersecretary of State for War] to a sense of urgency."[157]

Pemberton-Billing's polemics led to a judicial inquiry into the administration and command of the RFC, but they had also, as Spooner feared, alienated those he hoped to assist. Brancker wrote Trenchard on 28 March that "Pemberton-Billing is murdering more pilots in the House this afternoon. . . . It would be very amusing if it was not such a hopeless waste of time."[158] Trenchard considered the man and his speech appalling and later suggested to Major General Henderson that "Pemberton-Billing should be made to fly his own machine every day for a year. He would not fly for more than two days . . . because he would be either killed or broken up."[159] Henderson, an Army Council member who was drawn increasingly into aviation politics, later suggested that Pemberton-Billing, while "striving to do evil," had done some good since the government would now have to place the two aviation services on a better footing.[160] While the parliament debated murder charges and established investigatory commissions for the RFC and the Royal Aircraft Factory, the Asquith government attempted to manage the increasingly acrimonious interservice conflict over aviation with little if any changes to the system.

In 1916 the CID War Committee was the initial arena in which the Admiralty and War Office grappled over aviation. Both services complained that the other interfered with its duties and supply source, particularly that of high-powered engines. On 28 January Major General Henderson pleaded for the government to halt the wasteful army-navy competition for powerful engines that resulted when their allocation to the navy conflicted with the RFC's need for them in daily fighting on the Western Front. He suggested allocating first specific duties and then materiel to a particular service. On 10 February Balfour defended the Admiralty's need for powerful engines for seaplanes and the interservice competition for supplies, which he believed had led to improved design.[161]

When War Committee secretary Lt. Col. Maurice Hankey suggested on 9 February that the Ministry of Munitions control aircraft supply, both services demurred, stating that those responsible for production needed to be in close contact with the fliers. The War Committee did not support an air ministry, although the lack of a systematic aviation production program caused by orders from independent services convinced it that something such as a ministry was necessary for efficiency, coordination, and control.[162]

Confronted with this impasse, Hankey proposed a revival of the prewar CID air committee, and on 15 February the Joint War Air Committee

(JWAC) was created to guide British air priorities. Edward Stanley, the Earl of Derby, was its chair; air advocate Lord Montagu of Beaulieu was his deputy. Service representatives included Major General Henderson and the naval director of air services, Rear Adm. C. L. Vaughan-Lee. Its aims—to ensure that the manufacture, supply, and distribution of material accorded with the government's air war priorities, to coordinate the supply and design of materiel, and to avoid clashing or overlapping demands on manufacturing resources—were grandiose, especially in the absence of a governmental policy on air warfare and any executive power for the committee.[163] The JWAC became the next stage for the services' struggle to determine aerial priorities.

By mid-March the War Office and Admiralty had stated their priorities in aviation: the RFC wanted control of all air operations in land theaters, including long-range bombing; the RNAS wished to coordinate long-distance bombing, coastal patrol, fleet reconnaissance, and even assistance to the army. The army objected that naval encroachment in long-range bombing would interfere with the military's plans to expand the RFC, while the RNAS objected to granting exclusive responsibility for bombing to one service.

When the army pointed out that the RFC was short seven squadrons and 275 aircraft and pilots, the navy averred its willingness to loan the army RNAS units, but viewed the crux of the problem as the Royal Aircraft Factory's failure to fulfill expectations regarding airplanes or engines. Henderson accepted personal responsibility for stopping the army's design of high-powered engines in 1914, when he assumed they would be developed by private industry, but then he retorted that the Admiralty depended for its engines on firms that the army had developed. Derby took the army's positions that airpower was primarily a tactical weapon and the government needed to specify the functions of the two services and extend the JWAC powers to allocation. The navy, which continually defended an ad hoc basis of determining air policy for fear that it would lose its autonomy of operation, preferred to prioritize operations, to select the service to perform them in committee, and to wait until after the war to allocate duties to services.[164]

The JWAC foundered during the debate. Some six weeks after its formation, the JWAC was defunct. Derby resigned on 3 April with the explanation that the lack of executive power and authority rendered the committee unable to determine policy during the breach between the two services. He proposed joining the two air services to Asquith, but feared a potentially disastrous dislocation in wartime.[165] Lord Montagu, who had hoped that the committee would become the nucleus of an air board and ultimately of an air ministry, had resigned because the committee had no power. *Flight*, believing that the government had formed the committee simply to forestall public agitation for an air ministry, welcomed the resignations.[166] Historian Malcolm Cooper partially agreed with Hankey's later claim that the committee's failure stemmed from the unfortunate choice of civilian personnel. Hankey thought that Derby was overextended and insufficiently strong-willed, and that Lord Montagu's campaign for an independent air service made him unpopular with service representatives. Yet the main failure was that the committee lacked power to effect change, as both the official historian and Cooper, writing 50 years later, concurred, and that the government lacked a policy on air warfare, as Cooper argued.[167]

The JWAC's failure and the committee hearings to examine the Royal Aircraft Factory prompted Brancker to lament to Trenchard, "I get more and more impressed with the rottenness of our system and our institutions and a large portion of our people every day. The Boches will beat us yet unless we can hang our politicians and burn our newspapers and have a dictatorship." Trenchard replied, "Our institutions badly want revising, and I am afraid we shall not move until things get worse."[168]

In February and March Lord Curzon, Lord President of the Council, had badgered Prime Minister Asquith to grant him responsibility for aviation and suggested the formation of an air board preliminary to an air ministry. After the JWAC's demise, Montagu publicly proposed an experimental draft of an imperial air service and air board that would combine control of materiel design and supply. To the unanimous acclamation of a Navy League meeting early in May, he acknowledged opposition from the government but countered that in important things during the war, "the country had been first, the Houses of Parliament second, and the Government a bad third."[169]

The War Committee decided to establish an Air Board on 11 May. Yet the board under Curzon, as with the former JWAC, was merely an advisory body that could discuss policy, make recommendations to the army and navy, and attempt to coordinate materiel supplies, but with no executive power or authority over policy. Thus it became the next stage of the ongoing debate between the army and navy.

Both services continued to claim control over bombing and preferential rights to high-powered engines. The army continued to maintain that army expansion and tactical operations on the Western Front should have priority over strategic bombing for the production of aircraft, while the Air Board should control supply.

The Admiralty, War Office, and Air Board were united in their continued opposition to the proposed special engine section in the Ministry of

Munitions, which would control aero engine manufacturers. Yet both services were reluctant to discuss limiting engine types, Brancker believing that "useless ones will die of themselves."[170] In May William Weir, director of munitions in Scotland and the owner of firms that produced shells, airframes, and cylinder blocks for aircraft engines, had urged Minister of Munitions Lloyd George to remove aircraft design, production, and supply from the two services and take them under his control.[171] In July, when the board requested of the Ministry of Munitions an absolute priority for steel, machine tools, and labor for aviation, Lloyd George replied that the ministry should control both services' supply.

In August the navy bypassed the Air Board in securing a treasury sanction of nearly three million pounds for naval aviation and curtly dismissed the board's protest by informing it that the matter was navy business. Henderson then pointed out that the military placed all proposals before the board.[172]

By the fall the board failed to heal the breach between the army and navy; instead the board's president and the military representatives were now arrayed against the Admiralty. Curzon's 23 October report to the prime minister and War Committee was an indictment of the Admiralty, though Curzon, fearing wartime dislocation as did Derby before him, was not prepared to recommend the formation of an air ministry. After five months, Curzon concluded that the Admiralty's attitude prevented the board's fulfillment of its charge and condemned the Admiralty for its unjustified demands on aviation resources and lack of cooperation and communication with the board. Curzon believed that Britain needed a single, coordinated policy and that the Air Board should unify supply. First Lord of the Admiralty Balfour replied that he had "little to say" about the Air Board's work, as "they have not much to say themselves," and he lambasted the board for "abusing the Admiralty."[173]

The army and navy dispute over strategic bombing continued. In a visit to the board on 24 October, French aviation commander Commandant Barès proclaimed the increasing importance of bombing, advocated reprisal raids on German cities, and recommended that Britain order Hispano-Suiza and Clerget engines from France for a strategic force. The navy, enthused at the extension of Anglo-France bombing operations and bombing open towns, advocated a 200-plane bomber force in France and the need for 1,000 Hispano-Suizas and 1,000 Clergets in addition to army requirements. The army representatives contested Barès's assertions about bombing's importance, objected to the bomber force proposal, and advised that the army's unfulfilled requests for aircraft took precedence over these new ones. At Trenchard's behest, Douglas Haig opposed the plan and protested naval interference in what he considered a military matter. At the next Air Board meeting the Commander in Chief of the expeditionary forces in France (Haig), the Chief of the Imperial General Staff (Sir William Robertson), and the military representatives on the board agreed that air fighting, reconnaissance, bombing in connection with military operations, and occasional long-range bombing, in that order, were the priorities. Even after Curzon had informed the War Committee of this decision on 9 November, in December the Admiralty was still defending the RNAS request for a bombing force and planning to secure 8,000 Hispano-Suizas from France before 31 March 1918 if the Ministry of Munitions would allot the necessary raw materials. The army, meanwhile, was asking for 20 extra fighting squadrons, 4 of them from the navy. By this time, however, political events had overtaken the Air Board, which was about to undergo a radical transformation.[174]

Contemporary and historical assessments of the Curzon Air Board abound. The 24 October 1916 *Times* recalled that it had wanted an air ministry earlier and said that the Curzon Air Board lacked the authority to solve the problem of interservice rivalry.[175] In early November *Flight* judged the Air Board a failure, and while acknowledging the "rumors" that the Admiralty blocked the board's progress, it considered the crux of the matter the board's constitution and its lack of executive power, which was "wrong from the start" and a "stopgap . . . foredoomed to failure."[176] Historian Barry D. Powers judged the board a halfway measure toward an independent air ministry;[177] Malcolm Cooper believed it was a preliminary stage in the establishment of political control over the air effort.[178] According to the official history the board did useful work under Curzon,[179] but in fact it appears that the board was simply a third stage for reiterating the same arguments that had been circulating early in the year, an exercise in futility, as Brancker had feared in June,[180] that was necessary only because the Asquith government would not take decisive measures in aviation.

In November Curzon opposed granting control of aircraft supply to the Ministry of Munitions because it was primarily a manufacturing and production department and not attuned to the relationship between user and producer that was necessary in aviation. He considered it best for the services and the manufacturers if they emulated the French air service, in which the air department controlled its own supply while the munitions department provided labor and materials.[181]

On 7 December David Lloyd George succeeded Asquith as Prime Minister. He established a smaller War Cabinet to supersede the War Committee and then replaced Balfour with a First Lord of the Admiralty, Sir

Edward Carson, who accepted the separation of supply in the Ministry of Munitions. The 22 December War Cabinet meeting expanded the Air Board's allocation powers and created a fifth sea lord at the Admiralty who would represent aviation on the board. The Ministry of Munitions, which also had a board representative, now assumed control of aircraft design and supply in addition to managing the labor and materiel for aviation construction.[182] The army and navy remained directors of air policy, but they were to coordinate their policies in consultation with the Air Board. The board, whose new president was Lord Cowdray, had the authority to mediate between the Admiralty and War Office in case of conflict or competition and would adapt their programs to available resources in placing orders with the Ministry of Munitions. Lloyd George appointed William Weir to the crucial position of controller of aeronautical supplies in the Ministry of Munitions and also to a seat on the Air Board. The new government had used its control of the material and labor supply in the Ministry of Munitions to exert some initial influence over military aviation, but it had taken a year of repetitive debates under the previous government to reach this point.[183]

During that time the two committees investigating the administration and command of the RFC and the Royal Aircraft Factory had finished their tasks. The committee investigating the RFC met from 18 May to 1 August, issuing an interim report on 3 August and its final report on 17 November. The committee comprised legal professionals but no technical experts, and Major General Henderson's presence dissuaded manufacturers from testifying. Pemberton-Billing, whose allegations had led to the investigation, refused to appear on the grounds that the RNAS should also have been investigated. By July *Flight* suggested that the inquiry was merely retracing ancient history.[184] The final committee report in November charged lack of foresight in the factory's failure to anticipate and provide for the production of high-powered engines and proposed one supply department for both services, but deemed Pemberton-Billings's charges of murder and criminal negligence entirely unjustified.[185] The committee's report on the Royal Aircraft Factory, which was issued on 12 May and then on 19 July with an Air Board critique, noted the everpresent possibility that the factory might become a government arsenal and recommended a management board and a controller of aircraft supplies independent of the factory and in direct contact with the contractors.[186] The Air Board, at Henderson's urging, proclaimed construction at the factory to be minimal, a board of management as inappropriate for a military organization, and a controller unnecessary given the presence of the Directorate of Military Aeronautics at the War Office. Henderson informed the Air Board in mid-June that he was not renewing O'Gorman's contract, and in September Henry Fowler, the forceful and indefatigable former chief mechanical engineer of the Midland Railway and deputy controller of production in the Ministry of Munitions, became the new superintendent of the Royal Aircraft Factory.[187]

Central to these political debates and the frontline difficulties were the conditions in aviation procurement and ultimately the aviation industry, as inefficiencies in Britain's procurement system compounded the industry's inadequacies. The Directorate of Military Aeronautics under General Henderson had been reformed and expanded in early April 1916, its departments becoming subordinate directorates with Brigadier General Brancker as the director of air organization, and Brig. Gen. Duncan McInnes as the new director of air equipment in charge of the critical design, supply, and maintenance of aircraft. Yet McInnes's directorate was in an impossible position, increasingly less able to supply the quantity and quality of aircraft the RFC stipulated, and by September it was sending planes to the front at the expense of the training schools. An overburdened McInnes suffered a breakdown in fall 1916.[188]

Lack of more centralized, coordinated, and uniform controls contributed to problems in procurement. Military and naval representatives' opposition to the Ministry of Munitions' control of aero engine manufacture, their reluctance to limit engine types, and Brancker's belief that civilians could not produce the right type of aircraft[189] had led to a situation in which, according to Christopher Addison, Minister of Munitions, the "chief impediment to large scale supply" arose "from the enormous multiplicity of types resulting from too much expert zeal unchecked by practical considerations."[190] In December 1916 the army and navy had on order 9,483 aircraft of no fewer than 76 varieties and 20,000 engines of 57 kinds.

Rolls Royce complained about subcontractors who took contracts from a variety of works, placed no priority on aviation orders, and insisted on cost-plus-profit contracts while the government contractors were bound to fixed-price contracts. The Admiralty acknowledged that the Ministry of Munitions was legally empowered to control subcontractors, but preferred to use personal influence in these matters rather than surrender control of its manufacturers to the ministry.[191]

Manufacturers complained about the delays caused by constant modifications stipulated by the RFC and RNAS. The navy ordered its modifications because the engines had been put into service before they completed tests—a highly debatable policy but understandable in the difficult

TABLE 2.

British Aviation Production: Firms and Labor, August 1916

	Firms	% Dilution	Total	Men	Women	Boys
Airplanes	27	24.0	18,809	14,288	3,032	1,489
Seaplanes	21	26.1	3,576	2,640	585	351
Engines	114	30.7	19,692	13,633	3,711	2,348

SOURCE: Walter Raleigh and H. A. Jones, *The War in the Air*, app. vol., app. 33.

circumstances—while the War Office sought to ensure the standardization of parts.[192]

British dependence on French materiel compounded such problems. The French were hard-pressed to meet both their own requirements and those of their allies. For example, the British received only 24 of 130 Le Rhône 110-hp engines requested early in 1916. While every French engine in use was built in Britain by mid-1916, British output remained small and the dependence on France for Hispano-Suiza and Clerget engines continued. A joint army-navy purchasing commission under the naval attaché failed to ameliorate relations between the two British service representatives in France, while in the summer the British ambassador expressed concern that a mission of two young men should control such large sums of money.[193]

The foundation of the entire aviation effort was the British aviation industry (see Table 2). Domestic firms produced 5,716 airplanes in 1916, while the government imported another 917 planes, 659 of them from France. Britain's manufacture of aero engines, 5,363, was particularly inadequate, and the French supplied 24 percent of Britain's 7,227 engines in 1916.

Forty-one of those firms, including 10 aeronautical pioneers and 8 major automobile manufacturers, formed the Society of British Aircraft Constructors (SBAC) on 29 March. Other small wartime aviation manufacturers and engine producers formed the Association of British Motor and Aircraft Manufacturers. Rolls Royce joined neither group. The SBAC's main aim was to revise excess-profits duties that were based on prewar figures, to the disadvantage of the small aviation manufacturers who had ploughed profits back into the firms to finance a wartime expansion that would be of little use after the war when demand for aircraft had subsided.[194]

As these firms struggled to get their finances in order, they experienced many difficulties in increasing production. The limiting factor in accelerating aircraft production was engine production, which required more raw materials, machining capacity, trained workers, and erecting and testing facilities. The supply of skilled labor remained the determining factor in aircraft and particularly engine output, and in June the army and navy were requesting 5,400 skilled workers in the next months.[195]

Obtaining skilled labor was difficult. Volunteer workers in the Ministry of Munitions system, which guaranteed them the same wage and an allowance if they went to a specified district, often caused friction with other workers. One firm, Arrol Johnston, refused to employ trade unionists; another firm, Gwynne, found trade unionists and army individuals apathetic. Crossley Manchester, new to aero engine manufacture, was shifting automotive workers to aviation engines.[196]

Firms found it difficult to develop engines and increase output simultaneously, to secure a reserve of materials, particularly nickel chrome alloys, and to weed out defective materials. The magneto shortage became most acute in the summer, when the British had exhausted their supply from Germany. Only in the fall did British firms begin to deliver 20 to 30 magnetos weekly after 12 months of trying to compensate for Britain's lack of suitable materials such as magnets, hard rubber insulating material, and fine copper-enameled wire.

Certain solutions to production problems were, however, problematic in themselves. Claude Johnson, the outspoken managing director of Rolls Royce, suggested that the government select a moderate number of engine types and establish central factories with subcontractors to produce them, but Henderson believed that this concentration would limit improvement.[197] He was concerned about excessive dependence upon Rolls Royce and its superlative combat engines, the 275-hp Eagle and the 200-hp Falcon.

Yet Rolls Royce's engines suggested that the British aviation industry was beginning to hit its stride. Although the Royal Aircraft Factory's replacement for the BE2, the RE8, suffered a series of fiery crashes caused by failures in the factory's RAF4a engine and its proximity to the fuel tank, it produced the prototype fighter SE5 for the Hispano-Suiza engine in late November. The rapidly expanding Sopwith company followed the 1½ Strutter with the small single-seat scout, the Pup, which first flew in February and arrived at the front in the fall; then the Triplane, which was tested in the summer and would begin to arrive at the front early in 1917; and ultimately with the prototype of the famed Camel, which first flew on 26 December. The first prototype Bristol fighter underwent highly successful preliminary trials in September 1916. Britain's three most famous fighters of the war—the Camel, the SE5, and the Bristol fighter—thus first appeared in 1916.[198]

The British industry also progressed in bomber and observation plane development. Airco finished its first prototypes of the DH4 single-engine day bomber, one of which used the 250-hp Rolls Royce Eagle, while Handley Page, after a year of development, managed to deliver the first two operational twin-engine 0/100 bombers to RNAS Fifth Wing in November. The pilot of the third bomber would lose his way in overcast weather and present the Germans with an intact model on 1 January 1917. Armstrong Whitworth's stolid observation craft, the FK3 and FK8, better known as the Little Ack and Big Ack, also appeared in early 1916.[199]

The state government's role in aviation design and production changed. Although the government hearings defended the Royal Aircraft Factory's position, Henderson's removal of the factory's flamboyant and influential head, Mervyn O'Gorman, would significantly lessen its role. While some recent interpretations minimize the importance of the investigation, the quid pro quo for the favorable report was obviously the resignation of O'Gorman, who had served as a lightning rod for all the dissatisfaction with inadequate production. The aviation manufacturers no longer needed to fear the factory's competition, as they began to reach their objectives in aircraft and engine development.

The Lesser Powers

Russia

The German air arm regarded the Eastern Front as a reprieve for its Western Front aircrew, since the small Russian air service and front's vast expanse made aerial encounters infrequent. On 1 June the Russian air arm had 383 aircraft, of which 250 were in good condition and the other 133 were being repaired. By September it had 716 aircraft and 502 pilots in 75 aviation sections.[200]

Russian naval aviators were active in the Baltic and Black seas, flying both domestic Shchetinin flying boats designed by D. P. Grigorovich and imported Curtiss boats, despite defects in the latter's construction and engines. In the Black Sea Russian fliers, operating mainly from the station at Sevastopol and seaplane tenders, reconnoitered and bombed Turkish forts on the coast and in Anatolia, while in the north from their base at Reval, they scouted and spotted for ships bombarding German coastal batteries. By November they had 121 Shchetinin and 40 Curtiss boats.[201]

In 1916 the army air service became indispensable in preparing for large-scale offensives like the Brusilov breakthrough. To map the region, reconnaissance crews photographed all enemy advance positions from the Baltic to the Black seas, even using General Staff officers or artillery commanders where necessary to compensate for the grave shortage of trained observers. Each of the 12 Russian armies had one fighter squadron in June; in August the army formed the first large fighter group at the 11th Army and a second on the Southwestern Front in September.[202] Although overall land-air cooperation in the World War I Russian army was poor, in the summer of 1916 the Southwestern Front command staged bombing operations in cooperation with its attacks. The command recognized the necessity of coordinating the activities of air and ground forces in large operations, and in preparations for attacks in April and August it concentrated its aircraft forces and ordered long- and short-range reconnaissance missions.

Sikorskii's giant planes continued their operations all along the Eastern Front, in the north near Riga, near Minsk, and in the southwest near Galicia, although German fighters made their work more difficult and dangerous in 1916. In the May offensive in Galicia, two Muromets flew reconnaissance missions deep into enemy territory and bombed railroad stations and warehouses. On the Bay of Riga's western shore in the north, four Muromets destroyed a German seaplane station on 4 September. Despite the Sikorskii's strength and defensive armament, German fighters and antiaircraft fire began to inflict losses on them. In a 26 April attack on a railroad station near Friedrichstadt, IM-10 was hit by antiaircraft fire that wounded the pilot. After regaining control of the diving plane, the copilot managed to return. A number of the crew won medals for this mission, including Sgt. Maj. Marcel Pliat, a black Frenchman who spent a half hour on the plane's wing during flight while repairing a damaged engine. In a 23 September mission over the Bay of Riga, the IM-6 managed to return to base despite being hit 293 times by a German fighter. Three days later on the Central Front, four German fighters shot the IM-16 down in flames, killing its four-man crew. The Sikorskii airplanes were tough opponents, but even they could not survive massed fighter strength.[203]

Despite the air arm's growth, the picture in aviation was grim. Grand Duke Aleksandr, commander of the aviation directorate, complained of the official neglect of aviation, which resulted in slow promotions and low morale (in 1916 the air service had only one colonel).[204] The commander of 12th Army lamented to the Stavka in September: "We don't have engines, airplanes, machine guns—there is total unpreparedness."[205] Commissioned officer pilots suffered between 25 and 50 percent casualties up to October 1916.[206]

Undoubtedly prompted by these losses, in mid-1916 the Russian War Ministry adopted a new flight-training program that emphasized the practical and military aspects of flying more than the theoretical, which was characteristic of previous training. It established a chief of military flying schools to expand the training program, and by 1 September four government training schools were functioning—two new schools at Odessa and Moscow in addition to the two at Sevastopol and Gatchina.[207]

In general Russia's lack of development limited the pool of skilled individuals available for the technical services. The shortage of personnel for the technical cadre was particularly acute. At the end of 1916 less than a third of the air force's mechanics had a technical education.[208] Furthermore, the air arm needed trained artillery observers, but only on 31 August did General Alekseev, the Stavka chief of staff, organize special training and assign second lieutenants to the artillery as observers, resulting in 132 artillery officers in air arm units by late 1916.

The army suffered from a shortage of battle-worthy aircraft, since its wastage was nearly 50 percent of combat aircraft monthly from accidents and action. By mid-1916, 73 percent of the planes the Russian army received were domestically made, and most of the rest came from France. However, the French sent obsolete craft. Major General Pnevskii complained:

> New airplanes did not come at all. . . . If the airplanes were good, then the first big consignments went to the French Army. Our need was attended to only when the airplanes became obsolete and did not satisfy the army.[209]

The Russians lacked sufficient aircraft machine guns and were unable to develop a synchronizing gear for their fighters—except for a Duks factory gear for the Le Rhône engine that was manufactured only in small numbers.[210]

At the aviation commission of the Extraordinary Conference on State Defense, Duma representative A. F. Polovtsev observed that aviation's poor condition stemmed partially from the inadequate aircraft supply. Yet engine production was even less sufficient. In 1916 1,769 aircraft and 666 engines of seven different types were produced. In summer 1916 the Stavka established specifications for airplanes, dividing them into tactical craft for

long-range reconnaissance and bombing, corps aircraft for frontline observation and artillery spotting, and fighter aircraft. The Aviation Directorate
reasoned that the development of a national aircraft industry, which was
necessary to break dependence on foreign supplies, was possible only if it
established certain basic aircraft types for mass production.[211]

The War Department and the Aviation Directorate asked in vain for
huge financial subsidies to assist factories with securing plants, technical
personnel, workers, and materials but secured only 500,000 rubles from the
Extraordinary Conference of State Defense at the end of 1916. By the
year's end the 61 million rubles worth of airplanes ordered would require a
considerable expansion of the industry, yet the Aviation Directorate was unable to relax restrictions on procuring machine tools abroad, and it had to
fight hard to retain skilled workers exempted from the front in November.
The training of skilled workers, technicians, foremen, and aviation engineers
remained inadequate. The aircraft factories did receive some priority to acquire scarce metals and trucks for transport. The War Department's technical commission, which had aviation scientists for consultants and a central
science and technological laboratory for testing aviation materials, standardized manufactured goods used in aviation production, but was unable to
standardize the construction of the same aircraft types built at different Russian factories.[212]

The five Russian aircraft factories—Russko-Baltiiskii, Shchetinin,
Lebedev, Duks, and Anatra—could produce 205 planes monthly, a significant improvement from 37 per month in 1914. In addition to the Muromets, Russko-Baltiiskii was building an escort fighter in collaboration with
the Muromets squadron. By the end of 1916 Russko-Baltiiskii employed
nearly 1,000 aircraft workers. Yet because the War Department had only
paid for 3 of the 40 Muromets delivered by 17 October, the factory was
working at 40 percent capacity. In early September Sikorskii tested a new
Muromets with four Renault engines totaling 740 horsepower.

With 1,600 and 1,500 workers respectively, Duks of Moscow and
Anatra of Odessa could deliver 50 foreign-designed planes in 1916. By the
year's end the Shchetinin firm had shifted from Voisin to the production of
designer D. P. Grigorovich's flying boats. Both Shchetinin and Lebedev
could deliver 30 craft monthly. Lebedev produced Sopwiths and Farmans,
as well as a mediocre plane of its own design patterned after the Albatros.[213]

The Russian aviation industry's weakness remained engines. The
Gnome factory's 100 workers produced unreliable engines, but the War Department could not nationalize the factory because the latest methods of mechanical and thermal treatment of materials used in engine construction were

not known in Russia. From the war's beginning to 1 November 1916, Russia had imported 883 airplanes and 2,326 engines, while domestic factories had delivered 1,893 planes and 920 engines.[214]

Austria-Hungary

The small Austro-Hungarian air arm worked to capacity on the far-flung fronts. On the Western Front one unit patrolled 8 kilometers of territory, on the eastern front a unit patrolled 32 kilometers of war zone, and a unit in the Balkans monitored 70 kilometers of front. In Macedonia a four-plane Fokker unit was responsible for 200 kilometers of war front. On the Eastern and Balkan Fronts, supply was particularly difficult. In the Balkans aviators contended with mountains and disease; on the Southwestern Front in Italy they confronted mountains and violent storms. By the end of 1916, with Serbia defeated and Russia and Rumania collapsing, the Southwestern Front against Italy on the Isonzo River became the main emphasis of Austria-Hungary's air arm and army.[215]

The air arm continued to expand slowly. At the beginning of 1916 the army was 22 flight companies short of Conrad von Hötzendorff's prewar goal of 40 by early 1916. Soon the army raised its goal to 48 companies and managed to have 44 of at most eight planes each by the year's end.[216]

Austro-Hungarian naval aviators were increasingly engaged on the Italian Front. Italian Capronis could not reach the 420 kilometers to Vienna from the Isonzo River, but escorted by Nieuports they could and did bomb Pola, Trieste, Fiume, and Cattaro. Naval aviators had to defend against these raids, fly reconnaissance and bombing missions against ships, submarines, and harbors, and escort cruiser sorties against the Otranto blockade. They also attacked troop assembly points and supply dumps on the Isonzo battlefield starting in March 1916.[217]

Austria-Hungary's heroes included army aces Capt. Godwin Brumowski, who became a pilot in July 1916 and commanded a fighter unit on the Italian Front, and Sgt. Julius Arigi, a noncommissioned officer pilot who began his career in 1916 as a two-seater Brandenburg C1 pilot stationed in Albania. There Sergeant Arigi and his observer intercepted six Italian Farmans and shot down five in a 30-minute fight on 22 August. Gottfried Banfield, who had been in aerial combat since July 1915, commanded the naval air station at Trieste from February 1916 until the war's end. Flying Lohner boats, and ultimately the Brandenburg CC boat, he continued to down enemy aircraft despite the Allies' increasing aerial supremacy on the Southwestern Front.[218]

As the Italian war effort put more pressure on Austria-Hungary's limited aviation resources, the army and navy sought to increase their forces. On 22 January a high command committee of representatives from the General Staff, War Ministry, and the aviation troops command met to set guidelines for aircraft procurement. The navy was allowed to dispense a total of 264 aircraft contracts among four Austrian firms, while the army could rely on domestic factories and Hansa-Brandenburg. These guidelines presumed a tremendous increase in production during 1916 over the 281 airplanes produced domestically in 1915, yet raw-material and skilled-worker shortages meant that the industry was not likely to perform much better in 1916.[219]

The skilled-labor shortage was one of the most severe impediments to production, and the air department and the industry only narrowly averted disaster by preventing the War Ministry from inducting exempted personnel born between 1878 and 1897. In response to requests for 5,126 skilled workers in 1916, the aviation department received 2,857, and even then the industry was receiving primarily woodworkers when it urgently needed metalworkers. Despite these problems, the industry produced 807 aircraft in 1916, a substantial improvement over the 281 produced in 1915, while by January 1917 the firms employed nearly 6,000 workers, a tremendous increase from the 200 to 300 in August 1914. This growth, however, did not keep pace with the escalating air war.

To compensate for these deficiencies, in April 1916 the army high command established an aircraft acceptance section under its plenipotentiary in Berlin. As this procurement bureaucracy was formalized, the German armed forces' increasing demand for aircraft reduced its exports to Austria-Hungary from 186 in 1915 to 95 in 1916. Camillo Castiglioni's connection to Germany consequently became more important for procurement than official military channels, as his three companies—the German parent firm, Hansa-Brandenburg, and its licensed producers, Austrian Albatros and the Hungarian Aircraft Works—became the primary channel for the flow of German aircraft technology to Austria-Hungary.

After spring 1916 the Austro-Hungarian air arm relied primarily on the Castiglioni conglomerate. The Brandenburg C1 was the army's standard reconnaissance plane from spring 1916 to the war's end, while the D1 was the mainstay of the fighter force from fall 1916 until mid-1917, despite its early reputation as a *Sarg*, or coffin. The navy relied on the Brandenburg CC flying boat fighter and the large bomber-reconnaissance K-boat in 1916 and 1917. As alternatives the navy had only a few Lohner L-boats; the army possessed Lloyd and Aviatik products.

When the conglomerate attempted to capitalize on this dependence by raising prices, the navy accepted a price increase from 38,000 to 60,000 crowns in July 1916, while the army permitted only minuscule increases, thus allowing little or no profit on its planes. These disparate responses exacerbated the interservice rivalry, as Brandenburg attempted to cancel its army contracts to tend to the more lucrative naval offers. After lengthy disputes, the Austrian High Command merely confirmed its adherence to the 1916 norms granting the army all of Brandenburg's production, which made little difference, since in 1917 and 1918 the German navy would monopolize Brandenburg's production and the Austro-Hungarian forces would buy only from its subsidiaries.

Skilled-labor and material shortages also impeded engine production in the dual monarchy. Stoppages in deliveries of Austro-Daimler and Warchalowky Hiero engines resulted from copper, tin, and nickel shortages. When Austro-Daimler chief Ferdinand Porsche developed a 250-hp 12-cylinder V engine and a 360-hp six-cylinder engine in 1916, a license had to be negotiated with the Rapp engine works in Munich in November 1916 to build the engine for naval K-boats.[220]

Italy

Italian aviation expanded in 1916, its first full year of war. At the end of the first trimester it comprised 30 squadrons, including 7 Caproni bomber squadrons. By the year's end it had 44 squadrons, including 5 more Caproni squadrons.[221]

Italian development of the bomber arm stands out in comparison with other air arms. In 1916 Italy had the most operational multiengine bombers of all the powers. Italy's single, relatively limited, and stalemated front encouraged Guilio Douhet to seek dominance in the air, and the Capronis gave the air service the potential to do so. Enemy air attacks in January and February prompted the Italian supreme command to order an attack on Ljubljana on 18 February, in which Capronis dropped 1,800 kilograms of bombs. Symbolic of the Italian bomber force's preeminence was that in this attack Italian aviators won their first gold medal, Italy's highest award for valor. Two enemy planes killed the observer and wounded the pilot. Captain Balbo, the copilot, operated the machine gun until wounded in the arm and unable to fire. He then shielded the wounded pilot with his own body until he was hit and killed. Balbo's sacrifice enabled the wounded pilot to return to the base with his crew's bodies. The Capronis proved tenacious foes, but as losses mounted, they were forced to raid at night.

The June Italian counteroffensive in the Trentino-Alto Adige region included a raid by 34 Capronis on the Pergine Valsugana station. During the sixth Battle of the Isonzo, on 9 August 58 Capronis escorted by Nieuports bombed railway stations with 4,000 kilograms of bombs and repeated the raid on 15 August with 14 Capronis. On 13 September 22 Capronis bombed Trieste in response to Austrian raids on three Italian cities.

As the Capronis proved their worth, the Italian airship fleet, which lost 4 of 11 dirigibles in 1916, staged fewer missions. Reconnaissance crews received improved radiotelegraphy apparatuses and cameras, and played critical roles in locating Austrian artillery in the various battles during the year. Italian fighter aviation was born in early 1916, and its future ace of aces, Francesco Baracca, scored his first victory on 8 April, one of a few that month. After experiencing constant gun jams the previous months, Baracca downed an Aviatik, wounding the pilot lightly in the head and hitting the observer three times, so gravely that the plane was completely soaked with coagulated blood at the observer's position. He gained his second victory on 16 May, but achieved only two more in 1916.[222]

In February naval aviation was reorganized into two directorates, one at Taranto and the other at Venice. As it improved its defense against Austrian attacks and reconnaissance against mines and submarines, the navy supplemented Macchi's copies of the Lohner flying boats with 38 FBA boats from France. It used Capronis for bombers, and small (2,500 cubic meters) and medium-sized dirigibles for scouting.

Gabriele D'Annunzio staged aerial reconnaissance flights over the enemy coast and particularly over Trieste. But on 23 February he suffered a serious eye injury in an accident that disabled him for months. Thrown sharply against the machine gun when his plane landed, he sustained permanent loss of sight in one eye and temporary loss in the other, forcing him to spend several months in bed in the dark until his vision healed. Though instructed not to fly again at the risk of injury to his one good eye, he returned to participate in a 13 June bomber raid.[223]

The construction program of the Supreme Command and the General Directorate of Military Aviation, despite having to secure raw materials from the United States and build hydroelectric plants and electrical furnaces to produce aviation steel, became productive in 1916. Italy mounted a focused aviation mobilization by progressing from French to domestic aircraft designs based on a strong domestic engine industry, whose nucleus was Fiat. Production rose from 382 in 1915 to 1,255 aircraft, including 136 Caproni Cals. Most of the aircraft produced were copies of French Farmans (462) and 80-hp Nieuports (204). During 1916 the Caproni factory delivered 136 Ca1s powered by three Fiat 100-hp in-line engines and 9 Ca2s with a 150-hp Isotta-Fraschini replacing one of the Fiats. By the summer the Caproni factories near Milan were building more powerful versions using three 150- and 200-hp engines.[224]

The Technical Directorate played the central role in industrial development. It permitted one of its engineers, Ottorino Pomilio, to start a factory that opened in February. Italian engine firms concentrated on developing the six-cylinder in-line, and the engine labeled the deciding factor in Italian aviation appeared in 1916. Fiat's A12 of 250 horsepower had passed its bench tests in mid-1915, and its mass production, which began in 1916, had risen to 100 a month by the year's end. At that time the Technical Directorate and Fiat's aircraft company SIA began designing a two-seat reconnaissance plane using the A12 to replace the Farman. From 100 workers in 1915, the industry grew to some 40,000, as it worked toward producing 900 planes and 1,400 engines a month by the end of 1917.[225]

While Giulio Douhet believed that the authorities desired only defensive aviation and not the offensive bomber, the Capronis clearly were playing a significant role in Italian aviation. Their role, however, did not satisfy Douhet, who became increasingly convinced that only the airplane could break the military deadlock. Yet if the Caproni's fortunes were rising, Douhet's personal fortunes plummeted. He was overlooked when an engineer colonel was appointed director of aviation in Turin in 1916. Then he was arrested in September for leaving a memorandum criticizing the Italian war effort on a train. Found guilty on 15 October, he was sentenced to one year in prison. Though he would be exonerated in 1920, strategic bombing's staunchest advocate found himself in jail, where at least he might find time to write.[226]

Conclusion

Historians have considered 1916 a watershed in the first World War, as Verdun and the Somme dashed both sides' hopes for imminent victory. These battles also marked the true beginning of aerial warfare, with both sides committing to larger air arms to attain aerial superiority. Warfare in 1916 was as much an industrial as a military affair, and the production capacity in aviation of all the combatants, the major powers in particular, was rising. Although the major powers' aviation mobilization was marred by political and administrative friction, aviation production and technology developed to meet the rapidly escalating demands of the front. France was winning the race for industrial mobilization. Germany actually produced more airplanes than France (8,182 to 7,549), but French aero engine production far outdistanced Germany's (16,875 to 7,823) because of France's early and superior industrial mobilization of the automotive industry. Since British production was gaining ground rapidly (5,716 planes and 5,363 engines), Germany was in danger of being overwhelmed on the Western Front if the Allies could translate this industrial superiority into aerial mastery.

The aerial policies of the major powers on the Western Front reflected these industrial realities and their basic military strategies. British and French air policy and overall military strategy were offensive, and the British pursued the air offensive more unrelentingly and inflexibly than the French. The Germans husbanded their resources, fought defensively, and planned to concentrate their aviation forces to seek an occasional mastery limited in time and space. With the aircraft and engines under development in 1916 for the 1917 campaign, the aerial prospects for the Allies were excellent. The Germans, well aware of this potential, took steps to mobilize their industry to its fullest in the fall, and they already had a superior fighter in the Albatros to begin the campaign. Meanwhile, the lesser powers—Russia, Italy, and Austria-Hungary—who had depended on their more powerful allies for aviation materiel, now had to improve their domestic production capacity.

In 1916, after the grinding battles at Verdun and on the Somme, hopes for a decisive end to the war disappeared. The conflict seemed likely to continue to the exhaustion of one or all of the combatants, or, as some soldiers predicted, forever. In 1916 the air services provided Europe with its most revered heroes—aces like Ball, Boelcke, and Guynemer—youth who epitomized the national will to sacrifce in the monstrous struggle on the Western Front. The era of the individual ace would last into 1917, but the individual would have less impact in the growing war of attrition in the air. In 1917 mobilization would become even more critical for aviation, for the airplane had now become indispensable to the conduct of the war.

CHAPTER FIVE

1917

"The question of engines dominates entirely the problem of aviation."

J. L. DUMESNIL, AERONAUTICS BUDGET REPORTER TO

THE BUDGET COMMISSION, 28 JUNE 1917[1]

"I desire to point out that the maintenance of mastery of the air, which is essential, entails a constant and liberal supply of the most up-to-date machines, without which even the most skillful pilots cannot succeed."

GEN. DOUGLAS HAIG, DISPATCH OF 29 DECEMBER 1916[2]

The grinding war of attrition continued in 1917, as the combatants mobilized further and fought on. The British, who now bore the brunt of the conflict on the Western Front, pounded away at the Germans. The French army's disastrously abortive attack at the Chemin des Dames in April ended in mutiny, the French troops' refusal to attack, and a change of command at the general headquarters that would benefit the troops. The conflict drew in the United States, which entered the war on 6 April, and it exhausted and revolutionized Russia, while an increasingly debilitated

Austria-Hungary struggled on against Italy on the mountainous Southwestern Front. Beyond Europe, the British effort against the Ottoman Empire in the Middle East became more effective. Aviation played an increasingly important role on all fronts in 1917.

The Greater Powers

France

French aviation began 1917 in critical condition. The situation at the Somme in 1916 was now reversed, as German planes ranged over the French lines with impunity and the French infantry cursed French aviation. A struggle between GQG and the War Ministry for control of aviation in the post-Joffre era forced General Nivelle to remove Colonel Barès as director of aeronautics at GQG. Barès, an inspiring presence on airfields during the Battle of Verdun and the apostle of aviation to the army commands, was gone. Six days later Nivelle appointed the 10th Army's air chief, Commandant du Peuty, a former officer of Moroccan spahis who had become a fighter pilot in 1915, to concentrate on pursuit aviation.

Nivelle was preparing to launch his ill-fated assault on the Aisne, at the Chemin des Dames, where the Germans, expecting a French attack, had withdrawn to new defensive positions in the Hindenburg Line. As at Verdun and the Somme, French aviation took the offensive, and on 11 April, five days before the attack, GQG exhorted: "The aerial victory must precede the terrestrial victory of which it is both part and pawn. It is necessary to seek out the enemy over his own territory and destroy him."[3]

Fighter aviation was concentrated in a reserve army group (GAR) totaling some 150 single-seaters, leaving each army only one fighter squadron to protect its observation planes. On 15 April, Commandant du Peuty urged a maximum offensive effort to destroy German aviation. Yet in the week before the attack, the Germans avoided French offensive patrols of 10 to 20 planes and contested only fighter attacks on their barrage balloons, thereby thwarting the French effort to engage them in an air battle as a preliminary to the land advance.[4]

On 17 April the French Third Army headquarters emphasized that daily photo reconnaissance missions should be executed with diligence and fighter protection.[5] Yet gusting snow hindered observation, and violent wind currents threw some observers out of their planes. More critically, the GAR lacked sufficient fighters to maintain a "permanent" presence in its scheduled patrols over a 60-kilometer front. Small groups of German planes consequently slipped through the net and took a heavy toll of the obsolescent French observation planes. Army commanders' recriminations about inadequate liaison, which the GAR conceded on 29 April, stemmed from their assumption that French fighters should have been protecting their observation planes. Concerned only about the airspace directly above the battle, the commanders cared little about French fighter victories that had no direct effect on land operations.

Historian A. P. Voisin, who concurred with the commanders' perspective, judged the Aisne offensive the culmination, and the failure, of the offensive doctrine in aviation in 1917.[6] In June, parliamentary deputy J. L. Dumesnil proclaimed that the Germans had become masters of the sky during Chemin des Dames.[7] Although the French official history of aviation has more recently contended that the army fostered the legend of German aerial mastery at the Chemin des Dames to exculpate its failure,[8] the German air service did dominate the French and the British in April.

At the front and in the zone of the armies the French air arm lost 25 killed, 46 missing, and 59 wounded in combat, 59 killed and 93 injured in accidents in April. In May the toll dropped to 16 killed, 24 missing, and 45 wounded in combat, 48 killed and 49 injured in accidents. In both months the casualties from accidents exceeded those from combat. The air war consumed materiel at an even more ferocious pace. In April the French lost 47 planes and 57 engines destroyed, and 266 planes in accidents attributed to poor construction, age, inadequate maintenance, and pilot inexperience and fatigue. Another 385 planes and 133 engines had to be scrapped.[9]

The death toll dropped in May because the French air arm, and the French army, came under new command. The unmitigated disaster at the Chemin des Dames led to mutinies in the French army and to Nivelle's fall. His successor, Gen. Henri Pétain, confined the army to limited offensives for the rest of the year, husbanding his infantry while seeking to crush the Germans with superior firepower and artillery, aviation and assault tanks. Pétain informed Minister of War Paul Painlevé on 28 May: "Aviation has assumed a capital importance; it has become one of the indispensable factors of success. . . . It is necessary to be master of the air." To his intelligence agencies he predicted, "The obligation to seize aerial mastery will lead to veritable aerial battles."[10]

Yet Pétain interpreted mastery of the air in a limited fashion. On 10 May GQG decentralized fighter aviation under the control of the armies to support their limited attacks, escort observation planes, and prevent enemy reconnaissance.[11] Army Group Central had tested such a decentralized policy in preliminary attacks at the end of April, and Pétain pursued it in successful limited offensives in Flanders on 31 July, at Verdun on 20 August, and at La Malmaison on 24 October. His orders of 19 July restricted the air operations to the battle zone and ordered the direct and coordinated intervention of observation, bombardment, and fighter aviation in the land battle to destroy enemy ground forces. Army corps planes were to strafe trenches and batteries, while bombers attacked the battlefield and the reserves and batteries behind the front. Pétain noted the "capital importance" of aerial information in battle and the value of aviation work for troop morale, particularly if the troops could "feel and see that it is done."[12] As of August, Pétain advocated that aerial observation, not rigid plans, should regulate future artillery barrages, while fighters should protect attacks by assault tanks.[13]

On 2 August Pétain appointed a new aviation commander, Colonel (soon General) Duval, to organize the air arm. Duval, who had served as commander of the 314th Brigade and then staff chief of the Sixth Army at the Somme, was one of Pétain's closest collaborators, and his appointment confirmed that Pétain considered aviation of primary importance. Although they wanted du Peuty to command the fighter units, a role for which he would have been admirably suited, he left aviation and, in the spring of 1918, died in combat.[14]

By December Pétain sought certain aerial superiority in 1918.[15] GQG, anticipating the German offensive in 1918, expected to use the bomber defensively, for "employed in great mass, systematically, with continuity, on the enemy's rear along the front of attack, it is perfectly capable of paralyzing the offensive." In a 25 December letter to Gen. John J. Pershing, Pétain emphasized the tactical use of aviation to spot for the artillery and to strafe and bomb enemy reserves. By attacking enemy lines of communication during an Allied offensive, "aviation could be decisive if pursued with sufficient means," as it would prevent the Germans' massing their troops to block a successful attack by the Allies. If the Allies developed aviation to the maximum, Pétain mused, "one can wonder if it would not become a decisive arm . . . in rendering the adversary blind, in paralyzing his communications and in demolishing his morale."[16]

As GQG evolved its aerial strategy, its rapidly expanding frontline force, the largest of the major combatants, suffered from constant problems. The French had 1,420 frontline aircraft in January, 2,172 on 1 June, and 2,335 in early August. Although they outnumbered the Germans and the British, who had 1,980 and 1,200 aircraft, respectively, in August, they lacked the fighter strength to protect their obsolescent observation planes. In the summer, French fighter commanders, who admired Germany's light two-seat fighters, requested two-seat fighters for low-level and long-distance escort operations to replace the two-seat Spad, which was plagued by engine troubles.[17]

On 25 July, Pétain complained that only 715, or 55 percent, of the 1,292 airplanes manufactured had arrived at the front, a number inadequate to maintain the present units, much less increase the force.[18] The planes came without maintenance instructions and in shoddy condition. The Spads' 200-hp Hispanos had problems, and their armament was often poorly installed.[19] In November and December GQG continued to complain about insufficient supplies of replacement parts and accessories, constant breakdowns of Le Rhône 120- and Hispano 200-hp engines, defective construction of Moranes and Nieuports, even planes delivered without guns, motors, carburetors, tanks, or radiators.

In early March, the 150-hp Spad was faster than the German Albatros in level flight and in the dive, but inferior above 13,000 feet. The Albatros's ability to maintain a tight circle while climbing gave it a "decided advantage," forcing French pilots to break off combat. The 180-hp Spad was superior to the Albatros, but Stork commander Brocard believed that they would soon need the 200-hp Spad, which in prototype was very fast (over 130 mph), and ultimately a 300-hp engine for speeds over 180 mph.[20] The French had planned to increase the engine power quickly, yet serious problems with the 200-220 geared Hispano-Suiza disrupted Spad production throughout 1917. From mid-May through early July, du Peuty at GQG reported a steady decrease in Spad deliveries, from 423 in April to 346 in May and 155 in June.[21] The Nieuport with a 120-hp Clerget continued in service, though its speed and power were considered inadequate, and midyear expectations that the new Gnome 150-hp single-valve rotary engine would improve its performance were dashed when the engine was not ready.

As the Germans concentrated their fighter forces in steadily larger formations, the French countered with combat groups, patrolling sectors with 15 to 20 planes in three or four levels. Yet the French discarded their revered individualism reluctantly. The great aces of Squadron Spa 3 of Brocard's Storks were part of a combat group of four squadrons. The Storks epitomized French fighter aviation. Its fine pilots included the quiet, 23-victory ace René "Père" (father) Dorme and the cold and reserved 20-victory ace Albert Deullin. Deullin, returning from patrol in mid-February with his windscreen, face, and suit covered with blood, explained to his upset mechanic, "It is nothing. I shot from very close."[22]

The technique of closing to point-blank range, preferred by so many aces, was risky.[23] Alfred Heurtaux, a 21-victory ace who downed planes with as few as seven or eight rounds, always sought to get as close as 30 meters, "to shoot planes the way you shoot a cow in a corridor." On 3 September his war ended as he brought down a German two-seater; its observer shot him twice in the left thigh, severing his femoral artery. He revived from a dead faint in time to land and survived only because the phosphorus from the two incendiary bullets cauterized the wound and saved him from bleeding to death in the air.[24]

The legendary Georges Guynemer was the star in this firmament of aces. In eight months in 1917, the fragile youth shot down 28 planes, including a quadruple victory on 25 May, for a total of 53 victories. Unlike fliers who broke off combat once they lost the advantage of surprise, Guynemer refused to release a prey. This self-proclaimed "killer of Germans" was consequently wounded twice and shot down eight times.[25]

Keenly interested in his airplane, Guynemer became friends with Spad designer Louis Béchereau and often wrote from the front and visited the factory to describe his combats and suggest improvements to the planes. He even had his own personal Spad 12 with a 37mm Hotchkiss cannon firing through the propeller axis.[26]

To speak of Guynemer in knightly metaphors may not be hyperbole. In June, after some 20 minutes in inconclusive combat with an Albatros D5, Guynemer noticed that his adversary's gun had jammed. He waved farewell and broke off the fight, leaving his opponent (the source of this account), six-victory German ace Ernst Udet, so stunned and then disturbed that he had to take extended leave. Militarily speaking, Guynemer's gesture proved absurd. Udet later shot down 52 more Allied aircraft, became Germany's second-highest-scoring ace, and survived the war.

Guynemer expected to die in the service of France. When Guynemer's father warned in the summer of 1917 that there were limits to human powers, he replied, "Yes, limits that it is necessary to exceed. So long as one has not given everything, one has given nothing."[27] In early September a tired and depressed Guynemer, visiting his wounded squadron mate Heurtaux in the hospital, predicted that he would be the next to die. Two days later, on 11 September, Guynemer disappeared over Poelcapelle, as the Battle of Flanders (7 July–6 November) claimed another victim. Ill, possibly with tuberculosis, and under excessive nervous strain, he should not have been flying, but he refused to stop. French schoolchildren were told that he had flown so high that he could not descend. On 19 October the National Assembly and Senate enshrined "Capt. Guynemer, symbol of the aspirations and enthusiasm of the army of the nation," in the Pantheon, "whose cupola alone has sufficient span to shelter such wings."[28] The slender youth embodied the victory of the spirit over the flesh, of France's will to endure despite her grave wounds.

Guynemer's self-appointed avenger, his successor as French ace of aces, René Fonck, was a study in contrast to Guynemer. The short, stocky Fonck took no risks,[29] attacked only when he had the advantage, and sped away as quickly as he had struck, his own aircraft, by his account, never touched by bullets. He did not have to get close to his target. An extraordinary shot with tremendous reflexes and remarkable eyesight, he honed his aim by shooting 50-centime coins thrown into the air at 10 paces with a carbine.[30] Cold-blooded and arrogant, he never seized the imagination of his countrymen as Guynemer had. Not even the indomitable ace Charles Nungesser, who walked with a cane and occasionally had to be lifted into the cockpit, could equal the mythological Guynemer. In death the slender youth became greater than anyone could in life.

American volunteers in the Lafayette Escadrille also fell to the Grim Reaper in 1917, among them James R. McConnell, who had written of his experiences, and Edmond Genêt, the great-grandson of the French revolutionary government's ambassador to the United States. On the Aisne the squadron claimed seven Germans for the loss of four pilots in 66 combats, and at Verdun, five for the loss of three pilots in 150 engagements. Raoul Lufbery emerged as its ace, a sturdy and determined fighter who often flew an exhausting three or four times a day.[31]

In 1917 the squadron could not include all the U.S. pilots in the French air arm. Dispersed among French units were some 200 Americans of the Lafayette Flying Corps, including the first black combat aviator, Eugene "Jacques" Bullard, a decorated and wounded veteran of the French Foreign Legion who flew with Spa 85 and Spa 93. After the United States entered the war, the U.S. army invited these pilots to join the U.S. air service at higher ranks, but it did not extend the invitation to Bullard.[32] The U.S. army, reflecting the racism of U. S. society, was accepting no blacks in aviation. On 1 January 1918, the Lafayette Escadrille became the first U.S. fighter squadron, the 103rd Squadron, the nucleus of the future U.S. air service.

The fighter pilots were the darlings of France. They never had to request leave; if bad weather halted frontline operations, they simply flew to Bourget and were driven to Paris, where they were idolized and feted.

Worshipful women wrote them constantly, and once, as Guynemer and Heurtaux left a restaurant, they found the jewels and the addresses of adoring female patrons stuffed in their coat pockets.[33]

In his memoir *Notes of a Lost Pilot*, Jean Villars labeled all aviators "bourgeois," because the air arm was a privileged group, with "clean hands, interesting work, individual combat," a "knightly" group in which personal valor still counted. The fighter pilots were the youngest, the most ardent and capable. They were reproached for their independence, their youth, costumes, camaraderie, and, above all, for their unmilitary demeanor.

Addicted to their deadly pursuit, they did not speak of death; rather, they spoke euphemistically of being volatilized or evaporated *(volatilisé)*, or iced *(refroidi)*.[34] They also recognized the sporting aspects of aerial warfare. As Dorme once observed, his sportive combats provided "a gala spectacle" for the "brave infantry in the trenches."[35] They affected a nonchalance toward and a contempt for death. In the knightly tradition, they desired an exceptional, "clean" death in combat, not an anonymous one, or the bad luck *(la guigne)* of dying in an accident. These pilots, worshiped by the public, became the focus, even the prisoners, of a cult of heroism, fostered by journals like *La Guerre aérienne*.[36]

Yet the very independence and individuality of pursuit missions might impair the continued effectiveness of the French fighter arm in a war of mass operations. Villars pointed out that flying in a group gave fighter pilots every advantage, increasing the means of attack and defense and diminishing the chance of surprise. Yet after warning that lone sorties over the lines meant "playing the game of the Boche and . . . putting [oneself] at his mercy," he lamented:

> But no one wants to understand that; the veterans want to hunt individually, through overconfidence and a desire to work on their own; the novices imitate them through vanity and ignorance. And both finish by being killed, the young by a lack of address and training, the veterans because the pitcher that often goes to the well gets broken at last.[37]

The great aces' persistence in flying alone and their concentration in a few elite squadrons meant a lack of role models for new pursuit pilots.

The elite fighter arm was better off than observation and bomber units. Army corps crews flew planes that were cannon fodder. The best available army corps plane in 1917 was the fragile, obsolescent Sopwith two-seater—a judgment that damned the rest: ARs, Farmans, and Caudrons. Politicians and GQG particularly reviled the AR, but since no

French aircraft manufacturer Gabriel Voisin. (Courtesy of the National Air and Space Museum, Smithsonian Institution)

A lecture at the aviation school at Ambérieu. (Courtesy of the Service Historique de l'Armée de l'Air)

A wounded pilot is helped from a cannon-armed Breguet-Michelin 5 after a 1916 raid. (Courtesy of the Service Historique de l'Armée de l'Air)

A French AR1 reconnaissance plane. (Courtesy of the Service Historique de l'Armée de l'Air)

A French Nieuport 17 CI pursuit plane. (Courtesy of the Service Historique de l'Armée de l'Air)

A Nieuport 17's Le Rhône rotary engine. (Courtesy of the Service Historique de l'Armée de l'Air)

French ace Georges Guynemer. (Courtesy of the Service Historique de l'Armée de l'Air)

Guynemer in his Spad 7, "Vieux Charles." (Courtesy of the Service Historique de l'Armée de l'Air)

French ace Charles Nungesser and his father. (Courtesy of the Service Historique de l'Armée de l'Air)

French Undersecretary of State for Air Jacques-Louis Dumesnil with ace René Fonck. (Courtesy of the Service Historique de l'Armée de l'Air)

A French Salmson 2A2 observation plane. (Courtesy of the Service Historique de l'Armée de l'Air)

Mounting a Canton-Unné radial on a Salmson 2A2. (Courtesy
of the Service Historique de l'Armée de l'Air)

A French Breguet 14B2 bomber. (Courtesy of the Service Historique de l'Armée de l'Air)

Installing a French Renault 12-cylinder engine. (Courtesy of the National Air and Space Museum, Smithsonian Institution)

A Hispano-Suiza V8 engine. (Courtesy of the National Air
and Space Museum, Smithsonian Institution)

A French Spad 13 in U.S. colors. (Courtesy of the United States Air Force Museum)

U.S. ace Eddie Rickenbacker with his Nieuport 28. (Courtesy of the National Air and Space Museum, Smithsonian Institution)

The German Aviatik factory. (Courtesy of Peter M. Grosz)

Captured German plane on the Place de la Concorde, Paris, in 1918. (Courtesy of the National Air and Space Museum, Smithsonian Institution)

The wing-construction shop of the German LFG factory at Kaiserdamm. (Courtesy of the
Deutsches Museum)

The LFG works' assembly shop. (Courtesy of the Deutsches Museum)

Aircraft manufacturer Anthony Fokker, the "Flying Dutchman." (Courtesy of the National Air and Space Museum, Smithsonian Institution)

German ace Max Immelmann with his Fokker monoplane. (Courtesy of the United States Air Force Museum)

German ace Oswald Boelcke with his Fokker D3. (Courtesy of the Deutsches Museum)

German ace Werner Voss with his triplane. (Courtesy of the National Air and Space Museum, Smithsonian Institution)

German ace Manfred von Richthofen, the "Red Baron." (Courtesy of the National Air and Space Museum, Smithsonian Institution)

German aces Ernst Udet, at front left, and Bruno Loerzer, center. (Courtesy of the National Air and Space Museum, Smithsonian Institution)

other plane used the Renault 170- to 190-hp engine, the plane remained in service into 1918. Finally, at the end of 1917, the Breguet 14A2 and the Salmson 2A2 offered some hope of salvation.

Poor liaison with ground units often compounded this materiel inadequacy. Some commanders failed to use aviation competently. Captain de Lavergne, aristocratic commander of the C6 Squadron, commented of the general to whom he reported in mid-April at Chemin des Dames:

> He was the type of jovial peasant that one meets at the fairs. He could never get it in his head the difference between two-seat, biplane, or twin-engine *[biplace, biplan, ou bimoteur]*; for him, these terms were identical and he was quite surprised to learn of the first plane of my squadron that passed overhead that it was simultaneously biplane, two-seat, and twin-engine; the messages by wireless that his antenna received from the same plane surprised him most; aviation had come too late in his life for him to understand what it was and thus to use it. [38]

In May the 13th Army corps staged infantry training exercises to demonstrate the importance of collaborating with air observers, but inadequate liaison at the top was still occasionally evident. On 7 June the commanding general's failure to inform his air units of a German attack the previous night prevented them from targeting new German positions during the morning artillery barrage. [39]

Poor materiel also kept French bomber aviation in crisis throughout 1917. Ungainly single-engine Paul Schmitts proved too slow for daylight group raids and carried only 100 kilograms of bombs. French day bomber units fought in Sopwiths, night squadrons in lumbering Farman 40s, Breguet-Michelins, and Voisin 8s. One night all 20 of the Voisin squadron sharing the field with the Lafayette Escadrille crashed attempting to land in Flanders' impenetrable fog. Fortunately, no one was killed. [40] In August and September in the Verdun area these planes conducted an inconclusive airfield bombing war with the Germans. [41]

Until the end of 1916 GQG had controlled all air operations. In 1917, with governmental concern for the diplomatic implications of bombing cities and factories in Germany and occupied France, on 12 March General Lyautey, the minister of war, ordered raids on open cities only in reprisal for German attacks and at the express order of the government. GQG concentrated on battlefield aviation, but bomber commanders still yearned to strike Germany. In April Captain Kérillis regretted the feebleness of French strategic aviation and longed for reprisal raids to "strike the morale of the enemy, to intimidate him." Kérillis believed that a 50-plane raid on Munich "would have flung enough German entrails on the pavement of the city to give the torpedoers of the Lusitania and the arsonists of Reims pause for reflection."[42] In August Captain Laurens of the Second Bomber Group acknowledged that the bomber arm's primary role was attacking the battlefield and rail, supply, and troop centers and aviation fields in the enemy rear, yet he suggested that its secondary aim should be to weaken the enemy economy and to dissuade the enemy from attacking Allied cities.[43] Strikes on German industrial targets, however, invariably resulted in heavy losses to the poorly equipped raiders.

Consequently, the targets of the French air staff's "Plan of Bombardment Operations during the Winter of 1917–1918" were accessible and vulnerable. The French air arm renounced distant objectives in favor of the region within 100 miles of Nancy and acknowledged that the difficulty of daylight raids and the limited efficacy of night raids made destruction of the metallurgical shops in the Saar-Luxemburg-Lorraine region "problematical." They planned to blockade the ore mines and works of Lorraine and Luxemburg with night bomber strikes at railway stations and communications in Metz and Luxemburg. An American Expeditionary Force (AEF) assessment concluded that the plan was the "result of general experience rather than strategic conception."[44] Though Pétain secured government authorization to stage reprisal raids on Trier and Saarbrücken, he did not want such raids to degenerate into a cycle of atrocities and did not consider German morale susceptible to retaliatory raids.[45]

The arrival of the Breguet 14B2 at the end of 1917 enabled Pétain to anticipate day bombing in continuous group raids on railway stations to impede industrial production and rail traffic and to force German fighters to defend them. Armed with the Breguet 14 and the Spad, the French air arm planned to operate offensively en masse in 1918.

Naval aviation continued its minor role in 1917, patrolling the coast with 159 flying boats and four dirigibles at the beginning of the year. During 1917 it bought 297 seaplanes, introduced four flying boat types with 200-hp engines that could carry two to four bombs. In the fall Le Tellier was building a boat armed with a 47mm cannon, while in November the service was testing 280-hp Renaults in its flying boats.[46]

The division between the front and the rear and governmental instability complicated the development of the air arm and the aviation industry, and French politicians continued to criticize it. On 17 January parliamentary deputy P. E. Flandin condemned the debilitating schism between GQG and the War Ministry for destabilizing technological programs and disorganizing production. Flandin wanted a single director of military and naval aviation and an inter-Allied aviation office to coordinate a strategic plan. On 2 February aviation budget reporter Daniel Vincent wrote that the air arm had not met the programs formulated in 1916 for 1917 and had only 1,420 mostly obsolescent planes at the front instead of the 1,950 stipulated.[47]

The struggle of GQG and the War Ministry for supremacy in aviation in January and February exemplified Flandin's condemnation. On 12 January Col. H. J. Régnier, chief of the War Ministry's Twelfth Directorate, proposed the elimination of Colonel Barès's position of GQG Director of Aeronautics, a move that would simultaneously enhance the power of the War Ministry over aviation and remove a severe critic of its aviation bureaucracy. On 10 February the minister of war, General Lyautey, appointed artillery general Guillemin director general of aeronautics, with extended authority over the front air chiefs in technical matters. Barès protested vociferously, and GQG chief, Gen. Robert Nivelle, refused to allow the new agency frontline visits without permission. The GQG–War Ministry conflict ended in a draw, but with two casualties. The War Ministry forced Nivelle to remove Barès on 15 February, but in turn replaced Commandant Stammler as director of the SFA with Colonel Guiffart on 26 February.[48]

In this highly charged atmosphere, the parliament's aeronautical subcommission commented of Guillemin's inexperience in aviation that the "illnesses of aviation are too grave to wait for cure until the surgeon has learned to use his instruments."[49] In a secret committee meeting on 14 March, deputy and aviation officer Raoul Anglès excoriated the War Ministry's recent changes as an "empty sham," describing most French machines as planes "with which aviators can only die."[50] He feared that Guillemin, an artilleryman, would continue Régnier's treatment of aviation, when France needed new planes and coordination of the front and the rear. A silent Lyautey allowed Guillemin to reply to the deputies' interpellation, but later complained that even in secret committee the debate and disclosure of technical details threatened French national defense. In the ensuing uproar over this challenge to parliamentary rights, Lyautey resigned on 15 March, followed by the fall of Aristide Briand's ministry.[51] Aviation had truly arrived; it had occasioned the fall of a ministry.

On 20 March, the new ministry of Alexandre Ribot, with Paul Painlevé as minister of war, eliminated the general director's position in the Twelfth Directorate and returned to an undersecretariat of aeronautics, appointing as undersecretary Radical Socialist deputy Daniel Vincent, who had been a second lieutenant observer in Voisin V113 Squadron and a budget reporter in aviation in the chamber since 1915. Vincent, prodded by the expectations of the chamber's aeronautical subcommission of a unification and centralization of aviation command, moved quickly toward reforms.

As a parting shot, however, Guillemin upped the ante dramatically with regard to aircraft programs. On 15 March the War Committee passed a program proposed by General Nivelle at GQG of 2,665 frontline planes for the end of 1917, which was actually fewer than the parliament's army commission proposal in October 1916 of a 2,690-plane force. On 20 March, the day he left office, Guillemin advised the War Committee that a further increase, to 4,000 planes, would be necessary by 1 April 1918. His proposal would require production increases, higher allocations of personnel and materials, and the transfer of automotive factories, which used a labor force and primary materials nearly identical to those needed for aviation engines, to aircraft production. To compensate for reduced automotive production, automotive materiel could be requested from U.S. factories.[52] Guillemin was gone, but his 4,000-plane program would linger as a panacea, clouding all future debate.

General Nivelle informed Vincent that the 4,000-plane program "seemed to him neither necessary nor possible" and insisted on his program of 2,665 up-to-date planes. Vincent concurred, since France lacked the labor to produce 4,000 planes.[53]

Vincent's knowledge of the front and rear enabled him to provide a remarkable assist to aviation production, as he worked to improve the directorate's administration, secure additional factory labor, and ease the relationship of the rear to GQG. He halted the STAé's design and construction of planes, and limited it to research, judging designs, and providing technical assistance to the aviation industry. At the directorate Vincent replaced nonfliers with fliers returning from the front. He wanted to establish a regular rotation between the front and the rear, but GQG refused to release its officers and to accept officer pilots from the rear.[54]

During the last week of March, Vincent met with aircraft and engine manufacturers to standardize production. In response to their many complaints, he simplified the directorate's administrative procedures and assured the builders of labor, raw materials, and orders on a quarterly basis if they accepted the licensed production of aircraft designed by other manufacturers. Factories that refused licensed production would face the reassignment of their conscripted labor force. In order to achieve production of two engines for every airframe, he sought to draw new firms from artillery production, while the SFA chief, Colonel Guiffart, recruited subcontractors.[55]

Under armaments minister Albert Thomas, appointed in December 1916, subcontracting became essential to increasing production in 1917 and 1918. The number of airframe and engine firms rose from 39 at the end of 1916 to 62 by late fall 1917, while the expanding labor force averaged 90,000 workers in 1917. Subcontractors were the main source of this expansion; they produced 45 percent of the aircraft market in 1917 and most Hispano-Suizas, though Gnome and Rhône, Renault, and Salmson manufactured their own engines. The original manufacturers concerned themselves with invention and innovation, their expansion discouraged by the war profits tax of 1916, which took effect on 1 January and levied a 75 percent tax on war profits that exceeded prewar profits by more than 25 percent. Gabriel Voisin decided to leave the industry rather than become a licensed producer, partly because of pride but also because payment of the tax for 1917 would have consumed nearly one-third of his resources.[56]

Vincent strove mightily to reduce prices, but the aviation firms, particularly the engine producers, enjoyed a strong position relative to the French state. Even after interminable price negotiations, Hispano-Suiza, Salmson, and Gnome and Rhône never submitted price information. The government aeronautical contracts commission judged engine prices and license fees excessive but had no remedy beyond Vincent's policy of increased serial production, because it could not force the collaboration so necessary for accurate price assessment upon the manufacturers.[57]

In early August Vincent took further steps to improve the administration of aviation. He became Undersecretary for Military and Naval Aviation on 8 August and increased the allocation of new aero engines to the navy from 10 to 15 percent. He promoted Guiffart to Director of Military Aeronautics, replacing him at the SFA with his deputy, Commandant Guignard, a bridge-and-road engineer. The SFA reorganized its aircraft services according to type, while the engine service became autonomous under the directorate.[58]

While Vincent reorganized the procurement bureaucracy, in late June he complained to GQG and the War Ministry that he had yet to receive the labor promised to him earlier. Although on 25 June Minister of Armaments Louis Loucheur agreed to send Vincent 3,410 workers from artillery and automotive parks and armaments factories, only a comprehensive budget commission report on the state of French aviation on 28 June by Radical Socialist deputy J. L. Dumesnil, reporter of the aeronautics budget, secured more concrete assurances.[59]

Dumesnil deemed the army's total of 2,172 planes—690 fighters, 1,186 army corps planes, and 296 bombers—at the front as of 1 June entirely fictitious, as most of the planes, particularly the bombers and observation planes, were obsolescent. To "reconquer mastery of the air" France needed to increase the number and quality of airplanes, reduce the 37 aircraft types on order, and eliminate the AR. Dumesnil wanted two- or three-seat fighter types for long-range reconnaissance and bomber escort and for army corps aviation. The few remaining single-seat fighters could continue to operate as they wished, but the commission viewed mass as the central principle of war, and wanted aviation to achieve an aerial breakthrough by means of discipline, homogeneity, and leadership.

Dumesnil urged the War Committee to remedy immediately the grave shortage of labor in aviation factories, where 25 to 30 percent of plant was currently unused after a recent induction of 3,700 workers, with some 10,000 additional workers to implement the 4,000-plane program.[60] Though the War Committee could not guarantee the number of workers, it decided on 28 June to assign sufficient labor to assure full production, switch more large automotive factories to aviation production, reduce the number of aircraft types in service, and standardize the best two types of plane in each category.[61]

During the late spring and summer Vincent had kept Pétain informed about his progress. With Pétain's appointment on 2 August of Colonel Duval as director of aeronautics at GQG, Duval and Vincent arranged regular monthly meetings. Pétain now wanted a new minimum program to improve army corps aviation and insisted on priority for aviation production programs over certain artillery programs. On 2 September Duval and Vincent set a new program, targeting 2,870 planes for 1 March 1918—1,520 reconnaissance planes, 900 fighters, and 450 bombers.[62]

Vincent had clearly improved conditions in aviation, but by August War Minister Painlevé was hearing reports from parliamentary deputies and frontline officers of a crisis caused by supply deficits. Vincent was running afoul of politics, as had his predecessor, Bernard, as Painlevé became increasingly intrusive about aviation matters. On 5 September Vincent admitted to Painlevé that supply was problematic and industrial conditions fragile but denied the existence of a crisis. Supplies of superior planes were improving. His negotiations to reduce materiel prices had delayed contracts but had lowered Breguet prices, for example, by 6,000 francs, to 28,000. He paid the manufacturers' bills more promptly and collaborated well with GQG, but he conceded that he had probably interfered with the cliquish intrigues of some parliamentary deputies.[63]

Seven days later, in another change of government, Painlevé replaced Ribot as prime minister, and Vincent became Minister of Public Instruction, replaced as air undersecretary by J. L. Dumesnil.[64] In his five months as undersecretary Vincent had fulfilled the wishes of the parliamentary commission to unify and centralize the aviation command and guide the improvement of the technological and industrial program, yet achievement afforded no immunity against the vicissitudes of French political life.

Dumesnil, like Vincent, was a former aviator who had served in Squadron C13 from April to June 1917 and who shared Vincent's ideas, as well as the same uncomfortable position between GQG and the politicians. GQG remained dissatisfied with the progress toward the 2,870-plane program. Late in September a parliamentary commission report condemned the poor quality of airplanes and the state of disrepair in the squadrons. GQG attributed deficiencies of quality and supply to the poor organization of repair and production, and retroactively condemned Vincent for failing to impose sanctions on firms to halt delays in production and for promoting Colonel Guiffart, whom it considered responsible for the delays. Dumesnil contended that the report exaggerated the difficulties and estimated that not only would the 2,665-plane program be realized by the end of 1917 and the 2,870-plane program in the first trimester of 1918, but also a surplus of production would be achieved in the fourth trimester of 1917. GQG and Dumesnil then proposed a 4,000-plane program.[65]

On 8 October the War Committee granted absolute priority to aircraft production and approved the 2,870-plane program. It further sanctioned GQG and Dumesnil's proposal of a 4,000-plane program for October 1918 as a step toward unlimited production, although it acknowledged the impossibility of providing the labor theoretically necessary to produce 4,000 planes.[66]

Later all parties descended to a more realistic level. At October's monthly meeting with the undersecretary, Duval, dissatisfied with Dumesnil's projections of three months of deliveries, wanted six-month projections, assurances of steady production increases of Breguets, Salmsons, and Spads, and the development of a suitable night bomber. Duval also wanted more aircrew in 1918. In 1917 aviation schools had sent to the front an average of 200 pilots monthly from 380 student pilots. In 1918 they would need a minimum of 400 breveted pilots monthly from assignments of 500 student pilots.[67]

On 26 October the parliamentary subcommission advised the president of the War Council of their serious concerns about insufficient programs, the engine crisis, and France's loss of aerial mastery. On 5 November Duval warned Pétain that the 4,000-plane program would not necessarily ensure the advantage over the Germans unless the four causes of

French weakness—obsolescent aircraft, poorly built aircraft and engines, insufficient supplies of replacement parts and accessories, and insufficient and inadequately trained pilots—were eliminated. Yet he expected no improvement from a production organization that had yet to deliver the Breguet in large numbers.[68]

On 10 November Dumesnil replied to GQG that he was taking all possible measures to provide Breguets, Salmsons, and Spads. He hoped to achieve the 2,870-plane program by April, and despite production problems, he envisaged "the preponderant role" that the bomber wings would be called upon to play in 1918.[69] On 3 November Dumesnil had reorganized the SFA's engine production service to resemble the aircraft service, around eight officers in charge of various engine types,[70] but his efforts and repeated assurances did little to assuage the fears of GQG or the politicians.

At this juncture, Georges Clemenceau became prime minister on 15 November and promptly injected further complexity into aviation organization. Decrees on 19 and 22 November made the undersecretary responsible to two heads, the Ministry of Armaments in production and the War Ministry in technical and military matters. A Central Service of Aviation Production (SCFA) in the Ministry of Armaments directed the SFA, while Clemenceau's air adviser, Colonel Dhé, who had been a cabinet officer under Painlevé and was a trusted associate of Pétain, became Director of Military Aeronautics in the War Ministry.[71]

On 21 November and 2 December Pétain vigorously protested this new organization on the grounds that its vague delineation of power and responsibilities would impede close liaison with the front and would fragment authority over the manufacturers. Now he too, like Duval, expected no improvement in aviation in 1918.[72] Duval believed that the reorganization would only aggravate the "very grave" aerial situation and the failures of the technical (STAé) and production (SFA) services. He attacked the STAé for its insistence on constant minor modifications and its failure to perfect designs and to complete definitive drawings for mass production and the SFA for its feeble authority over the manufacturers, its lack of liaison with the industrial service that furnished raw materials, and its general lack of foresight and overview.[73]

Although GQG's condemnations indicated a continuing penchant for blaming all problems on the rear bureaucracy, regardless of the efforts of undersecretaries like Vincent and Dumesnil to improve procurement, its objections to Clemenceau's new organization were well founded. On 19 December Colonel Dhé became director of the Central Service of Aviation Production as well as director of aeronautics. Dumesnil and armament minister Loucheur, who had called aviation "a very sick child" on 7 December, empowered Dhé to represent both the armaments ministry and the under-secretariat where their spheres of authority overlapped.[74] The crucial link now lay in Dhé's hands—and thus Clemenceau's—exactly where the old Tiger wanted all power to reside in his civilian dictatorship.

Resolving matters at the top, however, was easier than correcting deficiencies of production, and Dumesnil answered Duval's criticisms of the directorate on 6 December, reiterating his earlier statement that he sought to prepare aviation for a "preponderant and decisive role" in the spring of 1918. He reminded Duval that his actions since September would influence production next spring at the earliest, while their present circumstances stemmed from decisions made early in 1917 with the agreement of GQG, whose program modifications often delayed serial production. Aviation, because of its incessant progress, was in "a crisis of perpetual childbirth," and so some frontline materiel would always be obsolescent.

Dumesnil defended the STAé's repeated tests, likening them to the front's time to determine the value of new machines, and explained that shortages of duralumin and Renault engines had delayed Breguet deliveries, while GQG had decided definitively on the Salmson only on 28 November. Dumesnil expected that all single-seat fighter squadrons would comprise only Spads by spring 1918, but he offered no specific prospects for bomber development or for the two-seat fighter. He did plan to meet the demand for pilots and to achieve the 2,870-plane program six weeks ahead of time, on 15 February, and was aiming for a monthly production of 3,000 airframes and 6,000 engines by 1 July 1918.[75]

GQG's demands and condemnations of the rear were understandable. Yet while GQG could not understand the lengthy delay in receiving new planes, the STAé considered Duval's accusations of interminable tests exaggerated; the perfection of new types, completion of production drawings, and modifications for serial production were always time-consuming and complex processes.[76] In fact, the example of the Breguet 14 and its Renault 300-hp engine indicated that while duralumin and raw material had posed problems, the directorate's hesitation in committing to mass-produce the machine before Daniel Vincent's arrival was primarily responsible for the delay.[77]

The end of the year witnessed the formation of various committees to expedite procurement. An aviation committee comprising General Duval, Colonels Dhé and Dorand, and Dumesnil convened daily and met with aviation manufacturers to ascertain their raw material needs, set priorities, and standardize machines and parts. Dorand chaired a joint SFA-STAé commission that met monthly to study the reports of the frontline technical adjutants in order to determine and correct defects in assembly and materials. On 21 December the SCFA established a permanent commission to inspect airplanes from the SFA and repair workshops before delivery to the front.[78]

This ever-changing French bureaucracy also had to contend with waves of strikes at the end of May and again in September, led by the trade union of metalworkers and workers in automotive and aviation factories. The latter strike, starting on 11 September, spread across Paris, from Morane-Saulnier to Salmson and Farman and ultimately to Renault on 26 September. Some 32 aviation factories and 57,000 workers stopped production, and Minister of Armaments Loucheur had to meet with labor leaders to resolve the differences.[79]

Amid the turmoil of bureaucratic instability and labor unrest, the French aircraft industry produced 14,915 planes in 1917, as monthly aircraft manufacture rose from 846 in January to 1,576 in December. Production increased most between February and March, when it jumped from 832 to 1,225 following the appointment of Daniel Vincent as undersecretary. It continued to rise through the year, fluctuating slightly. Aero engine production increased from 1,579 in January to 2,715 in December. It fluctuated wildly through March, then rose steadily through August and rapidly thereafter, to total 23,092 for the year.[80]

The emphasis on limiting the number of types resulted in the concentrated production of Spads, Hispano-Suizas, and, late in the year, Breguets and Renaults. Gnome and Rhône produced some 7,000 engines with 5,000 workers in 1917, but after June almost all the Le Rhône engines produced, 7,188 110-hp rotaries, were replacements for Nieuport fighters or training engines, while the firm's difficulties in perfecting the new Gnome single-valve 150-hp engine limited its deliveries in 1917 to only 86 of the 4,000 ordered.[81] Renault's engine production declined from 3,680 in 1916 to 2,470 in 1917, during the transition to the 300-hp engine.[82] Yet as the front's complaints indicated, the problem stemmed not so much from the number of planes and engines produced as from the quality. The key to success lay in the perfection of the engines, particularly the Spad's Suiza 200- to 220-hp Hispano-Suiza.

Germany

In 1917 Germany countered its manpower and material shortages and the assaults of the Allies with continued total mobilization in the Hindenburg Program. On the Western Front the German army retreated to the fortifications of the Hindenburg Line in February and March to shorten its line of defense. The United States' entry into the war in April 1917 portended the further deterioration of Germany's circumstances, particularly in the air, and anticipation of a U.S. aerial onslaught combined with the Allies' mounting aerial supremacy on the Western Front to prompt further mobilization.

The German air force, like the army, continued a defensive strategy in the west. Early in 1917 Kogenluft ordered more and longer reconnaissance forays to prepare for the Allies' expected assaults. Outnumbered in the air as well as on the ground, the air arm husbanded its resources. The balloon observers, protected by fighters and antiaircraft, ranged their guns from behind their own lines. To get information of events behind the enemy front, lone reconnaissance craft flew high-altitude photographic missions over the lines.[83]

Starting in April, the Germans had to fend off French attacks on the Aisne and British attacks at Arras. Against the French attack at the Chemin des Dames on the Aisne, the Germans chose not to oppose French pursuits but fought only over their own lines, attacked French observation planes in small groups, and protected their own observation planes. A new aircraft-warning service in the antiaircraft units, which connected aircraft observation posts at the front to fighter units through a telephone center for each army corps, informed German units of approaching enemy aircraft and confirmed German victories. Distinctive markings helped the posts to identify aircraft and encouraged the fantastic array of color schemes on German fighter aircraft.

The Battle of Arras is usually associated with German fighter aviation in general and Manfred von Richthofen in particular. German fighter units covered the army's withdrawal to the Hindenburg Line and were at their peak when the British attacked. In January the Albatros D1 and D2 fighters accounted for some 67 percent of the fighters at the front, and by March 137 of the latest-model Albatros, the D3, had arrived.[84] The British attacked at Arras before their new generation of fighters—Sopwith triplanes and Camels, SE5s, and Bristol two-seaters—was available in any number. German fighter forces, organized into Jastas equipped with the Albatros and led by Richthofen, took a frightful toll of British airmen, who pressed their offensive patrols regardless of risk.

On the front, the Germans arrayed 195 planes, one-half of them fighters, against 365 British, one-third of them fighters, while the main German force of 480 planes initially remained on the Aisne against the French. The Germans had fewer than half the number of fighters—114 to 385—and all aircraft—264 to 754—of the British along their contiguous front in April.

They compensated for this inferiority by shooting down 151 British planes for losses of 66 of their own during "Bloody April."[85] The British official history concluded that German dominance demonstrated the importance of aircraft performance in gaining aerial supremacy and that an air offensive would not necessarily ensure local superiority against a determined and skillful enemy that was numerically weaker but better equipped.[86]

Richthofen, who was awarded the *pour le mérite* on 16 January, had 16 kills at the end of 1916. In January he left Jasta Boelcke to assume command of his own squadron, Jagdstaffel 11, at Douai. By April he had molded his squadron into a formidable fighting unit and had nearly doubled his number of victories, to 31, in his red Albatros D3. During April Jagdstaffel 11, presented with abundant targets, particularly undefended two-seaters, scored continually, among the victories the first Bristol two-seat fighters to reach the front. On 13 April Richthofen downed 3 planes to reach 43 victories, thus surpassing Boelcke; he amassed 21 victories that month, including 4 on 29 April, before he went on leave.

By the time Richthofen returned on 14 June, the air war was about to reach a new level of intensity with the Allied attacks in Flanders, first at Messines and then at Ypres. At Ypres between 31 July and 10 November, the Allies concentrated 840 planes, 350 of them fighters, against the Germans' 600, 200 of them fighters, in an aggressive aerial campaign.[87]

The British attack at Arras in April also witnessed the debut of "infantry fliers," who had evolved from the protection flights for army co-operation planes (Schutzstaffeln or Schustas). These battle fliers (Kampfflieger) or, as they preferred to be called, storm fliers (Sturmflieger), supported the infantry with machine guns and grenades. That summer the Schusta became an effective offensive and defensive weapon, attacking enemy batteries, strong points, and infantry reserves with machine gun fire and light fragmentation bombs. Captain Wilberg, commander of fliers of the Fourth Army in Flanders, introduced wireless telegraphy to direct operations over the battlefront. During the British attack at Messines on 6 to 14 June, despite Allied numerical aerial superiority, the German infantry fliers controlled the enemy breakthrough on the evening of the first day.[88]

The infantry fliers took high losses in their dangerous work, as they ranged over the front at 600 meters altitude, buffeted by the drafts of passing shells, and then descended to strafe British troops from 100 meters above the trenches, in the dead zone between the artillery fire from both sides. In these units only the commander was an officer. The crews were almost entirely noncommissioned officers and soldiers. Capt. Friedrich Ritter von Krausser, commander of Bavarian Schutzstaffel 23, recalled the fine spirit of his men, particularly one Swabian Sergeant Schaefer, who reported to him after one mission in blood-soaked pants. When Krausser observed that Schaefer needed to have his wound treated, the sergeant reached down, pulled a shrapnel ball from his knee with his dirty hands, and then refused to go to the hospital. Krausser had to take Schaefer himself, only to have the sergeant return early to continue flying above the *rue de merde*, or "shit street," as they called the front. On 20 September, when heavy rain and low cloud grounded other units, Schutzstaffel 23 flew alone under the low ceiling below 100 meters and returned with their planes so badly riddled that they were out of action for eight days until they received new ones.[89]

As the storm fliers asserted themselves over the battlefield, German fighter units found their task in the heavens above more difficult. In May and June the British, equipped with new fighters, began to regain the advantage. The German fighter force was ill-prepared to meet the challenge, its most modern plane being the D5, which was merely a lightened Albatros D3. On 23 June, in an attempt to offset Allied superiority by concentrating its forces, Kogenluft grouped four Jastas into Jagdeschwader 1 under Richthofen at Courtrai. The mobility of what would soon be called the Richthofen Circus enabled the unit's colorful planes to appear at key points at the front with unprecedented rapidity.

Richthofen had barely assumed command of JG1 when he was shot down on 6 July, wounded in the head from long range by an FE2 observer. While convalescing, he attested to the serious condition of German fighter forces in a letter of 18 July to his close friend, Lieutenant von Falkenhayn of the Kogenluft staff:

> I can assure you that it is no longer any fun being leader of a fighter unit at this army [Sixth Army]. . . . For the last three days the English have done as they please . . .
>
> Our airplanes are inferior to the English in a downright ridiculous manner. The triplane [Sopwith] and the two-hundred-horsepower Spad, like the Sopwith single-seater [Camel] play with our D5s. Besides better quality aircraft they have quantity. Our fighter pilots, though quite good, are consequently lost! The D5 is so antiquated and laughably inferior that we can do nothing with it.
>
> . . . [T]he English even have C-planes [Bristol fighters], thus two-seaters, that the Albatros is not capable of overtaking, that overtake it in a curve with the greatest of ease, against which one is simply powerless.
>
> You would not believe how low morale is among the fighter pilots presently at the front because of their sorry machines. No one wants to be a fighter pilot any more.[90]

Richthofen lamented that shooting down planes was becoming more difficult, an enervating and thankless task, and that 50 percent of fighter pilots were dead before they received recognition or medals; JG1 had lost eight pilots since Richthofen had fallen. He resumed command on 25 July, just before the British attack at Ypres.

At the end of August Richthofen and a youth who was probably Germany's most gifted flier, Lt. Werner Voss, commander of Jasta 14, received two of the first Fokker triplanes. Though the triplane lacked speed, its exceptional maneuverability would make it a deadly weapon in the hands of Richthofen or Voss. Richthofen left for convalescence leave with 60 kills on 6 September, while Voss rapidly amassed victories. On 23 September, after claiming his forty-eighth victim, Voss gave combat to seven SE5As of the 56th Squadron, the RFC's finest, led by ace James McCudden. In a truly epic encounter, he fought them for 10 minutes, putting bullets in all of their craft, before one of them, Arthur Rhys-Davids, managed to bring him down. Voss had "out-Englished" the English with his daring attack, and he paid with his life.

When Richthofen returned late in October, he had to revert to the D5 because the triplanes had been temporarily grounded when wing failure killed two aces within two days at the end of the month. At the end of the year the German fighter arm still relied primarily on the Albatros D5. Such difficulty notwithstanding, the circus, with 20 fighters in April, then 36 in July, and occasionally 72 in the fall, held its own, in part because of the stability of its leadership.

Rudolf Berthold commanded his own Jagdgeschwader in 1917, as he accumulated victories and wounds. On 24 April he was shot in the right lower leg, leaving his right arm his only uninjured limb. On 10 October, after his twenty-ninth kill, a bullet splintered the bone of his right upper arm. Promoted to captain on 4 November, he chose to return to combat rather than to wait for the arm to heal. If he was killed, he reasoned, healing was superfluous; if he survived, he would recuperate after the war. He returned to the front on 3 January 1918.[91]

German storm fliers were no less valiant in their efforts. The most noteworthy aerial aspect of the last major struggle of 1917, the Battle of Cambrai (20 November to 12 December), was the fliers' performance in the successful German counterattack on 30 November. Their effective strafes of the battlefield immediately in front of attacking infantry "caused many casualties and proved very demoralising" to British troops. According to the British official history, their attacks on British infantry in the front and rear trenches from altitudes lower than 100 feet were executed with "skill and daring" and were undeterred by ground fire. When the British counterattacked, German low fliers raked the ground in front of the attacking troops and directed artillery fire on them.[92]

Despite their extremely hazardous work, the storm fliers' esprit de corps remained high, fueled by their desire to help the hard-pressed infantry. Operating from forward airfields close to the front, they attacked in squadron or group strength to increase their effect, particularly on the enemy's morale. Armed with machine guns, grenades, and fragmentation bombs, they would often approach the front from behind enemy lines, swoop in low over the battlefield in organized fashion, and then range up and down the trenches repeatedly. They flew under bad weather at 100 meters and were occasionally the only means of communication for frontline infantry.[93] This was the air war at its grittiest, as these anonymous fliers from the ranks flew into massed machine gun and rifle fire from the ground to help their anonymous kin, the frontline infantry.

One of the reasons for the storm fliers' success was their aircraft. Beginning in the summer the Schutzstaffeln received the CL-types, Halberstadts and Hannoveranas, light, strong, and maneuverable two-seaters with a communal cockpit for better communication between pilot and observer. They also received AEG, Albatros, and Junkers' J1 armored infantry planes. Powered by the 200-hp Benz Bz4, the AEG and Albatros were modified C-types with 860 to 1,078 pounds of additional armor plate for the crew and engine compartments, while the Junkers was all metal and ideally suited to low-altitude operations. Aircrews praised the slow and ungainly Junkers Möbelwagen, or "furniture vans," for the absolute security they offered from machine gun fire from the ground. Though they were vulnerable to enemy fliers above, their operational altitude of 100 meters was too low for flak, which was ineffective under 200 meters.

German long-range reconnaissance crews also received superior aircraft. Top crews flew over the lines alone and at high altitude in high-performance machines, using their skill and the planes' ability to evade the enemy. At the beginning of 1917, they would climb to their operational ceilings of 15,000 feet behind German lines and do the reconnaissance at full speed, losing 6,000 feet on the way.[94] By the end of the year their planes were capable of 20,000-foot ceilings on such missions with little loss of altitude. Albatros C7s, DFW C5s, LVG C5s, Rumpler C4s and 7s enabled the best crews to hold their own even against the new British fighters. The aircraft firms steadily refined these types and equipped them with more powerful engines, the first three types with the Benz Bz4 200-hp engine and the Rumpler with the Maybach high-compression 240-hp engine.

British aces had a healthy respect for these two-seater crews, some of whom were formidable. Naval 8 squadron commander Johnstone found it difficult to attack LVG, Albatros, and Aviatik two-seaters successfully because of their performance at altitudes above 17,000 feet. In December DFW, LVG, and Rumpler two-seater crews proved challenging opponents even for ace James McCudden. McCudden's modified SE5A could reach 20,000 feet, where craft like the Rumpler, whose heavily cambered airfoil was far more efficient at high altitude than the SE5A's flat one, usually operated with impunity. In McCudden's accounts of combats with four two-seaters at high altitude, three escaped, while in an encounter at low altitude a lone DFW forced him to break off combat for fear of being shot down.[95] Billy Bishop's patrol of six once jumped a lone German two-seater, who turned in a flash, attacked them head-on, hitting Bishop and another member of his squadron, and escaped, earning Bishop's accolade a "very fine pilot and a very brave man."[96]

Although heavy losses in planes and crews in 1917 forced the air arm to send aviators to the front with less training and shortages were affecting the quality of materials in aircraft and engines, the best and most-experienced crews and their airplanes remained highly effective. German observers in particular were an elite, much better trained than their Allied counterparts. While pilot training took two months, observer training took three and was much more comprehensive. It cost less to produce pilots than observers, who seldom became pilots. Within the air arm, congenial relations reigned between commissioned and noncommissioned aircrew and between pilots and observers, nicknamed Emil and Franz, who formed a close-knit team.[97]

In 1917, as air support became essential to the successful prosecution of land combat, the air arm became an integral part of the army. Each division had a flight unit and, if possible, a battle unit; each corps headquarters had two flight units for reconnaissance and artillery observation; and each army headquarters had a flight unit for long-range reconnaissance and three special photographic planes, a flight unit for observation for long-range artillery, and a fighter wing or group.

The high command continued its strategic operations in 1917, but without the Zeppelin. In June the army abolished its airship service, turned its two large Zeppelins over to the navy, and transferred army airship crews either to the navy or to the tethered-balloon units at the front. Its weapon of choice had become the bomber, for in the fall of 1916 Kogenluft had decided to attack England in a bomber campaign named Turk's Cross.[98] The 36 Gotha bombers of Kampfgeschwader 3 commanded by Capt. Erich

Brandenburg, to be joined later by the R-planes of Unit 501, were to crush the island's will to fight by disrupting war industry, communications, and supply in southeastern England. The large Gothas (78-foot wingspan, 39-foot length) and huge R-planes (138-foot wing-span, 73-foot length) were prodigious feats of technology and industry in those early years. The first, powered by two Mercedes 260-hp engines, cruised at 80 mph, had a defensive armament of three machine guns, and was equipped with cylinders of compressed oxygen for the crew of three. The Staaken R6, the most-produced giant plane, was powered by four 245- to 260-horsepower engines, cruised at 80 mph, had a crew of seven to nine, and carried a defensive armament of up to six machine guns.

The raids began on 25 May and struck London on 13 June. Ironically, Captain Brandenburg was seriously injured in a crash as he returned from receiving the *pour le mérite*. In late summer, after two disastrous raids, the Germans shifted to night attacks. The R-planes began their attacks with individual sorties in September. In six raids on eight nights at the end of September, of a total of 92 Gothas taking off, 55 reached Britain and fewer than 20 reached London, for the loss of 13 Gothas. The British struck back by raiding the Gotha bases. Although Ludendorff supported the further development of a heavy bomber arm, Kogenluft rejected the plans of Brandenburg's successor, Capt. Rudolf Kleine, for large-scale raids on Britain and in the fall gave fighters priority in the allocation of materials. Kleine mounted two incendiary raids, on 31 October and 5 December, but the incendiaries failed to ignite and the raiders suffered serious losses to barrage fire or crashes upon landing. Kleine was killed in a daylight raid on British troop camps near Ypres on 12 December, but the raids on England continued.

Meanwhile, Naval Airship Commander Peter Strasser forged ahead with Zeppelins, buttressed by Adm. Reinhold Scheer's appreciation of the value of the airships as scouts.[99] Airship attacks on England, in Strasser's judgment, remained valuable because of their potential to disturb transport, cause dread, and draw British defenses home from the Western Front. On 17 January he recommended lightening the two-million-cubic-foot Zeppelin to achieve a 16,500-foot ceiling with war load. This type, the "v" class, or "height-climbers," as the British called them, appeared in August to raid Britain at altitudes of 16,000 to 20,000 feet. The ships were too lightly built for full-speed maneuvers at low altitude, and above 15,000 feet navigation was more difficult, northerly gales raged that were undetectable at lower altitudes, and crews suffered from the cold and oxygen deprivation. Four abortive or ineffective raids in March through September were compounded by the loss of 2 Zeppelins on reconnaissance missions to British flying boats in May and June. In what became the last big Zeppelin attack of the war, on 19 October, 5 of 11 Zeppelins were lost, scattered all over western Europe from their bases to Thuringia to the French Riviera. Yet Strasser refused to yield. The naval airship command received its first Zeppelin equipped with new Maybach high altitude engines early in November, and in December Strasser ordered an even larger Zeppelin with seven engines and a volume of some 2.19 million cubic feet. At a time of increasingly scarce resources, the German armed forces thus waged two uncoordinated strategic campaigns against Britain, the army with airplanes and the navy with airships—neither with decisive success.

Naval aircraft development concentrated on two types—a fighter and a multi-engine seaplane. Naval agencies, pressed by raw material and industrial shortages, dropped their few single-seat floatplanes in September in favor of Ernst Heinkel's Hansa-Brandenburg W12 two-seat twin-float monoplane, as fast and maneuverable as a single-seater, though larger and heavier. In the hands of such accomplished pilots as Lt. Friedrich Christiansen, commander of Seaplane Unit 1 at Zeebrugge, the W12 took command of the air from the English over the Flanders coast from Zeebrugge to Ostende.[100] When Curtiss flying boats appeared in force over the North Sea in the summer, the Heinkel floatplanes would fly out to sea, alight to save fuel, and rise to attack them. In these encounters Christiansen earned the *pour le mérite* on his thirty-eighth birthday in December 1917.

The navy had far less success with multi-engine aircraft, because of the technological difficulty of setting giant craft on floats and because of disagreements among naval aviation agencies on the merits of the various types of large aircraft. Early in 1917 the Chief of the Admiralty Staff wanted torpedo planes; the Chief of Naval Flight Units, R-planes. Gotha and Brandenburg T-planes proved underpowered, although the Gothas were produced in small numbers to the end of the war. R-planes remained a subject of debate primarily among naval aviation agencies, which considered them either essential or too difficult to build. Staaken sought to set its R-planes on duralumin floats, and Zeppelin Lindau designer Claudius Dornier's third metal-flying-boat design won a naval contract in April 1917.

In the rear the total mobilization begun in the Hindenburg Program continued. The factories delivered 900 aircraft in September 1917, advancing rapidly toward the Hindenburg Program's spring 1918 production goal of 1,000 planes monthly, but the winter's coal and material shortage and transportation crisis sent deliveries plummeting to 400 aircraft in January.

The aviation inspectorate, under Maj. Wilhelm Siegert, responded with a flurry of activity.

The inspectorate concentrated on reorganizing its procurement bureaucracy and the aircraft industry and then coordinating procurement. In January 1917 it reorganized its aircraft depot under Maj. Felix Wagenführ and established an R-plane command to monitor the growing number of firms manufacturing the giant bombers. The two most noteworthy features of the new depot were its Scientific Information Bureau (Wissenschaftliche Auskunftei für Flugwesen, or WAF) and its department for evaluating captured aircraft.

Under the direction of Lt. Wilhelm Hoff (Res.), the WAF sought to coordinate all efforts in aviation science and to disseminate aeronautical information to the inspectorate, the Imperial Naval Office, research institutes, individual scientists and aircraft firms. Unfortunately Hoff neglected aircraft engines until late 1917. The department evaluating captured aircraft distributed its findings to the German industry and aviation press, and the captured aircraft also served as propaganda, displayed in a prize hall in Berlin.

In response to widespread manufacturers' complaints about material shortages, Siegert insisted in January 1917 that the War Trade Association of the German Aircraft Industry (Kriegsverband der deutschen Flugzeugindustrie) be formed. By centralizing material procurement, he ultimately forced the syndication of the industry, as all the large companies joined to ensure material supplies and contracts. The association also agreed to place its members' research at the WAF's disposal and to establish a commission to set standards for aircraft parts. The war association thus further centralized aviation procurement, science, and technology.

After the formation of the War Trade Association, the inspectorate unleashed a barrage of orders intended to coordinate the efforts of army and aircraft industry contractors and subcontractors to increase deliveries. On 12 January the inspectorate announced plans to centralize all material procurement for the industry—for example, contracting with one firm for the production of all the sheet brass. Such coordination was not always successful: in early April the depot advised factories to send their airplane linen, unpainted and bleached, to one cotton factory for painting, only to rescind the order two weeks later because German railways were already overtaxed.

The inspectorate was further determined to rationalize the industry's work methods and to match aircraft firms with prospective subcontractors. On 24 March Wagenführ instructed the construction inspectorates to avoid "absolutely" every "illogical" relationship (such as pairing north German subcontractors and south German factories) and to include the many capable metalworking and woodworking factories that were without contracts. He further instructed the aircraft industry to simplify work methods to save material and increase profits. The implementation of mass-production methods would improve licensed production, solving the problem of parts made by different licensed producers for the same craft still not being interchangeable.

Wagenführ prodded the manufacturers to maximize production, admonished them not to undertake more contracts than they could actually deliver, and chided them for competing with each other for designers, insisting that he be allowed to determine if their job changes were in the interest of the military.

By April the inspectorate had formulated a list of firms that would receive prior consideration in materials allocation and an aircraft and motor construction schedule prescribing optimum production for each factory. Factories performing well were assured of contracts and possible increases in orders; others would have their quotas reduced and contracts given to other factories. In order to prevent delays in engine deliveries from affecting aircraft production, every tenth C- and D-plane would be delivered without an engine.

Increased standardization, licensed production, and exchanges of vital information encouraged further military control over patent law. In 1916 the War Ministry's experts in the patent office prevented the publication of certain patents and then refused to discuss license fees or indemnities with the inventors on the grounds that they had no rights until the patent was published. After numerous complaints, on 8 February 1917 the Imperial Council (Bundesrat) modified aviation patent law to enable the patent office to place unpublished patents on the war rolls and distribute them only to the army and navy if the armed services deemed them in the interests of national defense. There were now two classifications of patents: those with war worth, which could be distributed without publication, and those without war worth, to be distributed after publication and protection of the inventor's interests. The first category entailed no public notice or claims proceedings and practically ensured the annulment of later claims. The new ruling had increased the War Ministry's power to regulate patent matters and legalized the military's arbitrary patent measures, allowing it to ignore patent law and civil courts for the last two years of the war.

The army could increasingly interfere in and control the affairs of the aircraft industry, but its policies either exacerbated or could not cure the materials and labor shortages, the consequent inflationary spiral of raw material prices and wages, and the transportation delays resulting from the deterioration of rail service.

At the expense of making the inflation worse, the War Ministry ensured aircraft workers' superior wages and demonstrated the army's continued appreciation of the importance and special nature of the airplane and aviation industry. On 9 March, however, the high command insisted that wage increases be slowed because they caused strikes and were detrimental to troop morale. In April 1917 workers in the aircraft industry in Berlin, including some 5,000 from AEG's Hennigsdorff aircraft works, and 2,000 at Staaken Luftschiffbau's R-plane factory, played prominent roles in a wave of strikes. Contrary to the high command's belief, the aircraft workers probably struck despite, not because of, their wage increases, as the general conditions of insufficient food rations and inflation provided sufficient cause.

The Hindenburg Program exacerbated Germany's raw material shortage. The high placement of the aviation industry on priority lists could not protect it from rising prices. The average price of 63 raw materials essential to aircraft production rose, from August 1914, 98.7 percent to 1 October 1916, 148 percent to 1 December 1916, 184 percent to 1 January 1917, and 232 percent to 1 July 1917. Subcontractors and large metal suppliers were late with deliveries and refused to guarantee their products because of the poor quality of raw materials. Aircraft prices spiraled upwards. A twin-engine G-plane ordered in October 1916 for April 1917 cost between 38,000 and 41,000 marks on order and between 75,000 and 85,000 marks upon delivery—in May or later.

The new air force bureaucracy failed to halt the conflicts that had previously impaired the efficiency of aviation mobilization. Particularism's effect on mobilization was complex, indissolubly linked with other factors, such as different regional levels of industrialization, tensions between the demands of the front and those of the rear, the effect of exemptions and female labor on production quality, and the problems of establishing branch factories of major Berlin firms in other areas of the empire. Because of a relatively high level of industrialization, for example, Württemberg had a surfeit of skilled workers, yet the Swabian War Ministry was reluctant to release its citizens to work elsewhere. Instead of sending more workers to Staaken, near Berlin, for R-plane construction, the ministry kept them in the state, at Flugzeugbau Friedrichshafen, on Lake Constance.

Prussia, Bavaria, and the Bavarian Aircraft Works (BFW) factory, which built Albatros aircraft under license, provided the best example of the impact of particularism. In February 1917, when the Prussian aviation inspectorate complained to the Bavarian construction inspectorate that monitored BFW's production about fatal crashes resulting from poor work-manship, BFW's director attributed the problems to the excessive induction of factory's male skilled workers and their replacement by female labor un-trained in the handicraft techniques of aircraft construction. On 3 March 1917 Kogenluft telegraphed the Bavarian War Ministry about the matter and threatened peremptorily to ban BFW aircraft unless the Prussian in-spectorate controlled the surveillance of the factory. The Bavarian war min-ister was convinced that Kogenluft was using the threat of closing BFW to eliminate Bavarian agencies from aircraft procurement. After securing an apology from general headquarters, he removed the construction inspec-torate's chairman and formulated new exemption guidelines similar to those of the high command to bring the composition of BFW's labor force more in line with that of north German factories. He refused, however, to sub-ordinate the construction inspectorate to the Prussian inspectorate.

Ultimately, progress in fighter development and overall production would determine the success of the Hindenburg Program in aviation. The evolution of the fighter illustrates the benefits and dangers of standardization and of the use of information gleaned from the evaluation of enemy aircraft, two techniques that the aviation inspectorate emphasized in its mobilization of the industry.

The Albatros D3 replicated the wing design of the French Nieuport in fall 1916. Like the Nieuport, recurrent lower-wing failures plagued its service, until the lower wing was strengthened in April and May 1917. The D3 enjoyed a long career—with some still serving in 1918—because the German air force and aircraft industry were slow to develop a better fighter. Given the inferiority of other fighters available in early 1917, Bloody April amply demonstrated the wisdom of reliance on the Albatros. Yet a com-placent aviation inspectorate had undertaken little developmental work in the nine months since the introduction of the Albatros biplanes. Albatros's successor for the D3 in April 1917, the D5, was a lightened D3 airframe on which the aircraft depot had tested only the fuselage and rudder, al-though the fuselage-wing interface differed from that of the D3. The omis-sion proved fatal. When the D5 reached the front in May 1917, wing fail-ures began immediately. Nevertheless, with no better aircraft, the aviation inspectorate ordered 200 D5s in April, 400 in May, and held out the pros-pect of contracts for 1,500 D-planes to Albatros over the next six months.

The final criterion of the Hindenburg Program's success was whether monthly production attained the 1,000 mark by the spring and the air ser-vice was able to increase its complement of airplanes by 500. Alex Imrie's work on the air service mentions that as of the summer of 1917, the fall 1916 program had not been completed, while Hilmer von Bülow, writing in the early 1930s, concluded that despite immense difficulties, the "great program was successfully carried out almost completely through the early year of 1917."

One German military history of the war credits the German air arm with 2,271 airplanes early in 1917, which would mean the program's success. Yet these figures, if correct, are quite amazing, because the aircraft industry did not attain its production goals. In January the factories delivered only 400 planes, while production may have dropped to only some 260 planes in February. Production figures for March and April are lacking, but official production deliveries from May through September were 789, 1,012, 731, 927, and 915 airplanes. Production reached the 1,000 mark only once. Under such conditions, the air service could have reached the program's stipulated frontline strength only by sacrificing the production of training planes or depleting its aircraft reserve, expedients that it frequently used later in the war.

The aviation mobilization of the Hindenburg Program had thus only partially succeeded. The air service did increase its effective strength, but shortages, which organizational measures could at best only mitigate, prevented the industry from meeting its production goals. Requested exemptions of some 3,500 skilled workers for the entire aviation industry were probably insufficient to achieve intended production increases. Finally, and most critically, the air force's lapse in fighter development and its apparent mortgaging of the future for the present were premature at a time when the army had no plans for winning the war on the Western Front. When the panacea of the submarine failed to win the war, the air force was doomed to face the Allies at a severe disadvantage numerically and, in fighter planes, qualitatively, during the second half of 1917.

In the spring, as Germany struggled against heavy British and French attacks, Ludendorff proceeded to plan a great German offensive to win the war in the spring of 1918, before U.S. might fell on Germany. An enlarged air force was essential to his success, so on 3 June Kogenluft and the aviation inspectorate met to discuss a new expansion plan, the America Program. While the absence of a U.S. aircraft industry would prevent a rapid buildup of U.S. squadrons, they anticipated that the United States would send engineers, businessmen, and even workers to raise the Allies' industrial capacity, which would in turn help to develop an U.S. aircraft industry. By early 1918, Kogenluft concluded, Germany could expect greatly increased aerial opposition over the Western Front. Within a week, Ludendorff endorsed Kogenluft's expansion plan and set it before the Prussian War Ministry on 25 June 1917:

> America's entry into the war compels a considerable strengthening of the air force by 1 March 1918. In order to be somewhat equal to the combined English-French-American air fleet, I order the formation of an absolute minimum of forty new fighter groups (Jagdstaffeln 41–80) and seventeen new flight units (Fliegerabteilungen 184–200).

The aim of monthly production of 2,000 planes and 2,500 engines by January 1918 would necessitate the allotment of 2,000 men for the aircraft factories and 5,000 for the engine factories by 1 December 1917 and priority in raw material allocation second only to the submarine manufacturers, with special consideration in the allotment of aluminum.

To the War Office Ludendorff insisted on the complete fulfillment of the program, which he considered of extraordinary importance, even if the task required the "use of the last reserves." Yet as early as 19 July, the War Ministry advised that fulfillment of the program would seriously impair other armaments production and suggested a reduction of monthly production goals to 1,600 planes and 1,800 engines. The high command allowed the latter figures to stand, while striving for the original limit, and informed Kogenluft on 25 July that "a certainty of fulfilling the America Program completely no longer exists in our economic situation."

The Bavarian and Austro-Hungarian representatives at the inspectorate believed that a "ruthless" use of the factories would enable the program to overcome raw material shortages, the dispersal of engine production in small factories, and the "surprisingly small" number of workers requested. Maj. Wilhelm Siegert moved ruthlessly to the task. On 31 July he issued to the aviation industry a rousing dual challenge—from the U.S. aircraft industry and the German frontline troops—that showed a willingness to disregard all but military considerations in the execution of the America Program. Most essentially he insisted upon the industry's complete and unquestioning participation in the War Trade Association and its subordination to a single will—his own—as he contended that shortages necessitated a system of rationing and allocation in order for Germany to continue the struggle.

Yet no single agency, including the War Office, could set a coherent price policy or resolve wasteful conflicts over procurement among various service and state agencies, so raw material prices continued to rise rapidly as new procurement programs made additional demands on already limited reserves. With no laws that forced firms to abide by military regulations, the indispensable aircraft engine companies refused to submit detailed information of their production costs to procurement agencies for profit and price checks. The industry's resistance to rationing assumed significant proportions by the late fall of 1917. Firms were hoarding gasoline, spare parts, and materials, responding to the controls and shortages by circumventing the former, thus exacerbating the latter.

The air service's fuel allotment, instead of doubling to 12,000 tons, plummeted in November to 1,000. The aircraft industry could not receive its demands for metals, rubber, and coal without severely damaging the rest of the armaments industry. Disaster compounded the problems, when in November, fire totally destroyed the North German Aircraft Works in Teltow, and the flooding of the Dillinger foundry interrupted the supply of armor plate for Junkers all-metal airplanes.

Perhaps the ultimate example of military intervention was the inspectorate's arrangement in October, after 10 months of negotiations, for the formation of the Junkers-Fokker Works in Dessau with a capital of 2.6 million marks. The partnership sought to couple Junkers's technical abilities with Fokker's flying and mass-production experience in the manufacture of the Junkers armored biplane. Although Junkers considered Fokker a wily, ruthless, and ambitious—if capable—competitor and resented the army's pressure to bind him to Fokker, his personal fortune was at stake and he ultimately succumbed.

While the J-plane entered serial production, Junkers continued development of a low-winged monoplane, substituting duralumin for steel and finishing a single-seater in September and a two-seater in December. Two naval fighter aces, Theo Osterkamp and Gotthard Sachsenberg, were quite impressed with the single-seater. The thick wing of Junkers's metal planes required no external bracing and thus reduced resistance and required less fuel and engine horsepower.

In the America Program, Kogenluft focused on the Bavarian aircraft industry and fighter development, which offered better possibilities for significant increases in production than north German factories. Prussian authorities consequently abandoned their efforts to gain control of the Bavarian administration and allotted proportionately more labor to it. From the beginning of the program in June to October, production rose steadily as the industry grew. Fighter producer Pfalz's labor force, for example, rose from 835 to 1,370. Winter weather and materials shortages, however, halted further progress.

Of Kogenluft's recommendations to the inspectorate on aircraft and engine development in the America Program, the most significant was development of a new fighter. Richthofen suggested on 18 July that replacement of the "lousy" Albatros was long overdue:

> We must unconditionally support and use every firm that produces a type merely somewhat better than this damn Albatros. As long as Albatros encounters no energetic competition, we will remain sitting in our D3s (D5s).
>
> What's going on with Fokker? He has two machines that are superior to the Albatros, and neither has been produced. There is his unbraced biplane with the stationary engine. It is unquestionably faster and has better qualities in the curve than the Albatros D5, and yet is not built. I believe Schwarzenberger [official of the aviation inspectorate] is behind this.
>
> Furthermore, he [Fokker] has a triplane that is certainly no longer in the formative stages and has already shown exceptional climb and speed, that must be unreservedly supported and sent to the front in large numbers as soon as we have rotary engines.

The inspectorate was well aware of the D5's shortcomings, describing the plane on 24 July as merely a lightened D3 whose performance was not sufficiently improved to warrant its production. Yet produce it they did; the parts and subcontractors were available, and D5 orders increased to more than 1,000 in October from Albatros's Johannisthal and Schneidemühl factories.

Richthofen, who was convinced that the solution to German fighter inferiority lay with Fokker's triplane, had shown Fokker a captured Sopwith triplane at the front in April 1917 before sending it to the inspectorate. Fokker instructed his chief designer, Reinhold Platz, to design a triplane using a rotary engine. The inspectorate had a supply of captured 110-hp Le Rhônes, while Fokker had a controlling interest in the German rotary engine firm Oberursel. After test flights in July demonstrated amazing maneuverability, the inspectorate ordered 320 Fokker Dr1s without awaiting the final results of its structural tests.

The army air service officially accepted the Fokker triplane after its structural tests. Its fame ascended meteorically with Richthofen and Werner Voss, but after crashes in October, an investigative commission found evidence of faulty workmanship in the wings and limited its use. The monthlong restrictions severely disrupted production, and instead of the 173 triplanes scheduled to be in service by December, only some 30 arrived. Other than the triplane and the Albatros, the German air arm had only the Pfalz D3, which began service in Bavarian units in the fall. Pilots, however, tended to prefer the Albatros. Pfalz's superb wood construction did not warrant duplication because it took longer than welded-steel frames, produced heavier fuselages, and required woodworking skills that were unavailable to other manufacturers.

By then Richthofen was interested in securing Fokker's "unbraced biplane with the stationary engine." At Richthofen's insistence, Lt. Konrad Krefft, the Richthofen squadron's technical officer, assembled the fighter leaders to petition for an open competition among all German factories for fighter prototypes. Fourteen days later Kogenluft agreed to the pilots' request and stipulated that the Mercedes 160-hp engine would be available to all entrants at a January competition at the Adlershof inspectorate.

Fighter development during the America Program to the end of 1917 was thus quite uneven, with the reliance on the obsolescent Albatros, the appearance of the Fokker triplane, and by the end of the year, the increasing role of the fighter pilots in the selection process. It depended on the outcome of a struggle between two informal alliances—the inspectorate and Albatros on the one hand and Richthofen and Fokker on the other. The inspectorate supported Albatros too long, probably because of Fokker's previous shoddy construction and a reluctance to disrupt mass production. Richthofen was instrumental in the evolution of the triplane and in securing for the fighter pilots a formal role in type selection, hitherto the prerogative of the aviation inspectorate. Richthofen's belief that there was a conspiracy in the inspectorate to prolong the Albatros monopoly and ruin Fokker at the pilots' expense provoked him to quick and effective action, as he mobilized the fighter pilots and approached Kogenluft directly with his plea for open competition. Richthofen, whose maneuvering shows a touch of the politician, emerges as a worthy successor to Boelcke. For him the responsibilities of command went beyond frontline service; they encompassed securing the best materiel possible for German fighter pilots.

The course of the America Program's fighter development illustrates that significant technological advances in aviation could not be created on command. The major types that came to fruition in the latter half of 1917— the two-seat attack fighter and the long-range bomber—were the products of gestation that antedated the America Program and even the Hindenburg Program. The CL-type—light, maneuverable, fast two-seaters used in attack and fighter roles—had been designed to meet an inspectorate specification of September 1916. The Halberstadt CL2 entered service in the summer of 1917; the Hannover CL2, the first design of the Hannoversche Waggonfabrik, in the fall.

Kogenluft's planned expansion of the bomber arm to 104 planes in the Hindenburg Program coincided with the production of the Gotha G4, the first plane capable of bombing England. Material shortages, transportation crises, and unsatisfactory tests of the first production model delayed the arrival of the first Gotha G4s until March, in time for the raids to begin on 25 May 1917. The R6, the only giant bomber to enter serial production, was the product of the Zeppelin works at Staaken and the inspectorate's efforts. Beginning in June, 18 were built—4 by the parent firm, 6 by Aviatik, 5 by Schütte-Lanz, and 3 by the east German Albatros works.

The America Program also entailed the development of new engine types and the expansion of the engine industry. The War Ministry and the aviation inspectorate had clung to the six-cylinder in-line, their major prewar aims of improved reliability and lower fuel consumption essentially unchanged. Authorities on aero engines acknowledged that the German engine industry's limited capacity encouraged the concentration on six-cylinder engines of 150 to 250 horsepower, but they believed that German firms could have made the transition to V engines if they had had the inspectorate's support.[101] When the Hispano-Suiza's appearance prompted consideration of the development of similar engines, it was already too late, because it took one and a half to two years to ready any engine for the front. The War Ministry and the inspectorate only belatedly moved beyond the original four engine firms, adding Opel at the end of 1916 as a first step to alleviate the growing engine shortage.[102]

At least the army did reconsider proposals from firms for high-altitude, high-compression engines, which it had earlier rejected on the grounds that the throttle arrangements preventing such engines from running at full power at low altitude were too complicated for service pilots. Maybach's work on Zeppelin engines culminated in the high-altitude 250-hp MB4a, the first high-compression engine able to be mass-produced. Though too large for fighters, it enabled Rumpler C6 and C7 long-range reconnaissance planes to operate at 20,000 feet and powered G- and R-planes and the last 14 five- to seven-engine military airships, the height-climbers. Benz and Daimler modified their successful six-cylinder in-lines into high-compression engines with throttle controls. In January 1917 former Daimler designer Max Friz began development of a high-compression engine at the Rapp engine works in Munich. In July Rapp became the Bavarian Motor Works (BMW), in September the BMW3a ran on the test stand, and the new firm's director, F. J. Popp, persuaded the inspectorate to allow it to produce the new engine. [103]

In rotary engine development, the Oberursel's nine-cylinder 120- and 145-hp versions passed their tests in 1917, although inadequate numbers of the latter engine meant that in 1918 Swedish Thulins (Le Rhône copies) and captured Le Rhône and Clerget engines would be used in German rotary-engine craft. Siemens Halske introduced a nine-cylinder geared rotary in which the crankcase and crankshaft rotated in opposite directions at the same speed for its D1 fighter, but both the engine and the plane required much further work. [104]

Demand for engines during the Hindenburg and the America programs rose faster than production. The shortage of skilled workers made it difficult to expand factories, although 9 factories began aero engine production in 1917, raising the total number of factories to 13. Production started at 619 engines in January and peaked in November at 1,307, but in early and late 1917 coal, raw material, and transport shortages resulted in production bottlenecks. During the year workers at Daimler and Benz refused to work a 12-hour day and 12-hour night shifts and engaged in work stoppages and sitdown strikes. Engine production in 1917 totaled 12,029; aircraft production, 13,977. The imbalance was crucial, as air arms required more engines than they did airframes, although the reliability and long service of German in-lines partially compensated for the shortage. [105]

These difficulties notwithstanding, by the end of 1917 the America Program, the climax of German industrial mobilization in aviation, focused all efforts on the great offensive planned for spring 1918, in order to bring the war to a victorious conclusion before the full weight of the United States fell upon the Central Powers.

England

In the war on the Western Front, the British staged four attacks in 1917, at Arras in April, Messines in June, Ypres in July, and Cambrai in November. RFC Headquarters reiterated in March the importance of gaining aerial ascendancy through offensive action and seeking out and destroying the enemy force—the guiding principle of air, land, and sea combat. Trenchard anticipated German aggressiveness in spring 1917, and although unable to secure enough up-to-date fighters, he nevertheless decided to counter with a more vigorous offensive, since air operations were essential to British success at Arras. In the belief that the "moral" effect on enemy troops far exceeded the considerable material damage that it could inflict, RFC head-quarters planned to thrust offensive patrols farther behind the enemy front to raid supply and troop collection points. [106]

Yet even as Trenchard prepared to step up his offensive, he reported to General Henderson on the rapidly growing German air strength. On 12 February increasing numbers of superior German planes "completely out-classed" British planes and threatened to drive them behind their own lines. In March still greater concentrations of German planes caused serious British losses. For only four aerial victories the British had lost 27 officers killed, wounded, or missing on 9 March and a total of 48 officers in two days. At the end of the first week in April Trenchard reported that they were "getting on top of the Huns," with 25 victories for 20 casualties, [107] but in fact the British had achieved no such victory tally and were entering the worst month of their air war.

At the Battle of Arras, which lasted from 9 April to 17 May, the RFC arrayed 365 aircraft, one-third of them fighters, against 195 German aircraft, one-half of them fighters. In April this smaller German aerial contingent, equipped with superior fighter aircraft, took a heavy toll of insufficiently trained British aircrews in obsolescent aircraft. [108]

British artillery spotting machines suffered heavy casualties from lack of fighter escort, while the fighter squadrons themselves took a beating. Two Nieuport squadrons, numbers 29 and 60, stationed at Izel le Hameau opposite Richthofen's Jasta 11 at Douai, lost more than 100 percent of their flying strength in April, with a total of 27 killed, missing, or taken prisoner, and 4 wounded and injured in crashes. Canadian Billy Bishop, who had arrived at the 60th Squadron in March with an unusually high 75 hours' flying time, emerged as the 60th Squadron's ace during this time, but over-all the picture was bleak. The British fought on, sustained by the erroneous belief that their toll of Germans exceeded their losses, when in fact the Germans, who kept a rigorous accounting of their own casualties and victories, accounted for 176 British planes in the Sixth Army area at Arras between 31 March and 3 May for losses of only 21 killed, 15 wounded, and 4 missing. British casualties rose to an all-time high. In the four-week period ending on 27 April, the RFC lost 238 killed or missing and 105 wounded, and the pilots' average flying hours before falling casualty diminished from 295 in August 1916 to 92 in April 1917. [109]

Some British aircrew had the misfortune to be transitioning into new planes during the battle. In the first sortie of the two-seat Bristol fighters of the 48th Squadron, its commander, Zeppelin killer Capt. William Leefe-Robinson, a Victoria Cross winner, and his entire five-plane patrol fell victim to the Albatrosses of Richthofen's squadron. The Bristol crews, unfamiliar with a plane that they feared was structurally weak, flew it like a two-seat reconnaissance plane. In time they would learn that this two-seater was superior to most single-seat fighters if flown aggressively, with the gunner merely to protect the tail and not as the main armament. Frequent gun stoppages with the new Constantinesco synchronizing gear on SE5s frustrated the pilots of 56 Squadron, while the RE8, the Royal Aircraft Factory's successor to the BE2, gained an evil reputation for crashing frequently in flames and spent the winter and spring "under a cloud."[110]

The RFC's offensive efforts did impress BEF commander Douglas Haig, who informed the War Office on 18 May that the success of the artillery and infantry depended largely on the efficiency of the RFC's artillery, photographic, and contact patrols, whose protection in turn depended on fighter squadrons equipped with sufficient superior machines to seek out and destroy enemy fighters in a sustained, vigorous offensive. Haig wanted the RFC to have at least two fighters for each artillery plane, to increase corps squadrons from 18 to 24 planes, and to have new units before the end of the year to prepare for spring 1918.[111] The number of army cooperation squadrons peaked in spring 1917, and the demand for fighting aircraft absorbed all production increases for the rest of the war.[112]

In the limited siege operation at Messines (7 to 14 June), air-artillery cooperation reached its peak in preparation for the battle, and both sides intercepted the other's air-ground wireless transmissions to locate enemy targets. British fighters provided continuous cover for army corps planes and sought to keep the enemy behind their own stationary observation-balloon line six miles behind the front. In June the shortage of reserves impeded the RFC's continuous offensive, and Trenchard's determination to make all patrols offensive fighting efforts without concentrating his force undermined the attack's effectiveness. At least by July, 37 of his 51 squadrons, as opposed to 22 of 51 in May, were equipped with new types, just in time for the climactic attack at Ypres.[113]

Before the Battle of Ypres (31 July to 10 November) the RFC once again sought to keep the Germans behind their balloon line. In the assault on 31 July, the weather and poor communication with ground units limited the RFC's artillery cooperation, photoreconnaissance, and contact patrols. The offensive army wing squadrons staged random, uncoordinated strafing attacks on the German rear but failed to check for German units advancing to counterattack.[114]

In August and October memoranda on air policy, RFC headquarters continued to preach the offensive, noting that since early 1916 the evolution of air fighting, the main task of the army (offensive) wings and the head-quarters wing, had determined RFC expansion. It relegated reconnaissance to an increasingly minor role and did not even discuss the corps squadrons' crucial responsibilities of infantry cooperation and contact patrols. The memorandum of 12 October, echoing Haig's of 18 May, sought two fighters for every corps squadron and then suggested 30 squadrons of long-range bombers with Bristol fighter escort in 1918.[115] British fighters, following the German lead, operated in units of ever larger size. By the end of August formations functioned in three layers, and as many as 60 machines engaged in lengthy skirmishes.[116]

Casualties were high during the summer. The RFC lost 434 officers in the 50 days from 31 July to 19 September. In mid-1917 it assumed the following aircrew "wastage": The life of a night bomber or corps pilot was 4 months; of fighter reconnaissance and bomber pilots, 3½ months; and of a fighter pilot, 2½ months.[117] By August, overtaxed aircrew suffered serious morale problems, as RFC brigade commanders added ground support tasks to Trenchard's constant offensive patrols. Though most squadrons stayed the course, not all did. On 28 September, Naval 10, ordered to bomb and strafe Rumbeke airfield at low level, did not descend below 300 feet. When ordered to repeat the mission, the commander informed Wing Command that the squadron was "not for it," a direct disobedience of orders that led to the squadron's transfer to the Fourth Wing RNAS at Dunkirk. Yet the worst was already past, as the RFC was gaining aerial ascendancy over the Germans, and its losses fell to 247 in the 60 days before the Battle of Cambrai, from 20 September to 20 November.[118]

Haig, in correspondence to the Army Council on 20 November, the day the Battle of Cambrai began, continued his support for further development of the RFC. Noting that he had 54 squadrons with 997 planes—compared with 52 with 794 planes on 5 June and 39 with 717 planes on 8 January—he assumed completion of the December 1916 program of 86 squadrons in June 1918. Most critically, he required 20 fighter squadrons and 10 long-range bombing squadrons to make up the deficit. For the summer of 1919 he would need 113 squadrons of 24 planes each for the front and 66 bomber and long-range fighter squadrons for strategic operations.[119]

At the Battle of Cambrai, which lasted from 20 November to 7 December, the British dispensed with a preliminary bombardment in order to surprise the Germans; the RFC planned to locate enemy batteries and bomb and strafe from low altitude during the attack. The day of the attack, however, misty weather limited air operations and prevented artillery cooperation, so the RFC repeated its roving ground attacks of Ypres. Its low-level missions suffered high casualties, as four scout squadrons assigned to ground attack lost 26 of 72 aircraft (35.5 percent), with 14 officers dead, missing, or wounded. On 22 November low-flying single-seaters suffered 40 percent aircraft losses, and the next day, with better weather, more than 30 percent casualties in combat against the Richthofen Circus. The RFC finished this difficult period by failing to detect the concentration of German troops for a counterattack on 30 November, when the Germans unleashed masses of low-flying aircraft in coordinated attacks immediately in front of their infantry that "caused many casualties and proved very demoralising." In contrast to the success of the German ground attack planes, British attacks at the beginning of the battle had been too diffuse, with excessive casualties. [120]

As this last major battle of 1917 raged, RFC headquarters advised its brigade commanders on 28 November to husband their resources and train crews for the spring 1918 campaign. They were to maintain 10 serviceable machines per squadron, reduce work over the lines to the absolute minimum necessary for training and operations, and refrain from operations in bad weather. New pilots being prepared for combat were not to cross the line for three weeks. [121]

At the end of the year the artillery and the RFC were concerned about inadequate communications, continuity among experts, and standardized procedures, as the quality of cooperation had declined from the level of Messines. Peter Mead, authority on British air observation, contended that Trenchard had avoided the mistake of making aerial fighting an end in itself instead of the means to the end of protecting observation craft. [122] In fact, air fighting had become the main goal of two-thirds of the RFC, while the corps squadrons were overburdened with many duties—artillery observation, contact and photographic patrols, bombing and ground strafing, infantry protection, even leaflet dropping.

Veterans of the 1917 campaign, some of them squadron commanders who later rose to air marshal's rank, have severely criticized RFC policies during the spring and summer. Joubert considered the RFC attempt to maintain strength all along the front in order to provide individual army commanders with their own private air force inferior to the German policy of concentrating at the decisive point of struggle. Sholto Douglas, commander of 43 Squadron, which suffered over 100 percent casualties in April, condemned the cost of the RFC's rapid expansion and the shortsighted policy of the relentless offensive, which pressed insufficiently trained aircrews and obsolescent airplanes into service. In Balfour's opinion, the moral ascendancy gained from rigidly scheduled, two-hour, twice-daily patrols on "terribly obsolete" Sopwiths was not worth the cost in lives, while the use of BE2Cs for artillery spotting was "a reckless waste of human life." Arthur Gould Lee cursed the "irrational obduracy" of Trenchard's Distant Offensive Patrols (DOPs), while Norman Macmillan recalled bitterly the belief among junior officers that casualty lists had no effect on Haig, Trenchard, or their brigade commander, Brig. Gen. T. I. Webb-Bowen. Macmillan and Douglas condemned Webb-Bowen and Trenchard, respectively, for refusing escorts for Sopwith two-seaters and accepting the ensuing losses.[123]

RNAS ace Canadian Raymond Collishaw commanded Naval 10 from 26 April until late July, when constant combat during the summer led to high casualties—10 of 15 pilots killed, wounded, or captured—and a decline in the squadron's fighting efficiency. While Collishaw recognized that commanders occasionally had to be ruthless, he believed that theirs were asking them to do too much. One or two senior officers without recent combat experience seemed firmly convinced that the more casualties a fighter squadron suffered, the better its performance. In June, when Trenchard ordered brigade commanders to conserve resources yet maintain the offensive spirit, Collishaw wryly commented that their brigade commander either did not receive the message or read only the last part, as they experienced no lull in operations.[124]

The high toll of new aircrew stemmed from their inadequate training for frontline combat through mid-1917. Although the RFC training establishment had grown by that time to 32 schools, with 15 under construction, the rapid expansion of frontline units and the severe casualties led to shorter training time for replacement crews. Macmillan recalled the crudeness of even advanced instruction and the "so many needlessly killed" in flight training with ineffective instructors. In May 1917 Lee observed that most new pilots had 15 to 20 hours' flight time and "can't even fly, let alone fight."[125]

Robert Smith Barry's sorely needed Gosport flight school for instructors began operations in 1917, but it would take time for the techniques to filter down to the training of all the service pilots. At Gosport pilots were encouraged to fly Avro 504 dual-control trainers powered by 120-hp Clergets adventurously in order to master the techniques of aerial combat and then to transmit those skills to their pupils. By summer 1917 all instructors spent two weeks at Gosport, and by fall pilots arriving at the front had many more hours' flight time than in April.[126]

Once the pilots got to the front, the stress of aerial combat manifested itself in stomach ulcers, insomnia, nightmares, and frayed nerves. Late in

May, Lee wrote that the average life of a scout pilot at Arras was three weeks, while six months of combat was all the average fellow could stand. [127] All pilots feared fire in the air and tended to blame a callous RFC command, directorate, and Air Board, all too old to fight, for the absence of parachutes. Tests in January had judged available parachutes too bulky, heavy (40 pounds), and difficult to operate, and the authorities failed to press their development, apparently afraid that parachutes might diminish the pilots' fighting ardor. [128]

Fliers fought on to preserve their "collective self-respect," their standing in their own eyes and the eyes of other units. They dealt with the constant danger in various ways. Balfour cultivated an impersonal detachment, a pose of cynicism about death, and did not discuss his most intimate thoughts with others. In his spare time he read frivolous literature and played bridge and emphasized that the heavy drinking depicted in the memoir *War Birds* by the American Elliot White Springs was not typical. [129]

According to ace Ira Jones, most RFC pilots regarded aerial combat as a "game . . . , just like rugger," which continued regardless of injuries to the players. Jones, like Balfour, could not share his most intimate thoughts, fears, and sorrow, because the RFC's aggressively offensive spirit could not tolerate such sentiments. "In the Mess, it was an unwritten law for pilots to forget their sorrow and assume a cheerfulness which gave the impression of 'living for the day.' " Canadian ace Billy Bishop and Australian ace R. A. Little viewed air fighting as a "wonderful game," a "gloriously exhilarating sport," exemplifying Norman Macmillan's categorization of certain RFC types as "devotees of sport" and "killers." [130]

Off-duty sports helped units relax and develop a corporate identity. Yet football games and "rags" in the mess had their minor risks of bloody noses and lips, blackened eyes, and the occasional broken limb. Philip Fullard, a former public school athlete who shot down more than 40 planes from May to November 1917, broke his leg in a football match in November. Fullard, who possessed all the ideal qualities of the ace—flying experience, mechanical aptitude, quick reactions, concentration and control under stress, a perfectionism about his air armament—believed that he was immune to nerves. Yet when his leg had to be reset repeatedly, his nerves "gave way completely," and he was unable to resume even light duty until September 1918. [131]

No one was immune to nerves, and not all pilots accepted the analogy to sport. Britain's greatest ace, Edward "Mick" Mannock, was a complex and temperamental Irishman who rejected the notion of combat as sport, hated the Germans, and sought to kill as many of them as he could. Blind in one eye, he had memorized the eye chart to enter the RFC, then developed a reputation for being a coward because of his early caution in the air. Mannock's socialist leanings and dislike of class divisions and officers' privileges further made him unpopular with some of his colleagues.

Mannock was often physically sick before patrol and suffered two temporary nervous breakdowns, and his constant gun jams and engine failures, even the loss of his right bottom wing once while on patrol, made such bouts understandable. Yet his flight and he, indicating no concern for the nerves of others, amused themselves occasionally frightening "crawling quirks" (British artillery fliers), by diving vertically on an unsuspecting observer at 160 mph and banking away just before shearing off the plane's tail. A peerless patrol leader, he took pains to help initiates in his squadron survive the difficult early days at the front. [132]

Albert Ball, whose dash and daring epitomized the RFC image, continued to attack enemy formations alone and often head-on in either his Nieuport or his SE5, counting on surprise, daring, and dead aim to strike quickly and extricate himself from tight situations. Yet as Ball's score mounted to 47, he tired of the killing and began to feel like a murderer. [133] His death in a crash after combat with the Albatrosses of Richthofen's Jasta 11 on 7 May cast a pall over the entire RFC. [134]

Regarding a pursuit as relentless and deadly as aerial fighting as a sport became increasingly difficult. Ace Arthur Rhys-Davids, formerly captain of Eton School, who shot down Werner Voss in September and lamented that he had not brought him down alive, exemplified that generation of public school boys whose loss Britain mourned. Initially he took walks at night quoting poetry with Cecil Lewis, flew with Blake's poems in case he was brought down alive, and planned to attend Oxford after the war. Yet Maurice Baring at RFC headquarters recalled that the last time he saw Rhys-Davids alive, the youth knew he would be killed. He was shot down chasing German two-seaters. [135]

By 1917 recruits of Rhys-Davids's and Lewis's social station were scarce. The War Office prevented the RFC from taking a disproportionate share of public school boys, and in the fall the pilot candidates had included very few graduates of the great English public schools. [136] A few men from the lower classes, like Mannock and McCudden, the sons of army noncommissioned officers, and many from the Dominions, like Bishop, Collishaw, and Little, filled the ranks of the RFC during the last two years of the war with capable and aggressive, if—in the eyes of the British middle and upper classes—somewhat undisciplined and uncivilized men. As Naval 8 commander G. R. Bromet, who was blessed with Australians and Canadians, said of his Canadians, "Wonderful chaps, breath of the wide open spaces, great pilots, likely to destroy a Mess or anything in five minutes at a guest night."[137] The Australians were probably even more rambunctious. Finally, there were the RFC's Americans, 210 American university volunteers who would see most of their service in 1918.[138] Despite the manpower squeeze, when the Army Council raised the question of noncommissioned pilots in August, the commander in chief was more concerned about separate messes for them than about their prospects for alleviating the shortage of aircrews.[139]

As the nature of the air war and the composition of the RFC changed, British aviation magazines continued to romanticize both the corps and the sporting, chivalric, heroic, and sacrificial images of the air war. As casualties mounted, *Flight*'s obituaries of officer aviators became less elaborate but adhered to a certain form, containing comments such as "a keen sportsman, a good shot, and a good rider to hounds," or "a keen big-game shot." Reports about fliers maintained a jaunty, sportsmanlike air, such as that of the famous polo player whose chief regret about aviation was that polo would hardly thrill him again.

The Times correspondent on 15 April reported of the lone airman who returned, riddled, from a long-distance mission, to make his report, and apologize for a rough landing caused by his smashed foot, "then, duty done, he died."[140] The *Aeroplane* of 30 May carried "The Lament of the Broken Pilot," who bid farewell to France, "the land of adventure and knightly deeds,/where the pilot faces the foe/in single combat as was of yore—/giving him blow for blow." No longer among the "throng of chivalry, youth, and pride," where his comrades entered "the airy lists in the name of Freedom and Right," our broken pilot would now keep their "armour bright."[141] Exclusive London stores like Abercrombie and Fitch advertised aviation clothing intended to dress the wealthy young sportsman-knight stylishly and appropriately for the airy lists.

In Arthur Gould Lee's opinion, the false image of the RFC created by the press—of intrepid, daredevil, hell-bent, fearless aviators—left pilots "cynically amused." Flying, he mused, gave "a sense of mastery over space, over nature, over life itself" to that "winged aristocracy of warriors"—Lee was not entirely immune to the heroic imagery himself—but the rest was bunk.[142]

In the brutal war of 1917, chivalry and sportsmanship were gone. James McCudden, who attacked when he had the advantage and broke off combat when he did not, lamented that shooting down unsuspecting Germans opposed what little sporting instinct he had left.[143] Sporting attitudes did not interfere with his meticulous and calculating approach to aerial combat. Balfour observed, "Of the chivalry of the air which is fatuously and ignorantly written about, neither side could afford to indulge in did it involve any risks."[144] Despite some evidence of chivalry, Macmillan asserted, "more often there was just the sheer bloody murder of the headhunter."[145] In Raymond Collishaw's opinion, chivalry was exaggerated, for air combat was a serious, deadly, and ruthless business that some confused with the tourneys of the Middle Ages.[146]

Though chivalry was dead, that "winged aristocracy," their exploits romanticized by the press, became the source of heroes to rally the masses during the slaughter of 1917. The RFC command, seeking to secure its niche as part of a mass army in which most soldiers would never receive individual recognition, initially eschewed such attention. The gloom from Ball's loss convinced Maurice Baring that it was better to keep aces incognito. When the War Cabinet desired to publish the names of outstanding pilots in October, Trenchard opposed such special treatment on the grounds that differentiation among RFC squadrons and between the RFC and the rest of the army would be unwise and invidious.[147] Yet the very impersonal nature of mass warfare required publicized heroes and ensured the lionization of these men as the war continued.

The quality of materiel provided left much to be desired, particularly the two-seater army cooperation planes. BE2s, which Trenchard termed a machine for the "indifferent pilot,"[148] remained in service, obsolete cannon fodder for German fighters, in part to complete production runs but also because many RFC pilots could not fly higher performance aircraft like the rotary-engine Sopwith.[149] The "Quirks," BE2 and RE8 crews, flew straight to their target and back at low altitude. An awed Arthur Gould Lee presumed that they were so accustomed to being "ruthlessly archied" at low altitude that they had become fatalistic, like infantrymen.[150] It never occurred to Lee that inadequate training may also have limited their ability to perform intricate maneuvers.

Pilots like Balfour and Macmillan condemned Sopwith two-seaters. Trenchard considered them "bad fighting machines" and expected "very large wastage" in pilots and materiel because their inadequate strength for artillery work caused them to "break up quickly." Sopwiths were delightful to fly, but their losses were severe on unescorted missions deep behind enemy lines. Used inappropriately for tasks beyond their performance, the Sopwith 1½ strutters served beyond their usefulness.[151]

Even ammunition was suspect. Buckingham incendiary bullets, which ammunition experts proclaimed dependable for four months, failed to set fire to balloons after two months, prompting Trenchard to wonder whether ammunition experts believed that bullets were like cheese, "better for keeping."[152]

In the realm where performance meant the most, fighter aviation, the British introduced three superior fighters in 1917—the Sopwith Camel, the SE5, and the two-seat Bristol F2 fighter. The rotary-engine Camel was reputedly the war's premier dogfighter, yet many British fighter pilots preferred the SE5A. The SE5A was faster and easier to land, its performance at altitude better, and its in-line engine quieter. The SE5A's steadiness in a fast dive made it a better gun platform, while its speed enabled it to break off combat at will.[153]

The skilled Camel pilot, though unable to run, had an aerobatic, unstable, and sensitive mount of unexcelled maneuverability. The Camel was potentially as dangerous to an inexperienced pilot or to one unaware of its vices as it was to the enemy. To counteract the engine torque on takeoff the pilot had to use right full rudder until he gained sufficient speed for the tail fin to be effective, otherwise the machine would ground loop and crash on its starboard wingtip. Its sensitivity also made it tiring to fly on long patrols. A design flaw that was recognized only after the war was the failure to pin the center section struts to the top wing, and violent maneuvers created such tension on struts and wings that they sometimes came loose, causing a crash.[154]

The Bristol fighter was indisputably the best two-seat fighter reconnaissance craft, and all three planes served until the end of the war, their performance enhanced by larger engines, the Camel's Bentleys, the SE5A's 200-hp Hispano-Suiza, and the Bristol's Rolls Royce Falcon.

England's circumstances in the tactical air war thus improved in 1917, but it had no effective strategic riposte to the German air assault on England that began in May. Army tactical day bomber crews in 1917 were gradually equipped with the DH4, an aircraft superb in speed and service ceiling and deficient only in the location of its main fuel tanks, which separated pilot and observer, making communication difficult. Night bomber crews, like their French counterparts, flew obsolescent types like FE2s, although naval crews had a few Handley Page 0/100 twin-engine giants.

The Admiralty halted the paltry strategic effort of the Third Wing RNAS late in March in order to help the RFC on the Western Front. The commander of the Dunkirk squadrons and the Third Wing's armaments officer, barrister Maj. Lord Tiverton, contended that bombing had the potential to be an extremely powerful weapon. Their superior Adm. Reginald Bacon, commander of Dover patrol, did not concur. Historian Neville

Jones and the official history praised the Third Wing's offensive against chemical, explosives, and munitions factories and iron foundries in the Saar-Lorraine-Luxemburg region for exerting an effect disproportionate to the number of raids. In their opinion, the force, which acquired DH4s and Handley Pages in spring 1917 to increase its striking power, could have shaken the morale of the population, adversely affected munitions output, and compelled the Germans to divert planes, labor, and materials to home defense.[155]

Contrary to such assertions, the most recent research on strategic bombing questions its effectiveness. Historian George Kent Williams has labeled the idea that bombing could lower the population's morale and will to resist to the point that they would force a peace a "peculiarly British obsession."[156] In his view, the Admiralty, assuming a priori that bombing was effective and hoping to undermine civilian will to continue the war, attributed a tremendous effect on enemy morale to every bomb that fell on Germany, a notion that most government officials came to accept. Yet postwar surveys of the results of RNAS raids on the Saar blast furnaces between January and March indicated that the British overestimated damage to both German material and morale.[157]

After the Third Wing disbanded in May, the German air raids on England encouraged the British public and politicians, who equated material destruction with undermining morale, to retaliate. At the War Cabinet's insistence and over the opposition of Trenchard, the RFC formed the 41st Wing under Lt. Col. Cyril Newall, which arrived at Ochey on 11 October.[158] A month and a half later, in a memorandum of 26 November to the War Cabinet on long-distance bombing, Trenchard accepted the premise that an unrelenting offensive would adversely affect enemy morale. Trenchard, assuming that the cabinet wanted raids "at any price, regardless of weather," lost 4 of 10 Handley Pages before the cabinet informed him differently.[159] BEF commander Haig considered morale irrelevant and assessed bombing effectiveness on the military results, but both Haig and Trenchard increasingly believed in the potential of night bombing.[160]

Although the night operations of 41 Wing's Handley Pages and obsolescent FE2s were hampered by bad weather and inexperience through January 1918 and fell short of expectations, the British continued to overestimate the damage they inflicted. In weather conditions varying from crystal clear to solid overcast, the 41st Wing had difficulty hitting targets smaller than a large town.[161]

As the RNAS ceased its strategic bombing effort, strides in flying boat technology enabled the improvement of its over-water operations. The

British navy had been buying Glenn Curtiss flying boats since 1914, at the instigation of naval officer J. C. Porte, who had worked with Curtiss before the war to develop the "America boat" for a transatlantic flight. Porte designed improved hulls for the boats at the Royal Navy Air Station at Felixstowe. The first battleworthy boat, the Curtiss H12 "Large America" of 1917, had a wingspan of nearly 93 feet and a length of 46 feet and was powered by Rolls Royce Eagles. These giants and their Felixstowe variant, the F2, with Porte's greatly strengthened hull, put an end in April to "spasmodic, uncoordinated, and ineffective" aircraft antisubmarine operations with the "Spider Web" system of patrols from Felixstowe,[162] and later Yarmouth and Killingholme, which systematically covered some 4,000 square miles of sea. They also shot down two Zeppelins in May within 150 miles of the British coast, reducing the Zeppelin's effectiveness in reconnaissance.[163]

In February the Grand Fleet, doubting that its three seaplane carriers could provide an aircraft screen for the fleet, began tests flying Sopwith Pups first from fixed 20-foot platforms on cruisers and then from turntable platforms on the top of turrets of capital ships. By October work was under way on an aircraft carrier.[164] Given these developments in heavier-than-air flight, the navy debated the value of airships. Although fleet exercises in September demonstrated the value of airship reconnaissance, nonrigids lacked the strength and endurance for extensive service over the North Sea. In airship policy debates from August through October, Churchill opposed them because an airship program would show no results before late 1918 at the earliest and would divert skilled workers and aluminum from airplanes. Fifth Sea Lord Godfrey Paine, however, believed that rigid airships would be useful in naval reconnaissance, convoy work, and submarine scouting.[165] While Paine's argument was correct for waters in which airships would encounter no aerial opposition, Churchill's argument of time and priorities was more telling. The navy continued to use nonrigid blimps for patrol.

While the RFC concentrated more than 50 RFC units in Europe, 7 served abroad, 2 each in Egypt and Salonika, and one each in Mesopotamia, East Africa, and India. In the Middle East, where a small Australian flying corps was stationed, German disinterest limited aerial fighting. The British prepared in the spring for the battle to enter Palestine, and the Germans, who had superior aircraft, attacked undefended patrols aggressively during the summer, displaying "daring tempered with much discretion."[166] By the fall of 1917 the British Bristol fighters and SE5s had gained aerial mastery and a numerical superiority of 30 to 40 aircraft to 4, a clear indication of the minor nature of the air campaign in the Middle East, particularly for the Germans.

As the British air war thus moved from disaster in the spring to ascendancy in the fall, the administration of aviation mobilization at home underwent dramatic and complex changes. Beyond the new Air Board under Lord Cowdray, the management of aeronautical supplies effectively rested foremost with the Ministry of Munitions' chief of the aeronautical department and controller of aircraft supply, William Weir, former director of munitions in Scotland, and then with engine supply chief Percy Martin, formerly Daimler's managing director.

As the civilian agencies assumed control of aeronautical supplies, the army and navy heads of aviation supply departed. Brig. Gen. D. S. McInnes left the Directorate of Air Equipment in the winter of 1916–17 to return to the Royal Engineers. In January, Murray F. Sueter stepped down as director of the Air Department in the Admiralty to command naval aviation in the Italian theater. The RFC and RNAS staffs merged in the Ministry of Munitions technical department under Brig. Gen. James Weir, William Weir's half brother, and the location of the Air Board and ministry air officials in the Victorian Hotel Cecil on the Strand gave rise to its nickname "Bolo House," a center of intrigue and animosity.[167]

The Air Board and the Ministry of Munitions succeeded in doubling aviation production by the summer of 1917, and the organization might have endured for the rest of the war, given the reluctance of many, including Cowdray, to undertake major administrative change in wartime, but for the Gotha raids, especially those on London of 13 June and 7 July. The parliament and the public clamored for defense, retaliation, and victory through air power. In an interview with the *New York Tribune* in August, George Bernard Shaw proclaimed, "This war will be won in the sky, not in the trenches" and said that air raids would attack civilians in capital cities, killing the nation by striking child-bearing mothers.[168] Victory through air power required an independent air arm and Air Ministry.

After the first raids, the Chief of the Imperial General Staff, Sir William Robertson, ordered the return of one or two squadrons from the Western Front, despite Haig's and Trenchard's vociferous objections to any such diversion of resources.[169] With the July raid the War Cabinet, expecting a likely German air campaign against London, wanted to double the size of the RFC and RNAS, thus increasing the former to 200 service squadrons. It formed a two-man committee of Lloyd George and South African soldier-statesman J. C. Smuts to study home defense, air organization, and operations. Smuts wrote two reports in just over a month. The first, voicing the existing consensus, recommended a unified defensive command and a strengthened air defense for Britain. The second and more far-reaching one, of 17 August, advocated an independent air service to carry the war to Germany, thereby preempting further German attacks on England.

Smuts sought an end to the division between military and naval aviation, which had caused "competition, friction, and waste," in order to use aviation as an independent arm of operations. Future aircraft production programs would yield by spring 1918 a "great surplus available for independent operations," which, to be employed effectively, required an independent staff and ministry. The next summer, Smuts envisioned, when the Western Front would be moving forward "at a snail's pace," the air battle would be far behind the Rhine, its pressure on industrial centers and lines of communication possibly the "determining factor" in ending the war. The progressive exhaustion of manpower in the war of arms and machinery meant victory would belong to the side that gained industrial superiority. England needed to establish a unified air service, ministry, and air general staff immediately in order to gain the overwhelming aerial predominance that would be important to winning the war, and in the long run possibly as important as naval supremacy. [170] Smuts based his conclusions on discussions with Henderson, who advocated a separate air department, and Weir, who estimated that a surplus air fleet would be available for a strategic bomber force in 1918.

The War Cabinet accepted Smuts's report in principle on 24 August and later appointed him chair of an aerial operations committee to set aviation allocation priorities that included Secretary of War Derby, Minister of Munitions Churchill, Air Board President Cowdray, and First Lord of the Admiralty Eric Geddes.

Yet a unified air arm was still not a given. When the Gotha daylight raids halted on 22 August and aircraft production encountered serious snags, the impetus for change flagged. At the 18 September War Cabinet meeting, Smuts expressed alarm that slow preparations were jeopardizing achievement of even the 86-squadron RFC program passed in mid-1916; he called for its immediate execution and for aviation to be assigned the same priority as shell production had had in 1915. Weir pointed out that fulfillment of the production program in aviation, the most recent service to make demands on the country's resources, would necessitate the diversion of industrial resources, in particular skilled labor, to aviation. [171] As if to emphasize the importance of the task, the Gothas staged six night raids between 24 September and 2 October.

Smuts's aerial operations committee requested and received power to set priorities for all munitions programs, and this war priorities committee then recommended on 28 September a priority for aviation second only to shipbuilding and sufficient to justify reducing the output of other munitions. The measure took effect even before the War Cabinet officially passed it on 14 November, and Smuts assured a 2 November War Cabinet meeting that the enlarged program could be carried out completely. [172]

By this time the War Cabinet had formed the nucleus of a strategic air arm in the 41st Wing RFC in early October, goaded by a memorandum from Rear Adm. Mark Kerr on 11 October claiming that the Germans were building a monstrous bomber force that would win the war unless Britain took immediate action. [173] Haig opposed the formation of the new air service at the 15 October meeting of the War Cabinet, and Trenchard and Henderson indicated that they could not launch a bombing campaign in earnest until summer 1918. But in November and December naval voices Tiverton and Wing Commander C. J. R. Randall of the naval air staff averred that bombing of chemical, explosives, aero engine, magneto, iron, and steel plants would have a decisive effect on the war. Trenchard cited the damage to material and morale possible from attacking large industrial centers, and future plans for the campaign reflected his opinions in their inclusion of cities as possible targets. By the end of November the cabinet had caught up with parliamentary and public opinion, and the Air Force Bill became law on 29 November. [174]

The dislocations so feared even by those who desired a separate air arm began to take place. The Secretary of State for War Derby wanted to replace the aging Henderson with Trenchard in the fall, but Haig refused to release his RFC commander. When Henderson left the position of Director General of Military Aeronautics to assist Smuts in October, the Chief of the Imperial General Staff, Robertson, and the Army Council attempted to regain control over air policy. They replaced Henderson with Maj. Gen. John M. Salmond, the 36-year-old director of training, who tended to rely on Trenchard, and sent Brancker, who had essentially run the directorate under Henderson, to command the small aviation brigade in Egypt and Palestine because they considered him a proponent of an air ministry. When Salmond considered resigning, Trenchard counseled, "You cannot resign in war."[175]

On 15 November Lloyd George approached Lord Northcliffe to be the new air minister, but Northcliffe refused in a published letter, which prompted Cowdray's resignation as president of the Air Board. [176] Lloyd George then turned to Northcliffe's younger brother Lord Rothermere. Trenchard, when the prime minister asked him to be chief of air staff, initially wanted to stay in France, but under Rothermere's and Northcliffe's threat of a press campaign against Haig, he returned in December. Salmond replaced him as the commander of the RFC in Europe. On 8 December U.S. military intelligence reported of the circumstances:

> Reports reaching us show that great disorganization exists in the British air service.
>
> British officers themselves complain bitterly of the inefficiency of their aircraft administration and of the lack of unity of control, as well as of the stupidity of those higher up.
>
> . . . Self-interest and party politics are said to dominate the situation.[177]

The historical debate over this messy political and administrative process has focused on Smuts's second report, one of the most important documents in the history of British air power. Historian Malcolm Cooper considered its premises—that the airplane was a weapon of strategic importance that the Germans planned to use extensively against Britain, that the aviation industry could support a strategic bomber force in addition to army and navy tactical air arms, and that the existing organization was inadequate to direct the air effort—mistaken. He condemned Smuts's proposal as an "overreaction" based on an inadequate appreciation of recent progress toward a unified air policy. The report led to dislocation and the formation of the Royal Air Force (RAF), an organization that did little to alter existing priorities. The British air effort faced 1918 in disarray, under an inexperienced operational commander (Salmond), a reluctant chief of staff (Trenchard), and a political head unequal to the task (Rothermere).[178]

Author David Divine judged that the RFC expansion plan far exceeded Britain's industrial resources, rendering Weir's and Smuts's premise of the surplus air fleet highly fallacious, and that the memorandum originated in the "irrational and unbalanced state of the Cabinet mind" immediately after the Gotha raids. Yet he concluded that Smuts's proposal of a separate air department was the correct solution, though arrived at by incorrect advice and methods, to the problems of waste, bickering, delay, and the inefficiency of "private empires," specifically Trenchard's in the RFC.[179]

Barry D. Powers believed that historians have overemphasized the importance of Smuts's report, as the RAF stemmed from a long trend of halting progress toward unity. The Gotha raids did convince General Staff chief Robertson and commander in chief of the Home Force Lord French of the need for the strategic air arm, but the factors leading to the formation of a

single independent air arm—the wasteful RFC-RNAS rivalry over industrial output and the desire to retaliate with an offensive air arm against Germany—antedated the raids.[180]

Powers correctly placed Smuts's report in the broader context of other
long-standing factors moving toward an independent air arm. The arguments of Cooper and Divine against Smuts's decision focus on the state of
aeronautical supplies and the potential for a surplus air fleet, though without
discussing aviation procurement and the industry throughout 1917 in any
detail. A discussion of the state of aviation procurement is essential to a
judgment of the report's wisdom and the formation of the Royal Air Force.

The transfer of aeronautical supply to the Ministry of Munitions was
the largest single addition to the ministry's responsibilities after its inception.
Aviation procurement was more complex than other war munitions because
of the airplane's rapid evolution, its high wastage, and the difficulty of cor-
relating aircraft and engine supply.[181]

In the ministry, William Weir saw his task as a "straightforward matter of industrial rationalization . . . to reduce the number of types of aircraft
and engines without hindering the development of new types."[182] He sent
efficiency production officers with engineering expertise, workshop practice, and organizational ability to each factory to improve planning and
management. With the backing of the Minister of Munitions, Christopher
Addison, he restricted the Royal Aircraft Factory (now the Royal Aircraft
Establishment) to laboratory work and prototype testing, leaving design and
production entirely to the industry. As of 14 March, airplanes and aero
engines headed a group one priority list that also included guns, tanks, railroads, and motor vehicles. Starting on 1 April the ministry licensed aviation
experiments to prevent wasteful expenditure of labor and materials, and
on 25 August it commandeered and distributed all flax to spinners at
fixed prices.[183]

The appointment of Winston Churchill, who wanted to replace the attrition of men with a war of machines using "masses of guns, mountains of
shells, clouds of aeroplanes,"[184] to be Minister of Munitions on 20 July further strengthened Weir's position as Controller of Aeronautical Supply.
Within the year Weir reduced the number of types from 55 aircraft and
33 engine to 30 and 25, respectively. By year's end he could offer low-
interest loans and even grants up to 50,000 pounds to firms to develop
production.[185]

In the first months of 1917, 65 firms on aircraft work took on some
7,000 new hands, increasing their work force by almost 10 percent. Dilution by women and boys in 28 representative aircraft firms increased from

TABLE 3:

Quarterly Aircraft and Engine Deliveries, 1917

	First	Second	Third	Fourth	Total
Domestic aircraft	2,402	3,167	3,548	4,649	13,766
Domestic engines	2,191	2,701	3,199	3,672	11,763
Imported aircraft	328	423	172	93	1,016
Imported engines	513	866	1,143	2,380	4,902

SOURCE: Walter Raleigh and H. A. Jones, *The War in the Air*, vol. 3, app. 7.

19.6 percent in January to 37.5 percent in June and 44 percent in December. In November the total aviation industry (771 aircraft, engine, and accessories firms) employed 173,969 workers—104,102 men, 52,734 women, 17,133 boys—making it the largest in the world.[186]

Aircraft and engine production increased during 1917, but aircraft production continued to exceed engine production, which necessitated continued dependence on French Hispano-Suizas, Clergets, and Rhônes to make up the deficit (see Table 3). Aircraft deliveries increased from 6,633 in 1916 to 14,382 in 1917, yet the figures for 1916 represented complete airplanes, while after June 1917 they represented airframes, partially assembled and often without engines.[187]

Dilution and material priorities yielded no solutions. Most firms still faced shortages of skilled labor, raw materials, factory space, machine tools, and components, especially ball bearings. In September labor priority meant little because the labor supply was "altogether inadequate." Although aircraft firms received trainees from government instructional factories, they lacked sufficient skilled labor to set up the jigs and machine tools for unskilled workers. In September the ministry decided to erect three national aircraft factories, an experiment that ultimately proved unproductive.[188]

Labor unrest and strikes compounded the difficulties of production. The aviation industry lost 281,600 workdays from strikes in London, Cowes, Birmingham, Coventry, and Wolverhampton over the food and coal shortage and the wrongful dismissal of shop stewards. In the second week of May a strike of workers in Sheffield, Manchester, and Coventry intensified the shortage of crankshaft and steel forgings. Late in 1917 woodworkers opposed to the piecework system of wages initiated strikes that required Smuts's mediation to restore negotiations. The sheet metal workers union in The Midlands staged a particularly disastrous strike over wages, and 2,000 woodworkers at Bristol also struck for higher wages. That strike, which began on 26 November, seriously affected aircraft manufacture, for as late as mid-December 50,000 workers in the aircraft factories were still striking.[189]

Yet manpower was only the second of two key factors limiting the wartime expansion of aircraft production. The major factor—engine development and supply—was particularly crucial because the French and British relied on engine power more than aircraft design to boost performance. As of spring 1917 it took some 64 weeks from approval of an engine design to mass production; consequently, the standardization of engine production preoccupied the Air Board and the Ministry of Munitions.[190]

Rolls Royce concentrated on increasing the output of the Eagle and the Falcon from 275 and 190 horsepower to 360 and 270, respectively, but its production of these handcrafted and unstandardized engines was inadequate. The Air Board did allow the firm to build a small repair plant, but late in July it declined Rolls Royce's proposal to acquire another factory. It also ceased attempts to arrange licensed production by a dozen British contractors when Rolls Royce general manager Claude Johnson threatened to tear up the drawings and go to prison rather than allow licensed production. In April the board concluded that technical considerations and the firm's "peculiar characteristics" presented "insurmountable difficulties" to sufficient production. Rolls Royce, Weir observed in the fall, had made it practically impossible for other firms to manufacture its engine.[191]

In January, in addition to confirming orders of 8,000 Hispano-Suizas from France, the board cast about for new domestic designs. For the 108 service squadrons stipulated in the December 1916 RFC program, it needed 8,000 engines in six months and production increases from some 600 engines monthly to 2,000. The board asked the internal combustion engine subcommittee of the Advisory Committee for Aeronautics to determine which two of four 200-hp water-cooled engine designs—BHP and Sunbeam six-cylinder engines and Hispano-Suiza and Sunbeam eight-cylinder types—would be most suitable for mass production.[192]

On 24 January the engine subcommittee judged the eight-cylinder Sunbeam and the six-cylinder BHP designs superior. The Sunbeam eight, later named the Arab, was touted as more reliable and stronger, with a better-designed crankcase than the Hispano-Suiza, and "practically certain" of success. The ministry's Director of Engine Supply, Percy Martin, had warned on 10 January that Britain's lack of forges for quality steel to be used in crankshafts made increasing output to 500 engines weekly and producing a suitable crankshaft for the six-cylinder BHP by May impossible. The subcommittee concluded, however, that any difficulty in producing

BHP crankshafts did "not appear to be insuperable." In February, without tests, the government ordered 4,400 Arabs from Sunbeam, Lanchester, and Austin and 2,000 six-cylinder BHPs from Siddeley Deasy, as well as Hispano-Suizas from Wolseley, only to learn shortly afterward that foundries could not guarantee suitable aluminum castings for the base chamber of the Arab. In mid-March, with almost 20,000 engines on order, Weir warned of the new engine designs' possible failure when 62 percent of their crankcases failed to meet quality standards. In April, though, the board assured the cabinet that it could overcome any problems.[193]

Engine deliveries exceeded 1,000 monthly for the first time in May, and from May through July Weir predicted a monthly production of first 2,500 and then 2,000 engines by the end of 1917, 2,400 and then 3,000 engines in March 1918, and 4,000 in the summer of 1918. He anticipated a surplus of 3,000 engines by the end of the year. On 21 June the Air Board even recommended to the War Cabinet that the RFC expand from 108 to 200 service squadrons, adding 92 squadrons of fighters and bombers; a month later, however, on 23 July, Weir acknowledged that the lack of skilled tool room labor, alloy steel, and ball bearings imposed limits on the program.[194]

In fact, the reality was much worse. At the end of May weekly engine output plummeted to 166, primarily because of defects in Hispano-Suiza crankshafts. Tests of the Sunbeam Arab revealed such serious cylinder and crank chamber weaknesses that the Air Board considered substituting the Hispano-Suiza, until Martin explained that the firms could not switch. The BHP, extensively redesigned for mass production after its first air trials, no longer fit its intended plane, the DH4, and in July more than 90 percent of its aluminum cylinder blocks were defective. The RFC received only 81 Sunbeam Arabs, which had been neither bench- nor air-tested as of September. High-powered engines—BHPs, Arabs, Rolls Royces, and Hispano-Suizas—ultimately contributed only 21 percent of British engine production in 1917 (2,417 of 11,763).[195]

The one bright spot occurred where it was least expected: in rotary engines, which Martin, early in 1917, had wanted to phase out because of their short life span. The design of the Hispano-Suiza had much impressed naval Lt. W. O. Bentley, the Admiralty's technical liaison with the Gwynne company, the British licensee for the Clerget rotary. He made a set of aluminum pistons for the Clerget that gave it a higher compression ratio and improved its cooling by replacing the cast iron cylinders with steel-lined aluminum cylinders, which spread heat more evenly. In early July the Bentley AR1 rotary engine passed its air tests, yielding 150 horsepower. The board promptly renamed the engine the BR1 in honor of Bentley and, in order to avoid problems with the Clerget license, had the Humber company produce the engines, which were immediately installed in Sopwith Camels. In October the BR2 delivered 230 horsepower, so the Air Board contracted for 1,500 monthly by July 1918.[196]

In October Martin ordered off the drawing board 100 300-hp Napier engines, a simple, robust design capable of 420 horsepower but 140 pounds lighter than the Rolls Royce. The Napier engine, a 12-cylinder W-type, with three banks of 4 cylinders each, developed 450 horsepower and proved to be a magnificent engine when it appeared after the war.[197]

At least the Napier was perfected. But fiascoes with untried engines continued. The Air Board nearly compromised Bentley production in November by committing to the untried All British Company (ABC) radial, the Dragonfly. Weir and the board became enthralled with this nine-cylinder design that would allegedly produce more than 300 horsepower for a weight of 380 pounds, a fantastic power-to-weight ratio. The board issued contracts for more than 10,000 for delivery in 1918 and began to phase out Bentley BR2 contracts in order to free manufacturing capacity.[198]

The Aircraft Inspection Department (AID), which had cautioned in January against relying on untried designs, warned that the Dragonfly's very simplicity and the shortcuts in production demanded prolonged testing; AID was thus incredulous to learn that the Dragonfly was to absorb all of British production in 1918 except Rolls Royce. After the production of some 1,000 Dragonflies in 1918, the engine, which remained 45 horsepower below and 56 pounds over its projected statistics, displayed an unfortunate tendency to disintegrate in the air. The government frantically fell back on BR2 production, and G. P. Bulman of AID later claimed, had the war continued into 1919, "the Dragonfly would have lost it for us in the air; we should have been beaten out of the sky."[199]

The failures in engine technology and inadequate engine production compounded disruptions in aircraft development and supply. In January delays in delivery of Bristol fighters actually panicked Trenchard, who fretted that things were "too hopeless" and "comic opera" and that "we deserve to lose the war." In September the Rolls Royce shortages prompted the modification of Bristol fighters for Hispano-Suizas, which in turn became unavailable, and the Sunbeam-powered Bristol fighter was inferior to the Rolls-powered Bristol.[200]

The SE5 and the 150-hp Hispano-Suiza proved a potent combination, but production of the 200-hp SE5A was arrested, first because of modifications and then, in September, because the Wolseley Hispano-

Suiza, named the Viper, which was already 70 to 90 pounds heavier than French versions, kept breaking down. The British often found French Hispano-Suizas flawed by "bad workmanship," "bad material, and faulty treatment of gears," and spare parts from the nine different French contractors occasionally were not interchangeable. In November the British government complained to the French that Hispano-Suizas from the French Brasier firm were not engines but "so much material which requires complete reconstruction" in England. Yet the situation was so desperate in October 1917 that defective Hispano-Suizas were sent to the front with notations in their logbooks about "incomplete efficiency"—which obviously dampened the morale of the pilots who got them. Hilary St. G. Saunders's history of the RAF, *Per Ardua*, labeled this a "shocking, indefensible solution," an "admission of defeat," of confusion and incompetence. In January 1918 some 350 to 400 SE5A airframes lay idle, awaiting engines.[201]

In September 1917 Brooke-Popham, quartermaster general of the RFC, commented, regarding engines, "We appear to be going downhill." While the Germans were developing 260-hp Mercedes for artillery machines, the British had no prospects for new types and were not obtaining enough of their highest-powered ones.[202]

The engine fiascoes affected day bombing disastrously. The Rolls Royce–powered DH4 enjoyed high speed and service ceiling, but shortages forced the use of BHPs and Fiats, none of which performed as well as the Rolls. Geoffrey de Havilland's successor to the DH4, the DH9, powered by the 230-hp BHP, proved so inferior to the DH4 that in November Salmond and Trenchard predicted disaster in day bombing, but production was too far along to stop it. The Air Board decided that the DH9 would be a stopgap until a twin-engine bomber, the DH10, could be produced; it would still use the BHPs. When Salmond posed the choice of using the Rolls Royce Eagle in flying boats or day bombers, Weir allocated the Eagles to large aircraft—flying boats and Handley Page bombers—and said it was "a question of either the DH9 with a BHP engine or nothing else."[203]

The failures of engine types made a shambles of delivery plans and longer-range intentions to phase out aircraft. Deliveries fluctuated wildly in May and June, and one week in late July the Ministry of Munitions received 18 instead of the 275 stipulated. The declining deliveries prevented a definite program of fitting engines to specific planes in mid-September.[204]

Ludicrous positions from members of the board compounded engine problems. Early in the year, delays in Armstrong Whitworth production because of Beardmore engine problems combined with the RE8's crashes to prolong the RFC's reliance on the BE2. On 27 April, when Air Board president Cowdray questioned the large numbers of obsolete BE2 in Weir's production program, Weir pointed out that its casualties were low compared to those of the RE8. Henderson would not admit that the BE2 was obsolete, later reporting that Brooke-Popham and Brancker advised retaining the BE in production because it was a better artillery spotter than the RE8. What the BE required, Henderson alleged, was adequate protection, which, of course, Trenchard's offensive policies denied.[205]

As of late March, Weir planned to end the production of RE8s and SE5s in September, Bristol fighters in October, Sopwith Camels in November, and DH4s and Armstrong Whitworths in December, although their replacements did not yet exist. On 17 August, Henderson first asserted that the Bristol fighter was "not very superior" to the RE8, and five days later, after talking to officers, he suggested that they drop the RE8 because it was "not altogether satisfactory." Ultimately, production failures of the Sunbeam Arab and the Hispano-Suiza postponed the intended reequipment of RE8 squadrons in France with Bristol fighters until September 1918.[206]

Yet, after all the setbacks, Weir proclaimed in November and December that the Rolls Royce expansion scheme would provide a surplus of Eagles in the last six months of 1918, and in mid-December he was planning for an RFC of 240 service squadrons, one-third of them equipped with the Rolls Royce or Liberty, one-third with the BR2, and one-third with the Hispano-Suiza, Sunbeam, and BHP.[207]

In 1917 the Air Board stumbled forward uncertainly, confronted with problems of development and production that its members did not understand and could not solve. The lack of priority for aviation production before 1917, the selection of untried engines for mass production, and the failure to expand Rolls Royce to the maximum prevented achievement of the July 1917 program during the war.[208]

Assessments of Smuts's recommendation of an Air Ministry that judge that Weir's enthusiasm outran his discretion, that there would be no surplus air fleet, that supply was not up to the task, thus were correct. Weir certainly appeared unduly sanguine about the prospects of supply throughout 1917. Yet Cooper cannot assert, on the one hand, the inadequacy of supply and, on the other, sufficient progress by the organization in 1917 not to warrant the drastic change to an Air Ministry. Furthermore, Divine's condemnation of the logic and process of judgment seems to miss certain essential points.

Haig's and Trenchard's approach to operations on the Western Front ensured that the front would always consume the available supply of airplanes, yet proponents of an independent strategic air arm and its potential to end wars had first to promise to fulfill the tactical air needs of the army and navy in order for the new arm to be militarily palatable. In attempting to placate the existing forces while arguing for the creation of new ones based on production that was inadequate even for current tactical needs, supporters of strategic aviation appeared irrational. In retrospect, an effective strategic air arm was at best remotely possible and at worst technologically impossible in World War I. Yet the long war, itself considered inconceivable in some circles before 1914, had rendered many apparent impossibilities possible. If the War Cabinet was "unbalanced" in the summer of 1917, if Kerr was "hysterical" in the fall, the Germans *were* bombing Britain, causing panic and loss of production, with relative immunity to air defense, and a heightened aerial assault was not out of the question.

It seems odd to argue that perhaps the organization divided between RFC and RNAS would have sufficed to meet future challenges, when it had not met present or past ones. The very failure to achieve a surplus made unified control even more imperative. The board and ministry did reduce the number of types in production and increase the supply. Better than the Admiralty, the War Office, and the Air Board, the Ministry of Munitions could prioritize labor and materials as necessitated by the extensive demands on the industry for tanks, transport, and agricultural machinery. It was making the difficult choices that the services had failed to make: standardizing some types, eliminating others, and killing bad procurement programs.

The new and untested technology of aviation engines and the wartime pressures for haste resulted in repeated errors and dead ends and made many of the board's decisions appear unwise, even irrational, in retrospect. On the other hand, the unfortunate condition of British engine development in 1917 would have tempted a realist to despair of ever achieving effective engine supply and to conclude that the air war was lost. Weir's optimism led to panacean expectations of engine designs, but the alternative might have yielded conclusions too painful to bear. Design was unpredictable, but at least Britain was now ready to produce successful designs in greater numbers than ever before.

The achievement of a surplus ultimately depended on increased production and a redefinition of the needs of the tactical air arms, and only an independent ministry might be able to do both. Both services had resisted bureaucratic change, and Trenchard and Haig showed no inclination to redefine their needs. General Staff chief Robertson and the Army Council were scheming to reassert the army's control over aviation. Under such circumstances, the decision for the Air Ministry appears neither illogical nor irrational but necessary, given past problems and future prospects.

Finally, political-military relationships in 1917 directly influenced the formation of the Air Ministry. Lloyd George had difficulty controlling the military establishment, as he struggled with Haig over the costly war on the Western Front. The formation of an independent air arm and the Air Ministry killed two birds with one stone: the air minister was a civilian, not a soldier, and the air arm offered the possibility of vaulting the "snail's pace" of the Western Front and Douglas Haig, to end the war more quickly.

The Lesser Powers

Russia

At the end of February the Russian air service's 91 frontline units had 545 serviceable airplanes—105 on the Northern Front, 112 on the Western, 222 on the Southwestern, 83 on the Rumanian, and 23 in the Caucasus. The 545-plane force included 118 Nieuports, 90 Farmans, 11 Voisins, 66 Moranes, and 37 Spads. Inadequate maintenance and supply meant that some units had only two engines for every 5 or 6 airplanes. Hastily trained and poorly equipped, the air arm's 500 frontline fliers suffered high losses—some 25 to 30 percent of commissioned personnel. The arm could conduct only limited and generally ineffective operations. In June units flew some 52 sorties daily during the offensive on the Southwestern Front, although the 10th Tactical Air Force lacked fighters to protect reconnaissance missions. The 24 fighter squadrons of 8 Nieuports each posed little threat to their German opponents. The Russian air arm lost one of its few aces, 15-victory ace E. N. Kruten, when he crashed at the end of a 4 June mission. In July Russian air strength had declined to 461 planes.[209]

The army had 38 Muromets under the general headquarter's direct control on 1 February, and the War Department intended to build 80 more in 1917. The giants continued to serve effectively in the spring, but in mid-April the provisional government relieved Gen. M. V. Shidlovskii of command of the squadron, and on 26 May, after the crash of a Muromets, a technical committee of the directorate of aviation declared the planes unsafe to fly. The supreme commander stopped further orders.[210]

By 1917 the naval air service had grown to 300 pilots in 35 flying boat units, with 88 planes and one seaplane tender in its Baltic fleet and

152 planes, four small dirigibles and three seaplane tenders in its Black Sea brigades. Their reconnaissance, combat, bombardment, and artillery spotting proved valuable in both seas, and the Grigorovich flying boats were also effective weapons.[211]

Russia's 16 aviation factories employed some 10,000 workers in 1917. The 11 aircraft factories had managed to increase their monthly production from 205 in 1916 to 352 in February 1917. After the March revolution, production levels declined 50 percent in some factories. The 5 engine factories, though supposedly capable of 110 to 150 engines monthly, actually delivered only 450 engines in all of 1917. Because of "the dislocation of the state economy," in the last three months of the year the government received only 90 engines from Russian factories. The number of imported engines varied, depending upon the source cited, from none in the second half of 1917 to 320 in the last three months—inadequate, in any case. The week before the Bolshevik Revolution, the chief of the air force directorate lamented that the lack of engines disrupted aircraft manufacture and restricted it to obsolete foreign types.[212]

The Boshevik seizure of power in November occasioned the disintegration of the army and navy air services, as production and maintenance ceased. The Bolshevik Military Revolutionary Committee understood the importance of preserving the army's technical cadres, established a bureau of commissars for aviation, and nationalized the aviation factories at the end of the year, but in fact there was no air arm or industry to govern.[213]

Austria-Hungary

The Russian collapse left the small Austro-Hungarian air service with an intensifying air war against Italy on the Southwestern Front, where it was outnumbered and confronted with Caproni attacks. Austrian battle fliers saw their first action in the tenth Battle of the Isonzo, in May and June, while the best fighter pilots, Godwin Brumowski, Julius Arigi, and Frank Linke-Crawford, continued to score as they shifted from the Hansa-Brandenburg D1 to the Austrian-built Albatros D3. For the twelfth Battle of the Isonzo, in October, 150 Austrian aircraft, reinforced by 90 German planes, including bomber units, were pitted against 320 Italian aircraft, including 85 Capronis. Though short of aircraft, the air arm fought well and routed the Italians. By the fall the air arm had grown to 66 flight companies and one G-plane squadron, only 5 units short of the planned expansion, but no company had more than 60 percent of its designated aircraft or pilot complement.

In 1917 a newly created naval aviation command had its arsenal at Pola with stations along the Adriatic coast. Naval aviator Gottfried Banfield, commander of the Trieste naval air station, fought Italian ace Francesco Baracca to a draw in his flying boat on New Year's Day 1917, then went on to score the first night victory and attack Italian motorboat patrols. Naval aviators were forced on the defensive during the summer over the Adriatic, and the navy had to order landplanes, since flying boats could not reach the altitude of the Capronis that were striking Pola and other targets. During the Isonzo battles, Austro-Hungarian naval fliers attacked harbors and supply bases and performed reconnaissance missions over land.[214]

In 1917 the Castiglioni conglomerate supplied the Austro-Hungarian army with C1 observation planes and D1 fighters, and the navy with CC flying boat fighters and K-boats for reconnaissance and bombing. The navy intended to rely on planes from Hansa-Brandenburg and engines from Rapp, later BMW in Munich, which Castiglioni acquired in July to increase deliveries of Porsche's 350-hp engine. Yet the German army and navy monopolized the services of Brandenburg and BMW, with catastrophic effects on engine, and consequently K-boat, production. By fall the naval air arm had only fighters and no bombers.

As German mobilization reduced the flow of German supplies to 32 planes for the entire year, Austro-Hungarian aviation forces were forced to rely on their own limited resources and Brandenburg subsidiaries Ufag and Albatros. The Hindenburg Program prohibited the previous system of exporting aircraft frames, while the Prussian army was more reluctant to grant export permits for aircraft materials and plant machinery.[215]

The army's policies generally did little to solve production problems. In 1917 the aviation arsenal and a special military price commission determined that aircraft price increases were needed to keep pace with rising labor and material costs, but the War Ministry granted none because it was not assured of sufficient funds to cover raises. Such stringency impeded production and robbed the industry of the reserves accumulation necessary for postwar survival. Profit per plane in Austria-Hungary, where serial deliveries were small and production problems great, needed to exceed that in Germany, but it did not.

The deficient organization of exemptions compounded the aircraft factories' problems in the summer of 1917. In the absence of an oft-requested central agency to distribute workers to industry, ordinary carpenters performed intricate work in the factories while skilled furniture makers and carpenters passed their time in frontline companies "making ingenious war me-

mentoes to amuse themselves," and large-scale-lathe hands did the precision work of turning motor cylinders while precision-lathe hands did large-scale work in metal factories.

In September the high command established a General Inspectorate to assume control of aviation in the rear from the War Ministry. In Germany the high command had granted the air force a procurement bureaucracy with some autonomy from the War Ministry. The Austro-Hungarian method of superimposing a new agency on top of the existing hierarchy was more comparable to the German high command's superimposition of the War Office on the War Ministry in the Hindenburg Program. It yielded similar results, as the General Inspectorate merely complicated command in aviation.

In light of such rampant military and industrial inefficiency, monthly aircraft deliveries in 1917 were low and erratic. Starting at 37 aircraft in January, deliveries rose to 135 in May, plummeted to 67 in June because of strikes and shortages, peaked at 211 in August, gradually declined to 142 in November, and stopped altogether in December because of severe winter shortages. Despite this dismal ending, the industry did increase its deliveries of aircraft from 732 in 1916 to 1,272 in 1917 and of engines from 854 to 1,230.

In July, the army aviation arsenal was determined to reach 400 aircraft monthly in 1918, but could secure only 4,500 workers through October to add to the existing labor force of nearly 6,000, when it estimated needs at a grandiose and unattainable 28,000 workers. The technological prerequisites for the expansion were also lacking. German firms adamantly refused to allow the dissemination of German technical reports in Austria. Austrian factories were reluctant to exchange information, and the arsenal's research institute did not share its proceedings with the firms. In any case, Theodore von Karman, one of the arsenal's best scientists, was preoccupied with the development of helicopters rather than war planes.

Despite the difficulties, in the fall the AOK stipulated the production of 750 planes and 1,000 engines monthly in 1918 and further insisted on having twin-engine G-planes and armored infantry J-planes. The aviation arsenal, aware of insurmountable difficulties yet reluctant to contradict the high command, concluded that the numbers were attainable. Ultimately, the disastrous effects of the winter coal shortage in December brought the arsenal to its senses, and it revised expectations to only 125 to 200 planes monthly through April 1918. Conceding that its reach had far exceeded its grasp, the arsenal grimly prepared to face what would be the final year of the war.

Italy

From January through April the Italian army air arm grew gradually.[216] In May Gabriele D'Annunzio, at the invitation of General Cadorna, advocated repeated and massed bomber attacks on enemy artillery batteries and reinforcements and on Austro-Hungarian bases at Pola and Cattaro. In the tenth Battle of the Isonzo, on 23 May, 30 to 40 Capronis became the nucleus for repeated wave attacks in support of infantry attacks against enemy troops at the front and in the rear. Though the attacks' imprecision limited their material results, an enemy officer's war diary recounted that Italian planes flying so low that the bombs dropping from the fuselage were clearly visible spread fear and panic among Austro-Hungarian troops.

Italian dirigibles performed bombing raids in the spring and summer, but the Capronis held center stage. On the night of 2 to 3 August 36 Capronis took off at one-minute intervals to bomb Pola, with D'Annunzio aboard the first bomber. Twenty Capronis attacked the objective, and though intense antiaircraft fire struck 10 of them, they repeated the attack the next night, dropping a total of eight tons of bombs, and again on the night of 8 August.

On 19 August, the second day of the eleventh Battle of the Isonzo, 85 Capronis accompanied by more than 100 fighters and observation planes supported the infantry attack. For the 10-day period 19 to 28 August, an average of 225 planes raided enemy positions daily, for losses of 81 of the 300 Italian aircrew participating. The Italian bombing effort so impressed the American Bolling Commission that it concluded: "In Italy alone, of allied countries, do the conceptions of this subject appear at the present time to be on sufficiently broad and sound lines," with "real and effective airplane bombing planned and in course of application."[217] A French observer, Commandant Le Bon, confirmed in September both the marked progress of Italian aviation in 12 months and the good results of bombing from Capronis, notwithstanding that conditions on the Southwest Front differed from those on the Western.[218]

On 4 October 12 Capronis flew 400 kilometers over the sea to bomb Cattaro, but the end of the month witnessed the disastrous twelfth Battle of the Isonzo, the Italian collapse at Caporetto and retreat to the Piave, and the installation of a new director of aeronautical services. In the retreat from 25 October to 14 November, the air arm lost 47 dead of 886 aviators engaged, as they staged repeated ground attacks in the effort to stem the tide. Confronted with German as well as Austro-Hungarian units, Italian aviation was hard-pressed from October through December, when 5 British and

10 French squadrons arrived as reinforcements. Italian fighter aviation, led by ace Francesco Baracca, who shot down his thirtieth plane in December, fought aggressively, and the first large aerial battle involving as many as 150 planes occurred on 8 December.

In the intensifying air war, the total number of army air squadrons rose from 47 to 73 in 1917, with 2 to 3 stationed in Albania and one in Macedonia, while Italian naval aviation, engaged in continual raids and counterraids against Austria-Hungary, gradually won superiority using FBA flying boats supplemented by Macchi's modified Lohner boats.

The air arm's growth was based on the Italian industry's production of 3,861 planes and 6,276 engines in 1917. Bolling, Le Bon, and British visitor Wing Commander Wilfried Briggs, head of the Admiralty's engine section,[219] attested strongly to the technological and industrial progress of Italian aviation. Bolling found their advancement "remarkable" from a condition as marginal as the United States' in 1915 to a system of production and development in 1917 that he judged better organized than the French system and as that of good as the British. The large engine factories of Fiat and Isotta-Fraschini were more like U.S. establishments than plants elsewhere, and he compared Italian directors, who worked in close harmony with the military, favorably to the most energetic U.S. businessmen.

In the rear the Technical Directorate under Lieutenant Colonel Ricaldoni, monitored production, received machines, trained pilots and mechanics, and had the planes flown to the front. The military technical staff had done considerable work on standardization of fittings. A Turin factory, for example, made all the bolts and turnbuckles, 12,000 and 15,000 daily, for the Italian air service.

Le Bon praised the aviation program for its thoroughness and simplicity, the Italian engine program for "remarkable unity of . . . conception," and Italian engines as "remarkable for their strength, their simplicity, reliability, and small consumption." The Italians, like the Germans, concentrated on perfecting six-cylinder engines. The well-organized factories had laboratories for mechanical, chemical, and analytical tests to ensure rigorously standardized production. The engine factories produced everything— radiators, tanks, and instruments—themselves. Fiat even made its own machine tools. Fiat's Turin workshops led the engine industry with a daily production of 20 engines, including accessories, while Isotta-Fraschini in Milan, Turin's SPA factory, Ansaldo at Genoa, and smaller factories around Milan contributed perhaps a total of 20 more engines. Ricaldoni expected to receive 100 engines daily by the spring of 1918.

The most crucial development in the aero engine industry was the modification of the Fiat A12 six-cylinder in-line, which developed 250 horsepower in 1916, to develop 300 to 320 horsepower in 1917. Production of the A12bis rose from 100 monthly in 1916 to 300 in 1917 and to more than 500 in 1918. Fiat would manufacture more than 13,000 of the type, nearly 50 percent of wartime Italian engine production.

Italian aircraft factories, in close collaboration with the Technical Directorate, made great strides in technological development and production. The wings of many Italian aircraft had the same chord, practically the same span, with little or no stagger. The firms emphasized the woodworking skills of Italian boatbuilders while avoiding metal as much as possible and reducing piano wires and turnbuckles to a minimum.

The aircraft types built in greatest number were 543 Pomilio and 448 SAML reconnaissance planes, and 367 FBA flying boats, the last by Macchi at Varese and SIA on Lake Maggiore. The Pomilio factory had 1,500 workers and was building 7 reconnaissance planes daily. Fiat's aircraft branch, SIA, developed a two-seat reconnaissance plane for the A12, the 7b1, which was sufficiently fast and maneuverable to hold its own against enemy fighters. Ansaldo bought the SIT factory in the fall of 1917 to produce the SVA, an all-wood fighter designed by the Technical Directorate that was an exceptionally fast single- or two-seat aircraft, ideal for the strategic reconnaissance role. The Caproni works at Taliedo was building one biplane and one triplane daily. Wing Commander Briggs found the Capronis, with their standardized wing ribs, bays, spars, and struts, designed with a view to ready production rather than ultimate aerodynamic efficiency and minimum weight, and he estimated that although the Handley Page bomber would be aerodynamically superior, a firm could build five Capronis to three Handley Pages.

Meanwhile, Giulio Douhet and Gianni Caproni were agitating for an Allied fleet of strategic bombers. Writing from prison in June, Douhet called for an Allied air fleet to bomb enemy cities in his essay "The Great Aerial Offensive" and urged Italy to build 1,000 planes, France 3,000, England 4,000, and the United States 12,000. In a July essay, "The Resistance of Peoples Facing the Long War," he underlined the effect on morale of the German raid on London, the inadequacy of antiaircraft defenses, and the necessity of massive force. He further congratulated Caproni for the bomber raids on Austrian territory. Douhet was released from prison on 15 October, one week before the disaster at Caporetto, and he returned to aviation in 1918.[220]

In an interview with *Le Petit Parisien* in October, Caproni advised that the war was one of materiel, which made it necessary to curtail enemy production. He lamented the excessive importance attached to aerial duels, the inadequate emphasis on raids on enemy bases, and suggested that the Allies needed a fleet of 200 to 300 bombers capable of carrying bomb loads of 2,000 kilograms.[221]

United States

The U.S. declaration of war on 6 April 1917 found U.S. aviation in a woefully unprepared state. The army air service had 65 officers, only 26 aviators among them, and 1,100 enlisted and civilian personnel; naval aviation, only 48 officers and 239 enlisted men. The Signal Corps had procured only 142 aircraft before 1917. The Mexican campaign against Pancho Villa from 1914 through 1916 had demonstrated the inadequacy of the tiny U.S. air service and provoked the criticism of aviators, Congress, and the press. Pershing praised his airmen and blamed the Signal Corps for inadequately supporting them.

During 1916 Gen. George O. Squier, returning from his post abroad as military attaché in London, became chief of the aviation section of the Signal Corps, while in June the National Defense Act authorized the formation of eight army aero squadrons, an increase in officers to 148, and an allocation of some $13 million to military aeronautics. Squier, appointed chief signal officer in February 1917, worked to persuade the civilian government agencies of aviation's importance, and the Secretary of War's annual report stressed the need for stimulating military aviation.

In March 1915 the navy had received $1 million for naval aviation, but the chief of naval operations paid little attention to it and the navy failed to specify who would be responsible for the aviation program. In June 1916 the navy's General Board foresaw the use of planes primarily for scouting and patrolling from ships and land bases and suggested an experimental airship program, and a naval appropriations bill at the end of August provided $3.5 million for aviation.[222]

The U.S. aircraft industry comprised 9 to 12 firms employing 10,000 workers by 1917. The two largest firms, Curtiss and Wright-Martin, each had capital of $10 million and were controlled by Wall Street syndicates dominated by automobile manufacturers like Howard Coffin of Hudson and Sydney Waldon of Packard. Coffin cavalierly commented in 1916 that "the problems confronting the aircraft industry are wonderfully simple compared with those of the automobile industry."[223]

The industry was wracked with patent disputes stemming from a federal court decision in January 1914 that the Wright patent on wing warping applied to any controls of the rolling motion of an airplane. In an attempt to settle the dispute and to facilitate the entry of the automobile industry into aviation production, Coffin and Waldon engineered the formation of the Aircraft Manufacturers Association in February 1917 to manage a patent pool. Wright-Martin, which held the key patent, promptly undermined the venture by refusing to join.

The 1 April 1917 edition of *Aviation and Aeronautical Engineering* decried the United States' neglect of aviation but recalled consolingly that England had been worse off in 1914 than the United States was then and had made "almost every conceivable mistake" in its efforts to obtain airplanes. The United States, the editor perhaps implicitly believed, would avoid such pitfalls, and he concluded that its greatest need was for more aircraft production facilities. Charles D. Walcott, Secretary of the Smithsonian Institution and chairman of the National Committee for Aeronautics (NACA), which President Wilson had formed in 1915, proclaimed that "no amount of money will buy time" and that the industry required governmental and military support as it standardized its products and resolved its patent disputes. Since the army had received only 64 of 366 aircraft ordered from 9 factories in 1916, Walcott reminded the journal's readers, industrial production from the 12 factories existing in 1917 was bound to fall far short of the need.[224]

With the declaration of war, the navy sent the United States' first military unit to Europe, an aeronautical detachment of 7 officers and 122 enlisted men, who arrived in France on 8 June. Late in September they began flying French Le Tellier seaplanes from U.S. naval air stations on the French coast to escort convoys from Quiberon to Saint-Nazaire.[225] In the United States the formation of a mighty military air service took center stage.

After the declaration of war, Squier requested the advice of air experts from abroad, and foreign military missions began arriving in Washington in April to obtain materials and stir enthusiasm for aviation and a U.S. air fleet that could "permanently cloud Germany's place in the sun."[226] In May French premier Alexander Ribot telegraphed suggesting a gigantic U.S. air arm of 4,500 airplanes; to achieve that goal would require the production of 2,000 aircraft and 4,000 engines monthly.[227] At Squier's urging, the Joint Army and Navy Technical Board recommended in June the production of 12,000 fighting planes, 5,000 trainers, and 24,000 engines and the training of more than 6,200 pilots by 1 July 1918. Yet the United States had neither the governmental organization nor the industry for such an immense program.

Authority over aviation was diffuse. Coffin and NACA proposed the creation of an Aircraft Production Board, which was formed on 16 May to assist and advise the services and manufacturers on design and production. The Joint Army and Navy Technical Board was to make final decisions in aircraft selection and procurement, and the Aircraft Production Board was responsible for aircraft requirements and placing contracts. In the army, the Signal Corps Aviation Section recruited and trained aviation personnel. The very governmental structure of the United States precluded close military-industrial ties. Law did not even allow the military to arrange advance payments and cost-plus contracts until later in 1917. The opposition of the secretaries of the army and navy killed proposals in Congress for a department of aeronautics. Initially Coffin preferred the loose organization because he wanted to limit governmental and military control of the industry. Yet by June he preferred to control aviation production himself and sought exclusive power for the board to grant contracts. *Aviation* was calling for clear statements of the function and authority of NACA, the army-navy joint boards, and the Aircraft Production Board. While *Aviation* considered the advisory powers of the Aircraft Production Board inadequate, it and aircraft manufacturers were concerned that the board would attempt to concentrate the industry in Detroit.[228]

Not everyone was convinced that such an enormous aviation program had merit. General Kuhn, chief of the war college, was doubtful that the plans could be executed within the time frame, but he considered aerial supremacy too important to be deterred by the magnitude of the problem.[229] Confronted with the concerns of the War Department's General Staff about the materials and industry required for the program, Squier went directly to the Secretary of War, Newton Baker, who in turn persuaded Woodrow Wilson of the importance of aviation.

Aviation advocates like Walcott, Coffin, and Squier unleashed a barrage of publicity. Squier predicted that in the postwar world armies would shrink but aviation would develop, on the foundation of the knowledge accumulated in wartime. At an 8 June luncheon in New York, Coffin proclaimed, "America's great opportunity lies before her. The road to Berlin lies through the air. The eagle must end this war."[230] In the press campaign to make the United States air-minded, the airplane became a miracle weapon, "the sling of the unprepared David against the militaristic German Goliath."[231]

Grandiose rhetoric punctuated the congressional hearings, as Squier invoked images of "winged cavalry sweeping across the German lines and smothering their trenches with a storm of lead, which would put the 'Yankee Punch' into the War."[232] Baker, who observed that the aviation program "lived up to America's traditions of doing things on a splendid scale," averred after the war: "We were dealing with a miracle. The airplane itself was too wonderful and too new, too positive a denial of previous experience, to brook the application of any prudential restraints which wise people know how to apply to ordinary industrial and military developments."[233] Or, as Col. T. DeW. Milling, chief of First Army air service, observed more prosaically after the war, the air service programs at the conflict's beginning were based on the "idea that has always seemed to exist in the United States, namely, that money can do anything."[234]

On 14 July the House unanimously approved the $640 million appropriations bill, which passed into law on 24 July. Only six months earlier a production of 1,000 planes annually was considered barely feasible. Now the industry would have to double that in a month. The expectations facing the military and the industry had reached wildly unrealistic heights.

Naval air appropriations increased to $3 million on 14 April, $11 million on 15 June, and $45 million on 6 October. The navy began flight training at the Massachusetts Institute of Technology and in Canada, and on 27 July authorized $1 million for a naval aircraft factory in Philadelphia that was completed in late November to accumulate data on the cost of private contracts. After considerable reductions from the initially grandiose estimates, a seaplane construction program in October set a target of 1,700 planes—235 twin-engine H16 and 825 single-engine HS1 Curtiss seaplanes and 640 training aircraft. If the United States had little else, it did have the Curtiss boats, and the navy had ordered its first one in 1916.[235]

The aircraft industry expanded to meet the expected mass production contracts, increasing its factory floor space from 740,000 square feet in July to 5.3 million in December. On 1 May Coffin called for standardization before investing millions in machinery to diminish the chaos of rapid expansion.[236] On 26 July the manufacturers agreed to a cross-licensing scheme proposed by NACA and the Aircraft Production Board in which they relinquished their patents to a new Manufacturers' Aircraft Association.

The key to the U.S. industry's fastest production of combat planes lay in copying European types. Yet from the start U.S. efforts to establish such arrangements were dogged by the difficulty of producing rapidly changing materiel and by fundamental differences of industrial approach between European serial production by skilled craftsmen and U.S. standardized, assembly-line mass-production techniques using unskilled labor and detailed blueprints and specifications for machinery.[237]

In May Baker decided to send a mission abroad to determine the best European materiel for production in the United States and to coordinate a production program with the Allies. Maj. Raynal C. Bolling, former chief counsel for the United States Steel Corporation, who had helped lobby the congressional appropriations, led 11 military, naval, and industrial experts, including army aeronautical engineers Capt. V. E. Clark and Capt. E. S. Gorrell. They sailed from New York on 17 June to spend nearly five weeks visiting England, France, and Italy. The mission encountered "princely courtesy" in Italy, no pressure to do business in England, and French offers to sell large amounts of materiel, which led to a contract on 30 August for 5,000 planes and 8,500 engines.

Convinced that the Europeans would retain supremacy in aviation design for the duration of the war, Bolling arranged for the immediate shipment of each ally's best materiel to the United States for possible licensed production. A preliminary 10 July report advised sending U.S. materials and engines to England and France and establishing large assembly plants there for English and French planes built in the United States. The mission's final report of 15 August suggested the free exchange of all patents, except for a payment of $100,000 to the French for three planes and three engines deemed immediately and vitally necessary. Bolling believed that the United States needed to supply the Allies with raw materials for their production of sufficient planes to sustain the United States until July 1918, the earliest possible date for substantial U.S. manufacture of frontline materiel. The United States would provide materiel first for its own training program, then for a tactical force for the AEF, and finally for special air forces comprising 37.5 percent fighters, 25 percent day bombers and 37.5 percent night bombers, the last of which he believed "might determine the whole outcome of military operations" through large-scale and continuous operations. Among other possibilities, the mission recommended for stateside production the Bristol fighter, Spad, DH4, and Caproni combat planes, and the Hispano-Suiza engine, but advised that such production should not interfere with shipments of materials and engines to Europe. Inter-Allied coordination, which the mission considered minimal, was an "absolute necessity" to the United States, as it arranged for the training of U.S. aviators and mechanics abroad and initiated the Inter-Allied Aircraft Committee, which met monthly in an attempt to coordinate production. Its work done, the mission disbanded, and Colonel Bolling became assistant to the chief of the air service in command of aviation in the zone of the interior in France.[238]

The Bolling mission's recommendations set in motion a variety of initiatives. The Italian army, which had directed much of Italy's aeronautical development, agreed to relinquish royalties after initial objections; the British, with the notable exception of Rolls Royce, concurred; the French government, however, which had high royalty agreements with its own firms, was unable to concur. The Italians sent sample materiel first, then the British, and finally the French, who were delayed by the fall of the Ribot government. Most of the materiel lacked complete drawings, specifications, and the information necessary for U.S. machine shop methods.

The task of aviation mobilization was more difficult than anticipated, requiring better organization and even military intervention in far-flung realms. In late August the Signal Corps Equipment Division was formed under Col. Edward Deeds and Sydney Waldon, who left Coffin's Aircraft Production Board for this source of real power over contracts. Both the Joint Army and Navy Technical Board and the Aircraft Production Board lost power, the former when AEF commander John J. Pershing insisted on final authority to determine aircraft types, the latter in October, when it became the Aircraft Board and was absorbed by the war and navy departments. In order to secure sufficient spruce from the Pacific Coast, the Signal Corps formed a spruce production division in the fall. On 19 September Waldon acknowledged the difficult undertaking ahead of the Curtiss company, as European designers and manufacturers honed their parts "to a degree of perfection that we know nothing about in this country at the present time. . . . [w]e have quite a problem ahead of us to educate our workmen to entirely new standards."[239] Squier did establish an experimental engineering organization in aviation in September at McCook Field in Dayton, Ohio, a research and development organization responsible for adapting European designs to U.S. production methods.

The institutions were new, the task immense. Colonels Deeds and Waldon of the Signal Corps Equipment Division decided to concentrate on the development of "one type of standardized engine designed especially to suit U.S. quantity production methods."[240] They enlisted E. J. Hall of Hall Scott Motor Company and J. G. Vincent of Packard to design a line of engines of 4, 6, 8, and 12 cylinders, the 8- and 12-cylinder engines to produce 225 and 330 horsepower. The two men required only four days to establish the engine's basic characteristics, which they drew from contemporary models. The steel cylinder and crankshaft design followed European practice, the die-cast aluminum alloy pistons were Hall Scott inventions, and the ignition system a Delco contribution. Packard built the V12 with the assistance of other automobile companies. Ford, for example, developed a method of making cylinders from steel tubing that saved the labor and material required to machine them from forgings and would allow daily production of 2,000 rough cylinders. The first 12-cylinder, which ultimately became the standard engine, passed its 50-hour endurance test on 25 August, after a remarkably short gestation, and the first 22 were delivered in December.

Aircraft development proceeded more slowly. The Dayton-Wright Airplane Company redesigned the De Havilland 4, which arrived in late July without engine or accessories, for the Liberty 12-cylinder engine. It flew in late October 1917, but the first U.S.-built prototype was still under construction at the end of the year.

A $30 million Spad contract with Curtiss entailed the redesign of the Spad for production using the Liberty 8-cylinder engine. The engine proved unsuccessful, and the subsequent reversion to the Hispano-Suiza aborted when Wright-Martin failed to deliver the engines. Such problems combined with premature fears of the Spad's impending obsolescence to halt the venture on 7 November. Pershing cabled on 14 December to leave single-seat fighter production to the European Allies, and the contract was canceled on 28 January 1918. Curtiss, teetering on the brink of bankruptcy from its rapid expansion and the introduction of mass-production techniques, received a new contract for 2,000 Bristol fighters in December.[241]

Bolling was interested in either the Caproni or the Handley Page for his all-important night bomber. Confronted with British recalcitrance in providing a Handley Page and Italian vacillation in choosing between the biplane and the triplane Caproni and slowness in providing engineers and drawings, Bolling played the British and Italians off against each other. After four months of negotiations, British representatives arrived on 30 December 1917 and the Italians on 16 January 1918.[242]

In Europe, the command structure of the embryonic U.S. Air Service was in flux. Col. Billy Mitchell had become aviation officer on Pershing's staff on 30 June, and in August, when Bolling took command of aviation in the rear in France, Mitchell assumed command in the zone of advance. Sources invariably cite Mitchell as a major influence on the Bolling mission in his advocacy of Trenchard's offensive use of aviation.[243] According to historian James Hudson, in May Major Mitchell, who was in Europe as Squier's personal observer, learned from Trenchard about the importance of strategic bombardment and unified air command.[244]

The Italian airmen and Caproni certainly advocated strategic bombardment and an inter-Allied unified air command to Bolling and Gorrell, and Major General David Henderson had discussed with Bolling the use of bombers to sever communications and sources of supply. But at that time Trenchard had not progressed beyond the offensive to embrace strategic bombardment; the unified command he was advocating was within the RFC, not the inter-Allied force the Italians supported. Mitchell could not have adopted from Trenchard ideas that the latter did not yet espouse, and Bolling and his mission were eminently capable of grasping and advocating the idea themselves.

The absence of a single U.S. aviation commander resulted in confusion and lack of cooperation between the front and rear, which did not abate entirely even when Brig. Gen. W. L. Kenly became chief aviation officer at the end of August. On 27 November Kenly in turn was replaced by Brig. Gen. Benjamin Foulois, who became chief of the air service, AEF, bringing with him a staff from Washington, whom Billy Mitchell disparagingly called carpetbaggers. Foulois assigned Bolling to coordinate inter-Allied industrial relations on 12 December. The new organization in late December set a goal of a 190-squadron air service by July 1918.

The first group of 47 flight candidates arrived in France in late June 1917, but the bulk of trainees did not arrive until fall, missing the best training time and crowding the French and embryonic U.S. training facilities in France. They often encountered such primitive conditions and such menial assignments at the facilities that one flier, when asked after the war about his treatment as a prisoner of war in Germany, acerbically answered, "A damn sight better than I got in France as a cadet."[245] A first detachment of 46 U.S. cadets arrived at the Italian flight school at Foggia on 28 September, to be joined by another detachment in October that included first-term congressman from New York Fiorello H. La Guardia.[246]

Perhaps the ultimate evidence of the disarray was the absence of agreement on the very nature of the future air service. In a statement of general principles on the use of the air arm in the fall, Col. Billy Mitchell emphasized the organization's tactical mission. It would help to destroy the enemy's military force in the field, and strategic aviation would strike supply and communications more than 25,000 yards, or a little more than 14 miles, behind the front.[247] In the rear in France, Bolling and Gorrell, influenced by Caproni, Douhet, and RNAS experts wing commander Spencer Grey and Lord Tiverton, became enthusiastic advocates of strategic bombing. In a memorandum of 28 November, Gorrell advocated wrecking Germany's commercial and manufacturing centers more completely than the anticipated German strategic campaign would wreck theirs. He accepted RNAS advice, suggesting as targets the Düsseldorff, Cologne, Mannheim, and Saar Valley groups and emphasizing the moral and material effects of bombing. He stressed the importance of concentration on selected targets and of U.S. initiative in coordinating an Allied bombing campaign.[248] In October the War Department General Staff decided that the air arm should have a ratio of 5:3:1 in pursuit, observation, and bombardment, which corresponded to neither Gorrell's notions of a ratio of 5:3:6 based on Italian observations nor Pershing's insistence of 3:2:1.5.[249]

In 1917 stipulations of the nature, composition, and size of the force remained hypothetical, depending ultimately on the success of embryonic training and production schemes. Creating an air arm with a front in Europe and a rear 3,000 miles away would be no mean feat, especially given the dramatic contrast between grandiose expectations and the confused and chaotic mobilization.

Conclusion

The air war in 1917 witnessed the evolution of massed fighter tactics over the Western and then the Southwestern Front, of close air support, and of bombers used in a German strategic campaign against Britain and in tactical raids on the fronts. The airplane was rapidly evolving from a means of tactical reconnaissance and artillery spotting into a multifaceted weapon of war.

The differing nature of the major air arms emerged clearly during the year. The RFC was an aggressive offensive arm that emphasized fighting and, increasingly, bombing and carried the fight to the Germans regardless of circumstances. It passed through its most serious crisis in the spring and summer, a crisis that stemmed in part from its offensive nature. When its reequipment with superior new fighters was delayed, primarily by engine problems, and the crews in its rapidly expanding force were inadequately trained, the RFC's insistence on the unrelenting offensive resulted in cruel losses among new airmen. Those who remained formed a core of battle-hardened survivors, who condemned their leaders, ignored newcomers in the certainty that few would survive, and fought on, sustained by their conviction of moral superiority. The British sometimes appeared driven by the notion that the higher the casualties, the higher the air arm's value. The RFC's offensive policies denigrated the significance of the high losses to the aircrews, while touting them as proof of the service's contribution to the war effort. The RFC replaced the losses with men from the Dominions, took delivery of the new fighters, and surmounted the crisis by the fall.

The French pursued an offensive, if more circumspect, policy in the effort to conserve their dwindling manpower. Acknowledging the limitations posed by inadequate materiel and serving an army that confined itself to limited offensive actions after the Chemin des Dames debacle, the French air arm as a whole did not go after the Germans aggressively, although its star fighter units relentlessly pursued the "Boche."

The German air arm, like its army, fought essentially a defensive war, husbanding its crews through such tactics as using one specialized plane for long-range reconnaissance rather than several with escort. But the high command combined the defensive stance with a strategic air offensive against Britain rather comparable to its submarine offensive in 1917.

With the development of large airplanes capable of striking at enemy heartlands, the question of appropriate targets and the notion of the vulnerability of civilian morale to such raids appeared everywhere. The bomber meant the demise of the airship as an offensive weapon, but Peter Strasser's justification for continued use of the Zeppelin—to strike British morale as much as any material target—echoed that of his bomber counterparts in Britain. While authorities differed on the mix of military, industrial, and civilian population targets, the question was on the table for discussion.

George Williams asserts that most British histories examining strategic bombardment underestimated or oversimplified the French bombing policy.[250] The French command under Pétain approached strategic bombing pragmatically, setting target priorities and assessed bombing effectiveness based on military results, not calculations of the effect on morale.

The various forces tended to view their Allied and enemy counterparts with both contempt and admiration. German pilots captured in the late spring invariably admired the courage and aggressiveness of British fliers, but they also knew that British losses were "very high," since the British fought over German lines in ridiculously inferior craft like the BE2. Manfred von Richthofen commented in February that "Englishmen see in flying nothing but a sport. . . . Therefore, the blood of English pilots will have to flow in streams."[251] Villars complimented the English on their discipline and pluck on patrol, but considered the Germans infinitely less "aviators" and fighter pilots than the French,[252] while Richthofen considered French attacking spirit like "bottled lemonade. It lacks tenacity."[253]

The British remained partially dependent upon French materiel and had appropriated the fundamental premises of the aerial offensive from the French. Though they had a smaller air arm than the French, they now assumed the main burden on the Western Front. As they pursued the offensive more aggressively and inflexibly than the French, they came to believe that the French were not carrying their fair share of the air war.

In a secret memorandum to the War Cabinet on 24 August, Trenchard judged that French aviation "excels in conception, but fails in execution." It suffered from too rapid an expansion, a lack of standardization and a multiplicity of machines in the same units, an unwise decentralization, and a lack of discipline. A limited number of star pilots did most of the work but were a law unto themselves, while many pilots did less work over the lines than the

British would expect of their pilots. The more rigid French system of promotion kept commanders and pilots too long in rank. The French were six months behind the Germans and a year behind the British in undertaking low-altitude operations. The lack of training in formation flying disinclined them to go over German lines, and they were more reluctant to attack against the odds than the British. French supply problems were complicated by the firms' political agitation, frequent changes in command and organization, and difficulties in procuring new materiel. The want of discipline and insufficient care of the machines were reflected in indifferent fittings, from gun mounts to bomb sights, and understrength units.[254]

Trenchard's harsh assessment was, in many respects, equally applicable to his own force. The RFC also suffered from rapid expansion, inadequate concentration of its force, a certain indiscipline, and difficulties getting new machines. On 4 August U.S. military intelligence reported: "As regards discipline, . . . the flying corps caused the British the most trouble, in view of the fact that the service, owing to its picturesque nature, is very likely to attract the wrong class of men."[255] Yet perhaps the most absurd of the disparaging remarks came from David Henderson in the Air Board meeting of 16 October, when he charged, "When the French had adopted any machine or engine on a large scale they had been proved to be wrong,"[256] while English engines self-destructed all around him.

French fighter pilots, most of them bourgeois like their counterparts in all the air services, appropriated the terminology of the knight, the military aristocracy. Unlike the mass slaughter below, they fought an individual war that they considered a true test of their personal ability and valor, for fighting alone or in small groups they had the choice to attack or flee. The British fighter pilots added to this the notion of teamwork, the Germans that of discipline. British teamwork in the air derived from their attitude toward sport, German discipline from the realization that the air war was a military endeavor. In both cases the approach to aviation enabled an effective transition to mass aerial combat, as pilots acknowledged and accommodated themselves to the new circumstances.

The French fighter pilots' concept of air combat clearly became increasingly detrimental to the effectiveness of French single-seater units. In the aerial environment of 1917, very few were capable of surviving, much less killing, alone, as the demise of Voss, Guynemer, and Ball demonstrated. German and British aces like Richthofen, Mannock, and McCudden were squadron leaders. The great French aces, however, those in the Storks and in other squadrons like Nungesser, remained loners, while the great French squadron leaders were usually father figures. Concentrating so many of the best fliers in the Storks left the other squadrons at a disadvantage. The German circus threatened to affect the German fighter arm similarly, but the Germans used first the Boelcke Jagdstaffel and then Richthofen's units as a training ground for squadron leaders. The French increasingly risked condemning their revered pursuit pilots to relative ineffectiveness, compared to fighter arms that understood that mass, not individuals, determined the course of the war in the air as it did on the ground.

This cultural bias also helps to explain why French fighters did not engage in ground attack. Reentering the ground war would soil the clean hands of those bourgeois aviators and expose them to the random death of the infantryman. Single-seat fighters were for aerial combat, and nothing less. Only after witnessing the effectiveness of German two-seater fighters did the French decide to develop their own, so that they might have low-level fighter operations while the single-seat elite continued to devote themselves solely to aerial fighting.

By 1917 the British and German commands believed that low-flying attacks were a powerful weapon in battle. British fighter pilots assumed the responsibility of ground attack as well as aerial fighting, as much as they reviled the latter duty. The Germans developed suitable planes for ground attack; the British simply threw in their fighters to supplement their army corps planes; the French did neither, and lagged far behind in effective ground attack operations.

In a recent study of battlefield aviation, *Strike from the Sky*, historian Richard Hallion praises the effectiveness, despite high casualties, of the RFC's use of fighters for ground attack.[257] A closer examination of British and German ground attack practices in 1917 suggests that the German approach was more effective and used aircraft and crews more efficiently than the British. The Germans profited from the Somme experience to develop specialized armor-plated ground attack planes and highly maneuverable light two-seaters for trench strafing. Their noncommissioned officer crews displayed high morale and great determination in their organized strafes en masse over and behind British lines and further disproved British claims about the inadequacy and even cowardice of noncommissioned officer pilots.

The memoirs of RFC fighter pilots who were assigned to low-flying duties and more immediate assessments of the Battle of Cambrai present a less favorable picture than Hallion does using secondary sources and the official history. Squadrons of Camels and second-rate DH5s assigned to low-flying work at Cambrai suffered prohibitive 30 percent losses. Arthur Gould Lee, who was shot down three times in seven low-flying sorties over Cambrai, considered it a wasteful employment of highly trained pursuit pilots for the "poor and uncertain" results of their actions.

Random, uncoordinated, and individual attacks were ill suited to have a critical effect on the mass battlefield. The RFC's resort to fighters for ground attack reflected its emphasis on fighters and then bombers to the denigration of army cooperation planes. It had not developed specialized types for trench work, although the single-seat fighter of World War I, unlike its successor of 1939–45, was an unarmored wooden contraption exceedingly vulnerable to ground fire. In haphazard fashion the RFC simply launched its fighter pilots with roving missions in keeping with the very individualistic notions that they were discarding in aerial combat.

As the airplane expanded its military roles, 1917 became a time of heightened aviation mobilization in all powers, occasioned by attrition and shortages and accompanied by heightened political strife in England and France.

The German army exerted more control over its aviation industry than did England or France, as its arbitrary methods in patent matters indicated. Yet the indispensability to the war effort of successful engine manufacturers gave them tremendous leverage in their relationship with the government, as their refusal to submit to state policies demonstrated.

Of the lesser powers, the Italian aerial mobilization was notable for the focus provided by the directorate, which compensated for severe material shortages by rigorous standardization and the utilization of wood and woodworkers. The Russian aerial effort, never substantial, disintegrated in revolution, while Austria-Hungary, beset by overwhelming shortages, careened toward collapse though its aviators fought as best they could. A U.S. aerial presence lay in the future.

Concerted efforts to improve aircraft performance bore fruit, in the fighter realm with increases in speed, climb, and maneuverability and in the bomber realm with large, lumbering, multiengine night raiders and single-engine day types. The Germans and British had evolved two-seat fighter types that could combat single-seaters, although the Bristol was intended primarily for fighter-reconnaissance operations, while the German types were intended for battlefield operations. For ground support the Germans had further created armored planes. Overall, the quality of German two-seat observation craft was far superior to that of the Allied powers, who fought in 1917 with largely obsolescent, poorly performing planes and tended to rely on fighter protection for their survival.

Everywhere the evolution of airpower demonstrated the signal importance of aero engines. Nineteen seventeen was a year of crisis in aviation for England and France, a crisis at bottom of aero engine production, which manifested itself differently in each country. The French were turning out more engines than any other power, but mastering the new technology of producing the geared 220-hp Hispano-Suiza proved difficult even for them in 1917 and consequently delayed the introduction of higher-performance Spad 13s and of British SE5As. The British and French relied primarily on increased horsepower rather than aircraft design to provide the essential margin of difference, and their problems with engine production impaired progress toward aerial mastery. Nevertheless France, effectively enlisting its automobile industry, outdistanced England and Germany in its development of high-powered engines.

Yet the very difficulties experienced in all the countries in engine development and production revealed the crucial position of high-powered engines. The engine was the heart of the airplane. The race here concerned quality and quantity, and France displayed the best combination of both. Germany, mired in material shortages, was unable to move beyond the six-cylinder in-line or to increase its production sufficiently, although its engines were marvelously reliable and durable. In Britain Rolls Royces were superb engines and Bentleys prolonged the operational effectiveness of rotaries at unbelievably high horsepower, but the Rolls Royce Eagles and Falcons, which could have been the backbone of British production from bombers to two-seat fighters, could not be mass-produced.

Among the lesser aviation powers, Italy's success in engine development and production set it apart from Austria-Hungary, which lacked the industry to produce Porsche's designs, and Russia, which never developed a significant engine industry. In United States the automobile industry was not only coordinating the development of combat engines but further threatening to dominate the embryonic aircraft industry as well.

French efforts to seek an ever more rational organization of the bifurcated aviation bureaucracy combined with governmental instability to condemn them to constant and debilitating changes and conflicts. Both in the rear and at the front, individuals entered and exited the aviation scene rapidly, bringing bureaucratic and programmatic modifications. Ironically, when Pétain, Duval, and Dumesnil finally achieved a semblance of autonomy, stability, and cooperation in the leadership of the front and rear, Clemenceau, a supporter of aviation but not of its autonomy, subordinated the undersecretary to the ministries of war and armaments. Yet the bifurcation made sense, as the War Ministry handled technical matters, the Armaments Ministry controlled material and labor allocations, and Colonel Dhé's role as coordinator between the two ministries assured Clemenceau of the control he required.

The British administration of aviation was as highly politicized and personalized as the French, as the transition to the Air Ministry amply demonstrated. But the British system was not racked by ministerial instability. In 1917 the Air Board, however oddly it seemed to perform its tasks, and the Ministry of Munitions Air Department were relatively stable entities. The RFC, Trenchard's empire, had had only one chief from 1915 to the end of 1917. The French system seemed constantly shifting; the British muddled about, reluctant to change, and then changed the system dramatically to create a new muddle.

In France and Britain the parliament played important roles in aviation, as parliamentary deputies wanted strategic air arms. In France, the army's control of aviation was a given, so the politicians sought the solution not in an air ministry but through secret committee interpellations and intrigues to affect the War Ministry and the undersecretary or director, whom the parliament could and did bring down, but to no avail in the pursuit of strategic aviation. In Britain the air lobby in parliament pressed the government for a separate air arm, to which the Lloyd George government resorted to resolve the army-navy conflict over aviation and to give the prime minister an ally in his struggle with the generals.

Compared to these complex situations, the German military bureaucracy in aviation was a paragon of stability, as the same officers—Hoeppner, Lieth-Thomsen, Siegert, Wagenführ—continued in control of aviation. Control over production and use of airplanes was more unified in Germany than in England or France, and it needed to be, given the shortages of materiel and manpower.

In 1917 possibilities of inter-Allied cooperation increased with the United States' entry into the war. The Allies depended on France for engines, but on the Western Front the lack of coordination between the British and the French enabled the German air arm to survive despite the Allies' increasing numerical superiority. Coordination would be necessary to bring the United States' forces to bear against Germany as soon as possible. English pleasure at securing a new ally mingled with fears that U.S. aircraft production would threaten the supply of silver spruce and other materials and that U.S. demands on French production might interfere with large orders long overdue. The British Air Board was willing to pay British firms royalties for materiel manufactured in the United States. Of course, the board was obviously going to recommend the manufacture of British types. Northcliffe planned to rely on the United States for aerial preponderance in late 1918, as he calculated that U.S. manufacturers would produce airplanes like automobiles, but by early November the United States' entry into the war had produced only interference in fulfilling its contracts, especially spruce, with England.[258]

In June 1917 Commander Tulasne, chief of the French aviation mission in the United States, reported that the United States was a tremendous reservoir of manpower, raw materials, and machinery, but time, French engineers, and aircraft prototypes would be necessary to adapt them to the new task. Yet the French delayed sending specimens of their best engines to the United States for fear of industrial espionage, while U.S. builders were surprised to have to pay license fees to build planes for the defense of France.[259]

Ideas of a strategic air offensive brought Italy more center stage than previously. France and England were preoccupied with the Western Front, which consumed nearly all their aviation production and effort. Both powers were casting about desperately in 1917 for materiel, particularly engines, and materials. The United States could offer the materials but not materiel, though the Liberty seemed a future possibility. Italy's engine industry, specifically Fiat, offered a present source of additional suitable engines. The Caproni, which was already produced under license in small numbers in France, might just be the night bomber the Allies would require. Inter-Allied cooperation and coordination in strategic aviation was more the product of the economic considerations, Caproni to carry the war to Central Powers via his bombers, the United States to translate its wealth in materials into some effective strike force as quickly as possible. French political and military leaders, regardless of the strategic air advocates in parliament, were not prepared to wage strategic air warfare, while the British cared little for inter-Allied strategic coordination. It remained to be seen how effective the Inter-Allied Aviation Committee, which formed in November to meet once a month in Paris to discuss supply and production of the Allied countries' aviation programs, would be.[260]

CHAPTER SIX

1918

"Aerial mastery is a matter of method and organization more than heroism."

HENRI CHAMPOMIER, *LA GUERRE AÉRIENNE*, JANUARY 1918[1]

Since the airplane had become the instrument to be used en masse over the battlefield, 1918 promised a continuation of 1917's tremendous development in military aviation and a heightened mobilization of the aviation industry. Although winter weather caused a relative lull in operations, both sides prepared for another year of siege warfare. With Russia no longer a factor and Austria-Hungary near collapse, the war was focused mainly on the Western Front, where the United States was expected in force in 1918, but only if the Allies could withstand the coming German spring offensive. If the Allies survived, then they expected the war to continue into 1919, when U.S. arms would enable them to crush the Central Powers.

The Greater Powers

France

In the 14 February *La Guerre aérienne*, former undersecretary of air Daniel Vincent advocated forming a doctrine for aviation, a "chain linking the past to the future." Early in the war, he recalled, aviation had lacked organization and doctrine, and had thus fallen into the excessive individualism of "sporting" aviation, with "as many principles as chiefs."[2] At GQG Gen. Henri Pétain and Gen. Maurice Duval planned for the French air service to achieve a new level of organization, doctrine, and operations in 1918. With sufficient resources to form larger formations, it planned to annihilate enemy aviation and gain definitive aerial mastery in tactical offensive operations. GQG's 11 February and 2 March orders prescribed aviation's principal role to be the destruction of enemy aviation.

Pétain, emphasizing the importance of concentrating aerial forces, ordered the formation of combat and day- and night-bomber wings. The day bomber, however, with its relatively small bomb load, would serve mainly to force enemy aviation into battle with its fighter escort. Pétain wanted to wield aviation en masse against the coming German attack. "The action of the cannon will be extended by all disposable aviation," he advised on 15 February. "With bombs and machine guns our planes will set upon columns in march, convoys, bivouacs, and parks day and night. . . . Army group commandants will assure the concentration of aeronautical means necessary to demoralize troops destined to lead and feed the attack."[3] Massive, concentrated, and precise bombing attacks on carefully selected military and industrial targets behind the front would aim primarily at material destruction, although GQG expected the attacks on troops to affect principally their morale. In the 2 March directive to combat aviation, Pétain advised that its concentrated assault on enemy aviation to secure aerial superiority and mobility over the battlefield would be one of the land operations' conditions of success.[4] Pétain's air chief, General Duval, would serve under the direct orders of the general commanding the armies. By March GQG had thus formulated the doctrine and command arrangement for using mass aviation in future battles.

In late February French military intelligence noted a German aviation buildup in preparation for the coming battle. The French air service, which had increased aircraft supply 17 percent between November 1917 and March 1918, was equal to German aviation by itself. Since October 1917 the French had forced fighter and bomber production at a feverish pace, and by the beginning of the German offensive on 21 March they had 11 fighter groups, 5 day-bomber groups, and 7 night-bomber groups. Compared to the September 1917 2,870-plane program and the October 4,000-plane program, on 1 April the army had 2,750 planes at the front (1,400 observation and 1,350 combat planes), while the aviation reserve had 581 planes on 21 March. The fighter and day-bomber wings were equipped with Spad 7s and Spad 13s and Breguets, a combination that would simplify production, repair, and training.[5]

In the March 1918 battle, Pétain used airplanes to deter the German offensive. In constant operations over the battle zone between 21 March and 12 June, 400 bombers dropped 1,200 tons of bombs, over 200 tons greater than in 1916 and 1917 operations combined.[6] During the German assault from 21 to 31 March, fighter aviation supported the ground forces and did not seek air combat. From 1 April to 14 May, General Duval emphasized the aerial battle and would not let fighter reserves be used for the observation planes' immediate protection. The wings entered action on 2 April, when a fighter wing and a bomber wing, named after their chiefs Philippe Féquant and Victor Ménard, formed a combat group. In the raids on the attacking German army, coordinating fighter escort with the bombers proved difficult, and Féquant's fighters sometimes seemed disinterested in bomber escort. By 5 April complaints from the armies reminiscent of the 1916 and 1917 offensive abounded. The air reserve's liaison with the armies lessened; sweeps behind enemy lines did not help the front; patrols were too high to attack low flying enemy aircraft and unable to protect reconnaissance airplanes near the lines.[7]

The GQG's next organizational measure, which marked a significant milestone in the concentration of French aviation, was forming the autonomous Aerial Division (Division aérienne) under General Duval on 14 May. The division was not a strategic arm, as GQG considered strategic aviation premature, but rather a tactical one.[8] It included all the day bombers and half the fighters, the other half going to the armies. For bomber escort the division gradually replaced single-seaters with heavily armored and armed three-seat twin-engine Caudron R11s or Breguets, and it shortened the distance of the raids when German Fokker D7 fighters appeared. Ultimately, on 15 June the first and second aerial brigades were formed, the first under the command of Major de Goÿs, who had escaped from Germany after more than two years of imprisonment, the second under Féquant.[9]

The Aerial Division's critics, such as A. P. Voisin, judged that the airplane still lacked the offensive capacity to be more than an auxiliary to the ground forces. The division did not wreak much destruction on its land targets, while the Germans did not necessarily challenge the fighters.[10] In general, the Aerial Division could not simultaneously fulfill the two contradictory demands of a combined fighter and bomber offensive and an air reserve to reinforce the armies' air units. Voisin's guiding assumption remained that

the air arm serve as the army's immediate auxiliary protecting army cooperation planes, while Pétain and Duval intended the Aerial Division for
wider-ranging duties in support of the army.

Between the spring and summer the air arm and, more crucially, the
proportion of its newer-model aircraft, grew. Sen. Gaston Menier, visiting
Féquant's second group at the front on 23 April, detected improvements
since 1917: fewer unusable planes, reinforced frames and better motor-
mount attachments that decreased the Spad's engine vibrations, and better-
trained pilots.[11] On 25 April, however, Pétain noted that the implementation of the 5 April 1917 2,870-plane was not yet completed, while the 8
October 1917 4,000-plane program had not yet begun. He still needed
more new fighters and observation planes, as Sopwiths and ARs still
served in frontline squadrons.[12] By the summer these circumstances improved. In April the air arm had 797 fighters, 1,605 artillery and army
corps planes, and 413 bombers; in July it had 1,090 fighters, 1,733
artillery and army corps planes, and 438 bombers. The force in April
comprised 1,723 modern and 1,092 obsolescent types, and in July it had
2,827 new types and 434 old models, an increase in modern types from
61 to 87 percent.[13]

As the French army took the offensive that summer, in the 12 July
Directive number 5 the air arm described its principles of attack, which
emphasized simplicity, audacity, and rapidity to gain tactical surprise. After
secret preparations, the preliminary artillery and bomber strikes would be
as brief and violent as possible to enable tanks to rupture enemy lines. Aviation would thus assure aerial superiority. This document also emphasized
the importance of air-artillery cooperation, but did not envisage liaison between tanks and airplanes.[14] When Allied commander Gen. Ferdinand
Foch stated the necessity for better communication between the Aerial Division and the army on 23 July, Duval blamed inadequate liaison on the
army commanders, who had made no effort to improve communication with
the division's small staff, gave his officers no information, and did not respond to his liaison efforts. The army commanders did not understand the
division's purpose, General Duval concluded, and viewed it merely as a
reservoir of reinforcements to protect their observation planes, rather than
understanding its offensive mission in connection with the armies. General
Duval believed that the army commanders wanted to control the division
and use it to protect their observation planes.[15] Army commanders also ignored the division's efforts. In July Gen. Charles Mangin complained to a
visiting parliamentary deputy about the insufficient use of bombers during
the intensive bombardment of battlefield targets.[16] Despite the criticisms

and problems, the Aerial Division continued its offensives in 1918 and later formed the nucleus of Billy Mitchell's 1,400-plane force in the fall Saint-Mihiel offensive.

If Commander Foch had concerns about Aerial Division liaison, he was pleased with the quality of aerial reconnaissance for the high command. The Weiller group—three squadrons of Breguets commanded by Paul-Louis Weiller—served directly under Foch as of 28 July. Each day they flew over the lines in groups of three at altitudes of nearly 8,000 meters to take a photographic map of enemy territory from 20 to 100 kilometers behind the rear. Every evening at GQG Foch used these photos to choose targets. For his unit's work, Weiller was awarded the *légion d'honneur*, becoming one of its youngest recipients.[17]

In August observation units theoretically comprised Breguets, Salmsons, and the Caudron R11. However, inadequate Salmson and Breguet-Renault engine production left Petain six squadrons short of the 2,870-plane program, while 24 of 53 Breguet squadrons were equipped with Fiat engines that were inferior to the Renault. Consequently, on 20 August, of 142 observation squadrons only 29 were equipped with Renault Breguets and 55 with Salmsons; two-seat Spads continued in service as a stopgap. During another visit to army corps squadrons on 13 August, Senator Menier observed that while army corps planes were supposed to protect themselves, they in fact required fighter protection over the German lines and did not always receive it; though pilots were skilled, gunners and mechanics tended to be inexperienced.[18] At least the Breguets and Salmsons, valued for their strength and performance, gave army corps crews a chance against German fighters.

In bomber aviation, inadequate Breguet deliveries caused large gaps in the 15 day-bomber squadrons. Two Caproni night bomber squadrons needed refitting, while production of the Farman F50 night bomber, which already equipped two squadrons, needed to be stopped until the planes could be perfected.[19] By September a Breguet with a 450-hp engine was under test. General Duval advised Dumesnil that the Caproni giant with 900 total horsepower was nose heavy, carried a small bomb load, and was not ready for wartime service. Most critically, exhaust flames from the engines threatened to set the gas tanks on fire.[20] Night bombers remained a weakness of French aviation to the war's end, but it was clear that the air arm was obtaining more and better tactical aircraft for daylight operations throughout 1918, though not as quickly as desired.

The emphasis on mass aviation required substantial expansion of training to increase aircrews and to replace losses. The French trained 6,909 pilots in 1918,[21] and although they claimed that in 1919 they would be training 1,000 pilots a month, the number breveted annually from 1914 to 1918 (134 in 1914, 1,484 in 1915, 2,698 in 1916, and 5,609 in 1917) suggested that the rate of increase had peaked in 1917. French casualties in the war's last six months, from May through October, totaled 2,327 killed, wounded, and missing at the front and in the rear. Combat casualties at the front reached 1,324, while 632 casualties were from accidents at the front and 371 were from accidents in the rear. Casualties peaked in June at 470, after which they declined steadily to the war's end.[22]

For massed tactics in aviation, the French fighter force had to relinquish some of its individualism to function effectively in 1918. In January Daniel Vincent advised that "the extreme individualism that gave aerial mastery in 1915 is no longer useful today." This sentiment was echoed later by Jacques Mortane, editor of *La Guerre aérienne*, when he indicated that aviation was no longer a sport but an "arm" with rigid discipline and prepared operations similar to an infantry assault.[23] Vincent attributed the change to the sense of discipline brought by newer recruits from other branches, although he might have acknowledged the importance of GQG's leadership. However, individualism was too ingrained to be eliminated, and Mortane's article was probably intended as much to remind pilots of the new order as to show the modification of tactics.

French ace of aces René Fonck exemplified the continued emphasis on individual tactics. In 1918 he firmly established himself as Guynemer's heir in victories. He had 19 confirmed kills at the end of September 1917, 32 by the end of March 1918, and ultimately 75 by the war's end, although he claimed 127. He twice shot down six planes in one day. Fonck continued to prefer individual combat, although at the war's end he acknowledged that German group operations "compelled us to do one thing that was formerly exceptional, that is to fly in groups of generally four fighters. A lone encounter against ten would be too unequal."[24] In 1918 the Germans and English were operating in units of far more than 10 airplanes.

French bomber aviation emerged in 1918 as a tactical arm. At a conference with the British on 22 December 1917, General Duval had disagreed with the British policy of bombing enemy industrial centers and warned that the French did not intend to join British operations. He feared German reprisals and contended that neither Britain nor France had sufficient forces to conduct an effective strategic bombing campaign.[25] The French revised their bombing scheme on 18 November 1917 and 5 January 1918, noting that their ideas were a "result of evolution during action, rather than a strategic plan." Attempting to curtail railroad traffic in iron ore from the Saarbrücken and Lorraine basins, the French designated nine railroad stations within 45 miles of the line as targets. In January, following German simplification of their rail network into two independent traffic systems, economic and strategic, the French decreased the number of targets to four stations in the more vulnerable economic network to blockade the iron ore.[26]

In May debates with the British, the French opposed both strategic aviation and aviation's autonomy. General Duval commented on 31 May that "if we are defeated on land, the bombardment of Cologne is without interest." Duval continued to judge Allied aviation insufficient to act both strategically and tactically at once and thus emphasized the tactical role in subordination to land forces. The French, though dismayed about Trenchard's independent bomber force, were willing to provide it with airfields. However, when the Supreme War Council established an Inter-Allied Independent Air Force on 24 September, they insisted that requirements for land operations take precedence over any independent operations.[27]

In 1918 French bomber crews in Breguets, usually carrying 24 10-kg bombs, aggressively raided across the lines in massed formations. Protected initially by single-seaters and later by a few heavily armed and armored Caudron R11 three-seaters or Breguet 14 escorts, the Breguets manned by skilled crews, their gunners armed with twin Lewis guns and carrying six circular drums of 97 cartridges for each gun, were not easy prey, even when alone. Gunner Sergeant André Duvau, at age 32 often called "Père Duvau" by squadron mates, had spent nearly 10 months in the back seat of Sopwiths and then Breguets. Returning from a raid in mid-July, he and his pilot lost their squadron in clouds. Duvau spotted five German fighters climbing to meet them, warned his pilot, who then did a climbing banked turn to give Duvau a clear shot at them. As German bullets struck the Breguet, Duvau fired only seven shots in two short bursts at the leader, who spun and then plunged earthward, while the others turned away. Duvau survived those raids without incident, but he recalled the risks—of frostbite, antiaircraft fire, German fighters, accidents—and the fears engendered by witnessing the fate of other aircrew, fears of crashing in flames just off the field and of being badly burned.[28]

During the spring and summer Pétain and Duval apprised Undersecretary Jacques-Louis Dumesnil of their rapidly escalating goals for aviation. On 24 April, emphasizing the necessity for more and better airplanes, Pétain proposed a 6,000-plane air arm of new types, including 300-hp fighters, night bombers, two-seat fighters, three-seat battle planes, improved Breguet day bombers, and armored Salmson observation planes. They would require 26,000 personnel, including 800 officers and 9,000 trained technicians.[29]

On 24 May Pétain asked for the following aircraft types: high- and medium-altitude single-seat fighters; a long-range reconnaissance plane to penetrate 200 kilometers into the enemy rear; a well-armed, fast, high-altitude, medium day bomber that could operate from unprepared airfields to extend the artillery by attacking railroads and troops; a medium night bomber; and a long-range heavy bomber to attack German industrial centers as far as the Ruhr. The last was intended to "paralyze the economic life of Germany and its war industries by methodical, massive, and repeated action against principal industrial cities, important marshalling yards, and to weaken the morale of its population by giving them a feeling of insecurity in a zone extending as far as possible into enemy territory." Pétain's priorities, in order, were to obtain new model two-seat combat planes, heavy and medium night bombers, armored assault planes, and three-seat combat planes, and to perfect present single-seat fighters and then day bombers.[30]

On 24 August Pétain insisted, as "an absolute necessity," that he have the 148 squadrons of Renault-Breguets and Salmsons with more powerful engines by 1919's first trimester. He hoped to use the Breguet models and more powerful 200-hp Capronis as night bombers.[31]

Fulfilling these requests depended on either unpredictable technological progress or increased production. For the latter, however, the French also had to consider the Allies' air arms. Although the War Committee on 27 May determined to assure that Allied requests for materiel did not injure French interests, on 17 September Dumesnil contended that they would have been able to realize the 4,000-plane program if they had not had to deliver large amounts of equipment to the Allies.[32] The United States, given the same priority as the French army, received 1,430 first-class planes (Spads, Breguets, and Salmsons) between 1 April and 16 September. If the United States were self-sufficient by early 1919, the French could achieve the 6,000-plane program, which they had initially intended for 1 April 1919.

Another reason for France's failure to achieve the 4,000-plane program on schedule was the underestimation of aircraft losses. The expected 33 percent monthly wastage of bombers had reached at least 50 percent in recent battles, and replacements dominated the supply. By late September supplies sufficed to create the new units, since Renault-Breguet production increased.

In 1918 German fighter aviation's progress required simultaneously increasing craft quality and quantity. Several excellent 300-hp single-seaters were likely to appear in 1919. By mid-September 300-hp Nieuports and Sopwith Dolphins were in production; the prototype Spad Herbemont had recently completed "extremely brilliant" tests; and the Béchereau airframe showed great promise.[33] The 2,870-plane program had stipulated 60 Spad squadrons by spring 1918; the 4,000-plane program required 84 by 1 October, which seemed unlikely since in mid-September fighter aviation had only 64 squadrons. Two-seat types were undergoing final tests in the fall. Two-seat fighters—the SEA (Société d'études aéronautiques) with a 375-hp Lorraine engine, the Breguet with a 450-hp Renault or Liberty, and the Morane with a Bugatti 420-hp engine—were under development, but in 1919 fighter aviation's fate depended entirely upon future developments. Only in November would the army begin to receive the first Hanriot and Spad Herbemont two-seat fighters, with another (the first machine of the new firm SEA created by young designers Henri Potez and Marcel Bloch) offering further prospects. On 19 September GQG determined its needs based on a 4,200-plane program.[34]

Aviation's politics and administration stabilized considerably in 1918. Daniel Vincent's February article posited that the press constantly raised public concern about aviation because the air arm lacked a doctrine of industrial production.[35] Jacques Mortane followed Vincent's editorial with a call for an air ministry, noting that Britain had an air ministry and Germany possessed a "dictator of the air" in Hoeppner.[36] The call for an air ministry would make no progress during the war. The political clamor for change remained focused on the lack of strategic bombers, though some key air advocates implied the need for an air ministry by attributing all deficiencies to the absence of unified control.

While 1918's battles confirmed the French high command's use of bombers against battlefield objectives and enemy transport, the GQG still faced vigorous and persistent criticism in parliament and the public arena from advocates of strategic air power. Premier Georges Clemenceau and Minister of Munitions Louis Loucheur supported the high command before parliament. On 5 April Loucheur, emphasizing the importance of strafing enemy columns, asserted that French and British aviation had retarded the enemy's arrival on the battlefield by one to two days, while Clemenceau on 3 June gave bomber attacks on the battlefield partial credit for halting the recent enemy advance. On 3 August, after the first summer offensive, Loucheur stressed the importance of demoralizing the Germans by bombing their rear.[37]

Still, parliamentary deputy Pierre Etienne Flandin continued to advocate strategic bombardment in 3 July and 18 September reports. Clemenceau had written him that concentration of forces was essential to victory, and that operations against enemy cities, though possibly of economic and morale importance, were only secondary. Flandin criticized the limited scope of France's military chiefs and the "narrow doctrine of conduct of the war" that attributed only moderate importance to attacking the industries that produced war materiel. All parliamentary deputies and the high command as well, as General Pétain's requests indicated, regretted the industry's inability to perfect a long-range bomber.[38] The deputies, however, had placed top priority on the bomber, but for the high command the long-range bomber was only one of many desired types.

In the military administration of aviation technology and production, 1918 was the era of the technocrats. Martinot-Lagarde of the aero-engine section and Legras of the propeller service—both graduates of the École Polytechnique—were joined in 1918 by another polytechnician, 38-year-old Albert Caquot, whom Colonel Dhé and Dumesnil appointed director of the STAé on 11 January 1918. In 1914 Caquot, a bridge builder, specialist in reinforced-concrete construction and aviation, and an advocate of organizational solutions to problems,[39] had designed a stationary observation balloon, whose streamlined form made it superior to the German Drachen in its ability to remain steady in high winds. After having created an observation balloon for the British fleet in 1916, Caquot had been sent to Britain in 1916 to direct the British fleet's use of captive balloons against submarines. Caquot balloons formed barrages above London and Paris to protect against German bombers.

At STAé Caquot now dealt with airplanes, at a time when the inability to perfect new materiel threatened to compromise the Allies' opportunities for aerial supremacy. The problem lay, as it had in 1917, in the Spad 13 and its 220-hp Hispano-Suiza engines. The prototype engine had passed its tests, but some 10,000 production engines had failed their 10-hour acceptance tests, usually through a seizure that left a "salad" of connecting rods or destroyed the crankcase. Caquot ordered the tests of 10 engines. He stopped the first after one hour, the second after two, and so on, to open the crankcase and dismantle the moving pieces. After four hours the cause of the problem became apparent. The oil pipe in the crankcase had broken under pressure, though the engine continued to run for a time.

Caquot attributed the difference in performance between the prototype and the series to weather. The prototype had been tested in warm weather, while the series appeared in the winter. The viscosity of the oils used in 1917 varied greatly with the temperature, and their thickening in the winter led to excessive pressure in the Hispano-Suiza's oil-circulation system. Technicians had to decrease the oil flow to limit its pressure to a level that the pipe could withstand. After Caquot designed a simple, inexpensive safety valve for the end of the oil pump, Hispano-Suiza production continued.

Caquot's solutions did not always work. His addition of bracing struts to correct the Morane fighter's weakness in dives reduced its performance so that it was relegated to training. Yet in most crucial situations, his genius for diagnosing a problem and finding a simple solution benefitted the air arm. When the front complained about excessive Breguet 14 modification, Caquot settled on a mass production aircraft, which was then license produced by large manufacturers such as Michelin. Caquot's transmission of U.S. propeller research to French manufacturers enabled them to improve their airscrews. Ultimately, Caquot generously surrendered all his rights to the French state at no charge and received medals from all the major Allied powers and gratitude from the French government.[40]

Caquot praised Minister of Munitions Loucheur's further mobilization of aviation. Between three and five times a week the directors of the technical and production sections met with Dhé, Duval, and Loucheur or Loucheur's adviser, engineer Ernst Mercier, to plan the air service's development. They then met with the industrialists once a week to set production schedules.[41] By May an editorial in *La Guerre aérienne,* "L'Arme à deux têtes" (the arm with two heads), praised the division of labor between the undersecretary and the munitions ministry. The undersecretary, as the client, selected and perfected types and then, in consultation with GQG, determined the quantity needed, while the ministry, as the supplier, managed serial production.[42] From the spring to the war's end *La Guerre aérienne* tended to praise the rear's organization. An editorial in early June lauded the STAé's efforts in converting theoretical programs from the front into technical specifications for engineers and builders and asserted that the STAé had clearly outdone its less organized German counterpart and a German industry that was more dispersed and less standardized than the French. In an early August editorial it recognized that fundamental to aviation's "new phase of its evolution"—collective effort as opposed to individual action—was the French industrial effort, which enabled the new doctrine.[43] In September the journal concluded that quality and quantity determined the command's aerial tactics, which had left the realm of improvisation and had now become part of a methodical plan, in which aviation was indispensable as an arm of military intelligence and destruction.[44]

In 1918 Loucheur and the aviation agencies attempted to control prices and increase licensed production.[45] In mid-April he considered the aviation service's contract justifications absolutely insufficient to determine whether prices were too high and insisted that the contract service under Commandant Guignard be placed under Colonel Weyl in the munitions ministry, who would collaborate with Guignard.[46] The prices of Hispano-Suiza 200-hp engines dropped from 18,000 to 22,500 francs at the end of 1917 to 17,500 to 18,000 in mid-1918.[47]

A report in October 1919 contended that the Hispano-Suiza should have cost 8,500 francs, allowing for a net engine cost of 4,500, 15 percent profit, a 10 percent allowance, and 150 percent for general costs and labor.[48] Yet such postwar calculations appear unrealistic, and Dhé justified the prices with the state's wartime need to develop aero engine production. Builders had used their profits to remunerate capital invested in the enterprise and to expand plant capacity, while continually rising material and labor costs made such calculations of net cost purely theoretical. The aviation service could not requisition engines or militarize factories because it lacked qualified technical personnel to assure production at commandeered factories, so the directorate had emphasized engine quantity and quality above all else.[49] While the French airplanes lacked the finesse of the German Fokkers with their thick cantilever wings, Capt. Albert Etévé of the STAé emphasized the quality, officially called *rusticité*, characterized by the adoption of very simple construction procedures allowing numerous airframes to be built quickly and cheaply.[50]

With further increases in licensed manufacture, in 1918 subcontractors played a decisive role in aviation production. They reaped 61.9 percent of the total business in 1918, up from 27.3 percent in 1916 and 35.1 percent in 1917. In airframe manufacture the subcontractors' market share rose from 16.2 percent in 1916 to 43.7 percent in 1917 to 61 percent in 1918. In engine manufacture, it declined from 32.9 percent in 1916 to 27.2 percent in 1917, because of Hispano-Suiza's introduction of its 200- to 220-hp engine and Salmson's launching of its 200- to 260-hp series engine, but then it rose to 62.7 percent in 1918. Thus, in 1918 the dominant or parent manufacturers had 38.1 percent of the market: the aircraft producers and engine manufacturers had 39 percent and 37.3 percent of their markets, respectively.[51]

Circumstances within the industry varied. Hispano-Suiza built 14.8 percent of its 25,741 engines in 1918; its 14 subcontractors, which included Peugeot, constructed 85.2 percent. The parent firms Spad and Blériot reaped 17 and 26 percent of the profits respectively on Spad production in 1918, and their subcontractors gained 57 percent. Breguet earned 13.7 percent of the profits from Breguet 14 production in 1918; its subcontractors, which included Michelin and Renault, obtained 86.3 percent. Firms like Renault and Salmson, however, did not subcontract their production.[52]

The aircraft industry remained centered in Paris and its suburbs, where 90 percent of French planes were built, despite limited decentralization in 1918 during the German advances toward Paris. Among the largest factories were Farman, with some 5,000 workers, and Nieuport, with 3,600 workers. The general condition of the factories was good, and most of them were entirely or partially fireproof. The larger companies had assembly plants, and the smaller ones had assembly shops. Women painted, varnished, stretched cloth over frames, and did light woodwork. Assembly rooms were well ventilated to release varnish fumes that could cause eye inflammation, headaches, or stomach trouble, and employees who worked in the varnish room fortified themselves with milk. Large factories had surgical stations staffed by trained nurses. The ordinary working day was 10 hours. Employees were paid 1.5 to 3 francs an hour or by piece, while foremen and staffs were paid monthly. Generally, the number of engines obtainable determined production. French standardization and coordination of production impressed American attaché H. Barclay Warburton in July as offering the potential for large-scale inter-Allied standardization of Spad production, despite enormous difficulties with political and industrial interests.[53]

In 1918, of 41,336 engines manufactured in France through November, 29,461 were stationary engines (V types or in-lines), 5,526 were radials, and 6,349 were rotaries, a dramatic change from the 1917 proportions, in which rotaries and stationary-engine deliveries were nearly comparable (10,757 to 11,395) and radials were relatively scarce (1,223).[54] As orders for rotary engines declined, Gnome and Rhône shifted to producing the Salmson Canton-Unné radial.

In August it took an average of 6.29 workers per month about 250 hours to manufacture a Hispano-Suiza engine. The Hispano-Suiza was one of the most easily constructed wartime engines, since in its parts design Birkigt had been preoccupied with ease of production and had created special machine tools and machines to produce complicated and delicate parts. In 1918 15,108 Hispano-Suiza 200- to 220-hp engines were delivered, only 956 by the parent company; the largest numbers, 4,451, 2,239, 1,784, 1,470, and 1,410, were delivered by Peugeot, Mayen, Brasier, Fives Lille, and Delaunay, respectively. Another 2,166 300-hp engines were delivered in 1918, 814 by the parent company.[55]

In 1918 Renault doubled its engine production from 2,470 in 1917 to 5,050 and nearly trebled its aircraft production from 290 to 870 in its second year of aircraft assembly. From 1 October 1917 to 30 September 1918 Renault's sales of aero engine and airframes came to 29.3 and 5.5 percent respectively of its total business.[56]

Even with the most successful aviation production apparatus in the world, the French still needed imports in certain categories. France needed more Breguets than Renault could deliver engines and secured Fiat A12bis 300-hp engines from Italy, although the Fiat Breguet was inferior to the Renault-Breguet. France received some 2,200 Fiats. The undersecretary in late August was still seeking a firm agreement on an order of 1,800 Fiats placed the previous month, although France had only delivered 800 of the promised 4,200 tons of raw materials to Italy in return. English and U.S. competition for the Italian engines, since Italian firms were already preparing for peacetime, made arrangements difficult.[57] In September Martinot-Lagarde was in Italy to secure more Fiat A12bis engines as quickly as possible and to remedy the engine's defects. Aircraft expert Dorand looked to Italy and England as potential sources for Caproni and Handley Page night bombers respectively.[58]

Yet the search for engines indicated a temporary decline in powerful-engine production, not a lack of their development. At the Armistice the French were introducing the next generation of lighter, more powerful, mostly water-cooled engines: the 300-hp Hispano-Suiza V8, 450-hp 12-cylinder Renault, and the 400-hp Lorraine-Dietrich, as well as a 16-cylinder, 450-hp Bugatti, and a 500-hp Salmson twin-row radial.

In 1918 the French aviation industry produced 24,652 airplanes and 44,563 engines. Its monthly aircraft production rose from 1,714 in January to 2,362, its peak, in October. Its monthly aero engine production increased from 2,567 in January to a high of 4,196 in October.[59] In November 1918 it employed 185,000 workers. Twenty-three percent were women, who were most numerous as textile workers in the airframe factories, where they composed a third of the work force. At the Armistice the production service, which had grown from fewer than 20 officers before mobilization to 540 officers and 3,000 personnel, was delivering a plane, completely equipped, armed, and with replacement parts, every 15 minutes, day and night, and a motor, complete with all accessories, every 10 minutes.[60]

On 19 November parliamentary deputy D'Aubigny assessed the state of French aviation at the Armistice. He charged that France had not fulfilled its promises to the United States, which had only 642 planes in line at the Armistice, 50 percent fewer than promised for 1 July. In October

France had only 2,639 planes at the front, all of them what he termed obsolete Spad 7s and Spad 13s and obsolescent Breguet 14s. The absence of heavy bombers to perform reprisal raids on German territory particularly annoyed him, since the army subcommission had long advocated them. The quality of French observation planes was inferior, with no hope for improvement in 1919. The new Nieuport and Sopwith fighters did not fully benefit from the 300-hp engine, while the Béchereau frame was still not ready. His previous 3 May report had criticized the absence of unified direction for aviation, and he now attributed all of aviation's problems to its lack of guidance.[61] The politicians of the aviation commission, still dissatisfied with France's failure to develop strategic airpower, thus ended the war on a negative note.

Yet D'Aubigny's assessment was excessively negative. Perhaps the service lacked unified leadership, perhaps its aircraft were not as modern as the politicians and General Pétain desired. Still, its procurement apparatus had obtained more materiel from its industry than any other country. At the 11 November Armistice, French aviation comprised 247 squadrons with 3,222 aircraft on the Western Front (France's Northeastern Front): 1,152 fighters, 1,585 observation planes, 285 day bombers, and 200 night bombers. The Aerial Division had 6 combat groups of 432 Spads, 5 bomber groups of 225 Breguets, and 4 squadrons of 60 long-range escort Caudron RIIA3s, for a total of 717 planes. Independent combat units comprised 42 squadrons of 720 Spads, 5 night bomber groups totaled 200 bombers, mostly Voisins, and 148 squadrons of 1,585 observation planes included 645 Breguets, 530 Salmsons, 305 two-seat Spads, 30 Caudrons, and 75 Voisins. The air arm had fallen 348 fighters and 575 bombers short of the 4,000-plane program, which anticipated having 1,500 fighters, 1,000 bombers and 1,500 observation planes at the front. Yet in depots there were nearly 2,600 airplanes waiting in the General Aviation Reserve. On all fronts the French air service had 336 squadrons, operated by 6,417 pilots, 1,682 observers, and 80,000 nonflying personnel.[62] In air strength it was the world's largest air force.

Germany

In the beginning of 1918, the German air force was preparing for the March offensive on the Western Front, hoping to end the war before the United States could affect its outcome. Meanwhile Germany continued its strategic air campaign against England. For the Naval Airship Division the year began inauspiciously, when five airships blew up and burned at the

Ahlhorn base on 5 January. Since the division only received a ship every two months, the disaster could have been crippling. Yet Peter Strasser was still determined to strike England, though three raids in March and April were ineffective. By then Zeppelin-Staaken and Schütte-Lanz had stopped airship production for R-plane manufacture, portending the ultimate end of the campaign. On May 4 Strasser fell in the L70, which was struck by fire from a DH4. His death ended the Naval Airship Division's campaign against England, and the dirigibles ended the war spotting for the fleet, which was relying increasingly on seaplanes for reconnaissance.[63]

German bombers continued their raids on England until May 1918 and also attacked Paris and French ports, initially with two wings of 30 planes and then four wings. In January the British War Office anticipated raids of over 100 German bombers by early summer. The Germans struck London for the first time in 1918 on 28 January, a raid punctuated by a 660-pound bomb from the giant plane R.39 that killed 38 and seriously wounded 85 people who had sought refuge in the basement of a printing works. The raids on England and on French ports took their toll on the bombers, and when Comdr. Ernst Brandenburg, on artificial leg and cane, returned to command the England wing in February, he halted combat flights until late March to refit. The six R-planes of Squadron 501 and naval Zeppelins continued the attacks. On 16 February R.39 dropped the war's largest bomb, a one-ton monster.[64]

During the week of the March offensive and again in April, when the Germans renewed their attack, Brandenburg's Gothas bombed French ports. On 9 May, a night when heavy fog grounded the Gothas, R-plane Comdr. Richard von Bentivegni sought to strike England with four planes before the fog settled, and lost two of his huge craft. The raids culminated on four nights in mid-May, when Brandenburg had amassed 43 Gothas and lost 6 of them. From the end of May the high command committed the bomber units to army support, dashing Brandenburg's hopes of returning to England in July. The R-planes' dropping of 30 tons of bombs on England may not have been worth the effort necessary to field the unit, although they and the Gothas did divert significant British forces to home air defense. It was evident by May that the strategic air campaign against England had failed in its first and most grandiose aim, to drive the nation from the war.

The challenge of the America Program's plan for mobilizing aviation lay not in the strategic offensive, but in the German air force's tactical role in the spring campaigns of the west. In March 1918 the air force had 153 flight units, 38 battle flights or Schlachtstaffeln for ground attack, 81 fighter units, and 7 bombing squadrons. The expansion had not adhered entirely to the program's plans. Instead of forming 17 new flight units to increase their number from 183 to 200, the air force had reorganized them, differentiating battle flights from flight units and then increasing the number of planes from 6 to 9 in 36 of the existing flight units. The new fighter units were often equipped only at half or three-quarters of their pilot strength, while two new Jagdgeschwader of four squadrons each were formed.[65]

On 21 March frontline aircraft in the west totaled 3,668—a substantial increase over the 2,271 planes the German air force had had in early 1917—while 307 were stationed in Italy, Macedonia, and the Middle East. Against the Allies' 4,500 frontline planes, the German army intended to use 2,000 and hold the rest in reserve, concentrating 49 flight units, 27 battle squadrons, 35 fighter units, and 4 bombing squadrons to support the attacking armies. To camouflage the attack's location only units already in the sector performed reconnaissance missions, while new squadrons arrived at night and assembled their craft two days before the attack. In the sector of the March offensive, the Germans initially managed to outnumber the Allies 820 to 645 craft.

When the infantry attacked on 21 March, low cloud cover over the battlefield prevented aerial support until noon. Then the battle units, flying at low altitudes, attacked enemy troops within 10 miles of the lines with machine guns and hand grenades. For the battle's first two days, the air umbrella was impervious to enemy opposition, as the fighter units effectively protected ground support fliers, who in turn monitored the German infantry advances marked by white cloths. By the third day enemy opposition was more effective, inflicting casualties on the battle flights and attacking German infantry from low altitudes, dissuading German troops from marking their advance for their own air support. German fighters were unable to prevent the RFC's ground attacks, and by 24 March they had lost aerial superiority in the area of attack.[66] During the week of the March offensive and again in April when the Germans renewed their attack, Brandenburg's Gothas bombed French ports. The night of 26–27 March German bombers bombed Doullens airfield, where the British were concentrating their formations, greatly reducing the next day's enemy air activity. Despite these efforts, by 28 March the great assault had ended.

The air arm had kept its units up to strength, actually adding six new flight units and five fighter units by the end of March. The battle and army cooperation units performed well over the front, but did not intensively bomb retreating British columns or British communications.[67] The German air service needed more operational units to deploy during the

March battle, better fighters to prevent enemy encroachment into the battle's airspace, and more day bombers to disrupt enemy ground operations.
Both its casualties and its inadequate replacements of personnel and aircraft
limited its effectiveness.[68]

The intense struggles in the spring at Armentières, Kemmel Hill, and
Reims were costly in German aircraft and crews. In the 18th Army sector,
losses of C- and D-planes from mid-March to mid-May were 324 and 135
respectively, of which 60 percent were not caused by enemy action. In January alone the air service lost 779 planes and 241 pilots and observers (179
of them killed) of approximately 4,500 aircrew at the front. These losses
increased during the spring offensives, and historian Alex Imrie calculated
that, based on 2,551 planes at the front in May 1918, one-seventh of this
pilot strength would have to be replaced every month—a burden beyond the
rear's capacity.[69]

In late May the high command committed the bomber units to army
support, and for the rest of the war the Gothas bombed continental ports
and then rear areas behind the enemy lines. Bomber crews, carrying as
heavy a bomb load as possible, often flew three raids a night against targets
such as munitions dumps behind the lines. German night bombing against
the British rear on the Western Front culminated in the spring and summer
of 1918, and the British judged them especially effective against railroad
communications. The frequent alerts in response to these disruptive raids
disturbed the British troops' rest. In raids on two nights in May, German
bombers destroyed some 11,500 tons of ammunition in depots, and their 11
August destruction of the base depot at Calais would have seriously affected
the supply of spare parts had the British not had such vast reserves.[70]

Unlike the British, the Germans had a limited supply of materiel and
thus absolutely required qualitative ascendancy. Yet the condition of the
German air force in the spring of 1918 gave little cause for optimism, as it
faced growing Allied numerical superiority. The quality of its aircraft in
service varied widely, while complaints about spare-part shortages and "the
careless work of the aircraft factories" on everything from the welding
on Albatrosses to poor motor installation in Friedrichshafen G3 bombers
were rife.[71] Among the observation planes in service, the Rumpler C7 remained superlative, its photoreconnaissance version, the Rubilt, capable of
flying 100 mph above 20,000 feet and virtually immune to interception by
Allied fighters.

The Rumplers and their 260-hp high-compression Maybach engine
advanced the state of aerial observation. They could reach 6,000 meters in
43 minutes, where they were beyond the reach of all but the most deter-

mined, skillful, and well-equipped of fighter pilots. Yet the physical stress of high-altitude flight in an open cockpit, particularly in the winter, was devastating, even on younger pilots who were selected for their physical conditioning. Crews often died of the bends or in spasms and fits after landing. One pilot recalled that his hands had begun to shake so badly that he could not eat soup with a spoon. To counter such stress and make observation more efficient, the Rumplers came equipped with both small bottles of oxygen for the crew, which they used above 3,500 meters, and serial automatic cameras, which could take three photos a minute after the observer started them with a lever. The test of an observer's excellence was determining what to photograph from such height, but once the camera was triggered, the observer could expend energy not on the camera but on the skies and earth below.[72] Thus, the receipt of the Rumplers was an event in a squadron's experience, since they gave their crew feelings of unconditional superiority and patriotic pride in such technological achievement.

The Albatros C12, the LVG, and the DFW C5s were efficient medium-range observation craft. The light C-types—Halberstadts and Hannoveranas—were quality aircraft. The Halberstadts were exceptional, but the Hannoveranas were hampered by the unreliability of their Argus engines. Of the three infantry, or J-planes, the all-metal Junkers remained highly praised, while the Albatros and AEG J-planes were now considered average. Of the fighters in service in April, the Fokker triplane maneuvered and climbed well but lacked speed, while the Albatros D5a and Pfalz D3a were inferior to enemy fighters.[73] During April 1918, in the tactical air war the fighter units, increasingly important to an air force on the defensive, had no superior airplane.

Steadily rising attrition among German combat pilots allowed a pilot who shot down five planes to become either the commanding officer or second in command of a squadron, while ace noncommissioned officers were rapidly promoted to commissioned officer status in the reserves.[74] Yet, against overwhelming odds that steadily worsened and in aircraft that failed to provide qualitative superiority, German fighter pilots continued to take a toll on the enemy. Jagdgeschwader 1 was particularly successful in early April, but then had to move to another airfield, amid rain and clouds that often curtailed operations. Manfred von Richthofen scored eight kills from 24 to 28 March, including a double victory on 26 March and a triple the next day to increase his total to 74. While the frequency of his kills was reminiscent of earlier times, Richthofen was war weary, driven only by duty. On 20 April he scored two victories to bring his total to 80, and then the next day, in pursuit of a Camel low over the lines, he fell to ground fire from Australian machine gunners. Richthofen's death cast a pall on the German air service.[75] On 1 March Rudolf Berthold, now a captain, had returned to the front, his latest wounds unhealed. On Richthofen's death he wrote, "Richthofen has fallen, daily friends fall; the British are superior to us. I must show the boys that duty remains above all."[76] Suffering horribly, as bone splinters continually had to be plucked from a festering wound, he fought on determinedly.

Long before Richthofen's death, it was evident that the German air service needed a new fighter. The Fokker Triplane was now eclipsed by Richthofen's passing, but at the end of April, just days after his death, a superlative new fighter, the D7, began arriving at the front. The plane was tested in January at the Type-D competition, arranged by Richthofen, at Adlershof. Anthony Fokker entered five biplanes and two triplanes, and Albatros entered four D5as. After flying one of the biplanes two days before the competition, Fokker decided that it was too sensitive for the ordinary pilot. Working 48 hours without rest he, designer Reinhold Platz, and a small crew lengthened the plane's fuselage and added a vertical fin. The result was a superb aircraft, fairly easy to fly yet responsive and extremely maneuverable at high altitudes. After four days of comparison tests, the frontline pilots unanimously judged the Fokker prototype the outright winner. General Hoeppner personally informed Fokker that he wanted 400 of the new planes immediately.

The D7 possessed, as one authority noted, "an apparent ability to make a good pilot out of mediocre material," which was a tremendous asset, considering the shortage of trained fighter pilots.[77] The plane, like all new types, was not entirely problem-free. In early June inadequately dried wood caused some wing-rib breakage in dives, and the summer heat occasionally resulted in exploding fuel tanks, until a better coolant was introduced. None of these difficulties grounded the D7, which became quite indispensable after rotary-engine fighters were grounded in May because of unreliable engine performance attributed to inferior engine oils.

As German military fortunes declined, the Fokker D7 remained the mainstay of the fighter forces until the war's end. Its appearance at the front coincided with gasoline rationing to the fighter units of 3,080 gallons monthly, thus limiting squadrons to fewer than 10 individual flights daily. By May and June the fuel crisis was severe—despite work on substitute fuels—as the air arm's use of nearly 10,000 tons exceeded its monthly supply by over 50 percent. When it climbed to a maximum of over 11,000 tons in July, the army satisfied the needs of a few important units at the expense of the rest of the frontline formations. Starting in August the air arm re-

A German Albatros D3. (Courtesy of Peter M. Grosz)

German Fokker D7s. (Courtesy of
Peter M. Grosz)

Readying a German Junkers J1 infantry plane for a mission. (Courtesy of the National Air and Space Museum, Smithsonian Institution)

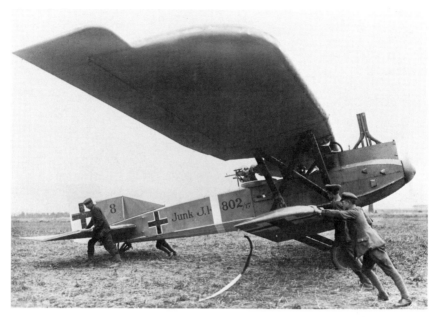

Positioning a J1 for takeoff. (Courtesy of the Deutsches Museum)

A Halberstadt gunner furnishes his cockpit. (Courtesy of Peter M. Grosz)

A German ground crew loads grenades into racks for Halberstadt trench fighters. (Courtesy of Peter M. Grosz)

A Halberstadt ready for take-off. (Courtesy of the National Air and Space Museum, Smithsonian Institution)

German Gotha bombers of Bogohl 3. (Courtesy of Peter M. Grosz and the United States Air Force Museum)

A German AEG G4 bomber with its Mercedes engines uncowled. (Courtesy of the United States Air Force Museum)

A German Flugzeugbau Friedrichshafen FF33 floatplane. (Courtesy of Peter M. Grosz)

Seaplane repair workshop at a German imperial dockyard. (Courtesy of Peter M. Grosz)

A German Flugzeugbau Friedrichshafen FF49c seaplane at sea. (Courtesy of the Royal Air Force Museum)

A British Avro 504 training plane. (Courtesy of the United States Air Force Museum)

The RFC on campaign in 1914. (Courtesy of the Royal Air Force Museum)

A dead British aviator and German spectators. (Courtesy of the National Air and Space Museum, Smithsonian Institution)

A Rolls-Royce Eagle engine. (Courtesy of the Royal Air Force Museum)

British ace Edward "Mick" Mannock, seated in chair at right, with his squadron. (Courtesy of the Royal Air Force Museum)

A British Sopwith Camel. (Courtesy of the United States Air Force Museum)

A British Bristol Fighter. (Courtesy of the United States Air Force Museum)

SVA fuselages in the Italian Ansaldo works. (Courtesy of the United States Air Force Museum)

Royal Air Force SE5A squadron. (Courtesy of the Royal Air Force Museum)

SVAs outside the Ansaldo works. (Courtesy of the United States Air Force Museum)

Sergeant Major Marcel Pliat, mechanic and gunner on Il'ia Muromets X. (Courtesy of the National Air and Space Museum, Smithsonian Institution)

Russian War Minister Sukhomlikov, fourth from left; General Shidlovskii, fifth from left; Igor Sikorskii, seventh from left; in front of an Il'ia Muromets aircraft. (Courtesy of the National Air and Space Museum, Smithsonian Institution)

Crash site of the Il'ia Muromets I on 11 May 1917. (Courtesy of the National Air and Space Museum, Smithsonian Institution)

Red Air Fleet personnel in front of an Il'ia Muromets aircraft during the Russian civil war. (Courtesy of the National Air and Space Museum, Smithsonian Institution)

ceived a monthly ration of 7,000 tons for the rest of the war, which radically restricted flight operations.[78]

In addition to such limitations, the Fokker D7's pilots were outnumbered by a foe whose morale was rising rapidly. Occasionally, German Jagdgeschwaders countered overall allied aerial superiority by rising in strength over the battlefield with four squadrons totaling 50 to 60 fighters. Each squadron remained a distinct unit, the first directly following the Geschwader commander in front at the lowest altitude, the second above to the right, the third above to the left and further behind, and the fourth above as reserve and top cover. The lead squadron attacked the enemy unit directly, attempting to shatter it for individual combat, while the next two sought to surround and split the enemy as the top squadron protected the fighters from outside intervention or dove on individual opponents who straggled away from the fight. After the fight the squadron leaders circled over a specific spot to collect their units and then assembled in the initial formation. If they won and controlled the air, they then attacked ground targets, spreading out in an extended front to dive on enemy columns, artillery, and tanks.[79]

Allied opponents never bested the Fokker D7, because the BMW engine vastly improved its performance, virtually halving the climbing time to 5,000 meters from 31.5 minutes with the Mercedes to 16 minutes. According to the official British history of the air war, the BMW gave the Fokker D7 a better climb rate than any contemporary Allied plane in service and exemplified the maxim that "technical superiority, not necessarily of great degree, is a dominant factor in air warfare."[80] The D7 was, and still is, widely regarded as the best fighter airplane of World War I.

In early June Kogenluft completed its plans for expanding the air arm from 1 July 1918 to 1 April 1919, conceding that numerical superiority was hopeless and planning to concentrate on technological advancement. The plan focused on increasing the number of battle units, given their field success and the necessity of even stronger ground-attack forces, and increasing flight units for reconnaissance, despite the strong enemy forces. Meanwhile, Kogenluft discarded an earlier idea to increase the fighter pilots in a squadron from 12 to 15 because of training shortages. Gradually it had to scale down a planned expansion of bomber units to one wing because of the aircraft industry's limitations.

A second single-seat fighter competition was held in June and July. The participating aces included Bruno Lörzer, Hermann Göring—soon to be the new commander of the Richthofen squadron—and naval landplane pilots, since naval landplane units in Flanders had a fighter force of 70 to 85 planes by the summer. The inspectorate asked the pilots to evaluate the planes according to their engines, particularly the 160-hp Mercedes, the 185-hp BMW, and the Oberursel rotary. This time the inspectorate, not the pilots, ultimately decided which aircraft types and engines would be produced. The pilots, however, recommended that the Mercedes go to Fokker D7s and Pfalz D3as, the BMW to D7s and the Pfalz D12, and the Oberursel rotary to the Fokker E5 monoplane. They considered the D7 and the Pfalz D12 equal, and thought the Pfalz would perform well when it arrived at the front in September 1918. The Fokker E5 monoplane and the SSW D4 were both deemed superior to the Fokker D7. The E5, which was cheaper, lighter, smaller, faster, easier to operate and to manufacture than the SSW D4, was to be the future mainstay of the German fighter arm. The SSW D4, which was the better high-altitude fighter, provided that its Siemens-Halske engines could be produced in quantity, would be an excellent top-cover interceptor. All believed that the Zeppelin metal biplane, the Dornier D1, which had shed its top wing in flight, killing Lt. Wilhelm Reinhard, then commander of the Richthofen squadron, was superior to most of the other craft.[81]

Fokker rushed the E5 into production in July, and the first few arrived at the front for evaluation in August, only to be hastily withdrawn later that month because of engine seizures and wing failure. These circumstances proved fortunate for the Allies. After an SE5 patrol had encountered Fokker monoplanes, British General Brooke-Popham had warned the Air Ministry on 17 August of the danger of a recurrence of the talk of 1915 that described British craft as fodder for Fokkers: "They absolutely made rings around the SE5s as regards speed, climbed considerably quicker and had a ceiling of 3 or 4 thousand feet above the SE5."[82] The monoplane, redesignated D8, did not reappear at the front until the end of the conflict and in numbers too small to affect the air war's course. By the war's end the poor quality of oil necessitated phasing out rotary-engine fighters such as the Fokker D8 and the SSW D4.

In the summer the German air arm continued to fight against a tremendous number of Allied aircraft. The training schools could no longer meet the front's needs. Although German aircrews still inflicted higher losses on the enemy than they suffered, gaining 487 victories for 150 losses in June, the Germans could not replace these losses, while the Allies could. By August personnel and material shortages jeopardized the effectiveness of the German air arm.

After 8 August, when the British attack near Amiens put the Germans to flight, the German army was forced on the defensive without respite. On a 25-mile front the British and French amassed 1,904 airplanes, including 988 fighters, against 365 German planes, including only 140 fighters, since the Germans had lacked sufficient knowledge of the attack's location to concentrate their units. The allies sought to bomb the Somme bridges to halt German reinforcements, and the Germans sought to prevent the bombing. In four days of ferocious fighting the Germans lost 30 planes, downed 144 Allied planes, prevented the bombers from destroying the bridges, and managed at least to contest Allied aerial superiority. The available German fighter units, among them the Richthofen squadron, had performed admirably. During the first week of the attack German night bombers dropped nearly 60 tons of bombs on Allied positions. The British official history, while acknowledging high British casualties, claimed that "the German air service was so roughly handled that it was never able fully to recover."[83]

By late August German fighter units found the Allied superiority oppressive, and shortages prevented sufficient training to maintain their effectiveness. They survived by dispersing their machines on the ground and rising to fight only in concentrated numbers.[84] Yet historians Alex Imrie and S. F. Wise disagree with the view that the German air force never recovered, contending that the British official history generalized incorrectly from the case of the Richthofen wing, which was withdrawn after the debacle.[85] The formation, with only 21 serviceable planes of its complement of 52, was already far under strength on 8 August and played little role during the rest of the war. Jagdgeschwader 2, however, downed 81 enemy planes in seven days after 12 September, losing only two of its machines. The effectiveness of some of the 14-plane Jagdstaffeln actually increased in the war's last three months. Jasta Boelcke registered 46 confirmed victories in September, losing only two of its pilots and scoring its highest total since forming in August 1916. Jasta 50 recorded over 50 percent of its victories at this time. Some German fighter forces thus continued to exact a higher toll of Allied aircraft than was inflicted on them, and bombing and reconnaissance planes performed their missions, despite stringent fuel rationing and irreplaceable losses of personnel and materiel, until the war's end.

The air service, its spirit unbroken, continued to fight, but aircrews knew that the war was drawing inexorably to a dismal end for Germany. Driven back from airdrome to airdrome, they found themselves under frequent surprise attacks from British planes on their own airfields.[86] Night bombers were pressed into service as tactical reconnaissance and ground-strafing machines, though the planes and crews were ill-suited to the tasks. Bomber units retreated from their bases near Ghent in October to finish the war near Brussels, continuing to bomb targets behind enemy lines as they went. Squadrons lacked suitable material for aircraft repairs, and exhausted fighter pilots, who were too tired to maintain good flight formation, lacked the fuel to fly in squadron strength. Fuel often contained so much water that the engines coughed. Although aggressive pilots occasionally found their peers so reluctant to engage the enemy that they did not follow the command to attack, some pilots continued to amass high victory scores.[87] Aces such as Ernst Udet and Lothar von Richthofen were effective to the very end, while Erich Löwenhardt amassed 53 kills before succumbing to a collision with another German pilot in August. On 10 August, after downing 44 aircraft, Rudolph Berthold crashed, breaking his arm anew. This time was final, however, as Kogenluft ordered him to the hospital until he was discharged.[88] All the air force's efforts were futile, for the conflict's outcome was a foregone conclusion.

The last fighter trials, held on 15 to 31 October, confirmed the demise of the rotary-engine fighter. Because of severe material shortages, the German air force intended to produce only one fighter type, equipped with the BMW 3a engine. The Armistice came before a final selection was made, but Fokker's parasol version of the D7 was the front-runner, while the Rumpler D1, the only plane to attain 8,000 meters, would join it in service in 1919.[89] The war's end, however, was less than two weeks away.

German naval aviation technology enabled naval fliers to compete over the North Sea until the war's end, despite their inadequate numbers. Ernst Heinkel's successor to the W12, the W19, a longer-range and larger plane with a 260-hp Maybach engine, appeared in January 1918. Most of the 53 W19s delivered to the navy did not arrive until May and June, when the Borkum seaplane station reported that not only was the big Brandenburg able to handle the English flying boats but it was faster and more seaworthy than anticipated. Despite temperamental engines, the W19 was clearly a success, and during 1918 these fighters from Zeebrugge and Borkum, often accompanied by W12s, regularly engaged large British F2a flying boats from Felixstowe and Yarmouth.[90]

Yet the best of Heinkel's creations was the W29. Early in 1918 Friedrich Christiansen advised Heinkel that they needed a successor to the W12 to maintain aerial superiority. Time was scarce, and only the 150-hp Benz was available, so Heinkel created a monoplane version of the W12 by dropping the top wing and increasing the chord and span of the bottom one. The reduction in frontal area and drag allowed a 10-mph increase in speed to 110 mph and a 50 percent increase in climb. Christiansen was so pleased with the plane that he insisted on flying one of the first production series directly from the test station at Warnemuende to Zeebrugge for immediate operational use. The 28 W29s produced enabled the Germans to preserve a competitive edge over the English. Later in 1918 Heinkel repeated the process used in enlarging the W12 and designed the W33 monoplane, a larger version of the W29 with a 245-hp Maybach engine, of which 26 were built.[91] All of the W-series floatplanes were clean and functional designs of superior performance. Heinkel's close relationship with Christiansen, reminiscent of Fokker's with Richthofen, was instrumental in his ability to fulfill the naval pilots' wishes.

Though the navy had excellent single-engine planes, it never had enough to guard minesweeping flotillas, guide submarines through cleared mine fields, and impede English minelaying expeditions. In the southern part of the North Sea, where air warfare was continuous during 1918, Christiansen's Seaplane Unit I in Flanders grew from 29 craft in 1917 to only 30 in 1918 because of inadequate supply.

Ultimately, beyond personnel reserves, of which Germany's did not compare to those of the Allies', success in the war of attrition was a function of production and supply. From the start in 1918, production had not sufficed to supply all the units planned in the America Program. In the first seven months of 1918, 1,009, 890, 1,360, 1,202, 930, 1,189, and 1,478 planes were delivered to the air force. Deliveries thus fluctuated wildly and in July 1918 were only beginning to approach 1,600—the War Ministry's minimal figure in July 1917. Monthly engine production from January through July was 1,445, 1,145, 1,290, 1,530, 1,390, 1,430, and 1,420.[92] Average engine production of 1,379 and average aircraft production of 1,151 compared unfavorably to the 1,800 and 1,600 figures for engines and aircraft production in the original minimum program. In April, one of the best production months in the first half of 1918, engine production was 1,530 and aircraft production was 1,360. Thus at the deadline for the America Program's completion, aircraft production in a good month still missed the minimum goal by 240 planes and 270 engines.

The War Ministry offered 1,000 mark bonuses to six aircraft firms for each plane accepted in March, because of the "extraordinarily large need for fighter planes expected in the coming offensive"[93]—a desperate measure for a hopeless offensive. The German homefront, taxed to the utmost, summoned its last reserves in the America Program, yet inadequacy—of labor, raw materials, transportation, personnel, and production—was the keynote of the program. The aircraft industry and the aviation inspectorate could not attain even the program's minimum goals. Thus, the original aim of doubling aircraft and engine production to 2,000 and 2,500 appears even more utopian. Ruthless memoranda, proclamations, and organizational measures could not overcome irremediable shortages and exhaustion. Ironically, after all the prodigious effort, the threat of an American aviation industry and aerial armada never materialized.

On 8 April, after the America Program's failure, Kogenluft and the aviation inspectorate emphasized improving their airplanes, especially fighters, and maintaining aerial strength rather than increasing it as they had sought in the Hindenburg and America programs. Although it would take two months to formalize the program, the air force received Ludendorff's support on 11 April, when he informed the War Ministry that its reductions in the arms industry were not to affect aircraft manufacture.[94] The industry, beset with shortages of fabric and metals and hampered by continued coal and transportation crises into June, sorely needed such preferential treatment.[95]

The industry's most salient problems were labor unrest and shortages. The emergency induction of eligible reserves in the late spring irreparably worsened the skilled-labor shortage in the industry's subcontractors. Some of the remaining skilled workers, who were already demanding higher wages, more food, and reduced hours, took time off without permission, knowing that their sorely needed skills made them indispensable. The industry, air force, and aviation associations were attempting to recruit and train more skilled aircraft workers and engineers, but the war would have to last far into 1919 before these remedies could take effect.[96] By the early summer, German aviation technology proved capable of matching the Allies', but material and labor shortages and employee unrest made prospects of dramatic increases in production uncertain. The Junkers-Fokker works, for example, had increasing difficulty securing administrative and engineering staff, labor, and particularly materials for the mass production of metal airplanes. Junkers and Fokker compounded these problems with their own personal disputes. Mistrustful of each other and communicating only through lawyers, the two strove to break up their union in the war's last months.[97]

Despite shortages, Kogenluft issued a new expansion program, a continuation of the America Program from 1 July 1918 to 1 April 1919. A fighter-pilot shortage prevented increasing the size of the fighter arm, but Kogenluft planned to increase the number of battle planes and bombers. Besides prescribing 40,000 additional personnel for the air force, the plan required 9,000 skilled workers for the industry to raise monthly production to 2,300 planes and 2,875 engines. Finally, Kogenluft proposed to split the aviation inspectorate into three separate ones for personnel, aircraft, and aerial photography.[98]

Still anticipating that American support would bolster the Allies' numerical superiority, Kogenluft—despite the increasing shortages and its failure to achieve its previous programs—planned to double production from its June figures while fragmenting the agency that had executed the previous programs. Yet it remained uncertain where the air force hoped to obtain 40,000 unskilled and 9,000 skilled workers when German labor reserves were approaching exhaustion. If the magnitude of the planned expansion seemed remarkable, the drastic modification of the bureaucracy appeared even more so. Kogenluft planned to intervene more directly in the aviation inspectorate's affairs, while divesting an exhausted Siegert of the immense burden of heading an agency that had mushroomed from a few hundred employees in 1915 to some 50,000 in 1918.[99] Kogenluft's concentration on aviation helped to improve transportation and the supply of raw materials, coal, and food, while seven new factories entered aero engine production in 1918.[100]

As both the army's and navy's experience in aviation indicated, production, not technology, was the Achilles' heel of the German air effort. By September shortages of precision machines for mass production, textiles, wood, and certain metals such as nickel were irremediable. The labor situation was rapidly becoming more unstable. Management-labor disputes intensified, as workers sought shorter hours while employers refused such requests. Irritated by food shortages, workers made food forays into the countryside under the guise of "sick leave," while serious strikes over food appeared inevitable in the coming winter.[101]

Despite such problems, some aircraft manufacturers such as Rumpler remained optimistic through September, though apprehensive about overextension in the coming peace. The firms were also able to increase their production from April to October while obtaining skilled workers, though probably not the 9,000 necessary. Aircraft production actually increased dramatically during the warm months, as the industry's production rose from 1,500 in July to 2,195 in October.[102] Aircraft production in October fell only some 100 units short of its projected goal for April 1919. Although it is impossible to ascertain what influence the changes in the inspectorate had exerted, sustaining such a production pace during the coming winter of 1918–19 would have been impossible. The industry had been on the verge of producing 1,000 planes in the early winter of 1916 before its production was halved by January 1917. A near total collapse of aircraft production was likely during the winter, when coal, material, and food shortages would have crushed productivity.

German engine production proved more fragile than aircraft manufacture, despite some successes. As the increasing reliance of the fighter trials on the BMW3a engine indicated, this 185-hp model became the key to German fighter performance in 1918. BMW began serial production in February, delivered nearly 150 engines a month at peak production, and became Germany's third largest aircraft engine factory with 3,500 employees, while Opel began production in June and would deliver 140 engines a month. More than 700 BMWs were delivered during the war, their only disadvantage being their "all too late birth," in the words of German ace Ernst Udet.[103]

A severe shortage of some 400 150- to 200-hp engines in early 1918 necessitated the delivery of most trainers without engines and ultimately interrupted aircraft production in April. Only the front's well-organized repair system mitigated the damage caused by the stoppage. From mid-1918, engine production progressed despite the fuel crisis.[104]

The aviation inspectorate had to militarize engine factories twice during the war. In a January week-long strike, which caused a four-month disruption of engine production (since a single engine was built over a six-month period), the inspectorate took control of the Argus works for 10 days. More significantly, it later temporarily militarized the Daimler works when its director threatened to stop night shifts if the army did not increase engine prices. A recent interpellation in the Reichstag had established that Daimler's large production enabled it to reap extraordinary profits despite charging lower prices than the competition. The inspectorate consequently refused to raise its prices, and when Daimler would not provide information to calculate the prices and prepared to carry out its threat, the army arrested the business director for a few days, then released him but forbade him to reenter the plant, after which it took little time to restore order.[105]

By 1 August only five German firms used their entire labor force on engines. The most important of these were Argus (967 employees), BMW (2,123 employees), and Maybach (2,680 employees). Sixty-five percent of Daimler's work force (16,315 employees) and 89 percent of Benz's (6,007) worked on aero engines. The industry achieved maximum production of 2,024 engines in October 1918, with Daimler delivering 635 (31.4 percent), Benz delivering 360 (17.8 percent), BMW delivering 140 (6.95 percent), and Opel and Maybach each delivering 130 (6.45 percent). Daimler and Benz delivered nearly 50 percent of German engines, supplemented by firms such as BMW and Opel that had more recently entered engine production.[106]

Aero engine production climbed during 1918, as the individual firms continued to increase production despite difficulties. Daimler's monthly production rose from just under 480 engines in March to peak at over 700 in September and then decreased to some 640 in October, while Benz's production fluctuated around 300 monthly before reaching 360 in October. Of the other firms, none of whose monthly production ever exceeded 150 engines, BMW showed the greatest increase rising from under 10 in March to almost 140 in October.[107]

Collapse and revolution in the rear indicated the end for Germany, while the Allies steadily advanced toward the German borders. The revolution was gaining momentum when the War Ministry on 4 November restricted aircraft use against revolutionary forces to reconnaissance missions, most likely because the rear echelons of the air service at the Fliers' Replacement Units and the industrial workers were no longer reliable.[108]

On the morning of 6 November, several companies of armed men from the infantry replacement battalion in Schwerin marched to the Fokker factory, ordered the workers to strike, and together formed a workers' and soldiers' council. Similar events occurred throughout Germany, as workers and soldiers at Daimler in Stuttgart/Unterturkheim and troops of various Fliers' Replacement Units, such as those in Brunswick, Böblingen, and Gotha, initiated the formation of workers' and soldiers' councils in early November.[109] On 9 November a general strike affected nearly all the factories in Berlin, and on 11 November World War I ended.

The German air force and naval air arm, though outnumbered, exacted a toll of Allied aircraft to the very end, because the German aircraft industry continued to develop superior single-engine aircraft. Conditions placed a premium on entrepreneurs such as Anthony Fokker, whose team under Reinhold Platz designed craft that could be easily mass-produced within the limits of the available materials. Remarkably, during the war's final months, the Fokker factory developed planes that could be flown by average pilots but were superior to Allied craft. Designers who operated more scientifically, like Junkers and Dornier, proceeded with all-metal construction, even though raw material shortages prevented the mass production of their planes, and their efforts placed Germany far beyond the Allies in metal aircraft construction.

Five factors allowed production to expand at the war's end: the increasing concentration on small airplanes; the more widespread use of new and speedy construction techniques, such as Fokker's welded steel tubing fuselage; the rationalization of the industry; the introduction of more machinery suitable for unskilled workers; and finally centralized controls on the industry, which enabled the transfer of supplies from less to more productive firms. Given sufficient food for the workers, materials for the factories, and transportation for supplies and finished materiel, the industry could have continued to increase its production. Yet the seasons largely determined these conditions, and once the favorable summer and fall months yielded to another cruel, cold winter, the German air arm's supply system, and ultimately the arm itself, would have ceased to be effective in 1919.

In November 1918 the German aviation industry, its expansion limited by skilled-labor shortages, probably employed approximately the same number of workers it had in the summer of 1917—40,000 in the aircraft factories, 30,000 in the engine plants, and 40,000 to 70,000 in subcontracting firms. A 1921 French document estimated the German industry at just over 100,000 workers, 45 factories with some 61,000 workers building airplanes and dirigibles, and 14 engines factories with nearly 24,000 workers, with other firms employing a total of some 16,000 workers producing accessories, instruments and weapons.[110]

On 11 November the German army's air arm comprised 284 units of some 4,500 aircrew and 2,709 combat aircraft, some 1,200 (48 percent) D-type single-seat fighters, 228 (8 percent) CL two-seat fighters, 1,000 (38 percent) C-type two-seat reconnaissance and all-purpose craft, 162 (6 percent) G-type twin-engine bombers, and 6 R-type giant planes. While these totals differed from those in August 1918 primarily in a slight shift toward D-types, they showed a drastic decline from the 3,668 frontline aircraft in the west during March 1918.[111] Losses in the spring offensives had been too severe for the industry to recoup, though the army's return to the defensive in August enabled the stabilization of the situation, if at a level over 25 percent below the early spring. Although the army had fought effectively to the end, its fighter arm equipped with capable airplanes, it was overwhelmed in the air. Its personnel and material reserves were dwindling, its flight operations circumscribed by fuel shortages, and its ability to contest the incursions of growing Allied air strength diminished. The German air service lost the war of aerial attrition.

Britain

In early 1918, as British aviation prepared to change to the Air Ministry and the Royal Air Force (RAF) in April, a 16 January memorandum from Trenchard on the RFC's defensive role indicated his continued advocacy for the offensive. The RFC was to detect and disrupt German preparations for attack through artillery cooperation and strafing and bombing attacks on enemy reinforcements and communications, and then, in preparation for a counterattack, conduct an offensive against enemy aviation.[112] Two days after releasing the memorandum, on 18 January, Trenchard became Chief of Air Staff. Thus the RFC in the field would be under new leadership when the anticipated German offensive struck.

To prepare for the German attack, Gen. John M. Salmond, who replaced Trenchard as RFC field commander on 20 January, ordered an increase in landing fields, trucks, and trailers to facilitate a retreat. He planned to concentrate low-flying aircraft in attacks on enemy infantry and the enemy rear to relieve pressure on British troops.[113] British night raids before the German attack failed to disrupt the German buildup, and in an 18 March day raid, British fighters and bombers lost 11 planes to some 50 German fighters—including Richthofen's squadron—scoring only four German losses. British aerial reconnaissance did not detect any significant activity behind the German front on the evening of 20 March.[114] When the Germans struck on 21 March, the RFC had 1,232 planes on the Western Front, compared to 961 at Cambrai the previous November.

Although the Germans had 1,000 planes along the British Front, they initially outnumbered the British at the point of attack, 750 to 580 aircraft. General Salmond, however, remained "cool and unfussed," having "not the slightest doubt we shall win, but the price is heavy, needlessly so."[115] During a 10-day period in April the RFC lost 478 airplanes, more than the previous two months combined; by 29 April it had lost 1,302 planes. The losses, particularly in the assault or ground-attack squadrons, were heavy, although the RFC could replace both the planes and pilots. It dissipated its strafing effort among a wide range of targets, while its artillery cooperation remained ineffective. Still, the flying corps's aggressive attacks harassed and ultimately helped to stem the German advance. One fighter plane flew so low that it ran over a German company commander. In the air the RFC increasingly nullified the German air arm's impact on the battle,[116] and by 24 March it had regained numerical superiority and was winning aerial ascendancy.[117] When the German advance on Amiens tapered off, the RFC assault squadrons countered a new German offensive south of Ypres.

In May the Germans shifted most of their air arm south to attack the French, but in heavy fighting north of the Somme throughout the summer, British fighter and ground-attack squadrons suffered severe losses. The corps squadrons benefitted from the pressure applied to the Germans by their more offensive colleagues and suffered far fewer losses in their daily artillery observation and infantry contact work.

In July the Army Council deemed aerial operations "an essential factor in the offensive military operations which are envisaged during the coming year." It specifically noted that low-flying fighter squadrons had proved highly effective in supporting troops and emphasized the need for the RAF's continuous and frequent attacks during land battles.[118]

In early August the British Fourth army attacked Amiens, assigning all the air brigade's fighter units to ground attack. British low fliers pressed German troops constantly and reduced severe tank casualties by laying smoke screens in front of advancing tanks and strafing German antitank gunners. In early July Maj. Trafford Leigh-Mallory's squadron of two-seat Armstrong Whitworths, joined in mid-August by a Sopwith Camel squadron, were assigned to the tank corps to develop aircraft-tank liaison and to protect the tanks against German antitank guns. For the remainder of the war, the two units operated successfully to locate and neutralize German antitank artillery.[119] Meanwhile, the RAF's long-range reconnaissance failed to detect German reinforcements in the August struggles, while its continual bombing attacks on 11 Somme bridges destroyed none, though they stirred a hornet's nest of German fighters in the bridges' defense. The RAF lost 847 aircraft in August. One hundred of them—the war's highest one-day toll—were lost the first day of the attack, 8 August, when the air force suffered 86 casualties, including 62 killed, missing, or taken prisoner.[120]

As the British army, coordinating its tank, artillery, and airplane use, advanced inexorably for the rest of the war, the RAF concentrated on offensive patrols, ground attacks against frontline enemy positions, and bombing attacks against the Somme bridges and occasionally German airfields. In early September the army gave the fighter units a respite, reducing fighter activity over the lines to a minimum, although fighter reconnaissance and bombing raids continued. As late as 30 October the British encountered heavy resistance from the German air arm, losing 41 planes while scoring 67 kills. From 1 August to 11 November the RAF lost 2,692 airplanes, but received 2,647 from British industry.[121]

In 1918 the RAF's tactical air war on the Western Front was more grueling and costly than on other fronts. In Italy the RFC/RAF's Seventh Brigade gained air dominance because of its superior fighter aircraft and experienced pilots, who regarded flying in Italy as "a holiday" compared to flying in the Western Front.[122] The RFC's fighter ascendancy, won by such fliers as William Barker, enabled British corps aircraft to perform their duties effectively. As on the Western Front, Camels were used for extensive low-level operations, particularly during the Austrian attack on the Piave Front in mid-June. Camel fliers machine-gunned Austro-Hungarian troops crossing bridges and ultimately helped to force the Austro-Hungarians to withdraw. During a long respite along a stationary front until late October, RAF units continued their offensive patrols, reconnaissance missions, and artillery cooperation. In the attack at Vittorio Veneto on 24 October they added ground strafing to their duties, and as the Austro-Hungarian army disintegrated in full retreat, the Camels wreaked havoc on the withdrawing columns, just as they had on a much smaller scale a month earlier in Macedonia and in Allenby's victory in Palestine.[123]

In Palestine the RAF had aided Allenby's breakthrough. Allenby had secured three squadrons of up-to-date airplanes that had allowed him to seize superiority from the small German force. This superiority, which Allenby acknowledged was one of the great factors in his success, allowed the English to conceal the concentration of their ground forces and gave them the advantage of surprise. In the attack in September the RAF blockaded the few enemy airfields and annihilated the fragmented Turkish Seventh and Eighth Armies in the pursuit after the battle, just as it destroyed the Second Bulgarian Army on the Macedonian Front on 21 September and the Italians after the Vittorio Veneto attack.[124] These victories would have been impossible against a first-rate enemy with a modicum of air support, as events on the Western Front, where the Germans remained well-equipped for aerial combat, demonstrated.

The relentless tactical air war over the Western Front claimed some of the best pilots. Maj. James McCudden, credited with 57 victories, fell prey not to the enemy but to a 9 July accident. His engine stopped as he was taking off, and he attempted to turn downwind to glide back to the field—a fatal error, and one that McCudden, a former flight instructor, must have understood. He died of a head injury from the ensuing crash.

Edward "Mick" Mannock swore to avenge McCudden's death. After a stint as an instructor, Mannock had returned to action on 12 April. An extraordinary deflection shot, he had little difficulty with Albatrosses and Halberstadts, and he countered the Fokkers' superior turn and climb capabilities with zoom and dive tactics. He took command of Billy Bishop's 85th Squadron after the Canadian Victoria Cross recipient had been spirited home with 72 victories on 19 June, to the consternation of some who remained.[125] Susceptible to nerves and fears of being flamed, a tired Mannock knew that "there won't be any 'after the war' for me." On 26 July 1918, he followed his 73rd official kill down to 200 feet and was shot down in flames by ground fire. He carried a pistol to avoid burning to death. From that altitude he probably had no chance to use it. Though he was Britain's ace of aces, Mannock remained relatively unknown to the public during the war, and received the Victoria Cross posthumously on 18 July 1919 only after fighter pilots led by ace Ira Jones had petitioned the government for recognition.

In 1918 Ira "Taffy" Jones reflected the changing character of the RAF. A former clerk and telegraph operator in civilian life, the feisty five-foot five-inch youth had served first as an air mechanic and then an observer. He arrived at the front in the 74th Squadron on 10 April 1918 and early concluded that air fighting was "really just a dangerous game . . . of kill or be killed," in which there was "no room for any of this chivalry of the air we hear so much about." He unabashedly idolized the ruthless Mannock as a modern hero. After Mannock's death, he ceased to care if he died and fought to avenge the deaths of his friends. While Jones traced British offensive spirit to the self-reliance and aggression bred in sports, he shunned sportsmanship. Officers of the "Eton and Sandhurst type" condemned his shooting of "Huns hanging in parachutes" as "unsportsmanslike." Jones, no public school graduate, was "unhampered by such considerations of 'form' " in his search for vengeance. He ended the war a 40-victory ace, his soul so gripped by the "thrill of fighting and sport of flying" that he was disappointed at the Armistice and signed to fly in north Russia. [126]

While the RAF received some fighters of Jones's caliber from the British Isles, R. S. Worley recalled that by mid-September, if the Germans' new recruits no longer possessed the fighting quality of their dead predecessors, a comparable situation existed in the RAF: "I suppose England is down to the dregs; at any rate, . . . the majority of the best pilots in the Wing hail from Canada, Australia, South Africa, and so forth."[127] Tom Cundall, the protagonist of V. M. Yeates 1918 novel about combat flying, *Winged Victory,* shared this impression, judging that "the Canadians were very much to be thanked for" British air supremacy in early 1918.[128] By 1 March nearly a quarter of RAF fliers in France were Canadian,[129] and by the war's end a disproportionate number of Canadian pilots ranked among the top aces: Billy Bishop with 72 kills, Raymond Collishaw with 60, William Barker with 59, Donald McLaren with 54, and six others with 30 or more victories each.[130] Some 300 Americans served, primarily in 1918, with British flying units during the war. Nearly 30 became aces and 51 were killed in combat, 32 were wounded, 32 became prisoners of war, and 8 were missing.[131]

Despite the RAF's changing composition, squadron command remained the English middle class's preserve, as an analysis of 37 squadron commanders who applied for permanent commissions at the war's end showed that they came from solidly middle-class prewar occupations and included 13 public school graduates.[132]

By 1918 the combatants were introducing standards in the selection of pilots and attempting to characterize types that would be successful in aviation. Captain T. S. Rippon of the Royal Army Medical Corps and Lt. E. G. Maxwell, pilot and air medical officer, both prefaced their research by observing that flying was no longer confined to the public school student, cavalry officer, or athlete, since the British were taking recruits from the lower-middle and working classes. The connection between introducing discriminating standards and the need to reach into the lower social orders was evident.

Rippon and Maxwell were convinced that temperament indicated the successful aviator. This potential ace had the attributes of the sportsman and athlete and would be "keen on flying," because it appealed to the "sporting instincts." Such qualities, by definition, were seldom found in the ranks of sedentary workers. Other characteristics, such as "good hands," unspoiled by the "heavy-handedness" necessary for automobile or motorcycle racing and ignorance of the mechanics of aircraft would have eliminated aces like Billy Bishop and James McCudden respectively. It was difficult for the British to divorce the criteria from subjective notions about class and the requirements of a good pilot.[133]

In 1918 the fighter pilots flew essentially the same pursuit types, but with more powerful engines, that they had flown in 1917. Of the British aircraft, John Slessor regarded the Bristol Fighter as 1918's most formidable combat aircraft.[134] Walter Noble, a Bristol pilot who emphasized that the RAF's raison d'être was to secure information on enemy activities and to prohibit knowledge of theirs, believed the Bristol fighter could hold its own even against the Fokker. In June 1918, a month of perfect flying weather, they flew 80 to 100 hours in two or more offensive patrols daily. A veteran of the trenches, Noble believed that the pressure on the infantry did not compare to that on combat fliers, who "went over the top" once or twice, occasionally three or four times, a day and had to contend with "Archie," "scraps," and the ever-present nightmare of engine trouble and bad weather conditions.[135]

The BMW powered Fokker D7 remained superior to all British single-seaters, including the last to appear at the front. The Dolphin, unusual among Sopwith craft for its use of the Hispano-Suiza in-line instead of a rotary, was fast and well armed, with two Vickers and two Lewis guns. It was unpopular because the pilot's head rose above the top wing. If the plane turned over, its weight, as one pilot suggested, rested on one's head, thereby breaking one's neck. In a crash, "the gas tank is right at your back like in a Camel and your legs are up under the motor. There's not much hope for the pilot."[136] Even Sopwith's successor to the Camel and Dolphin, the maneuverable Snipe that appeared in October, could not match the Fokker's speed, ceiling, or climb. The Snipe, however, was Canadian Maj. William G. Barker's mount on 27 October as he took a last flight over the Western Front before being posted home. At 21,000 feet, he attacked a lone Rumpler, which broke up in midair, but he was wounded in the right thigh by a Fokker climbing to the attack. Spinning down 2,000 feet, Barker leveled off in the middle of 15 Fokkers and set one on fire while the others wounded him in the other thigh. He fainted, and the Snipe spun down to 15,000 feet before he recovered consciousness amid more Fokkers. He flamed another, but one behind him further riddled the Snipe and shattered his left elbow. Barker fainted again, the Snipe spun to 12,000 feet, where he revived to find more Fokkers. He shot down a fourth and plunged for the British lines, with his engine smoking, to crash at a British balloon unit. This combat, the most epic of all the war's aerial encounters, won a riddled but alive Barker the Victoria Cross. [137]

The single-seat fighters—SE5As, Dolphins, and Camels—continued to carry the war to the Germans. A U.S. flier, one of many serving in British units during the war, explained that "a Camel pilot had to shoot down every German plane in the sky in order to get home himself, as the Camel could neither outclimb nor outrun a Fokker."[138] While the Camel has won praise as the war's preeminent dogfighter, its essential task in 1918 was ground attack in high-risk assault squadrons. Novelist V. M. Yeates, who survived 248 hours and four crashes in Camels during 1918 before being discharged with tuberculosis in the summer, termed it "the last occupation on earth for longevity" and "the great casualty maker."[139] Pilots' chances of surviving continuous low-altitude work for over a fortnight were "not great," and "big pushes" occasioned much strafing, reconnaissance, and casualties. Yeates considered ground strafing the most dangerous and valuable work that scouts performed, though they received little credit for it.

From March to November, the 80th Squadron, with a strength of 22 officers, suffered 168 casualties from all causes, about 75 percent monthly, with almost half killed.[140] A U.S. pilot who flew with the British, after surviving training in which three pilots practicing on Camels were killed in one day, commented that fighting Fokkers in Camels during the summer was exhausting and caused high losses, because the craft were deficient and concluded that it was "only a question of time until we all get it."[141] September 1918 casualty reports from RFC Headquarters record large numbers of Camel crashes on takeoff and landing due to pilot inexperience, while some planes that had been in service over 100 hours were too slow to maintain formation.[142] At the war's end a small number of armor-plated Sopwith Salamanders arrived to replace the Camels, although the Salamander's clumsiness and poor flying characteristics, according to one pilot, made it more lethal to its pilots than to the enemy.[143]

Of the observation crews' mounts, the Armstrong Whitworths and RE8s, the latter outgrew its initial negative reputation only with difficulty. Ira Jones referred to them as "flaming wafers" because of their tendency to burn in crashes.[144] RE8s crashed frequently when landing in gusty winds, though crews emerged unhurt from most of those accidents. Yet some RE8s survived over 300 hours of flight time and five months of service, becoming ever slower and more decrepit.[145]

From the beginning of 1918 to the Armistice, the RAF on the Western front continued its offensive over enemy territory, suffering total casualties of over 7,000, of which more than 3,700 were due to combat. Casualties increased through September, when they peaked at 1,023 (588 in battle and 435 from other causes), falling back to 941 in October.[146]

The relatively high number of missing personnel indicated the intensity of the offensive over enemy airspace, while casualties from other causes, which included such ailments as nerves and battle fatigue, took a toll of fliers in numbers nearly equal to that of combat. British Staff College notes on pilot casualties on the Western Front from January through September confirmed this proportion and indicated that of the average wastage per squadron of 6.3 pilots monthly, 3.8 of them were lost to battle casualties.[147] Pilot casualties remained heavy to the very end. According to fighter-pilot Duncan Grinnell Milne, a pilot's life in France during 1918 averaged under six weeks, to be terminated by nerves, crashes, injury, capture, or death. In the nine weeks before the Armistice his fighter unit lost, of an average of 18 pilots actively engaged, 6 killed, 4 injured in crashes, and 4 captured.[148]

To determine the average pilot life span, the RAF traced the careers to 31 October 1918 of all new pilots, a total of 1,437, sent to France from July to December 1917: 260 (18 percent) had been killed; 382 (26 percent) had been injured or sick and admitted to hospital; 287 (20 percent) were missing; 358 (25 percent) had been transferred home; and 150 (11 percent) were still in France. Of the 358 transferred to Home Establishment, 24 percent had returned home within three months of beginning active service,

TABLE 4.

The RAF's Western Front Casualties, 21 March to 11 November 1918

	Killed	Wounded	Missing	Total
Pilots	278	728	1,230	2,231
Observers	174	517	482	1,168
Total	452	1,245	1,712	3,409

13 percent within three to six months, 36 percent within six to nine months, and 27 percent had remained over nine months. Since pilots were generally transferred home after an average of eight to nine months of continuous service overseas, the 37 percent returning to Home Establishment within six months left the front early.[149] Overall, then, 64 percent of those 1,437 pilots were killed, wounded, or missing, and of the surviving 36 percent, about a quarter returned to England early in their tour. Only about a fourth of all the pilots completed a tour of duty, a chastening thought should one ever be tempted to minimize the toll of flying in World War I (see Table 4).

Although it is impossible to establish training casualties in Britain, Adm. Mark Kerr, commander of the southwest air force training area in 1918, observed that preventable accidents at Home Training Stations were numerous and that nearly 300 pilots were killed during one quarter (three months), 75 percent of the accidents coming from stunting low and other follies.[150] In 1917 and 1918 Britain's casualty rate in training of one student pilot every 606 hours of flight training was higher than the France's (1:931 hours) and the United States' (1:2,960 hours).[151] Only in late March did William Weir advise that the state needed to assume the funeral expenses of officers and cadets killed in Britain, after a mother of a recently killed cadet had written that the first intimation of her son's death was the bill for his funeral expenses.[152]

Although in 1918 the tactical air war absorbed the bulk of the RFC's and the RAF's attention and resources, strategic bombing often receives the most attention today because of its controversial and political nature, particularly because a key justification for the very creation of the RAF and the Air Ministry had been to enact the popular policy of bombing the German homeland. While the RNAS had cooperated with the French in its formulation of strategic targets, the RFC did not. On 22 December 1917 Trenchard informed the French that the British bomber force would not necessarily cooperate with them, and through mid-January 1918 the 41st

Wing's three bomber squadrons struck different targets from the French in operations limited by weather and inexperience.[153]

On 17 January the Chief of the Imperial General Staff planned to increase the strength of RFC bomber squadrons at Nancy from 3 to 31 squadrons by the end of October 1918 and to strike systematically German industrial towns on or near the Rhine. Regardless of losses or adverse conditions, the squadrons would concentrate on a town for successive days until they had thoroughly destroyed the target or so shaken worker morale and "public confidence" as to interfere seriously with production.[154] Yet the absence of a plan of attack on the German war industry left the RFC with 250 possible cities as targets,[155] not including targets of military import in Belgium.[156] The army's refusal to cooperate with the French and inability to limit its targets threatened to dissipate any strategic effort it mounted. This approach set the tone for the future strategic air campaign, for on 1 February 1918 the 41st Wing became the Eighth Brigade, which in turn became the nucleus of the Independent Force formed in June.

Trenchard, having set the policy, returned to join the Air Council, which was formed on 3 January. Lord Rothermere as Secretary of State for Air headed a strong committee that included Henderson as vice president, Trenchard as chief of staff since 18 January, Adm. Mark Kerr as his deputy, and William Weir from the Ministry of Munitions. Rothermere, reflecting the demands of the people and government for retaliation, advocated an enlarged bombing program to punish Germany for its raids and to defend Britain in a counteroffensive. Trenchard, who disliked his civilian bosses and resented Rothermere's penchant for asking advice on aviation from others, considered Lloyd George's ideas on airpower hazy and Rothermere's expectations excessive given the small size of the force, although his own desire to attack the large Rhine industrial centers was no more feasible.[157] Rothermere found Trenchard an intolerant know-it-all "of dull, unimaginative mind."[158]

By April the Air Council unraveled. After a disagreement with Trenchard, Kerr went to training command. After an argument with Rothermere, Trenchard abruptly resigned on 12 April, thereby violating his December 1917 advice to Salmond that one should not resign during war. Trenchard's archrival, Maj. Gen. Frederick Sykes, returned from the Supreme War Council at Versailles to become Chief of Air Staff, but Sykes's appointment led to Henderson's resignation. Henderson, who disliked Sykes, "earnestly desired to escape from the atmosphere of falsehood and intrigue which had enveloped the Air Ministry."[159] Undersecrtary of State Maj. J. L. Baird, a Trenchard supporter, then informed Lloyd George that he could no longer support Rothermere. Rothermere, suffering from poor health and the shock of losing a second son killed in action, resigned on 26 April to be replaced by William Weir.

Weir, now age 41, Secretary of State for Air, and soon to become a peer, believed that the long-range bomber was the weapon of the future,[160] because it was potentially more devastating to the enemy than the U-boat to England.[161] Weir wanted to develop a long-range bomber to "seriously worry Germany in centres where she felt herself perfectly safe from aerial attack." In November 1917 he had sent Handley Page a rough specification of the necessary type and then arranged its production in Belfast, since the Handley Page works was occupied with the 0/400 production. Thus had begun development of the giant four-engine V1500.[162]

Weir planned to build the Independent Force to conduct a massive aerial offensive against German cities to destroy key German war industries. He believed that the Air Ministry should control general air policy except operations that were navy or army related. He considered Trenchard's resignation unjustifiable and insubordinate, but recognized the indispensability of the RFC's key figure. He persuaded Trenchard to take command of the Eighth Brigade in mid-May by allowing the general to report directly to him. On 6 June Trenchard assumed command of the Independent Force under an arrangement that essentially enabled him to bypass Sykes and to treat his rival as he believed Rothermere had dealt with him when he had been Chief of Air Staff.[163]

Historian George Williams identified three competitive forces shaping British bombing policy in 1918: the War Cabinet, which planned expansion and strategy; Trenchard, the executor of strategy; and the Air Ministry in the middle.[164] Yet Trenchard, now the reluctant commander of only a part of his original force, was the unpredictable factor. He had never wanted the air force divorced from the army and was convinced that the split in the RAF would lower cooperation with Haig's army.[165] Of the Independent Force, he wrote in his diary that "a more gigantic waste of effort and personnel there has never been in any war."[166]

While lamenting these circumstances, Trenchard established an Independent Force staff, which duplicated the Air Staff bureaucracy, and effectively removed himself from control of the Air Ministry. He also viewed the Secretary of State for War Lord Milner's requests that the War Cabinet be kept informed of the bombing offensive's progress as a lack of trust.[167]

From the start Trenchard virtually ignored the War Cabinet and Air Ministry. He initially appropriated the bombing policy of Col. Cyril Newall (his predecessor at the Eighth Brigade) which emphasized iron and coal mines and railway materiel. Although Trenchard's aide Maurice Baring asserted that in late June Trenchard decided that British aviation was strong enough to defeat the Germans in France and to attack German industrial centers, the evidence indicates otherwise.[168] In June, to keep the initiative in the air war and bolster morale, Trenchard added enemy airfields to the force's objectives without informing Weir. Instead of striking the Air Ministry's priority targets—chemical factories and iron and steel works—the Independent Force concentrated on airfields and railroads from June through September, ultimately devoting 84.6 percent of its effort to these targets in September.[169] In the Air Ministry's Directorate of Flying Operations Major Lord Tiverton wrote numerous memoranda condemning the use of the Independent Force for such targets as a dissipation of force on missions that could have been better undertaken by regular army air units, but to no avail.

Trenchard concentrated on bombing enemy airfields in the attempt to cut his daytime losses to enemy fighters. Given effective German air defenses and the "marginal proficiency" of his aircrew, airfields and railroads were the only targets Trenchard could raid on a sustained basis. Throughout 1918 the British bomber forces were unable to bomb accurately, as day bombers preferred not to use their bombsights, while night bombers occasionally preferred targets of their own choosing to assigned ones. Both historians George Williams and Neville Jones considered the army aircrew's lack of training the probable cause of such problems.[170]

The training deficiency was compounded by the day bomber squadrons' poor equipment, as the DH9s proved true to the previous year's dire predictions. The six-cylinder 230-hp Beardmore-Halford-Pullinger (BHP) engine or the Siddeley Puma engine, not only gave the plane dramatically inferior performance compared to the DH4 (91 mph at a 5,000-meter service altitude compared to 122 mph at 7,000 meters) but also suffered constant mechanical problems. In May nearly 30 percent of DH9s performing bomb raids in the 99th Squadron had to abort their missions before takeoff. The first DH9s powered by the 400-hp Liberty engine arrived in September, but the squadrons never received enough of them to fly as a unit before the Armistice. Battle casualties to day-bomber units in five months amounted to 257 aircrew, 178 percent of its force strength in November, while its monthly wastage was just under 70 percent, eclipsing many scout squadrons. In the summer and fall operational losses forced three of Trenchard's four day-bomber squadrons to interrupt their operations because of personnel and materiel shortages. If night units flying FE2Ds and Handley Page 0/400s were twice as vulnerable to aircraft accidents as day units, they were four to five times less likely to become battle casualties.[171]

Between 6 June and 10 November the Independent Force dropped 550 tons of bombs, 160 by day and 390 by night, including 220 tons on airfields.[172] Historian George Williams rejects the unsubstantiated claim that the bombing greatly strained German resources by causing a great buildup in German air defenses, which in turn accounted for the Independent Force's losses. Williams concludes that aircrew inexperience, unreliable aircraft, and adverse weather frustrated the day-bombing campaign more than enemy countermeasures, demonstrating that "sustained long-range day bombardment was manifestly an unrealisable goal."[173]

Yet the sanguinary expectations at home occasionally intruded. On 10 September Weir, seeking some decisive results, wrote Trenchard:

> I would very much like it if you could start up a really big fire in one of the German towns. If I were you, I would not be too exacting as regards accuracy in bombing railway stations in the middle of towns. The German is susceptible to bloodiness, and I would not mind a few accidents due to inaccuracy.[174]

One week later Weir suggested concentrating on a West German city and advised Trenchard that reports of bombing railroads were harming their cause. The public, impatient for results and believing that too much labor had been invested in air operations, wanted to hear of raids on munitions works and other industrial targets.[175] On the other hand, Churchill considered it unlikely that terrorizing the population would compel the German government to surrender and that an air offensive alone was unlikely to finish the war. He believed that attacks on bases and communications should be related to the main battle with civilian casualties inevitable but incidental to these targets.[176]

All authorities acknowledged that the Independent Force was incapable of causing significant material damage but assumed that it could injure morale. Trenchard posited to Weir that "the moral effect of bombing stands undoubtedly to the material in proportion of 20 to 1." Yet postwar surveys of those regions of Germany under Allied occupation indicated that the raids had "only minor impact upon civilian morale and productivity." The raids only affected the morale in England, where they raised it through Trenchard's reports to the Air Ministry and the press.[177]

The postwar U.S. Air Service bombing survey concluded that the "lack of a predetermined program carefully calculated to destroy by successive raids those industries most vital in maintaining Germany's fighting forces" was the bombing campaign's greatest failure, and suggested that while the wish to " 'bomb something up there' might have appealed to one's sporting blood, it did not work with greatest efficiency against the German fighting machine."[178]

U.S. statistical analysis of British raids in the first half of 1918 judged the predominance of attacks on communications as "an apparent lack of concentration against particular objectives." The failure to select specific targets for concentrated attention was especially ironic, given the Chief of the Imperial General Staff's recognition in January of the need for such a strategy. Perhaps most chastening, in raids for material destruction where the bomber functioned like long-range artillery, from January 1 to May 15 all 19 British bombing squadrons—nearly 300 planes—dropped an average daily weight of explosives almost equal to the average expenditure of eight 155mm guns during the same period. Thus, it took two squadrons of bombing planes to equal the work of one 155mm gun. The average daily performance of the three long-distance bombing squadrons alone was slightly over that of five 75mm guns.[179]

British strategic bombing in 1918 was full of such paradoxes. Trenchard's position of chief of the "strategic" Independent Force, which he used primarily for tactical missions, gave him a claim to be the RAF's founding father. Lord Beaverbrook later observed, "He was a father who tried to strangle the infant at birth though he got credit for the grown man."[180] Weir's biographer W. J. Reader paraphrased more gently, "If Trenchard was, as he is often called, the father of the Royal Air Force, he was a notably unwilling one, and Weir deserves the credit for thrusting fatherhood upon him."[181]

Yet, as Lord William Beaverbrook cogently suggested, what was at stake was whether Lloyd George or the military would run the government.[182] The very arm that the War Cabinet hoped to control, the Independent Force, was controlled by an officer who highly valued loyalty to his army colleagues. After resigning from the Air Staff, Trenchard, out of allegiance to Salmond, had rejected command of the air force in France. Yet Trenchard's actions when chief of Air Staff—and those of his allies in the House of Commons (RFC subalterns Sir John Simon and Lord Hugh Cecil, both on Trenchard's staff)—in attacking Lord Rothermere and flouting disciplinary codes, and his lack of candor in dealing with Weir when chief of the Independent Force, indicate that he held no similar predisposition toward his civilian superiors.

From Weir's civilian perspective, the aim of the bomber force was to remove it and air policy from control of the army and navy, and also from the Allies.[183] To that end he had chosen Trenchard, the only person prestigious enough to command the force. Weir's plan was to persuade Trenchard to assume the command, but to do so he had to grant Trenchard independence. He exhorted his bomber commander to strike German cities and destroy German morale, the latter their common aim. Trenchard, however, saw his first priority as supporting the army and its air arm and his second as raiding Germany. Given the fact that his meager and ill-trained force was barely capable of its first task, which expended the forces necessary for its second, the reality of the Independent Force did not correlate with its image.

On 29 October Trenchard became commander of the Inter-Allied Independent Air Force, which the Supreme War Council had established on 24 September. The very commander who refused to coordinate bombing policy with the French would command this joint force. The French now insisted that supporting land battles take precedence over any independent air operations, thus taking a stance similar to Trenchard's position regarding British strategic air operations in 1917.[184] The war thus ended with the stage set for a final scene of transcendent irony, a scene that would never come to pass.

The Independent Force did divest naval aviation of its focus on bombing in 1918, although the navy managed to preserve the Dover Patrol air units' independence from the army and to continue its own aerial struggle against the Germans on the coast. Naval aviation now focused on fleet and antisubmarine patrol work. The long-range reconnaissance of its giant flying boats carried British aerial superiority far over the North Sea. On these six-hour patrols, the physical exertion, stress from navigating in bad weather, and fears of engine failure undermined the pilots' health and enabled them to stand only two to three patrols weekly.[185]

With the success and increasing importance of convoys, in the war's last six months nearly 200 airplanes, 300 seaplanes, and 75 airships operated from home stations on antisubmarine patrol. Airships accompanied convoys their entire route, while the planes relieved one another.[186] To protect maritime routes in the Mediterranean, five shorthanded naval groups escorted convoys, patrolled the Otranto barrage, and bombed U-boat bases in the Adriatic Sea and occasionally Constantinople.

By March 1918 the fleet had three carriers, while many warships carried fighting landplanes, which could take off from turret tops and decks to ditch in the sea after their mission. In general the Admiralty wanted to substitute landplanes for seaplanes and had concluded by February that in sighting submarines, seaplanes and flying boats were far more efficient per mile of flight than dirigibles. Yet the Admiralty continued developing rigid and nonrigid airships because it could not acquire sufficient floatplanes or flying boats for antisubmarine duties, much less secure sufficient landplanes to substitute for seaplanes.

Late in July the Admiralty told the War Cabinet that the Independent Force seemed to take precedence over naval requirements. The Admiralty did not receive the Sopwith Cuckoo torpedo planes and complained to the Air Ministry in August that inadequate supplies of large U.S. seaplanes, T-planes, and antisubmarine craft were handicapping naval operations. Later in the month the Air Ministry limited the growth of naval aviation from its current 55 squadrons to 95 by 30 September 1919, not the 130 the navy desired.[187] Naval aviation had been outflanked.

The success of English airpower, engaged on far-flung fronts from western Europe to the Middle East, depended on the materiel that the homefront provided. The formation of the Air Ministry had led to changes in the structure of aviation procurement. Under the old Air Board, design and supply had been separate, with the board's technical department managing the former while the Ministry of Munitions regulated the latter, though Munitions' aircraft and engine chiefs Weir and Percy Martin were also members of the Air Board and had offices in the Hotel Cecil with the board.[188] This bifurcation was less than ideal, as Minister of Munitions Churchill suggested on 25 April:

> The union under one authority of design and supply is the foundation of production on a great scale, and this is especially true when the character of the product is continually varying and developing. The interests of design and supply are naturally at variance, design seeking a swift and immediate road to perfection, and supply succeeding only through standardized output.[189]

The Air Ministry became the central authority in aeronautical supply. The Air Staff was the consumer, and the ministry's equipment division was the link to the Ministry of Munitions aircraft production department, which incorporated the Air Board's old technical department staffed with active air force personnel. The two ministries were tied by the Ministry of Munitions Director General of Aircraft Production (first Weir and then Sir Arthur Duckham), who also served on the Air Council, and the head of the Ministry of Munitions technical department, who since June was an officer in both ministries.[190]

In the year ending 1 March 1918, the Ministry of Munitions decreased engine types from 33 to 25 and aircraft types from 39 to 18 and concentrated on production by larger units. The government was never able to obtain competitive prices for engine production, because of the high demand and inadequate supply, though it examined company books from the beginning of the war.[191] The government's attempt to launch national aircraft factories also failed to contribute much to aviation production.[192]

On 7 March the War Cabinet approved a program formulated in late 1917, raising the RFC to 240 squadrons and the RNAS to 52, with a third of the squadrons to be powered by Rolls-Royce engines, a third by Bentley, and the rest with Hispano-Suiza, Sunbeam, and BHP engines. At the 23 March Air Council meeting on the future of the aviation program, Weir indicated that he hoped to have Arab engines for Bristol fighters and to standardize Rolls-Royce Eagle and Falcon production by October 1919.[193]

The January to July 1918 production program dated 25 December 1917 called for monthly average production of 2,420 planes, 200 seaplanes, and 2,300 engines; actual output through June averaged 2,500 planes, 120 seaplanes, and 2,670 engines from both domestic and foreign sources. In February the production program for the remainder of 1918 sought the monthly output of 3,800 planes, 190 seaplanes, and 3,440 engines; third-quarter monthly averages were 2,850 planes, 127 seaplanes, and 2,670 engines.[194] Production could not keep pace with the program, which had set relatively low goals for engine production the first semester, but quarterly engine production peaked in the year's first three months at nearly 8,300 engines.

On 28 January Weir, Director General of Aircraft Production, acknowledged to Brancker that British aviation would always be somewhat dependent on imported engines, including Clergets and Liberties. Certain engine firms were also problematic, such as Austin, which he described as "unproductive," and Sunbeam, which the government had mistakenly allowed to concentrate on too many engine types.[195] In January engine supplies were below anticipated deliveries, as three quarters of Hispano-Suiza 200-hp engines received recently had broken under test.[196]

Labor-management strife, strikes, and particularly labor shortages—specifically toolmakers and mechanical draftsmen—caused production problems. In the industry the struggle over wages continued in 1918, as trade union restrictions on piecework clashed with the manufacturers' insistence on maintaining the practice. The Alliance Works dismissed workers for calling a meeting during working hours, which mushroomed into a strike of 10,000 workers from 25 London factories on 27 June. The London Aircraft Committee agreed with the Ministry of Munitions that a resumption of work should precede arbitration, but unofficial workers' committees repudiated the agreement. After ministry warnings and negotiations, in which Winston Churchill participated, the strike at Alliance was settled by a government takeover.[197]

The government did not consider strikes its most serious problem; in 1918 the work force was its key concern. On 7 March Churchill asserted that production would soon outstrip labor. The gravity of the labor situation following the German offensive caused the Ministry of Munitions to release from service over 100,000 skilled workers by July. The serious repercussions on aircraft and particularly aero engine output resulted in a production of only 688 engines instead of the 1,132 expected the first week in July.[198]

Throughout 1918 Churchill advocated reducing reliance on infantry and artillery and increasing airpower, tanks, and poison gas supplies to move toward mechanical and chemical warfare. In late August from the front, Gen. Henry S. Rawlinson acknowledged that aviation and tanks were necessary but stated the real requirement was infantry. Advising Lloyd George in the fall, Churchill conceded that air force demands on personnel and materiel might be excessive for the results produced. Haig, he knew, would prefer 50,000 men in the infantry to the same number in the air force, because the air arm required 50 to 100 people for every person in the air. The search for new sources for army personnel, Churchill concluded, might necessitate cutting back plans for the air force.[199] In a 11 September Air Council meeting Weir explained that personnel and engines were the weak points in the future progression to September 1919. On 26 September the Air Council even discussed using a minimum number of carefully selected Indian pilots, a desperate measure dropped at the war's end.[200]

Fluctuating engine production from April through July (2,370, 2,080, 3,401, and 2,122 respectively) produced a severe disparity between aircraft and engine deliveries, and by August over 4,200 airframes were in storage awaiting engines. Engine repairs often could not compensate for manufacturing shortages, because of serious difficulties in obtaining spare parts.[201]

The contrast between the summer appearance of the Fokker monoplane at the front and British engine problems prompted Brooke-Popham to comment:

> People in England are living in a fools paradise at present, thinking that we are so far ahead of the Hun in all technical matters that we can develop new types of engines in our own time. Believe me, we have not got the time and every moment is of importance.[202]

Production in 1918 continued to suffer from earlier decisions. According to J. C. Nerney of the 1935 Air Historical Branch, the failure to develop the Rolls-Royce engine fully in 1916 "was felt most keenly when the shortage of high-power engines precluded the full expansion of the strategical bombing offensive against Germany." He judged the decision to concentrate on the abortive Royal Aircraft Factory design rather than the Rolls-Royce "one of the most vital in the air war," as belated attempts in 1918 to standardize the Rolls-Royce engine and increase its production 200 to 300 percent were fruitless.[203]

In January the engine supply branch formed a separate Rolls-Royce branch, enlisting both private and national factories for Rolls-Royce production, but too late to have any effect on the war. The Eagle's intricate hand fitting still made its production difficult and uneconomical, and government priorities for the company could not avert serious problems, given the engine's prominence in the 1918 programs. In October Rolls-Royce employed 8,342 workers with a relatively high dilution ratio of 39 percent, and it agreed to extend dilution if the aircraft production department did not induct more skilled hands. The weekly production of Rolls-Royce Eagle and Falcon engines rose from an average of 24 and 16 respectively at the end of 1917 to 38 and 18 in the war's last five months but never attained desirable levels.[204]

In the five weeks beginning 1 July and ending 3 August, the RAF expected to receive 3,619 aircraft from the industry. It received 3,479, but 1,334, or 38 percent, came without engines. Fifty-five percent of the DH9s, 59 percent of the SE5s, 74 percent of the Dolphins, and 72 percent of the Armstrong Whitworths were delivered without their BHP and Hispano-Suiza engines. Thus, statistics indicating that actual production of 18,538 aircraft for 1918's first seven months lagged behind that expected by only some 400 planes must not be taken seriously, since many came without engines.

Weekly airframe deliveries averaged 696 planes in July and 598 over the first seven months of 1918. Average weekly deliveries of domestically produced engines in July were 363, since only 50, 51, and 66 percent of expected deliveries of Rolls-Royce Eagles, Sunbeam Arabs, and Bentley BR2s were actually received. Over the seven-month period Eagle engine deliveries attained 78 percent of expected totals; Arab engines, 66 percent; imported Hispano-Suiza 200-hp engines, 77 percent; and the imported Le Rhône engines, 82 percent. Production was not improving, as the July figures indicated, and by October deliveries of Hispano-Suizas of both British and French manufacturers were in significant arrears, while efforts to secure more U.S. Liberty engines proved abortive.[205]

Despite the magnitude of these problems, the Ministry of Munitions succeeded in mobilizing the aviation industry in 1918. From 173,969 workers in aviation production in November 1917 the labor force had grown to 347,112 by October 1918—an increase of 99.5 percent, making the British aviation industry the world's largest. Even if one excludes raw material firms, the labor force for aircraft, engine, propeller, and parts manufacturing totaled 268,096, a 74.1 percent increase from 1917. Of the work force, 99,362 toiled in the engine industry and 112,385 built airplanes and seaplanes, up from 57,549 and 71,485 respectively in November 1917. Dilution attained 42.7 percent in the engine industry and 37.8 percent in the aircraft industry, up from 38.2 percent and 36.4 percent in industries that were already relatively highly diluted from earlier measures in 1916 and 1917.

In 1918 the aircraft industry delivered 30,671 airplanes and 1,865 seaplanes and flying boats, more than doubling its 1917 totals of 14,832 and 982. British engine manufacturers delivered 22,088 in 1918 and 11,763 in 1917; foreign manufacturers supplied 9,181 engines in 1918 compared with 4,902 in 1917. All the increases were substantial, approximately doubling the previous year's production. But this increment meant that aero engine manufacture, which had always lagged behind airframe production, fell further behind in 1918; only the import of foreign engines restored the balance. Despite such problems, in 1918 Britain, with the world's largest aircraft industry, supplied the largest air force, which totaled 291,175 officers and other ranks in November 1918.[206]

The Lesser Powers

Russia

Bolshevik Russia officially departed from the war in March 1918 with the Treaty of Brest Litovsk. After the Revolution aircraft production ceased and the air service nearly disintegrated. The Squadron of Flying Ships had to destroy 30 giant Sikorskii airplanes to prevent them from falling into German hands. Igor Sikorskii fled to Paris, where Albert Caquot asked him to design a bomber. When the Armistice ended its construction, Sikorskii migrated to the United States.[207] Squadron Commander Shidlovskii would be shot in 1919 while attempting to escape from Bolshevik Russia with his son.

By March 1918 a small but resurgent Soviet air arm probably had 100 to 150 airplanes formed into 30 squadrons, some formed from earlier tsarist units. The flight school at Gatchina was reopened, and by the summer a Red Aerial Fleet under the land forces' command was serving in the Battle of Kazan in the Civil War. An assortment of 260 old and captured aircraft equipped its formations by early fall 1918. The naval air service had collapsed after the revolution, but reappeared during the Civil War in fleet service and on the rivers against the white forces. In October 1918 it had 61 seaplanes, which sufficed for naval air superiority until the whites obtained British assistance. The Bolsheviks seized the Duks plant in Moscow and the Lebedev plant in St. Petersburg, and in late June they nationalized what remained of the aircraft industry, which lacked labor and materials.[208]

Austria Hungary

Russia's departure from the war gave the Austro-Hungarian air service no reprieve, since it was outnumbered in 1918 in the Italian and Balkan theaters. Fighting a defensive war against superior numbers, its fighter pilots at least possessed the Austrian Aircraft Factory's (Osterreichische Flugzeugfabrik AG, Offag) improved Albatros D3, with a strengthened airframe and more powerful engine that enabled it to compete against the Camels, Nieuports, and Hanriots that were its primary opponents on the Southern Front. Flying the D3, aces like Capt. Godwin Brumowski, who finished the war as commander of all the Isonzo Front's fighter squadrons and with 35 confirmed victories, remained effective to the war's end. Still, as the Armistice approached, in a force lacking adequate reserves and planes, losses often had a chilling effect. The death of ace Frank Linke-Crawford on 31 July effectively ended flight unit 60J, which was disbanded to replenish other units.[209]

Strong enemy air attacks at night against the Adriatic's coastal cities—especially Trieste, Pola, and Kumbor—forced the naval air arm, which lacked sufficient fighters, on the defensive. In small low-level raids, its few 350-hp flying boats struck Venice and coastal areas and Italian troops in Albania and northern Italy. Though the naval air arm had begun the war dominating its opponents, the Allies overwhelmed it by the war's end, because it had failed to develop modern fighters to preserve its superiority.[210]

From January through March 1918 the Austro-Hungarian aircraft industry, crippled by coal and transport shortages, inadequate aircraft prices, and skilled-worker inductions, delivered 506 airplanes, below the fall program to produce 750 planes and 1,000 engines monthly in 1918 but in accord with the aviation arsenal's anticipation of only 500 to 800 aircraft because of problems in engine production and machine-gun installation. In January the General Inspectorate considered the coal and transport situations "insupportable": the Lohner plant closed at the beginning of January; the Phoenix works, Albatros's successor, was rotating workers around ovens to keep them warm; and other factories were close to shutting down. On 2 March the Austro-Hungarian High Command (AOK) assured the Inspectorate that it recognized aviation's importance and would place the aircraft industry on the coal priority lists, but considering the inefficacy of similar high command gestures during 1917, only spring weather would alleviate the coal shortage's effects.[211] The industry lost skilled labor in a general induction of workers from January to April, as the AOK, robbing Peter to pay Paul, inducted workers from the industry to staff its air units. The aviation industry felt the full brunt of the War Ministry's refusal to increase prices in early 1918, as manufacturers contended with escalating material prices and labor union demands for higher wages as well as the War Ministry's intransigence. The Budapest factories' threatened "strike of capital" finally forced the War Ministry in March to raise aircraft prices.

During these crises, the navy suffered for having based its entire construction program, costing 29.5 million crowns, on untested and in part undetermined materiel from Castiglioni and his firms in Germany and Austria-Hungary. When the 350-hp flying boat failed, the navy's program disintegrated, since unlike the army, which had alternatives such as the Offag's Albatros D3 and the Aviatik Berg types, the navy had no other adequate craft. In March the AOK learned of Camillo Castiglioni's plan to unite all Austro-Hungarian aircraft companies in a monopoly. The aviation command immediately denounced Castiglioni, demanding the entrepreneur's induction and assignment to a post in Palestine where he could no longer transact business. Instead the command resolved to promote Offag as a counterweight to Castiglioni's firms and turned to Germany for prototypes of competitive aircraft.[212]

In 1918 the AOK's highest priority was procuring G-planes, armored infantry planes and all-metal aircraft such as the Junkers, and the Fokker D7. Yet Austria-Hungary lacked the metal and metalworkers to build the Junkers, could not manufacture or import steel tubing to build the Fokker, and did not have the expertise or capacity to build G-planes. As the AOK sought planes that were beyond the domestic industry's capacity, the aviation agencies, the General Inspectorate, the aviation command, and the War Ministry delayed embarking on them until they were no longer feasible.[213]

After many failures of projected new types, the aviation arsenal had become reluctant to encourage firms to produce new types. By August 1918, when it actively sought to develop new planes, it was too late. Austrian aircraft designer Julius von Berg protested the acquisition of licenses for German planes, believing that it would crush Austrian creativity and reduce their firms to mere branches of the German industry. Yet Berg was protesting a fait accompli; since 1914 the domestic industry had essentially been an adjunct to German firms.[214]

The army's aviation agencies were so desperate for planes that they even attempted to procure them from the Anatra works of Odessa, in the Ukraine, after the Treaty of Brest Litovsk, but their efforts were fruitless, because Anatra could neither control its workers nor obtain raw materials.

The AOK had received only 627 planes from March through May and in June it had only 67 companies with 684 planes, instead of its intended 100 companies with 1,080 aircraft. Late in August, as the air service suffered heavy casualties, the high command was exhorting the expansion of the air arm and industry even at the expense of other forces. Such appeals, however, were worthless. The flight companies fought at only 50 to 60 percent of their strength during the summer. After the collapse of the June Piave offensive, in which the air arm participated effectively, the war would soon end.[215]

As the aviation agencies visited the factories to estimate their production potential for future programs, they found unused equipment and unreliable, unruly labor. In a final desperate and irrelevant measure in September, the AOK assumed control of all aviation agencies and eliminated the General Inspectorate. The aviation industry's total deliveries for the 10 months of 1918 were 1,989 planes and 1,750 engines, which, though an increase of a third over 1917, barely kept pace with attrition.[216] At the front the aviators paid for the inadequacy and ineptitude with their lives. Fortunately for them, the war ended on 4 November 1918.

Italy

On 11 March 1918 the aeronautical service of Italy's supreme command became the Superior Command of Aeronautics under Gen. Luigi Bongiovanni, while a General Commissariat centralized the supply of material and military equipment but not personnel. Italian air service officers, who were recruited from all arms, continued to belong to their original regiments, which created disparities in rates of promotion. Aviators who sought promotion often had to return to their former regiments for a time.[217]

The air arm's materiel improved in 1918, as reconnaissance units replaced their ancient Caudron G3s with Pomilio biplanes, powered by Fiat 260-hp engines, that could fly 100 mph at low altitudes. The pursuit units flew Spads and Hanriots, and the bomber units gradually shifted from Caproni 450-hp to 600-hp bombers. Gianni Caproni shifted his construction from the biplane to a stronger and lighter, higher-hp triplane and then back to the biplane. The installation of Isotta-Fraschini engines—which were proving more reliable than Fiats—on Caproni triplanes improved their ability to perform missions over the Adriatic Sea, over which they sometimes flew as low as four meters altitude.[218]

In 1918 Italian aviation's major flaw lay in its artillery squadrons, whose Società Italiana Aviazione (SIA) 7B1s powered by Fiat 300-hp engines tended to lose their wings in flight. In August 1918 only 60 percent of the arm's craft were combat ready, partially because the army support units had had to abandon the SIA 7B and transition into the Pomilio. Later the speedy SIA 9B with the 600-hp Fiat engine lacked strength and lost wings in flight. Although the Italian air service preferred to use the multi-engine Capronis for day and night bombing, which made it potentially less reliant on single-engine types such as the SIA 9B, these failures left gaps in the air service.[219] Perhaps the best craft in the Italian air arsenal was the Ansaldo works' speedy SVA5, which lacked the maneuverability to serve its intended role as a fighter but in February became a successful long-range reconnaissance plane.

With the unified aviation command and the ability to mass Capronis and some 150 fighters either for patrol or escort, the Italian air service bombed selected targets, particularly hydroelectric stations, in daylight. The SVA's strategic reconnaissance of enemy rail traffic as far as Lake Constance enabled the Italian high command to detect enemy preparations early, while short-range missions located enemy air concentrations and rail movements. At the outset of the Battle of the Piave, which began on 15 June, Italian aviation had 553 planes at the front—221 fighters, 56 bombers, and 276 reconnaissance planes—supplemented by 20 French and 80 British reconnaissance and fighter planes. The morning of the attack, Italian aviators bombed and strafed the Piave River bridges to the front to prevent Austro-Hungarian reinforcements and munitions. Austro-Hungarian reports credited Italian planes flying at 50 meters altitude with causing grave losses among attacking troops. The next day the Italians' absolute aerial control enabled their bombers and artillery spotters to prevent communications between Austro-Hungarian troops on opposite sides of the river. Later at the Battle of Montello Italian aviation, superior in quantity and quality, continued domination of its Austro-Hungarian opponent, attacking the Piave River bridges and demoralizing Austro-Hungarian troops. During the victorious battle, in a squadron attack on Montello from 150 meters altitude, Italy's ace of aces Francesco Baracca fell to ground fire on 19 June.[220]

D'Annunzio climaxed the summer campaign on 9 August with a raid on Vienna, his goal for nearly three years. Now the SVAs of the Serenissima Squadron gave him the means to reach the enemy capital, though only to bombard it with leaflets in a symbolic gesture befitting the poet's style. He announced to the pilots before the flight that if they did not reach Vienna, they would not return. The eight SVAs completed the 1,000 kilometer round-trip to Vienna with the loss of only one to engine failure over Wiener Neustadt.[221]

Preparations for the climactic Battle of Vittorio Veneto occurred from August to mid-October, as the air arm attacked railroads and airfields, and the 21 October battle plan emphasized ground attack by all aircraft. From 22 October to 11 November the air arm had 407 to 478 planes, including over 200 of both fighter craft and reconnaissance planes and 38 to 56 bombers. General Bongiovanni used the SVAs for long-distance reconnaissance and light bombing, the Capronis to bomb airfields and the Vittorio Veneto munitions depots, and the fighters for air-combat and ground-attack missions. The battle ended on 4 November with complete victory and Austro-Hungarian capitulation. The army air service's 504 frontline airplanes on 4 November represented nearly a tenfold increase from its 58 unarmed airplanes at the declaration of war in May 1915.[222]

Italian naval aviation, which grew to 600 seaplanes, 17 dirigibles, and 500 pilots at 36 seaplane stations, also dominated its Austro-Hungarian opponent in 1918. Naval aviators, operating from their center at Venice, attacked Austro-Hungarian naval bases and shipping and railroad stations. They also cooperated with the army in the Piave battle.[223]

Italian aviation's success on the Southwest Front stemmed from its rear agencies' ability to mobilize the industry. The government department regulating the air service had evolved from a General Inspectorate in the War Office to a General Directorate of Military Aviation in the Ministry of Munitions and finally to a General Commissariat, established in April 1918 by a parliamentary act under Minister Eugenio Chiesa who was directly responsible to parliament and accountable for all aviation matters except field operations.[224] Giulio Douhet served as director of aviation at the commissariat from January to June 1918 but, frustrated, he retired from the army at age 49 to write.[225]

The Technical Directorate, working closely with industry, had successfully engineered the air arm's expansion. Although Italy depended on France for its fighters throughout the war, the domestic industry supplied reconnaissance craft and bombers. The air arm needed more SVAs and Capronis and had only 58 Capronis in the final battle compared to 62 in August 1917. Caproni had difficulty securing sufficient Isotta-Fraschinis for production, although it managed to produce 40 CA3s 450-hp biplanes, 255 600-hp CA5 biplanes, and 35 CA4 triplanes. In 1918 the Italian aviation industry manufactured 14,840 engines and 6,488 planes, including 1,183 SVAs, 1,073 Pomilios, and 577 FBA flying boats.[226]

Italian engine production had been particularly successful. All the engine firms—Fiat, Isotta-Fraschini, and Ansaldo—had followed identical programs of perfecting six-cylinder engines to obtain the maximum power for the minimum weight. Early in 1918 they were beginning to develop 12-cylinder V engines of 500 to 600 horsepower. Fiat, in addition to its 600-hp engine, was testing a promising 400-hp engine, the A15.[227] In September Fiat was building 37 to 38 engines daily and moving toward 40 to 42, or 1,000 to 1,200 monthly.

Fiat's production enabled Italy to build a reserve of 1,000 A12bis engines, which its allies sought in return for raw material supplies. The Italians complained that France's failure to deliver their stipulated raw materials was delaying production.[228] Yet the French, despite their desire to secure engines, were concerned about implications of Fiat's engine production for their postwar economy.

In August the French air undersecretary's office contended that large Italian war industries, more independent of the Italian government than their French counterparts, were already beginning their transition to peacetime production and using war production as a means to secure raw material, buildings, and equipment for postwar construction. Fiat intended to use its new large aircraft factory for railroad production, while the firm also studied agricultural machinery and automobile production, the latter with the aim of inundating postwar French markets while French automobile factories continued their aviation and artillery production. Fiat had reduced its 1,400-engine program to 1,000 to prepare for postwar automobile production. The Italian government believed that it was better to obtain tanks from the French while furnishing them with automobiles. As positioning for competitive positions in the postwar industrial world began, the French air undersecretary's office warned its government to be careful about giving Fiat automobile contacts.[229]

The United States

In 1918 the United States, still inexperienced in modern warfare, rushed to field an effective air arm for the European war, while struggling to establish an industry to support the new service and the logistics to transport supplies to the front. The optimistic predictions and expectations of 1917 yielded to the chastening realities of coordinating an effort to fulfill them in 1918.

At the front the U.S. Air Service command was riven with internal rivalries, which the May appointment of Brig. Gen. Mason M. Patrick as chief to replace Gen. Benjamin Foulois did not resolve. Only when Col. Billy Mitchell became the top American air combat commander, with considerable independence in establishing objectives despite the army's ultimate control, did these tensions ease.[230] Yet certain problems continued to plague the new arm. The command of fliers by nonfliers and the army's ignorance—from division staff officers to troops of the line—regarding the air service and its work remained dilemmas.

Colonel Mitchell, as his mentor Trenchard, was determined to take the aerial offensive. June's strategic bombing and independent air operations, the formation of the RAF's Independent Force, and Trenchard's refusal to acknowledge any superior—even Marshal Foch, Allied commander in chief—prompted the United states to switch from assisting the British campaign to supporting Foch's coordinated plan.[231] Meanwhile, Pershing's chief of staff warned air service officers "against any idea of independence."[232] The American air war would be a tactical campaign.

U.S. units saw action in the quiet sector around Toul in the spring. Ninety-three Lafayette Escadrille members transferred to the U.S. Air Service and 26 went to naval aviation. The escadrille's aces took command of U.S. units. For example William Thaw was commanding the 103rd Squadron of mostly former escadrille fliers when it transferred into the U.S. Air Service in May. Raoul Lufbery, the escadrille's ace, after a short stint flying a desk at the huge U.S. training base at Issoudun, returned to the air only to be shot down in flames in May by a German two-seater. Lufbery had shared his knowledge with Eddie Rickenbacker, a 27-year-old new pilot of the 94th Squadron and former race-car driver. Rickenbacker scored his first victory on 29 April and ultimately gained 26 victories to become the United States' leading ace.

By the end of June, 13 squadrons were operating at the front—6 pursuit, 6 observation, and 1 bomber squadron—when they transferred to the fighting around Château-Thierry during the Aisne-Marne offensive in July. Over Château-Thierry U.S. pursuit pilots encountered for the first time large concentrations of Fokker D7s, which fought aggressively and tenaciously in teams and made attacks on German observation planes dangerous.[233] The inexperienced pilots of the First Pursuit Group, mounted on France's second-line fighter, the Nieuport 28, found that they could not yet compete with the D7. In their three-plane incursions over German lines, they were barely able to defend themselves, much less U.S. observation planes.

The first U.S. day-bomber units, flying Breguets, began operations in June attacking railroad yards. On 10 July six Breguets of the United States' only bombing squadron, the 96th Squadron, got lost and were forced to land behind German lines. They compounded the disaster by failing to burn their aircraft, prompting the German message, "We thank you for the fine airplanes and equipment which you sent us, but what will we do with the Major?"[234]

By fall circumstances had improved markedly. When the AEF First Army attacked the Saint-Mihiel salient on 12 to 16 September, Colonel Mitchell had under his direct command or on call 1,481 airplanes—701 pursuit, 366 observation, 323 day bombers, and 91 night bombers—the largest concentration of Allied air forces during the war, nearly half of which belonged to the United States. Despite poor weather conditions, this overwhelming mass retained aerial control as the fighters penetrated over German airfields and day bombers struck targets on the battlefield and in the rear. Saint-Mihiel marked the meteoric ascent of the 27th Squadron's Arizona balloon-buster Frank Luke, who concentrating on observation ballons shot down 18 Germans in 17 days, but was downed by the Germans on 28 September as the Meuse-Argonne offensive began. In an unusual gesture for a downed pilot, Luke, rather than surrender, pulled his pistol to fight on the ground and was killed. His wingman and protector, Joseph Wehner, an ace in his own right, had fallen 10 days before.[235]

American bomber crews, whether flying Breguets or DH4s, suffered severe losses during the offensive when operating in small formations of 3 to 6 airplanes but far fewer in larger tight formations. The United States' use of virtually unprotected day bombers on raids 10 to 20 kilometers behind German lines—a French and British practice—resulted in such heavy losses that the U.S. Air Service resorted to bomber escorts in the Meuse-Argonne campaign. In that campaign from 26 September to the end of October, Mitchell pursued the same tactics as over Saint-Mihiel. He sent 100 aircraft-pursuit groups strafing over the lines, and staged his largest daytime raid on 9 October with 200 bombers and 100 fighters attacking German troop concentrations. Mitchell also further increased the size of his fighter patrols to counter German formations at the point of the U.S. attacks. The corps observation planes had the most difficult task—keeping pace with the infantry in contact patrols performed at tree-top level, often in fog and ground mist—in addition to their artillery observation tasks. Ultimately 18 observation squadrons would serve army or corps headquarters in what the army regarded as aviation's most essential task.[236]

Losses in the intensive fighting in the war's last three months offset the influx of new units to the front, and many of these approximately 31 units were understrength. On 26 September the air arm had 646 airplanes; on 15 October it comprised 579; and at the Armistice it could muster 45 squadrons with only 457 serviceable planes, less than half the authorized program. Supply remained a problem throughout the war, and was particularly grave during the Meuse-Argonne campaign. At the end of October the three pursuit groups could assemble only a little over half their listed strength of 300 Spads.[237]

The U.S. Air Service received 6,624 combat planes—4,879 from the French, 1,440 DH4s from the United States, 272 from the British, and 19 from the Italians. Of its French planes, 1,644 were Nieuports, 893 were Spad 13s, and 678 were Salmsons. At the war's end some 80 percent of the air service's planes were French made.[238] The Spad 13, France's first-line fighter, though not particularly maneuverable, was strong and the fastest fighter at the front. It was more difficult to keep in operation than the Nieuport 28 because the geared Hispano-Suiza 220-hp engine was more difficult to adjust and repair than the Nieuport's 160-hp Gnome rotary. In the August Saint-Mihiel buildup, problems with the 220-hp Spads of the 22nd Squadron made concentration on combat difficult, and at Saint-Mihiel some pilots could fly only one mission a day because mechanics were able to keep only 65 percent of the planes serviceable.[239]

U.S. squadrons judged the DH4 inferior to the Breguet for bombardment and the Salmson for observation. Similar average losses of Breguet, Salmson, and DH4 squadrons in the war's final months were misleading, since squadrons in quieter sectors used the DH4. The Breguet was faster, its metal-tubing fuselage stronger than the DH4's wood frame, and possessed better load and altitude capability. The sturdy Salmson 2A2 was overall the best observation craft. Although corps observation missions—especially infantry-contact patrol—suffered serious losses to enemy pursuit in the absence of fighter protection, on army observation missions above 15,000 feet the Salmson with its 260-hp radial could outrun the Pfalz, Albatros, and Fokker D7 and outclimb both the Pfalz and the Albatros.[240]

There were numerous complaints about faulty materiel, particularly engine assembly and magnetos. The DH4 frame was too weak for the Liberty engine to run at full throttle without shaking the plane to bits. One U.S. engineer officer considered Liberty planes unprepared for service and often replaced their shock absorbers and wheels with Breguet parts. Beyond such construction flaws, the absence of self-sealing gas tanks offering some protection against fire in the DH4s did not help the morale of bomber crews. French plane tanks had asbestos-rubber coatings that automatically sealed bullet holes. The DH4's nickname, "Flaming Coffin," stemmed from its unprotected gas tanks and pressure-feed gas system. If a bullet punctured the gas tank, the pressure system forced fuel out of the unsealed hole over the airframe. A single incendiary bullet or spark made the plane a flaming funeral pyre for its crew.[241]

Such potential fate did not deter American aircrews. Second Lt. W. J. Rogers, a DH4 observer of the 50th Aero Squadron, commented:

> Aerial observation is neither a bed of roses nor the path to glory that the man on the ground imagines it to be. The wind behind a Liberty is terrific, and it taxes the strength of the strongest to fight it for three hours. If the ship is rolled and tossed about very much, . . . the occupants sometimes get sick . . .
>
> But I like it. I'm sorry we had war, but since we did, I'm glad I was an aerial observer.[242]

Aircrew members underwent training at home and in Europe. The Signal Corps adopted the Canadian method, establishing ground training units at eight universities that ultimately put more than 17,000 cadets through an 8- to 12-week course. Although the army increased its flying fields for primary training from 3 in 1917 to 27 by the war's end, airplane and instructor shortages in the United States caused many aircrews to receive their primary and advanced training in Europe.[243]

The most noted training grounds in France were the pursuit school at Issoudun and the bomber school at Clermont-Ferrand. The French fighter-training method emphasized individual tactics rather than teamwork and formation flying, although "gang" or "collective and cooperative" fighting, perhaps the "exact antithesis of the 'sporting attitude,' " was most efficient and appropriate in 1918. The U.S. fliers did not fully appreciate the necessity for formation training until after the Battle of Saint-Mihiel, when they modified their instruction. Meanwhile, trainees and instructors in the bombardment school at Clermont-Ferrand suffered from dissatisfaction and poor morale. School commanders complained that pursuit aviation received excessive publicity, and that training for observation and bomber aviation was undervalued, neglected, and used as a threat for poor fighter-pilot trainees.[244]

Casualties of U.S. Air Service personnel attached to all armies in Europe mounted steadily from four in March to 537 in October. Of the total 583 casualties, 235 were killed in action, 130 were wounded, 145 taken prisoner, 45 were killed in accidents, 25 were wounded, and 3 were interned. Accidents at the front and in flight training were as lethal for the American air arm as other air arms. The figures show that 681 flight personnel died in the air service, 508 (74.6 percent) of them in accidents (263 training in the United States, 203 in AEF training schools in Europe, and 42 at the front), 169 (24.8 percent) in combat, and 4 (.6 percent) from disease. In 1920 Lieutenant Colonel Rowntree of the Medical Reserve Corps concluded that "for every flier killed in combat three succumbed to accidents."[245] In addition, 72 were missing, 137 taken prisoner, 127 wounded, and 3 interned at the front. Of the 2,034 flight personnel—1,281 pilots and 753 observers—who reached the front, for every 100 trained fliers 24 had been killed; for every 100 pilots 33 had been killed; and for every 100 observers 4 had been killed.[246] Pursuit training took the highest toll, followed by night bombing, day bombing, and then observation.[247]

On 6 April 1917 the navy had 21 seaplanes in use, and on 14 October it had over 500 seaplanes at U.S. naval stations and 400 abroad. U.S. naval aviators flew Capronis in the northern bombing group at Calais-Dunkirk. However they received only 18 Capronis in July and August 1918 instead of the 140 promised, and the planes' Fiat engines were so poorly built that they had to be completely reconstructed. The first Caproni with the superior Isotta-Fraschini engines arrived just after the Armistice. The group's day bomber DH4s flew with RAF units. The naval operation remained small, and at the Armistice it had only 17 serviceable aircraft—6 Capronis, 12 DH4s, and 17 DH9s—instead of the 40 Capronis and 72 day bombers planned. By the war's end naval aircraft would be based at 27 naval air stations from Ireland to Italy, and for their overwater operations they would rely increasingly on U.S.-made seaplanes—Curtiss boats with Liberty engines.[248]

In the United States, the disarray in the aviation industry continued in 1918. By January the production program's failures led President Wilson secretly to authorize sculptor and air enthusiast Gutzon Borglum to investigate the existence of an "aircraft Trust." Borglum's attacks forced the resignations of Col. Edward Deeds and Howard Coffin. By mid April aviation manufacturers, members of the Senate Committee on Military Affairs and particularly a president's special committee investigating the industry recommended placing the aircraft program under a powerful civilian executive separate from the Signal Corps. Builders complained about the lack of definite orders; the Senate committee decried the delays in the provision of training aircraft, the "gravely disappointing" production of Liberty engines, and combat-plane production that was "a substantial failure and constitutes a most serious disappointment in our war preparations." The committee majority believed that production needed to be removed from the Signal Corps entirely, although a minority insisted that the program was doing well given its difficult circumstances.[249]

In May the president appointed Brig. Gen. William Kenly, Pershing's former aviation chief, director of the Division of Military Aeronautics directly subordinate to the Secretary of War. President Wilson selected John D. Ryan, a director of the Anaconda Copper Company, to direct the army's Bureau of Aircraft Production and chair the Aircraft Production Board. The two offices proceeded to operate independently, since Secretary of War Newton Baker was too overburdened to serve as liaison between Kenly and Ryan. On 22 August a report by a subcommittee of the Senate Committee on Military Affairs recommended establishing an independent air secretary with a seat in the cabinet over a department of aviation, as existed in both England and France.[250] In August 1918 President Wilson placed Ryan in charge of aviation, appointing him a second assistant secretary of war and director of the U.S. Army's air service, but Ryan then left on a six-week tour of Europe, and the war ended before the new arrangement took effect.

As the government struggled to correct matters, rumors spread. The 22 March *New York World* carried part of Gutzon Borglum's report to the president, and Wilson referred the matter to the Justice Department. Charges of profiteering and conflict of interest led to an investigation of aircraft production by Charles Evans Hughes, Wilson's opponent in the 1916 election and a former Supreme Court justice. The investigation, which was completed in October, yielded evidence of confusion and conflict of interest though none of corruption or conspiracy. The matter was dropped at the war's end.[251]

During this political turmoil, the U.S. aviation industry strove to develop and produce combat airplanes. DH4 production began to accelerate in May, when 153 were manufactured, and culminated in October with the production of 1,097. Only 67 had reached the battlefront by 1 July, but tests showing them to be structurally weak and defective forced a temporary suspension of contracts. In 1918 Liberty-engine production increased dramatically from 39 in January to 620 in May to 1,102 in June and finally to 3,878 in October.[252] In July some aircraft plants were shut down or running below capacity.

The failure to manufacture foreign designs in the United States resulted from production problems. The government's cancellation of Spad production at Curtiss in January necessitated providing large advances to prevent the firm's collapse.[253] In late April the Joint Army and Navy Technical Board recommended SE5 production at Curtiss, but the prototype, an SE5a with a 200-hp geared Hispano-Suiza, arrived with incomplete drawings that mixed the SE5a and the SE5 with a 180-hp Hispano-Suiza. Later, on 20 August, the official test of the U.S. SE5 revealed engine and radiator problems. When the order was canceled at the Armistice, Curtiss had produced only one SE5.[254]

The 2,000 Bristol fighters ordered from Curtiss in January met a similar fate. Curtiss initially believed that the plane required extensive redesign and strengthening to contain the Liberty, but later abandoned these reservations. The first plane crashed in test on 7 May, then another crashed nose first on 7 June, killing the crew, as did a third in a 15 July test. The overpowered plane was deemed "unsafe, overloaded, and [of] no military value." On 20 July the order was canceled.[255] The United States would build no frontline fighters, only fighter trainers.

In February the Aircraft Production Board decided to produce both Handley Pages and Capronis and placed contracts in April with the Standard Aircraft Corporation in Elizabeth, New Jersey. By late June Army Chief of Staff Gen. Peyton C. March was studying the United States' ability to produce the Handley Page four-engine giant V1500. In late July the plant began to ship unassembled Handley Page 0/400 bombers without engines to England for assembly. It ultimately sent fewer than 100, none of which reached the front. Meanwhile, after much delay, misunderstanding, and trouble, the Caproni flew on 4 July and proved to be overpowered by the Liberty engines. In October the government decided that Capronis and Handley Pages were a stopgap measure until the manufacture of U.S. Martin bombers, a new design by Glenn L. Martin and Donald Douglas that would prove to be the world's best light bomber in 1920. The Armistice, however, led to the cancellation of all Caproni and Handley Page orders.[256]

Capt. Frank Briscoe, assigned to manage Caproni production, attributed the long delay and great expense to the serious problems of adjusting metric plans for skilled woodworkers to production by machine methods using U.S. measurements. He considered the greatest obstacle of all to be "the military method of handling industrial projects," specifically the absence of a single authority to manage the project.[257]

A report on U.S. aircraft production submitted on 22 August by a subcommittee of the Senate Committee on Military Affairs ascribed the disappointing results in aircraft production to the automobile manufacturers' control of the program. Their lack of experience in aircraft production and the emphasis on the Liberty engine, which was thought capable of powering all aircraft types, were largely responsible for production delays. The committee rejected as reasons for delays the difficulty of measurement conversion and of securing sufficient engines, and accused the board of being mainly concerned with adapting planes to the Liberty engine, referring to the abortive attempts to adapt the engine to the Bristol fighter and the Spad. It condemned the organization under the Aircraft Production Board as unsystematic and inefficient, and believed that the board should have heeded the 1917 recommendations of Colonel Clark and Colonel Bolling to produce foreign planes and engines. The committee also suggested that the board should have adopted the Italian approach of selecting the best French types for production and then gradually moving to domestic designs. It judged that a substantial part of the $640 million appropriation had been wasted, citing the $6.5 million expended on the Bristol fighter and the over $6 million expended on 1,200 standard J-trainers that had to be condemned.[258]

The navy's seaplane procurement was highlighted not just by Curtiss's success but also by that of the Naval Aircraft Factory in Philadelphia, which had begun deliveries in April. The first Naval Aircraft Factory plane flew in March, only 228 days after the factory's ground-breaking ceremonies. By the war's end the factory employed 3,750 workers, a quarter of them women, and by 31 December 1918 it had built 183 twin-engine flying boats, the last 33 of them Felixstowe F5Ls, the final version of the British boat powered by a Liberty engine.[259] A critical difference between the circumstances of naval and military procurement was the navy's foundation of the Curtiss designs, which compared favorably to those abroad and were probably the United States's true aircraft production success story. The military had no domestic landplane design of comparable standing.

Conclusion

In 1918 Aviation played a significant role in the war's outcome. The air arm was, as Pétain proclaimed, of capital importance, in the sense that no power could afford to be without it. All the powers had invested substantial resources to build their air arms. The importance of aviation's tactical role on the battlefield in support of the army was beyond dispute.

The quantity and quality of aircraft were essential to success in the aerial war of attrition. Balancing the two had posed one of the most difficult dilemmas in aviation's development. Through superior production, particularly French engine manufacture, the Allies had achieved an overwhelming numerical superiority in the air. Their inability to cooperate had prevented them from bringing this potentially oppressive ascendancy to bear against Germany—whose technical superiority had allowed it to hold its own on the tactical battlefront—until the U.S. fall offensive at Saint-Mihiel.

Strategic aviation in 1918 revealed the lack of cooperation among the Allies at the front. The Inter-Allied Aviation Committee neglected issues of supply and production at beginning of the year to debate general aviation policy, focusing on the formation of an inter-Allied bombing force to strike enemy production, communications, and morale. Beyond concerns expressed by all parties about the Allies' ability to produce a sufficient surplus of materiel for the bomber force, the French opposed an inter-Allied strategic force that would be independent of the Allied Commander in Chief Ferdinand Foch and thus violate their principle that the air force should be subordinate to the army. Furthermore, the French had no strategic bomber like the Caproni or Handley Page, so they would have had to produce Handley Pages or Capronis under license until they could build their own heavy night bomber. Trenchard's appointment as commander of the proposed inter-Allied bomber force in October represented a compromise: the greater size of the proposed British contingent underlay his appointment, and he would be nominally under the Commander in Chief but in fact the Supreme War Council would decide the force's general policy, although Foch could use it to support major army operations in progress.[260] The war ended before the force could be formed, and the Germans escaped a strategic campaign against their homeland.

If the quality of Allied aircraft design was not comparable to leading German efforts, Allied engine designers, particularly the French, more than compensated for any inferiority. Any differential in aircraft or engine quality remained too small to offset the huge quantitative gap. Designs by Fokker, Rumpler, Dornier, and Junkers gave the Germans the edge in airframe technology, which they appeared likely to keep in 1919, although such new fighters as the Nieuport-Delage 29 offered the Allies excellent prospects. German high-compression engines, the BMW 185-hp and the Maybach 260-hp power plants, endowed German fighter and reconnaissance craft with performance equivalent to and often superior to their Allied counterparts in 1918. Yet the Allies—who already possessed the Hispano-Suiza 220-hp and Bentley 230-hp fighter engines and Renault 300-hp, Rolls-Royce 360-hp, and Liberty 400-hp reconnaissance and bomber engines—were increasing engine horsepower, progressing even to 600-hp engines, while the Germans made no strides in producing more powerful engines. Aerial superiority in such a close technological competition went to the side with the numbers.

Quantity depended on production, and the Allies, with the French central to their effort, won the battle of production in 1918. Severe labor and materiel shortages limited the growth of the German air service, while Allied resources grew in 1918 and were bound to increase in 1919 when the United States exercised its industrial prowess. The German air arm had no additional labor reserves. Even if it could have produced more aircraft, it could not have trained the aircrews to operate them. The Allies had the Dominion and the United States, both virtually ready-made sources for materiel and military and industrial personnel.

Denis Winter's study of fighter pilots, *The First of the Few*, asserted that the single-seat fighter became "the crucial aeroplane of the Great War." To support his claim he cited the RAF's June 1918 proportions—58 percent fighter, 27 percent reconnaissance, and 15 percent bombers.[261] The comparative status of the air forces in 1918 provides information for a more comprehensive assessment of their character (see Table 5).

The U.S. War Department examined the air arms on the Western Front in August 1918 to determine "the properly balanced Air Force."[262] The French, with 2,820 planes, were 51 percent of Allied air strength, the British, with 1,644, were 30 percent, the Italians, with 614, were 11 percent, the United States, with 270, were 5 percent, and the Belgians, with 160, were 3 percent. In the Central Powers, it estimated that the Germans had 2,592 airplanes and the Austro-Hungarians had 717.

The ratio of pursuit planes to total service planes in the RAF was three-fifths greater than the French ratio and nearly a third more than the German. The British attached less importance to reconnaissance than the French and German services, whose ratios were nearly the same. In the French, Italian, and German air services, the percentages of observation and bombardment aircraft were greater than pursuit aircraft; the reverse

TABLE 5.

Composition of Allied and Central Power Air Forces, August 1918

Air Service	Pursuit	Observation	Bombardment
France	34.0%	51.0%	15.0%
Britain	55.0	23.0	22.0
Italy	46.0	45.0	9.0
United States	46.5	46.5	7.0
Germany	42.0	50.0	8.0
Austria-Hungary	63.0	28.0	9.0

was true for the British and Austrian services. While the British proportion of bombers to total force was marginally larger than the French and growing, the two similarly apportioned their forces between day and night bombers: the British had 53 percent day and 47 percent night bombers, and the French had 52 percent day and 48 percent night bombers.

The report interpreted the nonuniformity in proportions to indicate the absence of a common theory about aviation's function in military operations and, in some cases, particularly in the United States', difficulties in obtaining equipment. After noting that the British air service was primarily a "fighting arm" in which pursuit played "the preponderant role," it observed:

> It is a striking fact that, as respects the relative distribution of fighting and reconnaissance machines, there was a closer resemblance between the French and German Air Services than between the British and the French.[263]

The War Department report considered this disparity in distribution indicative of "a fundamental difference in policy, presumably based on a theory of the chief function of aviation in warfare not held by other allied armies."[264]

Overall, the report categorized the services in three groups: the Austro-Hungarian and British, with a very small proportion of observation planes; the U.S. and Italian, with an even distribution of pursuit and observation craft; and the German and French, with the proportion of observation craft equal to or greater than other types. The War Department report concluded that craft distribution indicated the existence of "two widely divergent theories" on the "chief function of aviation in warfare." The British practice, in which "the air service is primarily a combatant arm" whose "principal duty is to seek out and destroy the enemy forces by attack from the air," contrasted with the French and German applications, in which the air arm's principal function was "reconnaissance for the purpose of securing information on enemy positions and movements to be used in directing troop operations and artillery fire."[265] The report drew no conclusions about the Italian air service, while it erred in assuming that the organization of the Austro-Hungarian air service reflected a perspective similar to the British. In fact, Austria-Hungary's air arm was lacking in defensive capabilities.

Despite these 1918 force-composition differences, plans for the future makeup of the U.S., British, and French air arms all emphasized the two-seat fighter. The U.S. War Department report noted that the AEF's plans for the composition of the U.S. air service in mid-1919 more closely approximated the French air arm proportions; the U.S. Bureau of Aircraft Production's projected figures for 1919 approximated the British. Although the RAF had 87 percent single-seat and 13 percent two-seat fighters in August 1918 and was receiving 6 single-seaters for every two-seater in the summer of 1918, British and U.S. aviators anticipated in late 1917 that the two-seater would supersede the single-seater. The U.S. program for 1919 thus planned for a ratio of two-thirds two-seater pursuit to one-third single-seater. The report did not mention that the French in 1918 also planned to increase substantially the proportion of two-seaters for escort and ground support. The three Allied forces on the Western Front all planned to shift their resources from single- to two-seat fighters, undoubtedly because of the latter's versatility in long-range bomber escort, ground strafing, and fighter reconnaissance roles, leaving the single-seat pursuit to concentrate on interception.

A French assessment described two different definitions of the roles of aviation:[266] the German air arm's defensive role that subjected aviation to other arms' control and was necessitated by a strict economy of forces rigorously adapted to the moment's circumstances; and the British and French air arms' roles that were essentially offensive and less restricted, better designed to force the enemy to consume his material and labor reserves. In this interpretation, unlike the statistical analysis, the French aligned themselves with the Allies—the Germans on the defensive and saddled with scarcity of resources and the Allies on the offensive and endowed with prodigious resources. This was a fair assessment of the air war in August, since the German strategic air offensive against Britain had ceased in May 1918.

André Voisin emphasized yet another disparity between the French and British, supported by his belief that the best way to combat the enemy air arm was aviation in the service of other arms, not by forcing the hypothetical air duel. He disputed the use rather than the concept of a powerful air reserve such as France's Aerial Division and preferred the RFC approach elaborated in Salmond's 15 February 1918 memorandum, which emphasized the defensive and particularly the reconnaissance role of aviation before an enemy attack and then artillery observation and troop strafing during the attack. Voisin deemed this approach better focused and coordinated with other arms than the French search for aerial battle, which might dissipate its force.[267] Voisin, in drawing general conclusions about British operations from their response to the March offensive and in seeking to discredit the use of the Aerial Division, idealized British tactics and overlooked the RFC's and later the RAF's focus on aerial combat.

The RAF was the most aggressively offensive of the air arms in 1918, a policy that required a preponderance of fighters and was also reflected in its having the highest proportion of bombers and the lowest proportion of observation planes of any air force. Ironically, the most defensive and least aggressive air service of all, the Austro-Hungarian, was the only one to have a higher proportion of fighters than the British, but for the defensive role.

The similarity of the United States' and Italy's ratios seems surprising given Italy's emphasis on bombing and the Caproni, yet engine-supply problems and the relative expense of the bombers compared to single-engine tactical planes limited the number of Capronis in 1918. In the United States, the confused and uncoordinated state of U.S. doctrine and procurement makes it speculative to suggest that the proportions stemmed from policy rather than circumstances. In any case, both forces had air arms balanced nearly equally between pursuit and observation.

Finally, the preponderance of reconnaissance planes in both the French and German air arms reflected the great importance of observation to their long-established land armies. While the French regretted not having more pursuit planes in 1918, their aggressive use of the Aerial Division's bombers with or without fighter escort enabled them to keep offensive pressure on the Germans, who, faced with British, French, and U.S. air strength, had no choice but to fight defensively to the end. The Germans had used their battle and bomber squadrons offensively during their attacks early in 1918, but after midyear, such use was impossible. They were beaten on the ground and in the air.

CHAPTER SEVEN

Aftermath & Conclusion

"I think . . . of all who sacrificed their lives on the flying and battle fields for the steep ascent of the young creation [the airplane].

The work of a decade is ruined.

However, as the legend according to which the phoenix was able to rise from his ashes, so will the airplane rise from the dead, out of the world of conflagration, out of the rubble of the instrument of destruction to bind people together as the symbol of a new future."

LT. COL. WILHELM SIEGERT UPON HIS RESIGNATION FROM THE GERMAN
AVIATION INSPECTORATE AND THE ARMY, 13 DECEMBER 1918[1]

After four and a half years of titanic struggle, the Great War had ended. The Western Allies stood victorious, if exhausted, and ready to pursue the struggle to complete victory with U.S. forces in 1919 if necessary. The Central Powers were defeated and prostrate, Austria-Hungary disintegrating and Germany threatened with political collapse. The Armistice brought an end to the fighting in the west; in the east conflict continued, in the Russian Civil War of 1918–21 and the Russo-Polish War of 1920–21.

Postwar Demobilization and Contraction

The Red Aerial Fleet had few airplanes, 260 in the fall of 1918 and 350 in November 1919; the factories produced only 669 new airplanes from 1918 to 1920, although they reconditioned 1,574 planes and 1,740 engines. The Bolsheviks began to promote the rebirth of the aircraft industry through aid to scientist Nikolai Zhukovskii's aerodynamic research institute and his Moscow Air Technical College, both of which became state agencies. They also reopened the military flight school, and despite frequent accidents in training because of the haste and the low educational level of the students, the number of aviators increased from 302 in June 1919 to perhaps 700 by the end of 1920.[2]

The small number of aircraft on both sides of these eastern European wars limited air operations primarily to reconnaissance, ground attack, and communications. In the Russian Civil War, the Allies sent small volunteer aerial units to aid the white forces. In the Russo-Polish War, a force of some 150 Polish planes, including American and British volunteer pilots, faced some 200 Russian planes along a five 500-mile front. Though too few in number to have had a decisive effect on the war, airplanes did effectively harass Bolshevik forces.[3]

In other European countries and the United States, the end of the war brought demobilization of the armed forces and the contraction of the aviation industry. The postwar reduction in Austro-Hungarian aviation was disastrous. With the dissolution of the monarchy, the new national governments assumed military authority within their borders. In Austria the government asked the factories to continue work without profit in order to assure their workers of wages for a minimum of six months. The industry had to complete aircraft contracts for civil aviation, but as of March 1919 its attempts to sponsor commercial aviation had failed, and the firms either turned to other pursuits or collapsed. The Hungarian aircraft factories did not survive their nationalization by Bela Kun's communist regime.[4]

In Germany preparations for postwar military procurement and civil aviation had begun in 1917. In the fall Ludendorff advocated military control of civil aviation. The Deutsche Bank sponsored conferences on commercial aviation through the postal ministry, while in December AEG founded the air transport company Deutsche Luftreederei. Kogenluft, determined to assure Germany a leading position in postwar commercial aviation, began experimental airmail flights in February 1918. Early in the spring it permitted AEG, whose efforts received encouragement from the Imperial Naval Office and the Office of the Interior, to contact Scandinavian companies about forming air transport lines. The highest government agencies thus planned to promote commercial aviation to compensate for the impending drastic reduction of military contracts.[5]

The collapse of the imperial government on 9 November and the abdication of Kaiser Wilhelm, the formation of a provisional government on 10 November, and the spontaneous sprouting of workers' and soldiers' councils around Germany created a tense and uncertain atmosphere. In a Germany haunted by the specter of imminent revolution, the air force and aircraft industry groped for survival.[6]

The Armistice treaty of 11 November prescribed the immediate demobilization of the German air force and the surrender of 2,000 fighters and bombers, particularly Fokker D7s and night bombers. Hindenburg, maintaining that there were only 1,700 war planes at the front, asked that the Allies accept that figure, which they later did. Yet the Germans did not surrender even that number. By 12 December, at the first meeting of the Allied Armistice Commission in Trier, the Allies had received only 730 usable aircraft. The German army attributed its perfunctory compliance with Allied demands to disorganization during demobilization, mutinous conditions, and continued fighting in the east. Yet the inspectorate later confided to civilian agencies that the army had some 9,000 planes after the surrender. The army was simply refusing to cooperate with the Allies.[7]

In revolutionary Berlin on 10 November, a Soldiers Council of Flying Troops demanded the inspectorate's transformation into the German Air Office. Despite these orders, the inspectorate continued to function under its old title, convening the manufacturers to prod them toward peacetime production, advising them that the government would limit nonprofit contracts to the minimum necessity for relief and retention of workers. The firms, left largely to their own devices, found themselves in the grips of a "fearful depression," as designer Hermann Dorner advised air force Capt. Kurt Student when the latter inquired about employment in mid-November.[8]

On 26 November the government announced the formation of an Air Office in the Office of the Interior to regulate civilian aviation and help the military liquidate military aviation. The undersecretary, August Euler, a prewar aviation pioneer and marginal aircraft manufacturer, thought only in terms of reducing German aeronautical enterprises to small research workshops, relics of the age of his successes before 1912 but inadequate for postwar development. He soon learned that the government's mandate did not ensure the cooperation of the military authorities or the federal states.[9]

In the midst of the confusion, on 13 December 1918, Lt. Col Wilhelm Siegert resigned from the inspectorate after nearly 10 years in aviation.

Siegert's replacement, Maj. Wilhelm Hähnelt, whose illustrious wartime career had culminated in his command of aviation of the Second Army in 1918, exemplified the tendency to fill the positions in the rear echelon bureaucracy with officers who had served in the air force staff chain of command at the front. Hähnelt, Lieth-Thomsen at Kogenluft, and the War Ministry brooked no interference from the civilian air office in the liquidation of military aviation. [10]

Furthermore, since the Air Office had no ability to issue contracts, all Euler could do was suggest to the industrialists that they accept the inevitability of drastic shrinkage. His own small firm in Frankfurt was now quarters for French troops and horses. Some factories continued aircraft production, while others produced furniture and machine equipment. The Pfalz factory was also located in the occupied zone. The Hannover Railroad Factory built some 200 more light two-seat fighters after the fighting had ended. Fokker's venture into boat manufacture and commercial scales failed, and only the diversity of his industrial empire—the aircraft factory at Schwerin, an armaments factory at Reinickendorff, the Oberursel Motor Works near Frankfort, and a small seaplane factory in Travemünde—forestalled collapse. His losses, and fear for his life during the revolution, convinced the Dutchman that he should leave Germany. In contrast, Hugo Junkers, undaunted by defeat, assembled his design and engineering staff on 11 November to inform them that the firm would now concentrate on civil air transportation. Junkers, the world's foremost authority on all-metal airplane construction, emerged from the war with the capital, plant, and experience to look to the future. [11]

The future looked grim at the beginning of 1919, given sporadic violence in the Spartacist rebellion in January, communist risings in March and April, and a disastrous economic situation. At least the government of the Weimar Republic came into existence in early February, to reign in international limbo until 8 May, when its representatives received the terms of the Versailles peace treaty. [12]

Kogenluft was dissolved on 21 January, but its heart, Col. Lieth-Thomsen, became head of the War Ministry's aviation department. Lieth-Thomsen and Hähnelt decided to use 500 planes suitable for air transport to form four permanent airlines and a military air courier service from major cities to Weimar. Since the aircraft industry and civilian air agencies were establishing their own commercial aviation ventures, Euler was shocked at these military ventures, which he feared would obstruct the development of civil aviation. Even the objections of the finance, economics, and postal ministries to the courier service did not deter the army, which planned to use the service to maintain military readiness. No resolution of the civil-military conflict in this "internal air war" had been reached by May; the army ignored distinctions between the civilian and military spheres, while the civilians considered that postal and transport aviation were civilian matters to be conducted by the Air Office and the aircraft industry.[13]

Meanwhile, the industry found itself in an inescapable dilemma: neither aircraft manufacture nor conversion provided profits, since demand was lacking in all industrial spheres. Factories generally attempted to continue aircraft production, as those who built G- and R-planes tried to modify them for commercial use. Despite the absence of outright bankruptcies and collapse, the industry was in distress. Anthony Fokker fled to Holland, smuggling six trains carrying over 400 engines, 120 D7s, 20 D8s, 60 observation planes, and tons of parts and equipment with him. Junkers continued to be the exception. When the Junkers-Fokker Works dissolved in December 1918, Junkers assumed all the shares and in April increased the capital of the joint-stock company. That spring the company delivered all-metal fighters to the army and developed the prototype Junkers F13, an all-metal six-seater cabin monoplane that was destined to become the most widely used transport plane in the world in the 1920s.[14]

The disclosure of the Versailles Treaty terms on 8 May ended the discouraging limbo disastrously. Five articles—numbers 198 through 202 in part 3 of the treaty—were devastating, forbidding and demobilizing naval and military aviation and ordering the surrender of materiel, prohibiting the production and importation of aircraft and parts for six months after the treaty took effect, and giving Allied aircraft free passage through and landing rights in Germany. The Inter-Allied Control Commission stipulated by article 210 would ensure adherence to the treaty's provisions.[15]

The terms convinced the army that civil aviation was useless for its purposes, as the Allies would simply commandeer equipment from the civilians, so elements within the army began to contemplate the politically perilous course of resurrecting an air force. Meanwhile, discussion of commercial aviation enterprises, steered by AEG, proceeded along the lines of collective economy enlisting the united efforts of state governments, communities, and private interests. The treaty initially appeared to foster the separation of German military and civil aviation and thus to offer the opportunity for a civil aviation and aircraft industry independent of the military. But all of the debates came to naught when the Allies presented the final peace terms on 17 June, allowing Germany six days to accept them.[16]

The signing of the Versailles Treaty on 23 June signaled the death knell of the German air force and aircraft industry of World War I. By the time the treaty became effective, on 10 January 1920, the remaining old guard of Germany's first air force had followed Siegert's precedent and retired, Lieth-Thomsen on 11 August 1919, General Hoeppner on 30 September, and Major Hähnelt on 31 October. Gen. Hans von Seeckt, chief of the German Troop Office, proclaimed the official dissolution of the German air force on 8 May 1920 with the epitaph "The arm is not dead; its spirit lives." Seeckt knew well how alive military aviation was in the imagination of his aviation experts.[17]

The dismantling of German military aviation was the central occurrence of 1920. Although the Allies had allowed Germany 199 airplanes for commercial and military use through January 1921, they did not grant the request to establish a militarized aerial police, which would have been merely a small air arm in disguise. The Allies extended the initial six months' limitation on production because the German government had not complied with the aerial clauses of the Versailles Treaty since 10 June 1919. Factories had been building materiel that the German government was not surrendering or destroying. Informers provided precise information on a large amount of hidden materiel in Berlin and Bavaria. Despite the Allies' Boulogne decision of 22 June 1920 to stop German aircraft production, German firms continued to build aircraft. The control commission waited to stop production of the Zeppelin-Staaken four 4-engine 1,000-hp giant until they saw its performance and obtained information about the firm's program. Reports from the Scientific Society for Aviation (Wissenschaftliche Gesellschaft für Luftfahrt) in September 1920 included discussions on metal aircraft from Junkers, on R-planes, seaplanes, engines, and Ludwig Prandtl's test institute at Göttingen.[18]

A Swiss engineer reported in 1921 that German factories, which had undergone a violent crisis after the Armistice, were back in operation, working to restore their position. AEG, Rumpler, LVG, and others were building slower and higher-payload planes to use civil aviation as a means to rebuild military aviation and establish commercial supremacy.[19] The Air Office, which became the aviation department in the transport ministry, was no longer in August Euler's hands, as he had resigned in December 1920. His successor, Capt. Ernst Brandenburg (Ret.), unlike Euler, was perfectly willing to use German civil aviation as a vehicle for military aviation. The air office coordinated and funded aviation science institutes, the industry's research offices, aviation clubs and associations. A network of associations linked aviation manufacturers, engineers, and veterans.

The similarities between civil and military aircraft necessitated the imposition of limits on the ceiling, speed, range, and load of all German aircraft in an Allied ultimatum of 1 May 1921. The Allies continued their prohibitions of aircraft manufacture into 1921, as it was evident that German firms, which kept their design offices in Germany but established branches abroad for manufacture, had not ceased production. The French, in particular, were sorely disturbed by the continuing progress of German aviation technology. The French Undersecretary of State for Aviation concluded an 18 January 1921 report on German aviation:

> From the time the Junkers and Zeppelin corporations can put their aircraft on the market, commercial aviation will progress with an incredible swiftness. . . .
>
> To place the enormous number of factories capable of producing aviation equipment on a footing to produce new material will require no more than three months; to enable them to produce again at full capacity, no more than nine months to one year. Consequently, the terms of the Treaty of Versailles which forbid all aeronautical construction in Germany for six months will have no appreciable effect on the subsequent volume of Germany's aeronautical production. The only present restriction to Germany's assuming aviation supremacy is her financial and economic situation.[20]

The French sought to postpone the inevitable resurgence as long as possible. Yet in 1921 the French undersecretary was more sanguine about the prospects for the German aircraft industry's revival than most German manufacturers. In fact, much of the industry, including many prominent firms, collapsed or left production. The Rumpler works was dissolved in June 1919, and Rumpler turned to automobile construction; Halberstadt and Aviatik attempted to produce agricultural machinery, failed, and were dissolved in 1920 and 1921, respectively. By 1921 the major aviation firms Rumpler, Aviatik, Halberstadt, LVG, Gotha, and Zeppelin-Staaken had disappeared, while AEG, SSW, and the Hannover Railroad Factory had disbanded their aircraft departments. The Inter-Allied Control Commission confirmed that practically all the old firms, if they survived at all, were producing other implements. By 1921 the World War I German aircraft industry was no more.[21]

The continued aviation restrictions ultimately benefitted the German army, as the German Defense Ministry's secret rearmament in Russia enabled it to evade the total ban on military aviation, while the limitations on commercial aviation forced the few remaining German aircraft firms, such as Junkers, Albatros, and Heinkel, back into contact with the army to get contracts. Junkers, for example, after constant French harassment forced him to suspend operation of his airmail line late in October 1921, agreed to construct an aircraft and aero engine plant in Russia for the army. In 1922–23 the army approached Albatros, Heinkel, and the new Arado company for the Russian venture, and though their deficiencies forced it to rely temporarily on Anthony Fokker in Holland, the future connection was established. The Allied bans restored the symbiotic relationship between the military and industry much more rapidly than might have occurred had German civil aeronautics been left alone to prosper in peace. The restrictions had severely crippled the industry and the air arm, but the few firms that survived and the new ones that arose in the 1920s were invariably and indissolubly linked to the German army in the clandestine rearmament of the Reich.[22]

The contraction in the victor states was more gradual and less severe. In Italy military aviation stagnated, and the industry virtually ceased production until the revival of military aviation with the coming to power of the Fascists in 1922 coincided with increasing orders for civil aircraft. Douhet's publication of *The Command of the Air* in 1921 also helped to renew interest in the airplane. Yet Italy, like France and England, was quick to seek markets abroad for its aircraft and to use aviation for propaganda to secure commercial benefits. In mid-1919 all three western powers were competing to develop aviation in Argentina, where the Italians made the biggest display, sending a large commission, famous aviators, mechanics and engineers, and 20 aircraft ranging from giant Capronis to flying boats.[23]

In France the air arm diminished in size from 90,000 officers and men in November 1918 to 39,055 in October 1920. Its number of aircraft shrank from 11,023—3,437 at the front, 3,886 in reserve, 3,000 in the schools, 700 in the interior and overseas—in November 1918 to 3,940 in March 1920, of which 3,050 were in storage. With the dramatically reduced need for procurement, that part of the French aviation bureaucracy diminished from some 4,000 to 40 persons. Of the air arm's 119 flights, 20 were in occupation in Germany and 18 in the Near East and Morocco, where, in the postwar turmoil and military campaigns, the airplane served as an instrument of reconnaissance, communications, evacuation, as well as a means for control and pacification of rebellious tribes. Military airlines in 1919 opened the way to civil aviation, while military aviators participated in competitions and in pioneering flights to the East and Africa.[24]

The penchant for bureaucratic reorganization so evident during the war continued in the postwar era. Air undersecretary Dumesnil resigned at the Armistice for reasons of ill health, and the undersecretariat was abolished on 10 January 1919, its functions reverting to the Directorate of Aeronautics under Colonel Dhé in the War Ministry. In April General Duval assumed command of the directorate, which, like various other governmental ministries—colonial, transport, and postal—added a commercial aviation agency. In June the directorate formed an Office of General Coordination of Aeronautics, which was transferred in January 1920 to an Undersecretariat for Aeronautics and Air Transport under P. E. Flandin in the Transport Ministry.

The coordination office acquired civilian and military aviation materiel. Flandin, who served as undersecretary until February 1921, was determined to prevent the industry's disappearance and granted funds for its rebirth. On 26 June 1920 Flandin and the aviation trade association, the Chambre Syndicale, negotiated the formation of a group to liquidate aviation stocks for the next six years. In order to avoid the unemployment of aviation workers and to secure the new engines being built, the government had not halted manufacture abruptly after the war. Labor remained mobilized until May 1919, so the firms delivered some 5,000 airplanes and 15,000 engines that were not sold or turned over to neutral powers. In 1919 more than 8,000 airplanes and 11,000 engines, which were expensive to preserve and whose value diminished quickly, became available for liquidation. By selling materiel at prices beginning at 60 percent of the original price and giving 60 percent of the profits to the state and 40 percent to the manufacturers, the group cleared the market by 1923. Through Flandin the army issued contracts for new airplanes such as the Farman F60, the Spad 20 and 33, and the Nieuport 29, and he provided 14.5 million francs in subsidies for the embryonic air transport industry. The number of civilian airlines increased from 4 companies with 27 pilots and 46 airplanes in 1919 to 12 companies with 72 pilots and 185 planes in 1920.

With the curtailment of orders to the industry, the work force fell from 183,000 in 1918 to 100,000 in June 1919, 5,200 in 1920, and 3,700 in 1921. The number of manufacturers fell from some 50 in 1918 to 10 in 1920, and first subcontractors, then the aviation manufacturers themselves, turned to other industries. The engine manufacturers converted, Hispano-Suiza to luxury automobiles, Salmson to everything from automobile chassis to typewriters. Renault closed its aviation design office in September 1919. Gnome and Rhône barely escaped liquidation in 1921, while Clerget collapsed after an unsuccessful venture into automobile production and the suicide of its designer Eugene Blin. Surviving firms entered commercial aviation, as Blériot-Spad, Farman, Breguet, Caudron, Nieuport, Morane-Saulnier, Gnome and Rhône, and Salmson founded lines across western Europe.

Germany, though beaten and disarmed, continued to strike fear in the hearts of Frenchmen. Dorand, who was president of the production subcommission of the Inter-Allied Control Commission, was increasingly consumed before his death in the early 1920's about the resurgence of Germany, as his position afforded him a bird's-eye view of German aviation developments.

After a trip to Germany, René Fonck, now parliamentary deputy of Vosges and member of the army commission, warned in the 4 June 1920 *Écho de Paris* of its resurgence in aviation, particularly its progress in metal and giant aircraft construction. In June and September 1921 Dorand advised the French War Ministry similarly and contrasted German progress with the stagnation and lethargy he perceived in the French industry since the Armistice. He proposed a research center in Paris that would emulate the Zeppelin establishment at Friedrichshafen to study and build metal airplanes. Dorand even attempted to lure Claudius Dornier to France, but French industrialists refused to employ the German designer. After Dorand's death, his son published his warnings in the 5 October 1922 and 31 May 1923 *La Vie au Pétrole*. But the idea of the study center and plans to build a giant transport died with Dorand.[25]

In England a Civil Aerial Transport Committee appointed in 1917 recommended in 1918 the expansion of civil aviation after the war, with state aid if necessary, as a prosperous civil aviation would encourage the development of modern airplanes and indirectly benefit military aviation. The recommendations were ignored.

At the Armistice, Lord Weir returned to private business, and in 1919 Gen. Frederick Sykes, nearly the lone advocate among high-ranking officers of a separate air force, resigned as Chief of Air Staff when Churchill, the new Secretary of State for Air, persuaded Trenchard to return to the Air Ministry as Chief of Air Staff. Sykes's plans to maintain a permanent home defense force were too grandiose and expensive for Churchill and the budget, while Trenchard planned to reduce the force to the minimum essential for overseas garrisons and a small home reserve. RAF strength of 30,122 officers and 263,410 other ranks had already declined by 18 October 1919 to 6,005 and 31,976, respectively.[26]

After the war RAF volunteer units were still engaged in the Allied intervention in Russia. The RAF sent 400 officers and men and 277 aircraft to help the white army in south Russia.[27] The 47th Squadron of the RAF, for example, transferred at the end of the war from the Middle East. Using Sopwith Camels and DH9s under the command of RNAS/RAF ace Raymond Collishaw from June 1919 to March 1920, it operated successfully with white cavalry to bomb and strafe Bolshevik cavalry into disarray, after which the white cavalry would attack. Apparently airplanes struck terror among the red peasant troops.

The outskirts of the empire provided a major arena for the RAF to prove its continued worth. It survived the postwar reductions through a policy of "air control," policing the far corners of the British Empire more cheaply and successfully than the army could. The first use of the policy, on the Afghan-Indian border in May through August 1919, was not particularly successful because the decrepit BE2cs could not fly high enough to get above the Afghan tribesmen in the mountains of the north-west frontier or carry enough bombs to strike them effectively. Against the "Mad Mullah" in Somaliland in 1919 and 1920, however, a flight of eight RAF DH9s first operated independently to locate, bomb, and strafe the Mullah's camp and then in combined operations with the army, drove him into Ethiopia, where he soon died. The success of the operation, the novel use of airplanes as the main weapon, and the cost of only 77,000 pounds enabled Trenchard and Churchill to argue successfully at the Cairo Conference of 1921 for the RAF's larger role in policing the Middle East. Air Vice Marshal Sir John Salmond headed the RAF's first peacetime independent command in Iraq in 1922.[28]

The RAF stationed two squadrons in Ireland, where they were also used for population control to "fly low over the small villages and inspire considerable fear among ignorant peasantry, some of whom still believed that the machines can swoop down and pick them up at will."[29] Events in Ireland, Africa, and the Middle East indicated that the prewar visions of the airplane to preserve dominion over the empire had come to pass. The Great War had presented the opportunity to perfect the instrument of domination.

After the war the government was concerned with disposing of its airplane stocks and planes on order. It sought to minimize unemployment by forbidding a general discharge of munitions workers, although it ordered the abolition of all overtime work and a reduction of the work week. As it was also cheaper to complete work on airplanes and engines than to abandon production of half-completed equipment that would have no disposal value, the Ministry of Munitions allowed "war break clauses" of three months for aircraft companies and four for engine companies. The firms consequently delivered nearly 14,000 planes and engines. The government was accepting weekly delivery of more than 250 airplanes and engines in May 1919, and as of late July was still due more than 3,600 planes and 5,000 engines.[30]

A Ministry of Munitions Disposal Board could not manage the problem, so the government, at the urging of Frederick Handley Page, sold the surplus stock in 1920 to the Aircraft Disposals Company for 1 million pounds and half of future profits, which would total 6 million pounds. Some firms sold the materiel abroad, while the government also gave surplus aircraft to the Dominions in 1919 and 1920.[31]

Given the small demand for aircraft during the severe postwar contraction, aviation firms attempted to diversify. Airco, part of Holt Thomas's giant aviation empire that included engine, airship, and parts production, needed more contracts—45—to survive than the government planned to buy from the entire industry. The company sent a design team to the United States to study automobile mass production, while Sopwith tried to produce motorcycles. Handley Page, Airco, and Blackburn tried to start air transport ventures. Two aircraft firms, Bristol and Armstrong-Whitworth, bought aero engine firms, which were reasonable investments since the British government paid for developing military engines between the wars.

In 1920, the year of crisis for the British aircraft industry, a disastrous slump crushed most of the economic ventures of aviation manufacturers. By 1921, for example, all British civil airlines had stopped flying, to resume only when the government began to subsidize their operation. With the poor economy and seriously diminished demand, final payment of the wartime excess profits tax came due. Major pioneering companies like Sopwith and Airco collapsed under the burden, although in collapse they often gave birth to heirs, as Sopwith did to Hawker and Airco to De Havilland. Handley Page would have collapsed had Frederick Handley Page not been on the Aircraft Disposals Company board. Although the Society of British Aircraft Constructors claimed to have 28 airplane and 12 engine manufacturers on its rolls in 1920, the Air Ministry indicated that only 13 aircraft firms were active and manufacture was limited.

At this point the Air Ministry became concerned that the industry might become too small to meet the needs of national defense, so through arrangement with the Society of British Aircraft Constructors, it aided the industry by preserving a ring of 16 competing aviation companies. The early 1920s would be difficult times for the aviation industry, but the agreement ensured the survival of a nucleus of firms. This last statistic is the best indication that the contraction in England was less severe than in Germany, as the German industry shrank to four firms. The efforts of the English and French governments to ease the contraction were more effective because the victors could establish break clauses unaffected by domestic political and economic collapse and international constraints.

In the United States the air service shrank from 190,000 men at home and abroad to 27,000 in June 1919 and some 10,000 to 12,000 men in 1920.[32] In the industry 90 percent of the plant had already been liquidated by 1919, as the air arm sought to dispose of huge amounts of surplus equipment. The industry collapsed after the Armistice, as aircraft production dropped from 14,000 in 1918 to 328 in 1920.[33] Glenn Curtiss had been planning a transatlantic flight in 1914; in 1919 a navy Curtiss boat performed the feat.

In all the countries the air arm and aviation industry survived, if barely. Aviation commanders and productive industrialists continued in their professions, but what happened to the aviators? Despite the stress and losses of wartime, the exhilaration of flight and aerial combat left the survivors with no regrets about their participation in the great war in the sky. The problem for the thousands of trained aviators was what to do after the war and demobilization. Some of them never flew again, but others stayed in the air force, and a few would rise to command positions, in time for another world war. Some turned to civil aviation, if not aerial transport or airmail flying, then barnstorming, participating in cross-country flights, air shows, and contests, sometimes seeking to re-create artificially the highly charged atmosphere of aerial combat.

For some, particularly those in Germany, the defeat and collapse were nearly as stressful as the front. One German ace, Fritz Ritter von Roth, committed suicide on 1 January 1919. A number of aviators joined the "Freikorps" to fight the Bolsheviks within and outside of Germany, both in the air and on the ground. Rudolph Berthold, his right arm withered and useless, formed his own paramilitary unit, the Eiserne Schar Berthold, fighting in Germany and in the east. On 15 December 1920, in Harburg, Germany, the Iron Knight, as he was known, met a brutal end at the hands of his communist opponents. Others, like Hermann Göring, served abroad either as agents for aircraft manufacturers or as advisers to foreign airlines and air forces. Ernst Udet, Germany's greatest surviving ace, became a playboy and stunt flier, perfect material for the filmmakers of the postwar era who romanticized aerial combat to a generation of moviegoers in the 1920s and 1930s.

Germany differed from the Allies in that elsewhere the aviators had the possibility of remaining in the contracted air forces of their respective countries. Otherwise, the conditions were much the same for aviators in other countries. In England Ira Jones and Raymond Collishaw stayed in the air force and volunteered for service in south Russia, while Cecil Lewis entered civil aviation in Britain and gravitated to China.

In France, René Fonck turned to politics, but Charles Nungesser epitomized the difficulties of postwar adjustment. Counting among his wartime injuries a fractured skull, shattered right arm and palate, broken jaw (seven times) and legs, dislocated knees, clavicle, left wrist, and right foot,

Nungesser believed that he had become the symbol of combat. Toward the end of the war he had swum in a Paris meet to demonstrate to survivors that they could hope to readapt to civilian life. Yet he himself could not, until air undersecretary Flandin suggested that he start a flight school at Orly airfield. There the 45-victory ace sought to re-create the atmosphere of the front, the "familiar decor of the heroic act."[34] Still discontent, Nungesser wondered why death had spared him during the war. He flew in Cuba and then in the United States in exhibitions and movies, but remained dissatisfied. Transatlantic flight ultimately offered deliverance, and Nungesser and his navigator, another wartime flier, took off in their plane, *l'Oiseau Blanc*, (White Bird), on 8 May 1927 from Le Bourget to fly the Atlantic nonstop. They disappeared without a trace. Had they succeeded, they would have beaten Lindbergh by 12 days.

Conclusion

In August 1914 the European powers had gone to war with rudimentary air services, each comprising at most a few thousand personnel and 300 service aircraft, and embryonic aviation industries of a few thousand workers. During the war of movement, airplanes delivered valuable information, and when the conflict on the Western Front settled into the trenches, the airplane became the sole mobile means of reconnaissance and artillery spotting. In the west in 1915, air commanders decided upon two important interrelated policies: They were going to prevent enemy reconnaissance efforts and they required airplanes en masse for effective aerial operations. The first aim led to armed airplanes and to the first pursuit planes—single-seat single-engine craft armed with a machine gun synchronized to fire forward through the propeller. The struggle for aerial supremacy began, as armies required more and better airplanes.

The Battle of Verdun and the Battle of the Somme in 1916, which forced the codification of aerial combat tactics, brought home the importance of mass. As air services required increasing numbers of aircrew and aircraft, aviation bureaucracies expanded to train larger numbers of men for combat flying and ground maintenance and to spur the growth of an aviation industry and its development of high-performance airplanes and engines. The growth of the air force and the aviation industry spiraled rapidly upward.

At the front the organization of the air arms and aircraft types evolved. As the war expanded in scope, the basic tactical unit, the French escadrille of 6, the German Flieger-Abteilung of 6, and the British squadron of 12 planes, expanded in size to 12, 9, and 18 planes, respectively. These units were subsumed under increasingly larger ones, like the German fighter Jagdstaffeln of 14 planes and the circuses of 60, as the attempt to achieve aerial superiority led to concentration of forces. The ultimate unit was the French aerial division of 1918, with more than 700 bombers and fighters. Although aircraft became more specialized, the basic types remained the two-seat single-engine all-purpose biplane—the backbone of all air arms for reconnaissance and bombing—and the single-seat single-engine pursuit biplane. Other important categories were variants of those types, ground support and fighter reconnaissance craft, and also two- to six-engine night bombers.

In regard to the nature and composition of the three major air arms by 1918, the English emphasized pursuit over reconnaissance, the French reversed the emphasis, while the Germans fell in between. All three major powers, and the lesser powers as well, considered the air war essentially an army cooperation war; they differed on how best to conduct it.

The French high command concentrated on reconnaissance and artillery spotting and regarded the bomber force primarily as a tactical weapon, as long-range artillery and a means to force the German air arm to fight to prevent their incursions. Armed with the Breguet 14, a superlative plane for daylight raids en masse of limited range into the enemy's rear areas, the aerial division was a potent tactical force. French fighter planes flew protective cover, but the persistence of individualist French fighter tactics condemned the French pursuit arm to relative ineffectiveness compared to the squadron and circus operations of the English and German air arms in 1918.

The German air service essentially waged a defensive struggle throughout the war, particularly in 1918, using its single-seat fighters primarily for interception. Yet the use of special two-seaters for ground attack enabled battle units to fight effectively on offense or defense, while the reliance on highly trained crews and superior airplanes for lone reconnaissance missions enabled them to conserve their resources far better than their opponents.

Two factors explain the large proportion of fighter planes in the RAF: the policy of incessant offensive patrols in squadron strength over enemy lines and the use of fighters in the ground attack role. The increasing number of bombers in the RAF at the end of the war reflected British efforts—primarily tactical in fact, though increasingly strategic in intention—to strike Germany.

All the aviation commands considered strategic bombing potentially effective in disrupting industrial production, damaging enemy morale, and drawing forces away from the front. After an initial abortive effort in 1915, the French high command decided to postpone another until it had more suitable airplanes. But French industry did not develop an operational heavy bomber during wartime, and in 1918 the French high command still considered strategic aviation premature.

Only the absence of sufficiently long-range aircraft prevented the Germans from striking England as early as 1915. Later they attacked with dirigibles, then twin-engine bombers, and ultimately with their giant four- to six-engine R-planes. Their strategic effort diverted limited resources from other tasks, and in May 1918 they gave up the campaign when the Western Front demanded their concentration of forces in support of the land war.

The German attacks did not drive England out of the war; they provoked the English to attempt to retaliate in kind. The RNAS was strongly interested in strategic bombing, the RFC only in the Western Front. By 1917 British policymakers posed two criteria for undertaking a strategic campaign—a production surplus and suitable airplanes. They anticipated having both in 1918 in their Independent Force, but did not achieve the first and had too few of the second. The RAF planned a full-scale campaign against Germany in 1919.

The very fact of the dramatic growth of air forces and aviation industries proves that governments believed that aviation was sufficiently important to engage in an aerial armaments race. In 1917 and 1918 all three major powers placed aviation at the top of their priority lists in the allocation of manpower and materiel. The size of the air forces in personnel at the Armistice, while small compared to the total in the armed forces, represented an enormous expansion in four years. The British air arm had grown from 2,073 officers and men in both the RFC and RNAS in August 1914 to a total of 291,175 officers and men to become by far the largest air force in the world.[35] The U.S. Air Service, the last air arm to enter the war, had grown from 1,395 officers and men to 195,024 at the Armistice.[36] The French air force had grown from some 3,500 to 90,000 in comparison.[37] In November 1918 the Italian air arm had 3,180 officer and enlisted pilots, 1,157 officer engineers and observers, and 96,000 enlisted men.[38]

These air arms did not determine the outcome of World War I. That was essentially decided on the earth's surface, not in the air. Fighters, except when pressed into service for ground attack, played an indirect role in the ground war of protecting reconnaissance planes and bombers, while strategic bombing was too embryonic to affect the outcome of the war.

The airplane established its real significance in support of the army on the battlefield. Aircraft reconnaissance made it difficult for armies to achieve surprise and forced the movement of men and materiel behind the lines at night. Then, in 1917 and 1918, in its increasingly aggressive strikes against troops and supplies on and behind the battlefield, it became even more effective. Politicians and generals such as Churchill, Ludendorff, and Pétain recognized the importance of airpower. Control of the skies over the battlefield had become essential to victory in World War I, just as it would be 20 years later. Strategic aviation, if it had played little role in the 1914–18 conflict, seemed to offer the key to victory in future wars. The fighter pilots of 1914–18 evolved the basic techniques still used today and became the commanders of the second Great War. In both strategy and tactics the air war of 1914–18 portended the larger aerial struggle of 1939–45.

The war of the masses bequeathed to them a new individual hero, the aviator. Lloyd George praised his airmen, that "cavalry of the clouds":

> They skim like armed swallows, hanging over trenches full of armed men, wrecking convoys, scattering infantry, attacking battalions on the march. . . . They are the knighthood of the war, without fear and without reproach. They recall the old legends of chivalry, not merely the daring of their exploits, but by the nobility of their spirit, and, amongst the multitude of heroes, let us think of the chivalry of the air.[39]

Laurence Goldstein's book, *The Flying Machine and Modern Literature*, considered the postwar memoirs of air aces the closest approximation to knightly tales of old, catalogs of warriors' repeated trials by combat with an avowed moral purpose.[40] Felix Philipp Ingold in *Literatur und Aviatik* pointed out that wartime aviation provided the means and theater for a contemporary re-creation of the duel: Actions were visible and had certain moral norms, the pilots received certain privileges, such as being invited to dine with a victorious opponent or a burial with full military honors. The success of pilots could be quantitatively measured through their number of kills, the measure of the new hero. They were celebrated as popular heroes, honored as demigods, objects of an unparalleled secular holy cult. These air heroes were convinced that they were personally responsible for saving or increasing the honor of their nation; they believed that God watched over them and occasionally even likened themselves to gods, elevated above everything earthly.[41]

The exhilaration of flight, the conquest of space and speed, the sense of mastery over others and the environment that was absent in land warfare were all part of the attraction of military aviation. In many respects the airplane established itself as the ideal weapon for western man, who regards his technical mastery as proof of his superiority over others. Air warfare was the apotheosis of warfare in modern, technological, and industrial society. It literally and figuratively enabled its combatants to rise above the anonymity of mass society and modern warfare to wage a clean and individual struggle. It allowed the preservation of notions of sport and individual combat in a war in which land and naval conflict amply demonstrated that modern warfare had rendered such ideals obsolete and ludicrous. Finally, it made it possible to bomb enemy cities and civilians with relative impunity and in such impersonal fashion that the prospect of future aerial depredations on civilian populations became attractive to air planners after the war.

The melding of man and machine was striking. That aerial fighting was furthermore a small man's preserve illustrates the idea of the airplane as extending, or enhancing and equalizing the ability of some to participate in warfare. The cramped cockpits and small load-carrying of aircraft placed a premium on smallness. The ranks of the aces were studded with men who were a little over five feet in height, who were sometimes too frail, like Guynemer, to enter the infantry, or who had been invalided by wounds from the ground war.

This is not to imply that only the feeble flew. The fitter the flier, the better he was able to endure the severe physical and mental stress of aerial fighting, especially at higher altitudes. And the toll of aviation was severe, as casualty figures in training and at the front confirm.

The merging of man and machine meant that if one or the other was fatally struck, the lives of both ended. The use of the airplane also intensified man's dependence on technology, as it required other modern technology—trucks and trains for transport, optics for cameras, an array of weapons from machine guns and bombs to rockets—to make it effective. The air fighters also became vulnerable to the vicissitudes of technology. A significant factor in the nervous strain associated with aerial warfare arose from the unpredictability of the materiel, the ever-present threat of mechanical failure.[42]

War flying was dangerous, as illustrated by the most accurate figures available of the losses in aviation of the great powers (see Table 6). Of Britain's casualties, officers composed 12,787 of the 16,623 total, while in Germany they composed 6,893 of the 16,054 total. The German loss totals seem the most complete, as they include losses at the front and in the rear, accounting also for sickness, accidents on the ground, and even losses on the

TABLE 6.

British, German, and French World War I Aviation Casualties

	British	German	French
Killed or died	6,166	5,953	2,872
Wounded or injured	7,245	7,350	2,922
Missing or interned	3,212	2,751	1,461
Total	16,623	16,054	7,255

ground in bombing raids. The British follow in completeness, and the French are last in detailed compilation.[43] France trained 16,458 pilots and 2,000 observers in the five years from 1914 to 1919, so 7,255 casualties of 18,458 aircrew mean that some 39 percent of aircrew fell casualty. The RFC and RAF trained nearly 22,000 pilots during the war;[44] figures for observers trained are not available. Yet since 12,787 of the above casualties were officers and 3,836 noncommissioned officers and men, if one assumes that most of those officers were pilots, more than 50 percent of British pilots became casualties. In the absence of figures for aircrew trained in Germany, one can assume that their percentage of casualties was at least as high as that of the French, and perhaps higher than that of the British, since they were running out of manpower in 1918 and their force was proportionately smaller. Yet the Germans, for their losses, exacted a high toll from the other two major powers, in particular the British, whose exceedingly offensive policies rendered their aircrew particularly vulnerable. The toll in all countries is ample proof that aviators paid no less a price in wartime sacrifice than infantry. The airman's claims of equal significance in the war effort rest ultimately on these figures.

Above these fliers in their operational units, an aviation command attached to general headquarters and subordinate commands attached to armies or army corps directed the air war. Yet the overall command apparatus in the major powers differed in organization and stability. The German aviation command under Lieth-Thomsen, Siegert, and in 1916 Hoeppner was the most stable. It controlled the hinterland bureaucracy, which reached down to the aviation industry at home, although particularistic conflicts among the German states impeded its most efficient functioning. Since the army was the most powerful institution in Germany, the army air command did not have to contend with challenges either from civilians or from a naval air arm.

The English and French commands functioned under the control of civilian governments. In England a civil-military command arose, which, though beset by personal antagonisms, proved capable of great extension. Trenchard at the front and Henderson and Brancker at home provided continuity for the RFC from 1914 through 1917, but they had to contend with the RNAS for supremacy in the allocation of resources at home. By 1917 the division between War Office and Admiralty, RFC and RNAS, led to such confusion and competition for resources that the government instituted first the Air Board and then the Air Ministry to coordinate aircraft production at home and the RAF to fuse the two air arms at the front.

French aviation, like its British counterpart, had no single chief over the fighting and home front, but in France this lack of coordination allowed a debilitating schism to develop between front and rear. Although the undersecretaries of state for aviation were quite successful in reorganizing the rear bureaucracy and spurring the industry to great efforts in the service of the front, they found themselves caught in a web of political and industrial intrigue and government changes that led to their removal from office.

Despite the instability of the French political scene, French manufacturers outproduced their competition. The procurement bureaucracies in all countries helped their industries to expand and rationalize their plants, secure labor and raw materials, and coordinate scientific and industrial efforts to hasten air progress. The French and German aviation industries were smaller and more productive than the British because they employed less unskilled labor. The key to French aircraft manufacturing success lay in the procurement bureaucracy's initiation of a policy of standardization of aircraft types beginning in October 1914. The English also standardized aircraft types, but not as rigorously and with a less well-developed industry than the French, while the Germans attempted to standardize types only in 1917. France consequently produced 264 prototypes for 38 service types; England, 309 prototypes for 73 service types; and Germany, 610 prototypes for 72 service types.[45]

French supremacy in engines was based on two primary types—first the Gnome and Le Rhône rotary engines and then the Hispano-Suiza V8 engines—and stemmed from the procurement bureaucracy's 1915 decisions to press for higher-horsepower engines and to include the automotive industry in engine production. The Hispano-Suiza, despite production problems in 1917 and early 1918, is still considered the outstanding engine of the war from a technical standpoint. The French army received more than 18,000 Gnome and Le Rhône rotaries and 25,000 Hispano-Suizas during the war, in addition to other quality engines from Clerget, Renault, and Salmson.

As only one French company, Salmson, built radial engines, the water-cooled V engine, which was designed and produced primarily by automotive firms, became the backbone of French aero engine production. Hispano-Suiza became the nucleus of the French air arm's major production group, and the 200- to 220-hp version was license-produced by 14 French firms, of which 7 were automotive manufacturers like Peugeot. Automotive companies developed or produced 49,184 engines, and of 23 French industrialists building complete aero engines at the end of the war, 12 had manufactured automobiles before the war.[46]

The English produced excellent Rolls Royce engines, improved the Clerget rotary in the Bentley, and license-produced the Hispano-Suizas, but their premature reliance on abortive experimental designs in 1917 seriously disrupted their wartime engine production. The Admiralty instigated both Rolls Royce's aero engine production and Wilfred Bentley's improvement of the rotary engine. The Rolls Royces—the 12-cylinder 280-hp Falcon and the 360-hp Eagle—were outstanding engines, but their unsuitability for mass production and easy repair meant that only 4,080 Eagles and 1,969 Falcons were manufactured, as the War Office refused to extend the works while the firm refused to allow licensed production.[47]

The lack of suitable aero engines remained Britain's Achilles' heel, and the British ultimately had to rely on France for some 16,000 additional engines. Of the five largest prewar British car companies—Wolseley, Humber, Sunbeam, Rover, and Austin—only Sunbeam developed its own aero engines, and they were not particularly successful. The others, and automobile firms like Lanchester and Standard, built French engines under license.[48]

The German military aviation procurement bureaucracy, saddled with material, fuel, and manpower shortages, feared the disruption of engine production. It consequently did not deviate from one engine type—the water-cooled in-line with six separate cylinders built of welded steel construction. In 1914 their 120-hp Austro-Daimler designed by Ferdinand Porsche was the world's most efficient and reliable aircraft engine, the progenitor of not only the excellent Mercedes and BMW 6-cylinder types but also the Allies' 6-, 8-, and 12-cylinder in-lines.

The Germans relied primarily on two producers, Daimler and Benz. Of total German wartime aero engine production of 43,486, Daimler delivered 19,876 Mercedes (45.7 percent of the total); Benz, 11,360 (29.2 percent); and Opel 2,260 (5.2 percent). Daimler's large share of the market and the procurement bureaucracy's hesitation in requesting more powerful and different engine types and in recruiting more firms to produce them limited German engine production.[49]

If the French experience showed that a combination of an enlightened and enabling policy on the part of procurement agencies with independent initiatives by engine producers was critical to the development and production of aero engines during the war, the German illustrates how the restrictive policies of procurement agencies, control by two producers, and wartime shortages could combine to limit the evolution of aviation engines.

Wartime Italy's leading manufacturer of aircraft engines was Fiat, which built 15,380 six-cylinder water-cooled in-line engines and 1,336 airplanes in its aircraft production branch in Turin. All Italian combat engines, from automobile manufacturers Fiat and Isotta-Fraschini, and from Ansaldo, a shipbuilding firm that built automobiles and aero engines, were six-cylinder in-lines. Production of their powerful fuel-efficient engines was rigorously standardized.[50]

The unity of concept and effort enabled Italy to mount a creditable aerial effort, particularly in comparison to Austria-Hungary and Russia, whose wartime aero engine production was so small that it merits little comment. In both eastern empires, automobile firms produced aircraft engines, but neither state had the finances or the industrial base for much aviation development in addition to other war materiel. The Austro-Hungarian industry manufactured only 4,346 engines and became increasingly dependent on the Germans, while Russia was dependent on the French for its materiel.[51]

The last power to enter the war, the United States produced one combat engine, the Liberty 400-hp V12, a product of the American automobile industry, which delivered 15,572 Liberties from December 1917 to December 1918. The industry could point to the Liberty with pride, but it lacked an airframe truly suitable for the big engine.[52]

In Germany, Italy, and the United States, the automobile industry bore the burden of aero engine development and manufacture and concentrated on one type of combat engine—the six-cylinder in-line in Germany and Italy and the V12 in the United States. Such standardization impeded experimentation but proved wise under wartime conditions, especially in light of England's chastening experience in contracting for experimental types. Ultimately, in all countries the combination of both governmental policies and industrial capabilities that focused increasingly on the automobile industry determined the success of aero engine production. The French combination was far superior to the rest.

French relative simplicity and standardization of aircraft types accompanied the diversified development of high-powered engines with superior levels of production of both. German near uniformity of engine development contrasted sharply with its proliferation of aircraft types for lower production totals, even more so in engines than aircraft. Substantial British aircraft development and production contrasted with uneven performance in the development and production of aircraft engines. Concentration on standardization of construction techniques in aircraft and engine production enabled Italy to outpace the other lesser powers, Austria-Hungary and Russia, whose limited production meant that they remained dependent on their greater allies. And the United States, last to enter the air race and the war, was essentially dependent on the Allied powers for its materiel during the few months that it participated in the war to end all wars.

By 1918 the English were surpassing the French in monthly airframe production, occasionally exceeding 3,000 planes a month as opposed to the French maximum of 2,700, but the French were delivering some 4,000 engines at peak production, more than double British manufacture. The Germans, reaching exhaustion in manpower and materials in 1918, topped out at 2,200 planes and 1,900 engines. French, German, and English aircraft manufacture was 52,000, 48,000, and 43,000, respectively, but the French produced some 88,000 engines to English and German totals of 41,000 each.

Yet in Europe the industry's essential dependence on skilled labor and its wartime shortages of labor, machine tool, and material could not be completely offset by governmental priorities in the allocation of materials and skilled labor and the government's promotion of licensed production and the hiring of unskilled workers. Ultimately, had the war continued, U.S. mass-production techniques and the absence of labor or material shortages would have enabled the United States, with its single product (the Liberty), to outproduce the European powers.

The Central Powers were doomed to lose the manufacturing race. Germany had no recourse in Austria-Hungary, an ally whose industrial weakness meant that while its designers might develop capable engines, the dual monarchy could not produce them in any significant quantities. Germany had even less recourse in its client states, as it had to send Turkey a total of 390 aviators, 1,740 ground crew, and 415 airplanes to maintain a small Turkish air arm during the war.[53] In the Allied powers, on the other hand, France could secure the Hispano-Suiza in neutral Spain, use its own automobile industry to produce "Hissus" in numbers sufficient to shore up even British production, and rely on the United States to compensate for deficiencies in its automotive production. The Allies had only to equip a small Belgian air force of some 100 airplanes in 1918 beyond their own air arms, and at least the Belgians supplied their own aviators. The Allies' aviation superiority was consequently overwhelming.

The use of the airplane as a new weapon in the arsenals of the belligerents of World War I entailed the creation and evolution of new technology, a new industry, and a new branch of the military. Aviation mobilization in some respects became the ultimate test of a state's ability to wage modern warfare.

The difficulties of aviation mobilization were enormous. Governments, for example, had to set targets for aircraft production based on estimated and rapidly changing wartime requirements. In the later years of the war, establishing production goals became standard practice, and invariably the powers did not achieve the targets they set. Shortages of labor, materials, and transportation thwarted the German high command's aviation mobilization in the Hindenburg and America programs. In England Weir never realized his sanguine predictions for English aero engine production in 1918, because the British aviation industry had been starved of resources too long to permit its rapid expansion and was consequently just approaching full capacity at the end of the war.[54] Even the French, the most successful aviation manufacturers of the war, were unable to secure prescribed skilled manpower and raw materials despite the priorities granted to aviation production and the proliferation of production targets from the high command and the undersecretary. Thus it was not surprising that the United States encountered serious problems in its attempt to put a force in the air and vastly overestimated its capacity. The gap between predicted and actual production was so enormous that it led to allegations and investigations of corruption in an attempt to understand how the monumental sum invested in aviation had yielded such paltry returns.

Yet the failures to achieve the targets must be put in perspective. These powers were developing a unique weapon under wartime conditions that forced substantial risk taking to keep pace in the new military-technological-industrial arms race in aviation. Estimating requirements and production, mastering new and rapidly developing technology, and producing constantly changing materiel in the face of increasing shortages of skilled labor and materials were enormously complex challenges. Furthermore, no one could predict the success of airplane designs that took six months from conception to production and engine designs that took at least nine—provided all went well.

The targets certainly served as a very real spur to increase production. They represented what governments believed was essential to defeat the enemy as well as the planners' claims for scarce manpower and materials in the competition on the home front with other government agencies. And although there were real disadvantages to stoking expectations to fever pitch only to fall short constantly, aircraft production did increase in all countries to the end of the war, even in Germany.

Overall, and at the risk of oversimplification, certain powers passed the test of aviation mobilization better than others. Among the great powers, the French achieved the highest marks, with the Germans and British in nearly a dead heat for second. The French won because they recognized the importance of the airplane, particularly the engine, and mobilized first and most extensively. The Germans made the most effective use of severely limited resources of the great powers, and thus deserve second place before the British, whose wartime mobilization often seemed a muddle, though they began from a lower level than France and Germany, since their air arm and aviation industry were not as advanced as those of France and Germany in 1914.

Among the lesser powers, Italy focused its aviation resources far better than the rest, certainly outdistancing Russia and Austria-Hungary. Of these last two, both had gifted individual designers such as Sikorskii and Porsche, but neither could surmount industrial backwardness to the extent necessary to field an extensive air arm. The United States was in a class by itself, without the time to develop a focused aviation mobilization.

Judgments of the war's effect on air progress vary greatly. East German aviation historian Gerhard Wissmann contended that the war retarded advances because capitalist systems and imperialistic wars of necessity impede scientific progress. Progressive concepts that offered no immediate dividends interested neither manufacturers nor the military, and the emphasis on large-scale serial production limited the possibilities for further technological progress.[55] British aviation historian Harald Penrose offered a more balanced point of view. Mathematical calculation, wind tunnel diagnosis, and four years of intense experience allowed a better understanding of aircraft strength, stability, and controllability. Both sides did much research in such fields as airfoil shapes, but the Germans tended to apply the results in their efforts to improve aircraft performance, while the English and French relied primarily on more powerful engines for improved performance. Penrose concluded that much progress occurred despite a lack of change in basic aircraft structures.[56]

A random sampling of participants in aviation in the war reveals a great diversity of attitude. The most accomplished scientist of the German manufacturers, Hugo Junkers, was convinced before the war that a conflict would hasten technological and industrial development enormously,[57] and while his wartime and postwar success would probably have done little to change his opinion, some of his struggles to secure funds and labor to develop his metal cantilever-wing aircraft in the midst of wartime shortages might have given him some pause for reflection. German designer Ernst Heinkel suggested that four and a half years of wartime development equaled six years of peacetime evolution, though he did not elaborate on his calculations.[58] General Duval, chief of the French air arm in 1918, stated unequivocally that "engineers and builders have realized, from a technical point of view, progress that would have required, in normal times, a half century."[59]

Albert Etévé, aircraft expert in the STAé, was more circumspect. The dizzying pace of development imposed by the "imperious law of daily combat" left insufficient time to verify details prudently and to comprehend industrial and technical difficulties. The policy of *rusticité*, the adoption of simple construction processes permitting the fastest and cheapest production of the most airplanes, took precedence over technological finesse.[60] In the summer of 1917, Lt. Col. Mervyn O'Gorman of the Royal Aircraft Factory lamented that wartime pressures had forced aeronautical engineers away from their normal wide outlook and habit of detached thinking and toward a concentration on details.[61] Yet the former head of the Metal Design Department of the Air Ministry declared in 1919 that it would probably take 10 or more years before metal construction would reach the state of development it would have attained in 10 months under wartime conditions.[62]

The great conflict had hastened aviation progress, although the pressures of time did not allow either for reflection or for incorporation of some of the scientific progress in the aircraft produced. A major reason for the progress was that the war provided a focus for and stimulated the coordinated efforts of all institutions—government, industry, and science—which were involved in aviation. The Prussian aviation inspectorate's scientific information bureau coordinated all efforts in aviation science and disseminated scientific and technical information to the industry and the military. In England the prewar cooperation between the Royal Aircraft Factory and the National Physical Laboratory was supplemented by a government privy council committee for scientific and industrial research and its deliberations with the Society of British Aircraft Constructors. In France, the STAé collaborated with the military aviation laboratories at Chalais-Meudon, the Eiffel Laboratory, and commissions of the aviation industry's syndicate, while in Italy the Technical Directorate coordinated the various agencies.[63]

German aircraft technology emerged superior, as English and French observers noted after the war.[64] Airframes were stronger structurally, airfoils had better aerodynamic quality, and in this realm the Germans undoubtedly led with their work on metal aircraft and the cantilever wing. Yet some of this progress occurred in spite of wartime conditions. Junkers, for example, refused to compromise his all-metal construction with wartime demands of simplicity for mass production,[65] and he and Claudius Dornier did not allow wartime shortages to arrest their pursuit of advanced construction techniques, contrary to Wissmann's judgment that immediate profit was the sole motive for development.[66]

Engine development had also progressed rapidly in wartime. In 1918 aero engines were more powerful, more reliable and lighter than their prewar ancestors. They could generate four to five times the horsepower of prewar engines at weights of two pounds per horsepower compared to weights of four to five pounds per horsepower for prewar power-plants. If German airframe technology was superior to that of the Allies, the latter had gained the advantage in engine technology. In a sense, the English and French could afford the simplicity, or *rusticité*, of airframe construction that Albert Etévé described because they could rely on more powerful engines to provide the increased performance that the Germans required more sophisticated aircraft structures to obtain. The Hispano-Suiza's lightness, high power, simplicity of design, and relative ease of manufacture meant that it required less labor and raw materials than any power plant of similar capacity. The German Mercedes, for example, had some 900 parts to the Hispano-Suiza's 400, and the material in the Hispano-Suiza weighed about one-third less than that in a Mercedes of the same power.[67]

Despite these distinctions, some salient similarities of development should not escape notice. In all countries designers and companies that had prewar experience in airplane and engine construction produced the wartime strides in aviation. Builders such as Fokker, Dornier, Heinkel, Sopwith, Barnwell of Bristol, Béchereau, Breguet, Caproni, Sikorskii, and Curtiss were prewar aviation pioneers, while companies such as Daimler, Hispano-Suiza, and Rolls Royce built upon successful backgrounds in automotive production.

Wartime markets fueled the tremendous expansion of air forces and aviation industries. Although total figures are elusive, Emmanuel Chadeau calculated that the French spent 2.193 billion francs on aviation from 1914 through 1918, compared to 136 million from 1909 through 1913.[68] Russia's wartime outlay for aviation production totaled approximately 216 million rubles.[69] In 1918 air arms and aviation industries that had had only a few thousand personnel before the war numbered hundreds of thousands of soldiers and workers, numbers scarcely imaginable in 1914, not to mention 1909. At the Armistice German, English, and French aircraft industries were each manufacturing 2,200 to 3,000 aircraft monthly, twice as much as their annual prewar deliveries in 1913–14. What war granted, however, peace rescinded, at least in terms of size. Three years later, in 1921, the air arms had shrunk, but not to their prewar size, while industries once again employed only a few thousand workers.

Yet some changes were not undone. Though European aero engine production remained primarily a matter of skilled workmanship, the use of rational work methods and the employment of machine tools and jigs to ensure uniformity of production had transformed aircraft construction. The war had accelerated air progress despite the drawbacks and waste occasioned by the haste of wartime pressure. Planes could reliably carry heavier loads at higher speeds and altitudes than before the war. There had been no prospects for the commercial or sporting development of the airplane in 1914; the war prepared the industry to develop these markets in the 1920s. Yet the cost in manpower, materiel, and money—in death and destruction—had been enormous.

For that price, the war left a rich legacy for the future of airpower, yet, the factual lessons of the battlefields of 1914–18 have often been lost in theory and wishful thinking. The airplane had certainly proved its worth as a tactical weapon whose major purpose was to affect the ground war, despite the disproportionate attention devoted to fighter operations. Observation, bomber, and ground attack aircraft were the tools for this direct action.

Theory and wishful thinking after the Great War, however, focused on strategic aviation and actually threatened to drive the lessons on tactical success from the minds of observers.

After the failure of the French attacks on the west German war industry in 1915, the Germans were the only power in World War I to mount a strategic air campaign, against the British in 1917 and 1918. The French and British both struck strategic targets, but not in a concerted campaign intended to knock Germany out of the war. The French used bombers in tactical attacks on the battlefield effectively in 1918, yet French inferiority in strategic aviation overshadowed the success of these combined operations, even to aviators who had participated in the victorious campaign of 1918. General de Goÿs much later regretted his inability to bomb south German cities after the armistice with Austria-Hungary in hopes that a taste of the horrors of war might lead to a victory and their detachment from Germany.

After 1921 Commandant Orthlieb, in his course at the war college on the lessons of the air war, said that what prevented aviation from playing a decisive role in the war was the lack of a powerful long-range bomber. At the same time that he demonstrated the positive results of French battlefield aviation and the mediocre ones of German attacks on Paris, he believed that the night "cruiser" capable of carrying several tons of explosives against cities would change everything.

The more these officers speculated on the ability of strategic bombardment to force enemy capitulation by bombing cities, wrecking war industry and the morale of the population, the less they recognized the contributions of battlefield aviation. Of course, this combined with the views of some infantrymen, who had complained of aerial inactivity during the entire war whenever they did not see their own planes directly over their positions and who had not understood the merits of battlefield aviation. The result, according to historian Philippe Bernard, was that after using aviation well tactically, the French army failed to draw the lessons of the war methodically and fell prey to the myth of strategic bombardment, despite evidence from German and British strategic bombardment that it had not achieved their objectives.[70]

Postwar surveys acknowledged that the RAF's limited capabilities precluded significant material effects, and the German authorities asserted that the raids had minor impact on production and civilian morale. The postwar U.S. Air Service survey criticized the lack of a bombing program and a sustained focus on particular targets. Yet as historian George Williams concluded, the Air Ministry report of January 1920 simply "institutionalize[d] the optimistic view of bombing that had been promoted during hostilities," just as the April 1919 parliamentary paper, "Synopsis of the British Air Effort during the War," emphasized the moral and material effect of the raids. Of course, the RAF's existence was at stake, and stressing the unique contribution and significance of strategic aviation was certainly a critical factor in its preservation as an independent service. Perhaps most interesting was that Air Staff memorandum number 11.A of March 1924 acknowledged that while "the lessons of military history seem to recommend" the use of strategic forces to attack first enemy aerodromes to gain superiority and then the homeland, the Air Staff was convinced that the "correct" approach was to bomb military objectives in populated areas to gain a decision from the effect on morale and the dislocation of civilian life. Civilian morale had become the target, but without any realistic assessment of what the bombers could do, because the estimates were removed from the historical reality of what they had done in World War I.[71]

These examples indicate just how difficult it is to glean lessons from history that are rooted more in the facts than in wishful thinking and myth. Those divining lessons from warfare often have preconceived notions of what they seek or are impelled by diverse imperatives—political, military, economic, and cultural—to perceive certain lessons while ignoring others. The lessons of the war attributed to strategic bombing a prowess based not on wartime experience but on extrapolations of that experience by airpower theorists that enabled them to claim for airpower decisive significance in future wars. Giulio Douhet was the most eminent of these theorists, and *The Command of the Air* encapsulated in 1921 the claims for airpower that its proponents everywhere asserted. The willingness of strategic airpower advocates to contemplate striking directly at civilian centers with bombs or chemicals was founded on the preconception, however reasonable it appeared, that civilians would be less able to withstand such pounding than soldiers. Furthermore, enemy civilians would "squeal" before one's own populace, as Trenchard suggested in the early 1920s. All these notions sprang from the limited experience of striking civilians from the air in World War I without conclusive results, thus leaving theorists to speculate inductively about the future applications and effects of strategic airpower, speculations that continue to this day.

At the turn of the twentieth century the airplane, the genie of powered flight, was unleashed and then turned to destructive purposes in World War I. At the war's conclusion, the airplane became an instrument of peace but continued to enthrall society with its potential for greater destruction. Twenty years later, World War II provided ample opportunity for the realization of this potential. Military aviation has continued to grow ever more powerful since its inception in the Great War of 1914–1918, and society remains in its thrall.

Notes

CHAPTER ONE

To 1914

1. Henry S. Villard, *Contact! The Story of the Early Birds*, 21–22.
2. Felix P. Ingold, *Literatur und Aviatik: Europäische Flugdichtung 1909–1927*, 104–5.
3. Lee Kennett, *A History of Strategic Bombing*, 8–9.
4. Charles Christienne et al., *Histoire de l'aviation militaire française*, 20–25. Albert Etévé, *Avant les cocardes: Les Débuts de l'aéronautique militaire*, 15–16.
5. Michael Balfour, *The Kaiser and His Times*, (New York: W. W. Norton and Company, 1972), 290.
6. KAdL, *Die Militärluftfahrt bis zum Beginn des Weltkrieges 1914*, 1:1–73 passim.
7. The following paragraph, unless otherwise noted, is based on Alfred Gollin, *No Longer an Island*, 276–77, 282–83, 336–39, 402–4.
8. Ibid., 193.
9. On Wells, see also Stephen H. Kern, *The Culture of Time and Space, 1880–1918*, 242–43.
10. Ibid., 193.
11. Christienne et al., *Histoire de l'aviation*, 29–31. Etévé, *Avant*, 17–18. Patrick Facon, "L'armée française et l'aviation 1891–1914," 3–5.
12. Antoine Odier, *Souvenirs d'une vieille tige*, 117. Etévé, *Avant*, 21–23.

13. On the Wright brothers, see Fred Howard, *Wilbur and Orville*.

14. John H. Morrow, Jr., *Building German Air Power*, 14. Alfred Gollin, *The Impact of Air Power on the British People and Their Government, 1909–1914*, 170–73.

15. Villard, *Contact!*, 55–60.

16. Etévé, *Avant*, 15–16. Facon, "L'Aviation," 5. Christienne et al., *Histoire de l'aviation*, 31–34.

17. Facon, "L'Aviation," 5–6. Christienne et al., *Histoire de l'aviation*, 31–34. Etévé, *Avant*, 15–16. Odier, *Souvenirs*, 128–29.

18. Gabriel Voisin, *Men, Women, and 10,000 Kites*, 31, 45, 75, 106, 140, 169.

19. Christienne et al., *Histoire de l'aviation*, 36–37.

20. Ibid., 37.

21. KAdL, *Militärluftfahrt*, 3:10.

22. Morrow, *Building German Air Power*, 17–19.

23. Ibid., 103.

24. Gollin, *Impact of Air Power*, 309–11.

25. Robert F. Futrell, *Ideas, Concepts, Doctrine: A History of Basic Thinking in the United States Air Force, 1907–1964*, 15. Kennett, *Strategic Bombing*, 9–11.

26. Edmond Petit, *La Vie quotidienne dans l'aviation en France au début du XXe siècle (1900–1935)*, 79.

27. Louis Morgat, "L'Aviation en Berry avant la Grande Guerre," *RHA*, 1980, no. 1:159–60.

28. Hilmer von Bülow, *Geschichte der Luftwaffe*, 3. Ritter, 25.

29. Facon, "L'Aviation," 3.

30. Charles H. Gibbs-Smith, *The Aeroplane* 66.

31. On the French aircraft industry, see Petit, *La Vie quotidienne*, 1–53. Emmanuel Chadeau, "L'industrie Française d'aviation à la veille de la Première Guerre Mondiale," *RHA*, 1981, no. 2:61–81, and ibid., no. 3:181–206, passim. James Laux, "The Rise and Fall of Armand Deperdussin," *FHS*, 8, no. 1 (Spring 1973): 95–104, passim.

32. Odier, *Souvenirs*, 190–91.

33. James Laux, "Gnome et Rhône: Une Firme de moteurs d'avion durant la Grande Guerre," 171–74. Herschel Smith, *A History of Aircraft Piston Engines*, 58–60.

34. Petit, *La Vie quotidienne*, 80.

35. On early French military aviation, see Facon, "L'Aviation," 4–10. Christienne et al., *Histoire de l'aviation*, 26–27, 38–46. Félix Marie, *Les Origines de l'aéronautique militaire (novembre 1909–novembre 1910)*. Etévé, *Avant*.

36. Marie, *Origines*, 26–27, 42, 49–53.

37. Ibid., 87–89.

38. Facon, "L'Aviation," 15.

39. Etévé, *Avant*, 177–78.

40. Philippe Bernard, "A propos de la stratégie aérienne pendant la Première Guerre Mondiale: Mythes et réalités," *RHMC* 16 (1969): 354–55.

41. Marie, *Origines*, 23.

42. Chadeau, "L'Industrie," 198.

43. On the competition, see Colonel Rougevin-Baville, "Le Concours," *RHA*, 1969, 30–38. On Breguet, see Claude Breguet, "Dix Ans d'avions Breguet 1909–1919," *RHA*, 1969, 102–5. On Deperdussin, see Laux, "Deperdussin."

44. Petit, *La Vie quotidienne*, 52.

45. On German aviation, see Morrow, *Building German Air Power*, 14–47. Jürgen Eichler, "Die Militärluftschiffahrt in Deutschland 1911–1914 und ihre Rolle in den Kriegsplänen des deutschen Imperialismum," *ZFM* 24, no. 4 (1985): 350–60; ibid., no. 5 (1985): 403–12. Douglas H. Robinson, *Giants in the Sky: A History of the Rigid Airship*, 40–62.

46. On England, see, in general, Gollin, *No Longer an Island*, 433–68; Gollin, *Impact of Air Power*, 1–190 passim; Harald Penrose, *British Aviation: The Pioneer Years 1903–1914*, 145–331 passim.

47. S. W. Roskill, ed., *Documents Relating to the Naval Air Service*, 1:14.

48. Gollin, *Impact of Air Power*, 183.

49. *Flight 3*, passim but particularly no. 46 (18 November 1911): 994.

50. *Flight 3*, no. 51 (23 December 1911): 1100.

51. On Austria-Hungary, see Morrow, *Building German Air Power*, 104–8. Ernst Peter, *Die k.u.k. Luftschiffer- und Fliegertruppe Österreich-Hungarns, 1794–1919*, prewar chapters.

52. Peter, *Luftschiffer- und Fliegertruppe*.

53. On Russian aviation, see David R. Jones in Robin Higham and Jacob W. Kipp, *Soviet Aviation and Air Power: A Historical View*, 16–17. Robert A. Kilmarx, "The Russian Imperial Air Forces of World War I," *AH* 10 (July 1963): 90–91. Von Hardesty, "Aeronautics Comes to Russia: The Early Years, 1908–1918," 23–33.

54. On Italian aviation, see Angelo Lodi, *Storia delle origini dell'aeronautica militare 1884–1915*, 1:61–177 passim. On Douhet, see Frank J. Cappelluti, "The Life and Thought of Giulio Douhet," 31–46.

55. Villard, *Contact!*, 8.

56. See ibid., passim. Roger E. Bilstein, *Flight in America, 1900–1983*, 16–29. Eugene Emme, "The American Dimension," in United States Air Force Academy Symposium, 1978, 58–60. On Navy, see Richard Knott, *The American Flying Boat: An Illustrated History*, 8–9.

57. Ingold, *Literatur und Aviatik*.

58. Ibid., 86–87.

59. Ibid., 89–90.

60. Ibid., 216–17.

61. Ibid., 104–5.
62. Ibid., 104.
63. Ibid., 116–17.
64. Ibid., 104.
65. Ibid., 218.
66. Gollin, *No Longer an Island*, 328–29. Ingold, *Literatur und Aviatik*, 96.
67. Ingold, 97.
68. Ibid., 148–51.
69. Ibid., 29–47.
70. *Aeroplane* 1, no. 14 (7 September 1911): 323; ibid., no. 16 (21 September 1911): 375–76; ibid., no. 19 (19 October 1911): 462; ibid. 5, no. 23 (4 April 1912): 602.
71. Villard, *Contact!*, 127.
72. *Flight* 6, no. 10 (7 March 1914): 248–49.
73. Ibid. 5, no. 47 (22 November 1913): 1263–64. *Aeroplane* 5, no. 21 (20 November 1913): 550–52; ibid., no. 23 (4 December 1913): 598.
74. Chadeau, "L'industrie," passim.
75. Emmanuel Chadeau, *L'Industrie aéronautique en France 1900–1950: De Blériot à Dassault*, 58–66.
76. *Aeroplane* 6, no. 7 (12 February 1914): 152–54.
77. Christienne et al., *Histoire de l'aviation*, 55.
78. *L'Aérophile*, no. 6 (15 March 1914): 124–27.
79. Laux, "Gnome et Rhône," 177.
80. Morgat, "L'Aviation en Berry."
81. *Aeroplane* 6, no. 4 (22 January 1914): 85, 106; ibid., no. 7 (12 February 1914): 152–54.
82. Petit, *La Vie quotidienne*, 83–84.
83. Ibid., 95.
84. Morgat, "L'Aviation en Berry," 196.
85. On German aviation in the years 1912–14, on airplanes, see John H. Morrow, Jr., *German Air Power in World War I*, 7–11. Morrow, *Building German Air Power*, 48–103. On airships, see Eichler, *Militärluftschiffahrt*, passim, and prewar material in Douglas H. Robinson, *The Zeppelin in Combat: A History of the German Naval Airship Division, 1912–1918*. In general, see KAdL, *Militärluftfahrt*. On engines, see Kyrill von Gersdorff and Kurt Grassmann, *Flugmotoren und Strahltriebwerke*, 9–13.
86. KAdL, *Militärluftfahrt*, 2:86.
87. Eichler, *Militärluftschiffahrt*, 407–10.
88. Ibid., 410.
89. David Landes, *The Unbound Prometheus: Technological Change and Industrial Development in Western Europe from 1750 to the Present* (Cambridge: Cambridge University Press, 1969), 306.

90. *Flight* 5, no. 5 (1 February 1913): 107–8; ibid., no. 9 (1 March 1913): 243–44; ibid., no. 15 (11 April 1913): 415.

91. Ibid., 4, no. 16 (20 April 1912): 346–49.

92. *Aeroplane* 6, no. 3 (15 January 1914): 56–58; ibid., no. 4 (22 January 1914): 80–82.

93. *Flight* 6, no. 5 (31 January 1914): 105–6, 112–13; ibid., no. 9 (28 February 1914): 207–8.

94. Thomas A. Keaney, "Aircraft and Air Doctrinal Development in Great Britain, 1912–1914," 35, 176.

95. G. P. Bulman, "I ought to have been sacked," 28–32.

96. *Aeroplane* 6, no. 1 (1 January 1914): 14.

97. *Flight* 5, no. 49 (6 December 1913): 1315–16.

98. Ibid., no. 10 (7 March 1914): 248–49.

99. Keaney, "Aircraft in Great Britain," 288.

100. *Flight* 6, no. 26 (26 June 1914): 670–77; ibid., no. 27 (3 July 1914): 698–701.

101. Frederick Sykes, *From Many Angles: An Autobiography*, 114.

102. *Aeroplane* 3, no. 14 (2 October 1913): 374.

103. R. A. Mason, "The British Dimension," 22–25.

104. *Flight* 6, no. 7 (14 February 1914): 170–73; ibid., no. 24 (12 June 1914): 632–33.

105. Sykes, *From Many Angles*, 105–6.

106. On prewar Austro-Hungarian aviation, see Morrow, *Building German Air Power*, 108–14; Peter Schupita, *Die k.u.k. Seeflieger: Chronik und Dokumentation der österreichisch-ungarischen Marineluftwaffe 1911–1918*, 11–16; Peter, *Luftschiffer- und Fliegertruppe*, prewar chapters.

107. On Russia, see N. Kozlow, *A Study of the Military-Technical Supply of the Russian Army in the World War*, 86–93. Jones in Higham & Kipp, 18–20. Kipp in Higham & Kipp, 137–9. Chaney and Greenwood in Higham & Kipp, 266–7. Kilmarx, "Russian Imperial Air Forces," 90–92. On Sikorsky, see Igor Sikorsky, *The Story of the Winged S: An Autobiography*, and K. N. Finne, *Igor Sikorsky: The Russian Years*, 25–55.

108. On Italy, see Lodi, *Storia*, vol. 2 passim. On the aviation industry, see Piero Vergnano, *Origin of Aviation in Italy, 1783–1918*, passim. On Douhet, see Cappelluti, "Douhet," 45–66.

109. On American aviation, see Futrell, *Ideas*, 14–15; I. B. Holley, Jr., *Ideas and Weapons*, 28–33; Bilstein, *Flight in America*, 26–31, 34–35; Archibald D. Turnbull and Clifford L. Lord, *History of United States Naval Aviation*, 1–44.

110. Kern, *Time and Space*, 72, 194, 242–47, 287, 310–11, 317.

111. Keaney, "Aircraft in Great Britain," 221.

112. *Aeroplane* 3, no. 7 (15 August 1912): 159–60; ibid., no. 15 (10 October 1912), 359–60.

113. Keaney, "Aircraft in Great Britain," 247–48.

114. Henri Mirande and Louis Olivier, *Sur la bataille: Journal d'un aviateur français à l'Armée Bulgare au Siège d'Andrinople*, 333.

115. Keaney, "Aircraft in Great Britain," 252–53.

116. Ibid., 215–16, 242, 309–20.

117. Christienne et al., *Histoire de l'aviation*, 58.

118. Bülow, *Geschichte der Luftwaffe*. Peter Supf, *Das Buch der deutschen Fluggeschichte*.

119. Penrose, *Pioneer Years*, 513–15.

CHAPTER TWO

Into the Fray,
August to December 1914

1. René Chambe, *Au temps des carabines*, 53.

2. Christienne et al., *Histoire de l'aviation*, 56, 61–62.

3. Albert Etévé, *La Victoire des cocardes*, 143.

4. *L'Aéronautique pendant la Guerre Mondiale*, 391, 400; Georges Huisman, *Dans les coulisses de l'aviation 1914–1918: Pourquoi n'avons nous pas toujours garder la maitrise des airs?*, 21–23.

5. Huisman, *Coulisses*, 22–23; Christienne et al., *Histoire de l'aviation*, 163.

6. Gilbert Hatry, *Renault, usine de guerre 1914–1918*, 23.

7. Ibid., 23–24; Patrick Fridenson, *Histoire des usines Renault*, 1:93.

8. *L'Aéronautique*, 644; James Laux, "Gnome et Rhône: Une firme de moteurs d'avion durant la Grande Guerre," 179.

9. Etévé, *Victoire*, 143; Christienne et al., *Histoire de l'aviation*, 175; *L'Aéronautique*, 398.

10. Huisman, *Coulisses*, 20; DAeM MdG to CinC, 26 August 1914, A77, SHAA.

11. Etévé, *Victoire*, 147; *L'Aéronautique*, 385, 391, 398.

12. Huisman, *Coulisses*, 16–19.

13. Christienne et al., *Histoire de l'aviation*, 83–87.

14. Jacques Mortane, *Histoire illustrée de la guerre aérienne (1914–1918)*, 29–30; "L'Aéronautique militaire française pendant la Guerre de 1914–1918," vol. 1, "1914, 1915, 1916," *Icare, revue de l'aviation française*, no. 85 (Automne 1978): 16–17; "Notes sur l'aviation en 1914, particulièrement à la 5e armée," SHAA; Huisman, *Coulisses*, 28–29; Christienne et al., *Histoire de l'aviation*, 87–88.

15. Daniel Vincent's parliamentary questions, no. 3, 1A5, SHAA.

16. Philippe Bernard, "A propos de la stratégie aérienne pendant la Première Guerre Mondiale: Mythes et réalités," *RHMC*, 16 (1969): 357–58.

17. "L'Aéronautique," *Icare* 1:19.

18. Chambe, *Temps*, 33–35.

19. Dir. de l'Aéro to GQG, 25 October 1914, File Blériot, A75, SHAA.

20. Rapport Hirschauer, 8 October 1914, A14, SHAA; Chadeau, *L'Industrie aéronautique en France*, 119–20, 123–24.

21. Renault to Colonel Bouttiaux, 24 October 1914, 1A4, SHAA; Daniel Vincent's parliamentary questions, no. 11, 1A5, SHAA.

22. DAeM MdG no. 1738/12 to GQG, 18 October 1914, A85, SHAA.

23. *L'Aéronautique*, 95–96; GQG note to MdG, A14, SHAA.

24. Daniel Vincent's parliamentary questions, no. 11, 1A5, and question of 9 March 1916, 1A4, SHAA; Laux, "Gnome et Rhône," 78.

25. Fridenson, *Renault*, 1:91.

26. Bernard, "Stratégie aérienne," 358–59.

27. Alex Imrie, *Pictorial History of the German Army Air Service, 1914–1918*, 22–23.

28. On airships, see ibid., 23–24, and Neumann, *Luftstreitkräfte*, 346–50, 362–63.

29. Christienne et al., *Histoire de l'aviation*, 88.

30. Elard von Löwenstern, *Der Frontflieger aus Vorkriegs=, Kriegs und Nachkriegs=Fliegertagen*, passim.

31. John R. Cuneo, *Winged Mars*, 2:92–94.

32. Morrow, *German Air Power in World War I*, 16–17.

33. Ibid., 17–18.

34. Ibid., 18–19.

35. Ibid., 19–21.

36. Ibid., 21.

37. Imrie, *Pictorial History*, 26.

38. "L'Aéronautique," 1:77.

39. Maximilian von Cossel in Georg P. Neumann, ed., *In der Luft unbesiegt*, 20–22.

40. Morrow, *German Air Power*, 25–26.

41. Ibid., 27–28.

42. Ibid., 22–23.

43. Ibid., 28–31.

44. A. H. G. Fokker and Bruce Gould, *Flying Dutchman: The Life of Anthony Fokker*, 117–18.

45. Morrow, *German Air Power*, 31–33.

46. Frederick Sykes, *From Many Angles: An Autobiography*, 138.

47. David Divine, *The Broken Wing: A Study in the British Exercise of Air Power*, 52.

48. Malcolm Cooper, *The Birth of Independent Air Power: British Air Policy in the First World War*, 18–19.

49. Peter Mead, *The Eye in the Air: History of Air Observation and Reconnaisance for the Army 1785–1945*, 51–58.

50. Sir Philip Joubert de la Ferté, *The Fated Sky: An Autobiography*, 48.

51. Frank D. Tredrey, *Pioneer Pilot: The Great Smith Barry Who Taught the World to Fly*, 28.

52. Walter Raleigh and H. A. Jones, *The War in the Air*, 2:88.

53. Sir Roy Fedden in *A Century of British Aeronautics*, 169–70.

54. Harald Penrose, *British Aviation: The Pioneer Years, 1903–1914*, 532–60.

55. Cooper, *Birth of Independent Air Power*, 20.

56. Divine, *Broken Wing*, 67.

57. Sykes, *From Many Angles*, 144–46.

58. Neville Jones, *The Origins of Strategic Bombing: A Study of the Development of British Air Strategic Thought up to 1918*, 68.

59. Sir Philip Joubert de la Ferté, *The Third Service: The Story Behind the Royal Air Force*, 19, 28.

60. Randolph S. Churchill, *Winston S. Churchill*, 2:652–53.

61. *Flight* 6, no. 43 (23 October 1914): 1065.

62. Ibid., no. 47 (20 November 1914): 1129–30.

63. Raleigh and Jones, *War in the Air*, 1:370; Peter H. Liddle, *The Airman's War 1914–18*, 30–31.

64. Churchill, *Churchill*, 3:175.

65. Petr Dmitrievich Duz, *History of Aeronautics and Aviation in the USSR: The First World War Period (1914–1918)*, 13; N. Kozlow, *Military-Technical Supply*, 100; Jacob W. Kipp, "The Development of Naval Aviation, 1908–1975," in *Soviet Aviation and Air Power*, ed. Higham and Kipp, 139.

66. Duz, *Aeronautics and Aviation in the USSR*, 20.

67. Ibid., 22.

68. W. Bruce Lincoln, 57.

69. Ibid.

70. Duz, *Aeronautics and Aviation in the USSR*, 31; Lincoln, 58.

71. Duz, *Aeronautics and Aviation in the USSR*, 352.

72. Ibid., 350–53. K. N. Finne, *Igor Sikorsky: The Russian Years*, 57–72.

73. Duz, *Aeronautics and Aviation in the USSR*, 81.

74. Ibid., 260.

75. Ibid., 260–68; David R. Jones, "The Beginnings of Russian Airpower, 1907–1922," in *Soviet Aviation and Air Power: A Historical View*, ed. Robin Higham and Jacob W. Kipp, 22.

76. Kozlow, *Military-Technical Supply*, 107, 111–12; Jones, "," 20; Duz, *Aeronautics and Aviation in the USSR*, 471.

77. Ernst Peter, *Luftschiffer- und Fliegertruppe*, 113–28.

78. Ibid., 131; Schupita, *Die k.u.k. Seeflieger*, 161–66.

79. Morrow, *German Air Power*, 167–68.

80. Ibid., 168–69.

81. *Flight* 3, no. 41 (9 October 1914): 1026.

CHAPTER THREE

1915

1. Johannes Werner, *Boelcke. Der Mensch, der Flieger, der Führer der deutschen Jagdfliegerei,* 125.

2. Quoted in Peter H. Liddle, *The Airman's War, 1914–18,* 45.

3. *L'Aéronautique pendant la Guerre Mondiale,* 415. Jacques Mortane, *Histoire illustrée de la guerre aérienne (1914–1918),* 137.

4. Etévé, *Victoire,* 135, 152.

5. Christienne et al., *Histoire de l'aviation,* 90, 164.

6. George Huisman, *Dans les coulisses de l'aviation 1914–1918: Pourquoi n'avons nous pas toujours garder la maitrise des airs?,* 46.

7. On air operations in 1915, see Christienne et al., *Histoire de l'aviation,* 89–104.

8. On Garros, see ibid., 103–4. Garros memorandum, 3 November 1914, Morane file, A75, SHAA.

9. "Guynemer et les Cicognes," *Icare* 122, no. 3 (1987): 24.

10. Escadrille no. 57, 10e armée, 19 July 1915, Nieuport file, A75, SHAA.

11. DAeM MdG, "Procès Verbal," bomber prize commission, 26 July 1915, A14, SHAA.

12. Dorand to MdG, 20 January, 12 March, and 4 April 1915, Dorand Papers, Musée de l'Air.

13. *L'Aéronautique,* 125–29.

14. On French bombardment aviation, see Christienne et al., *Histoire de l'aviation,* 92–100.

15. Emmanuel Chadeau, "État, enterprise et développement économique: L'Industrie aéronautique en France (1900–1940)," 371.

16. DAeM MdG to GQG, 28 June 1915, A75, SHAA.

17. J. A. Gilles, *Flugmotoren 1910 bis 1918,* 78–79.

18. Emmanuel Chadeau, *L'Industrie aéronautique en France 1900–1950: De Blériot à Dassault,* 126–29.

19. GQG Service Aéronautique no. 2934 to 12e Directorate MdG, 7 July 1915, A82, SHAA.

20. Service Aéronautique 3e armée to GQG Service Aéronautique, 27 August 1915, A82, SHAA.

21. DAeM to MdG no. 8601 2/12 to GQG, 4 September 1915, A81, SHAA.

22. Voisin to Barès, 7 September 1915. DAeM to MdG no. 8878 2/12 to GQG, 11 September 1915, A85, SHAA.

23. GQG 2392 to MdG, 6 July 1915, A14; Daniel Vincent's parliamentary questions, no. 8, 2 August 1915, 1A5, SHAA.

24. Etévé, *Victoire*, 153, 157–58. Commandant Grard no. 45224/M to MdG, A77, SHAA.

25. C. Fayette Taylor, "Aircraft Propulsion: A Review of the Evolution of Aircraft Piston Engines," *Smithsonian Annals of Flight* 1, no. 4 (1971): 33.

26. Ibid., 33.

27. Philippe Bernard, "A propos de la stratégie aérienne pendant le Première Guerre Mondiale: Mythes et réalités," *RHMC* 16 (1969): 359.

28. Le Chatelier report to aviation commission, 5 July 1915, A81, SHAA.

29. Bernard, "Stratégie aérienne," 360.

30. Ibid., 361.

31. 2e Rapport présenté à la commission de l'armée de la Chambre des Députés par M. D'Aubigny (secretary of aviation committee), 23 September 1915, A81, SHAA.

32. Flandin to d'Aubigny, 21 September 1915, A81, SHAA.

33. Etévé, *Victoire*, 156–58.

34. Ibid., 158–59, 161–62, 167.

35. Ibid., 156–59. Huisman, *Coulisses*, 81.

36. Etévé, *Victoire*, 159–61.

37. Ibid., 160. Huisman, *Coulisses*, 73.

38. Huisman, *Coulisses*, 73.

39. Le Chatelier report, 5 July 1915, A81, SHAA.

40. Etévé, *Victoire*, 159–61. Huisman, *Coulisses*, 95–99.

41. Etévé, *Victoire*, 162.

42. Dorand, "Au sujet de la situation actuelle des avions militaires," DP, MdA.

43. Chadeau, *L'Industrie*, 86–87, 97.

44. Christienne et al., *Histoire de l'aviation*, 175.

45. Ibid. James Laux, "Gnome et Rhône: Une firme de moteurs d'avion durant le Grand Guerre," 182. Chadeau, *L'Industrie*, 89, 93.

46. Siegert in Georg P. Neumann, ed., *In der Luft unbesiegt*, 24–28.

47. Ibid., 126.

48. Morrow, *German Air Power*, 36–37.

49. Ibid., 48.

50. A. H. G. Fokker and Bruce Gould, *Flying Dutchman: The Life of Anthony Fokker*, 122–27.

51. Morrow, *German Air Power*, 40–41.

52. Immelmann, *Immelmann*, 93.

53. Immelmann, *Mes Vols de Combat*, 46, 49.

54. Werner, 107.

55. Ibid.

56. Immelmann, *Mes Vols de Combat*, 32.

57. Werner, 1–124 passim.

58. Morrow, *German Air Power*, 41–42.

59. Ibid., 42.

60. Neumann, *Luftstreitkräfte*, 463–65.

61. Morrow, *German Air Power*, 52–54.

62. Ibid.

63. On the Zeppelin campaign in 1915, see Douglas H. Robinson, *Giants in the Sky: A History of the Rigid Airship*, 92–113, and *Zeppelin in Combat*, 53–119. Alex Imrie, *Pictorial History of the German Army Air Service, 1914–1918*, 30. George H. Quester, *Deterrence before Hiroshima*, 24–26. Neumann, *Luftstreitkräfte*, 349–56, 363–68, 370, 391–92.

64. Robinson, *Zeppelin in Combat*, 64.

65. Gaissert in Neumann, *Unbesiegt*, 237–47.

66. Morrow, 50–52.

67. Ibid., 37–38.

68. Ibid., 39.

69. Junkers Notizbücher 1915 passim; Junkers to Prussian War Ministry, 30 August 1915; "Überblick" (of the development of all metal planes), 14 March 1918; Junkers Papers, Deutsches Museum. See also Richard Blunck, *Hugo Junkers: Ein Leben für Technik und Luftfahrt*, 90–102.

70. Morrow, 43–46.

71. Bullinger, "Erzeugung der Flugmotoren," report VI, 2, GC.

72. Ibid., 1–2. Kyrill von Gersdorff and Kurt Grassmann, *Flugmotoren und Strahltriebwerke*, 12, 21–23.

73. Morrow, *German Air Power*, 48–50.

74. Cooper, *Birth of Independent Air Power*, 27–29. Peter Mead, *The Eye in the Air: History of Air Observation and Reconnaissance for the Army 1785–1945*, 65–67.

75. Basil Collier, *Heavenly Adventurer: Sefton Brancker and the Dawn of British Aviation*, 47.

76. Cooper, *Birth of Independent Air Power*, 31.

77. Ibid., 27–28.

78. *Flight* 7, no. 29 (16 July 1915): 505–6.

79. Cooper, *Birth of Independent Air Power*, 21–23, 31–32.

80. Ibid., 29. Mead, *Eye in the Air*, 68–69.

81. Geoffrey Norris, *The Royal Flying Corps: A History*, 114–15.

82. Lewis A. Strange, *Recollections of an Airman*, 102, 111–12.

83. Ibid., 123, 132. Tyrrel M. Hawker, *Hawker, VC*, 53–125 passim. Liddle, *Airman's War*, 43–45.

84. Cooper, *Birth of Independent Air Power*, 30–31.

85. Air Ministry, "Synopsis of the British Air Effort during the War." Cmd. 100, April 1919, 4. MID 9793-295, RG 165, NA.

86. James T. B. McCudden, *Flying Fury*, 1–78 passim.

87. Sholto Douglas, with Robert Wright, *Combat and Command*, 55–97.

88. Ibid., 49.

89. Cecil Lewis, *Sagittarius Rising*, 7.

90. Douglas, *Combat and Command*, 29–30.

91. Winifred Loraine, *Robert Loraine: Soldier, Actor, Airman,* 217–18.

92. Peter Parker, *The Old Lie: The Great War and the Public School Ethos,* 266.

93. *Aeroplane* 9, no. 18 (3 November 1915): 542.

94. Col. W. S. Brancker, "HQ RFC Historical Notes," 10 June 1915, AIR 1/408/15/231/49, PRO.

95. S. W. Roskill, ed., *Documents Relating to the Naval Air Service,* 1:223.

96. Ibid., 230.

97. Arthur Longmore, *From Sea to Sky 1910–1945,* 47–48.

98. Roskill, *Documents,* x.

99. Richard B. Davies, *Sailor in the Air,* 75.

100. Air Ministry, "Synopsis," 6. Liddle, *Airman's War,* 41–46. Walter Raleigh and H. A. Jones, *War in the Air,* 2 (pt. 1).

101. Liddle, *Airman's War,* 149–51. Air Ministry, "Synopsis," 7. F. M. Cutlack, *The Australian Flying Corps in the Western and Eastern Theatres of War 1914–1918,* 5.

102. AIR 1/2319/223/29/1–18, PRO.

103. *Flight* 7, no. 21 (21 May 1917): 349–50.

104. Ibid., 7, no. 26 (25 June 1915): 446–48, 455; ibid., no. 30, (23 July 1915): 525–26, 539–42; ibid., no. 43 (22 December 1915): 798, 802.

105. JWAC 7, AIR 1/2319/223/27, PRO.

106. Raleigh and Jones, *War in the Air,* 3:253.

107. Harald Penrose, *British Aviation: The Great War and Armistice 1915–1919,* 28, 71, 77.

108. Ministry of Munitions, *History of the Ministry of Munitions,* 12 (pt. 1): 55–57.

109. Ibid., 54.

110. J. C. Nerney, "Aircraft Design and Production, 1914–1918," 4–6, AIR 1/678/21/13/2186, PRO.

111. Penrose, *Great War,* 345.

112. Peter Fearon, "The Formative Years of the British Aircraft Industry, 1913–1924," *Business History Review* 43 (1969): 485.

113. *Flight* 7, no. 49 (3 December 1915): 933–34.

114. Raleigh and Jones, *War in the Air,* 1:455. Neville Jones, *The Origins of Strategic Bombing: A Study of the Development of British Air Strategic Thought up to 1918,* 76. Trenchard CRFC 2000 to Asst. DMA, 6 December 1915; Trenchard to Innes Kerr, 8 November 1915; AIR 1/1071/204/5/6138, PRO.

115. Jones in Higham and Kipp, 22, 24.

116. Christine Holden, "The View from Furshstadtskaya Street: American Military Attaches' Reports on Russian Aeronautics," 20–24.

117. On the Sikorsky giants, see K. N. Finne, *Igor Sikorsky: The Russian Years,* 71–111. Petr Dmitrievich Duz, *History of Aeronautics and Aviation in the USSR: The First World War Period (1914–1918),* 359–65.

118. Holden, "View," 12–13.

119. N. Kozlow, *A Study of the Military-Technical Supply of the Russian Army in the World War*, 114–18, 121–27.

120. Duz, *Aeronautics and Aviation in the USSR*, 507.

121. Ernst Peter, *Die k̦.u.k̦. Luftschiffer- und Fliegertruppe Österreich-Hungarns, 1794–1919*, 123–28, 143–45.

122. Ibid., 131–37, 156–60.

123. Morrow, *German Air Power*, 169.

124. Ibid., 169–71, 213.

125. "Aviation Service in Italy," War College Division, 9520-E-1, 5 January 1917, RG 165, NA. In general, unless otherwise noted the discussion of Italy is based on Felice Porro, *La Guerra nell'aria*, 28–85 passim, 420.

126. H. H. Arnold, "Italian Aeronautical Status," stencil no. 246, 26 July 1916, RG 18, NA. On the Italian aviation industry, see Piero Vergnano, *Origin of Aviation in Italy, 1783–1918*, 89–90, 106, 110–11, 123–24.

127. Peter, *Luftschiffer- und Fliegertruppe*, 138.

128. Ibid., 138–40, 164.

129. Gabriele D'Annunzio, *Aviatore di guerra: Documenti e Testimonianze*, 94. Peter, *Luftschiffer- und Fliegertruppe*, 164.

130. Frank J. Cappelluti, "The Life and Thought of Giulio Douhet," 67–110 passim.

CHAPTER FOUR

1916

1. *Aeronautics* 10, no. 135 (17 May 1916): 317–18.

2. Alain Morizon, "L'Aviation en 1916," end chart, SHAA.

3. Etévé, *Victoire*, 199.

4. Jacques Mortane, *Histoire illustrée de la guerre aérienne (1914–1918)*, 137–39, 193.

5. On Verdun in general, see Christienne et al., *Histoire de l'aviation*, 105–9.

6. André P. Voisin, *La Doctrine de l'aviation française de combat au cours de la guerre (1915–1918)*, 2–3.

7. Etévé, *Victoire*, 203.

8. Voisin, *Doctrine*, 3–4.

9. Georges Thénault, *L'Escadrille Lafayette (avril 1916–janvier 1918)*, 1–51 passim. Philip M. Flammer, *The Vivid Air: The Lafayette Escadrille*, 5–59 passim.

10. "L'Aéronautique militaire française pendant la Guerre de 1914–1918," vol. 1, "1914, 1915, 1916," *Icare, revue de l'aviation française*, no. 85 (Automne 1978): 23.

11. Bernard Lafont, *Au ciel de Verdun: Notes d'un aviateur*, 165.

12. Ibid., 28–29.

13. Ibid., 29.

14. "L'Aéronautique," 1:49–53, 58.

15. Etévé, *Victoire*, 201. Voisin, *Doctrine*, 6–8. Christienne et al., *Histoire de l'aviation*, 109–10.

16. Voisin, *Doctrine*, 9–16.

17. Ibid., 19–20. Christienne et al., *Histoire de l'aviation*, 115–16. Notes on artillery aviation collected by M. Raiberti, deputy, 30 December 1916, 130 AP 6, DP, AN.

18. *L'Aéronautique pendant le Guerre Mondiale*, 46–47.

19. "Guynemer et les Cigognes," *Icare*, no. 122, p. 63.

20. *L'Aéronautique*, 47.

21. Flammer, *Air*, 61–103 passim. Thénault, *Lafayette*, 46–78 passim.

22. "Guynemer," 73–74, 135–36.

23. Christienne et al., *Histoire de l'aviation*, 116–17.

24. "L'Aéronautique," 1:81–83.

25. Christienne et al., *Histoire de l'aviation*, 118–20. See also AEF, "Account of the Aviation Plan of Bombardment by Airplane," 18 November 1917, AIR 1/1976/204/243/39, PRO.

26. Simone Pesquies-Courbier, "Le bassin ferrifère de Briey durant la guerre de 1914–1918," *RHA*, 1981, no. 2: 121, and "La politique de bombardement des usines sidérurgiques en Lorraine et au Luxembourg pendant la Première Guerre Mondiale," *RHA*, 1981, no. 44: 135.

27. Etévé, *Victoire*, 200.

28. Werner, *Boelcke*, 145.

29. Etévé, 200–4. Notes on aviation collected during deputy Lucien Klotz's visit to the northeast armies, 20 May 1916, 130 AP 6, DP, AN.

30. Louis Thébault, *L'Escadrille 210*, 29, 49, 53, 59.

31. Mortane, *Histoire illustrée*, 126–27.

32. Vincent, Report to Budget Commission on Aeronautics to 1 November 1916, 1 December 1916, 130 AP 9, DP, AN.

33. Mortane, *Histoire Illustrée*, 127.

34. Etévé, 200.

35. Commandant Roland, lecture on "Organization and General Principles of the French Flying Corps," 16 December 1916, AIR 1/997/204/5/1241, PRO.

36. Etat Numérique, October 1916, 130 AP 8; Etat Mensuel, October 1916, 130 AP 6; Vincent report, 1 December 1916, 130 AP 9; DP, AN.

37. 1, no. 7: 212–14.

38. Georges Huisman, *Dans les coulisses de l'aviation 1914–1918: Pourquoi n'avons nous pas toujours garder la maitrise des airs?*, 118, 129.

39. Mortane, *Histoire illustrée*, 102–4.

40. *Aeroplane* 10, no. 6 (9 February 1916): 232.

41. Huisman, *Coulisses*, 110.

42. Etévé, 199.

43. Christienne et al., *Histoire de l'aviation*, 166 44. *Aeroplane* 10, no. 10 (8 March 1916): 386.

45. GQG, Commandant de l'Aéronautique, Inspection du Matériel 1631 M to GQG CdA, 19 October 1916, A82, SHAA.

46. *L'Aéronautique*, 113–16. Etévé, 206–7.

47. DP, MdA.

48. Etévé, 201–2, 208.

49. 5770–154, Report 14, 15 December 1916, RG 165, NA.

50. D'Aubigny, "Rapport sur les Travaux de la Commission de l'Armée pendant la Guerre 1914–1918," 72.

51. Joffre 4909 to MdG, 7 March 1916, A75, SHAA.

52. Rapport du Capitaine Adrian sur les avions de bombardment, no. 607, 21 August 1916, A81, SHAA.

53. Mortane, *Histoire illustrée*, 127–28.

54. D'Aubigny, "Rapport," 68–69.

55. Etévé, 204.

56. Production figures in tables from *L'Aéronautique*, 394, 398.

57. Commission des Marchés 1369-M/C to DAeM, 13 October 1916, 1A4, SHAA.

58. "Rapport fait au nom de la commission chargé d'examiner les marchés conclus par l'état depuis le début de la guerre," par M. Pierre-Étienne Flandin, no. 3271, 5 April 1917, Chambre des Députés, 11e legislature, session de 1917, 1A3; Réponse au rapport Flandin, 12 May 1917, 1A4; SHAA.

59. Rapport Flandin, no. 4411, session de 1918, 6 March 1918, 1A3, SHAA.

60. MdG DAeM, 3e Bureau to President, 8 July 1916, 1A4, SHAA.

61. Rapport de M. Lelong, Ingénieur-Chef de le Marine, member de la Commission des Contrats de l'Aéronautique, "Au Sujet des prix des Moteurs d'Aviation," 16 June 1917. Doc. 3689 3/12 of 13 March 1918, 1A4, SHAA.

62. Huisman, *Coulisses*, 117–21.

63. Emmanuel Chadeau, *L'Industrie aéronautique en France*, 81–139 passim. Naval attaché report on French aviation statistics, A-1-Q 12616, RG38, NA.

64. James Laux, "Gnome et Rhône, Une firme de moteurs d'avion durant la Grande Guerre," 180–84. Office of Naval Intelligence, File A-1-Q/6136, Aeronautics—General Data, Dept. 5, 7 January and 29 February 1916, RG18, NA.

65. Patrick Fridenson, *Histoire des usines Renault*, 1:97–109.

66. J. Bitchakdjian, "Les débuts des industries françaises d'aéronautique: La Société des moteurs Salmson 1913–1917," 70–85.

67. Huisman, *Coulisses*, 135.

68. Ibid., 124–29, 135.

69. Etévé, *Victoire*, 214–19.

70. Alex Imrie, *Pictorial History of the German Army Air Service, 1914–1918*, 31.

71. Ibid., 31–32.

72. Ibid., 32–34. Hähnelt in G. P. Neumann, *Die Deutschen Luftstreitkräfte im Weltkriege*, 466–67.

73. Werner, 146–67, 159–60.

74. Imrie, *Pictorial History*, 33.

75. Peter M. Grosz, "The Albatros Fighters D1 to D5a," 3, GC.

76. A. H. G. Fokker and Bruce Gould, *Flying Dutchman: The Life of Anthony Fokker*, 192–93. Oswald Boelcke, *Hauptmann Boelckes Feldberichte*, 84–85.

77. Werner, 158–68.

78. John R. Cuneo, *Winged Mars*, 2: 245–54.

79 "L'Aéronautique," 1:87–89.

80. Interrogatories of German prisoners 1915–1917, AIR 1/1/4/26/1, PRO.

81. Siegert in Neumann, *Luftstreitkräfte*, 469–77.

82. Ibid.

83. Imrie, *Pictorial History*, 35–36.

84. Werner, 182–218 passim.

85. Ludwig Gengler, *Rudolf Berthold*, 31–73.

86. Cuneo, *Winged Mars*, 2:260.

87. Imrie, *Pictorial History*, 39–40. Neumann, *Luftstreitkräfte*, 356–57.

88. Neumann, *Luftstreitkräfte*, 65.

89. Imrie, *Pictorial History*, 37. Neumann, *Luftstreitkräfte*, 356–57.

90. Imrie, *Pictorial History*, 37–8. Neumann, *Luftstreitkräfte*, 344–45, 358–61, 368–69, 371–73.

91. On naval airship operations, see Douglas H. Robinson, *Giants in the Sky: A History of the Rigid Airship*, 113–25; Neumann, *Luftstreitkräfte*, 388–89, 392–93, 395–96. Robin Cross, *The Bombers: The Illustrated Story of Offensive Strategy and Tactics in the Twentieth Century*, 24–28.

92. Robinson, *Giants*, 122.

93. Quote in S. F. Wise, *Canadian Airmen and the First World War: The Official History of the Royal Canadian Air Force*, 241–42, and in Walter Raleigh and H. A. Jones, *War in the Air*, 3:237.

94. Sir Arthur Hezlett, *Aircraft and Sea Power*, 63.

95. Morrow, *German Air Power*, 87–88. Peter Gray and Owen Thetford, *German Aircraft of the First World War*, 68–71.

96. Siegert in Neumann, *Luftstreitkräfte*, 305–11.

97. Morrow, *German Air Power*, 66–68.

98. Neumann, *Luftstreitkräfte*, 305–11.

99. Ibid., 305.

100. Karl Köhler, "Auf dem Wege zur Luftwaffe," *Wehrwissenschaftliche Rundschau* 16, no. 1 (January 1966): 553.

101. Feldflugchef no. 548, 31 August 1916, MKr 1405, BKA.

102. Ludwig Wurtzbacher, "Die Versorgung des Heers mit Waffen und Munition," in Max Schwarte, ed., *Der Weltkampf um Ehre und Recht*, 6:115.

103. Morrow, *German Air Power*, 63–65.

104. Ibid., 56–59.

105. Ibid., 65, 75. Gerald D. Feldman, *Army, Industry, and Labor in Germany, 1914–1918*, 126.

106. Morrow, *German Air Power*, 75.

107. Ibid., 61–62. Grosz, "Albatros," passim.

108. H. H. Suplee, "Plywood in Aeroplane Construction," *Aerial Age Weekly*, 20 January 1919, pp. 945–47, 961. *Aviation and Aeronautical Engineering* 5, no. 2 (15 August 1918): 102.

109. Following material on Junkers from his diaries and correspondence with Prussian War Ministry in the Junkers Papers, Deutsches Museum.

110. The following material on engine production is from Kyrill von Gersdorff and Kurt Grassmann, *Flugmotoren und Strahltriebwerke*, 24–38. Bullinger, "Kriegserfahrungen in der Motorenabteilung der Flugzeugmeisterei," Part IV, p. 2 and app. chart 42. J. A. Gilles, *Flugmotoren 1910 bis 1918*, 72–74.

111. Raleigh and Jones, *War in the Air*, 2:147, 157, 165, 167.

112. Maurice Baring, *Flying Corps Headquarters, 1914–1918*, 139. Raleigh and Jones, *War in the Air*, 2:176–86.

113. Cooper, *Birth of Independent Air Power*, 77.

114. Ibid., 78. Aeroplane Wastage in 2nd Quarter 1916, 6 July 1916, AIR 1/878/204/5/586, PRO.

115. Cooper, *Birth of Independent Air Power* 76–77. Trenchard to Brancker, 13 March 1916, MFC 76/1/5, TP, RAFM.

116. Trenchard to Brancker, 7 and 9 March 1916; Brancker to Trenchard, 8 and 18 March and 19 April 1916; MFC 76/1/5, TP, RAFM. CRFC 2047G Trenchard to DMA, 4 April 1916; CRFC 2047G Trenchard to DAO, 15 May 1916; Maj. D. Powell no. 87/7094, 23 March 1916; AIR 1/997/204/5/1241, PRO.

117. Trenchard to Brancker, 14, 24, and 27 March 1916; Brancker to Trenchard, 22 March 1916; MFC 76/1/5, TP, RAFM.

118. Air Board minutes, 4th meeting, 29 May 1916, AHB, MD.

119. Maj. D. Powell no. 87/7094, 23 March 1916, AIR 1/997/204/5/1241, PRO.

120. John Laffin, *Swifter than Eagles: The Biography of Marshal of the RAF Sir John Maitland Salmond*, 74–77.

121. Trenchard to Brancker, 25 March, 11 and 17 April 1916; Brancker to Trenchard, 11 and 22 April 1916; MFC 76/1/5, TP, RAFM.

122. Trenchard, "Short Notes on the Battle of the Somme 1 July–11 November 1916," MFC 76/1/4, TP, RAFM. Christopher Cole, ed., *Royal Flying Corps 1915–1916*, 176–335 passim.

123. Trenchard, 2 July 1916, MFC 76/1/7, TP, RAFM. Cole, *Royal Flying Corps*, 176, 189.

124. Alan Bott, *An Airman's Outings with the RFC, June–December 1916*, 215.

125. Cross, *The Bombers*, 31–2.

126. Sir Philip Joubert de la Ferté, *The Fated Sky. An Autobiography*, 59. Basil Collier, *Leader of the Few. The Authorized Biography of Air Chief Marshal the Lord Dowding of Bentley Priory*, 105–20. Frank D. Tredrey, *Pioneer Pilot: The Great Smith Barry Who Taught the World to Fly*, 35. Sholto Douglas with Robert Wright, *Combat and Command*, 113.

127. Cecil Lewis, *Sagittarius Rising*, 52, 58, 75, 121–22, 138.

128. *Flight* 8, no. 5 (3 February 1916): 97; ibid., no. 33 (17 August 1916): 705–6.

129. Tyrrel M. Hawker, *Hawker, VC*, 182.

130. Peter H. Liddle, *The Airman's War 1914–18*, 47.

131. Interrogation, AIR 1/1/4/26/1, PRO.

132. Trenchard to Brancker, 9 September 1916, MFC 76/1/7; Trenchard to Robertson, 30 September 1916, MFC 76/1/8; TP, RAFM.

133. MFC 76/1/4, TP, RAFM.

134. Trenchard, "Short Notes."

135. Douglas, *Combat and Command*, 50.

136. Hawker, *Hawker, VC*, 128–87 passim. Liddle, *Airman's War*, 40–47.

137. Norman Franks, *Aircraft versus Aircraft: The Illustrated Story of Fighter Pilot Combat since 1914*, 27.

138. Chaz Bowyer, *Albert Ball, VC*, 20, 51, 53, 80.

139. Franks, *Aircraft*, 26–27.

140. Bowyer, *Ball*, 83.

141. Ibid., 86.

142. Cole, *Royal Flying Corps*, 312.

143. Trenchard, "Short Notes."

144. Raleigh and Jones, *War in the Air*, 3: 393–99.

145. Air Board minutes, 27th meeting, 26 October 1916; 30th meeting, 11 December 1916, AHB, MD.

146. 10 October 1916, AIR 1/997/204/5/1241, PRO.

147. Trenchard to Brancker, 24 November 1916, MFC 76/1/8, TP, RAFM.

148. Tredrey, *Pioneer Pilot*, 53–55.

149. Trenchard CRFC 2047G to DAO, 8 December 1916, AIR 1/997/204/5/1241, PRO.

150. John C. Slessor, *The Central Blue: Recollections and Reflections*, 643–55. Geoffrey Norris, *The Royal Flying Corps: A History*, 126, 132.

151. Robin Higham, *The British Rigid Airship, 1908–1931: A Study in Weapons Policy*, 11, 116, 121–22. Sir Alfred Pugsley, "Airships," *A Century of British Aeronautics* 70 (January 1966): 46–47. Guy Hartcup, *The Achievement of the Airship* (London, 1974), 117.

152. Neville Jones, *The Origins of Strategic Bombing: A Study of the Development of British Air Strategic Thought up to 1918*, 119, 124, chaps 3 and 4, to 126 passim.

153. Barry D. Powers, *Strategy without Slide-Rule: British Air Strategy 1914–1939*, 49. Raleigh and Jones, *War in the Air*, 3:244.

154. S. W. Roskill, ed., *Documents Relating to the Naval Air Service*, 1:269.

155. *Flight* 8, no. 8 (24 February 1916): 149–52.

156. Ibid., no. 13 (30 March 1916): 257.

157. *Aeroplane* 10, no. 8 (23 August 1916): 542.

158. 28 March 1916, MFC 76/1/5, TP, RAFM.

159. 3 April 1916, MFC 76/1/76; Trenchard to Brancker, 31 March 1916, MFC 76/1/5, TP, RAFM.

160. Henderson to Trenchard, 20 April 1916, MFC 76/1/76, TP, RAFM.

161. Roskill, *Documents*, 1:286–90.

162. Ibid., 293, 300.

163. Ibid., 293, 307–8.

164. Jones, *Strategic Bombing*, 85–89. Roskill, *Documents*, 319–35. JWAC 3, 7, and 9, AIR 1/2319/223/26-7, PRO.

165. Raleigh and Jones, *War in the Air*, 3:269–70.

166. *Flight* 8, no. 16 (20 April 1916): 325–26, 337–38.

167. Raleigh and Jones, *War in the Air*, 3:269. Cooper, *Birth of Independent Air Power*, 47–53.

168. Brancker to Trenchard, 13 April 1916; Trenchard to Brancker, 14 April 1916; MFC 76/1/5, TP, RAFM.

169. *Flight* 8, no. 18 (4 May 1916): 378.

170. Air Board minutes, 14th meeting, 26 June 1916, AHB, MD.

171. W. J. Reader, *Architect of Air Power: The Life of the First Viscount Weir of Eastwood 1877–1959*, 57.

172. Air Board minutes, 22nd meeting, 24 August 1916, AHB, MD.

173. Lord Curzon's "Report of the Proceedings of the Air Board, 1916," 23 October 1916; Balfour's reply, 6 November 1916; CAS Archives AIR 8/2, AHB, MD.

174. Air Board minutes, 26th meeting, 24 October 1916; 28th meeting, 1 November 1916; 29th meeting, 22 November 1916; 31st meeting, 30 December 1916; AHB, MD.

175. Raleigh and Jones, *War in the Air*, 3:277.

176. *Flight* 8, no. 44 (2 November 1916): 947–48.

177. Powers, *Strategy without Slide-Rule*, 46.

178. Cooper, *Birth of Independent Air Power*, 57–58.

179. Raleigh and Jones, *War in the Air*, 3:273.

180. Brancker to Trenchard, 14 June 1916, MFC 76/1/6, TP, RAFM.

181. Last Words on the Air Board Controversy, 15 November 1916, AIR 8/2, AHB, MD.

182. Roskill, *Documents*, 1:445–46.

183. Raleigh and Jones, *War in the Air*, 3:281–84. Reader, *Architect of Air Power*, 57–58.

184. *Flight* 8, no. 28 (13 July 1916): 179–80.

185. Final Report of the Committee on the Administration and Command of the RFC, Cmd. 8194, AIR 1/2405/303/4/5, PRO. Cooper, *Birth of Independent Air Power*, 43–45. *Flight* 8, no. 21 (25 May 1916): 431–32; ibid., no. 22 (1 June 1916), 461–71; ibid., no. 26 (29 June 1916): 551–56; ibid., no. 28 (13 July 1916): 587–90.

186. Report of the Committee on the Royal Aircraft Factory, 13 May 1916, AIR 1/2405/303/4/6, PRO.

187. *Flight* 8, no. 39 (28 September 1916): 826.

188. Trenchard to Henderson, 29 October and 1 November 1916, MFC 76/1/76, TP, RAFM. Cooper, *Birth of Independent Air Power*, 36, 78–79.

189. Air Board minutes, 14th meeting, 26 June 1916, AHB, MD.

190. Christopher Addison, *Politics from Within, 1911–1918*, 2:88.

191. Air Board minutes, 8th meeting, 7 June 1916, AHB, MD.

192. Ibid.

193. AIR 1/630/17/122/23, PRO. Air Board minutes, 16th meeting, 4 July 1916, AHB, MD.

194. Harald Penrose, *British Aviation: The Great War and Armistice 1915–1919*, 138–39, 142.

195. Air Board minutes, 14th meeting, 26 June 1916, 15th meeting, 30 June 1916; AHB, MD. Lord Sydenham memoranda in AIR 1/2306/215/17, PRO.

196. Ibid.

197. Air Board minutes, 8th meeting, 7 June 1916, AHB, MD. Johnson before the Air Board, 7 June 1916, AIR 1/2306/215/16, PRO.

198. Bruce Robertson, *Sopwith—The Man and His Aircraft*, 59. Penrose, *Great War*, 176, 182, 196.

199. Penrose, *Great War*, 165–68, 197.

200. Petr Dmitrievich Duz, *History of Aeronautics and Aviation in the USSR: The First World War Period (1914–1918)*, 307. Golovine, 150–51. Jones in Higham & Kipp, 22.

201. Duz, *Aeronautics and Aviation in the USSR*, 29–30. Christine Holden, "The View from Furshstadtskaya Street: American Military Attaches' Reports on Russian Aeronautics," 24–29.

202. Jones in Higham & Kipp, 22, 24. Duz, *Aeronautics and Aviation in the USSR*, 24, 116, 139–42.

203. K. N. Finne, *Igor Sikorsky: The Russian Years*, 123–38.

204. Jones in Higham & Kipp, 23.

205. Duz, *Aeronautics and Aviation in the USSR*, 115.

206. Von Hardesty, "Aeronautics Comes to Russia: The Early Years, 1908–1918," 19–20.

207. Duz, *Aeronautics and Aviation in the USSR*, 261, 371–72. Von Hard-

esty, Introduction to *Gatchina Days: Reminiscences of a Russian Pilot*, by Alexander Riaboff, 16–19.

208. Duz, *Aeronautics and Aviation in the USSR*, 61, 291. Jones in Higham & Kipp, 22, 24.

209. Duz, *Aeronautics and Aviation in the USSR*, 307.

210. Ibid., 93–102.

211. Jones in Higham & Kipp, 21. Duz, *Aeronautics and Aviation in the USSR*, 307, 319–20.

212. Duz, *Aeronautics and Aviation in the USSR*, 320, 332–39.

213. Ibid., 402, 436, 451–52.

214. Ibid., 510–11, 544.

215. Ernst Peter, *Die k.u.k. Luftschiffer- und Fliegertruppe Österreich-Hungarens, 1794–1919*, 170–83.

216. Morrow, *German Air Power*, 116.

217. Peter Schupita, *Die k.u.k. Seeflieger: Chronik und Documentation der österreichisch-ungarischen Marineluftwaffe 1911–1918*, 178–94.

218. See chapters on each aviator in Martin O'Connor, *Air Aces of the Austro-Hungarian Empire, 1914–1918*.

219. Material in the following paragraphs is from Morrow, *German Air Power*, 171–73.

220. Schupita, *Die k.u.k. Seeflieger*, 117–21.

221. Unless otherwise noted, the material on Italy comes from Felice Porro, *La Guerra nell'aria*, 90–150 passim.

222. Francesco Baracca, *Memorie di guerra aerea: Documenti e testimonianze*, 75–8.

223. D'Annunzio, *Aviatore di guerra: Documenti e testimianze*, 94. Anthony Rhodes, *D'Annunzio*, 183.

224. H. H. Arnold, "Italian Aeronautical Status," 26 July 1916, Stencil no. 246, RG18, NA. Apostolo & Abate, 37.

225. Piero Vergnano, *Origin of Aviation in Italy, 1783–1918*, 90, 111–12, 123–24.

226. Frank J. Cappelluti, "The Life and Thought of Giulio Douhet," 113–19, 128, 136.

CHAPTER FIVE

1917

1. Rapport présenté à la Commission du Budget, 130 AP 6, DP, AN.

2. *Aeroplane* 13, no. 1 (2 January 1918): 11.

3. "L'Aéronautique militaire française pendant la Guerre de 1914–1918," vol. 2, "1917–1918," *Icare, revue de l'aviation française*, no. 88 (Printemps 1979): 17.

4. On aviation at the Chemin des Dames, see Patrick Facon, "L'aviation française au 'Chemin des Dames,' " *Aviation Magazine*, no. 805 (1 July 1981): 80–87.

5. Accounts in aviation files labeled C.A., 3e armée, 13e C.A., Aéron. 251, 17 April 1917, SHAA.

6. André P. Voisin, *La Doctrine de l'aviation française de combat au cours de la guerre (1915–1918)*, 20, 33.

7. Rapport, 28 June 1917, 130 AP 6, DP, AN.

8. Christienne et al., *Histoire de l'aviation*, 128.

9. Etats Numériques; Etats Mensuels; Tués, Blessés, Disparus; statistics in 130 AP 6, DP, AN.

10. Guy Pedroncini, *Pétain: Général en chef 1917–1918*, 41, 57.

11. "L'Aéronautique," 2:23.

12. Pedroncini, *Pétain*, 59.

13. Ibid., 81–82.

14. George Huisman, *Dans les coulisses de l'aviation 1914–1918: Pourquoi n'avons nous pas toujours garder le matrise des airs?*, 224–27.

15. Pétain to Président, Comité de Guerre, 2 December 1917, 130 AP 7, DP, AN.

16. Pedroncini, *Pétain*, 41–42.

17. Voisin, *Doctrine*, 70–73.

18. GQG Pétain to MdG, 25 August 1917, A14, SHAA.

19. GQG M.I., 2 and 16 June 1917; Commandant du Peuty 12 August 1917, A82, SHAA.

20. Commandant Brocard, 10 March 1917 report, AIR 1/1/14/25, PRO.

21. GQG Aéro Pétain to Sous-Secrétaire, 29 May and 3 July 1917, 14, SHAA.

22. "Guynemer et les Cigognes," *Icare, revue de l'aviation française*, no. 122 (1987): 64, 97–98.

23. Ibid., 45–47.

24. Ibid., 43–44, 87.

25. Ibid., 59.

26. Ibid., 135–37.

27. Ibid., 27.

28. Ibid., 27, 74, 87.

29. Ibid., 101, 149.

30. "L'Aéronautique," 2:29.

31. Georges Thénault, *L'Escadrille Lafayette (avril 1916–janvier 1918)*, 96–114 passim.

32. P. J. Carisella and James W. Ryan, *The Black Swallow of Death*, passim.

33. "L'Aéronautique," 2:43–44.

34. Lieutenant Marc, *Notes d'un pilote disparu (1916–1917)* (Notes of a Lost Pilot), [Jean Béraud Villars], 165–74, 212–13.

35. Jean-Pierre Dournel, "L'image de l'aviateur français en 1914–1918," *RHA*, 1975, no. 4: 78.

36. Ibid., 1976, no. 1: 95, 116–22.

37. Villars, *Notes* (American translation of Marc, *Notes*), 211–21.

38. "L'Aéronautique," 2:19.

39. 3e armée, 13e corps d'armée, 3&7 June 1917, C.A., SHAA.

40. Thénault, *Lafayette*, 103.

41. Christienne et al., *Histoire de l'aviation*, 114–18.

42. Philippe Bernard, "A propos de la stratégie aérienne pendant la Première Guerre Mondiale: Mythes et réalités," *RHMC* 16 (1969): 363.

43. Ibid., 363–64.

44. AEF account of the aviation plan of bombardment, 18 November 1917, AIR 1/1976/204/273/40, PRO.

45. George Kent Williams, "Statistics and Strategic Bombardment: Operations and Records of the British Long Range Bombing Force during World War I and Their Implications for the Development of the Post-War Royal Air Force, 1917–1923," 94–98, 101–2. Pedroncini, *Pétain*, 58. Castelnau GAE HQ Aerons. S.C. no. 3954, 18 October 1917, AIR 1/1976/204/273/40, PRO.

46. *L'Aéronautique pendant la Guerre Mondiale*, 412–20.

47. P. E. Flandin, Rapport . . . l'Aéronautique, 17 January 1917, 130 AP 9, DP, AN.

48. Albert Etévé, *La Victoire des cocardes*, 203–4.

49. Ibid., 225.

50. Georges Bonnefous, *Histoire politique de la Troisième République*, vol. 2, *La Grande Guerre (1914–1918)*, 225.

51. "L'Aéronautique," 2:10. Christienne et al., *Histoire de l'aviation*, 141; *Aeroplane* 12, no. 12 (21 March 1917); Etévé, *Victoire*, 225–26.

52. Gen. Guillemin, DGAM 5594 2/12 to Président, Comité de Guerre, 20 March 1917, A14, SHAA.

53. Jacques Mortane, *Histoire illustrée de la guerre aérienne (1914–1918)*, 105. Pedroncini, *Pétain*, 56. Etévé, *Victoire*, 228.

54. Etévé, *Victoire*, 230–33, 235–36.

55. Emmanuel Chadeau, *L'Industrie aéronautique en France 1900–1950: De Blériot à Dassault*, 137.

56. Chadeau, "État, entreprise et developpement économique: L'Industrie aéronautique en France (1900–1940)," 430–34. Chadeau, *L'Industrie*, 99–116, 137–40.

57. Rapport . . . LeLong. "Au Sujet des Prix des Moteurs d'Aviation," 16 June 1917 in Document 3689.3/12 of 13 March 1918; Vincent no. 05739 3/12 to Président, 7 June 1917; 1A4, SHAA.

58. *L'Aéronautique*, 385–412.

59. Sous-Secrétaire, 25 June 1917; GQG Aero note, 25 June 1917; A14, SHAA.

60. Dumesnil, Rapport au commission du Budget, 28 June 1917, 130 AP 8, DP, AN.

61. Vincent to Président, 7 July 1917; parliamentary reporters to Président, 12 July 1917, 130 AP 9, DP, AN. Vincent reply to Pétain no. 27.428, 29 June 1917, and 34200 S.I.-O/12 to CinC, 11 July 1917, A14, SHAA.

62. Vincent 11469 2/12 to CinC, 16 June 1917 in answer to letter 27.705, 29 May 1917, A14; GQG Duval to SS, 22 July 1917, A78; GQG 13 August 1917, A14; GQG Aero to SS, 16 August 1917, A82; SHAA.

63. MdG to SS, 14 August 1917; SS no. 614/S, 5 September 1917 to MdG, 130 AP 6, DP, AN.

64. Christienne et al., *Histoire de l'aviation*, 142–43. "L'Aéronautique," 2:11.

65. Mortane, *Histoire illustrée*, 106. GQG, 7 October 1917, A81, SHAA; SS, 130 AP 9, DP, AN; analyse de la note, 6 October 1917, A14, SHAA.

66. MdG no. 81 SCG, 8 October 1917, 130 AP 6, DP, AN; Dumesnil no. 11136.4.C/12 to CinC, 20 October 1917, A14, SHAA.

67. GQG Aero GCC to SS, 22/10/17, 130 AP 7, DP, AN. CinC (general staff aero service) no. 30288 to SS, 25 October 1917, A14, SHAA.

68. GQG Aero note for CinC, 5 November 1917, A14, SHAA.

69. Dumesnil no. 2815 2/12 to CinC Pétain, 10/11/17, 130 AP 7, DP, AN; also in A14, SHAA.

70. SFA no. 252, 3 November 1917, A86, SHAA.

71. Huisman, *Coulisses*, 259. Chadeau, *État*, 382.

72. Pétain to President, CdG, MdG, 2 December 1917, 130 AP 7, DP, AN.

73. GQG Pétain no. 23887 to MdG, 21 November 1917; GQG Aéron Duval to Pétain no. 2237, 21 November 1917; 130 AP 7, DP, AN.

74. Chadeau, *État*, 347. *L'Aéronautique*, 385–412.

75. Dumesnil no. 12.950 4/12 to MdG, 6 December 1917; Dumesnil to Pétain, 21 December 1917; 130 AP 7, PD, AN. Dumesnil to Pétain, no. 13150 4C/12, 10 December and no. 26478 2/12, December 1917, A14, SHAA.

76. Etévé, *Victoire*, 242–45.

77. D'Aubigny, Rapport . . . Aéronautique, 3 May 1918, in Rapport sur les Travaux de le Commission de l'Armée, no. 6999 (Paris, 1919), 68–74, SHAA.

78. MdA CFAS, 21 December 1917, A75, SHAA.

79. Gilbert Hatry, *Renault, usine de guerre 1914–1918*, 123.

80. *L'Aéronautique*, 394, 398.

81. James Laux, "Gnome et Rhône: Une firme de moteurs d'avion durant la Grande Guerre," 179–80.

82. Patrick Fridenson, *Histoire des usines Renault*, 1:107.

83. Peter Mead, *The Eye in the Air: History of Air Observation and Reconnaissance for the Army 1785–1948*, 94–95.

84. Morrow, *German Air Power*, 90.

85. Ibid., 91.

86. Walter Raleigh and H. A. Jones, *The War in the Air*, 3:334–64.

87. Ibid., 4:114–18, 142–214.

88. Alex Imrie, *Pictorial History of the German Army Air Service, 1914–1918*, 45, 47.

89. Krausser in Georg P. Neumann, ed., *In der Luft unbesiegt*, 79–91.

90. Morrow, *German Air Power*, 109.

91. Ludwig Gengler, *Rudolf Berthold*, 73, 77, 81.

92. J. C. Nerney, "The Battle of Cambrai," passim, quotes are on 42, 49, AIR 1/678/21/13/1942, PRO.

93. Oskar Bechtel in Neumann, *Unbesiegt*, 166–75.

94. Interrogation of observation officer, 21 January 1917, AIR 1/1/4/26/1, PRO.

95. Peter Gray and Owen Thetford, *German Aircraft of the First World War*, 80, 177, 203.

96. William A. Bishop, *Winged Warfare*, 133.

97. Interrogations, 30 April and 1 May, 1917, AIR 1/1/4/26/1, PRO.

98. On the raids on Britain, see Raymond H. Fredette, *The Sky on Fire: The First Battle of Britain 1917–1918*; H. G. Castle, *Fire over England: The German Air Raids in World War I*; Christopher Cole and E. F. Cheesman, *The Air Defense of Great Britain 1914–1918*.

99. On the airship raids, see Douglas H. Robinson, *Giants in the Sky: A History of the Rigid Airship*, 127–38.

100. The following discussion of German mobilization to the topic of engines is based on Morrow, *German Air Power*, 73–120.

101. J. A. Gilles, *Flugmotoren 1910 bis 1918*, 87. Kyrill von Gersdorff and Kurt Grassmann, *Flugmotoren und Strahltriebwerke*, 34.

102. Bullinger, "Kriegserfahrungen," Bericht VI, "Erzeugung der Flugmotoren," 2–5, GC.

103. Gersdorff and Grassmann, *Flugmotoren*, 12–38 passim.

104. Ibid., 38, 40.

105. Bullinger, VI, 5–6.

106. Memorandum, "Fighting in the Air," Raleigh and Jones, *War in the Air*, 3:339, app. XI.

107. Trenchard, 6 and 8 April 1917, MFC 76/1/76, TP, RAFM.

108. Cooper, *Birth of Independent Air Power*, 81.

109. Ibid., 76. S. F. Wise, *Canadian Airmen and the First World War: The Official History of the Royal Canadian Air Force*, 407. J. C. Nerney, "Development of Aircraft Production," AIR 1/678/21/13/2138, PRO.

110. Brancker to Trenchard, 8 February 1917, MFC 76/1/10; Brancker to Trenchard, 29 March 1917, MFC 76/1/11; TP, RAFM.

111. Haig GHQ no. O.B./1826 to Secretary, W.O., 18 May 1917, AIR 1/2267/209/70/34, PRO.

112. Cooper, *Birth of Independent Air Power*, 80.

113. Raleigh and Jones, *War in the Air*, 4:114–18. Mead, *Eye in the Air*, 89–90, 95. Cooper, *Birth of Independent Air Power*, 75.

114. Mead, *Eye in the Air*, 90–1.

115. "Future Air Organization . . . ," 12 October 1917, MFC 76/1/4.

116. Sholto Douglas, with Robert Wright, *Combat and Command*, 176.

117. J. C. Nerney, "Expansion and Development of the Air Services, 1917–1918," 13, AIR 1/678/21/13/2100, PRO.

118. Wise, *Canadian Airmen*, 427–38.

119. Haig no. O.B./1826/E, 20 November 1917, AIR 1/2267/209/70/34, PRO.

120. Nerney, "Cambrai," AIR 1/678/21/13/1942, PRO.

121. AIR 1/522/16/12/5, PRO.

122. Mead, *Eye in the Air*, 94–97.

123. Douglas, *Combat and Command*, 122–46. Harold Balfour, *An Airman Marches: Early Flying Adventures, 1914–1923*, 77, 85. Arthur Gould Lee, *No Parachute: A Fighter Pilot in World War I*, 218. Arthur Gould Lee, *Open Cockpit: A Pilot of the Royal Flying Corps*, 91–92.

124. Raymond Collishaw, with R. V. Dodds, *Air Command: A Fighter Pilot's Story*, 90, 117.

125. Norman MacMillan, *Into the Blue*, 31–48. Lee, *Parachute*, 4.

126. John Laffin, *Swifter than Eagles: The Biography of Marshal of the RAF Sir John Maitland Salmond*, 77–81. Peter H. Liddle, *The Airman's War 1914–18*, 73–79.

127. Lee, *Parachute*, 7.

128. Liddle, *Airman's War*, 90. Penrose, *Great War*, 271. *Flight* 9, no. 35 (30 August 1917), 949, 972. *Aeroplane* 13, no. 26 (26 December) 1929.

129. Balfour, *Airman*, 77, 83, 95.

130. Ibid., 77. Frederick Oughton and Vernon Smyth, *Ace with One Eye: The Life and Combats of Maj. Edward Mannock*, 159. William A. Bishop, *Winged Warfare*, 141. Macmillan, *Blue*, 25.

131. Liddle, *Airman's War*, 64–69.

132. On Mannock, see Edward Mannock, *The Personal Diary of Maj. Edward "Mick" Mannock*. Oughton and Smyth, *Ace*.

133. Chaz Bowyer, *Albert Ball, VC*, 138.

134. Maurice Baring, *Flying Corps Headquarters, 1914–1918*, 221.

135. Ibid., 254–55. Cecil Lewis, *Sagittarius Rising*, 168–69, 186–88.

136. Air Board meeting, 14 December 1917.

137. Liddle, *Airman's War*, 63.

138. Laffin, *Swifter than Eagles*, 97.

139. J. C. Nerney, "Summary of Notes on Training RFC and RAF 1918," 11–12, AIR 1/678/21/13/2084, PRO.

140. *Flight* 9, no. 16 (19 April 1917).

141. *Aeroplane* 12, no. 22 (30 May 1917).

142. Lee, *Cockpit*, 43, 52–53.

143. James T. B. McCudden, *Flying Fury*, 236.

144. Balfour, *Airman*, 95.

145. Macmillan, *Into the Blue*, 102.

146. Collishaw, *Air Command*, 107–8.

147. Trenchard CRFC 2160 (G), 5 October 1917, AIR 1/522/16/12/5, PRO.

148. Trenchard to Brancker, 9 February 1917, MFC 76/1/10, TP, RAFM.

149. Douglas, *Combat and Command*, 133, 172.

150. Lee, *Cockpit*, 33–35.

151. Balfour, *Airman*, 66–84. Trenchard to Brancker, 9 and 21 February 1917, MFC 76/1/10, TP, RAFM. Macmillan, *Into the Blue*, 65, 75–77, 95–97.

152. Brancker to Trenchard, 28 August 1917; Trenchard to Brancker, 29 August 1917; MFC 76/1/16, TP, RAFM.

153. Douglas, *Combat and Command*, 189–90.

154. W. Geoffrey Moore, *Early Bird*, 133, 137, 141. Lee, *Parachute*, 160. Norman Macmillan, "British Aircraft Design," *A Century of British Aeronautics*, 125.

155. Neville Jones, *The Origins of Strategic Bombing: A Study of the Development of British Air Strategic Thought up to 1918*, 124.

156. Williams, "Statistics and Strategic Bombardment," 56.

157. Ibid., 45–64.

158. Wise, *Canadian Airmen*, 282–86.

159. War Cabinet 268, extract meeting 8 November 1917, AIR 1/2267/209/70/29, PRO.

160. J. C. Nerney, "Aircraft Production," 51–60, AIR 1/678/21/13/2138, PRO.

161. Williams, "Statistics and Strategic Bombardment," 186.

162. C. F. Snowden Gamble, *The Story of a North Sea Air Station*, 159.

163. Richard Knott, *The American Flying Boat: An Illustrated History*, 22–33. *Flight* 9 (22 November 1917): 1240.

164. S. W. Roskill, ed., *Documents Relating to the Naval Air Service*, 1:185, 532–33 and 193, 547.

165. Ibid.

166. F. M. Cutlack, *The Australian Flying Corps in the Western and Eastern Theatres of War 1914–1918*, 73.

167. G. P. Bulman, "I ought to have been sacked," 64.

168. *Aeroplane* 13, no. 7 (15 August 1917): 485–86.

169. Barry D. Powers, *Strategy without Slide-Rule: British Air Strategy 1914–1939*, 58, 63, 85–86, 96.

170. MFC76/1/1, TP, RAFM.

171. Nerney, "Aircraft Production," 79–83, AIR 1/678/21/13/2138; Weir in app. 2 to Smuts memorandum "Air Preparations and Offensives," 18 September 1917, AIR 1/719/35/6, PRO.

172. Nerney, "Aircraft Production," 87–88, AIR 1/678/21/13/2138; Nerney, "Expansion and Development of the Air Services, 1917–1918," AIR 1/678/21/13/2100; PRO.

173. Mark Kerr, *Land, Sea, and Air: Reminiscences of Mark Kerr*, 287–92.

174. Cooper, *Birth of Independent Air Power*, 115–17. Jones, *Strategic Bombing*, 152–63. Sir Maurice Dean, *The Royal Air Force and Two World Wars*, 26.

175. Cooper, *Birth of Independent Air Power*, 109–11.

176. H. Montgomery Hyde, *British Air Policy between the War, 1918–1939*, 34.

177. *United States Military Intelligence 1917–1927* 2:14.

178. Cooper, *Birth of Independent Air Power*, 99–107, 119–20.

179. David Divine, *The Broken Wing: A Study in the British Exercise of Air Power*, 104–24.

180. Powers, *Strategy without Slide-Rule*, 90–100.

181. Ministry of Munitions, *History of the Ministry of Munitions*, 12, pt. 1:60–61.

182. W. J. Reader, *Architect of Air Power: The Life of the First Viscount Weir of Eastwood 1877–1959*, 58.

183. Ministry of Munitions, *History*, 4:44; ibid., 7:35. Nerney, "Aircraft Production," 8–9, AIR 1/678/21/13/2138, PRO. *Flight* 9, no. 14 (5 April 1917): 311, 314; ibid., no. 29 (19 July 1917): 726; ibid., no. 38 (30 August 1917): 882.

184. Churchill, *Churchill*, 4:61.

185. Reader, *Architect*, 63. Ministry of Munitions, *History*, 12, pt. 1:88.

186. Cooper, *Birth of Independent Air Power*, 93. Raleigh and Jones, *War in the Air*, 6:84–85. Dept. of Aero Supplies, report no. 24, 18 August 1917, AIR 1/500/15/331/5, PRO. Ministry of Munitions, *History*, 12, pt. 1:183.

187. Statistics File, 47, AIR 1/686/21/13/2248, PRO.

188. Nerney, "Aircraft Production," 12–14, AIR 1/678/21/13/2186; reports of Dept of Aero Supplies, 29 June 1917; no. 27, 8 September 1917; no. 29, 22 September 1917; AIR 1/500/15/331/5, PRO.

189. Reader, *Architect*, 61. Brancker to Trenchard, 9 and 18 May 1917, MFC 76/1/13, TP, RAFM. Penrose, *Great War*, 333; Ministry of Munitions, *History*, 12, pt. 1:85. *Flight* 9, no. 49 (6 December 1917): 1269–72; ibid., no. 50 (13 December 1917): 1297–98; ibid., no. 51 (20 December 1917): 1326–28; ibid., no. 52 (27 December 1917): 1359–60. *Military Intelligence*, 2:21.

190. Ministry of Munitions, *History*, 12, pt. 1:62.

191. Air Board to War Cabinet, 17 April 1917, AIR 1/522/16/12/5, PRO.

192. Nerney, "Aircraft Production," 12, 17, 18, AIR 1/678/21/13/2138, PRO. Air Board minutes, 32nd and 33rd meetings, January 1917, AHB, MD.

193. Air Board minutes, 42nd meeting, 24 January 1917; 35th meeting, 10 January 1917; 48th meeting, 7 February 1917; AHB, MD. Nerney, "Aircraft

Production," 19–21, AIR 1/678/21/13/2138, PRO. Cooper, *Birth of Independent Air Power*, 88–89.

194. Air Board minutes, 101st meeting, 15 June 1917; 103rd meeting, 20 June 1917; 117th meeting, 23 July 1917; AHB, MD.

195. Nerney, "Aircraft Production," 23–26, 28–30, AIR 1/678/21/13/2138, PRO. Cooper, *Birth of Independent Air Power*, 91.

196. Air Board, 34th meeting, 8 January 1917; 113th meeting, 11 July 1917; AHB, MD. Nerney, "Aircraft Production," 102–4. Penrose, *Great War*, 227–28, 230.

197. Herschel Smith, *A History of Aircraft Piston Engines*, 34–35.

198. Nerney, "Aircraft Production," 104–6.

199. Bulman, "I ought to have been sacked," 79–81.

200. Brancker to Trenchard, 29 July 1917, MFC 76/1/17, TP, RAFM. Brooke-Popham to Pitcher, 13 July 1917, Reports on British machines, AIR 1/1/4/17, PRO.

201. Progress and Allocation Committee, Directorate of Aircraft Equipment, report no. 256, 21 December 1917; no. 180, 24 September 1917; no. 175, 18 September 1917; no. 174, 17 September 1917; no. 141, 9 August 1917; AIR 1/2303/215/13, PRO. Trenchard to Brancker, 11 August 1917, MFC 76/1/16, TP, RAFM. Nerney, "Aircraft Production," 26–27. Hilary St. G. Saunders, *Per Ardua: The Rise of British Air Power 1911–1939*, 215.

202. Brooke-Popham to Pitcher, 13 September 1917, AIR 1/1/4/17, PRO.

203. Nerney, "Aircraft Production," quote on 119, 110–22. Air Board minutes, 163rd meeting, 9 November 1917; 167th meeting, 21 November 1917; 168th meeting, 22 November 1917; 172nd meeting, 29 November 1917; AHB, MD.

204. Progress and Allocation Committee, Directorate of Aircraft Equipment, reports no. 112, 4 July 1917; no. 151, 21 August 1917; no. 159, 30 August 1917; no. 182, 14 September 1917; AIR 1/2303/215/13, PRO.

205. Air Board, minutes, 81st meeting, 27 April 1917; 83rd meeting, 2 May 1917; AHB, MD.

206. Air Board minutes, 68th meeting, 26 March 1917; 127th meeting, 17 August 1917; 129th meeting, 22 August 1917; 130th meeting, 27 August 1917; 132nd meeting, 31 August 1917; AHB, MD.

207. Nerney, "Aircraft Production," 120–21, 127. Raleigh and Jones, *War in the Air*, 6:51.

208. Raleigh and Jones, *War in the Air*, 6:98–99.

209. Jones in Higham and Kipp, 20–5.

210. K. N. Finne, *Igor Sikorsky: The Russian Years*, 145–50.

211. Kipp in Higham and Kipp, 142–3.

212. Petr Dmitrievich Duz, *History of Aeronautics and Aviation in the USSR: The First World War Period (1914–1918)*, 524, 527, 688.

213. Jones in Higham and Kipp, 26–27.

214. Schupita, *Die k.u.k. Seeflieger*, 194–221.

215. The rest of the material on Austro-Hungarian aviation comes from Morrow, *German Air Power*, 173–77, 213.

216. Unless otherwise noted, material on the Italian air arm comes from Felice Porro, *La Guerra aerea*, 151–246 passim, and that on the industry from Piero Vergnano, *Origin of Aviation in Italy, 1783–1918*, passim.

217. Bolling Report, 15 August 1917; Bolling to Coffin, 15 August 1917, box. no. 33, file no. 452.1; Bolling to Coffin, 15 October 1917, Aircraft Board File 1015, box no. 35, file 452.1, RG 18, NA.

218. Report on Italian aviation by Commandant le Bon, September 1917, HQ RFC, AIR 1/1073/204/5/1652, PRO.

219. Reports on French and Italian aviation engines, September 1917, AIR 1/703/27/4/10, PRO. Material on the factories and standardization comes from Briggs, Bolling, and le Bon reports.

220. Frank J. Cappelluti, "The Life and Thought of Giulio Douhet," 138–45.

221. *Aeroplane* 13, no. 16 (17 October 1917): 1142.

222. Archibald D. Turnbull and Clifford L. Lord, *History of United States Naval Aviation*, 47–67.

223. Quoted in Alex Roland, *Model Research: The National Advisory Committee for Aeronautics 1915–1958*, 2 vols. (Washington: NASA, 1985) 1:35.

224. *Aviation and Aeronautical Engineering* 2, no. 5 (1 April 1918): 213, 223.

225. Adrian O. Van Wyen, *Naval Aviation in World War I*, 13.

226. R. M. McFarland, "The Foreign Missions to the U.S.," 21.7.19, 336.91C, RG 18, NA.

227. Maurer Maurer, ed., *The U.S. Air Service in World War I*, 1:51.

228. *Aviation and Aeronautical Engineering* 2, no. 9 (1 June 1918): 391; ibid., no. 10 (15 June 1918): 448. Robert F. Futrell, *Ideas, Concepts, Doctrine: A History of Basic Thinking in the United States Air Force, 1907–1964*, 1:19. Jacob A. Vander Meulen, "The American Aircraft Industry to World War II," 30.

229. Frederick Palmer, *Newton D. Baker: America at War*, 1:291.

230. Ibid., 289.

231. Ibid., 290.

232. Ibid., 291–92.

233. Ibid., 279.

234. Maurer, *U.S. Air Service*, 4:5.

235. Turnbull and Lord, *United States Aviation*, 105–10. Knott, *American Flying Boat*, 32–34. Van Wyen, *Naval Aviation*, 34.

236. *Aviation and Aeronautical Engineering* 2, no. 7 (1 May 1918): 309.

237. Vander Meulen, "American Aircraft Industry," 13.

238. Bureau of Aircraft Production, History of the Bolling Aeronautical Mission by R. M. McFarland, 29 October 1919, 334.8, RG 18, NA. Raynal Bolling, "A Lesson in Timing," *Airpower Historian* 7 (1960): 222–32.

239. Mrs. A. B. Gregg, Bureau of Aircraft Production, "History of the Spad," 452.1, RG 18, NA.

240. G. W. Mixter and H. H. Emmons, *United States Army Aircraft Production Facts*, 16.

241. Vander Meulen, "American Aircraft Industry," 54–58. Mrs. A. B. Gregg, Bureau of Aircraft Production, histories of the Spad and Bristol fighter, 452.1, RG 18, NA.

242. Mrs. A. B. Gregg, Bureau of Aircraft Production, History of Caproni biplane, 452.1, RG 18, NA.

243. Futrell, *Ideas*, 18–19.

244. James J. Hudson, *Hostile Skies: A Combat History of the American Air Service in World War I*, 51.

245. Lucien H. Thayer, *America's First Eagles: The Official History of the U.S. Air Service, A.E.F. (1917–1918)*, 48.

246. Maurer Maurer, "Flying with Fiorello. The U.S. Air Service in Italy 1917–1918," *Air Power Historian* 11 (October 1964): 113–18.

247. Futrell, *Ideas*, 20–21.

248. Edgar S. Gorrell, "An American Proposal for Strategic Bombing in World War I," *Air Power Historian* 5 (April 1958): 102–17.

249. Draft, *Seventy-five Year History of the USAF*, 28.

250. Williams, "American Aircraft Industry," 110, 115–16.

251. Manfred von Richthofen, *Der rote Kampfflieger*, 89.

252. Marc, *Notes*, 220, 187.

253. Richthofen, *Kampfflieger*, 89.

254. Trenchard to CIGS, 24 August 1917, AIR 1/522/16/12/5, PRO.

255. *Military Intelligence*, 1: 8–9.

256. Air Board minutes, 152nd meeting, 16 October 1917.

257. Richard P. Hallion, *Strike from the Sky: The History of Battlefield Air Attack, 1911–1945*, 14–28.

258. Weir to Bolling, 4 August 1917; Cowdray note for Sir Frederick Black; Northcliffe to Cowdray, 10 August 1917; Northcliffe cable to War Cabinet, 31 October 1917; War Cabinet G.T. 2508, 2 November 1917; AIR 1/26/15/124, PRO.

259. Huisman, *Coulisses*, 305–17.

260. Weir Memo G.T. 4552 War Cabinet Inter-Allied Aviation Committee, 13 May 1918, AIR 1/27/15/1/127, PRO.

CHAPTER SIX

1918

1. Henri Champomier in *La Guerre Aérienne*, no. 62, 17 January 1918, p. 162.

2. Vincent, "Aviation a-t-elle une Doctrine?" *La Guerre Aérienne*, no. 88 (14 February 1918), 218–19.

3. Guy Pedroncini, *Pétain: Général en chef 1917–1918*, 209.

4. Ibid., 209–10.

5. Ibid., 207–9, 291.

6. Ibid., 285, n. 1.

7. André P. Voisin, *La Doctrine de l'aviation française de combat au cours de la guerre (1915–1918)*, 111–12.

8. Ibid., 82.

9. "L'Aéronautique militaire française pendant la Guerre de 1914–1918," vol. 2 "1917, 1918," *Icare, revue de l'aviation française*, no 88 (Printemps 1979): 59–64.

10. Voisin, *Doctrine*, 126–27.

11. Report, 130 AP 9, DP, AN.

12. Pétain to Dumesnil, no. 27.190, 25 April 1918, 130 AP 7, DP, AN. Etévé, *Victoire*, 267.

13. Pedroncini, *Pétain*, 402.

14. Ibid., 408.

15. Duval to Pétain no. 2565, 130 AP 7, DP, AN.

16. Philippe Bernard, "A propos de la stratégie aérienne pendant la Première Guerre Mondiale: Mythes et réalités," RHMC 16 (1969): 374.

17. "L'Aéronautique," 2:64.

18. Report, 130 AP 9, DP, AN.

19. Pétain to Dumesnil, no. 37594, 24 August 1918, 130 AP 7, DP, AN.

20. Report, 130 AP 10, DP, AN.

21. *L'Aéronautique pendant la Guerre Mondiale*, 96.

22. Christienne et al., *Histoire de l'aviation*, 159.

23. Jean-Pierre Dournel, "L'image de l'aviateur français en 1914–1918," *RHA*, 1975, no. 4: 75, 77.

24. Ibid., 75, 77, 81; ibid., 1976, no. 1: 108, 110.

25. George Kent Williams, "Statistics and Strategic Bombardment: Operations and Records of the British Long-Range Bombing Force during World War I and Their Implications for the Development of the Post-War Royal Air Force, 1917–1923," 121–22.

26. Ibid., 104–11.

27. Ibid., 228–29. S. F. Wise, *Canadian Airmen and the First World War: The Official History of the Royal Canadian Air Force*, 308.

28. André Duvau, "BR 29, Souvenirs d'escadrille," SHAA, 1976, 24–29.

29. Pétain to Dumesnil, no. 27.190, 25 April 1918, 130 AP 7, DP, AN.

30. Pétain to Dumesnil, no. 30605, 24 May 1918, 130 AP 7, DP, AN.

31. Pétain to Dumesnil, no. 37594, 24 August 1918, 130 AP 7, DP, AN.

32. Dumesnil to Pétain, 17 September 1918, 130 AP 7, DP, AN.

33. Dumesnil to Pétain, 17 September 1918, 130 AP 7, DP, AN.

34. Etévé, *Victoire*, 268.

35. Daniel Vincent, "Aviation a-t-elle une Doctrine?" *La Guerre Aérienne*, no. 88, 14 February 1918, 218–19.

36. Jacques Mortane, "Parlons d'ailes: le ministère de l'aviation est nécessaire," *La Guerre Aérienne*, no. 88, 14 February 1918, 219.

37. Bernard, "Stratégie aérienne," 370.

38. Ibid., 370–71.

39. "L'Aéronautique," 2:104.

40. Jean Kerisel, *Albert Caquot 1881–1976: Créateur et précurseur*, passim.

41. "L'Aéronautique," 2:106. Etévé, *Victoire*, 261.

42. *La Guerre Aérienne*, no. 78, 9 May 1918, 410.

43. Ibid., no. 82, 6 June 1918, 474; ibid., no. 90, 1 August 1918, 612.

44. Ibid., no. 96, 12 September 1918, 699–700.

45. "Aéronautique," 2:110.

46. Loucheur, 18 April 1918, 130 AP 7, DP, AN.

47. Charts, carton 1A3, SHAA.

48. Rapport . . . sur marchés de moteurs Hispano-Suiza, no. 7070, 11e. législature. Session de 1919, 8 October 1919, 1A3, SHAA.

49. Dhé at MdG, DAM, 3043 3/12, 15 March 1919, 1A3, SHAA.

50. Etévé, *Victoire*, 255.

51. Emmanuel Chadeau, "État, entreprise et développement économique: L'Industrie aéronautique en France (1900–1940)," 438–45.

52. Ibid.

53. Report 2081–5, American attaché H. Barclay Warburton to chief of military intelligence, 31 July 1918, NA.

54. James Laux, "Gnome et Rhône: Une firme de moteurs d'avion durant la Grande Guerre," 182.

55. Ministère des Travaux Publics, Sous-Secrétaire d'Etat de l'Aéronautique et des Transports Aériens no. 02033, 13 February 1920, 1A3, SHAA.

56. Patrick Fridenson, *Histoire des usines Renault*, 1:107, 111.

57. SSdA, 1106.64/AP, 27 August 1918, 130 AP 10, DP, AN.

58. Dorand, "Note au sujet de l'avion Caproni," 20 February 1918, Dorand to SSdA, 5 October 1918, DP, MdA.

59. Christienne et al., *Histoire de l'aviation*, 175.

60. Chadeau, "État," 2, 347, 434. Etévé, *Victoire*, 253.

61. Reports in 130 AP 9, DP, AN.

62. Etévé, *Victoire*, 292–95. Patrick Fridenson, "Bilan des Forces Aériennes 1914–1918," *Forces Aériennes Françaises* 23, no. 252 (November 1968): 475.

63. Douglas H. Robinson, *Giants in the Sky: A History of the Rigid Airship,*, 138–39.

64. See Raymond H. Fredette, *The Sky on Fire: The First Battle of Britain, 1917–1918*, passim.

65. Alex Imrie, *Pictorial History of the German Army Air Service, 1914–1918*, 51.

66. Wise, *Canadian Airmen*, 502–3.

67. Ibid., 509–10.

68. Walter Raleigh and H. A. Jones, *The War in the Air*, 4:363–65.

69. Morrow, *German Air Power*, 120.

70. AIR 1/678/21/13/2137, PRO.

71. Morrow, *German Air Power*, 123.

72. F. W. Radenbach, *Weit im Rücken des Feindes* (Berlin 1938), 122–25, 190.

73. Morrow, *German Air Power*, 124.

74. Peter Kilduff, trans. and ed., *Germany's Last Knight of the Air* (London: Kimber, 1979), 107.

75. Wise, *Canadian Airmen*, 514–15.

76. Ludwig Gengler, *Rudolf Berthold*, 84.

77. Morrow, *German Air Power*, 113.

78. Bullinger, Bericht IV: "Die Betriebsstoffversorgung," 8–10, GC.

79. Hermann Göring in Georg P. Neumann, *In der Luft unbesiegt*, 132–34.

80. Raleigh and Jones, *War in the Air*, 6:445.

81. Morrow, *German Air Power*, 128.

82. Brooke-Popham to Brig. Gen. Huggins, Air Ministry, 17 August 1918, AIR 1/1/4/11, PRO.

83. Raleigh and Jones, *War in the Air*, 6:435–36, 442–44, 491.

84. Wise, *Canadian Airmen*, 553–54.

85. Imrie, *Pictorial History*, 58.

86. Kilduff, *Last Knight*, 144.

87. Ibid., 155, 177. "Portrait of a Pilot, Paul Strahle, Jasta 57," *Cross and Cockade* 12 (Fall 1971): 193–231.

88. Gengler, *Berthold*, 84–87.

89. Morrow, *German Air Power*, 134.

90. Ibid., 135.

91. Ibid.

92. Ibid., 119.

93. Ibid.

94. Ibid., 121.

95. Ibid., 122.

96. Ibid., 123.

97. Notizbücher, JP, DM.

98. Morrow, *German Air Power*, 125.

99. Ibid., 126.

100. Bullinger, Bericht VI. "Die Erzeugung der Flugmotoren im Kriege . . . ," 6–8, GC.

101. Morrow, 136–37.

102. Ibid., 137–38.

103. Kyrill von Gersdorff and Kurt Grassmann, *Flugmotoren und Strahltriebwerke*, 36–37.

104. J. A. Gilles, *Flugmotoren 1910 bis 1918*, 117, 119.

105. Bullinger, "Erfahrungen und Vorschläge für die Militärisierung eines Betriebes," 1–3, GC.

106. Bullinger, Bericht VI. "Die Erzeugung der Flugmotoren im Kriege . . . ," 11–13, also app. 46.

107. Ibid., app. 45.

108. Morrow, German Air Power, 139.

109. Ibid., 140.

110. Fr SSdA, bulletin no. 19, "Germany. A compilation of information . . . ," 18 January 1921, NASM.

111. Imrie, Pictorial History, 59.

112. "Employment of the RFC in defense," CRFC 1957/1.G, 16 January 1918, AIR 1/522/16/12/5, PRO.

113. Cooper, Birth of Independent Air Power, 144–45.

114. Wise, Canadian Airmen, 483, 486–88.

115. John Laffin, Swifter than Eagles: The Biography of Marshal of the RAF Sir John Maitland Salmond, 98–105, 116.

116. Raleigh and Jones, War in the Air, 4:283, 316, 359.

117. Wise, Canadian Airmen, 499–510.

118. Air Ministry to Air Council, 57/Airc/1(MO4), AIR 1/2267/209/70/34, PRO.

119. Brereton Greenhous, "Close Support Aircraft in World War I: The Counter Anti-Tank Role," Aerospace Historian 21 (June 1974): 87–93.

120. Wise, Canadian Airmen, 518–41. See also John C. Slessor, Air Power and Armies, 131, 184.

121. Cooper, Birth of Independent Air Power, 141–51. See also Wise, Canadian Airmen, 479–576.

122. Wise, Canadian Airmen, 460.

123. Ibid., 455–78.

124. Slessor, Air Power, 10–13, 44, 102.

125. Ira Jones, Tiger Squadron: The Story of 74 Squadron, RAF, in Two World Wars, 140–41.

126. See Ira Jones's books: Tiger Squadron, An Air Fighter's Scrapbook, and King of the Air Fighters: Biography of Maj. "Mick" Mannock, VS, DSO, MC.

127. Rothesay Stuart Worley, Letters from a Flying Officer, 190.

128. V. M. Yeates, Winged Victory, 50.

129. Wise, Canadian Airmen, 481.

130. Denis Winter, The First of the Few: Fighter Pilots of the First World War, 22.

131. James J. Hudson, In Clouds of Glory: American Airmen Who Flew with the British during the Great War, 6–7.

132. Arthur Longmore, From Sea to Sky, 1910–1945, 86.

133. Flight 10, no. 49 (3 October 1918): 1105–6, 1117–18.

134. Slessor, Air Power, 50.

135. Walter Noble, *With a Bristol Fighter Squadron*, passim.

136. John M. Grider, *War Birds: Diary of an Unknown Aviator*, 105. Hudson, *Clouds*, 111–12.

137. Wise, *Canadian Airmen*, 566–68.

138. Quoted in Hudson, *Hostile Skies*, 202.

139. Yeates, *Winged Victory*, 22, 31.

140. Slessor, *Air Power*, 100.

141. Grider, *War Birds*, 221, 233–37.

142. RFC HQ casualty reports, 11–30 September 1918, AIR 1/859/204/5/419–20, PRO.

143. Sir Philip Joubert de la Ferté, *The Third Service: The Story behind the Royal Air Force*, 62.

144. Jones, *Tiger Squadron*, 70, 84.

145. RFC HQ casualty reports, 11–30 September 1918, AIR 1/859/204/5/419–20, PRO.

146. Jewel Case, AH.204/5/1170, AIR 1/686/21/13/2245, PRO.

147. Notes are found in GC.

148. Grinnell-Milne, *Wind in the Wires*, 211.

149. Folio 5, AIR 9/3, PRO.

150. Mark Kerr, *Land, Sea, and Air: Reminiscences of Mark Kerr*, 280.

151. Williams, "Statistics and Strategic Bombardment," 141. Sweetser, *The American Air Service*, 301.

152. Air Council, 21st meeting, 22 March 1918, AHB, MD.

153. Williams, "Statistics and Strategic Bombardment," 147, 151, 160, 166, 171, 179.

154. CIGS (Maurice) 121/SWC/39 to Gen. Wilson, 17 January 1918, "Memorandum on Bombing Operations for the Supreme War Council," AIR 1/2267/209/70/29, PRO.

155. Neville Jones, *The Origins of Strategic Bombing: A Study of the Development of British Air Strategic Thought up to 1918*, 162–63.

156. Army Council 0140/1490 (MO1), 12 February 1918, AIR 1/2267/209/70/29, PRO.

157. Williams, "Statistics and Strategic Bombardment," 203–6. H. Montgomery Hyde, *British Air Policy between the Wars, 1918–1939*, 34–36.

158. Beaverbrook, *Men and Power*, 236. W. J. Reader, *Architect of Air Power: The Life of the First Viscount Weir of Eastwood 1877–1959*, 68.

159. Beaverbrook, *Men and Power*, app. IV, letter 12.

160. Reader, *Architect*, 75.

161. Jones, *Strategic Bombing*, 172.

162. Weir, "Note on the History of the 'V' type," 15 July 1918, AIR 1/2302/215/10, PRO.

163. Reader, *Architect*, 67–68, 70–74. Williams, "Statistics and Strategic Bombardment," 211–14. Sir Maurice Dean, *The Royal Air Force and Two World Wars*, 31.

164. Williams, "Statistics and Strategic Bombardment," 207–10.

165. Beaverbrook, *Men and Power*, 220.

166. Hyde, *British Air Policy*, 39, 43.

167. Williams, "Statistics and Strategic Bombardment," 193–96, 211–14.

168. Maurice Baring, *Flying Corps Headquarters, 1914–1918*, 280.

169. Williams, "Statistics and Strategic Bombardment," 233–51, 257, 260–62.

170. Jones, *Strategic Bombing*, 170–71. Williams, "Statistics and Strategic Bombardment," 332, 335, 186–91.

171. Williams, "Statistics and Strategic Bombardment," 276–78, 286.

172. C. Gordon Burge, *The Annals of 100 Squadron*, 158.

173. Williams, "Statistics and Strategic Bombardment," 294–96, 298.

174. Weir to Trenchard, 10 September 1918, MFC 76/1/94, TP, RAFM.

175. Weir to Trenchard, 17 September 1918, MFC 76/1/94, TP, RAFM.

176. Hyde, *British Air Policy*, 42.

177. Ibid., 343–44, 346, 348, 350.

178. Williams, "Statistics and Strategic Bombardment," 350–51.

179. Statistical Analysis of Aerial Bombardment, p. 22, RG 18, NA.

180. Beaverbrook, *Men and Power*, 220.

181. Reader, *Architect*, 74.

182. Beaverbrook, *Men and Power*, 235.

183. Reader, *Architect*, 80.

184. Williams, "Statistics and Strategic Bombardment," 228–29. Wise, *Canadian Airmen*, 308.

185. C. F. Snowden Gamble, *The Story of a North Sea Air Station*, 348–49.

186. Wise, *Canadian Airmen*, 218–28.

187. S. W. Roskill, ed., *Documents Relating to the Naval Air Service*, 1:610–712 passim.

188. J. M. Spaight, *The Beginnings of Organized Air Power*, 108–10.

189. Ibid., 106.

190. Ibid., 198–203.

191. Ministry of Munitions, *History of the Ministry of Munitions*, 12, pt. 1:87–88.

192. Ibid., 157, 171.

193. J. C. Nerney, "Aircraft Production," 129–30, 159–61, AIR 1/678/21/13/2138, PRO.

194. Ibid., 128–29. Jones, *War in the Air*, 3: App. 7.

195. AIR 1/6A/4/42, Notes for Discussion . . . , 28 January 1918, AIR 1/6A/4/42, PRO.

196. Progress and Allocation Committee, Directorate of Aircraft Equipment, no. 277, 19 January 1918, and no. 282, 25 January 1918; AIR 1/2302/215/13, PRO.

197. *Flight* 10, no. 28 (11 July 1918): 761; ibid., no. 29 (18 July 1918): 815–16.

198. Nerney, "Aircraft Production," 129–32, 159–61, AIR 1/678/21/13/2138, PRO.

199. Churchill, *Churchill*, 4:67, 72, 136, 144.

200. Air Council minutes, 48th meeting, 11 September 1918; 51st meeting, 26 September 1918; AHB, MD.

201. Nerney, "Aircraft Production," 133–36, AIR 1/678/21/13/2138; Aircraft Supply Committee minutes, no. 33, 29 July 1918, AIR 1/2302/215/11; Directorate of Aircraft Equipment, AIR 1/2304/215/13/pt3; PRO. Ministry of Munitions, *History*, 12, pt. 1:77–79, 82.

202. Brooke-Popham to Brig. Gen. A. Huggins, 17 July 1918, AIR 1/1/4/11, PRO.

203. J. C. Nerney, "Aircraft Design and Production, 1914–1918," 6, 13; 5 February 1935, AIR 1/678/21/13/2186; PRO.

204. Department of Aircraft Production, no. 84, 28 October 1918, AIR 1/500/15/331/5. Nerney, "Aircraft Production," 162–63, AIR 1/678/21/13/2138; PRO.

205. Expected and actual output and issue, AIR 1/2302/215/10; Nerney, "Aircraft Production," 136–40, AIR 1/678/21/13/2138; PRO.

206. Raleigh and Jones, *War in the Air*, 3:app. 7; and ibid., app. vol.: apps. 33 and 35.

207. Igor Sikorsky, *The Story of the Winged S: An Autobiography*, 142–45.

208. Jones in Higham and Kipp, 27–30. Kipp in Higham and Kipp, 143. Robert A. Kilmarx, *A History of Soviet Air Power*, 35–67.

209. Martin O'Connor, *Air Aces of the Austro-Hungarian Empire, 1914–1918*, 222.

210. Peter Schupita, *Die k.u.k. Seeflieger: Chronik und Dokumentation der österreichisch-ungarischen Marineluftwaffe 1911–1918*, 222–24.

211. Morrow, *German Air Power*, 177–78.

212. Ibid., 179–80.

213. Ibid., 181.

214. Ibid., 182.

215. Ibid., 183.

216. Ibid., 184.

217. "The Italian War Effort," AIR 1/684/21/13/2237, PRO.

218. Felice Porro, *La Guerra nell'aerea*, 257–69. Gabriele D'Annunzio, *Aviatore di guerra: Documenti e testimonianze*, 229–30.

219. Dorand to SSdA, "Compte-rendu d'une mission en Italie," February, DP, MdA.

220. Porro, *La Guerra*, 278–301.

221. D'Annunzio, *Aviatore*, 261, 266.

222. Porro, *La Guerra*, 381–85.

223. Ibid., 257–300.

224. "The Italian War Effort," AIR 1/684/21/13/2237, PRO.

225. Frank J. Cappelluti, "The Life and Thought of Giulio Douhet," 149.

226. D'Annunzio, *Aviatore*, 229–30. Porro, *La Guerra*, 381–85.

227. Dorand, "Compte-rendu," DP, MdA.

228. Report of Martinot Lagarde mission, 14–19 September 1918, 130 AP 10, DP, AN.

229. SSdA, office of the allies, 1106 64/AP, 27 August 1918, 130 AP 10, DP, AN.

230. James J. Hudson, *Hostile Skies: A Combat History of the American Air Service in World War I*, 56.

231. Williams, "Statistics and Strategic Bombardment," 122–23.

232. Robert F. Futrell, *Ideas, Concepts, Doctrine: A History of Basic Thinking in the United States Air Force, 1907–1964*, 24.

233. Maurer Maurer, *The U.S. Air Service in World War I*, 1:292.

234. Hudson, *Hostile Skies*, 129.

235. Lucien H. Thayer, *America's First Eagles: The Official History of the U.S. Air Service, A.E.F (1917–1918)*, 176–203. Maurer, *U.S. Air Service*, 3:passim.

236. Thayer, *Eagles*, 204–30.

237. Ibid., 151–52, 213. Statistics Branch, General Staff, "The Balanced Air Force, Distribution of Service Planes as Related to Military Policies," RG 18.

238. Thayer, *Eagles*, 153.

239. Hudson, *Hostile Skies*, 126. Maurer, *U.S. Air Service*, 1:295, 311.

240. Maurer, *U.S. Air Service*, 1:185, 212–33, 263, 272.

241. Thayer, *Eagles*, 237, 241, 244, 246.

242. Maurer, *U.S. Air Service*, 4:171.

243. Thayer, *Eagles*, 59.

244. Maurer, *U.S. Air Service*, 4:1–362 passim.

245. *Aviation Medicine in the AEF*, 205.

246. Ibid., 217.

247. Thayer, *Eagles*, 70–71.

248. Adrian O. Van Wyen, *Naval Aviation in World War I*, 79–87. Richard Knott, *The American Flying Boat: An Illustrated History*, 35–36.

249. *Aviation and Aeronautical Engineering* 3, no. 6 (15 April 1918): 383–87.

250. Ibid. 5, no. 3 (1 September 1918): 161–69.

251. Jacob A. Vander Meulen, "The American Aircraft Industry to World War II," 67.

252. G. W. Mixter and H. H. Emmons, *United States Army Aircraft Production Facts*, 25, 48.

253. Vander Meulen, 58–59.

254. Mrs. A. B. Gregg, "History of SE5 single-seat pursuit plane," Bureau of Aircraft Production, 452.1, RG 18, NA.

255. ———, "Bristol fighter," Bureau of Aircraft Production, 452.1, RG 18, NA.

256. ——— , "History of the Caproni biplane," BAP, 452.1, RG18, NA.

257. Data on history of the Caproni project, 452.1, RG 18, NA.

258. *Aviation and Aeronautical Engineering* 5, no. 3 (1 September 1918): 161–69.

259. *Aviation and Aeronautical Engineering* 5, no. 7 (1 November 1918): 434–35. Knott, *American Flying Boat*, 35–36. Van Wyen, *Naval Aviation*, 35–37.

260. Interallied Aviation Committee, AIR 1/26/15/1/121 and AIR 1/27/15/1/127, PRO. Conseil Supérieur de Guerre, Représentants Militaires, Note Collective no. 35, Aviation de Bombardement, 3 August 1918, 130 AP 8, DP, AN.

261. Winter, *First of the Few*, 16–17.

262. "Distribution of Service Planes As Related to Military Policies," RG 18, NA.

263. Ibid., 2.

264. Ibid., 11.

265. Ibid., 14–15.

266. *La Guerre Aérienne*, no. 94, 29 August 1918, 674.

267. Gabriel Voisin, *Men, Women, and 10,000 Kites*, 88–90.

CHAPTER SEVEN

Aftermath and Conclusion

1. Siegert to August Euler, 13 December 1918, fol. no. 265, NE, BA.

2. Jones in Higham and Kipp, 27–31.

3. Richard P. Hallion, *Strike from the Sky: The History of Battlefield Air Attack*, 55–58.

4. Morrow, *German Air Power*, 184–85.

5. Ibid., 143–45.

6. Ibid., 145–66.

7. Ibid., 146.

8. Ibid., 147–48.

9. Ibid., 148–49.

10. Ibid., 150.

11. Ibid., 150–52.

12. Ibid., 153–54.

13. Ibid., 154–56.

14. Ibid., 157–59.

15. Ibid., 159.

16. Ibid., 160–62.

17. Ibid., 162–63.

18. DP, MdA.

19. Ibid.

20. Translation of Regular Information, Bulletin no. 19, "A Confidential Document of the French Sub-Secretary of State for Aeronautics, 18 January 1921," in *Germany: A Compilation of Information for the Period August 1914 to May 1920*, NASM, SI.

21. Morrow, *German Air Power*, 165–66.

22. Ibid., 166.

23. *United States Military Intelligence, 1917–1927*, 8:1072–73.

24. On the postwar French aviation bureaucracy, military and civilian, and the industry, see Christienne et al., *Histoire de l'aviation*, 213–28, and Emmanuel Chadeau, *L'Industrie aéronautique en France 1900–1950: De Blériot à Dassault*, 150–57, unless otherwise noted.

25. Note "l'aviation civile allemande . . . 15.9.21," 22.9.21, DP. MdA.

26. *Military Intelligence*, 11:2, 624.

27. Ibid., 11:2, 625; 12:2, 670.

28. Malcolm Smith, *British Air Strategy between the Wars*, 21–29.

29. *Military Intelligence*, 11:2, 626.

30. Ministry of Munitions, 2, pt. 1, Supplement: 20–21, 26.

31. On the British aircraft industry, see Peter Fearon, "The Formative Years of the British Aircraft Industry, 1913–1924," *Business History Review* 43 (1969):476–95. Peter Fearon, "The Vicissitudes of a British Aircraft Company: Handley Page Ltd. between the Wars," *Business History* 20, no. 1 (January 1978): 66–86.

32. Maurer Maurer, *Aviation in the U.S. Army 1919–1939*.

33. John B. Rae, *Climb to Greatness. The American Aircraft Industry, 1920–1960*, 3, 18.

34. Marcel Jullian, *Le Chevalier du Ciel: Charles Nungesser*, 33.

35. Walter Raleigh and H. A. Jones, *The War in the Air*, App. Vol., app. 35.

36. G. W. Mixter and H. H. Emmons, *United States Army Aircraft Production Facts*, 5.

37. Christienne et al., *Histoire de l'aviation*, 62, 156–57.

38. *Military Intelligence*, 7:804.

39. David Lloyd George, *The Great Crusade: Extracts from Speeches Delivered during the War*, (New York: Doran and Co.), 212.

40. Laurence Goldstein, *The Flying Machine and Modern Literature*, 89.

41. Felix P. Ingold, *Literatur und Aviatik: Europäische Flugdichtung 1909–1927*, 224–26.

42. Edwin C. Parsons, *I Flew with the Lafayette Escadrille*, 130–34.

43. German losses from *Statistisches Jahrbuch für das Deutschen Reich 1924–1925*, 30; compiled apparently from the War Ministry, Kogenluft demobilization office, and Idflieg. British losses from Walter Raleigh and H. A. Jones, *The War in the Air*, app. vol., app. 35. French losses from "Statistics regarding French avi-

ation during the war," U.S. Naval Attaché to Office of Naval Intelligence, 14 January 1920, NA. Italian losses from German offical source, GC.

44. Air Ministry, "Synopsis of the British Air Effort during the War." Cmd. 100. April 1919, 4. MID 9793–295, RG 165, NA.

45. Christienne et al., *Histoire de l'aviation*, 177.

46. On French government policy, see MdG (DAeM) to President du Comité de Guerre no. 5594 2/12. 20.3.17, 130 AP 7; Daniel Vincent to Président, 7.7.17, 130 AP 9: DP, AN. Patrick Fridenson, *Histoire des usines Renault*, 96. *L'Aéronautique*, 400.

47. J. A. Gilles, *Flugmotoren 1910 bis 1918*, 146. Kenneth Richardson, *The British Motor Industry, 1896–1939*, 134. Herschel Smith, *A History of Aircraft Piston Engines*, 61. On Rolls Royce, see "Aircraft," 5–7, 13, AIR 1/678/21/13/2138, PRO. Raleigh and Jones, *War in the Air*, 148. Ministry of Munitions, *History of the Ministry of Munitions*, 12, pt. 1, 78. For American assessment, see S. G. Averell, report of 1.11.18, box 112, RG 18, NA.

48. Engine production figures from Raleigh and Jones, *War in the Air* 2, app. 7; ibid., 3, 254. J. P. Bardou et al., *The Automobile Revolution*, 70, 81. William Hornby, *Factories and Plant*, 19. J. C. Nerney, "Aircraft Production," 1, AIR 1/678/21/13/2138, PRO. On British engine development in general, see Robert Schlaifer and S. D. Heron, *Development of Aircraft Engines. Development of Aviation Fuels*, 42–138, 200.

49. Gilles, *Flugmotoren*, 22, 23, 60–61, 87–88, 102–4. Smith, *Aircraft Piston Engines*, 29–30, 35–36. Morrow, *German Air Power*, 97, 193.

50. "Report on Italian Aviation," September 1917, AIR 1/1073/204/51/652; "Report on Italian and French aviation engines," September 1917, AIR 1/703/27/4/10; PRO.

51. On Austria-Hungary, see Gilles, *Flugmotoren*, 76–77, and Morrow, 213. On Russia, see Robert A. Kilmarx, "The Russian Imperial Air Forces of World War I," *Airpower Historian* 10 (July 1963): 90–95, and Jones in Higham and Kipp, 15–31.

52. Mixter and Emmons, *Aircraft Production Facts*, 15–27, 30. Philip S. Dickey, "The Liberty Engine, 1918–1942," *Smithsonian Annals of Flight* 1, no. 3 (1968): passim. I. B. Holley, Jr., *Ideas and Weapons*, 118–24.

53. B. P. Flanagan, ed. and trans., "History of the Ottoman Air Force: Reports of Maj. Erich Serno," *Cross and Cockade* 2, no. 2: 97–145; ibid., no. 3: 224–43; ibid., no. 4: 346–69.

54. Cooper, *Birth of Independent Air Power*, 91–95.

55. Gerhard Wissmann, "Imperialistischer Krieg und technisch-wissenschaftlicher Fortschritt," *Jahrbuch für Wirtschaftsgeschichte*, 1962, pt. 2, 145–58.

56. Harald Penrose, *British Aviation: The Great War and Armistice 1915–19 9*, 467.

57. Richard Blunck, *Hugo Junkers: Ein Leben für Technik und Luftfahrt*, 89.

58. Ernst Heinkel, *Stürmisches Leben*, 69.

59. Etévé, *Victoire*, 302.

60. Ibid.

61. Penrose, *Great War*, 304–5.

62. Ibid., 534–35.

63. On Germany see Morrow, *German Air Power*, 76–77. On Britain, Harald Penrose, *Great War*, 205. On France, *L'Aéronautique pendant la Guerre Mondiale*, 114, 499–500.

64. Penrose, *Great War*, 456–7. Bulletin no. 19, "A Confidential Document of the French Sub-Secretary of State for Aeronautics, 18 January 1921," in *Germany: A Compilation of Information for the Period August 1914 to May 1920*, 5, NASM, SI.

65. Blunck, *Junkers*, 105–10. A. H. G. Fokker and Bruce Gould, *Flying Dutchman: The Life of Anthony Fokker*, 147–48. JN, DM. Junkers File, GC.

66. Laurence K. Loftin, Jr., *Quest for Performance: The Evolution of Modern Aircraft*, 27–47.

67. *Aviation and Aeronautical Engineering* 5, no. 9 (1 December 1918): 549–53; ibid., no. 11 (1 January 1919): 675.

68. Emmanuel Chadeau, "État, entreprise et développement économique: L'Industrie aéronautique en France (1900–1940)," 1:75. Five francs equaled a dollar before 1914.

69. Archive no. 92, fond 493, opis 7, pp. 19–57.

70. Philippe Bernard, "A propos de la stratégie aérienne pendant la Première Guerre Mondiale: Mythes et réalités," 371–75.

71. George Kent Williams, "Statistics and Strategic Bombardment: Operations and Records of the British Long-Range Bombing Force during World War I and Their Implications for the Development of the Post-War Royal Air Force, 1917–1923," 343–44, 348, 350–51, 365, 370–71.

Selected
Bibliography

General Works

Official Histories

Allied Armies under Marshal Foch in the Franco-Belgian Theater of Operations. The Report of the Military Board of Allied Supply, vol. 1, pt. 1. Washington, D.C.: Government Printing Office, 1924.

Periodicals

Cross and Cockade.

Secondary Sources

Air Power and Warfare. The Proceeding of the 8th Annual Military History Symposium, United States Air Force Academy, 18–20 October 1978. Edited by Alfred F. Hurly and Robert C. Ehrhardt. Washington: Office of Air Force History. 1979. See especially paper by R. A. Mason, "The British Dimension," 22–35.

Angelucci, Enzo. *The Rand McNally Encyclopedia of Military Aircraft, 1914–1980*. New York: Military Press, 1981.

Bradou, J. P. et al. *The Automobile Revolution. The Impact of an Industry.* Translated by James M. Laux. Chapel Hill: University of North Carolina Press, 1982.

Campbell, Christopher. *Aces and Aircraft of World War I.* New York: Greenwich House, 1984.

Color Profiles of World War I Combat Planes. New York: Crescent Books, 1974.

Cross, Robin. *The Bombers: The Illustrated Story of Offensive Strategy and Tactics in the Twentieth Century.* New York: Macmillan, 1987.

Fitzsimons, Bernard. *Warplanes and Air Battles of World War I.* New York: Beekman House, 1973.

Franks, Norman. *Aircraft versus Aircraft: The Illustrated Story of Fighter Pilot Combat since 1914.* New York: Macmillan, 1986.

Gibbs-Smith, Charles H. *The Aeroplane: An Historical Survey of Its Origins and Development.* London: Her Majesty's Stationery Office, 1960.

Goldstein, Laurence. *The Flying Machine and Modern Literature.* London: Macmillan, 1986.

Gröhler, Olaf. *Geschichte des Luftkriegs 1910 bis 1980.* Berlin: Militärverlag der DDR, 1981.

Hallion, Richard P. *Rise of the Fighter Aircraft, 1914–1918.* Annapolis: Nautical and Aviation Publishing Co., 1984.

———. *Strike from the Sky: The History of Battlefield Air Attack, 1911–1945.* Washington, D.C.: Smithsonian Institution Press, 1989.

Hartcup, Guy. *The War of Invention: Scientific Developments, 1914–18.* London: Brassey's, 1988.

Hezlett, Sir Arthur. *Aircraft and Sea Power.* New York: Stein and Day, 1970.

Higham, Robin. *Air Power: A Concise History.* New York: St. Martin's Press, 1972.

Ingold, Felix P. *Literatur und Aviatik: Europäische Flugdichtung, 1909–1927.* Basel: Birkhäuser Verlag, 1978.

Jane's Fighting Aircraft of World War I. New York: Military Press, 1990 [1919].

Johnson, J. E. *Full Circle: The Tactics of Air Fighting, 1914–1964.* New York: Ballantine, 1964.

Kennett, Lee. *The First Air War, 1914–1918.* New York: Free Press, 1991.

———. *A History of Strategic Bombing.* New York: Scribner's, 1982.

Kern, Stephen H. *The Culture of Time and Space, 1880–1918.* Cambridge, Mass.: Harvard University Press, 1983.

Lamberton, W. M., and E. F. Cheesman. *Reconnaissance and Bomber Aircraft of the 1914–1918 War.* Letchworth, Herts.: Harleyford, 1962.

Layman, R. D. *To Ascend from a Floating Base: Shipboard Aeronautics and Aviation, 1783–1914.* Teaneck, N.J.: Fairleigh Dickinson University Press, 1979.

Loftin, Laurence K., Jr. *Quest for Performance: The Evolution of Modern Aircraft.* Washington, D.C.: National Aeronautics and Space Administration, 1985.

Millett, Allan R., and Williamson Murray, eds. *Military Effectiveness.* Vol. 1, *The First World War.* Boston: Allen and Unwin, 1988.

Norman, Aaron. *The Great Air War.* New York: Macmillan, 1968.

Nowarra, Heinz J. *Marine Aircraft of the 1914–1918 War.* Letchworth, Herts.: Harleyford, 1966.

Quester, George H. *Deterrence before Hiroshima.* New York: Wiley, 1966.

Reynolds, Quentin. *They Fought for the Sky.* New York: Holt, Rinehart and Winston, 1957.

Robertson, Bruce, et al. *Air Aces of the 1914–1918 War.* Letchworth, Herts.: Harleyford, 1964.

Robinson, Douglas H. *The Dangerous Sky: A History of Aviation Medicine.* Seattle: University of Washington Press, 1973.

————. *Giants in the Sky: A History of the Rigid Airship.* Seattle: University of Washington Press, 1973.

Schlaifer, Robert, and S. D. Heron. *Development of Aircraft Engines. Development of Aviation Fuels.* Boston: Harvard University Graduate School of Business Administration, 1950.

Smith, Herschel. *A History of Aircraft Piston Engines.* Manhattan, Kans.: Sunflower University Press, 1986 [1981].

Stokesbury, James L. *A Short History of Air Power.* New York: William Morrow and Co., 1986.

Taylor, C. Fayette. "Aircraft Propulsion: A Review of the Evolution of Aircraft Piston Engines." *Smithsonian Annals of Flight,* vol. 1, no. 4, 1971.

Villard, Henry S. *Contact! The Story of the Early Birds.* Washington, D.C.: Smithsonian Institution Press, 1987.

England and the Dominions

Primary Sources

AIR 1 and AIR 8 materials of the Public Record Office (PRO) and Air Historical Branch, Ministry of Defense. (AHB, MD)

Air Board, minutes of meetings, AHB, MD.

Trenchard Papers, Royal Air Force Museum. (TP, RAFM)

Published Documents

Air Ministry. "Synopsis of British Air Effort during the War." Cmd. 100. London: His Majesty's Stationery Office, April 1919.
Roskill, Stephen W., ed. *Documents Relating to the Naval Air Service*. Vol. 1, *1908–1918*. Publications of the Navy Records Society, vol. 113. London, 1969.

Memoirs

Addison, Christopher. *Politics from Within, 1911–1918*. Vol. 2. London: Jenkins, 1924.
Balfour, Harold. *An Airman Marches: Early Flying Adventures, 1914–1923*. London: Greenhill, 1985 [1935].
Baring, Maurice. *Flying Corps Headquarters, 1914–1918*. Edinburgh: Blackwood, 1968 [1920].
Bartlett, C. P. O. *Bomber Pilot 1916–1918*. London: Allen, 1974.
[Aitken, Max] Lord Beaverbrook. *Men and Power 1917–1918*. New York: Duell, Sloan and Pearce, 1956.
Bewsher, Paul. *Green Balls: The Adventures of a Night Bomber*. London: Greenhill, 1986 [1919].
Bishop, William A. *Winged Warfare*. Garden City, N.Y.: Doubleday, 1967.
Bott, Alan. *An Airman's Outings with the RFC, June–December 1916*. Elstree, Herts.: Greenhill, 1986 [1917].
Bulman, G. P. "I ought to have been sacked." Unpublished memoir, RAFM/B963.
Callender, Gordon W., Jr. and Gordon W. Callender, Sr. *War in an Open Cockpit: The Wartime Letters of Captain Alvin Andrew Callender, R.A.F.* West Roxbury, Mass.: World War I Aero Publishers, 1978.
Cobby, A. H. *High Adventure*. Melbourne: Kookaburra, 1981.
Collishaw, Raymond, with R. V. Dodds. *Air Command: A Fighter Pilot's Story*. London: Kimber, 1973.
Davies, Richard B. *Sailor in the Air*. London: Davies, 1967.
de Havilland, Sir Geoffrey. *Sky Fever*. London: Hamilton, 1961.
Douglas, Sholto, with Robert Wright. *Combat and Command*. New York: Simon and Schuster, 1963.
Gamble, C. F. Snowden. *The Story of a North Sea Air Station*. London: Oxford University Press, 1928.
Grinnell-Milne, Duncan. *Wind in the Wires*. Garden City, N.Y.: Doubleday, 1968.
Harvey, W. J. [Night-Hawk]. *Rovers of the Night Sky*. London: Greenhill, 1984 [1919].

Insall, A. J. *Observer: Memoirs of the RFC, 1915–1918*. London: Kimber, 1970.

Jones, Ira. *Tiger Squadron: The Story of 74 Squadron, RAF, in Two World Wars*. London: W. H. Allen, 1954.

——— . *An Air Fighter's Scrapbook*. London: Nicholson and Watson, 1938.

Joubert de la Ferté, Sir Philip. *The Fated Sky: An Autobiography*. London: Hutchinson, 1952.

Kerr, Mark. *Land, Sea, and Air: Reminiscences of Mark Kerr*. New York: Longmans, Green and Co., 1927.

Lee, Arthur Gould. *No Parachute: A Fighter Pilot in World War I*. New York: Harper and Row, 1968.

——— . *Open Cockpit: A Pilot of the Royal Flying Corps*. London: Jarrolds, 1969.

Lewis, Cecil. *Sagittarius Rising*. New York: Harcourt, Brace and Co., 1936.

Long, S. H. *In the Blue*. London: John Lane, 1920.

Longmore, Arthur. *From Sea to Sky, 1910–1945*. London: Bles, 1946.

McCudden, James T. B. *Flying Fury*. London: Hamilton, 1930 [1918].

MacLanachan, W. [McScotch]. *Fighter Pilot*. London: Routledge, 1936.

Macmillan, Norman. *Into the Blue*. London: Jarrolds, 1969.

Mannock, Edward. *The Personal Diary of Maj. Edward "Mick" Mannock*. Introduced and annotated by Frederick Oughton. London: Spearman, 1966.

Moore, W. Geoffrey. *Early Bird*. London: Putnam, 1963.

Noble, Walter. *With a Bristol Fighter Squadron*. Portway, Bath: Chivers, 1977 [1920].

Slessor, John C. *The Central Blue: Recollections and Reflections*. London: Cassell, 1956.

Strange, Lewis A. *Recollections of an Airman*. London: John Hamilton Ltd., 1933.

Sueter, Murray F. *Airmen or Noahs*. London: Putnam, 1928.

Sykes, Frederick. *From Many Angles: An Autobiography*. London: Harrap, 1942.

[Voss, Vivian] "Vee, Roger." *Flying Minnows*. London: Arms and Armour, 1977 [1935].

Worley, Rothesay Stuart. *Letters from a Flying Officer*. Gloucester: Sutton, 1982 [1928].

Yeates, V. M. *Winged Victory*. London: Buchan and Wright, 1985 [1934] (a novel based on the author's wartime experiences).

Official and Squadron Histories

Burge, C. Gordon. *The Annals of 100 Squadron*. London: Reach, 1919.

Cole, Christopher, ed. *Royal Air Force 1918*. London: Kimber, 1918.

————, ed. *Royal Flying Corps 1915–1916*. London: Kimber, 1969.

Cutlack, F. M. *The Australian Flying Corps in the Western and Eastern Theatres of War 1914–1918*. Sydney: Angus and Robertson, 1933.

Hornby, William. *Factories and Plant*. History of the Second World War. War Production Series. London: Her Majesty's Stationery Office—Longmans, Green, and Co., 1958.

Jones, H. A. *Over the Balkans and South Russia, 1917–1919, Being the History of No. 47 Squadron Royal Air Force*. Elstree, Herts.: Greenhill, 1987 [1923].

Ministry of Munitions. *History of the Ministry of Munitions*. 12 vols. London: His Majesty's Stationery Office, 1922.

Pattinson, Lawrence A. *History of 99 Squadron, Independent Force, Royal Air Force, March, 1918–November, 1918*. Cambridge: Heffer, 1920.

Postan, M. M., D. Hay, and J. D. Scott. *Design and Development of Weapons: Studies in Government and Industrial Organization*. History of the Second World War. United Kingdom Civil Series. London: Her Majesty's Stationery Office, 1964.

Raleigh, Walter, and H. A. Jones. *The War in the Air*. Vols. 1–6. Oxford: Clarendon, 1922–37.

Wise, S. F. *Canadian Airmen and the First World War: The Official History of the Royal Canadian Air Force*. Vol. 1. Toronto: University of Toronto Press.

Periodicals

Aeronautics.
The Aeroplane.
Flight.

Secondary Sources

Adkin, Fred. *From the Ground Up: A History of R.A.F. Ground Crew*. Shrewsbury: Airlife, 1983.

Bowyer, Chaz. *Albert Ball, VC*. London: Kimber, 1977.

————. *For Valour: The Air VCs*. London: Kimber, 1978.

Bruce, J. M. *The Aeroplanes of the Royal Flying Corps (Military Wing)*. London: Putnam, 1982.

————. *British Aeroplanes 1914–1918*. London: Putnam, 1957.

Castle, H. G. *Fire over England: The German Air Raids in World War I*. London: Secker and Warburg, 1982.

A Century of British Aeronautics. A Centenary Journal, Journal of the Royal Historical Society 70 (January 1966).

Churchill, Randolph S., and Martin Gilbert. *Winston S. Churchill.* Vols. 2–4. Boston: Houghton Mifflin, 1967, 1971, 1975.

Cole, Christopher, and E. F. Cheesman. *The Air Defense of Great Britain 1914–1918.* London: Putnam, 1984.

Collier, Basil. *Heavenly Adventurer: Sefton Brancker and the Dawn of British Aviation.* London: Secker and Warburg, 1959.

————. *Leader of the Few: The Authorized Biography of Air Chief Marshal the Lord Dowding of Bentley Priory.* London: Jarrolds, 1957.

Cooper, Malcolm. *The Birth of Independent Air Power: British Air Policy in the First World War.* London: Allen and Unwin, 1986.

Dean, Sir Maurice. *The Royal Air Force and Two World Wars.* London: Cassell, 1979.

Divine, David. *The Broken Wing: A Study in the British Exercise of Air Power.* London: Hutchinson, 1966.

Dixon, Ronald, ed. *Echoes in the Sky: An Anthology of Aviation Verse from Two World Wars.* Poole, Dorset: Blandford, 1982.

Fearon, Peter. "The Formative Years of the British Aircraft Industry, 1913–1924." *Business History Review* 43 (1969): 476–95.

————. "The Vicissitudes of a British Aircraft Company: Handley Page Ltd. between the Wars." *Business History* 20, no. 1 (January 1978): 63–86.

Fredette, Raymond H. *The Sky on Fire: The First Battle of Britain 1917–1918.* New York: Harcourt, Brace, Jovanovich, 1966.

Gollin, Alfred. *No Longer an Island. Britain and the Wright Brothers, 1902–1909.* Stanford: Stanford University Press, 1984.

————. *The Impact of Air Power on the British People and Their Government, 1909–1914.* Stanford: Stanford University Press, 1989.

Greenhous, Brereton. "Close Support Aircraft in World War I: The Counter Anti-Tank Role." *Aerospace Historian* 21 (June 1974): 87–93.

Hawker, Tyrrel M. *Hawker, VC.* London: Mitre, 1965.

Higham, Robin. "The Dangerously Neglected—The British Military Intellectuals, 1918–1939." *Military Affairs* 29, no. 2 (Summer 1965): 73–87.

————. *The British Rigid Airship, 1908–1931: A Study in Weapons Policy.* London: Foulis, 1961.

————. "The Peripheral Weapon in Wartime: A Case Study." *Air Power Historian* 8, no. 2 (April 1961): 67–78.

Hyde, H. Montgomery. *British Air Policy between the Wars, 1918–1939.* London: Heinemann, 1976.

Johnstone, E. G., ed. *Naval Eight.* London: Arms and Armour, 1972 [1931].

Jones, Ira. *King of the Air Fighters: Biography of Maj. "Mick" Mannock, VS, DSO, MC.* London: Nicholson and Watson Ltd., 1934.

Jones, Neville. *The Origins of Strategic Bombing: A Study of the Development of British Air Strategic Thought up to 1918.* London: Kimber, 1973.

Joubert de la Ferté, Sir Philip. *The Third Service: The Story behind the Royal Air Force.* London: Thames and Hudson, 1955.

Keaney, Thomas A. "Aircraft and Air Doctrinal Development in Great Britain, 1912–1914." Diss., University of Michigan, 1975.

Kemp, P. K. *The Fleet Air Arm.* London: Jenkins, 1954.

Kingston-McCloughry, E. J. *War in Three Dimensions: The Impact of Air Power upon the Classical Principles of War.* London: Jonathan Cape, 1949.

Laffin, John. *Swifter than Eagles: The Biography of Marshal of the RAF Sir John Maitland Salmond.* Edinburgh: Blackwood, 1964.

Liddle, Peter H. *The Airman's War 1914–18.* Poole, Dorset: Blandford, 1987.

Loraine, Winifred. *Robert Loraine: Soldier, Actor, Airman.* London: Collins, 1938.

Macmillan, Norman. *Offensive Patrol: The Story of the RNAS, RFC, and RAF in Italy 1917–1918.* London: Jarrolds, 1973.

Mead, Peter. *The Eye in the Air: History of Air Observation and Reconnaissance for the Army 1785–1945.* London: Her Majesty's Stationery Office, 1983.

Norris, Geoffrey. *The Royal Flying Corps: A History.* London: Muller, 1965.

Oughton, Frederick, and Vernon Smyth. *Ace with One Eye: The Life and Combats of Maj. Edward Mannock.* London: Muller, 1963.

Parker, Peter. *The Old Lie: The Great War and the Public School Ethos.* London: Constable, 1987.

Penrose, Harald. *British Aviation: The Great War and Armistice 1915–1919.* London: Putnam, 1969.

———. *British Aviation: The Pioneer Years 1903–1914.* London: Putnam, 1967.

Powers, Barry D. *Strategy without Slide-Rule: British Air Strategy 1914–1939.* London: Croom Helm, 1976.

Rawlinson, A. *The Defense of London 1915–1918.* London: Melrose, 1924 [1923].

Reader, W. J. *Architect of Air Power: The Life of the First Viscount Weir of Eastwood 1877–1959.* London: Collins, 1968.

Richardson, Kenneth. *The British Motor Industry, 1896–1939.* London: Macmillan, 1977.

Robertson, Bruce. *Sopwith—The Man and His Aircraft.* Letchworth, Herts.: Air Review Ltd., 1970.

Saundby, Sir Robert. *Air Bombardment: The Story of Its Development.* New York: Harper and Brothers, 1961.

Saunders, Hilary St. G. *Per Ardua: The Rise of British Air Power 1911–1939.* London: Oxford University Press, 1945.

Slessor, John C. *Air Power and Armies*. London: Oxford University Press, 1936.

Smith, Malcolm. *British Air Strategy between the Wars*. Oxford: Clarendon Press, 1984.

Spaight, J. M. *The Beginnings of Organized Air Power. A Historical Study*. London: Longmans, Green and Co., 1927.

Tredrey, Frank D. *Pioneer Pilot: The Great Smith Barry Who Taught the World to Fly*. London: Davies, 1976.

Williams, George Kent. "Statistics and Strategic Bombardment: Operations and Records of the British Long-Range Bombing Force during World War I and Their Implications for the Development of the Post-War Royal Air Force, 1917–1923." Diss., Oxford University, 1987.

Wilson, Trevor. *The Myriad Faces of War: Britain and the Great War, 1914–1918*. London: Polity, 1986.

Winter, Denis. *The First of the Few: Fighter Pilots of the First World War*. London: Penguin, 1983 [1982].

Wynn, Humphrey. *The Black Cat Squadron: Night Bombing in World War I*. Washington, D.C.: Smithsonian Institution Press, 1990.

Young, Desmond. *Member for Mexico: A Biography of Weetman Pearson, First Viscount Cowdray*. London: Cassell, 1966.

France

Primary Sources

Papers of J. L. Dumesnil, Archives Nationales (AN).

Papers of J.-B. E. Dorand, Musée de l'Air (MdA).

D'Aubigny. "Rapport sur les Travaux de la Commission de l'Armée pendant la Guerre 1914–1918." No. 6999. Chambre des Députés, 11e legislature, Session de 1919. Paris: Martinet, 1919.

Grand Quartier Général (GQG) des Armées du Nord et du Nord Est. Etat-Major. 3e Bureau et Aéronautique. "Instruction sur l'organisation et l'emploi de l'aéronautique aux armées." Mars 1918. Titre II, "Aviation de Combat." Titre III, "Aviation de Bombardement." Paris: Charles Lavauzelle, 1918.

Ministère de la Guerre. "Instruction du 28 décembre 1917 sur liaison pour les troupes de toutes armes." Paris: Charles Lavauzelle, 1920.

Memoirs

d'Arnoux, Jacques. *Paroles d'un revenant*. Paris: Plon, 1925.

Boulenger, Jacques. *En escadrille*. Paris: La Renaissance du Livre, 1918.

Chambe, René. *Au temps des carabines.* Paris: Flammarion, 1955.

Chaput, Jean. *Quelques lettres de Jean Chaput.* Paris: Tolmer, 1920.

Dassault, Marcel. *The Talisman.* Translated by Patricia High Painton. New Rochelle: Arlington House, 1971 [1969].

Duvau, André. *Br. 29: Souvenirs d'escadrille.* Vincennes: Service Historique de l'Armée de l'Air, 1976.

Etévé, Albert. *Avant les cocardes: Les Débuts de l'aéronautique militaire.* Paris: Lavauzelle, 1961.

———— . *La Victoire des cocardes.* Paris: Lavauzelle, 1970.

Forces Aériens Français. Spécial cinquantenaire de la victoire. *Revue mensuelle de l'Armée de l'Air* 23, no. 252 (November 1968).

JeanJean, Marcel. *Des ronds dans l'Air: Souvenirs illustrés.* Aurillac: Imprimerie Moderne, 1967.

———— . *Sous les cocardes. Scènes de l'aviation militaire.* Paris: SERMA, 1964 [1919].

Laffray, Jean. *Pilote de chasse aux Cigognes.* Paris: Fayard, 1968.

Lafont, Bernard. *Au ciel de Verdun: Notes d'un aviateur.* Paris: Berger-Levrault, 1918.

Marc, Lieutenant [Jean Béraud Villars]. *Notes d'un pilote disparu (1916–1917).* Paris: Hachette, 1918. Translated by S. J. Pincetl and Ernest Marchand, *Notes of a Lost Pilot.* Hamden Conn.: Archon, 1975.

Marie, Félix. *Les Origines de l'aéronautique militaire (novembre 1909–novembre 1910).* Paris: Lavauzelle, 1924.

Mirande, Henri, and Louis Olivier. *Sur la bataille: Journal d'un aviateur français à l'Armée Bulgare au siège d'Andrinople.* Paris: Ambert, 1913.

Nadaud, Marcel. *En plein vol: Souvenirs de guerre aérienne.* Paris: Hachette, 1916.

Odier, Antoine. *Souvenirs d'une vieille tige.* Paris: Fayard, 1955.

Thébault, Louis. *L'Escadrille 210.* Paris: Jouve, 1925.

Thénault, Georges. *L'Escadrille Lafayette (avril 1916–janvier 1918).* Paris: Librairie Hachette, 1939.

Violan, Jean. *Dans l'air et dans la boue: Mes missions de guerre.* Paris: Librairie des Champs-Elysées, 1933.

Voisin, Gabriel. *Men, Women, and 10,000 Kites.* Translated by Oliver Stewart. London: Putnam, 1963 [1961].

Official Histories

L'Aéronautique pendant la Guerre Mondiale. Paris: Maurice de Brunoff, 1919.

Christienne, Charles et al. *Histoire de l'Aviation Militaire Française.* Paris: Charles Lavauzelle, 1980.

Periodicals

L'Aérophile, 1914–19.
La Guerre aérienne, 1917–19.
La Guerre aérienne illustrée, 1916–19.

Secondary Sources

"L'Aéronautique militaire française pendant la Guerre de 1914–1918." 2 vols.,
"1914, 1915, 1916" and "1917, 1918." In *Icare, revue de l'aviation
française.* Special numbers, 1978, 1979.
Audigier, François. "Histoire de l'aviation militaire française des origines à
1939." In-house-work, Service Historique de l'Armée de l'Air, 1971.
Barthélémy, Raymond, ed. *Le Temps des Hélices.* Paris: Éditions France-
Empire, 1972.
Bénoist, Odile. "Le Recrutement des aviateurs Français pendant la Guerre
1914–1918." Mémoire de maitrise, Université de Paris I, 1974–75.
Bernard, Philippe. "À propos de la stratégie aérienne pendant la Première
Guerre Mondiale: Mythes et réalités." *Revue d'histoire moderne et contem-
poraine* 16 (1969): 350–75.
Bitchakdjian, J. "Les débuts des industries françaises d'aéronautique: La Société
des moteurs Salmson 1913–1917." Mémoire de Maitrise, Université de
Paris X—Nanterre, 1969.
Bonnefous, Georges. *Histoire politique de la Troisième République.* Vol. 2,
La Grande Guerre (1914–1918). Paris: Presses Universitaires de
France, 1967.
Cantener, Henri. *Hommage aux Ailes Lorraines.* Nancy, 1968.
Chadeau, Emmanuel. "État, entreprise et développement économique: L'Indus-
trie aéronautique en France (1900–1940)." 2 vols. Diss., Université de
Paris X—Nanterre, 1986.
———. *L'Industrie aéronautique en France 1900–1950: De Blériot à Dassault.*
Paris: Fayard, 1987.
———. "L'Industrie française d'aviation à la veille de la Première Guerre
Mondiale." *Revue historique des armées,* 1981, no. 2:61–81; no.
3:181–206.
Dournel, Jean-Pierre. "L'image de l'aviateur français en 1914–1918." *Revue
historique des armées,* 1975, no. 4:58–83; 1976, no. 1:95–123.
Facon, Patrick. "L'armée française et l'aviation 1891–1914." Paper presented
at the Southern Historical Association Meeting, November 1985.
———. "L'aviation française au 'Chemin des Dames.'" *Aviation Magazine,*
no. 805 (1 July 1981): 80–87.
Fridenson, Patrick. *Histoire des usines Renault.* Vol. 1, *Naissance de la grande
entreprise 1898–1939.* Paris: Seuil, 1972.

le Goyet, P. "Évolution de la doctrine d'emploi de l'aviation française entre 1919 et 1939." In Numéro spécial sur l'aviation française (1919–1940), *Revue d'histoire de la Deuxième Guerre Mondiale* 19, no. 73 (January 1969): 3–41.

"Guynemer et les Cigognes," *Icare, revue de l'aviation fançaise,* no. 122 (1987).

Hatry, Gilbert. *Renault, usine de guerre 1914–1918.* Paris: Lafourcade, 1975.

Hodeir, Marcellin. "L'Aviation militaire française de la Première Guerre Mondiale (1917–18): Étude du milieu social. Approche des mentalités." Mémoire de maitrise, Université de Paris IV, 1976–77.

Huisman, Georges. *Dans les coulisses de l'Aviation 1914–1918: Pourquoi n'avons nous pas toujours garder la maitrise des airs?* Paris: Renaissance du Livre, 1921.

Jauneaud, Marcel. *L'Aviation militaire et la guerre aérienne.* Paris: Flammarion, 1923.

Jullian, Marcel. *La grande bataille dans les airs 1914–1918.* Paris: Presses de la Cité, 1967.

——— . *Le Chevalier du ciel: Charles Nungesser.* Paris: Amiot Dumont, 1953.

Kaspi, André. *Le Temps des Américains: Le Concours américain à la France en 1917–1918.* Paris: Publications de Sorbonne, 1976.

Kerisel, Jean. *Albert Caquot 1881–1976: Créateur et précurseur.* Paris: Éditions Eyrolles, 1978.

Laux, James. "Gnome et Rhône: Une firme de moteurs d'avion durant la Grande Guerre." In *1914–1918. L'Autre front.* Cahiers du "Mouvement Social," no. 2. Paris: Les Éditions Ouvrières, 1977.

——— . *In First Gear: The French Automobile Industry to 1914.* Montreal: McGill Queens University Press, 1976.

——— . "The Rise and Fall of Armand Deperdussin." *French Historical Studies* 8, no. 1 (Spring 1973): 95–104.

Lissarrague, Pierre. *Memento d'histoire de l'aéronautique militaire française.* Vol. 2, *La Guerre 1914–1918.* École Militaire de l'Air, 1978.

Livre d'Or de la Société Française Hispano-Suiza. Paris: Draeger Frères, 1924.

Marchis, Lucien. *Vingt-cinq ans d'aéronautique française.* 2 vols. Paris: Chambre syndicale des Industries aéronautiques, 1934.

Morgat, Louis. "L'aviation en Berry avant la Grande Guerre." *Revue historique des armées,* 1980, no. 1: 158–216.

Mortane, Jacques. *Les As nous parlent.* Paris: Baudinière, 1937.

——— . *Histoire illustrée de la guerre aérienne (1914–1918).* Paris: L'Édition Française Illustrée, 1921.

——— . *Les Vols Émouvants de la guerre.* Paris: Hachette, 1917.

——— , and Jean Daçay. *La Guerre des nues racontée par ses morts.* Paris: L'Édition Française Illustrée, 1918.

Orthlieb, Commandant. *L'Aéronautique hier—demain.* Paris: Masson, 1920.

Pedroncini, Guy. *Pétain: Général en chef 1917–1918*. Paris: Presses Universitaires de France, 1974.

Pesquiès-Courbier, Simone. "Le bassin ferrifère de Briey durant la guerre de 1914–1918." *Revue historique des armées*, 1981, no. 2: 91–128.

———— . "La politique de bombardement des usines sidérurgiques en Lorraine et au Luxembourg pendant la Première Guerre Mondiale." *Revue historique des armées*, 1981, no. 4: 127–59.

Petit, Edmond. *La Vie quotidienne dans l'aviation en France au début du XXe siècle (1900–1935)*. Paris: Hachette, 1977.

Porret, D. *Les 'As' français de la Grande Guerre*. 2 vols. Paris: Service Historique de l'Armée de l'Air, 1983.

Quellennec, Jacques. *Roland Garros: Mémoires*. Paris: Hachette, 1966.

Renaud, Paul. *L'Évolution de l'aéronautique pendant la Guerre 1914–1918*. Paris: 1921.

Revue Historique de l'Armée. Special issue. *L'Aviation Militaire Française 1909–1969*. 1969.

Sahel, Jacques. *Henri Farman et l'aviation*. Paris: Grasset, 1936.

Truelle, J. "La Production aéronautique militaire française jusqu'en juin 1940." In Numéro spécial sur l'aviation française (1919–1940), *Revue d'histoire de la Deuxième Guerre Mondiale* 19, no. 73 (January 1969): 75–110.

Vincent, Daniel. *La Bataille de l'air*. Paris: Berger-Levrault, 1918.

Voisin, André P. *La Doctrine de l'aviation française de combat au cours de la guerre (1915–1918)*. Paris: Berger-Levrault, 1932.

Germany

For additional primary and secondary sources on German aviation, see the bibliographies in the author's two works cited below under Secondary Sources.

Primary Sources

Euler Papers, German Federal Archive, Koblenz.

Junkers Papers, Deutsches Museum (DM), Munich.

Army and Navy material on aviation, Federal Archive, Military Archive, Freiburg.

Bavarian documents in the Bavarian War Archive, Munich.

Memoirs

Boelcke, Oswald. *Hauptmann Boelckes Feldberichte*. Gotha: Perthas, 1917.

Bullinger. "Kriegserfahrungen in der Motorenabteilung der Flugzeugmeisterei." Reports in Peter Grosz Archive, Princeton.

Eddelbüttel, F. W. *Artillerie-Flieger.* Dresden: Das Grössere Deutschland, 1918.

Fokker, A. H. G., and Bruce Gould. *Flying Dutchman: The Life of Anthony Fokker.* New York: Holt, Rinehart and Winston, 1931.

Heinkel, Ernst. *Stürmisches Leben.* Edited by Jürgen Thorwald. Stuttgart: Mundus-Verlag, 1953.

Immelmann, Max. *Mes Vols de Combat.* Translated by Paul Stehlin. Paris: Librairie des Sciences Aéronautiques, 1930.

Löwenstern, Elard von. *Der Frontflieger aus Vorkriegs-, Kriegs und Nachkriegs-Fliegertagen.* Berlin: Bernard und Graefe, 1937.

Marben, Rolf. *Zeppelin Adventures.* London: Greenhill, 1986 [1931].

Neumann, Georg P., ed. *In der Luft unbesiegt.* Munich: Lehmanns, 1923.

Radenbach, F. W. *Weit im Rucken des Feindes: Kriegserlebnisse eines Fernaufklärers.* Berlin: Traditions-Verlag, 1938.

Richthofen, Manfred von. *Der rote Kampfflieger.* Berlin: Ullstein, 1917.

Schäfer, Leutnant. *Vom Jäger zum Flieger.* Berlin: Scherl, 1918.

Schleustedt, Franz. *Vollgas: Ein Fliegerleben.* Berlin: Steiniger, 1939.

Schröder, Hans. *A German Airman Remembers.* London: Greenhill, 1986 [1935].

Udet, Ernst. *Mein Fliegerleben.* Berlin: Ullstein, 1935.

Weltkoborsky, Norbert. *Vom Fliegen, Siegen und Sterben einer Feldflieger-Abteilung.* Vol. 80 of series *Deutsche Tat im Weltkrieg 1914–1918.* Berlin: Bernard und Graefe, 1939.

Official Histories

Kriegswissenschaftliche Abteilung der Luftwaffe (KAdL). *Die Luftstreitkräfte in der Abwehrschlacht zwischen Somme und Oise vom 8. bis 12. August.* . . . Berlin: Mittler und Sohn, 1942.

————. *Die Militärluftfahrt bis zum Beginn des Weltkrieges 1914.* 3 vols., 2d rev. ed., edited by Militärgeschichtliches Forschungsamt. Frankfurt: Mittler und Sohn, 1965–66.

————. *Mobilmachung, Aufmarsch, und erster Einsatz der Deutschen Luftstreitkräfte im August 1914.* Berlin: Mittler und Sohn, 1939.

Periodicals

Deutscher Luftfahrer Zeitschrift, 1909–20.
Flugsport, 1908–21.

Secondary Sources

Arndt, Hans. "Die Fliegerwaffe." In *Der Stellungkrieg 1914–1918,* edited by Friedrich Seeselberg, pp. 310–69. Berlin: Mittler und Sohn, 1926.

———. "Die Fliegerwaffe im Weltkrieg." In *Ehrendenkmal der deutschen Armee und Marine*, edited by Ernst von Eisenart-rothe, pp. 281–95. Berlin: Deutscher National-Verlag AG, 1928.

———. "Der Luftkrieg." In *Der Weltkampf um Ehre und Recht*, edited by Max Schwarte, vol. 4: 529–651. Leipzig: Finking, 1922.

Blunck, Richard. *Hugo Junkers: Ein Leben für Technik und Luftfahrt.* Düsseldorf: Econ-Verlag, 1951.

Bülow, Hilmer von. *Geschichte der Luftwaffe.* Frankfurt: Moritz Diensterweg, 1934.

Cuneo, John R. *Winged Mars.* 2 vols. Harrisburg: Military Service Publishing Company, 1942, 1947.

Eichler, Jürgen. "Die Militärluftschiffahrt in Deutschland 1911–1914 und ihre Rolle in den Kriegsplänen des deutschen Imperialismum." *Zeitschrift für Militärgeschichte* 24, no. 4 (1985): 350–60; no. 5 (1986): 403–12.

Feldman, Gerald. *Army, Industry, and Labor in Germany, 1914–1918.* Princeton: Princeton University Press, 1966.

Gengler, Ludwig. *Rudolf Berthold.* Berlin: Schlieffen, 1934.

Gersdorff, Kyrill von, and Kurt Grassmann. *Flugmotoren und Strahltriebwerke.* Munich: Bernard und Graefe, 1981.

Gilles, J. A. *Flugmotoren 1910 bis 1918.* Frankfurt: Mittler und Sohn, 1971.

Gray, Peter, and Owen Thetford. *German Aircraft of the First World War.* London: Putnam, 1962.

Haddow, G. W., and Peter M. Grosz. *The German Giants: The Story of the R-planes, 1914–1919.* London: Putnam, 1962.

Imrie, Alex. *Pictorial History of the German Army Air Service, 1914–1918.* Chicago: Henry Regnery Co., 1973.

Immelmann, Franz. *Immelmann. The "Eagle of Lille."* Translated by Claude W. Sykes. London: Hamilton, 1936.

Morrow, John H., Jr. *Building German Air Power, 1909–1914.* Knoxville: University of Tennessee Press, 1976.

———. *German Air Power in World War I.* Lincoln: University of Nebraska Press, 1982.

Neumann, Georg Paul. *Die Deutschen Luftstreitkräfte im Weltkriege.* Berlin: Mittler und Sohn, 1920.

Ritter, Hans. *Der Luftkrieg.* Leipzig: Verlag von Köhler, 1920.

Robinson, Douglas H. *The Zeppelin in Combat: A History of the German Naval Airship Division, 1912–1918.* London: Foulis, 1962.

Supf, Peter. *Das Buch der deutschen Fluggeschichte.* 2d ed., 2 vols. Stuttgart: Drei Brunnen Verlag, 1956, 1958.

Werner, Johannes. *Boelcke. Der Mensch, der Flieger, der Führer der deutschen Jagdfliegerei.* Leipzig: K. F. Köhler, 1932.

Zürl, Walter, ed. *Pour le Mérite—Flieger.* Munich: Pechstein, 1938.

Russia

Primary Sources

Material on Russian budgetary allocations for aviation in the Central State Military Historical Archive, Moscow, Archive No. 92, Fond 493, opus 7, pp. 19–57, located and translated by Von Hardesty.

Memoirs

Finne, K. N. *Igor Sikorsky: The Russian Years*. Edited by Carl Bobrow and Von Hardesty, translated and adapted by Von Hardesty. Washington, D.C.: Smithsonian Institution Press, 1987.

Riaboff, Alexander. *Gatchina Days: Reminiscences of a Russian Pilot*. Edited by Von Hardesty. Washington, D.C.: Smithsonian Institution Press, 1986.

Sikorsky, Igor. *The Story of the Winged S: An Autobiography*. New York: Dodd, Mead, 1938.

Official Histories

Kozlow, N. *A Study of the Military-Technical Supply of the Russian Army in the World War*. Part I, *From the Beginning of the War to the Middle of 1916*, pp. 86–148 on "Army Aircraft Equipment," translated by Charles Berman. Moscow: Government Military Publications Division, 1926.

Secondary Sources

Duz, Petr Dmitrievich. *History of Aeronautics and Aviation in the USSR: The First World War Period (1914–1918)*. Moscow: Oborongiz, 1960 (NASM translation from the Russian).

Hardesty, Von. "Aeronautics Comes to Russia: The Early Years, 1908–1918." Paper presented at the meeting of the American Association for the Advancement of Slavic Studies, November 1988. National Air and Space Museum Research Report 1985, pp. 23–44.

Golovine, Nicholas. *The Russian Army in the World War*. New Haven: Yale University Press, 1931.

Higham, Robin, and Jacob W. Kipp. *Soviet Aviation and Air Power: A Historical View*. Boulder: Westview, 1977. See especially introduction by Robin Higham and essays by David R. Jones (pp. 15–33), Jacob W. Kipp (pp. 137–65), and Otto Chaney and John Greenwood (pp. 265–87).

Holden, Christine. "The View from Furshstadtskaya Street: American Military Attaches' Reports on Russian Aeronautics." Paper presented at the meeting of the American Association for the Advancement of Slavic Studies, November 1988, 41 pp.

Kilmarx, Robert A. *A History of Soviet Air Power.* New York: Praeger, 1962.

——— . "The Russian Imperial Air Forces of World War I." *Airpower Historian* 10 (July 1963): 90–95.

Lincoln, W. Bruce. *Passage through Armaggedon: The Russians in War and Revolution, 1914–1918.* New York: Simon and Schuster, 1986.

Strizhevsky, S. *Nikolai Zhukovsky: Founder of Aeronautics.* Moscow: Foreign Languages Publishing House, 1957.

Austria-Hungary

Documents on military and naval aviation in the Austrian Military Archive, Vienna.

Secondary Sources

O'Connor, Martin. *Air Aces of the Austro-Hungarian Empire, 1914–1918.* Mesa, Ariz.: Champlin Fighter Museum Press, 1986.

Peter, Ernst. *Die k.u.k. Luftschiffer- und Fliegertruppe Österreich-Hungarns, 1794–1919.* Stuttgart: Motorbuch Verlag, 1981.

Peters, Klaus. "Zur Entwicklung der österreichisch-ungarischen Militärluftfahrt von den Anfängen bis 1915." Diss., University of Vienna, 1971.

Schupita, Peter. *Die k.u.k. Seeflieger: Chronik und Dokumentation der österreichisch-ungarischen Marineluftwaffe 1911–1918.* Koblenz: Bernard und Graefe, 1983.

Italy

Memoirs

Baracca, Francesco. *Memorie di guerra aerea.* Rome: Edizioni Ardita, 1934.

D'Annunzio, Gabriele. *Aviatore di guerra: Documenti e testimonianze.* Milan: Impresa Editoriale Italiana, 1930.

Official Histories

Molfese, Manlio. *L'Aviazione da ricognizione italiana durante la Guerra Europea (maggio 1915–novembre 1918).* Rome: Provveditorato Generale dello Stato Libreria, 1925.

Secondary Sources

Apostolo, Giorgio, and Rosario Abate. *Caproni nella Prima Guerra Mondiale.* Europress, 1970.

Bompiani, Giorgio, and Clemente Prepositi. *Le Ali della guerra.* Milan: Mondadori, 1931.

Camurati, Gastone. "Aerei italiani 1914–1918." *Rivista aeronautica,* vol. 48, nos. 6–8, 10–12; vol. 49, no. 1.

Cappelluti, Frank J. "The Life and Thought of Giulio Douhet." Diss., Rutgers University, 1967.

Lodi, Angelo. *Storia delle origini dell'aeronautica militare 1884–1915.* 2 vols. Rome: Edizioni Bizzarri, 1976–1977.

Ludovico, Domenico. *Gli Aviatori italiani del bombardimento nella Guerra 1915–1918.* Rome: Ufficio Storico Aeronautica Militare, 1980.

Mandel, Roberto. *La Guerra aerea.* 2d ed. Milan: Scrittori, 1933.

Porro, Felice. *La Guerra nell'aria.* 5th ed. Milan: Corbaccio, 1940.

Prepositi, Clemente. *I Cavalieri dell'aria nella Grande Guerra: Il primato italiano nella guerra aerea (1911–1912, 1915–1918).* Bologna: Cappelli, 1933.

——— . *Francesco Baracca.* Milan: Zucchi, 1937.

Rhodes, Anthony. *D'Annunzio. The Poet as Superman.* New York: McDowell, Obolensky, 1960.

Vergnano, Piero. *Origin of Aviation in Italy, 1783–1918.* Genoa: Intyprint, 1964.

United States

Primary Sources

Documents in Record Groups 18 and 165, National Archives (NA).

Documents in the Caproni Records, Air Force Historical Research Center, Maxwell Field.

Documents Collections

United States Military Intelligence, 1917–1927. 20 vols. New York: Garland, 1978.

Memoirs

Biddle, Charles J. *Fighting Airman: The Way of the Eagle.* New York: Doubleday, 1968 [1919].

Channing, Grace E., ed. *War Letters of Edmond Genêt*. New York: Charles Scribner's Sons, 1918.

Grider, John M. *War Birds: Diary of an Unknown Aviator*. Elliot W. Springs, ed. Garden City, N.Y.: Garden City Publishing Co., 1938.

Loening, Grover. *Our Wings Grow Faster*. Garden City, N.Y.: Doubleday, Doran and Co., Inc., 1935.

McConnell, James R. *Flying for France*. Garden City, N.Y.: Doubleday, Page and Co., 1917.

Mitchell, William B. *Memoirs of World War I*. New York: Random House, 1956 [1928].

Parsons, Edwin C. *I Flew with the Lafayette Escadrille*. Indianapolis: Seale, 1963 [1937].

Porter, Harold E. *Aerial Observation*. New York: Harper and Brothers, 1921.

Rickenbacker, Eddie V. *Fighting the Flying Circus*. New York: Doubleday, 1965 [1919].

Rossano, Geoffrey L. *The Price of Honor: The World War One Letters of Naval Aviator Kenneth MacLeish*. Annapolis: Naval Institute Press, 1991.

Rowe, Josiah P. *Letters from a World War I Aviator*. Boston: Sinclaire, 1986.

Springs, Elliott White. *Nocturne Militaire*. New York: Doran, 1927.

Winslow, Carroll Dana. *With the French Flying Corps*. New York: Charles Scribner's Sons, 1917.

Official Histories

Aviation Medicine in the A.E.F. Washington: Government Printing Office, 1920.

Maurer, Maurer. *Aviation in the U.S. Army, 1919–1939*. Washington, D.C.: Office of Air Force History, 1987.

———, ed. *The U.S. Air Service in World War I*. 4 vols. Washington, D.C.: Office of Air Force History, 1978–79.

Mixter, G. W., and H. H. Emmons. *United States Army Aircraft Production Facts*. Washington, D.C.: Government Printing Office, 1919.

"Seventy-five Year History of the United States Air Force," Draft by the Office of Air Force History, seen by the author in 1989–1990.

Thayer, Lucien H. *America's First Eagles: The Official History of the U.S. Air Service, A.E.F. (1917–1918)*. San José, Calif., and Mesa, Ariz.: Bender Publishing and Champlin Fighter Aces Museum Press, 1983.

Periodicals

Aviation and Aeronautical Engineering.

Secondary Sources

Bilstein, Roger E. *Flight in America, 1900–1983*. Baltimore: Johns Hopkins University Press, 1984.

Carisella, P. J., and James W. Ryan. *The Black Swallow of Death*. Boston: Marlborough House, 1972.

Coffmann, Edward M. *The War to End All Wars: The American Military Experience in World War I*. Madison: University of Wisconsin Press, 1986.

Cooke, David C. *Sky Battle: 1914–1918*. New York: Norton, 1970.

Davis, Burke. *War Bird: The Life and Times of Elliott White Springs*. Chapel Hill: University of North Carolina Press, 1987.

Dickey, Philip S. "The Liberty Engine, 1918–1942." *Smithsonian Annals of Flight*, vol. 1, no. 3, 1968.

Flammer, Philip M. *The Vivid Air: The Lafayette Escadrille*. Athens: University of Georgia Press, 1981.

Freudenthal, Elsbeth. *The Aviation Business: From Kitty Hawk to Wall Street*. New York: Vanguard, 1940.

Futrell, Robert F. *Ideas, Concepts, Doctrine: A History of Basic Thinking in the United States Air Force, 1907–1964*. Vol. 1. Montgomery: Aerospace Studies Institute, Air University, 1971.

Holley, I. B., Jr. *Ideas and Weapons*. Washington, D.C.: Office of Air Force History, 1983 [1953].

Howard, Fred. *Wilbur and Orville: A Biography of the Wright Brothers*. New York: Knopf, 1987.

Hudson, James J. *Hostile Skies: A Combat History of the American Air Service in World War I*. Syracuse: Syracuse University Press, 1968.

———. *In Clouds of Glory: American Airmen Who Flew with the British during the Great War*. Fayetteville: University of Arkansas Press, 1990.

Knott, Richard. *The American Flying Boat: An Illustrated History*. Annapolis: Naval Institute Press, 1979.

Palmer, Frederick. *Newton D. Baker: America at War*. 2 vols. New York: Dodd, Mead and Co., 1931.

Sweetser, Arthur. *The American Air Service: A Record of Its Problems, Its Difficulties, Its Failings, and Its Achievements*. New York: D. Appleton, 1919.

Turnbull, Archibald D., and Clifford L. Lord. *History of United States Naval Aviation*. New Haven: Yale University Press, 1949.

Vander Meulen, Jacob A. "The American Aircraft Industry to World War II." Draft diss., University of Toronto, 1989.

Van Wyen, Adrian O. *Naval Aviation in World War I*. Washington, D.C.: Chief of Naval Operations, 1969.

Index